D1462401

AVOIDING THE
APOCALYPSE
THE FUTURE OF THE
TWO KOREAS

AVOIDING THE APOCALYPSE
THE FUTURE OF THE TWO KOREAS

❖

MARCUS NOLAND

INSTITUTE FOR INTERNATIONAL ECONOMICS
WASHINGTON, DC
JUNE 2000

Marcus Noland, senior fellow, was the senior economist for international economics at the Council of Economic Advisers (1993-94). He has been a visiting professor at Johns Hopkins University, the University of Southern California, Tokyo University, Saitama University, the University of Ghana, and a visiting scholar at the Korea Development Institute. He has written many articles on international economics and is the author of *Pacific Basin Developing Countries: Prospects for the Future* (1990). He is coauthor of *Global Economic Effects of the Asian Currency Devaluations* (1998), *Reconcilable Differences? United States-Japan Economic Conflict* with C. Fred Bergsten (1993), and *Japan in the World Economy* with Bela Balassa (1988), coeditor of *Pacific Dynamism and the International Economic System* (1993), and editor of *Economic Integration of the Korean Peninsula* (1998).

INSTITUTE FOR INTERNATIONAL ECONOMICS
11 Dupont Circle, NW
Washington, DC 20036-1207
(202) 328-9000   FAX: (202) 328-5432
http://www.iie.com

C. Fred Bergsten, *Director*
Brigitte Coulton, *Director of Publications and Web Development*
Brett Kitchen, *Marketing Director*

Printing and typesetting by Automated Graphic Systems

The image on the cover of this book is that of a Buddhist guardian figure as portrayed on a temple gate in South Korea. Photograph source: Index Stock Imagery.

Printed in the United States of America
02 01 00   5 4 3 2 1

Library of Congress Cataloging-in-Publication Data

Noland, Marcus, 1959-
  Avoiding the Apocalypse : the future of the two Koreas / Marcus Noland.
    p. cm.
  Includes bibliographical references and index.
  ISBN 0-88132-278-4
    1. Korea (South)—Economic policy—1960- 2. Korea (North)—Foreign economic relations. 3. Korea—Economic conditions—1945-
4. Korea—Economic policy.   I. Title: Economic turmoil on the Korean Peninsula. II. Title.

HC467 .N658 2000
338.9519--dc21   00-038314

ISBN 0-88132-278-4

Contents

Tables

Figures

Boxes

Preface

Since its inception, the Institute has devoted considerable attention to developments in South Korea. We have published two major studies on the country by leading experts from South Korea itself, *Korea in the World Economy* by SaKong Il and *The Dynamics of Korean Economic Development* by Cho Soon. We have hosted six annual meetings of the Korea-United States 21st Century Council, jointly sponsored with the Institute for Global Economics in Seoul and the Korea Foundation, to bring together officials from the governments and private sectors of the two countries to discuss the key bilateral and global issues that they need to address together.

During the past decade, it has become increasingly apparent that events north as well as south of the 38th parallel have significant implications for the United States and indeed for all of Northeast Asia. The nuclear confrontation between North Korea and the United States, and the contemporaneous famine in North Korea, have dramatically raised the ante on the Korean peninsula. In recognition of these changing circumstances, in September 1997 we hosted a major international conference about issues on the Korean peninsula and published *Economic Integration of the Korean Peninsula*, edited by Senior Fellow Marcus Noland. The Asian financial crisis, which shook South Korea later that year, then called into question both South Korea's willingness and capacity to manage contingencies involving the North.

The present study represents the culmination of Noland's pathbreaking research on both North and South Korea. It integrates his extensive study of both countries into a single narrative, and pulls together the inextricably entwined economic and security aspects of the situation on the Korean peninsula. It provides both an overview of the two countries' economies and a careful analysis of the three crises (the North Korean nuclear confrontation, the North Korean famine, and the South Korean financial disruption) that frame the situation on the Korean peninsula today.

Noland analyzes possible future developments in terms of three scenarios: successful reform in the North, its collapse and absorption into the South, and an intermediate scenario in which the North muddles through, making ad hoc adjustments as circumstances dictate, supported financially in this endeavor by external powers which, for their own reasons, prefer the maintenance of a divided peninsula to unification. The study concludes with policy recommendations for South Korea, the United States, and others with interests at stake on the Korean peninsula. This truly unique study is particularly timely as the two Koreas have announced their first summit meeting since the formal partition of the peninsula in 1945, holding forth the prospects of significant changes in an unsustainable status quo.

The Institute for International Economics is a private nonprofit institution for the study and discussion of international economic policy. Its purpose is to analyze important issues in that area and develop and communicate practical new approaches for dealing with them. The Institute is completely nonpartisan.

The Institute is funded largely by philanthropic foundations. Major institutional grants are now being received from the William M. Keck, Jr. Foundation and the Starr Foundation. A number of other foundations and private corporations contribute to the highly diversified financial resources of the Institute. About 26 percent of the Institute's resources in our latest fiscal year were provided by contributors outside the United States, including about 11 percent from Japan. The Freeman Foundation and the Korea Foundation have provided generous financial support to this project.

The Board of Directors bears overall responsibility for the Institute and gives general guidance and approval to its research program—including the identification of topics that are likely to become important over the medium run (one to three years) and which should be addressed by the Institute. The Director, working closely with the staff and outside Advisory Committee, is responsible for the development of particular projects and makes the final decision to publish an individual study.

The Institute hopes that its studies and other activities will contribute to building a stronger foundation for international economic policy around the world. We invite readers of these publications to let us know how they think we can best accomplish this objective.

C. Fred Bergsten
Director
May 2000

Acknowledgments

The preface to historian Walter Rodney's book *How Europe Underdeveloped Africa* reads in part: "Contrary to the fashion in most prefaces, I will not add that 'all mistakes and shortcomings are entirely my responsibility.' That is sheer bourgeois subjectivism. Responsibility in matters of these sorts is always collective, especially in regard to the remedying of shortcomings." This book has had an unusually long gestation period, and as a consequence, a large number of people and institutions have thankfully participated in the collective remedying of its multitudinous shortcomings.

I have benefitted tremendously from the opportunity to present this book or its background papers in seminars sponsored by the American Economic Association, the Asian Development Bank Institute, the Australian National University, the Council on Foreign Relations, Claremont McKenna College, Columbia University, the Council on US-Korea Security Studies, Economists Allied for Arms Reduction, Georgetown University, Hitotsubashi University, the Hoover Institute, the Institute for Global Economics, the Institute for International Economics, the International Food Policy Research Institute, the Korea Development Institute, the Korea Economic Institute, the Korea Institute for International Economic Policy, Korea University, both the Economics Department and the Asia-Pacific Center of Stanford University, the University of California/San Diego, the University of Southern California, United States Forces Korea, and the World Bank.

Individually, Desaix Anderson, Brian Barna, C. Fred Bergsten, Thomas Byrne, Geoffrey Carliner, Choi Inbom, William R. Cline, William Drennan,

Nicholas Eberstadt, F. Gordon Flake, Morris Goldstein, James Gordon, Michael R. Green, Han Seung-soo, Peter Hayes, Gary C. Hufbauer, Kim In-june, Samuel Kim, Lee Doowon, Lee Yang-ho, Danny Leipziger, LiGang Liu, Warwick McKibbin, Anthony R. Michell, Kongdan (Katy) Oh, Pyo Hak-kil, J. David Richardson, Daniel Rosen, R.W. Sennewald, Jeffrey Shafer, Scott Snyder, Tao Wang, Robert Warne, John Williamson, Yoo Jung-ho, and Young Soogil offered enormously helpful comments on the manuscript or the background papers.

As befits a product so long in the making, I received help from a number of research assistants. Chi Zhang and Alexandra Harney were there at or near the beginning, and Hye Kyung Lee was there at the end, but it was Mina Kim who did the lion's share of the work in the middle, and my debt to her is considerable.

With good humor Ambassador (ret.) Robert J. Rich, Jr. took on the herculean task of making my prose both more comprehensible and more diplomatic, though I am not sure he would want to do it over again. Once the publication process was underway, Kara Davis designed a striking cover, and Marla Banov and Brigitte Coulton shepherded the whole thing through in record time.

Finally, I must acknowledge two enormous debts. Through the good offices of Dr. SaKong Il in 1991, I was able to spend time at the Korea Development Institute as a visiting scholar, and it was during this stay that I developed an interest in North Korea and what the unification of Korea might entail. I doubt that Dr. SaKong could have foreseen how his intervention on my behalf would eventually come to fruition, but I hope that he does not regret the assistance that he provided. My other debt is to Sherman Robinson, with whom I collaborated on a number of the papers that underpin this book analytically. This book could not have been written without that partnership.

Call me a bourgeois subjectivist, but with all this collective assistance, responsibility for the remaining shortcomings are mine alone.

Introduction

We attacked every type of target from culverts and railroad bridges to cars and trucks and tanks, and right on up through war supporting industries, both direct and indirect. We did some major damage out there . . . we smashed completely the high frequency steel installation at Songjin . . . we smashed entirely the entire chemical complex at Konan, which is far and away the largest in the Far East . . . . We completely destroyed the large fertilizer plant at Konan . . . . I would say the entire, almost the entire Korean Peninsula is just a terrible mess. Everything is destroyed. There is nothing standing worthy of the name.

—General Eugene O'Donnell, Jr., commander of the USAF's Far Eastern Bomber Command, testifying before the Committee on Armed Forces and the Committee on Foreign Relations, 1951.[1]

The Korean peninsula is a densely populated area with few natural resources save some mineral deposits in the North. Ethnically, the population is highly homogenous. In the first century BC three kingdoms were established with borders roughly corresponding to those of contemporary North and South Korea. One of these kingdoms eventually established its dominance, and the peninsula was unified politically in the 7th century AD. Nevertheless, the Korean state struggled to remain independent of foreign powers, including China to its north and west and Japan to its south and east. After repelling a 17th century Manchurian invasion, the

---

1. Committee on Armed Services and Committee on Foreign Relations, United States Senate. 1951. Military Situation in the Far East, Part 4, Washington: Government Printing Office, 3064, 3075.

Chosun (Yi) dynasty shut itself off from the rest of the world, earning the sobriquet of "the Hermit Kingdom."

Paralleling Japan, a reform movement emerged in Korea during the 19th century and with it a great interest in foreign intellectual and technological innovations. However, during the second half of the 19th century, this engagement took an ominous turn, with foreign powers including the United States, and most decisively Japan, attempting to forcibly open Korea to commercial exchange.

The Koreans repulsed initial forays by the French and the Americans, but the newly reemergent Japan, regarding Korea as "a dagger pointed at its heart," proved more resolute. In 1876 the Japanese succeeded in opening two Korean ports and began to intervene in Korean internal politics. Korea sought formal ties with the United States, hoping that this would deter the depredations of its neighbors, but this proved illusory. By the end of the 19th century, the situation had degenerated into a scramble in which Japan successively defeated first China (1894-95) and then Russia (1904-05). The United States was among the Western powers that acquiesced to Japan's seizure of Korea in 1905 and its formal annexation in 1910.

During the period of Japanese occupation, the Korean economy exhibited regional differences in its pattern of development. Mining and industry were mainly concentrated in the North, while the South remained the agrarian breadbasket. It has been estimated that, at the time of the Second World War, per capita output of mining and manufactures was three times as high in the North as in the South, only 35 percent of the colony's heavy industry was located in the South, and 80 percent of the South's electricity was supplied by hydroelectric dams in the North.[2]

At the conclusion of the Second World War in 1945, Korea was partitioned into zones of US and Soviet occupation. In the immediate aftermath of Japan's withdrawal, Koreans were able to maintain some production in all sectors of the economy, demonstrating that they had acquired or maintained a substantial base of relevant skills during the colonial period.[3] Unable to agree on a formula for unification, in 1948 the Republic of Korea (ROK) was proclaimed in the zone of US occupation in the South, while the Democratic People's Republic of Korea (DPRK) was established under Soviet tutelage in the North.[4]

---

2. See Kim and Roemer (1979), Eckert (1991), and Woo (1991) for informative analyses of Korean economic development during the colonial period. The North would later cut off electrical supplies to the South in May 1948, following the partition (Armstrong 2000).

3. See Kim and Roemer (1979), Jones and SaKong (1980), and Westphal et al. (1981).

4. Throughout this book, for simplicity's sake the Republic of Korea will be referred to as South Korea and the Democratic People's Republic of Korea as North Korea.

In June 1950, North Korea invaded South Korea. The initial success of the invading forces was reversed with the support of a US-dominated United Nations (UN) contingent, driving China to enter the war in October under pressure from Stalin in order to prevent a North Korean defeat. By March 1951, a stalemate emerged, and truce talks, which dragged on for two years, began in June. The conflict ended in 1953 with the original demarcation between North and South more or less reestablished, but ceding the Kaesong high ground to the North and thus arguably putting the South at a disadvantage by enabling the North to hold Seoul hostage militarily. The see-saw character of the war, involving armies from both sides traversing the peninsula, left both countries economically devastated and reliant on their respective patrons. While the pre-partition disposition of assets clearly favored the North, by the end of the war much of what had been inherited had been destroyed, and mass population movements (primarily from the North to the South) meant that relative endowments of human capital had been reshuffled as well. It is difficult to ascertain with any degree of accuracy relative capacities at the time of partition.[5]

In a period of less than two generations, Korea had been conquered, colonized, partitioned by foreign powers, and devastated by civil war. Understandably many Koreans blamed Japan, the United States, and the Soviet Union for their plight. Even in the South, such feelings festered despite the loss of more than 33,000 US casualties in the defense of South Korea (Drennan 1994).

Divergent Paths

After the war, the paths of the two Koreas diverged markedly. A capitalist economic system was established in the South, albeit one characterized by considerable state intervention in economic life. As described in chapter 2, after languishing for a decade, a series of fundamental economic reforms were initiated in 1963. The result was an explosion of economic growth during which South Korea experienced on average a 7 percent real per capita income growth for the next 25 years, resulting in a quintupling of real per capita income. Political modernization and democratization followed, and, by the 1990s, South Korea was surely one of the most democratic societies in Asia.

In the North, a thoroughly orthodox Soviet-type central planning model was adopted by the world's only example of dynastic Stalinism. As with many centralized planning systems, it achieved some early success in

---

5. See Kim and Roemer (1979) on the distribution of assets at the end of the war. In the two decades following the war, North Korea experienced considerable human capital inflow as the *Chochongryun*, an organization of pro-Pyongyang ethnic Koreans in Japan, organized the voluntary repatriation of more than 100,000 Koreans.

mobilizing resources. As described in chapter 3, the conventional wisdom is that per capita income in the North exceeded that in the South until the 1970s. However, by this time, opportunities to grow through "extensive" means of marshaling greater resources began to dwindle, and the North proved largely incapable of growing through the "intensive" means of raising the productivity of existing assets. Having borrowed extensively on international markets in the aftermath of the first oil shock, it defaulted on its loans and was effectively cut off from international capital markets, narrowing the regime's economic options and leaving it dependent on the Eastern Bloc for support.

The situation worsened in the mid-1980s as relations deteriorated with its principal benefactor, the Soviet Union, and aid from fraternal socialist allies began to dry up. The collapse of the Soviet Union and the subsequent breakup of the Eastern Bloc was a major macroeconomic shock that ushered in a period of as yet unabated decline. By the mid-1990s, the North's dream of unifying the peninsula began rapidly to fade, a casualty its own failing economy and the vibrancy of the South and its support from the world's sole superpower, the United States.

Three Crises

North Korea began a small nuclear program in the 1950s, receiving help from the Soviet Union and later from China. The motivations for this program are unclear: it could have been purely for research purposes or as a stepping stone to an energy program, or it could have been purely for prestige. Many developing countries in the 1950s and 1960s operated small research reactors, so in this regard North Korea was not unique. Of course, the fact that atomic bombings of Hiroshima and Nagasaki brought Japan to its knees undoubtedly made an impression on Kim Il-sung,[6] the former anti-Japanese guerilla and founding leader of North Korea—as did his own subsequent fight with the Americans. The North Korean nuclear program could have been intended as a weapons program from the start. Or, a program that was originally begun with one purpose could have been transformed into something else in the intervening years. We may never know.

Parallel to its nuclear program, North Korea began developing, producing, and exporting increasingly long-range ballistic missiles. Again, there are multiple interpretations. North Korea could have seen the development of missiles as enhancing deterrence on the peninsula, despite the

---

6. When the full names of Koreans are cited, they are given in the normal Korean sequence, with surname first. The surname is then followed by the generational and given names with a hyphen between them for ease in distinguishing the components. When citing a name only with surname and initials, it will be given in the Western pattern, as J.C. Kim, for example.

fact that its 10,000 forward-deployed artillery tubes already held Seoul hostage. Moreover, in its deteriorating economic circumstances missile exports were one of its few sources of hard currency earnings. But, as one former high-ranking US official put it, "the missiles only make sense if you have something to put on top of them."

This was not idle speculation. By the early 1990s, US intelligence analysts became increasingly convinced that the North Koreans were attempting to develop nuclear weapons. As recounted in chapter 4, an international confrontation ensued, involving the US, North Korea, and the United Nations. The upshot was that the United States and North Korea signed an "Agreed Framework" (reproduced in Appendix A) specifying a set of reciprocal obligations that involve the termination of the North Korean weapons program, the provision by an international consortium of new light-water nuclear power reactors by the target date of 2003, and the normalization of economic and political relations. This agreement, in essence, sought (through the provision of economic and political inducements) to halt North Korea's further development of nuclear weapons. This agreement is the centerpiece of North Korea's political and economic interaction with the rest of the world, and today official transfers exceed private transactions.[7] North Korea's economic and strategic relations are inextricably linked. For better or worse, it appears highly unlikely that the US-led consortium will complete construction of the reactors on the projected schedule in 2003. The failure to meet this target could mark a turning point in North Korea's relations with the West—either toward renewed confrontation or toward a new and ultimately more constructive engagement.

At the same time that North Korea was drifting into a nuclear confrontation with the United States, it was sliding into a famine that may have claimed roughly 10 percent of the precrisis population. As demonstrated in chapter 5, the famine was a product of decades of economic mismanagement, and actually preceded the highly publicized natural disasters of 1995 and subsequent years. The North Koreans adopted a number of coping mechanisms in response to this calamity, but the principal one was to demand aid from the international community. North Korea demanded money or food aid as a prerequisite to its participation in a variety of diplomatic forums, and given its growing capacity for wreaking havoc, assistance was forthcoming. In the case of the United States, negotiations relating to the North Korean missile program, its nuclear program, and the "Four-Party Talks" aimed at achieving a more durable basis for peace on the peninsula have all occasioned US assistance.[8] In effect, the North

---

7. Some have argued that the Agreed Framework is not an "agreement" in a legal sense in that it does not provide for any enforcement mechanism and can be regarded as non-binding.

8. The Four-Party Talks first convened in December 1997 and include China, the United States, and North and South Korea.

Koreans have used the external threat posed by the missile and nuclear programs to extort money from the rest of the world. By the late 1990s, North Korea was receiving aid from nearly fifty countries and had become the single largest recipient of US aid in Asia. Again, in the case of North Korea, it is impossible to separate strategic considerations from economics.

During the 1990s, South Korean policy toward the North swung from the relatively hard-line policy of former President Kim Young-sam and his predecessors to the engagement policy of current President Kim Dae-jung, illustrating the diverse attitudes toward the North within South Korea. The apparent costliness of German unification had already cooled the ardor of some South Koreans by the time the country was rocked by a financial crisis in late 1997. The crisis had its roots in a development model characterized by considerable government intervention in the economy. While this approach may have been reasonable for a late developer playing technological catch-up, the system became increasingly questionable as South Korea approached the world technological frontier. The state had encouraged the development of a state-dominated, bank-centered financial system that facilitated the channeling of capital to the state's preferred borrowers and projects. This policy of channeling government-directed capital effectively socialized risk. The system of capital channeling, combined with the lack of an effective mechanism for disciplining failure, created moral hazard on an enormous scale and gave rise to giant, highly indebted, conglomerates or *chaebol*, whose economically unjustified agglomerations of unrelated economic activities were justified only by the owner-managers' relationship with the state. The result was the development of a symbiotic relationship between the state on the one hand and the giant *chaebol* on the other.[9]

This system has been subject to periodic crises: one during the early 1970s, another during the early 1980s, and, of course, the recent crisis that has plagued the country from 1997 through 1999. The latest crisis, if not its timing, was foreseeable. Indeed, the crisis would have eventually occurred regardless of events in Southeast Asia, although contagion exacerbated the situation.

Starting in early 1996, South Korea suffered severe terms of trade shocks. As export prices fell, expectations of future corporate earnings were revised downward, and the prices of stock market shares and land fell.

---

9. As Leipziger and Petri (1993) presciently wrote, "Korea's policy goals are increasingly those of an advanced industrial economy—to become more competitive in advanced industries and to maintain market shares in key world markets. Yet the most visible instruments of Korean industrial policy, including especially credit policy, have been inherited from a simpler economy. These tools are not well adapted to addressing the country's new economic objectives and are rapidly becoming politicized . . . [T]he conflict between goals and means is undermining the credibility of industrial policy and is delaying the development of institutions that will have to be important in the economy's next phase of growths" (p.1).

With the combined falls in export and asset prices, the financial condition of the highly leveraged *chaebol* began to deteriorate as did bank balance sheets. During the spring of 1997, a series of economic and political crises hit the country—two former presidents, Chun Doo-hwan and Roh Tae-woo, were jailed on corruption charges, the sitting president's son was arrested on corruption charges, and Hanbo, ranked by sales as the seventeenth largest *chaebol*, collapsed under a mountain of bad debt.

In July 1997, the Bank of Thailand severed the Thai baht's link to the US dollar, setting off the Asian financial crisis. As the summer progressed, conditions in South Korea worsened both internally and externally. The South Korean won, which was informally fixed against the US dollar, came under downward pressure. In a vain attempt to vouchsafe the foreign debts of private institutions and to defend the value of the currency, the Bank of Korea spent tens of billions of dollars in foreign exchange reserves. By the third week of December, however, foreign exchange reserves were nearly exhausted, and the country stood on the precipice of an international default that was avoided only through emergency intervention by the International Monetary Fund (IMF).

The severe recession that followed and the liberalization measures that were adopted as the *quid pro quo* for the IMF standby package have had significant relevance both for the future prospects of the South Korean economy and for South Korean attitudes toward developments in the North. On the one hand, the crisis has strengthened feelings in South Korea that it is unprepared for the financial exigencies of early unification and has further cooled enthusiasm for integration with the North. At the same time, the resulting liberalization of the economy in response to the crisis will strengthen its ability to handle unification economically if a collapse in the North were to occur.

Prospects for the Future

On the Korean peninsula, the world confronts a face-off between what is surely one of the greatest success stories of the post-war era and what has been described as an "alienated" state—one fundamentally opposed to, and with no real stake in, the existing international order.[10] This situation creates fundamental policy dilemmas of enormous practical and ethical import for the rest of the world. Judged in terms of the share of population under arms or the share of military expenditures in national income, North Korea continues to maintain the most militarized society on earth. Its armed forces are the fifth largest in the world, exceeded only by those of China, the United States, Russia, and India. It produces and

---

10. Roy (1998) uses the term "alienated state." See Reese (1998) for a detailed and accessible overview of North Korean internal politics.

exports ballistic missiles and is thought to possess large stores of chemical and biological weapons as well as perhaps a few nuclear weapons. Unlike 170 other nations, it has refused to sign the Chemical Weapons Convention. In 1993 it became the first and only country to declare its intention to withdraw from the Nuclear Non-Proliferation Treaty (NPT), a move it later "suspended." It invaded the South once and in subsequent years engaged in state sponsored terrorism. Internally, it maintains a personality cult of religious proportions around the late Kim Il-sung and his son Kim Jong-il and has one of the worst human rights records of any state existent today.

If the North Korean regime is irredeemable, should not the rest of the world act to hasten its demise? If so, what policies should be considered and what risks contemplated? If not, how should the desire to provide humanitarian assistance to the innocent be weighed against the support to war-making capability that may be inherent in even the best designed humanitarian program? What, if any, conditions should be attached to aid? How should the world's response be coordinated? What should be the response if the situation in North Korea becomes unstable—if it experiences a coup, an implosion, or a civil war as an outcome of the current crisis?

The United States has enormous stakes on the Korean peninsula. Having already fought one war there, the United States continues to maintain 37,000 troops in South Korea. It is the one place on earth where the United States could become nearly instantly involved in a major ground war. Beyond this immediate security issue, North Korea looms large in US concerns about proliferation of weapons of mass destruction. Economic issues are a grave concern as well—South Korea is an important ally and trade partner, and, as will be subsequently demonstrated, the costs of unification in case of North Korean collapse could amount to hundreds of billions of dollars. Moreover, the Korean peninsula is a fulcrum on which relations between the United States and China, the United States and Japan, and China and Japan all turn.

The range of possible outcomes on the Korean peninsula is enormous. The North Korean leadership faces essentially three broad economic options: they can adopt fundamental economic reforms in an attempt to reverse the economic decline, recognizing that reform may unleash forces that threaten the essential character of the political regime; they can stand pat and try to ride out the current crisis, risking collapse; or they can seek to "muddle through," making ad hoc adjustments as the circumstances dictate.

The current regime (or some successor) could undertake the economic and diplomatic moves necessary to stabilize the economic situation and end the famine. Reform of the North Korean economy would have two profound effects: first, there would be a significant increase in exposure to international trade and investment (much of this with South Korea and Japan, two countries with which North Korea maintains problematic relations), and second, changes in the composition of output would be tremendous, involving literally millions of workers changing employment. Both of these developments could be expected to have enormous political implications and could present significant, perhaps insurmountable, obstacles to reform under the current regime.

As an alternative, the regime could stand pat and hope to ride out its difficulties. Although this holds the promise of short-run political stability, if current trends continue it eventually will put a significant share of the population at peril. Moreover, North Korea differs in some significant ways from other socialist regimes that were able to survive self-inflicted famines earlier in this century. First, unlike the others, the Kim Jong-il government is not a revolutionary regime, but the dynastic continuation of one that has now held power for more than 50 years. Surely, neither this government (nor the governed) have the same capacity for enduring hardship that would exist in a period of revolutionary fervor. Second, North Korea is a relatively industrialized, urbanized society, and this reduces both its government's ability to squeeze resources out of the agricultural sector and the populace's coping mechanisms. Third, previous socialist country famines have largely been precipitated by the introduction of counterproductive policies, and could be solved relatively straightforwardly by the removal of those policies. Less a function of bad weather or the sudden introduction of misguided policies, North Korea's current agricultural problems appear to be the culmination of policies undertaken for two generations.

How this plays out depends, at least in part, on the intentions of the North Korean elite. If this elite has given up hope of reunifiying the peninsula on its own terms, its may be amenable to a reform process that could amount to "unification through golden parachutes," in which the elite uses its control of the state to channel rents for their own "soft landing" through a kind of "*apparatchik* capitalism." This endgame would be consistent with the retention of some weapons of mass destruction capacity to maintain double-sided deterrence—and a withering of conventional military capability that would no longer be necessary.

Alternatively, the North Korean elite could retain hopes of forcibly reunifying the peninsula and simply regard recent diplomatic openings as an opportunity to "play for time" and channel economic gains into a broad program of military modernization. A diplomatic settlement, which could result in the removal of US troops from the peninsula, could get them a long way down this road. A third possibility is that the North Koreans have no aggressive intent, but are so paranoid and fixated on military security that they are quite literally willing to spend themselves into the grave in pursuit of external security. In the words of Pyongyang-affiliated journalist Kim Myong-chol, "the Americans remain the most serious security threat to the DPRK. This perception vindicates Kim Jong-il's decision to spend every single earned dollar on building up an awesome self defense against the Americans and Japanese" (M.C. Kim, 1999).

In this view, the avoidance of a military confrontation with the United States in 1994 has given North Korea an opportunity to develop more effective means of extorting resources out of the rest of the world and of pushing for unification on their own terms (or redoubling a defensively-oriented arms build-up). North Korea's August 1998 public announcement of its missile exports, its test of a multi-stage rocket, and its suspected continuation of nuclear weapons-related activities perhaps give some indication of the country's future course. North Korea could continue a strategy of attempting to extort resources out of the rest of the world, offering to abandon weapons development and export while continuing to make clandestine sales. In the simplest terms, the North Korean economy no longer works. It does not generate enough output to sustain its population biologically, nor, absent fundamental economic reforms, will it do so in the future. Under current conditions, North Korea will require external support for the foreseeable future. Yet the world community is unlikely to continue this support unless North Korea continues to pose a security threat to its neighbors. Economic collapse (presumably precipitating a significant alteration in or disappearance of the current political regime) would be disastrous in human terms and pose great risks to international political stability, especially if it were accompanied by civil war and military intervention by external powers. Surrounding countries—South Korea, China, and Japan—and the United States have demonstrated a willingness to provide this support and more for fear of North Korea's collapse, or, worse, an internal conflict or lashing out that could put millions of people in Northeast Asia in harm's way, including tens of thousands of US troops stationed in South Korea and Japan.

The provision of this aid is tied to the existence of this security threat. If North Korea was simply a country with a broken economy and 22 million impoverished citizens, it is extremely unlikely that a multinational consortium would be pouring in billions of dollars of aid in the form of food and infrastructural investments. There are plenty of such countries in Central Asia and Africa, but the rest of the world does not build them light-water nuclear reactors. Indeed, one could argue that the famine does not even distinguish North Korea—contemporaneous situations in Africa are as bad, if not worse. Rather, North Korea's ability to extract such resources from the world community is intimately related to the threat it poses, and, in this sense, the status quo more closely resembles extortion than charity. The threat that North Korea poses is its sole asset. It is unlikely to negotiate away this asset very easily.

The marriage of the rocket and nuclear programs would give the North Koreans impressive tools with which to intimidate their immediate neighbors and create proliferation nightmares for the United States. The truly frightening aspect of this reasoning is that this scenario would be a continuation of the status quo. Ironically, given obstacles to successful reform, such an externally high-risk strategy might be the path of least resistance internally to a weak and risk-averse regime.

Today the North Korean elite appears to be split in this regard.[11] Pyongyang's hesitant steps toward economic reform, for example, have a two steps forward, one step back character. But the question remains whether its system-preserving reforms in the form of tourism projects, mining enclaves, and special economic zones will be sufficient to maintain social stability and avert collapse. At some point, developments may force the North Koreans to make a fundamental choice: either to continue down the extortionist road (which requires periodic threat reminders) or to abandon this path and undertake the hard and uncertain task of economic reform. The first approach has yielded a stream of tactical payoffs, but these appear insufficient to reverse the secular deterioration of the economy. North Korea is winning the battles but losing the war. The problem is that care is required to make a convincing case for the second path that does not end with the North Korean elite either dead or working as janitors for Hyundai, and it is unlikely that this elite will commit class suicide.

The April 2000 announcement of the first North-South summit, three days before a South Korean general election in which Kim Dae-jung's ruling coalition trailed in the polls, is consistent with all of these hypotheses. It could signal that, having consolidated political power, a newly confident Kim Jong-il is ready to begin responding constructively to the overtures from the South. Or, it could be merely a tactical move on the part of the North, timed to extract maximum concessions from a pliant Kim Dae-jung. Only time will tell.

Tour de Horizon

The stakes are extraordinarily high for both North and South Korea and for countries such as the United States that have a direct stake in Korean affairs. The crisis is economically driven, but the economics are extremely

---

11. Former Defense Secretary William Perry, who led the Clinton Administration's policy review of North Korea, has testified that he believes the North Korean leadership is split on the issue of normalizing relations with the United States. Desaix Anderson, who as Executive Director of the Korean Peninsula Energy Development Organization (KEDO) has had extensive dealings with the North Koreans, asserts that just such a division does exist, and ascribes it to a split between those (most prominently associated with the foreign ministry and the economics ministries) who favor some opening to the outside world, and "hardliners" in the military and the Korean Workers Party (KWP) (Anderson 1999). Takesada (n.d.) asserts a similar split and discusses the increasing influence of the military in North Korean policymaking.

politicized—indeed, official transfers, not private transactions, are at the center of North Korea's external economic relations. It is impossible to separate economics and politics in this analysis.

Unfortunately, much of the existent work on these issues reflect a pie-in-the-sky wishful thinking that confuses hoped for "soft-landings" with policies designed to achieve desired goals or official formulas for unification with actual behavior. This book will argue that the economic future of the Korean peninsula can usefully be discussed in terms of three basic scenarios: successful economic reform of North Korea; collapse of the North Korean state and its absorption into South Korea; and an intermediate scenario of "muddling through" in which North Korea makes a series of regime-preserving reforms short of the fundamental transformation envisioned in the first scenario.[12] Obviously these three scenarios are neither exhaustive nor exclusive. It is possible, for example, that rather than the peaceful collapse and absorption that occurred in East Germany, North Korea could plunge into a civil war, possibly involving the intervention of external powers, or it could even lash out militarily. And of course it is possible that eventual unification of Korea on essentially South Korean terms could be preceded by a prolonged period of muddling through.[13] So little is known about North Korea, and the dynamics of the issues addressed in this book are so complex, that it would be foolhardy to predict any of these outcomes with a strong degree of confidence.[14] One could imagine a range of outcomes from significant reform and possibly successful transition into a market economy with enhanced national political status and capabilities to the economic equivalent of life-support and reversion to the status of a Chinese tributary state.

This book is organized into three parts. Part one, consisting of this introduction and the next two chapters, provides an overview of the South and North Korean economies. There has been so little interaction between the two Koreas in conventional economic terms, that the histories of each of these economies can be written with little reference to events in the

---

12. The term collapse, though frequently used, is seldom defined. Huh (1996), S.C. Kim (1996), Choi (1998), and Pollack and Lee (1999) are laudable exceptions. For the purposes at hand, collapse will be defined as an economic catastrophe that leads to the disappearance and replacement of the state. As discussed in chapter 9, it is logically possible, though unlikely, that the Kim regime could collapse and a successor regime could maintain North Korea as an independent state for an extended period of time.

13. Moon (1999) systematically analyzes a large number of these alternatives.

14. In one poll of scholars, 38 percent of the respondents predicted that the current regime would not last a decade (Y.S. Lee 1995). In a more recent poll, the respondents' mean subjective probability of collapse was 26 percent, while the mean estimate of significant reform was 40 percent (Noland 1998a, table 1). A survey of the professional literature on the topic (Oh and Hassig 1999) found that most analysts expect some kind of muddling through, around a quarter of the papers predict collapse in the near-term, and successful self-initiated reform appears to be the least expected outcome.

other half of the peninsula. The second part of the book, comprising chapters 4, 5, and 6, examines the three crises that frame the situation on the Korean peninsula today—the North Korean nuclear confrontation, the North Korean famine, and the South Korean financial crisis. Again, although South Korea's influence on the nuclear confrontation and famine are not inconsiderable, in an immediate sense, neither of the Koreas plays a central role in the crises affecting the other. Yet the two Koreas can be likened to strands of a braided rope—distinct but intertwined and ultimately part of a single thread. This is most clear in the third part of the book, which examines alternative future paths for the peninsula structured around three fundamental scenarios of successful reform (chapter 7), collapse (chapter 8), and muddling through (chapter 9) in the North. Obviously these alternative outcomes in North Korea will be partly shaped by, and have influence on, South Korea. A series of computable general equilibrium models are used to shed light on the critical issues that these alternatives pose to both North and South Korea. The book concludes with a summary of recommendations for policies both for South Korea and third parties, including the United States.

It will be argued that muddling through or some sustained period of North Korean decline before the regime's ultimate denouement are the most likely outcomes, though collapse remains a distinct possibility. Sadly, successful economic reform appears to be the least likely eventuality. Either way, the status quo is not viable in the long-run. Maintenance of North Korea as an independent state would involve varying mixes of domestic economic reform and external support and could imply varying degrees of national political autonomy depending on the degree of reliance on outside support. North Korea is already the largest recipient of US assistance in Asia. Maintaining this kind of largesse to an unreconstructed, vituperative, Stalinist dynasty is politically unsustainable in the donor countries, particularly in the United States. Indeed, the likely failure of the US-led multinational consortium to complete construction of the light-water reactors by 2003 as specified in the Agreed Framework may well trigger—for better or ill—a significant reorientation of relations between North Korea and the West. Ironically, this could encourage increased reliance on China and a gradual reversion of North Korea to a Chinese tributary state—the status quo for nearly a millennium and an inversion of the self-reliant dreams of Kim Il-sung.

2

The South Korean Economy until 1997

In the aftermath of the Second World War, the United States encouraged the development of a market economy in the South, though the state played a prominent role in what developed, perhaps reflecting the dirigiste character of Japanese colonial administration, Korea's lack of historical experience with capitalism, and President Syngman Rhee's use of state-generated rents to solidify his power base politically.[1] Indeed, an important theme that has run throughout South Korean economic history has been the critical role of the state, its role in the generation of rents, and the politicization of the distribution of these rents. This political-economic tendency will be relevant when possible South Korean responses to developments in the North are analyzed later in this book.[2]

Economic policy during the Rhee presidency lacked any overarching rationale or coherence. Following the Korean War (and a similar reform in the North), a major land reform was carried out in the South in 1954. This led to productivity gains in the agricultural sector, but these were undermined by the government's policy of "three lows"—low grain prices, a low (i.e., overvalued) exchange rate, and low interest rates (Cho 1994). The results were misallocation of capital and recurrent balance of payments crises. The trade regime was characterized by considerable barriers, including an import licensing system and multiple exchange rates for different activities. These policies, together with an export-import-link

---

1. See Jones and SaKong (1980) and Woo (1991) for examples.

2. SaKong (1993) and Cho (1994) both provide excellent overviews of postwar South Korean economic development.

system, encouraged rent-seeking behavior and the development of giant conglomerates, or *chaebol*.[3] The maintenance of negative interest rates inhibited the development of the banking sector (which was permitted little freedom from government control) and encouraged the channeling of capital to large politically influential borrowers. As the prominent South Korean economist Cho Soon observed: "The most notable feature of the [South] Korean economy during the 1950s was its dependence on US economic aid" (Cho 1994, 13).

This assistance was not entirely without merit, however. It helped reconstruct the physical infrastructure, which had been devastated during the war. South Koreans were able to expand their skill base through cooperation with the United States. American aid directly contributed to the rapid expansion of education within South Korea and made overseas training and education possible for thousands of Koreans (Westphal et al. 1981), including some of its future economic policymakers. Some transfer of technical skills and management techniques undoubtedly occurred through close contact with US military forces, but its significance is difficult to assess. Likewise, local firms certainly benefited from participation in local military procurement programs and later from offshore procurement programs during the Vietnam War (Rhee 1994). In the 1950s, the human capital embodied in the South Korean labor force was quite high relative to its low level of per capita income.[4]

Economic Policy in the 1960s

The Rhee government collapsed in April 1960 and was replaced by a government under Chang Myon, who in turn was overthrown in a coup by General Park Chung-hee in 1961. Park had a clear view of modernization through extensive contact with Japanese and American educational and military institutions.[5] However, his seizure of power lacked popular legitimacy, so he turned to economic development as a means of mobilizing

---

3. Leff (1978) defines these as "a multi-company firm that transacts in different markets but which does so under common entrepreneurial or financial control." The family-dominated nature of these firms and their non-transparent financial practices distinguished the *chaebol* from contemporaneous Western conglomerates. Rather, they appear to be more like the prewar Japanese *zaibatsu*, with which they share a Chinese ideograph and with which South Korean leaders were well acquainted. One major difference, however, is that the *zaibatsu* were typically built around a bank, while the South Korean *chaebol* are dependent on state-dominated financial intermediaries.

4. Jones and SaKong (1980) observed that, while in 1961 South Korea was ranked sixtieth among seventy-four developing countries in terms of per capita income, it was ranked fourteenth according to a measure of socioeconomic development.

5. For a highly readable account of economic policy during the Park years, see Clifford (1997).

popular support and used the threat posed by the North as a justification for the ruthless pursuit of his goals.

After two years of poor economic performance, the government began a fundamental reversal of policy in 1963. The basic philosophy underlying the revised First Five Year Plan reflected a strong commitment to industrialization and an important role for the state in this process.[6] Exports were seized upon as a barometer of success. As one observer put it, "they were the only statistics that couldn't be faked." The government would set the basic economic development goals and would selectively intervene to ensure their attainment. Although most economic activity would still be carried out by private firms, the state would complement or replace them as needed. Export targets were formulated in considerable detail by product, market, and exporting firm.

The most important reforms were the unification of the exchange rate and the devaluation of the currency in 1964. At the same time, the government began to introduce a wide range of export promotion measures. A government-subsidized organization, the Korea Trade Promotion Corporation (KOTRA), was established to promote exports and to perform market research. Exporters were provided exemptions from duties on imported intermediates, tax incentives, preferential access to capital, special depreciation allowances on imported capital equipment, and a variety of non-pecuniary awards.[7] These policies and institutions paralleled those that had been implemented in Japan.

While the trade regime was being recast toward emphasis on exports, reforms were also implemented in other areas of economic policy. In 1963 the military government revised the labor laws to discourage the establishment of independent labor unions. Instead, it encouraged the organization of unions within a centralized system that was established

---

6. As with the prior Rhee and Chang regimes, state intervention was also used to generate funds to consolidate political power. As Clifford (1997) describes it, the economy that Park and his followers built was in essence a continuing criminal enterprise. Criminal gangs often force initiates to engage in some ritualistic criminal activity (such as a violent attack on a random passerby). The purpose is to create a shared bond of criminality, reciprocal obligation, and organizational cohesiveness built around each member's shared vulnerability to exposure to the authorities. South Koreans operated in an environment characterized by a plethora of infrequently enforced laws which, if actually followed, would make economic (and indeed normal) social life virtually impossible. The result was to induce virtually everyone to run afoul of at least some stricture, becoming, in principle at least, a criminal. This creates an enormously powerful mechanism for social control and produces correspondingly large incentives to conform to the wishes of the powerful. The result is the rule of men, not of law. It also lends itself to abuse of the legal system as an instrument for political retribution. Kirk (1999) contains a detailed account of politicized prosecutions during the 1990s.

7. These provisions were calculated on the basis of gross, rather than net, export volumes, and thus encouraged the importation of semi-finished products for assembly and reexport.

Figure 2.1 Financial development

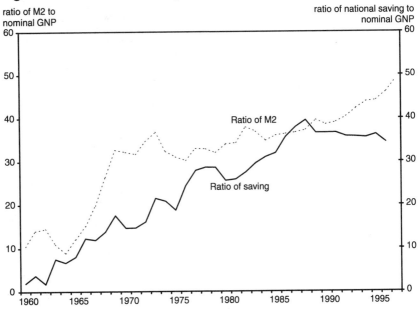

Sources: Bank of Korea; World Bank, *World Development Indicators*.

so as to facilitate government control. This system was tightened further in 1971 by legislation banning strikes, making virtually any form of collective bargaining or action illegal (Haggard 1990, Cho 1994).

The financial system still bore a strong imprint from the colonial period.[8] Financial reform began in 1965 when interest rates were raised, encouraging saving and financial deepening as well as more efficient use of capital. The national saving rate doubled in five years, and the ratio of M2 (a broad definition of the money supply) to GNP nearly tripled over the same period (figure 2.1).

This policy regime remained largely in place through the late 1960s and the Second Five Year Plan. There was an expansion of export promotion measures, including generous wastage allowances on duty-free imports and reduced prices for electricity and rail transport.[9] The export-import-link system allowed exporters to earn rents through the importation of restricted items. Overall, the trade regime could be characterized as modestly biased toward exports, with established industries receiving roughly

---

8. See Cargill (1999) for a comparison of the Japanese and South Korean financial systems.

9. The excess wastage allowances on duty-free imports for export production allowed export oriented firms to divert these duty-free inputs into the production of goods for local sale, to their competitive advantage in the domestic market.

neutral incentives, while a few infant industries were actively promoted (Westphal and Kim 1982).

Economic Policy in the 1970s

In 1972, President Park, who had been reelected for a third term, pushed through the repressive *Yushin* (Revitalization) constitution, which essentially made him president for life. This was followed in 1974 by the death of Park's wife, Yook Young-soo, who was killed in a botched assassination attempt on the President's life by a *Chochongryun* member. Park subsequently became increasingly withdrawn and, in the atmosphere of sycophancy that surrounded him, out of touch with South Korean reality. However, concerned with the threat from the North and unconvinced of the strength of the US military commitment to the preservation of the South, he launched a heavy and chemical industry (HCI) drive in an attempt to steer the composition of industrial output toward more engineering-intensive products. The aim was to upgrade South Korea's export profile and reduce reliance on imported arms. Opportunities for inefficiency, incompetence, cronyism, and corruption, which had always been present in the state-led model, now dramatically increased in scale. The government began attempting to orchestrate enormous capital-intensive projects, playing the *chaebol* off against each other while contending with the effects of the first Organization of Petroleum Exporting Countries (OPEC) oil shock. The result, not surprisingly, was a decline in macroeconomic performance.

The financial liberalization policy was reversed in 1972, when interest rates were lowered and direct government control of the banking system was increased in order to channel capital to preferred sectors, projects, or firms. The government had earlier implemented industrial promotion policies for selected industries, but in the 1970s these efforts were intensified. In order to finance large-scale projects, special public financial institutions were established, and private commercial banks were instructed to make loans to strategic projects on a preferential basis. By the late 1970s, the share of these "policy loans" had risen to 60 percent (Yoo 1994).[10] These loans carried, on average, negative real interest rates, and the annual interest subsidy grew from about 3 percent of GNP in 1962-71 to approximately 10 percent of GNP on average between 1972 and 1979 (Pyo 1989). The detrimental impact of credit rationing was moderated by short-term foreign capital inflows and the existence of a large curb market, which provided non-preferred customers with capital, albeit at high interest rates

---

10. The definition of "policy loans" is imprecise, and various sources report significantly different figures. See Cho (1994) for a discussion of this issue.

Figure 2.2   Real interest rates

percentages

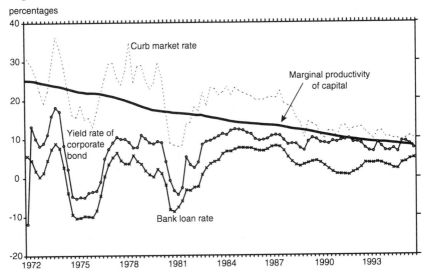

Source: Cho and Koh (1996).

(figure 2.2). Capital channeling policies were augmented by extensive tax incentives for the priority industries. It is estimated that the effect of the special tax measures was to reduce the marginal corporate tax rate from 50 percent to 20 percent for the targeted industries. These industries also received trade protection. As might be expected, allocative efficiency declined, and the marginal product of capital was lower in the favored sectors throughout the 1970s (Yoo 1994).

Although some of the more excessive incentive schemes were scaled down, export promotion remained a primary policy goal. Indicative export targets were reemphasized. Firms not achieving them were not subject to penalty, but the targets were sometimes negotiated jointly with wastage allowances. There is also some evidence that firms achieving their targeted goals could expect more favorable tax treatment (Westphal and Kim 1982).[11]

As a consequence of these credit, tax, and trade policies, Yoo estimates that during the late 1970s around 80 percent of fixed investment in the

---

11. The government also encouraged the establishment of general trading firms along Japanese lines, granting them special administrative and financial benefits and special allowances for foreign exchange. The notion was that these firms could capture scale economies in international information gathering and marketing and promote exports. In fact, the trading company share of exports did rise, exceeding 50 percent in the 1980s. Interestingly, these firms were almost exclusively *export* oriented. Unlike their Japanese counterparts, they did not intermediate large volumes of imports (Cho 1994).

Figure 2.3 Share of GDP due to top 10 *chaebol*

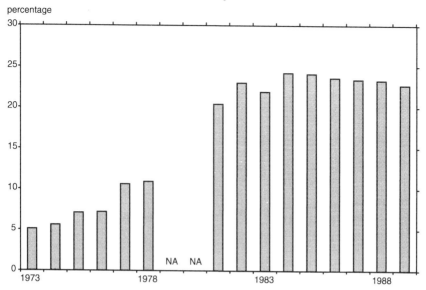

Source: SaKong 1993, table A.21.

manufacturing sector went to the favored heavy and chemical industries (Yoo 1994). During the first three years of the Fourth Five Year Plan (1977-81), investment in basic metals and chemicals was 130 percent and 121 percent, respectively, of the targets for the entire period, while textiles and other light industries received only 50 percent and 42 percent, respectively, of their planned investment (Balassa 1990).

These policies gave rise to serious moral hazard problems, as large *chaebol* could undertake ever larger investments, confident that the government would not permit large projects in priority sectors to fail. Statistics on the *chaebol* do not exist for the 1960s (because of lack of balance sheet data), but SaKong (1993) documents that the share of the top ten *chaebol* in South Korean GDP rose from 5 percent to 23 percent in the decade between 1973 and 1982 (figure 2.3). The system encouraged the *chaebol* to diversify by offsetting possible losses in some ventures with secure profits in others. As might be expected, allocative efficiency declined, and the marginal product of capital was lower in the favored sectors throughout the 1970s (Yoo 1994). Park and Kwon (1995) show that during the HCI drive the establishment of oligopolistic positions by the *chaebol* retarded technological change. Once scale economies were taken into account, total factor productivity (TFP), correctly measured, actually turned negative.

It is difficult to assess the welfare implications of the industrial promotion policies of the late 1970s, given the lack of counterfactual evidence on what would have occurred in their absence. Nonetheless, the fall of allocative efficiency and the relatively weak export performance of South Korea relative to similarly endowed economies have led even ardent proponents of the interventionist strategy (e.g., Pack and Westphal 1986) to conclude that the HCI policy was a failure. A more general evaluation of the selective intervention strategy concluded that in most cases the targeted sectors did not meet the criteria for successful intervention (Noland 1993a). There were also undesirable macroeconomic effects: The expansionary credit policy aggravated inflation, while low real interest rates encouraged disintermediation and stagnation of the financial sector. By 1978 the economy was overheating. In the following years, the economy was further rocked by the second oil shock. Export growth, which had begun to slow in 1978, actually turned negative in 1979. Social unrest began to increase, and in the fall of 1979 rioting occurred in Pusan and Masan—cities where rioting had preceded the fall of the Rhee government in April 1960—prompting the economic technocrats to formulate a stabilization plan.

Economic Policy under President Chun

The Park era came to a close on 26 October 1979 with his never fully explained assassination by Kim Jae-kyu, the head of the Korean Central Intelligence Agency, during what amounted to a palace coup. Over the course of the next year, a group of more junior military figures supplanted the generals of Park's generation, with General Chun Doo-hwan emerging as the authoritarian ruler. Given the condition of the economy at the end of the 1970s, economic technocrats were already attempting to introduce a stabilization policy and reverse the worst excesses of the HCI drive.[12] As the military men sorted themselves out, in January 1980 the economists initiated a textbook austerity plan.

Chun faced the same dilemma that Park had faced earlier: his rise to power lacked popular legitimacy (indeed, it had been accompanied by large scale violence, most notably in the city of Kwangju), and he needed prosperity to buy legitimacy. Park Chung-hee was brutal, but this was balanced by pragmatism and a strong sense of direction. The same could not be said about his successors. Chun Doo-hwan and his cronies more or less stumbled into power, driven more by intra-military rivalries and narrow career interests than by any real sense of where they wanted to take the country.[13] Facing deteriorating economic performance, which was

---

12. Yoo (1994) goes so far as to argue that the reversal of the heavy and chemical industries policy was the greatest policy achievement of the period.

13. See Clifford (1997), Gleysteen (1999), and Wickham (1999) for accounts of Chun's rise to power.

exacerbated by the second oil shock, Chun and his fellow officers turned to the technocrats to fix the economy and shore up their political legitimacy.[14] This group, led by Kim Jae-ik, director general of the Economic Planning Board's (EPB) planning bureau and later Presidential Secretary for Economic Affairs, implemented a policy of macroeconomic stabilization through which they began to liberalize and deregulate the South Korean economy. This policy shift was ratified in the Fifth Five Year Plan (1982-86), marking a movement away from interventionist strategy. The increases in trade protection that had accompanied the industrial promotion policies of the late 1970s were reversed. The government also undertook liberalization of the financial sector. Commercial banks were denationalized, but the state retained the right to appoint boards of directors and senior officers. There was, however, an easing of direct government control of banks and non-bank financial institutions. The share of "policy loans" in domestic credit was reduced from approximately 45 percent in the period 1974-82 to 35 percent in 1983-88. Commercial banks were required to extend at least 35 percent of their loans to small and medium-sized firms to compensate for the effects of the earlier policy. Interest rates were deregulated, resulting in renewed financial deepening as depicted in figure 2.1.

The nascent reform movement was dealt a tragic blow on 9 October 1983 when Kim Jae-ik and sixteen other South Koreans, including Deputy Prime Minister and EPB head So Sok-jun, Minister of Energy Suh Sang-chul, and Minister of Commerce and Industry Kim Dong-whie, were killed in Rangoon, Burma by North Korean commandos in a bombing aimed at Chun, who escaped unhurt. The predictable reaction in Seoul to the bombing and the Soviet downing of flight KAL007 in September 1983 was to hunker down. Though liberals within the government continued to press for change, the reform movement lost momentum. Without any overarching vision, corruption, present throughout the Park era, exploded.[15] Reformers continued to make progress in the trade and financial arenas, and in 1985 they attempted to rein in industrial policy interventions with the introduction of the Industrial Development Law (which replaced directed credits with research and development support as the

---

14. Chun literally scheduled early morning tutoring sessions. Perhaps there is something peculiarly Korean about this. It is hard to imagine the typical military dictator staying up late to study for his early morning economics lesson. See Clifford (1997) for details.

15. In the aftermath of the Rangoon bombing, the Chun government set up a foundation ostensibly to provide for the victims' families. As with previous governments, the private sector was used as a source of funding for political patronage. The Federation of Korean Industries estimated that quasi-taxes averaged between one half and one percent of sales during the administrations of Chun Doo-hwan and his successor Roh Tae-woo (Clifford 1997). Both were convicted on corruption charges during the presidency of Kim Young-sam, who later pardoned them—a decision that *his* successor, Kim Dae-jung, supported.

prime instrument of industrial policy) and the simultaneous repeal of selective intervention laws. Nevertheless, the government continued to intervene in the economy, restricting Samsung's entry into the automobile market, while rescuing *chaebol* heavily involved in shipbuilding, machinery, and other sectors of excessive investment (Leipziger and Petri 1993). Moreover, by 1986 the negative external shocks of the early 1980s had been reversed, and the South Korean economy received a boost in the form of the "three blessings"—the fall in the oil price, the fall in world interest rates, and the appreciation of the Japanese yen. As the economy again boomed, the enthusiasm for reform, never great, slackened.

The Democracy Pledge and Twenty-five Years of Development

Rising expectations politically and economically circumscribed Chun's room to maneuver. Ironically, the groundbreaking for authoritarian rule's grave had occurred in October 1979, when, during the closing days of the Park regime, Seoul Mayor and Park appointee Chung Sang-chon announced that the city would enter the competition to host the 1988 Summer Olympics. With national prestige on the line and his own legitimacy in question, Chun could hardly back away from Park's commitment. The organizing committee, led by Hyundai founder Chung Ju Yung, proceeded to apply itself to the task of winning the bid with a single-mindedness that would be a model for years to come. When the International Olympic Committee (IOC) voted in September 1981, Seoul won.

The securing of the 1988 Olympic bid had two implications. First, as surely was foreseen in 1979, it necessitated a further upgrading of Seoul's infrastructure, essentially raising it to developed country level. The second impact was perhaps more profound, and surely unforeseen: Hosting the Olympics made it effectively impossible for Chun to use his usual repressive tactics to handle social discontent. In 1987, with the Seoul Games only a little more than year away, rioting interrupted a number of sporting events. There was talk in the IOC of moving the games elsewhere.

Chun was already in trouble domestically. The world spotlight severely limited his options. His response was to call an election and introduce constitutional changes which essentially tilted the rules in favor of his long-time confidant and hand-picked successor, General Roh Tae-woo. The election of Roh would presumably reduce the building social pressures while allowing the highly unpopular Chun to live out his post-leadership life in relative peace. However, rather than acting as a safety valve, Roh's 29 June 1987 democratization pledge signaled a shift toward more permissive government and revealed a reticence on the part of the authorities to crack down due to international scrutiny associated with the upcoming Olympic Games. This gave rise to an unprecedented upsurge in

Figure 2.4   Purchasing power adjusted real GDP per capita

US dollars (constant 1985
international prices)

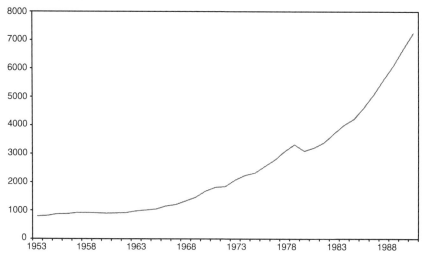

Source: Summers and Heston 1991.

social mobilization. In December 1987, Roh prevailed in a three-way contest against two longtime opposition civilian politicians, the more conservative Kim Young-sam and the more liberal Kim Dae-jung, and assumed the presidency in time to host the Olympic Games. From the Roh administration forward, economic policymaking in South Korea would be subject to far greater popular demands and scrutiny.

In this respect, the 29 June 1987 democratization pledge represented a watershed in South Korean economic history. What is undeniable is that, in the quarter century following the 1963 reforms, the South Korean economy had undergone a tremendous transformation. Real per capita income growth averaged 7 percent a year, and the level of per capita income more than quintupled (figure 2.4). The share of agriculture in the economy fell from more than 45 percent in 1964 to just over 10 percent in 1988, offset by the rise in manufacturing (which doubled its share of output over this period) and, to a lesser degree, services (figure 2.5). The share of exports in GDP increased from less than 5 percent in 1963 to more than 35 percent in 1988 (figure 2.6). Imports rose by a similar amount. The figures document a dramatic opening of the South Korean economy.

The question naturally arises as to what explains this performance. As noted earlier, South Korea in 1963 surely had a far higher level of human capital than suggested by the level of per capita income, and human capital accumulation, at least in part, had been financed by relatively

Figure 2.5   Structure of output

percentage of GDP

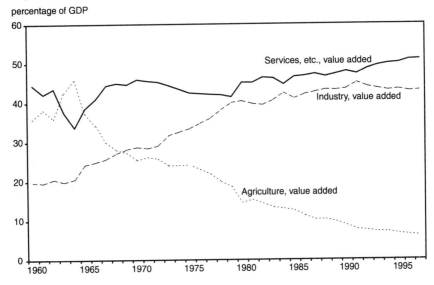

Source: World Bank, *World Development Indicators.*

Figure 2.6   Exports and imports as a share of nominal GNP

percentage

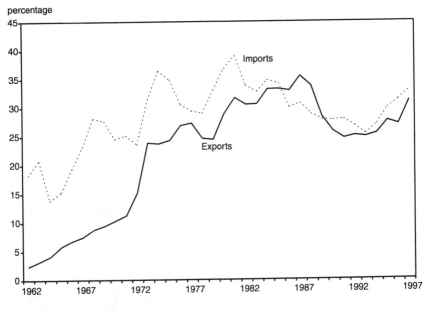

Source: Bank of Korea.

generous American aid.[16] In Park Chung-hee, South Korea had a leader with clear ideas of what he wanted to accomplish in terms of economic development and military preparedness. The institutional structures that Park created facilitated achievement of goals established by the government without a lot of expenditure on direct inducements or enforcement. The country was also blessed with a thin layer of highly competent technocrats, many of whom had been educated in Japan or the United States. (The importance of sheer competence at the top cannot be overemphasized. South Korea was lucky to have a small but enormously important cadre of decision makers who had some understanding of how a modern society was supposed to work—policymakers who through exposure to educational opportunities abroad had some notion of where they were heading and how to get there—an advantage that many other contemporaneously developing countries simply did not have.) Although there were considerable disagreements over policy (often between the US-educated economists on one side and Park and his fellow officers on the other), one gets the impression that these were disagreements over strategies to attain shared development goals—not fundamental differences about modernization.

The emphasis on exports was key because it offset two inherent dangers in the South Korean economy: the inability to exploit scale economies or technological development in a small, poor, domestic market and the inherent tendency for firms to build up anticompetitive positions in a small market. By emphasizing the world market over the domestic market, South Korean policy facilitated the exploitation of scale economies and the production of goods that might not have even had a domestic market (color televisions in the 1970s, for example). The world market also provided an incontrovertible yardstick by which success could be measured. Although firms might be able to exploit market power or political connections domestically, they would have a much greater difficulty doing this on the world stage.

The country then needed institutional mechanisms for transforming the latent productive potential of the economy into goods that the rest of the world wanted to buy.[17] Foreign direct investment (FDI) does not appear to have been very important in this regard. Until the late 1970s, South Korean policy effectively discouraged foreign direct investment by imposing minority ownership requirements, requiring technology transfers (in the absence of any intellectual property rights enforcement), and

---

16. Tuition-free primary education was made compulsory in 1949, and within a decade 96 percent of South Korean children were enrolled (Y. Lim 1999). During this period, the government devoted around three-quarters of its education budget to primary education. This had a low foreign exchange content. Aid was useful in financing higher education and study abroad, as well as acting as overall balance of payments support.

17. See SaKong (1993) for an overview of these issues.

imposing strict export performance requirements (SaKong 1993). Not surprisingly, most foreign investment in South Korea took the form of commercial loans, not direct investment. Even if it were assumed that all FDI went into the manufacturing sector, it would have accounted for less than 5 percent of the manufacturing capital stock in 1970 (Westphal and Kim 1982). Indeed, FDI flows into South Korea were small relative to those experienced by other developing countries such as Brazil, Mexico, and Taiwan, and there does not appear to be any strong correlation between sectors that attracted FDI and those that enjoyed subsequent export success.[18] Looking at detailed microeconomic data, Baily and Zitzewitz (1998) argue that the restrictions on FDI retarded technological development in South Korea, though they admit that the South Koreans achieved technological mastery in sectors in which comparators such as Brazil did not.

Similarly, the evidence on the importance of technological licensing in spurring exports is mixed (Westphal et al. 1981). Subcontracting unrelated to foreign direct investment and contact with foreign trading companies may have been of greater importance.[19] Rhee et al. (1984) reports surveys done in the 1970s indicating that capital goods suppliers and buyers of output were leading sources of technology transfer. With respect to the former, Westphal, Kim, and Dahlman (1985) report that South Koreans developed a considerable amount of technical competence through contact with capital goods suppliers, including the training of engineers abroad. Likewise, Westphal et al. (1981) gives several examples of foreign buyers assisting South Korean exporters with product design and process technology.

It is apparent that, through whatever channels, the South Koreans attained a certain level of technological and managerial competence that provided the basis for the exploitation of international trade opportunities. Government policy attempted to develop this base through a variety of supportive measures. Starting in the mid-1960s, potential exporters were granted access to inputs at world market prices and to trade finance through the previously described mechanisms, which were administered in a relatively non-discretionary and automatic way. Free trade zones, introduced in the 1970s, appear to have been of little importance, generating a de minimis share of exports. Bonded warehouses were of somewhat greater importance, accounting for roughly 10 percent of trade (Rhee 1994). The exchange rate was kept competitive, if not artificially underval-

---

18. Kim and Hwang (1998), who looked at more recent experiences in the semiconductor and pharmaceutical industries, ascribe a considerable role to FDI in technology transfer.

19. Although South Korean trading firms eventually came to intermediate more than half of South Korean exports, these were not established until 1975. Thus it is hard to argue that they facilitated exports in the early part of the export boom.

ued. South Korea also benefited from the rapid growth of world markets during the postwar period.

The resultant changes in the composition of trade were astounding. In 1963, non-fuel primary products accounted for fully half of South Korea's total exports, and the third largest export item was human hair wigs. Twenty-five years later primary product exports had fallen to 5 percent. Engineering products, which had made up only 5 percent of South Korea's exports in 1963, were more than 40 percent a quarter century later. Products such as motor vehicles, which were not even manufactured in 1963, were major export earners a generation later (Noland 1991a).

Once the economy was able to access world demand, it took off. Kim and Roemer (1979) estimate that total factor productivity increased 4 percent annually between 1960 and 1973, with 1.6 percentage points of this explained by human capital accumulation and the remaining 2.4 percentage points a pure productivity increase. Looking at a slightly longer and more recent sample period, Kwon (1986) similarly concludes that total factor productivity averaged 3 percent a year in the two decades from 1961 to 1980. Of this, 45 percent could be attributed to technological change, 38 percent to scale economies, and 17 percent to increased capital utilization. Baily and Zitzewitz (1998) estimate that TFP growth (unadjusted for changes in human capital or labor force quality) exceeded 3 percent annually in the 1980s. Across industries, this pattern of technological advance was correlated with success in global markets (Dollar and Sokoloff 1990). Indeed, Nam (1999) argues that access to world markets and avoidance of the domestic demand constraint causally explains TFP growth.

However, Kwack (1999), while obtaining the standard result of 3 percent TFP growth through the 1970s and 1980s, calculated that TFP growth began to slow around 1990, falling below one percent a year.[20] Moreover, he argues that this adversely affected export competitiveness and profit margins, ultimately contributing to problems the financial sector. We return to this issue in chapter 6.

Precrisis Economic Policy, 1987 to 1997

The Roh government and the successor government of Kim Young-sam continued a gradual process of liberalization both internally and externally. Internally, the focus was on product, labor, and financial markets, the latter also having an important external dimension. Trade and financial policies were the keys to South Korea's interaction with the rest of the world.

---

20. See this source for citations of additional estimates of Korean TFP growth.

Product Market Policy

The distinguishing feature of South Korean product markets has been the prominence of the *chaebol*. In positive terms, such organizations might be considered an institutional response to conditions of scarce managerial or human capital and limited financial markets. This organizational form could also have been derived from rent-seeking behavior generated through state intervention in the economy, and a number of the *chaebol* had originated from business-government relations during the Rhee regime of the 1950s.[21]

The *chaebol* really took off under Park, however, especially during the HCI drive of the 1970s (figure 2.3). Park's growth-oriented policy, pervasive regulations creating entry barriers (and thus protecting incumbents from competition), and penchant for sole-sourcing important infrastructural and other large-scale government supported projects in effect socialized risk and created opportunities for cross subsidization across different business ventures. This facilitated the *chaebol* tendency to enter otherwise unrelated lines of business.[22] Under Park, the number of subsidiaries of the top thirty *chaebol* grew from 126 in 1970 to 429 in 1979, indicating that diversification had been driven by growth. Just prior to the crisis, in July 1997, the largest five *chaebol* had on average 52 subsidiaries spread across 30 industries, a truly extraordinary degree of diversification (Yoo 1999, table 5).[23]

The government-business symbiosis had implications for finance, economic efficiency, and social equity. On the financial side, the development strategy of administrative guidance required state domination of the financial sector. The strategy required an emphasis on indirect finance, limitations on foreign participation in financial markets, and domestic firm access to foreign finance. If the government was going to channel capital, it had to limit capital markets to institutions that could be dominated if not controlled, and it had to limit the firms' financing options to those institutions. Presumptively less compliant foreign banks could not be allowed into the market in any significant way, for, if they were allowed to establish a significant presence, they would undermine the domestic banks operating under the burdens of "policy lending." Thus the financial

---

21. See Jones and SaKong (1980).

22. A study done by the Korea Fair Trade Commission (KFTC) in the late 1980s found that in nearly all 89 industries surveyed, incumbents were protected by some kind of governmentally created barrier to entry (Graham 1996). Cho (1994) argues that the establishment of government supported firms in upstream industries inevitably led to the creation of vertically integrated firms. He contrasts the South Korean experience with Taiwan's, where upstream industries were encouraged through publicly owned, not privately owned, firms.

23. The figures are not much different if the broader sample of the top 30 *chaebol* are considered; they averaged 27 subsidiaries spread across 20 sectors.

system had to be built around a relatively small number of South Korean financial intermediaries, and corporate finance had to be largely limited to borrowing from those intermediaries.

There were multiple implications of these policies. First, the firms emphasized growth, not profitability, since risk was socialized and increased borrowing made further borrowing advantageous under the "too big to fail" notion promoted by the government's routine interventions. From the standpoint of a lender, the bigger the firm the more credit-worthy the firm, since size increased the likelihood that the government would intervene in the event that the firm got into financial trouble (which the government did on a fairly routine basis, especially in the late 1960s and early 1970s).[24] The implication was that firms became extraordinarily leveraged as growth became the name of the game. Loans were the mechanism for growth, and, paradoxically, debt signaled credit-worthiness, a state of affairs that S.M. Yoo (1999) described as "survival of the fattest."[25] E.H. Kim (1990), in a study of corporate finance covering the decade 1977-86, found that "the largest firms have the weakest financial structure" as measured by the degree of equity in their capital structures (342). A corollary to this system of corporate financing was the encouragement of extensive cross-shareholding, cross-loan guarantees, and non-transparency, all of which served to facilitate borrowing. In July 1997, just prior to the crisis, the average debt-equity ratio of the thirty largest *chaebol* exceeded 400 percent (Yoo 1999, table 9).[26] The pattern of cross-finance is particularly pernicious as it sets up a set of private incentives for inside shareholders that are socially suboptimal and indeed disadvantageous to outside shareholders (S.M. Yoo 1999).

Given the self-reinforcing nature of the system, it is unsurprising that, over time, the favored conglomerates accounted for a growing share of national output and borrowing. As SaKong (1993) documents, the *chaebol* accounted for a steadily rising share of national output from the early 1970s to the mid 1980s. Moreover, the increase in share was positively associated with *chaebol* size. The share of national output accounted for by the top five *chaebol* grew more rapidly than the top ten's share did, which in turn grew more rapidly than the top 30's share. On average, the ten largest *chaebol* grew 28 percent a year during the 1970s. Hyundai, generally the largest in the late 1970s and 1980s, grew at 38 percent

---

24. See E.H. Kim (1990), Cho (1994), and E.M Kim (1997).

25. As E.H. Kim (1990) documents, this was reinforced by the tax code. Corporate interest payments are tax deductible, while dividends to shareholders are not. This reduces the after tax cost of debt relative to equity for the corporation. Likewise, the personal income tax code encourages the holding of debt instruments, since interest earnings are taxed more lightly than dividend earnings.

26. By the end of 1997, it stood at 500 percent, and 600 percent if the debt of subsidiaries were included on a consolidated basis (Claessens, Ghosh, and Scott 1999).

annually, while Daewoo, the youngest of the top five *chaebol* (founded in 1967), grew an astonishing 54 percent annually during this period (E.M. Kim 1997).[27] At the time of Daewoo's collapse in 1999, it alone reportedly accounted for 5 percent of South Korean GDP.

Economic policymakers were not unconcerned by this pattern of developments, and they responded by attempting to limit *chaebol* access to bank lending, to restrain their anticompetitive tendencies, and to encourage the growth of small and medium-size enterprises (SMEs). None of these attempts can be regarded as particularly successful.

In 1974, the government issued an emergency decree to attempt to limit *chaebol* access to bank finance and to encourage direct finance through capital markets. Later that year, the government adopted the Prime Bank System, reminiscent of the Japanese main bank system, in which the largest lender was given the responsibility of monitoring business performance and borrowing from all sources. In theory, the *chaebol* were supposed to get prime bank permission when they purchased real estate or entered new lines of business and were to sell off unused land holdings or issue new shares to obtain permission. In reality, these rules did little to constrain *chaebol* behavior.[28]

In 1984, the government moved to strengthen this regime by temporarily freezing bank credits to the top five *chaebol* and setting credit ceilings for the top thirty. As a result, over the next several years their share of borrowing dropped considerably. This was offset, however, by increased borrowing from non-bank financial intermediaries, with the share of non-bank borrowing by the top 30 *chaebol* reaching 45 percent by 1991 (SaKong 1993). In 1986, as part of its overhaul of competition policies, the government introduced new rules to limit cross-investment and cross-shareholding. The rules would also prevent the *chaebol* from creating new businesses and from inflating their capital base without actually increasing their equity base. The government further restricted the *chaebol* by introducing ceilings on the amount of equity investments that the top 30 could make in other firms and the amount of mutual debt guarantees that could be undertaken.

Despite these attempts to rein in the financial practices of the largest *chaebol*, these firms continued to expand to the point where their financial practices posed a systemic risk to the domestic financial system. Indeed, the *chaebol* share of bank lending actually increased in the aftermath of the financial crisis, as risk-averse bankers, faced with considerable

---

27. It should be noted that success is not guaranteed. There have been considerable changes in the size rankings of *chaebol* over time. See E.M. Kim (1997), table 4.1 for some evidence of this. However, prior to the collapse of Hanbo in January 1997, only one major *chaebol*, Kukje, had been allowed to fail (in 1985), and even then the government-led restructuring imposed no real burden on its creditors.

28. See Jwa and Huh (1998) for an analysis of the prime bank system.

uncertainty about South Korea's economic future, increased lending to the *chaebol* under the "too big to fail" theory. The effect can be seen in the travails of Daewoo, which, allowed to go bankrupt, reportedly doubled the amount of non-performing loans in the already weak South Korean banking system (to be discussed in greater detail in chapter 6). Indeed, as Leipziger (1988) presciently put it, "Korea had no satisfactory 'exit policy' and no institutions capable of managing it" (124).[29] The real defect in the *chaebol* system has been the lack of capital market discipline in the market for corporate control and ultimately the absence of an exit mechanism in the form of effective bankruptcy procedures.[30]

The growth of the *chaebol* had efficiency implications as well. Their dominance of a wide variety of products and sectors created anticompetitive possibilities, including mutual forbearance, reciprocal dealings, and other restraints on competition based on intra-group transactions of products, services, and financial resources. Park and Kwon (1995) show that the growth of the *chaebol* reduced competition in product markets, increasing markups and slowing technological change. According to the Korea Fair Trade Commission, 326 firms in 140 markets were designated in 1996 as "market-dominating" based on a criterion of market size and market share.[31] Moreover, considerable regulatory authority is granted formally or informally in South Korea, and investigation of the industry associations by the Korean government found a majority engaged in anticompetitive practices.[32]

Over the years, the government has attempted a number of policies to spur competition. Competition policy got its start in 1975 when the

---

29. The sad and disturbing thing about Leipziger's (1988) analysis of industrial restructuring is that it could have been written a decade later—nothing really changed.

30. As observed by the OECD (1999), the precrisis bankruptcy process was cumbersome and prone to abuse by delinquent firms. As an indicator of this, more than half the reorganization cases completed between 1993 and 1995 had been filed more than five years earlier, and less than a quarter of the firms had successfully emerged from reorganization. As a consequence, lenders often preferred to reschedule debt rather than going through the relatively ineffective legal procedure.

31. "Market dominance" is deemed to exist in markets of more than 50 billion won when the largest firm's share is greater than 50 percent or the top three firms' share is greater than 75 percent, when any firm with less than a 10 percent share is excluded from the calculation. It should be noted that "market-dominating" firms are not limited to the *chaebol*, and, in one recent year the top 30 *chaebol* accounted for less than half of the turnover in these highly concentrated markets (OECD 1996).

32. In 1994 South Korean authorities investigated 68 industry associations and found that 48 of the associations had been engaging in anticompetitive or unfair practices. The following year Korean authorities investigated 218 industry associations and ordered them to revise 369 anticompetitive or unfair measures or practices. In 1996, the Korean government announced that it would begin regulating not only collusion among rival firms, but among trade associations as well (USTR 1999).

government enacted the Price Stabilization and Fair Trade Act. This was introduced not to improve competition *per se*, but rather to limit the inflationary consequences of anticompetitive behavior (Leipziger and Petri 1993). Unfair trading practices were defined in terms of price movements rather than in terms of anticompetitive behaviors. The regime was strengthened in 1980 with the Antitrust Act, which outlawed a number of horizontal restrictions on trade (such as the formation of cartels) as well as vertical restraints on trade (such as retail price maintenance) and established the Korea Fair Trade Commission (KFTC) as an enforcement agency (a task it shares with the Antitrust Division of the Korean Department of Justice). In 1986, competition policy was further strengthened with rules designed to limit economic concentration by restricting intercompany ownership, and, for the first time, anticompetitive mergers by business groups.

Until 1994, however, the KFTC was under the authority of the Economic Planning Board (EPB), and competition policy concerns were subordinated to other economic policy goals. Graham (1996) argues that attempts to impose competition policy restraints on the *chaebol* were routinely undercut by industrial policy proponents who successfully inserted numerous exceptions into competition policy legislation. As one observer put it, "the laws had many loopholes," and KFTC enforcement proved toothless.[33]

The law was amended in 1986 and in 1994, when the Korea Fair Trade Commission (KFTC) became a legally independent regulatory body reporting to the Prime Minister. Its fortunes received another boost with the election of Kim Dae-jung. A revised Fair Trade Act passed the National Assembly in 1999 in the wake of the financial crisis. It is hoped that this will rejuvenate the KFTC, which has been generally regarded as lax in its enforcement of existing law. Since the crisis, the KFTC has stepped up its initiation of cases involving abuse of market power, collusive activities, trade association activities, unfair trade practices, and unfair subcontracting practices (Leipziger 1999, table 4).[34]

The government has repeatedly tried to get the *chaebol* to specialize in core competencies and to spin off some of their far-flung subsidiaries.[35] "Specialization policy" was introduced in 1991, strengthened in 1993 and 1995, and received a further boost with the financial crisis in 1998.[36] Yet

---

33. The June 1996 conviction of three senior KFTC officials for accepting bribes in return for favors did not strengthen the agency's image.

34. For example, the KFTC launched an extensive probe of 62 companies for unfair dealings with subcontractors in October 1999.

35. See K. Kim (1999).

36. According to the KFTC, through the first 18 months of the crisis the market seemed to be accomplishing what the government could not: The top five *chaebol* launched 451 new

the government's attempts to prune the *chaebol* have largely failed.[37] Perversely, the attempt to orchestrate the so-called "big deals" business swaps in response to the crisis would have the effect of further concentrating particular firms' dominance of certain sectors; Hyundai dominance in trucks is a case in point.[38] Likewise, beginning in the mid-1970s, the government introduced various measures to promote small and medium-sized enterprises, but these have not been particularly successful.[39]

The third implication of *chaebol* growth was political in a broad sense. The tight relationship between business and the state contributed to the perception that political connections (if not outright corruption) were the key to business success—not intrinsic competence. This was particularly true since the emphasis on bank finance, combined with the policy loans, interest rate ceilings (which existed until 1988), and administrative guidance (which continued thereafter) created excess demand for loans and credit rationing. Given the state dominance over the banking system, credit was in part allocated on the basis of personal and political connections, as well as outright bribery. This delegitimated the accomplishments of the *chaebol* (especially given the lack of popular legitimacy of their government counterparts). This surely has contributed to the sense of popular alienation and disaffection that has bedeviled South Korean industrial labor relations as discussed in the section on labor market policy that follows.

Labor Market Policy

During its period of rapid industrialization, South Korea experienced a rapid shift out of rural employment into manufacturing and services. Accompanying this was a rise in recorded female labor force participation.

---

firms through separation, with another 33 launched by *chaebol* ranked below the top five (*Korea Times*, 20 October 1999).

37. Leipziger and Petri (1993) discuss two interesting examples of this phenomenon. In 1989, the government became concerned that the *chaebol* were soaking up an excessive share of bank lending for speculation in the real estate market, exploiting their access to subsidized capital. Ultimately, the government bought their "excess land holdings" at "handsome prices." In 1991, having imposed a ceiling on *chaebol* access to subsidized bank loans, under the pressure of deteriorating economic conditions the government tried to increase the amount of credit available for productive investment by allowing each *chaebol* to exempt three "core sectors" from the ceiling. Not surprisingly, the *chaebol* selected their most capital-intensive sectors, leading to rapid increases in investments in petrochemicals and semiconductor fabrication.

38. USTR (1999) reports that US industries, including semiconductor and telecommunications firms, have raised concerns about precisely this anticompetitive impact of the "big deals."

39. Similarly, Graham (1996) cites another perverse case in which restrictions on *chaebol* entry into new sectors actually gave rise to monopolies.

Hours worked were quite long, and few envied South Korea's safety record. Yet South Korea appeared to achieve "growth with equity." Measured wage inequality was low by international standards, as might be expected in the case of an industrializing labor-abundant country rapidly increasing its exposure to international trade, though there is some reason to question the South Korean government statistics on this point (cf. Lindauer 1997).[40] In certain respects, South Korean labor markets developed a dualistic structure in which the industrial employees of the major *chaebol* occupied a privileged position relative to similarly skilled workers (i.e., they were able to capture some of the rents accruing to the *chaebol*).[41] Characterization of South Korean labor market rigidity has typically been focused on this part of the labor force, though at the macroeconomic level the South Korean labor market has been relatively flexible in terms of wage-setting compared to other OECD countries (Jeong 1997), and nowadays the frequency of turnover is reasonably high relative to OECD countries (D.G. Shin 1999). During the Rhee government, South Korea copied its early (and largely inappropriate and ignored) labor laws from those of developed countries. In the early 1960s, the Park regime enacted a series of changes that circumscribed union activities. As noted earlier, independent trade unions were effectively banned in 1971. The Korean labor movement subsequently developed a dualistic structure, with government-approved unions on the one hand and informal or underground unions on the other. Although the labor laws were revised in the early 1980s, the reforms did not adequately address this situation. "Third parties" were prohibited from intervening in labor disputes (some of the unofficial unions had grown out of religious organizations, and student radical groups were sometimes interested in inserting themselves into enterprise disputes). Industrial unions were reorganized along Japanese lines as company unions to discourage strikes. Union-shop clauses were abolished. The minimum number of workers required to organize a union was increased. Consequently, the official unionization rate fell from 20 percent of the labor force in 1980 to less than 16 percent in 1985 as these provisions took hold and workers became increasingly disaffected with the officially approved unions (figure 2.7). The labor laws underwent further revisions in 1986 and 1987, partially liberalizing unionization in the context of political democratization, but, after an uptick in the late 1980s, membership has continued to decline to the point that a smaller share of the South Korean labor force is unionized than is the case in the United States.

Roh's 29 June 1987 announcement of political liberalization set off an explosion of repressed labor discontent. South Korea experienced more

---

40. For analyses of broader labor market issues such as safety, gender roles, rural-urban migration, and income distribution not covered in this section, see C.S. Kim (1990), J.G. Yoo (1990), B.S. Lee (1994), Lee and Lindauer (1997), and Kim and Son (1997).

41. See Park (1999) for a nice discussion of labor market dualism.

Figure 2.7   Unionized workers and labor disputes

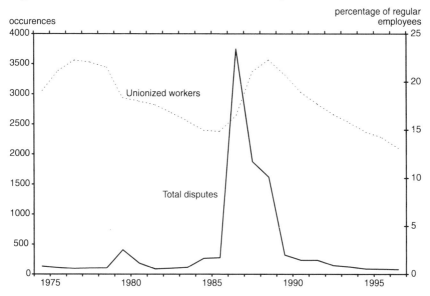

Sources: South Korean Ministry of Labor; National Statistical Office Database.

strikes in July and August 1987 than in the previous 25 years combined. Nearly 70 percent of manufacturing establishments with ten or more employees experienced some kind of labor dispute in the second half of 1987. The number of labor-management disputes surged from 276 in 1986 to 3,749 in 1987 before falling to 1,873 in 1988, to 1,616 in 1989, and back to the levels of a decade earlier by 1990 (figure 2.7).

Resolution of these disputes was impeded by the coexistence of *de jure* and *de facto* unions, and by the reluctance of public officials to enforce the highly unpopular laws on the books. The government's effective withdrawal from any attempt to guide the labor market outcomes left firms and workers to settle disputes without the benefit of a clear legal or institutional framework. Accordingly, various legal and extralegal means were used to settle disputes, sometimes causing the spread of conflict and distrust.[42] The problems were exacerbated by the fact that many of the disputes involved oligopolistic *chaebol*. The negotiations could be likened to those between bilateral monopolists, and thus involved the disposition of potentially enormous economic rents. Moreover, labor's fundamental dissatisfaction with existing aspects of industrial relations meant that union demands were far-ranging, calling not only for wage increases, but union autonomy, fair labor practices and legal reforms, and

---

42. See Cho (1994), Clifford (1997), and Vogel and Lindauer (1997) for examples.

liberalization of a management style characterized by one observer as "authoritarian paternalism" (Park 1990). The high stakes, the broad diversification of the *chaebol* (which obscured the relationship between the economic vitality of an individual enterprise and that of the firm as a whole), and the inexperience of the negotiators on both sides were all factors that contributed to difficulties in resolving these disputes. Passion was fed by an abiding sense of grievance. Some observers linked this to the rapid increase in wealth inequality and relative deprivation of the working class that occurred in the 1980s (Vogel and Lindauer 1997).[43]

By 1990 this turmoil had burned itself out, and the level of disputes had returned to their historical levels. However, the labor law revisions undertaken by the Roh government in the wake of this unrest left a number of contentious issues unresolved. At the national level, only one organization, the Federation of Korean Trade Unions (FKTU) formed under the Park regime, was recognized, despite the fact that the Korean Confederation of Trade Unions (KCTU), heir to the "unofficial" or "democratic" unions of the 1980s, boasted 1.5 million members and significant influence in some of South Korea's largest enterprise unions.[44] "Third parties" (including the KCTU) were still restricted from intervening in labor disputes, and industrial unions were restricted in their ability to take part in the activities of company unions. Teachers and most government employees were prohibited from organizing, and the definition of "essential service" workers who were prohibited from striking was relatively broad. Lastly, unions were prohibited from engaging in political activities. At the same time, employers regarded restrictions on layoffs and dismissals as impediments to economic restructuring and efficiency. (The restrictions on layoffs were justified by the lack of a state-provided social safety net. While this institutional arrangement was acceptable during periods of rapid growth, the privatization of the social safety net was more onerous in downturns. Moreover, it could actually work against the interests of workers. As Stiglitz (1999) points out, in a life-time employment system the labor market may interpret separation from a current employer as a signal of an individual's poor quality.)

Aspects of South Korean labor law were incompatible with the conventions of the International Labor Organization, which South Korea joined

---

43. As Lindauer (1997) observes, during the 1970s and 1980s, there was a considerable increase in the concentration of wealth, due largely to capital gains on land ownership. Between 1974 and 1989 land values appreciated at an estimated rate that was three times as fast as GNP, and in some years capital gains exceeded total GNP growth. These increases in wealth were enormous and were concentrated in a few hands—in 1988 the top one percent of the income distribution owned 44 percent of the total land value; the top 10 percent owned 77 percent of the land.

44. The KCTU was not granted formal legal status until November 1999, ending the FKTU's official monopoly on the trade union movement.

in 1991. In 1995 a presidential commission was appointed to review labor practices, and, in late 1996, the government unveiled a new set of labor law revisions. South Korean practices were also inadequate from the standpoint of the Organization of Economic Cooperation and Development (OECD), which the Kim Young-sam government wished to join. In 1995, a presidential commission was appointed to review labor practices, and the government unveiled a new set of labor law revisions in late 1996. These highly controversial revisions ran into significant opposition in the National Assembly, however. The ruling New Korea Party attempted to justify certain provisions of the legislation as required for OECD membership, though this was not the case. On 26 December 1996, the ruling party was reduced to calling a surreptitious dawn quorum of the National Assembly to pass the legislation without objection by the absent opposition Assembly members. After a nationwide strike ensued, the revision of the labor laws was canceled (Young 1997). This uneasy peace continued until the financial crisis forced further revisions in labor laws (as discussed in chapter 6).

Trade Policy

The domestic economy interacts with the world economy through the channels of international trade and finance. As the financial reforms in South Korea had an important international dimension, and international capital movements played an important role in the financial crisis, we will first discuss first trade and then finance in the following section.

Historically, the South Korean economy has been characterized by pervasive regulation, non-transparency of implementation, and rent seeking. Unsurprisingly, foreign firms have often found it difficult to penetrate this market. The metaphor "peeling an onion" has been used to describe the process of stripping away the layers of legal and bureaucratic impediments to access. Nevertheless, over the past two decades considerable progress has been made in liberalizing international trade.

Border Measures

The Sixth Five Year Plan (1987-91) reinforced the existing trend toward liberalization, which was given additional pressure from the United States and the successful conclusion of the Uruguay Round of global trade talks in 1993. In 1980, the average tariff was 24.9 percent, and nearly one-third of imported products were under some sort of quantitative restriction. By 1993, the import-weighted average tariff had fallen to 10.6 percent, and less than 2 percent of imported products were subject to quantitative restriction (PECC 1995, table A.3). As an outcome of the Uruguay Round negotiations, average tariff rates in the manufacturing sector were reduced to levels only slightly higher than those imposed by developed countries

Table 2.1 South Korean tariff rates (percent)

Sector	Pre-Uruguay Round	Post-Uruguay Round
Metal mining	2.05	2.05
Coal mining	9.21	2.79
Oil and gas extraction	10.71	10.79
Stone and other nonmetallic minerals	3.92	2.29
Food and other kindred products	14.76	8.98
Tobacco products	100.00	65.50
Textile mill products	27.64	18.05
Apparel products	29.48	19.05
Lumber and wood products	8.25	6.85
Furniture and fixtures	26.21	8.58
Paper and allied products	11.40	0.24
Printing and publishing	4.40	0.14
Chemicals and allied products	18.34	6.73
Petroleum and coal products	8.69	5.67
Rubber and miscellaneous products	27.88	9.15
Leather and leather products	22.09	10.40
Stone, clay, and glass products	25.29	12.50
Primary metal industries	16.61	7.71
Fabricated metal products	22.69	11.42
Industrial machinery	18.26	11.85
Electrical machinery	20.33	6.79
Transportation equipment	4.21	3.31
Instruments and related products	20.02	9.08
Miscellaneous manufactures	27.74	8.66
Total	16.29	7.71

Note: Data organized by Standard Industrial Classification (SIC).

Source: USTR.

(table 2.1).[45] Accompanying the tariff cuts were reductions in quantitative barriers. Outside of agriculture, the percentage of product categories covered by quantitative import restrictions is virtually nil (APEC 1995). South Korea also lowered, by as much as 30 percent, special luxury taxes that had the effect of repressing imports, though special taxes on problematic items such as automobiles remain.

---

45. Yoo (1993) has analyzed the determinants of South Korean protection. While the results varied somewhat depending on econometric specification, he found that in general the degree of protection depended on factors affecting the "demand for protection," the "supply of protection," and the government's own bureaucratic objectives. In particular, protection was positively associated with demand factors such as the number of workers in an industry and the industry concentration ratio. Protection was positively related to share of output exported and negatively related to share of output purchased by consumers, both reflecting domestic opposition to protection. The extent of protection also was related to the government's own agenda, with agriculture, infant industries, and sectors with high import penetration ratios all receiving protection.

Table 2.2 Estimates of tariff-equivalents of Korean agricultural NTBs, 1992 (percent)

Product	Collected tariff rate[a]	Nontariff barrier[b]	Tariff equivalent of tariff and NTB[c]
Beef	20.1	148.9	169.0
Pork	20.8	30.2	52.0
Poultry	20.1	44.9	65.0
Dried onions and garlic	52.5	206.9	259.4
Dried beans	30.0	463.8	493.8
Nuts	34.6	199.2	233.8
Peppers	38.9	261.1	300.0
Barley	34.9	389.5	424.4
Corn	2.6	362.4	365.0
Milled rice	5.0	590.0	595.0
Malt	35.1	263.9	299.0
Soybeans	3.0	538.0	541.0
Peanuts	40.3	215.8	256.1
Oilseeds	34.8	458.3	493.1
Dairy products	21.5	128.6	150.1
Leaf tobacco	19.9	51.1	71.0

a. Collected tariff rate is measured as tariff revenue divided by total import value, using average annual exchange rate for 1992 ($1 = 780 won).

b. The nontariff barrier equals the tariff equivalent of the total difference between domestic and foreign prices, minus the tariff rate.

c. The tariff equivalents of the product categories comprising several subitems with different tariff equivalents are derived by taking the weighted average of individual products' tariff equivalents based on their production values for 1992.

Source: N. Kim 1996, table 2.17.

Agriculture remains substantially protected, however. Although South Korea has been a major agricultural importer, most imports are accounted for by bulk commodities due to quotas and other barriers that effectively exclude foreign producers from markets for high value-added or processed agricultural products.[46] Indeed, calculations by N. Kim (1996) indicate that the tariff equivalents of non-tariff barriers in agriculture can be hundreds of times the nominal tariff rates (table 2.2).

---

46. Items of particular interest to the United States include fruits, vegetables, grains (e.g., rice and barley), poultry, and beef. In 1989 Korea agreed to improve access for orange juice, distilled spirits, and cherries, to disavow quantitative trade restrictions on 62 agricultural and fisheries products, and to remove 243 other restrictions over the period 1992-97 on a phased basis. Imports of several products were subsequently restricted by phytosanitary barriers (e.g., pecans and strawberries) or customs clearance problems (e.g., grapefruit).

In the case of beef, a General Agreement on Tariffs and Trade (GATT) panel ruled in 1989 in response to a complaint initiated by the United States that Korea's beef quota was inconsistent with the GATT balance of payments exception. In the following year the United States, Australia, New Zealand, and South Korea agreed to a phased opening of the Korean beef market, beginning with a relaxation of the quota and followed by the establishment

The implementation of tariff-rate quota (TRQ) schemes is an area of particular international concern. Under its Uruguay Round commitments, South Korea established TRQs to provide for minimum access in previously closed markets or to maintain pre-Uruguay Round access. In-quota tariff rates have been low, but foreigners have complained that over-quota rates have been prohibitively high.[47] In the politically contentious rice sector, South Korea agreed to a minimum market access commitment that would involve imports supplying one percent of domestic consumption in 1995, with this figure rising to 4 percent in 2004. The tariff equivalent is nearly 600 percent. In addition, South Korea was permitted to maintain state trading in a number of products, which potentially negated the impact of tariff cuts, and in other cases South Korea was able to negotiate increases in previously bound tariffs.[48] Consequently, the implications of the Uruguay Round for South Korean agriculture may prove slight (Johnson 1995). The OECD in its ongoing work on indicators of government assistance estimates that producer subsidy equivalents reached nearly 100 percent in some sectors (table 2.3).

Finally, the discussion thus far has mainly focused on nominal rates of protection. Effective rates of protection take into account the impact of protection of intermediate inputs on the incentives to produce finished products domestically. If, for example, inputs were to be more highly protected than the finished product, then that sector would receive reduced actual protection, since the protection afforded to the finished product would be more than outweighed by the high prices producers were forced to pay for intermediate inputs. More typically, tariffs would escalate (rise by degree of processing) such that effective rates of protection for sophisticated manufactures exceed nominal rates.

---

in 1993 of a buy/sell system linking certain large buyers directly with producers. The third phase of the beef market liberalization, involving the elimination of all non-tariff barriers and an end to state trading by 2001, was concluded as part of the Uruguay Round. The United States has since complained repeatedly about South Korean implementation of this agreement (USTR 1999).

Additionally, as part of its Uruguay Round commitments, South Korea agreed to phase out import restrictions on a variety of agricultural products of interest to the United States, including pork, chicken, oranges, orange juice, dairy and whey products, apples and apple juice, grapes and grape juice, and other fruit juices. In the same agreement, South Korea was permitted to raise its "bound" tariff rates on these goods to levels not to exceed the domestic-foreign price differential. These tariffs would then be reduced by 24 percent of the base level over a ten-year period.

47. See USTR (1999) for number examples.

48. The United States has raised complaints about the implementation of the tariff-quota schemes. In the case of oranges, for example, the South Korean government designated the country's only citrus cooperative as the sole importer of fresh oranges, creating what appears to be a clear conflict of interest. Similarly, in the case of rice, a state trading organization controls not only importation, but also internal distribution, preventing foreign producers from directly marketing high-quality rice to consumers (USTR 1999).

Table 2.3 Producer subsidy equivalents, 1997
(percent)

Product	Subsidy equivalent
Barley	93
Rice	92
Oilseeds	96
Other crops	92
Milk	71
Beef and veal	67
Pig meat	29
Poultry	73
Eggs	6
Livestock products	49
All products	75

Source: OECD (1999), *Review of Agricultural Polices in Korea.*

Yoo, Hong, and Lee (1993) have estimated the effective rates of protection in South Korea prior to the Uruguay Round (table 2.4). Their results affirm that variations in nominal rates of protection across sectors are manifested in even more highly dispersed rates of effective protection. In the extreme cases of wooden furniture and textiles, effective protection has actually been negative—inputs have been so highly protected relative to outputs that producers have been discouraged from engaging in those activities. On the other end of the scale, rates of effective protection in apparel and electrical machinery have been more than double their nominal rate, providing a big boost for domestic production of these products.[49]

Other Impediments to Trade

Tariffs and quantitative restrictions are not the whole story, however. South Korea has long been a target of antidumping suits brought by foreign competitors. In the early 1990s, South Korea began developing its own antidumping laws and has become an increasingly enthusiastic practitioner.[50] Unfortunately, negotiators have made little progress in reining in these impediments to trade. Although the Uruguay Round agreement contains language that should streamline the process, it has done

---

49. These results are pre-Uruguay Round. Presumably the impact of the Uruguay Round agreement would have been both to reduce levels and to narrow the range of effective protection afforded the manufacturing sector in South Korea. Unfortunately, post-Uruguay Round estimates for South Korea do not exist.

50. See Noland (1998b) for a more detailed discussion of South Korea as both a practitioner of and defendant in antidumping suits, as well as a discussion of other barriers that South Korean exports face.

Table 2.4 Effective and nominal rates of protection, selected sectors, 1990 (percent)

Sector	Effective rate of protection[a]	Nominal rate of protection[b]
Rice	499.6	311.0
Vegetables	13.1	15.4
Fruits	140.1	98.8
Livestock	144.3	43.5
Plywood	5.3	6.4
Wooden furniture	−2.3	4.2
Textiles	−8.5	5.2
Apparel	71.0	29.7
Industrial chemicals	13.6	11.3
Other chemicals	49.4	29.0
Glass and glassware	11.1	10.7
Ceramic products	6.2	7.7
Metallic household articles	18.7	12.9
Other metallic articles	29.0	16.0
General machinery	25.0	17.3
Electrical machinery	77.5	35.4
Automobiles	16.6	14.8

a. The effective rate of protection for sector j is defined as $[VA_j/VA_j^w-1]$, where VA_j is value added at domestic prices and VA_j^w is value added at world prices.

b. For industrial products, nominal protection is estimated by comparing domestic and foreign prices; for agricultural products, it is the sum of tariffs and the tariff equivalents of NTBs.

Source: Yoo, Hong, and Lee 1993, tables VI-1, VII-1.

little if anything to alter the fundamentally irrational nature of the permitted practices.[51]

The South Korean government also has been in the process of reviewing a variety of laws and regulations—such as the administration of import licenses; standards, testing and certification requirements; and quarantine inspections—which, although not designed to restrict imports, may have that practical effect.[52] For example, customs clearance delays for agricultural products can take a month or more, far higher than observed in

---

51. One obvious tack would be for the reinvigorated KFTC to engage in some joint international competition policy initiatives. These have been discussed between the United States and South Korea bilaterally in the Dialogue for Economic Cooperation (DEC), but participants in these negotiations believe that joint activities are a long way off, despite the KFTC's increased autonomy and the public unpopularity of the *chaebol*. On a regional basis, competition policy is the subject of discussion within the Asia-Pacific Economic Cooperation (APEC), though little progress has been made to date. Multilaterally, the European Union and Japan proposed discussing these issues at the 1999 Seattle Ministerial, but US opposition doomed this effort.

52. When the government began its review in 1996, these special laws covered 26 percent of import categories; by the end of 1988, coverage had been reduced to 19 percent (Young 1989).

Figure 2.8 Number of days required for customs clearance of agricultural products

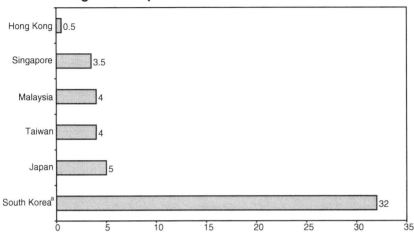

a. Settlement of B/L and application to customers and quarantine office 2 days, quarantine to be filed with Health Bureau 1 day, quarantine test 25 days, forwarding test results 1 day, clearance 2 days, importation stamps 1 day. Recent changes have reduced the number of clearance days for fresh fruit and vegetables.

Source: American Chamber of Commerce in Korea, *Korea: US Trade and Investment Issues 1996.*

other Asian countries (figure 2.8). In the mid-1990s, the South Korean Customs Service implemented a series of reforms designed to streamline procedures. Nevertheless, problems have remained.[53] However, many of the problems have appeared to arise not from the behavior of the Customs Service but rather from policies and decisions by the Ministry of Health and Welfare (MOHW) and the Ministry of Agriculture, Forests, and Fisheries (MAFF). The former agency appears not to have been sufficiently socialized in international norms, and the latter appears to have been captured by import-competing interests.[54]

---

53. USTR (1999) gives examples of arbitrary changes in customs classification, switching products from a tariff-only line to a restrictive TRQ, and rejections of customs clearance applications on administrative grounds (erasure marks on the application, wrong font, etc.). The USTR also alleges that South Korean regulations often require local trade associations to approve import documentation, which requires exporters to share confidential business information with their competitors.

54. USTR (1995) gives the example of an MOHW requirement that each importer of an identical product (e.g., the same brand of canned food in the same size container) go through a separate cumbersome registration procedure. Tarullo (1995) gives the example of medical equipment standards that deviate from international norms and the Customs Service practice of individually opening each device, thus subjecting it to possible contamination. The US medical equipment industry estimates that $200 million in sales are lost due to these practices. Problems have continued to fester, and the United States and Korea have been through multiple rounds of consultations through the WTO. See USTR (1999) for details.

Foreign observers have long identified standards, testing, labeling, and certification requirements apparently drafted without reference to international norms and effectively targeted only toward imported products as the most onerous secondary barrier (USTR 1999 and American Chamber of Commerce in Korea (AmCham) 1999). Although significant progress has been made in the 1990s, foreigners claim that these methods have still been used to discourage imports. Many of the complaints have related to agricultural imports, medical equipment, pharmaceuticals, and cosmetics. Exporters have reported unduly restrictive and arbitrary phytosanitary requirements. In many cases importers have been denied requests for scientific data upon which imported food shipments have been rejected (see box 2.1). Following the submission of a Section 301 petition by the US beef and pork industry in May 1995, the United States initiated formal consultations under the GATT's successor World Trade Organization (WTO) dispute settlement mechanism with particular regard to the shelf-life restrictions mandated by the South Korean government. In July 1995 this led to a bilateral settlement in which South Korea agreed to phase in the common international practice of manufacturer-determined sell-by dates for most food products. According to the United States Trade Representative (USTR), some problems still remain (USTR 1999).

In the past, South Korea maintained a variety of practices to encourage domestic firms in government procurement, but these have been narrowed by its implementation of the WTO Agreement on Government Procurement. South Korean authorities estimate that, of total government procurement of $3.8 billion in 1998, approximately $1.3 billion was covered by the WTO code.[55]

Trade reform has been pursued in other areas as well. In recent years, new patent, copyright, and trademark laws have been enacted, a patent court has been created, and resources devoted to enforcement have been increased. Even the USTR admits that "there has been some improvement over the past several years on the removal of pirated and counterfeit goods from the Korean market" (USTR 1999, 282), though, of course, problems remain.[56]

Liberalization of the automobile sector is an issue of great sensitivity in South Korea. In 1997, South Korea became the world's fifth largest manufacturer of automobiles and its third largest exporter. Although it

---

55. South Korea has been building a new international airport at Inchon, which has become a recent point of contention with the United States. The United States has asserted that the airport's construction should come under the government procurement code, while the South Korean side has argued that the airport authority is not subject to the WTO code. In February 1999 the United States sought formal consultations in the WTO, and, unable to reach an agreement with South Korea, requested in May the formation of a WTO dispute settlement panel. In May 2000 the panel ruled against the US.

56. See AmCham (1999) for a judicious discussion of this issue.

Box 2.1 The Strange Case of Sausages

In March 1994, South Korea barred entry of a shipment of frozen heat-treated pork sausages when the sausages were arbitrarily reclassified and the legal shelf life was reduced from 90 to 30 days. (The government-mandated shelf-life system, itself an anachronism practiced by few other countries, affected US exports of a variety of processed foods.) This action was the catalyst for the filing of a Section 301 complaint by US producers. (US officials were unwilling to take the case to the General Agreement on Tariffs and Trade (GATT) for fear that a US victory in this case would hurt chances of congressional passage of the Uruguay Round, where critics were claiming that the GATT's successor, the World Trade Organization (WTO), would be able to strike down US health and safety laws. Once the Uruguay Round passed Congress, US officials were willing to use the WTO to resolve the issue.) As for the sausages themselves, the South Korean importer who was stuck with them unloaded them in China.

The importer was less lucky in the popcorn case. The following year an export shipment by a small US producer was impounded for more than six months then rejected on the grounds that it had high levels of e-coli bacteria. No test results were furnished to substantiate this judgement, and the exporter was denied the right to resubmit new tests indicating that there were no bacteria present. The Korean authorities also dismissed the argument that the high temperatures needed to pop popcorn would kill any bacteria. South Korean authorities eventually announced that it was the fault of the importer who had self-certified the absence of e-coli bacteria, though, as it turns out, standards did not even exist for e-coli bacteria on popcorn. In the end, the importer was stuck with the popcorn and the exporter was out $50,000 (USTR 1996). The value of time spent by government officials and private lawyers attempting to resolve this undoubtedly exceeded the value of the shipment. These practices delay importation, contribute to deterioration (which ironically may be a potential public health concern), raise costs, and discourage imports.

Through the 1990s the South Korean government took steps to try to improve the transparency of its standards setting practices, and these have been subject to bilateral consultation under the auspices of the US-ROK Dialogue on Economic Cooperation (DEC). The Uruguay Round agreement on sanitary and phytosanitary restrictions and the improved dispute settlement mechanism have greatly increased the likelihood of resolving these issues. Indeed, the specter of a WTO case appears to have contributed to resolving the sausage dispute.

possesses the most rapidly growing market in Asia, it has continued to severely circumscribe access to its own market, where imports make up less than one percent of consumption. (In contrast, in the United States, non-North American imports account for 15 percent of consumption in the United States, with Korean imports alone accounting for 2 percent.) The importation of Japanese cars was banned until South Korea, in the context of bilateral negotiations with Japan in the WTO, agreed to lift the prohibition at the end of 1999. This date was brought forward six months to mid-1999 as part of the IMF package negotiated during the financial crisis. Importation of other, non-Japanese autos has also been discouraged.[57] More directly, the US government has been concerned about tariffs (currently 8 percent), discriminatory internal taxation (based on engine size), various standards and certification requirements, residual restrictions on US firms' consumer financing activities, and certain aspects of consumer auto loan financing in Korea. These were subject to bilateral Memoranda of Understanding concluded in 1995 and 1998.[58]

Services

In a relative sense, the services markets remain generally less open than the goods markets, though, as in the case of goods, there has been a trend toward significant liberalization, in large part through a combination of multilateral negotiation and bilateral pressure. (Discussion of crisis-driven financial services liberalization will be deferred until chapter 6.) There is a considerable overlap between services and investment, since often one cannot be efficiently undertaken without the other.

South Korea has historically restricted foreign providers' access to its services markets through a "negative list" system, but over time this list has been narrowed considerably. Private construction and engineering markets were opened to international competition in 1996, and the public works market was opened to foreign providers in the following year.[59] In advertising, foreign firms have historically complained about the state-affiliated monopoly, the Korea Broadcast Advertising Corporation (KOBACO), which allocates television and radio advertising time. However, the crisis has led to an excess of supply over demand, and both

---

57. In 1990 the South Korean government launched an "austerity" or "anti-consumption" campaign. Limitations were placed on promotional activities in response to government administrative guidance, and purchasers of imported automobiles were threatened with tax audits. South Korean officials explained that the campaign was against ostentatious and excessive consumption, not imports *per se*, but a number of examples suggest that this was not entirely the case. A lingering problem from this period has been the perception, publicly denied by the National Tax Administration in 1994 and reiterated in 1995, that the purchase of an imported car would result in a tax audit. President Kim Young-sam again publicly stated in 1996 that the purchase of a foreign car would not result in a tax audit, but in 1997 Korean negotiators admitted that the practice had continued, terming it a "mistake" (*Inside U.S. Trade*, 29 August 1997).

58. Under current law, South Korean banks are not allowed to hold title on cars as collateral on loans for auto purchases. As a consequence, some consumers default on the loans, and it is difficult for the banks to seize the cars. US automakers argue that this has impeded the development of a car loan market and thus has depressed the demand for cars, especially luxury cars.

59. AmCham (1999) and USTR (1999) report that difficulties encountered by US firms since liberalization have been largely "cultural," not legal, in nature, and they report few complaints about access.

AmCham (1999) and USTR (1999) report that KOBACO has shown considerable flexibility in dealing with foreign providers. Quotas on foreign content imposed on movie theaters, as well as on broadcast and cable television, continue to be a source of complaint.

The major area of current focus continues to be financial services, however. South Korea implemented a series of reforms in banking, securities, and insurance associated initially with its application to join the OECD, and later as part of its strategy for coping with the financial crisis. In banking, although a significant number of restrictions on foreign banks have been removed, foreign banks continue to complain that their activities have been restricted by South Korean assessment of capital reserves based on the local, rather than the parent, entity and the slow and nontransparent process of regulatory approval for the introduction of new products.

Investment

Restrictive policies toward inward FDI have been significantly liberalized. Historically, South Korea had discouraged foreign investment (and access to its services markets) through a "negative list." Foreign investment was restricted through equity participation or other requirements, though over the years the pervasiveness of these barriers has declined.[60] As a consequence of these restrictions, South Korea has stood out as one of the few countries in the world where minority participation (rather than majority ownership) is the dominant form of foreign direct investment.[61]

However, the government of Kim Dae-jung has made increased foreign investment a priority, both as a response to the financial crisis and as a way of diluting the pervasive presence of the giant *chaebol* in the South Korean economy.[62] In November 1998, the government enacted the Foreign Investment Promotion Act. It explicitly established the principle of

---

60. In 1980, less than half of five-digit Korean Standard Industrial Classification (KSIC) sectors were unconditionally open to foreign direct investment (FDI). Since 1989, 79 percent of these sectors were open to FDI, 16 percent were conditionally open, and five percent were closed. Openness has been highest in manufacturing (98 percent), lowest for agriculture (20 percent), and in between for services (62 percent). In 1994, 87 percent of these sectors were open to FDI, including 98 percent of manufacturing and 76 percent of service sectors. As a consequence of the financial crisis (discussed in more detail in chapter 6), a number of restrictions on foreign direct and portfolio investment, especially in the services sector, were lifted in 1998 and 1999. Remaining statutory foreign investment restrictions are mainly related to national security, cultural protection, and protection of the agricultural and fisheries sectors. See J.D. Kim (2000) for further details.

61. This has begun to change since the financial crisis and the liberalization of foreign investment laws, however. Indeed, much of the inward FDI surge has taken the form of foreign firms buying out their local joint venture partners.

62. See Ahn (1999), Beck (1999), J.D. Kim (1999), and Kang (1999) for analyses of these policy changes.

national treatment, further narrowed the "negative list," broadened the scope of tax incentives available to foreign investors, simplified approval procedures, and established foreign investment zones.[63] Once established, foreign firms are accorded national treatment.

Foreign investment ceilings in financial markets have been largely eliminated, with the exception of a few parastatal enterprises that are in the process of privatization and a few specified sectors, such as education, media, and beef wholesaling. Other recent reforms permit hostile takeovers and increase foreigners' ability to take significant minority positions in publicly traded South Korean firms.

Outside agriculture, restrictions on foreign land ownership, long a source of complaint, have largely been lifted. Because of these legal changes and the financial crisis, foreign investment in the South Korean economy has grown rapidly in recent years (figure 2.9).[64] Research by J.D. Kim (1999) demonstrates that this investment has had important beneficial spillover effects to the South Korean economy.

Several years ago, the present author wrote an evaluation of South Korean trade policies (Noland 1998b). This treatment is considerably shorter. The Uruguay Round agreement, bilateral pressure, the financial crisis, and the relatively liberal policies of the Kim Dae-jung government have contributed to considerable reform of South Korean trade policy. Many of the old barriers have been lowered, narrowed, or eliminated completely. In both the goods and services areas, trade liberalization has not only played its conventional role of improving the efficiency of resource allocation, but importantly may have served as a check on the exercise of market power by the giant *chaebol*, which have disproportionately received trade protection in the past. A similar trend of liberalization driven by both internal and external forces has been underway in the financial sector.

Precrisis Financial Policies

Since the founding of the republic, South Korea had maintained highly regulated and repressed financial markets, emphasizing indirect finance through the state-dominated banking system and capital controls to delink

---

63. The government can reject foreign investment not in "negative list" sectors only for one of five specific reasons and within sixty days of notification. Otherwise, the investment can proceed. These reasons include: protection of national security; maintenance of public order or the protection of public health, morality, or safety; fulfillment of obligations relating to international peace and security; prevention of monopolistic or predatory practices in the domestic market; and violation of Korea's Antitrust and Fair Trade Law.

64. The data in figure 2.9 are based on actual investment and are somewhat lower than the data on investment approvals released by the Bank of Korea. The recent experience with foreign direct investment is discussed in more detail in chapter 6.

Figure 2.9   Foreign direct investment

net inflows (billions of US
dollars)

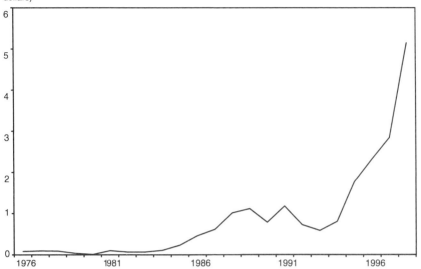

Source: World Bank, World Development Indicators; Korea Economic Institute of America,
Korea Insight Vol. 1, No. 5 August 1999.

domestic financial markets from the global market. These were the twin
pillars of President Park's state-directed, capital channeling model. However, pressure for liberalization developed over time from both from
domestic firms disadvantaged in international competition by high
domestic interest rates and limited options for corporate finance and
from foreign governments promoting the interests of their own financial
providers. Some South Koreans genuinely believed that the benefits to
be gained through more efficient financial markets were outweighed by
the potential destabilizing macroeconomic effects, or that South Korean
financial firms were not yet ready to compete with foreign firms (e.g.,
Park 1995, Park and Song 1996).[65] Others probably opposed liberalization
out of self-interest, since liberalization would erode their privileged posi-

---

65. For example, Park and Song (1996) write: "Korean policymakers have been reluctant
to liberalize the capital account rapidly. There is concern that devastating macroeconomic
instability would result from a sudden opening up of financial markets. In contrast, efficiency
gains to the economy from liberalization are considered to be relatively small, possibly even
insignificant, and at best realized in the long run" (p.14). Park (1995) states that: "Domestic
financial institutions have little competitive advantage over their foreign counterparts. At
best Korea's financial sector remains an infant industry and may need market protection"
(p.7). These authors were affiliated with the South Korean bank-supported Korea Institute
of Finance (KIF).

tion within the South Korean financial system. The outcome of this tension was a political compromise resulting in a gradual, uneven, and ultimately problematic liberalization program that lasted a decade before being overtaken by the 1997 financial crisis.

The Sixth Five Year Plan (1987-91) reinforced the existing trend toward financial sector liberalization. The process received a further boost in 1993 with the introduction of multiyear financial plans, including one that was promulgated in 1995 and was scheduled to run through 1999. Additional reforms were announced as part of South Korea's 1996 accession to the OECD. A Presidential Commission for Financial Reform was established in January 1997 to propose broad recommendations for the modernization of the financial system. It issued three reports that year.[66] The 1995 multiyear plan and South Korea's application to join the OECD became the focal points in the battle over reform.

The Structure of Banking

South Korean financial institutions include bank and non-bank deposit taking institutions, investment and insurance firms, and equity markets.[67] On the lending side, South Korean banks faced some competition from an underdeveloped commercial paper market, and in some areas, such as automobile finance, from consumer lending institutions. Historically, foreign banks' activities were highly restricted, though as part of the liberalization program they were allowed to open multiple branches.[68]

The trend was toward a diminution of overt state involvement. The share of state banks in lending fell over time and accounted for only 13 percent of loans in 1996. Policy loans, which contain a significant subsidy element, became less important over time, declining to 18 percent of bank credit and 5 percent of all lending in 1995.[69] Moreover, these loans were increasingly concentrated in the public financial sector, with the share at 39 percent and rising. However, the commercial banking sector was still

---

66. See Cargill (1999) for a summary of these reports.

67. Between 1994 and 1996, the government more than doubled the number of merchant banks, licensing 24 new ones. Of these, 15 were converted from relatively weak finance companies. Haggard (2000) reports the astonishing fact that three of these were insolvent *at the time that they were licensed.* These institutions were not subject to the same ownership limitations as the commercial banks, and some were controlled by *chaebol.* Moreover, they were subject to less regulatory oversight. These institutions later played an important role in the financial crisis, lending aggressively and speculating in financial markets in Southeast Asia, Russia, and other emerging markets.

68. In 1996 the government announced plans to permit foreign banks to establish wholly-owned subsidiaries around late 1998, as well as to let them into the credit card business.

69. Figures on policy loans vary from source to source due to the imprecise definition of a policy loan. The figures cited are from the Bank of Korea as reported by the OECD. Some South Korean analysts report significantly higher figures.

more dependent on policy lending than the rest of the non-state financial system, with policy loans accounting for 18 percent of commercial bank lending.

In parallel to the reduced state efforts to channel capital, the commercial banks were privatized in the mid-1990s. There was movement away from direct government appointment of senior bank managers, though the government still did not permit complete autonomy either in the selection of senior management or in operational decisions regarding portfolio allocation.[70] The legacy of state involvement was further manifested by overstaffing and an implicit guarantee of lifetime employment. Returns on assets were low, relative both to returns observed in other countries and to the returns achieved by foreign banks operating in the South Korean market.

Perhaps as a consequence of continued state involvement in the banks, it was widely believed that the government would not permit a bank to fail, and indeed none ever had.[71] A deposit insurance scheme involving non-risk-adjusted uniform premiums was introduced in 1996. (The possible moral hazards created by the implicit state guarantee and the provision of non-risk-adjusted insurance will be taken up in chapter 6.)

Commercial banks were supervised by the Monetary Board, the governing body of the Bank of Korea and the Office of Bank Supervision, which also regulated other financial institutions under the delegated authority of the Ministry of Finance and Economy. (Securities and insurance were supervised by similar boards under the Ministry.) The core commitments of South Korean bank regulation were the adoption of the Bank of International Settlements (BIS) capital adequacy guidelines and the CAMEL system (Capital adequacy, Asset quality, Management ability, Earnings quality, and Liquidity level), based on US regulatory practices. The 1993 introduction of a "real name" law relating to bank account and property ownership represented a significant step forward in that, as it would in principle give regulatory officials much greater information with which to combat malfeasance by bank insiders.

Interest rates have been deregulated over time, beginning in 1988.[72] Deregulation has appeared to have real effects on interest rates. There was a narrowing of the differential between interest rates and corporate

---

70. For example, as the stock market declined in late 1996, bureaucrats issued "window guidance" requiring that banks hold on to their stocks to support share prices. They did— and increased their ultimate losses.

71. In 1996, regulatory authorities were authorized to order poorly managed financial institutions to merge with other financial institutions. The Ministry of Finance and Economy (MOFE) or the deposit insurance agencies would also be authorized to force poorly managed firms to take self-defensive measures such as increasing capital or selling off stock holdings.

72. Prior to the crisis, only 17 percent of bank deposits (less than 5 percent of total deposits) and 3 percent of domestic loans were subject to direct rate regulation.

bond rates as shown in figure 2.2. Yet the impression remained that, although interest rates were formally deregulated, the commercial banking sector was still subject to administrative guidance. It was expected that additional international capital market liberalization would contribute to further interest rate reduction, and that real rates would continue to reduce gradually as the capital stock grew and the marginal product of capital declined (figure 2.2). The deregulation of banks and non-bank financial institutions, together with the growth in stock and bond markets, led to a withering of the curb market, which declined to less than 10 percent of domestic credit.

In 1993, the government expanded the scope for short-term foreign currency borrowing by allowing firms to borrow abroad directly or through South Korean banks to finance the importation of capital goods. With interest rates relatively high in South Korea, and continued restrictions on firms' ability to issue long-term bonds or secure long-term loans in foreign markets, firms were encouraged to increase their reliance on short-term foreign borrowing, and South Korean banks were encouraged to step up their won-lending activities. This was to play a significant role in the subsequent crisis.

Capital Markets

Although some government policies inhibited their development, long-term capital markets were large. (Short-term capital markets were relatively small and underdeveloped.) Daily turnover in the stock market was the sixth largest in the world. At its peak, stock market capitalization reached a quarter trillion dollars, making it the 16th largest in the world, and stock market capitalization as a share of national income was higher than in some OECD countries, despite policies that favored debt over equity finance.[73]

In 1990, the government established a quarterly quota on new issues. At times, more than 300 firms waited for permission to issue stock.[74] This

---

73. As noted earlier, tax policies encouraged the issuance of debt over equity shares. Figures on the valuation of the stock market should be taken with a grain of salt due to the extensive web of cross-holdings, which would tend to inflate valuations.

74. In February 1985, the Japanese yen began a rapid appreciation against other currencies, particularly the US dollar. As the relative cost of production in Japan rose, Japanese firms responded by moving production offshore, mainly to South Korea and Taiwan. As growth slowed, Japanese monetary authorities pursued a policy of aggressive monetary expansion, cutting the official discount rate to its then-historical low.

Rapid monetary growth and low interest rates, together with a still appreciating currency, facilitated the creation of an asset market bubble and an outflow of capital, much of it going to South Korea. At this time the won was pegged to the US dollar. The real depreciation caused by yen appreciation, combined with the inflow of capital and technology from Japan, created a kind of "hyper competitiveness" and emergent macroeconomic imbalances (Balassa and Williamson 1990). Soon South Korea was experiencing an asset bubble similar to Japan's; between 1985 and 1989 the money supply increased by 105 percent, the price

repression of the normal functions of the capital market gave rise to corruption as firms resorted to bribery to get their shares listed.[75] At the core was a positive list system through which anything not explicitly permitted was prohibited. This hampered the introduction of new instruments throughout the financial sector. The Ministry of Finance and Economy indicated that it would end the quota system, permit the listing of stock futures contracts, widen the permissible daily trading bounds for individual stocks, abolish fixed commissions on stock trades, and clarify the rules on mergers and acquisitions. Nevertheless, it prevented the introduction of derivative instruments that would enhance firms' ability to manage risk in both the foreign exchange and equity markets.

Foreign participation in the stock market was also restricted. The government limited the amount of shares that foreigners could hold in individual stocks in the aggregate and individually.[76] As a consequence of this segmentation, the shares held by foreigners often traded at a premium over the shares held by domestic residents. The government refused to permit screen-based trading for foreign held shares and did not allow publication of stock market price indices for those shares, creating an illiquid market that conveyed abnormal profits to dealers with price information.[77]

The long-term bond market was large, with the corporate bond market five times as large as the government bond market, in part due to favorable tax treatment. The government discouraged the development of an efficient auction and a secondary market for government bonds. No swap,

---

level rose by 3 percent, and the stock market went up by 458 percent, becoming the ninth largest in the world by 1989. Eventually, South Korea came under both market and political pressure to revalue. As it did, stock prices fell. The quota on new listings was in response to this.

75. In June 1996, the governor of the Securities and Exchange Commission (SEC) and a director of MOFE were arrested for taking bribes to get firms listed. Six other SEC executives were forced to resign.

76. Initially this was set at 10 percent in January 1992 and subsequently raised to 12 percent in December 1994, 15 percent in July 1995, and 18 percent in April 1996. In June 1996, the government announced a further phased opening that would increase the ceiling to 20 percent in 1996, and three additional percentage points annually thereafter to 29 percent by 1999. The MOFE added that it might abolish the ceiling entirely in 2000 if "economic circumstances" were appropriate. The ceiling was raised on schedule to 20 percent in October 1996 and to 23 percent in May 1997, but then the plan was overtaken by events and the ceiling was raised to 26 percent in November 1997, to 55 percent in December 1997, and finally to 100 percent in May 1998. A similar pattern occurred for the ceilings on ownership by individual foreign investors.

77. In an attempt to invigorate the over-the-counter (OTC) market, the government announced that it would begin to allow foreign investors to purchase shares "directly" in addition to the current practice of investing "indirectly" through a mutual fund reserved for foreigners. The OTC market, established in 1987, has had a yearly trading volume roughly equal to the daily volume on the Seoul stock exchange.

bond, or interest futures markets existed. Foreigners were only eligible to purchase a limited number of corporate bond issues. The government announced in August 1996 that foreign investors would be allowed to invest in convertible bonds issued by large corporations beginning in 1998, but that full opening of the bond market would be delayed until the differential between South Korean and overseas interest rates, at that time 6 to 7 percent, narrowed to 2 percentage points. Of course, there was no guarantee that this would ever occur.

Participation in South Korean capital markets by foreign firms was also limited. Foreign securities firms were permitted to own up to 10 percent of the paid-in capital of South Korean securities firms, and were allowed in 1995 to establish branch offices or joint ventures. In June 1996, the Ministry of Finance and Economy announced a new proposal to eliminate the 10 percent limit on ownership and to permit foreign firms to open wholly-owned subsidiaries in December 1998.

On the outflow side, capital outflow by residents was largely liberalized, though some restrictions have remained in place. Domestic residents were permitted to invest in foreign stocks in the 13 largest markets through mutual funds. In reality, actual investments were minuscule, and South Korean residents' portfolios were highly concentrated in won-denominated assets.

The Liberalization Plan

Out of the OECD application process came a multiyear, phased, financial liberalization plan to break down some barriers within the domestic market and to liberalize capital outflows before capital inflows. As planned, domestic residents would be free to purchase foreign securities and to establish foreign currency bank accounts in 1998. Domestic firms would no longer be required to obtain prior approval to be allowed to issue foreign currency-denominated equity-related securities (warrants), but rather would be subject only to a reporting requirement.

Non-residents would be allowed to issue won-denominated securities, and the ceiling on non-residential purchases of equities would continue to be raised. Also, friendly takeovers would be permitted by 1997. Restrictions on foreign purchases in the bond market would be partially removed, with restrictions on purchases of short-term debt lifted before restrictions on investment in long-term bonds. In respect to short-term capital flows, non-residents would be allowed to open won-denominated accounts at overseas branches of South Korean banks. This liberalization of short-term capital flows prior to lifting of similar restrictions on long-term flows created an incentive to rely on short-term financing and would come back to haunt South Korea, as discussed in chapter 6.

Restrictions on both inward and outbound direct investment would be partially eased. Foreigners would be allowed to buy land freely in some sectors (though they would still need the permission of local authorities in others). Limits on outbound FDI were to be lifted gradually.

With regard to the participation of foreign financial institutions in South Korean markets, foreign banks and securities firms would be allowed to establish more branches and offices, respectively. Foreign insurance companies would be permitted to hold own-currency-denominated cash or securities as well as won-denominated assets. Foreign equity participation in investment trusts and asset management companies would be introduced in a controlled manner, with all restrictions to be removed in 1998.

In short, the plan amounted to a continuation of the ongoing liberalization process on a variety of fronts, though many of its provisions would leave the government with significant discretion. It was unclear what controls would remain in 1999, the terminal year of the plan. At the end of 1995, domestic market interest rates had largely been freed (a year ahead of schedule). However, the government still regulated the portfolios of commercial banks. It still owned a large number of financial institutions (of which the Korea Development Bank was the largest), and state-owned financial institutions dominated some markets (such as mortgage lending). According to the OECD, remaining restrictions continued to impede the flow of capital from commercial banks to other financial institutions, including the privately owned non-bank institutions, which it identified as the most dynamic part of the Korean financial sector. Government control over the introduction of new instruments had retarded the adoption of innovations in the securities market, and would be expected to continue to do so under this plan. Despite the decline of policy loans, the central bank would still act as a source of subsidized lending to preferred borrowers. Foreign participation in South Korean financial markets would continue to be circumscribed, and access by residents to international capital markets would still be restricted. Under this plan, the South Korean financial system would have remained among the most repressed in Asia.

Reservations to OECD codes are permitted, and in the financial services area, the average acceptance rate of financial liberalization codes is 89 percent; South Korea used its exceptions remit liberally, accepting only 65 percent of the OECD's financial system codes (though in fairness, some of these exceptions were scheduled for phaseout by 2000) (Dobson and Jacquet 1998). As will be seen in chapter 6, events were to force a degree of liberalization which was unforeseen by South Korea's financial market architects.

Conclusions

In the four decades following the devastation of the Korean War, South Korea transformed itself into a prosperous democracy, becoming the first country in the postwar period to make the transition from a developing to a developed country. Yet the country's politics and economy still bore the imprint of the development model that President Park Chung-hee had forged decades earlier. Technological capability, capital accumulation, and access to world markets powered South Korea's rapid development and income growth. But the model, which had proved so successful in transforming a backward economy into a world beater, was of questionable value as South Korea approached the technological frontier. As the economy entered the 1990s, it possibly contained the seeds of its own destruction.

The *chaebol*, the product of the large-scale state intervention in the economy, posed a systemic risk to the increasingly fragile financial system that had been built around them, and the government had proved unable to formulate any effective response. Labor, repressed under Park, was restive, as a bubble in the asset markets generated increasingly obvious disparities in wealth and opportunity. And the foreigners, who had been willing to cut South Korea economic slack during the Cold War, increasingly demanded that South Korea play by the developed country rules appropriate to its newly achieved status. As we will see in chapter 6, this combination of fragile institutions and growing demands was to prove incapable of withstanding the internal and external forces at play.

3

The North Korean Economy

If one wants the prosperity of the national economy, he should thoroughly reject the idea of dependence on outside forces, the idea that he cannot live without foreign capital. . . . Ours is an independent economic structure equipped with all the economic sectors in good harmony and with its own strong heavy industry at the core. It is incomparably better than the export-oriented economic structure dependent on other countries. . . .We must heighten vigilance against the imperialists' moves to induce us to 'reform' and 'opening to the outside world.' 'Reform' and 'opening' on their lips are a honey-coated poison. Clear is our stand toward 'reform' and 'opening.' We now have nothing to 'reform' and 'open.' By 'reform' and 'opening' the imperialists mean a revival of capitalism. The best way of blocking the wind of 'reform' and 'opening' of the imperialists is to defend the socialist principle in all sectors of the economy. . . . We will never abandon the principle, but will set ourselves against all attempts to induce us to join an 'integrated' world.

—from a joint editorial published by *Rodong Sinmun*, the newspaper of the Central Committee of the Korean Workers Party, and *Kŭlloja*, the Central Committee's political theory magazine, 17 September 1998.

Physically, North Korea is about the size of Pennsylvania, with about twice as many people. Economically, it is about the size of Wyoming and is shrinking. At the time of the partition in 1945, nearly two-thirds of Korean industry was located in the North, which imported food from the agricultural South (Yeon 1993b, D. Lee 1993, 1995). The North undertook a productivity enhancing land reform in 1946, and after the 1950-53 war North Korea's development outpaced that of the South.[1] After visiting

---

1. On conditions in agriculture and the land reform see Jung and Park (1998); on subsequent developments see Hwang (1993).

North Korea in 1965, Joan Robinson proclaimed that "all the economic miracles of the [post-World War II] world are put in the shade by these achievements" and concluded that "as the North continues to develop and the South degenerate, sooner or later the curtain of lies must surely begin to tear" (Robinson 1974, 208, 215). Robinson's views, though perhaps melodramatic in tone, were far from unusual: the conventional wisdom is that the North's per capita income exceeded the South's until the 1970s, with one respected academic specialist dating it as recently as 1986.[2]

While South Korea has encountered the problems associated with increased prosperity and making the transition to developed country status, North Korea faces problems of both a different magnitude and character. Unfortunately, analysis of the North Korean economy is severely hampered by the dearth of reliable research materials, and thus is inherently more speculative than analysis of the South's economy. Perhaps in keeping with an earlier Korean regime's description as the "Hermit Kingdom," the North Korean government is incredibly parsimonious in the publication of economic data. Although it does release budget figures, external trade statistics are considered a state secret. As a consequence, what information does exist is often fragmentary, unconfirmable, or subject to the political agenda of its originator. Fortunately, with North Korea's recent membership in the United Nations, apparently reliable data are starting to trickle out through UN agencies.[3]

This chapter presents an overview of the North Korean economy. Because so little is known, and much of what is thought to be known is of questionable reliability, this requires a more careful examination of the basic "facts" than was necessary in the previous discussion of the South Korean economy. First, the basic institutions of the North Korean economy are reviewed. Then, the existing statistical data is analyzed. We then consider North Korea's coping mechanisms in the face of its current economic crisis. External relations are taken up next. These are examined in some detail for two reasons. First, North Korea's external economic relations are relatively observable and provide some insight into the state of the North Korean economy. Second, North Korea's external economic

---

2. On the conventional wisdom, see Eberstadt (1994a) and S.K. Kim (1994). This view would be consistent with the econometric evidence of Easterly and Fisher (1994), who found that centrally planned economies (CPEs) typically exhibit stronger than average performance in the initial stages of industrialization, which deteriorates into weaker than average performance as allocative inefficiencies become more and more costly. According to one of the two series calculated by Hwang (1993), South Korea's per capita income did not overtake that of the North until 1986.

3. An example is the demographic data provided to the UN and subsequently analyzed in the pioneering work of Eberstadt and Banister (1992a), who concluded that the data appeared to have been reported without adjustments or tampering. Eberstadt (1999a) reaches harsher conclusions in a later assessment of a broader range of official data.

relations are highly politicized. As a consequence, some discussion of the diplomatic environment is needed to understand the development of external economic relations. The chapter concludes with an analysis of the North's recent limited market opening moves, which sets the stage for consideration of the energy and food crises in the next two chapters.

Organization of the North Korean Economy

The North Korean economy is organized along lines similar to other centrally planned economies (CPEs).[4] Since the country's inception, property rights have resided primarily with the state, and resource allocation has been largely carried out through the planning mechanism, not through markets. The roles of money, prices, and other familiar institutional features of market economies have been severely circumscribed. The distinguishing feature of the North Korean case has been the extremes to which these policies have been taken.

The organizing principle of the North Korean economy is the ideology of *juche*, or national self-reliance. *Juche* was first proclaimed by Kim Il-sung in 1955 and represents the perhaps understandable response to Korea's historical status as a "shrimp among whales." It provided a convenient rationale for balancing off the Soviet Union and China. It also proved useful in the process of rebuilding the Korean Workers Party (KWP) (which had collapsed during the Korean War) and purging potential rivals for being too close to foreign interests (Koo 1992, Armstrong 1998). "*Juche* for the economy" was proclaimed in 1956, when North Korea encountered difficulty securing economic assistance from both the Soviet Union and China (see box 3.1).

The result has been the development of the world's most autarkic economy, with an international trade share (exports plus imports) of approximately 12 percent of GDP, well below the 50 to 55 percent observed in South Korea and a fraction of the even larger share that North Korea would exhibit were it a "normal" country, as demonstrated in chapter 7. The emphasis on self-reliance has been so great that North Korea never joined its communist brethren in the Council for Mutual Economic Assistance (COMECON). Indeed, its own central plans were timed to frustrate their linkage with those of the other planned economies (Hwang 1993).

In North Korea, economic assets are predominately in state hands. The Constitution establishes two basic categories of economic organization (state-owned enterprises and worker cooperatives) and appears to estab-

---

4. For basic overviews of the North Korean economy see Chung (1974), *Deutsch-Koreanische Industrie und Handelskammer* (DKIH) (1991), Hwang (1993), D. Lee (1997) and H.S. Lee (1999). Kornai (1992) is the classic work on CPEs.

Box 3.1 *Juche* as Theology

Contemporary North Korea is a wild mélange of an authoritarian Confucian dynasty, a Stalinist state, and a religious cult, complete with its own theology, *juche*. The dynastic characteristics of the regime are most apparent in the transfer of titular power from Kim Il-sung to Kim Jong-il. Now Kim Jong-il is reportedly grooming *his* eldest son, Kim Jong-nam, for power. As the *Economist* observed, something must have changed since the 1970 edition of North Korea's "Dictionary of Political Terminologies," which defined hereditary succession as "a reactionary custom practiced in exploitative societies" (10 July 1999). Indeed, its dynasticism has been demonstrated by its 1997 adoption of a "*juche*" calendar, proclaiming 1912, the birth year of Kim Il-sung, as the first year of the "*Juche* Era." S.S. Kim (1998) and H.S. Park (1998) explore the ideological basis of *juche*, Buzo (1999) examines the Stalinist origins of North Korean politics, and Armstrong (1998) analyzes the increasingly neo-Confucian nature of North Korean politics and the cult of personality surrounding Kim Jong-il.

This is no ordinary neo-Confucian state, however, and the cult of personality surrounding the Kims is extreme even by the disheartening standards of the 20th century. During a visit, the present author was struck by the apparent parallels between North Korean symbols and slogans and those of Christianity. It is known that Kim Il-sung's father attended a Christian missionary school in Pyongyang (Suh 1988), and Kim Il-sung wrote of having attended church as a child (Kang 1997). Indeed, the hagiographic mythology surrounding the birth of present-leader Kim Jong-il appears to draw upon Christian imagery. According to the legend, a swallow appeared to an elderly man on the slopes of sacred Mt. Paekdu, heralding the imminent birth of a great general. This was accompanied by three guiding stars leading the faithful to the log cabin where the infant Kim lay. Propaganda has been explicit in its religious content: Kim Jong-il is described as "a contemporary God," "superior to Christ in love, superior to Buddha in benevolence, superior to Confucius in virtue, and superior to Mohammed in justice," and, ultimately, "the savior of mankind." Snyder (1999b) and H.S. Lee (1999) provide religious interpretations of the North Korean regime, which H.S. Park (1998) likens to "a religious cult" (p.224).

Of course, as the history of religious cults demonstrates, such extreme authority invested in charismatic but fallible leaders often ends in tragedy, and it should come as no surprise that North Korea has an appalling record on human rights, as documented by Amnesty International (1996), the Research Institute on National Unification (1996), Gustavson and Lee-Rudolph (1997), the Citizens' Alliance to Help Political Prisoners in North Korea (1999), Karatnycky (1999), and the US Department of State (1999).

lish the goal of nationalizing the co-ops. The state retains ultimate property rights, and the co-ops are granted usage rights (Namkoong and Yoo 1994).[5]

The planning structure was reorganized somewhat in 1964 and again in 1981 to devolve greater power to provincial and local authorities.

---

5. A constitutional revision promulgated in August 1998 mentions private property and inheritance rights. These nascent changes are taken up in the next section on crisis response.

An uncertain degree of system-fraying decentralization appears to have occurred in response to the crisis of the 1990s. Enterprises are again classified as state-owned or worker cooperatives, and further classified by size. For administrative control purposes they are further categorized as central or local. Larger plants are under the control of the central party and the Economic Bureau of the Office of State Affairs. Local plants are under the control and guidance of local party and economic guidance committees at the provincial level (Hwang 1993). A new incentive system for enterprises (the "Independent Accounting System") was introduced in 1984, and in the 1990s a greater degree of multiplant integration under a common management structure with an associated domestic trading firm (similar to the East German *Kombinat* or South Korean *chaebol*) was permitted.[6] Worker remuneration is set on the basis of job classification and seniority among other factors, supplemented by a material incentive system.[7]

Agriculture was collectivized in 1953. Operations are organized into state farms and peasant cooperatives, with the County Farm Management Committee and the Central State Agriculture Committee responsible for economic management, and party organs providing management guidance (or interference, depending on one's perspective) (see box 3.2). On the state farms, peasants are paid fixed salaries. In the case of the cooperatives, which are theoretically owned by the members, members receive equal shares paid in cash and in kind, with bonuses going to work units over fulfilling targets. In 1996, the bonus system was expanded with subteam members freely allowed to dispose 10 percent of their harvest if they met the production target (Lee 1999).[8]

Recent tendencies embody two potentially conflicting initiatives. First, the regime has sought to increase the importance of state farms (which are considered ideologically more advanced) and to integrate the agricultural sector more firmly into the central plan. Advocates of the family responsibility system or other more incentive-compatible ways of organizing

---

6. See I.D. Koh (1998). However, there are indications that this integration may have been reversed or decentralized in the aftermath of the August 1998 constitutional reform.

7. A worker honorific incentive system, the *Chollima* movement, named after a winged mythological horse that could travel 250 miles a day, was introduced in 1956 when Kim Il-sung visited the Kangson Steel Plant and unburdened himself about the difficulty of leading the nation in the face of "the U.S. imperialists and the Syngman Rhee puppet clique growing wild with their 'march north' shriekings" (quoted in H.S. Lee (1999) p.50). So moved, the Kangson workers dutifully boosted output, producing their own Stakhanov, a smelter worker named Chin Ung-won, who was promoted as a model worker, upholding the policies of the party and state, strengthening the collectivist life, pursuing ideological work, and generally attaining lofty ideals.

8. For organizational descriptions of agriculture see Hwang (1993), S.C. Kim (1994), Y.S. Lee (1994a, 1997), H.S. Lee (1994a, 1999), and Moon (1998). Additional sources are cited in the discussion of the famine in chapter 5.

Box 3.2 A Tale of *Juche* Agriculture

What follows is meant as a cautionary tale for prospective planners everywhere. In 1962, in a Hooveresque moment, Kim Il-sung promised the North Korean people "meaty soup, steamed rice" and the other ingredients of the socialist good life. Soon thereafter a General Bureau of Poultry was established with the goal of fulfilling the Great Leader's promise by putting chicken in every pot.

The bureau began by importing a large number of baby chicks and establishing huge chicken plants, one allegedly larger than the biggest in the capitalist world. The bureau had neglected to secure adequate supplies of chicken feed, however, and in 1970 Kim Il-sung proclaimed "an all-people movement to raise chickens everywhere."

This mass mobilization was not entirely successful, as marauding chickens were eating feed meant for humans. In 1977, Kim Il-sung seized upon the idea of breeding earthworms, night crawlers, and even maggots to use as protein supplements for the nation's chickens and pigs. (The Great Leader admitted that raising maggots might attract flies, but nonetheless ordered chicken plants not located near populated areas to begin breeding maggots.) Indeed, the following year he decreed that each province and city should establish a dedicated earthworm breeding scientific facility.

Despite the high-level attention, all was not well on the earthworm front, and in 1980 the Great Leader admitted that the earthworm project had failed.

Night crawlers disappeared from the radar screen until 1992, when the official press began touting a protein feed breakthrough led by the Dear Leader, Kim Jong-il. On 7 May 1993—more than 20 years after his fateful promise—at the Sopo Chicken Plant in Pyongyang, Kim Il-sung proclaimed the triumphal achievement of the earthworm protein industry and his approval of the quality of meat and eggs produced using earthworm protein feed (H.S. Lee 1994b).

Unfortunately, as is discussed in chapter 5, Kim Jong-il's policy response to the famine was similar, emphasizing technical solutions, mass mobilization, and top-down hectoring, rather than a consideration of incentives and the possible advantages of decentralized decision-making.

production were reportedly punished. In 1994, Kim Il-sung stated his intention to nationalize all farms, a goal subsequently reaffirmed by Kim Jong-il.[9]

At the same time that the farming has been brought under more central control, there has been some loosening of control at the individual farm level. Under the stress of the ongoing crisis, reports have emerged of greater tolerance of small private plots, reductions in the size of farm work groups to seven or eight persons, expanded bonus systems, and fixed-rent tenancies or arrangements through which families are granted responsibilities for particular subplots as the regime tries to grapple with the current situation. It is impossible to determine the quantitative impor-

---

9. See Niksch (1996) and *Vantage Point*, March 1995.

tance of these new institutional arrangements, though D. Lee (n.d.) argues that productivity under these arrangements is higher than on the state farms. One gets the impression that the North Korean authorities regard their current difficulties as the product of technological backwardness or lack of revolutionary ideology on the part of the rural labor force, not a problem of organization or incentives, but that they are willing to tolerate a certain degree of experimentation in the face of a crisis.[10]

The central plan, specified in physical terms, is formed iteratively by the State Planning Commission (the central authority), the Office of State Affairs, and local committees from each plant and enterprise (see table 3.1, which summarizes North Korea's central plans). Prices, set by the central planners to reflect labor input, play an accounting, not a resource alloca-tion, role. There are three sets of prices, roughly corresponding to three types of markets (state-run, co-op, and farmers), which are applied depending on the organizational characteristics of the transacting parties. State-run markets, which handle mostly industrial goods, transact at "wholesale prices." A transaction between a state enterprise and a co-op would be priced at "industrial wholesale prices"—the "wholesale price" plus a transactions revenue tax wedge.[11] The third category of prices is retail prices charged at commercial outlets, where queuing is apparently the norm. In addition, there are limited farmers' and citizens' markets in which prices presumably reflect scarcity values, as well as black markets in consumer goods.[12] It is unclear to what extent the spread of farmers' markets, informal markets outside the central plan, and black markets are a tacitly approved coping response to the current crisis. Indeed as the Public Distribution System (PDS) for food has deteriorated, households are increasingly reliant on markets for food. Michell (1998) guesses that market transactions account for 20 percent of the actual economy.

All financial transactions are intermediated by designated state-owned banks as a method of control.[13] (In any event, money is basically only a means of exchange, since prices are irrational and resource allocation bureaucratic.) In the mid-1990s, the government allowed two joint venture

---

10. See, for example, Y.S. Lee (1996, 1997), Murooka (1999).

11. One implication of taxing enterprises differentially by ownership type (in addition to violating horizontal equity) is that it makes calculating *sectoral* tax burdens effectively impos-sible.

12. For a description of the formal pricing structure see Hwang (1993). For descriptions of black markets see Bazhanova (1992), Suh and Kim (1994), S.C. Kim (1996), D. Lee (1997), and Suh (1998). S.G. Hong (1999) and Ministry of Unification (1999) contain an analysis of farmers' markets and food prices. A freelance Japanese journalist surreptitiously videotaped some 4,000 people buying and selling everything from clothes to shampoo, to meat at one such market. Foreigners are barred from these markets.

13. For more on the North Korean financial system, see P.J. Kim (1995, 1998).

Table 3.1 North Korea's central plans

Period	Plan	Goals	Achievements (as announced by KWP)
1954-56	Three-year plan	1) Rebuild war damaged industrial facilities and structures 2) Reach pre-war level of industrial output	1) Industrial output increased 2) Grain output 2.87 million tons annually 3) Consumer goods output increased 2.1 fold
1957-60	Five-year plan	1) Stress heavy industry development 2) Solve food, clothing, housing problems 3) Socialization of private enterprises 4) Collectivization of agriculture	1) National income increased 2.2 fold 2) Industrial output increased 2.6 fold 3) Grain output 3.8 million tons annually 4) Targets met one year ahead of schedule
1961-67	First seven-year plan	1) National income to increase by 2.7 fold 2) Continue heavy industry development 3) Light industry and agricultural development 4) Grain output to reach 6 to 7 million tons 5) Innovation and technology revolution 6) Socialist cultural revolution 7) Increase in people's standard of living	1) National income achievement unpublished 2) Heavy industry output 72.2 percent of target 3) Light industry output 67.0 percent of target 4) Agricultural output 57.0 percent of target 5) Fishery output 58.0 to 70.0 percent of target
1968-70	Three-year plan	1) Military modernization 2) Strengthen military industrial complex 3) Advance technology and innovation	1) Military expenditure increased from 5 percent to 30 percent of government budget 2) Electricity and coal output target achieved
1971-76	Six-year plan	1) National income to increase 1.8 fold 2) Modernization of heavy industry—industrial output to rise 2.2 fold 3) Innovation and technology diffusion 4) National defense budget to increase to 30 percent of budget 5) Expansion of foreign trade	1) National income target increased 1.7 to 1.8 fold 2) Industrial output increased 2.5 fold 3) Grain output reached 8 million tons
1977	Extension	1) Attain missed targets for six-year plan	1) Oil refinery construction started

(continued)

Table 3.1 (continued)

1978-84	Second seven-year plan	1) *Juchehwa* scientific management and modernization of economy 2) Development of petrochemical industry 3) Reduce production costs 4) Modernize railway system and ports 5) Adopt independent accounting system 6) Expand foreign trade and joint ventures	1) "10 long-term goals" partly attained 2) Industrial output increased 2.2 fold 3) Grain output up to 10 million tons 4) Electric railway system 60 percent completed 5) National income unpublished 6) Independent accounting system adopted
1985-86	Two-year extension	1) Attain missed "10 long-term goals" 2) Priority on energy and transportation system	1) West coast tide control gates built 2) Industrial and grain output unpublished
1987-93	Third seven-year plan	1) Attain "10 long-term goals" 2) National income to increase by 1.7 fold; industrial output to increase 1.9 fold, grain output by 1.4 fold 3) Foreign trade volume to increase 3.2 fold 4) Technology investment 3 to 4 percent of government budget	"Due to the collapse of socialist countries and the socialist market, our country's economic cooperation and trade have faced setbacks. This has brought serious damage to our economic construction, and therefore our third Seven Year Plan has had a hard time achieving its goals . . ." Prime Minister Kang Song-san, 8 December 1993.

Source: Adapted from Kuark (1992) table 2.1.

banks to be established to facilitate FDI in the Rajin-Sonbong special economic zone (SEZ) in the far northeast. In 1995, the Dutch bank ING, which has developed a business niche operating in problematic markets, undertook a joint venture with the (North) Korean Foreign Insurance company, the monopolist for non-life insurance, to establish an investment bank that was 70 percent owned by ING, making the ING-Northeast Asian Bank the first Western bank in North Korea. Soon thereafter, the Hong Kong securities firm Peregrine and the North Korean government agreed to set up the Peregrine-Taesong Development Bank. It shut down, however, when Peregrine went bankrupt in January 1998, and ING Bank pulled out of its joint venture soon thereafter.[14]

One foreign banker who worked in North Korea indicates that by 1997 the inter-bank payments clearing system had completely broken down, and that banks were only accepting cash even for inter-bank transactions (Chiddy 1997). Understandably, most foreign banks refuse transactions with North Korean counterparts. Limited interest bearing accounts exist, with rates set by the planners, but these play no real role in determining the rate of capital accumulation, which is determined by the planners.[15] Likewise, interest rates play no allocative role, as capital is allocated by the central planners through government-controlled financial institutions in the form of investment grants (Hwang 1993). In March 1992, the government promulgated a 40 percent wage increase and in July 1992 issued new currency to eliminate currency overhang and to confiscate the returns to black marketeering (Eberstadt 1994a, P.J. Kim 1995, 1997, Oh 1996). Not surprisingly, foreign exchange certificates are preferred to domestic currency as a store of value and medium of exchange, and hard currency trades at an enormous premium on the black market[16] (see box 3.3).

Output is measured on a material product basis, which is basically incompatible with the system of national accounts used in market economies. Net material product covers value-added in the material product sectors (manufacturing, agriculture, construction, commodity transportation, productive communication, productive commerce, and a few others). Total material product multiplied by prices yields the gross output value of social production.

There are three outstanding problems with this definition. First, produced intermediates are doubled-counted. Second, non-material sectors (housing, health and welfare expenditures, education, science, art, personal services, state administration, etc.) are ignored. Third, the prices, which are calculated to reflect the labor theory of value, do not reflect true scarcity values. Even under the best of circumstances (such as having a cooperative government) concording material product accounts to a national accounts basis is difficult. Given the secrecy of the North Korean government, concordance is virtually impossible. Hwang (1993) makes a valiant effort, but the results are not fully convincing.

---

14. There are now no foreign banks operating in North Korea, though rumor has it that another bank affiliated with the Emperor property development group of Hong Kong, developer of the Rajin-Sonbong casino, may be licensed at some time in the future.

15. An underground curb market exists, however.

16. See Michell (1998) for a more extensive discussion of the twists and turns of North Korean currency policy.

Table 3.2 Composition of output, 1992-96 (millions of US dollars at US$1 = won 2.15)

	1992	1993	1994	1995	1996
Total	20,875	20,935	15,421	12,802	10,588
Agriculture	7,807	8,227	6,431	5,223	4,775
Industry	4,551	4,689	3,223	2,228	1,556
Construction	1,315	1,256	910	819	508
Other	7,160	6,762	4,858	4,532	6,748

Source: North Korean submission to the IMF.

Box 3.3   Black, Brown, and Blue Won

Officially the standard brown (*Choson*) won and the blue (foreign exchange certificate) won trade at the same 2.07 rate to the US dollar. Oh (1996) claims that the black market rate went from 80 won to the dollar in 1993 to 120 won to the dollar in 1996. During the author's visit to the Rajin-Sonbong Free Economic and Trade Zone in 1996, the black market rate appeared to be on the order of 50 to 70 won per dollar. A visitor to the Chinese border areas during the first half of 1997 reported that the black market rate peaked around 250 to 280 won per dollar, but had fallen to 220 won per dollar by June 1997. One got the impression that the penalties for black market currency exchange were quite severe, and that as a consequence it was a very fragmented, repressed market. Hence, significant disparities could contemporaneously exist between the rates on brown or blue won, or spatially in different locations, or even with respect to the ethnicity of the market participants. Black marketeers might be hesitant to be seen in the company of obvious foreigners.

In November 1997, use of the blue (foreign exchange certificate) won was abolished in the Rajin-Sonbong special economic zone, and the North Korean government took the unusual step of devaluing the brown (*Choson*) won from the official rate to 200 won to the dollar—roughly the black market rate—but only in the Rajin-Sonbong special economic zone. Rumors began to circulate that the blue won would be abolished, inasmuch as the Foreign Trade Bank did not have enough foreign currency reserves to back the blue won in circulation. Chiddy (1998) claims that the economy of Pyongyang is already effectively dollarized.

Historically, the sole significant piece of economic information published by the North Korean government has been its budget, though even this practice lapsed in the mid-1990s.[17] Under the strain of its ongoing crisis, North Korea hosted an informational mission from the IMF in the fall of 1997 and released to the Fund mission macroeconomic data which North Korean authorities had constructed with the assistance of the local United Nations Development Program (UNDP) office. Table 3.2 presents

---

17. See Cho and Zang (1999a) for a description of budgeting procedures.

Table 3.3 Government budget balance (billions of North Korean won)

	1994	1995	1996	1997	1998	1999
Revenues	41.6	24.3	20.3	na	19.8	na
Expenditures	41.4	24.2	20.6	na	20.0	20.4
Economic development	na	na	12.4	na	na	na
Social and cultural	na	na	5.0	na	na	na
Defense	na	na	3.0	na	3.0	3.0
General administration	na	na	0.2	na	na	na
Balance	0.2	0.1	−0.3	na	−0.2	na
Memorandum item:						
GDP	33.2	27.4	22.7			

Sources: North Korean submission to the IMF; The People's Korea webpage: http://www.Korea-np.co.jp/pk.

figures on the composition of output. The data suggest that the economy has collapsed around agriculture—that is, the fall in agricultural output has been actually less dramatic than the decline in output in other sectors. According to these figures, industrial output fell by nearly two-thirds between 1992 and 1996, and construction activity declined by almost as much. Taking construction as a proxy for investment, it is possible that investment may well have fallen below replacement level, and that the capital stock may have been shrinking. This notion is supported by the government expenditure data reported in table 3.3 (as well as by the extensive anecdotal evidence of North Koreans bartering scrap for food on the Chinese border).

Taking the economic development category as a proxy, investment has fallen by more than half from the values announced by the North Korean government in the early 1990s.[18] This point is further reinforced if one believes that certain military or military-related expenditures are hidden in the economic development budget. Estimates of North Korean military manpower and equipment do not show anything like this decline over the relevant period. Indeed, US and South Korean defense ministry figures show a slight increase in North Korean military deployment during this period. This suggests that the non-military part of the economy is being severely squeezed.

Two other things stand out in table 3.3. First, the government reports expenditures and receipts for 1994 far larger than GDP. This appears to violate the basic precepts of national income accounting. Second, it reports expenditures on defense that are far smaller than normally cited. Indeed, data on labor force participation provided by the North Korean authorities appear to omit the military entirely. All in all, these figures should probably be taken with very large grains of salt.

---

18. Data on capital goods imports from an earlier period reported by Eberstadt (1998a) suggest that the decline in investment may be a secular phenomenon going back decades.

Table 3.4 General government revenues, 1996
(millions of North Korean won)

Direct taxes	
Profits from state enterprises	6,290
User fees for working capital	2,250
Profits from cooperative farms	180
Indirect taxes	
Turnover taxes	8,080
Social insurance revenues	90
Other revenues	3,430
Total revenues	20,320

Source: North Korean submission to the IMF.

Data on government revenues are reported in table 3.4. The largest single source of revenue is turnover taxes, which is typical in CPEs.[19] These taxes present special problems for analysis because they are levied at differential rates depending on the legal status of the transacting parties. For example, the tax wedge imposed on an exchange between two state enterprises is different than the wedge imposed on a transaction between a state enterprise and a cooperative. Profits from state enterprises are the next largest source of government revenue. Excluding the problematic data for 1994, it seems that the government sector accounts for roughly 90 percent of activity controlled by the central planners—a large share, even by the standards of CPEs—with the caveat that these figures appear to apply only to activities undertaken under the plan.

A second, parallel, military economy exists outside the central plan, and does not appear to be considered in the data cited above. Its origins lie in a military modernization program adopted at the fifth plenary session of the Fourth Central Committee of the KWP in 1966 following the intensification of the Sino-Soviet split (Koo 1992, Namkoong and Yoo 1994). This parallel economy is highly secretive, even internally. According to Eberstadt (1994a), the State Planning Commission reportedly was deprived of access to information on it in the early 1970s. Meetings with outsiders are not held in the usual government ministries, but rather in unofficial locations such as hotels, etc. (DKIH 1991). This parallel economy amounts to autarky-within-autarky. The military maintains a completely integrated economic system, from farms and mines on up through facilities to manufacture uniforms and weapons, with separate administra-

---

19. North Korea abolished its personal tax system in 1973. However, a press report since the IMF mission indicates that the government has begun collecting a monthly wage tax (*Joong Ang Ilbo*, 5 April 1999). It has also been reported that the government is collecting half of the wages of North Koreans working abroad.

tive structures and foreign trade firms. DKIH (1991) estimates that half of the army is engaged in what elsewhere would be civilian economic activities, an estimate with which Sigal (1998a) concurs, as does a former senior US intelligence official. One might think of this as a giant US Army Corps of Engineers.

This would make the parallel military economy quite large: North Korea is the most militarized economy on earth, with 1.05 million men under arms, or 44 per 1000 people or fully one-fifth of men of working age (US Arms Control and Disarmament Agency (ACDA) 1998, Eberstadt and Banister 1992b, Eberstadt 1994b). Likewise, North Korea appears to devote a higher share of national income to the military than any other country in the world. ACDA puts this at 28.6 percent of GDP, though this would seem to be a stunningly precise estimate.[20] Although the economic crisis of the 1990s has resulted in some reduction in military expenditures in absolute terms, the military's share of the economy has probably risen as civilian activity has contracted precipitously. The parallel military economy has privileged access to technology and imports (including food). It actively exports and maintains its own trading channels outside the central plan.[21] This is potentially of enormous policy importance: To the extent that the proceeds from arms sales are going directly to the military, the military may have a purely pecuniary incentive to continue selling arms, even if other parts of the government would like to restrict sales for broader foreign policy reasons.[22] There is reason to believe, however, that the division between the civilian and military parts of the economy has been eroding under the pressure of the current difficulties. Indeed, the

---

20. Other estimates of the military's share of output range from 20 percent (CIA 1994) to 20-25 percent (Namkoong and Yoo 1994), to 30 percent (Trigubenko 1991), to 40 percent (Patrick 1991). Some of the discrepancies in these figures may be due to differences in definition: the defense budget versus military controlled production, for example, and other differences may be due to sample period since it appears that military expenditures have declined at a rate less than that of the overall economy. A former professor at Kim Il-sung University estimated that, while the defense budget directly consumes only 15 to 25 percent of output, the military gets a share of all government spending programs, and the true size of the parallel military economy was on the order of half of total output (Cho Myung-jae interview, 8 July 1995). However, Von Hippel and Hayes (1998) compute that energy use for narrowly defined military purposes (as opposed to all activities undertaken by the North Korean military) accounts for only 6 percent of total energy consumed in North Korea.

21. DKIH (1991) gives the example of an electronics technology that was used in the military sector for four years before being allowed into the civilian sector. The present author was told of one instance in which a foreign firm could not get mineral ore of the proper purity through civilian channels, but was sold the commodity by a military enterprise. See Lim (1999) and Takesada (n.d.) for more on the organization of the military economy.

22. North Korea has complained vociferously about the nearly annual joint military maneuvers undertaken by the US and South Korean militaries. During this period, the North Koreans undertake a variety of defensive responses which they argue have significant direct and indirect economic costs.

semi-official South Korean news agency *Yonhap* reported that Kim Jong-il had ordered the military "to take over the economy," and that military officials had been assigned to every major industrial facility and cooperative farm, apparently to prevent pilfering of materials and equipment by workers using these assets to barter for food.[23]

The Korean Workers Party controls considerable assets. There has also been mention of a "court" or "Kim family" economy, though the analytical significance of this term is unclear (C.S. Lee 1994). In the late 1960s, considerable effort was apparently devoted to investigation of the class background of the entire population and to the classification of the population on the basis of presumed political reliability (Hunter 1999). The "core class"—known colloquially as "tomatoes"—red to the core—are thought to account for perhaps 20 to 30 percent of the population, while perhaps 40 to 50 percent of the population are in the "unstable" or "apple" class—red only on the surface, and the "hostile" or "grape" class makes up the remainder.[24]

Clearly, there is considerable social differentiation, and the ruling elite live far differently than the mass of the common people, a pattern that has been accentuated by the crisis.[25] Although there is no data on income or wealth distribution in North Korea, and what fragmentary wage data that does exist appears relatively compressed, anecdotal evidence suggests that the income distribution is probably more unequal than in pre-reform Eastern European countries, largely due to the extensive non-wage benefits available to the elite, a situation that has been magnified under the famine.[26]

Statistical Comparison of the North and South Korean Economies

Some socioeconomic data for North and South Korea are reported in table 3.5. These data come from the national reporting authorities via the

---

23. *Yonhap*, 31 May 1999. See P. Kim (1999) for a description of pilfering and bartering as a famine response.

24. See Suh (1998) for an enlightening account of class conflict in North Korea.

25. Urban workers supposedly work six days a week, with 15 days paid vacation annually. Farmers have the first, eleventh, and twenty-first days of the month off. Every office worker is assigned one day of manual labor a week, with most white collar workers (except teachers) engaging in manual labor every Friday. Saturday is an education (indoctrination) day for everyone. Much of everyday life is organized by local "committees of public security." These groups control the distribution of biweekly food rations, and the quarterly and biannual clothing rations. They assign housing and can mete out punishment for such infractions as making an unauthorized visit to another area or region (DKIH 1991, Hwang 1993, Cho 1997). Of course this discipline has presumably eroded as a consequence of the crisis.

26. See D. Lee (1997) for discussion of distributional issues and P. Kim (1999) for speculation about the social impact of the famine.

Table 3.5 Socioeconomic indicators, 1992

	South Korea	North Korea
Life expectancy at birth (years)	70.4	70.7
Total fertility rate	1.7	2.4
Infant mortality rate (per 1000 live births)	21	25
Adult literacy (percentage)	96.8	95.0
Urban population (percentage of total population)	78.1	73.6

Sources: UNDP, Human Development Report 1994; UNESCO, Yearbook 1993.

UN. (In the case of the North Korean data it might be more accurate to describe it as estimates constructed by the UN.) What is striking about table 3.5 is the similarity of the figures. (It should be kept in mind that the data pertain to 1992—the figures have undoubtedly diverged since then.) South Korea appears to be further along in its demographic transition, as evidenced by the lower fertility and infant mortality statistics, but life expectancy, literacy, and urbanization are comparable for the two countries. The question immediately arises: how reliable are these data?

The answers are mixed. Eberstadt and Banister (1992a) subjected the North Korean demographic data to intense analysis and concluded that the data appear to be reported as collected, without invention, adjustments, or tampering, and that the quality appears comparable to that observed in developing countries (i.e., bad sampling methodologies, etc., but no obvious falsification). Eberstadt and Banister use demographic models to reconstruct the North Korean data and calculate estimates not radically different than those reported by the North Koreans: they estimate life expectancy for 1992 to be 69.5 years (versus the reported figure of 70.7), the infant mortality rate to be 29.5 per thousand (versus 25), and the total fertility rate to be 2.4, equal to the reported figure.[27] However, as indicated earlier, they then went on to use this data to count the "missing men" and concluded that North Korea was maintaining armed forces of roughly one million troops.

In 1994 North Korea conducted a census, the first since the partition. Eberstadt (1999a) analyzes this data and concludes that, unlike the earlier figures, the internal discrepancies are so large as to call into question the integrity of the data. Eberstadt identifies three major anomalies in the data: an apparent undercount of the total male population, the apparent undercount of the total female population, and the undercount of young females, and observes that these would be consistent with tampering to impede the estimation of "missing males," and hence inferential estimation of the size of the military, as done by Eberstadt and Banister (1992a).

---

27. Eberstadt (1995a) also notes that South Korea's demographic statistics are not always above reproach.

Table 3.6 Educational attainment rates

	Graduates and attendees of post-secondary schools (percentage of adult population)
North Korea 1987-88 (16 and above)	13.7
South Korea 1980 (15 and above)	9.2
Japan 1980 (15 and above)	18.5
China 1982 (15 and above)	0.9
Hong Kong 1981 (15 and above)	6.6
United States 1987 (16 and above)	36.0
East Germany 1981 (15 and above)	14.9
Soviet Union 1970 (16 and above)	9.4

Source: Eberstadt 1995a, table 31.

With respect to literacy, it should be recalled that North Korea has maintained longer compulsory education than the South and has a younger age structure of the population, both of which would presumably contribute to high adult literacy. Moreover, as indicated in table 3.6, reported rates of post-secondary education for North Korea are on par with those of East Germany and significantly higher than those for the Soviet Union, at least in the late 1970s. One gets the impression that North Korea has a relatively well-educated population, and thus the reported proximate universal literacy may not be far off the mark.[28]

The urbanization data may be subject to the greatest error, simply because the definition of an urban area does not appear to be well standardized either within North Korea or internationally. North Korea was probably more urbanized than South Korea at the time of partition, but the *juche* requirement of virtual self-sufficiency in agriculture must have slowed the rate of urbanization, as apparently confirmed by Eberstadt (1995a). It appears that the data may overstate the relative urbanization of North Korea, but it is difficult to determine the extent. It may also be the case that North Korea has been de-urbanizing in response to the current crisis, as urban residents migrate to the countryside to improve their access to food or through rumored involuntary relocation schemes.

Setting these uncertainties aside, the overall impression one gets is that North Korea is a relatively well-educated and urbanized country with a large military-industrial complex. In comparison to its communist or former-communist brethren, it is perhaps more similar to Eastern European countries like Romania or Bulgaria or some of the former republics of the Soviet Union than the more rural China or Vietnam (table 3.7).

---

28. Foreign business executives have indicated that literacy is "nearly universal." See Cho and Zang (1999b) for a description of North Korea's educational system.

Table 3.7 Distribution of labor force at time of reform

Country	Year	Sector Agriculture	Industry	Service
Czech Republic[1]	1989	11[a]	39	50
Slovakia[1]	1989	15[a]	34	51
Poland[1]	1989	7[a]	37	56
Hungary[1]	1990	15[a]	36	49
Soviet Union[2]	1987	19[a]	38[b]	43
Ukraine[3]	1990	20	40	40
Belarus[3]	1990	20	42	38
Romania[1]	1990	28[a]	38	34
Bulgaria[1]	1989	19[a]	47	34
North Korea[4]	1993	33	37	30
China[5]	1978	71	15	14
Vietnam[2]	1989	71	12	17

a. Agriculture and forestry

b. Industry and construction

Sources:
1. Commander, Simon and Fabrizio Coricelli. 1995. *Unemployment, Restructuring, and the Labor Market in Eastern Europe and Russia.* Washington: World Bank, tables 1.1, 2.2, 3.5, 5.1, and 6.11.

2. Eberstadt, Nicholas. 1995. *Korea Approaches Unification.* Armonk: M.E. Sharpe, table 6.

3. Bosworth, Barry P. and Gur Ofer. 1995. *Reforming Planned Economies in an Integrating World Economy.* Washington: Brookings Institution, table 3-1.

4. Eberstadt, Nicholas. 1998. A Quantitative Comparison of Current Socioeconomic Conditions in North and South Korea. Paper presented at the Second Conference of the International Interdisciplinary Project on Nation-Building for Korean Unification, Honolulu, Hawaii (21-25 January).

5. Sachs, Jeffrey and Wing Thye Woo. 1994. Structural Factors in the Economic Reforms of China, Eastern Europe, and the Former Soviet Union. *Economic Policy,* 18: 101-45, table 2.

Assessing the size of the North Korean economy or the level of per capita income is extremely difficult for several reasons. As indicated earlier, centrally planned economies (CPEs) use a fundamentally different set of national accounting principles than market economies. It is difficult to move between the centrally planned accounting system and the market accounting system in the best of circumstances. This task is made virtually impossible by the overwhelming secrecy of the North Korean regime and the extreme paucity of statistical material emanating from the North. Even if one can calculate North Korean income in the domestic currency, one faces the very difficult task of estimating the shadow price of foreign exchange in order to convert measured income into a common international currency. As previously noted, Hwang (1993) makes a heroic effort along these lines, but in the end the results are not entirely persuasive.

Table 3.8 Capital stock and GDP regressions

Dependent variable	Independent variables						Standard error	R²
	Constant	News	Energy	Cargo	TV	Life		
GDP per capita	−2.37	0.19	0.21	0.03	0.15	1.68	0.12	0.98
	(−0.97)	(2.77)ᵃ	(2.80)ᵃ	(1.51)	(2.18)ᵇ	(2.66)ᵃ		
	Constant	News	Energy	Radio				
Capital per worker	3.77	0.32	0.41	−0.08			0.24	0.90
	(10.20)ᵃ	(2.98)ᵃ	(2.53)ᵇ	(−4.02)ᵃ				

Notes: All variables are in logs. Corresponding t-statistics are in parentheses.

a. Statistical significance at the 1 percent level.

b. Statistical significance at the 5 percent level.

c. Statistical significance at the 10 percent level.

Legend:

NEWS = newsprint, writing paper consumption per capita (kilograms per 1000 inhabitants)

ENERGY = commercial energy consumption per capita (kilograms of coal equivalent per capita)

CARGO = air cargo per capita (unit of air cargo = ten million kilometers)

TV = television sets in use per 1000 inhabitants

LIFE = life expectancy (years)

RADIO = radios in use per 1000 inhabitants

Source: UNESCO, *Yearbook* 1993.

In response, a number of researchers have attempted to estimate North Korean income indirectly through the method of physical indicators (Chun 1992, Jeong 1993). In this approach, a statistical relationship is established between income and various indicators for a sample of comparator countries. Then North Korean values of the development indicators are plugged into the statistical model to derive an estimate of North Korean income.

The regressions estimated for this purpose are reported in table 3.8. In these regressions, income per capita is expressed as a double logarithmic function of air cargo volume, consumption of printed materials, ownership of radios and televisions, energy use, and life expectancy. The relationship between these variables and per capita income (measured in purchasing power-adjusted terms) is quite tight, with the regression explaining 98 percent of the variation in income levels across a sample of 30 countries.[29] A similar regression relating the amount of physical capital stock per worker is also reported in table 3.8.

29. The sample, determined on the basis of data availability, consisted of Argentina, Austria, Brazil, Canada, Denmark, Finland, France, Germany, Greece, Hong Kong, Indonesia, Israel, Italy, Japan, South Korea, Malaysia, Mexico, Norway, Pakistan, Peru, the Philippines, Singapore, Spain, Sweden, Taiwan, Thailand, Tunisia, Turkey, the United Kingdom, and the United States.

It might be desirable to estimate a regression using only data from CPEs. This proved problematic for two reasons. First, there were relatively few (seven) usable data points.

Table 3.9 International income and capital stock comparisons, 1990

Country	GDP per capita	Capital stock per worker	Capital-output ratio
South Korea	8,271	17,995	6.44
Bulgaria	7,529	na	na
Malaysia	5,997	na	na
Thailand	4,270	4,912	2.69
Romania	2,656	na	na
Indonesia	2,323	na	na
North Korea (regressions)	2,284	4,879	6.18
Philippines	2,112	3,698	4.39
China	1,536	na	na

Note: Romania's figures are for 1989. GDP per capita is in current international dollars, capital per worker in 1985 international dollars. Capital-output ratio reflects adjustment for investment price level change and the difference between total population and the economically active population. In the case of North Korea, the sample average was applied for the investment price change.

Source: Summers and Heston, 1991.

In table 3.9, the fitted values for North Korea are reported along with the actual values for several other Asian countries and two CPEs. According to the econometric model, per capita income (in purchasing power-adjusted terms) in North Korea in 1990 was $2,284, similar to Indonesia, the Philippines, and Romania (in 1989) and about one-quarter that of South Korea. Even with the relatively tight fit of the regression, the 90 percent forecast interval around this estimate (the values that would insure that the true value has a 90 percent chance of being within this interval) is quite broad: from $1,339 to $3,897.[30]

To facilitate comparison, table 3.10 reports estimates of the ratio of South Korean to North Korean per capita incomes (a common benchmark),

Second, the data for the CPEs has some strange characteristics, possibly due to mismeasurement or the economic decline of the European CPEs after 1989. A regression estimated solely on these data points had a lower coefficient of determination (0.89) than the regression reported in table 3.8 and an implausible pattern of estimated coefficients. The projected estimate of North Korean per capita income from this regression was $1394, lower than the estimate reported in table 3.9, but within the 90 percent confidence interval as indicated below.

30. Using a similar approach, Jeong estimates that North Korea's per capita income is $1,181 while Chun puts the figure at $1,273, but these figures are not directly comparable to those reported in table 3.9. Neither Chun nor Jeong use purchasing power corrected data, and as a consequence both obtain downwardly biased estimates of North Korea (and other low income country) incomes. Jeong, for example, estimates per capita income in India to be $52 and in the Philippines to be $339 (less than a third of his estimate for North Korea), while the estimates in table 3.9 indicate that per capita income in the Philippines and North Korea are roughly the same. Chun does not report any international comparisons.

Table 3.10 Ratio of South Korean to North Korean per capita income, 1990

Source	Per capita income
Hwang[a]	5.40
National Unification Board	5.23
Chun	4.48
Jeong[b]	4.23
Noland	3.62
Hwang[c]	2.49

a. Converted to a common currency using the North Korean trade exchange rate.

b. 1989.

c. Converted to a common currency using North Korean official exchange rate.

though even this normalization is not entirely adequate, as the figures unadjusted for purchasing power parity (PPP) exhibit spuriously high ratios. The estimates range from 5.40 (from Hwang 1993, using the North Korean trade exchange rate to convert to a common currency) to 2.49 from the same source using the official exchange rate to make the currency conversion. The estimate reported in table 3.10 implies a ratio of 3.62.

It is worth noting that these estimates pertain to 1990, which may well have been the peak of North Korean per capita income. It is virtually certain that the relative disparity between North and South Korean income has widened in the intervening period. If one updated these ranges on the basis of the Bank of Korea (BOK) real GDP estimates, then the ratio of South to North per capita income in 1997 would be between 8:1 and 11:1.[31] With the assistance of the UNDP, the North Korean authorities have recently attempted to make their own estimates of GDP, calculating that in 1996 GDP was $10.6 billion and per capita GDP was $480, based on the official exchange rate of 2.15 North Korean won per US dollar.[32] These estimates imply that South Korean incomes were more than 20 times higher than those in the North.

31. The prize for precision, North Korean division, goes to Shishido and Hamada (1998), who, without revealing their methodology, report a PPP-adjusted estimate of North Korean per capita income in 1995 of $3,596.90, which, given the South Korean estimate of $11,172.10, would yield a ratio of 3.106.

32. These figures should be regarded with skepticism: as Eberstadt (1999a) points out, the North Koreans released three widely disparate estimates of per capita income for 1989, implying that GNP declined anywhere from 11 to 70 percent between 1989 and 1995.

The North Koreans appear to take an especially relaxed approach to national accounting when there is money at stake. Shortly before releasing the figures cited above, the North Koreans told the UN that indicated that per capita GDP was $239 in 1995—the figure used in assessing their dues to that organization.

Figure 3.1 Estimates of North Korean GDP

growth rate (percentage)

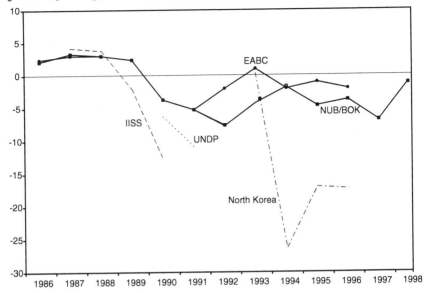

Note:
IISS = Institute for Strategic Studies
EABC = East Asian Business Consultancy

Some capital-output ratios are reported in the third column of table 3.9. As countries develop and accumulate capital, the additional capital needed to produce additional output rises. This is to say that the capital-output ratio tends to rise with income. The capital-output ratio also will rise with the degree of economic distortion as capital is misallocated into low productivity uses. CPEs tend to waste capital and, as a consequence, exhibit high capital-output ratios. As might be expected, North Korea exhibits a very high capital-output ratio given its apparent level of income, although given the quality of the underlying data perhaps this point should not be pressed too far.

The data discussed thus far pertain to the North Korean economy's level of development in comparison to other countries, including South Korea. A distinct issue is the time path of the North Korean economy. Figure 3.1 depicts estimates from several individuals and organizations as to growth rates of the North Korean economy. There is a general consensus that the North Korean economy suffered some severe shocks from 1989 on due to the withdrawal of Soviet assistance, bad harvests, and the collapse of the Commonwealth of Independent States (CIS) economies, which were North Korea's largest trade partners. There does not appear to be a consensus as to the depth and persistence of this slowdown.

As demonstrated above, it is no mean feat to estimate the level of North Korean output, much less its time path. The most widely cited figures come from the BOK, which puts out the official South Korean estimates of North Korea's economy. These figures are apparently derived by taking classified data on physical output generated by South Korean intelligence agencies and then applying South Korean prices and value-added weights to indices of physical production. Because the original estimates of physical output are classified, there is little opportunity to check their plausibility. Nor is it obvious that South Korean prices and value-added weights are the most appropriate. Moreover, the ultimate growth rate figure is reportedly subject to interagency bargaining within the South Korean government. Given these caveats, the BOK numbers are probably best regarded as coming with very large standard errors.[33]

For their part, the North Koreans report that industrial output increased by 5.6 percent annually from 1987 to 1993 (Han 1995), though privately they have admitted that the economy has shrunk about 30 percent since 1991. In July 1997, in an apparent attempt to obtain food aid, they presented figures to the UN that implied an enormous fall in output. The aforementioned national accounts constructed with the assistance of the UNDP's Pyongyang office indicate that GDP fell by nearly half between 1992 and 1996 (table 3.2, figure 3.1). At the other extreme is Michell (1998), who estimates that the economy shrank by less than 10 percent over the same period.

Moreover, while the slowdown shown in figure 3.1 looks quite grim, national income and personal welfare may diverge quite sharply. Momentarily setting aside this issue of the famine (which is taken up in greater detail in chapter 5), the decline in national income probably overstates the decline in household welfare (Illarionov, Layard, and Orszag 1994), as has been the case in other transitional economies such as Russia. It is unlikely that services (housing services and education, to give two examples), which are undercounted in the material product accounting system

---

33. Put another way, if we formed 90 percent confidence intervals around these estimates, they might well encompass zero—that is, we might not be reasonably certain whether the North Korean economy grew or shrank in 1996, much less that it shrank four percent. This is more than a purely theoretical consideration, as some contemporaneous visitors to North Korea (or at least to Pyongyang) have reported anecdotal evidence reporting positive growth relative to the early 1990s—more cars on the road, more goods in the shops, more air pollution, etc.—not the steadily shrinking economy portrayed in figure 3.1. (Indeed, in 2000 reports began emerging that the economy had possibly bottomed out and was no longer shrinking.) However, North Korea exhibits significant regional disparities, and reports from other parts of the country paint a very different picture. Pyongyang may not be indicative of the situation in the rest of the country. See Michell (1998) for more discussion of these issues and some alternative calculations.

and are not amenable to physical measurement (the basis for the figure 3.1 estimates), declined as much as manufactured output. (People may not be operating very efficiently due to power shortages and a lack of spare parts, but they are still living in the same apartment and their children are still attending school.) These considerations would appear to caution against interpreting the estimates displayed in figure 3.1 as indices of hardship or political discontent. Indeed, the subtle relationship between material deprivation and political change is a topic that will be taken up again in the third section of this book.

Crisis Response

The North Korean economy is, in essence, broken. It is beset with a variety of problems typical of CPEs, and is unable to generate enough output to sustain the population biologically (at least given the current regime's priorities). Its shortcomings have been exacerbated by the *juche* ideology and the extreme concentration of power in the hands of a single individual, first Kim Il-sung and now his son Kim Jong-il. Although the central planners were initially successful in mobilizing resources, in recent years economic performance has clearly deteriorated. Tremendous resources have been poured into costly "white elephants."[34] The North Koreans were forced to admit that in almost every industrial sector output had fallen significantly short of the third seven-year plan goal (Yoo 1996), and North Korea has not unveiled a new plan in more than a decade.

---

34. In a 1986 essay, which, among other things propounded a notion of immortality based on the trinity of the leader, the party, and the masses, Kim Jong-il proclaimed that "We must be firmly determined to carry out the revolution and construction in our own style. . .," a line that has since frequently cropped up in propaganda slogans. North Korea's own style of industrial development has long been characterized by a penchant for what one observer described as "monumental edifices." Among the more prominent:

- The never opened, slightly askew, 105-story Ryugyong Hotel dominates the Pyongyang skyline. "Under construction" for more than a decade, a delegation from the European Chamber of Commerce in Seoul inspected the site and deemed it "irreparable" (Flake 1999a).

- The longest dam in the world, the West Sea Barrage, cuts across the West Sea where the estuary of the Taedong River empties into it. According to one international aid official, one effect of the barrage has been to encourage silting, which has rendered the system of locks unusable.

- Vinalon is a multipurpose synthetic fiber developed in North Korea. Not content with the world's largest vinalon plant in Hamhung, in 1986 the regime broke ground on a new complex near Sunchon that would double Hamhung's capacity. H.S. Lee (1999) estimates the cost of the yet uncompleted project plant at over 12 billion won, or more than one-third of annual GDP.

The economy's worsening conditions did force a political response. During the 21st plenary session of the 6-term Party Central Committee on 8 December 1993, North Korea admitted that it had failed to attain the desired goals. As a stop-gap measure, the North Koreans decided to set the next three years as a buffer period during which it would concentrate on boosting agriculture, light industry, and foreign trade. These "three firsts" were again emphasized in Kim Il-sung's New Year's Day address on 1 January 1994 and reiterated in the official 1995 New Year's Day pronouncement following his death. However, as seen below, subsequent pronouncements appear to have backed away from this: while restoring agriculture remains a priority, policy statements since the death of Kim Il-sung appear to be more skeptical with regard to international economic relations, and there appears to be a renewed emphasis on heavy industry.

In an earlier attempt at righting the economy, in 1984 the government launched the "August 3 campaign for people's goods," so named for Kim Il-sung's proclamation date. The plan was to increase the availability of consumer goods by locally mobilizing underutilized labor (housewives, retirees, the handicapped, etc.) and waste materials.[35] It is claimed that more than 6,000 types of goods have been produced under this program, including chinaware, furniture, and some electrical goods (Kim and Koh 1994). Products were sold to consumers through direct sales stores outside the central plan, and sales in 1991 reportedly reached 13 percent of sales in the central plan (H.S. Lee 1991, 1994c, and 1999).[36]

It would appear that the significance of the August 3 campaign lies not in its actual accomplishments but rather on whether it represented the leading edge of more ambitious reforms. (After all, it is hard to believe that retirees fashioning handicrafts out of locally available scrap material would in itself be an adequate response to decades of neglect of the consumer goods market.) In this light, it is difficult to judge the August 3 campaign a success.

---

35. This was in keeping with the longstanding policy of producing 60 percent of consumer goods within each local region—another example of "autarky-within-autarky"! A recent article published in the North Korean press by Won To-hui, director of the cabinet secretariat, continues to propound on this theme of local areas producing a range of products for local needs (*Pyongyang Minju Choson*, 31 January 1999).

36. Although H.S. Lee's appraisal of this policy is relatively positive, observers associated with the South Korean government unification think tank have been more critical. Oh (1993) argues that the campaign has been a "means of mobilizing untapped local resources rather than an attempt to utilize any market mechanism, since it was designed to keep any deviations from the central planning system within carefully monitored limits" (p.147), while S.C. Kim states that the policy "was never meant to foster local autonomy," and that the emphasis on local production was followed by creation of a new organization to strengthen central control through the party apparatus (pp.5-6). Indeed, he argues that distribution of these products through state controlled stores fostered corruption in the late 1980s. Some have simply interpreted the movement as a blame-shifting exercise by the

The August 3 campaign and the crisis do appear to have led to a loosening of the distribution mechanism. There has been an increase in the number of direct sales outlets where co-ops sell directly to the public at non-controlled prices, as well as an increase in department stores selling imported Chinese consumer goods at non-controlled prices. Even state firms have begun to divert production into non-controlled distribution channels. Domestic trading firms have begun to arbitrage prices across markets. As a consequence, the central planners have begun to replace fixed prices with price ceilings or bands. Systemic failure has thus been met with a tactical reform.

The crisis in production has been further exacerbated by the inadequacy of the infrastructure. The telecommunications system is dilapidated. Air and sea transportation facilities are limited. According to the South Korean government, 90 percent of North Korea's cargo and 64 percent of its passenger travel is by rail. About 80 percent of the railway track is electrified, and much of the railway network is single track. Only eight percent of the roads are paved, and the road from Pyongyang to its port of Nampo, for example, is a bumpy single lane much of the way. As noted earlier, coal, oil, and electricity all appear to be in short supply, and manufacturing facilities experience periodic shutdowns due to power interruptions. Power shortages and lack of spare parts have reduced capacity utilization in the industrial sector to 10 to 15 percent or less (see chapter 7).

The agriculture sector is clearly in trouble due to the collapse of the industrial economy (as will be discussed in chapter 5) as well as failures of organization. Officially, there has been increasing emphasis on state farms, and the political leadership apparently views the problems in agriculture as stemming from a shortage of science and revolutionary fervor on the part of the peasantry, though a limited material incentive was introduced for the co-ops in 1996. Likewise, there are reports of new, more incentive-compatible forms of organization such as fixed rent tenancies being introduced. However, how widespread these developments are is unknown.

North Korea's agricultural difficulties are part of a larger pattern of environmental degradation, despite what it calls its "*juche*-oriented environment protecting ideology." Problems include severe industrial pollution, soil erosion and runoff due to problems in reforestation, inefficient use of energy and the highest per capita hydrocarbon emissions in the world, very high levels of fertilizer and pesticide use with their attendant problems, and a lack of institutional capacity to formulate, monitor, and implement environmental policies.[37]

---

central authorities, as in "don't look to us for those goods—produce them yourselves, like province X."

37. See Hayes (1994), Hayes and von Hippel (1998), and S.J. Hong (1999).

The emphasis on domestic production necessitates excessive diversification of the economy, and thus suboptimally small industrial plants. Outsiders estimate that the technology used in the industrial sector is generally two decades behind that of the rest of the world (Patrick 1991, Korea Development Bank 1998). However, in some particular sectors, especially those such as nonferrous metals that have relevance to military production, the technological gap appears to be less.

In response to these mounting difficulties, the regime has engaged in a number of coping mechanisms. Absent any real reform, the regime continues to rely on Stakhanovite exhortations and militaristic sloganeering of "total mobilizations" and "battle at missile speed," and invokes images of the "arduous march" of the communist anti-Japanese guerillas of the 1930s.[38]

A second response has been to try to generate desperately needed foreign exchange through one-off projects like the Rajin-Sonbong SEZ and the Mt. Kumgang tourism project—projects that can literally and figuratively be fenced off from the rest of the economy.

The third tactic is the use of threat and brinkmanship to extract resources from the rest of the international community.[39] But even the limited reforms have been undercut by North Korean actions—a submarine incursion immediately following the Rajin-Sonbong international investment conference in September 1996 and the detention of a South Korean visitor soon after the start of the Mt. Kumgang tours. Even the donation of 500 head of cattle to North Korea by Hyundai chairman Chung Ju-young was followed in June 1998 by a second submarine incident and the discovery of a dead North Korean frogman on a South Korean beach. This delayed, though ultimately did not derail, Chung's second visit and the initiation of the Mt. Kumgang tourist project, but led the South Korean government to suspend official assistance. After Chung's second visit in November 1998, a third sub was sunk by the South Korean navy in December, and a June 1999 naval clash in the Yellow Sea months after the start of Mt. Kumgang tours was the largest military encounter between the two countries since the signing of the Korean War armistice.[40] This was followed

---

38. Similarly, the "Red Banner" campaign begun in 1995 appears to be an intensification of the old orthodoxy. See Murooka (1999) for more details. Pollack and Lee (1999) cite an April 1997 speech by Kim Jong-il upon the 50th anniversary of Kim Il-sung University in which he argues that military concerns must take precedence over the economy, and that the way to solve the contemporaneous economic difficulties is to emulate the army's "undying and absolute sacrificing spirit" (p.36). In fairness to Kim, Park Chung-hee used to do the same thing in *South* Korea—in 1968 South Koreans were instructed to "Fight While Working, Work While Fighting."

39. See Snyder (1999b) for a sophisticated analysis of these tactics.

40. Some have argued that the submarine and frogman incursions are routine: without the means of electronic intelligence gathering the North must use agents on the ground for reconnaissance. Since the incursions are relatively frequent, a certain number are likely to

in the September 1999 run-up to the Berlin missile talks by a unilateral declaration by the North Korean military that it was redrawing the UN Command-designated border in the Yellow Sea and threatening to enforce its declaration "by various means."[41]

Similar mixed signals have emanated from Pyongyang with regard to more comprehensive reform. A constitutional revision promulgated in August 1998 mentioned "private property" (Article 24), "material incentives" (Article 32), and "cost, price, and profit" (Article 33) in an otherwise thoroughly orthodox elaboration of a planned, socialist, self-reliant, *juche* economy. Babson (n.d.) interprets a statement identifying as a goal of the economy "growth and prosperity of the Fatherland" instead of the "country's independent development" as signaling a shift toward greater pragmatism. J. Choi (1998, 1999), however, interprets both aspects of decentralization as well as the terminology mentioned above as simply ratifying practices already in existence and not indicating any move toward reform. Indeed, shortly after the constitutional revision, the *Rodong Sinmun* (the newspaper of the Central Committee of the Korean Workers Party) and *Kŭlloja* (the body's politico-theoretical magazine) published a joint editorial blasting reform (quoted at the beginning of this chapter). Also, a number of economic reformers were reportedly purged.[42]

In December 1998, ten North Koreans in Beijing took a week-long class in international business law taught by American professors in a program sponsored by the Asia Foundation, Beijing University, and New York University. Through the offices of the World Bank (of which it is not a member), the North Korean government arranged business training classes in China for its cadres. These were scheduled to begin in March 1999, but North Korea withdrew at the last minute. That spring it also pulled out of a professorial exchange program between the economics departments of Kim Il-sung University and the Australian National University (ANU).[43]

---

be intercepted. How these incidents play out is then as much a political issue as a military one. One former high ranking US military official has proposed sharing US satellite intelligence with the North Koreans on a real time basis, precisely as a means of reducing the need for physical incursions.

41. The North Koreans later threatened to "crush" any violations of the unilateral declaration "through various and cruel means."

42. See Jee Hae-bom, *Digital Chosun Ilbo*, 29 September 1998, and J. Choi 1999.

43. Earlier, in 1997, a handful of graduate students entered the Australian National University. After completing their program at ANU they returned home via China. In Beijing, they were permitted to visit the government agency responsible for special economic zones, but the North Korean embassy would not permit them to visit the government bureau handling economic restructuring, much to the amusement of their Chinese hosts. After their return to North Korea, the students were rumored to have gone through a very intensive reeducation program. See *Newsreview*, 13 February 1999, for a brief account of the Bretton Woods' institutions attempts at cooperating with North Korea on training issues.

In April 1999 the Supreme People's Assembly (SPA) passed a law elucidating the process of central planning. Given that North Korea had been practicing central planning for several decades, one might ask why such a law is necessary. According to Yang Hyong-sop, the Vice Chairman of the SPA standing committee, the "the law on the plan of the national economy is a revolutionary plan to thoroughly ban the wind of economic liberalization and to adhere to the principle of planned management . . . no attempts for the decentralization of power or liberalization will be allowed and the state's centralized and unitary guiding principle will be invariably adhered to." A *Rodong Sinmun* commentary described it as "our own-style revolutionary planning law, which thoroughly bars the wind of economic liberation and reflects the immovable will of the party, the state, and the people who adhere to the principle of planned management . . . [and will deal] a heavy blow to those who plot to destroy the socialist economy." The good news is that this implies that such souls exist. The bad news is that their actions have been criminalized.

A month later the regime arranged for a handful of female graduate students to take the Graduate Record Exam (GRE)—a prerequisite for entering a graduate business administration program in the United States. And then on 31 May 1999 the *Rodong Sinmun* and *Kŭlloja* published another joint editorial stating that:

> The ideological and cultural infiltration by imperialism is a means for aggression and interference that is being committed under the rubric of cooperation and exchange. . . . The collapse of the erstwhile Soviet Union and east European countries is entirely attributable to their flinging the door open to the imperialist ideological and cultural poisoning. The corrupt ideas spread by the imperialists are more dangerous than A-bombs for those countries in the process of socialist construction. . . . It is important to sternly smash capitalist and non-socialist factors in the bud. All catastrophic consequences originate in small things.

International Economic Relations

Traditionally, international trade has been regarded as a necessary evil, though at times the regime has paid lip service to international cooperation and exchange. In 1994, foreign trade was proclaimed one of the "three firsts" along with agriculture and light industry. Both the *juche* ideology and the planned character of the economy would appear to work against notions of comparative advantage and the exploitation of international trade for the purpose of increasing income and welfare. As Kuark (1992) observed:

> Foreign trade in North Korea was generally limited to the planned importation of domestically unavailable goods needed for building a socialist economy and the exportation of a sufficient volume of goods or "surplus goods" to cover the cost of planned imports. Foreign trade has been conducted mainly to obtain

essential imports. Exports have never been considered for economic gains in employment or income, but as a means to finance necessary imports (p.21).

The 1970s push for military modernization left the country heavily indebted relative to its meager export earnings, and the 1975 *de facto* default effectively cut it off from international capital markets. The economy suffered further negative shocks with the withdrawal of Soviet economic support in the mid-1980s and the subsequent collapse in the early 1990s of the CIS economies (which had been North Korea's largest trade partners).[44] Although increased Chinese support has partly offset the loss of Soviet aid, China too has indicated that there are limits to how far it will go to support the *juche* economy, especially in light of the liberalizing economic reforms undertaken in China. By all appearances, North Korea has been under significant balance of payments pressures with deleterious implications for growth prospects.

This section reviews North Korea's external economic relations. It begins with an overview of its trade and financial relations, and then discusses economic relations with its major trade partners in turn. The chapter concludes with a discussion of North Korea's current reform efforts, including the Rajin-Sonbong SEZ and the Mt. Kumgang tourism project, setting the stage for an analysis of alternative development scenarios in the later chapters.

International Trade and Finance

A variety of party and state organs handle trade policy matters. The governmental units were reorganized in the August 1998 constitutional revision into a ministry of trade. Historically, trade was funneled through a few large trading firms. This system was partially decentralized in 1984, and now roughly 100 trading firms are reportedly in operation. North Korea maintains a multiple currencies, multiple exchange rate system (see box 3.3).

The regime's obsession with secrecy ought to be less of a problem in analyzing the countries' external economic relations. In principle, "mirror

---

44. It would be interesting to compare the responses of North Korea and Vietnam to the common shock of the withdrawal of Soviet aid and the collapse of the USSR. My supposition is that the Vietnamese were able to far more effectively reform their more agriculturally based economy and boost exports to ease the balance of payments constraint, while, in the absence of greater export orientation, the North Koreans were forced to reduce the level of domestic activity. Unfortunately, the extreme uncertainty surrounding the North Korean balance of payments position (largely because of the issue of remittances addressed later in this chapter) effectively precludes quantitative inquiry along this line. However, Eberstadt (1997a) calculates that, between 1989 and 1995, the Vietnamese nearly tripled their exports (largely by liberalizing the price of rice, their major exportable, thus encouraging increased output), while North Korean exports fell by half. Similar possibilities for reform in North Korea are discussed in chapter 7.

Figure 3.2　North Korean trade

exports and imports
(billions of US dollars)

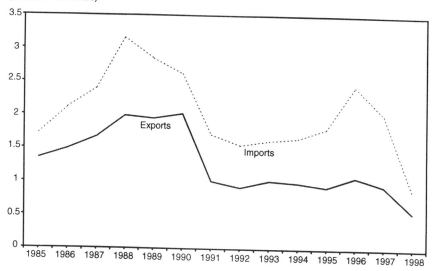

Source: Bank of Korea, KOTRA.

statistics" reported by North Korea's trade and investment partners can be used to deduce North Korea's external transactions. This data is subject to considerable uncertainty: the figures reported here are based on partner country submissions to the WTO, supplemented with data from the Korea Trade Promotion Corporation (KOTRA) in the cases of countries that do not report the commodity structure of their trade with North Korea to the WTO.[45] Finally, countries do not report barter or countertrade transactions; to the extent that North Korea has been able to successfully conclude barter deals, this trade may also be counted in the statistics.

Figure 3.2 displays the time path of aggregate imports and exports. The data show that imports have consistently exceeded exports, and that,

---

45. As with so much about North Korea, these statistics must be treated with care. The data underlying figure 3.2 are derived from the International Monetary Fund's *Direction of Trade Statistics*. Since North Korea does not release any data on external trade, the figures have been obtained by summing trade reported by North Korea's trade partners. According to standard accounting conventions, exports are valued "free on board" at the port of exportation, while imports are valued including cargo, insurance, and freight charges at the port of importation. Because North Korea's exports are derived from partner countries' reported imports, they have to be adjusted for the transportation and insurance charges that have been included in the import statistics. Following IMF conventions, in the absence of other information these are assumed to be 10 percent of the value of imports. Similarly, North Korea's imports, which are derived from its partner countries' exports, must be adjusted for the "missing" transportation and insurance costs.

Beyond this valuation issue, the data from the IMF (as well as the commodity composition of trade data gathered by the WTO and distributed through the UN) contain inaccuracies

after peaking in the late 1980s, trade has fallen substantially in the 1990s. Given the highly questionable nature of the GDP statistics discussed in the previous section, the falling volume of trade is probably the best indicator of the deterioration of the North Korean economy.

Historically, North Korea oriented its trade relations in a highly political (as distinct from economic) manner. The Soviet Union and its East Bloc allies were its most important trade partners, although during a development push in the 1970s North Korea greatly increased its trade and investment relations with the developed capitalist countries (with the exception of the United States). As outlined in Eberstadt, Rubin, and Tretyakova (1995), North Korea suffered an enormous trade shock when the Russian economy collapsed, and it subsequently reoriented its trade toward China. China initially tried to limit its exposure to North Korea (Eberstadt 1995b), but as will be discussed in chapter 5, the worsening famine forced their hand.

As can be seen in table 3.11, China is by far and away North Korea's main trade partner. It has allowed the North Koreans to run annual bilateral deficits of approximately one half billion dollars since 1995.[46] Indeed, China's prominence in North Korea's trade would be even larger if barter transactions and aid were counted in these figures. If North

---

due to misreporting by North Korea's trade partners. Currently the biggest problems appear to be with Mexico and Austria, whose national trade authorities have begun getting North and South Korea confused. Given the extremely low levels of North Korean foreign trade, misreporting of this kind can wreak havoc with the data. Indeed, it was misreporting of this type (along with mistreatment of the valuation issue outlined above) that led to South Korean newspaper reports in 1995 that North Korea was running a trade surplus.

A third potential problem involves North Korean trade with China. A growing share of North Korean trade consists of processing on consignment, much of which is transshipped through China. It may well be the case that these inflows and outflows are being double counted by the Chinese, who do not use the same trade accounting procedures as the rest of the world.

Finally, it should be noted that the figures reported here differ significantly from those reported by KOTRA. For one thing, unlike all other reporting authorities, KOTRA does not count inter-Korean trade as foreign trade. Moreover, it treats in-kind aid shipments as "exports," though more properly they should be considered official transfers. Second, KOTRA does not do the valuation adjustment properly (they adjust imports, but not exports). Finally, KOTRA's data for some bilateral flows differs significantly from that reported by the World Trade Organization, the United Nations, and the International Monetary Fund, for unknown reasons.

46. Some have questioned whether these figures accurately reflect China's trade with North Korea. It may well be that South Korea processing on commission trade, which is mainly routed through China, could be double-counted in the Chinese figures. Even if this were the case, however, the double counting would occur with respect to both imports and exports, and so would do little to boost the magnitude of China's trade imbalance with North Korea. Similar arguments could be made regarding smuggling and barter. If accurately counted, these activities would increase recorded trade *volumes*, but it is unclear how they would affect trade *balances*, if at all.

Table 3.11 North Korean trading partners, 1997 (millions of US$)

	North Korean exports	North Korean imports	Net exports
China (including Hong Kong)			
Raw	147	566	
Corrected	134	623	−489
Japan			
Raw	296	179	
Corrected	269	197	72
South Korea			
Raw	193	115	
Corrected	193	127	66
Russia			
Raw	17	74	
Corrected	15	81	−66
Germany			
Raw	43	43	
Corrected	39	47	−8
Global total			
Raw	954	1,545	
Corrected	993	1,829	−836

Notes: IMF, *Direction of Trade Statistics* import data (of partner country) adjusted for transportation and insurance charges.

IMF, *Direction of Trade Statistics* export data (of partner country) adjusted for "missing" transportation and insurance costs.

North-South Korea trade data from South Korean National Unification Board (NUB). NUB data based on a customs clearance.

North Korea-Iran and North Korea-Libya trade data from KOTRA. KOTRA data also adjusted.

1996 North Korea-Lebanon trade data used instead of 1997 numbers.

Sources: IMF, *Direction of Trade Statistics;* KOTRA; National Unification Board.

Korea's trade with China is regarded as politically determined, China is financing more than half of the North Korean deficit.

Following China, North Korea's largest trade partners are Japan, South Korea, Russia, and Germany. Noticeably absent from this list is the United States, which effectively maintains an embargo against North Korea despite a minor relaxation of restrictions in January 1995. However, while not engaging in much trade, the United States has been a major provider of assistance in the form of food, funding for the Korean Peninsula Energy Development Organization (KEDO), and payments for the remains of US soldiers missing from the Korean War. Indeed, North Korea is now the largest US aid recipient in Asia.

The commodity composition of trade for 1997 is reported in table 3.12. Again, interpretation is problematic. The data reported in table 3.12 by commodity does not match the data reported in table 3.11 by partner. Some countries may report overall trade with North Korea but not its

Table 3.12a North Korean exports by largest commodity groups, 1997

Exports (US$ millions)	Share (percentage)	Industry (SITC-4 Classification)
161.22	15.1	Gold, non-monetary
58.73	5.5	Parts of telecommunications and sound apparatus
54.86	5.1	Other outer garments of textile fabrics
49.72	4.7	Crustaceans and mollusks, fresh, chilled, frozen, etc.
47.48	4.5	Hay and fodder, green or dry
47.44	4.4	Gramophone records and similar sound recordings
38.81	3.6	Machines and appliances for specialized particular industries
36.24	3.4	Overcoats and other coats, men's
34.56	3.2	Thermionic, cold and photo-cathode valves, tubes, parts
25.72	2.4	Other fresh or chilled vegetables
1,066.18		Total, All commodities

Table 3.12b North Korean imports by largest commodity groups, 1997

Imports (US$ millions)	Share (percentage)	Industry (SITC-4 Classification)
96.43	7.7	Maize (corn), unmilled
65.49	5.2	Petroleum oils and crude oils obtained from bituminous minerals
65.47	5.2	Meal and flour of wheat and flour of meslin
53.80	4.3	Res: Petroleum products, refined
53.06	4.2	Iron ore and concentrates, not agglomerated
47.55	3.8	Rice semi-milled or wholly milled, broken rice
38.93	3.1	Passenger motor cars, for transport of passengers and goods
33.21	2.6	Mineral or chemical fertilizers, nitrogenous
26.55	2.1	Fabrics, woven, containing 85 percent of wool/fine animal hair
26.35	2.1	Fabrics, woven of continuous synthetic textile materials
1,259.13		Total, All commodities

Source: Statistics Canada, *World Trade Analyzer* (1980-97).

commodity composition, so the parts of the sample underlying table 3.11 figures are omitted from table 3.12. It is unclear how the arms trade is counted (if at all) in these figures (figure 3.3).[47] They could be misclassified (i.e., a missile is listed as "fabricated metals product" or put in the miscellaneous "non-identified products" category) or simply unreported. Barter transactions and aid also are omitted from these data.[48] With these caveats

---

47. That the military has its own trading channels is prospectively of enormous importance. They potentially could continue to engage in arms trade for pecuniary or strategic reasons, even if this were opposed by other parts of the state on diplomatic grounds. North Korea also sells military training and praetorian guard services and reportedly has sold tunneling technology.

48. Aid figures are summarized in a subsequent section. As discussed in chapter 5, North Korea has obtained significant international assistance to deal with its food shortage, both bilaterally from China and from other countries through the World Food Program. The quantity, value, and concessional component of food coming from China are unclear. Simi-

Figure 3.3   North Korean arms trade

millions of current US dollars

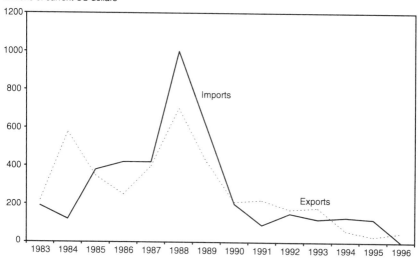

Source: US Arms Control and Disarmament Agency (1996), *World Military Expenditure and Arms Transfers Report.*

in mind, the data in table 3.12 indicate that natural resource products and light manufactures dominate North Korea's exports. On the import side, cereals, petroleum, and industrial intermediates are the largest import categories. Eberstadt (1998a) argues that the value of capital goods imports has been declining since the mid-1970s.

Data on North Korea's accumulated foreign debt and its debt/export ratio are displayed in figure 3.4. North Korea's debt is modest in absolute terms ($7.6 billion in 1994), and the vast majority of this figure ($6.2 billion) is long-term debt owed to former CPEs. (The South Korean National Intelligence Service valued this at $11.9 billion at the end of 1997, with $7.35 billion owed to former CPEs and $4.55 billion owed to Western countries.) It is questionable how much of the ruble-denominated debt will ever be repaid. Approximately $650 million is long-term debt owed to OECD countries. This figure has been relatively constant, reflecting the unwillingness of Western banks, governments, and multilateral institutions to increase their long-run exposure in North Korea. (The North Koreans reportedly owe another $2 billion in arrears to Western banks.) The remainder ($1 billion) consists of short-run loans that are generally rolled over. Given that in reality North Korea has defaulted on most of

---

larly, as discussed in chapter 4, North Korea has been receiving energy assistance in the form of oil and nuclear reactor construction through the Korean Peninsula Energy Development Organization (KEDO), a multinational consortium established as part of a 1994 nuclear agreement with the United States.

Figure 3.4 North Korean debt and debt service - export ratio

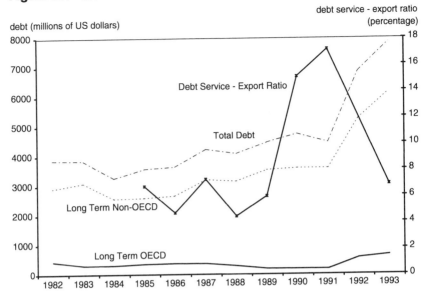

Source: OECD.

its long-term debt, its reservice payments are modest ($70 million) except for a spike in repayments during the period 1990-91 (see box 3.4). Compared to other CPEs, North Korea's debt to exports ratio (including the ruble denominated debt) is quite high (770.6 percent). However, the debt service to exports ratio is low (6.9 percent) since North Korea has essentially stopped paying its debt and no longer has access to long-term capital markets (table 3.13).

A thin secondary market exists for North Korean debt, and this market seems to move mainly on speculation and rumor (figure 3.5). The conventional wisdom has been that the possibility of collapse and absorption by South Korea (and hence the assumption of the debt by the government of a unified Korea) creates an effective price floor at around 10 to 20 cents on the dollar. Indeed, some traders regard the discount as an inverse indicator of regime viability—as the likelihood of collapse increases, the discount narrows, reflecting the increased likelihood of payoff by a unified Korea. However, the run-up in prices in late 1996 and early 1997 was ascribed to rumors that the South Korean government would permit South Korean firms to purchase the debt, and that the United States was considering removal of sanctions. The subsequent price decline has been attributed to the worsening of the country's diplomatic situation. An earlier spike in December 1994 reputedly reflected a surreptitious attempt by the North Korean government to buy back its own debt.

Box 3.4 Deadbeat Debtor

In 1975 the North Korean government gained the notoriety of being the first (and only) communist government to default on international debt. To the chagrin of Western financial institutions, it subsequently demonstrated that the 1975 episode was no aberration.

In 1976 a delegation of Japanese creditors negotiated a rescheduling, but the North Koreans again reneged, and in 1979 a second rescheduling was signed specifying a ten-year repayment period starting in 1980. The North Koreans kept up their payments until June 1983, and then requested another rescheduling. A third agreement was reached.

In 1983, after the Rangoon bombing, the Japanese government determined that North Korea had instigated terrorism and applied economic sanctions. In retaliation, North Korea stopped payment on the debt, which exceeds ¥80 billion (approximately $667 million) (Halloran 1998).

Following the failure of another rescheduling in 1986, Western private creditors declared North Korea in default and sought to have its assets (including gold in London) seized. In February a North Korean ship was detained in Indonesia for North Korea's failure to pay debts to North Korean rubber exporters. In October the Japanese government was forced to pay 32 export insurance firms a total of $196 million to bail them out of trouble caused by North Korean defaults, and that same month the North Koreans tried to pay other Japanese creditors in fish instead of cash.

The following year, a draft agreement was reached on a 12-year rescheduling, and in 1988 North Korea made the first installment on a repayment schedule that involved repaying a third of a $900 million debt, with the remainder to be cancelled. The North Koreans subsequently failed to keep up the payments, and in 1990 the French government froze North Korean assets in France (Koo 1992, Hwang 1993).

North Korea has been impervious to legal action by a consortium of over 100 banks in 17 countries and has ignored judgments by the International Court of Arbitration. When asked about the debt situation, Kim Mun-sung, then the chairman of the (North) Korean Committee for the Promotion of External Cooperation—the state organ charged with soliciting foreign direct investment—replied: "It is a morally negative thing for business people to make bad rumors and big noises about a few pennies of debt in this country. If you lose this time, you may gain next time" (*Financial Times*, 29 April 1995).

Given this lack of access to conventional channels of international finance, the question naturally then arises: how have they financed the chronic trade deficits? Given the politicization of North Korea's external economic relations, it is convenient to first examine exchange by partner and then attempt to construct a balance of payments for North Korea.

Economic Relations with Russia

Historically, the Soviet Union was North Korea's principal patron, largest trade partner, and, most importantly, its major source of oil and military

Table 3.13 Aid from the USSR

Year	Millions of US dollars
1980	260
1981	145
1982	130
1983	40
1984	55
1985	93
1986	6
1987	− 33
1988	− 41
1989	− 16
1990	0

Source: Central Intelligence Agency, Handbook of Economic Statistics (various issues).

Figure 3.5 North Korean debt prices in the secondary market

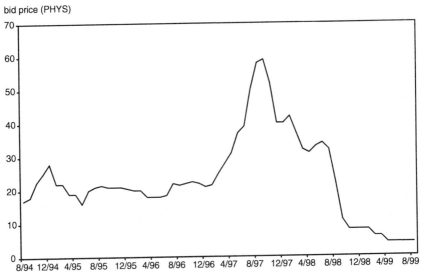

bid price (PHYS)

Source: Various Issues of International Financing Review, ANZ Bank, Cantrion Capital Markets.

assistance.[49] Eberstadt, Rubin, and Tretyakova (1995) report that the Soviet Union accounted for all of the increase in North Korean trade volumes in the 1980s. According to the South Korean government's National Unifi-

---

49. For more on relations between North Korea and the Soviet Union and Russia see Bazhanova (1992), Eberstadt, Rubin, and Tretyakova (1995), Zacek (1998), and Bazhanov (2000a).

cation Board, between 1948 and 1984 the Soviet Union provided North Korea with $2.2 billion in aid and credits (Hwang 1993, table 5.4).[50] Military goods played a prominent role in this. According to Zacek (1998), between 1981 and 1985 the Soviet Union supplied North Korea with $900 million in arms transfers alone, and Eberstadt (1997a) concludes that military goods accounted for one-third of North Korean imports from the Soviet Union. In addition to goods, the Soviets also supplied blueprints and technical assistance.

However, by the mid-1980s the disenchanted Soviets began pressuring the North Koreans to begin repaying the accumulated credits. In 1985, the Soviet Union and North Korea agreed on a repayment schedule that would involve the North Koreans repaying 60 million rubles in 1986 and 125 million rubles annually thereafter until the 560 million ruble debt was eliminated.[51] Repayment was to take the form of products, as well as processing on commission. Net resource transfers as estimated by the US Central Intelligence Agency (CIA) are reported in table 3.13.

As with nearly everything else having to do with North Korea, these figures need to be interpreted carefully. The Soviet Union reportedly provided oil to the North Koreans at two-thirds of the world price. This implicit subsidy is included in the CIA figures. At the same time, North Korea was sending products to the Soviet Union, and it is not clear what were the real terms of trade. It could be that, while the Soviet Union was underpricing its oil, it was also extracting imports from the North Koreans at less than world prices, so the net magnitude of the subsidy is unknown. With this caveat, the CIA figures show that by 1987 the net resource transfer had turned in favor of the Soviet Union. In 1988, the Soviet Union began actively reorienting its policy in favor of the South, and in 1990 Soviet Premier Mikhail Gorbachev and South Korean President Roh Tae-woo held a successful summit (Bazhanov 2000a).

That same year Soviet Foreign Minister Eduard Shevardnadze toured the Soviet Union's fraternal allies to inform them that the Soviet Union was ending barter trade arrangements and that, beginning in 1991, all transactions would be on a hard currency basis. According to Zacek (1998), the Soviet Union and North Korea signed a bilateral exchange agreement for 1991 in November 1990, but all deliveries were suspended between January and April. The two countries signed another agreement in April that recognized the North's inability to pay for the critically needed oil imports in hard currency and postponed the implementation of the hard currency plan until 1992.

---

50. It should be noted that this assistance was provided in rubles, and would have limited usefulness outside the Soviet bloc. Translating the ruble figure into US dollars should be done with extreme caution.

51. Lee (1996) puts the debt at 22 billion rubles, or $4 billion. These large discrepancies apparently reflect the difficulties of valuing non-convertible ruble debt.

The volume of trade between North Korea and Russia declined precipitously with the worsening of political relations and the implosion of the Russian economy. In 1989 the Soviet Union supplied North Korea with half of its coal and refined oil and a third of its steel, and trade with the Soviet Union accounted for more than half of North Korea's two-way trade. As far as can be determined, the fall in imports from Russia in 1991 was equal to 40 percent of North Korea's global imports, and by 1993 imports from Russia were only 10 percent of their average 1987-90 level (Eberstadt, Rubin, and Tretyakova 1995). In 1990, the Soviets delivered 410,00 tons of oil, but in 1991 this figure fell to 100,000 tons (Zacek 1998).

At the same time, the Russians demanded repayment of the accumulated debts, which they valued at $4.6 billion. Not surprisingly, the North Koreans refused and hinted that they would block the construction of an oil pipeline from Russia to South Korea. The Russians then recalled their technicians working in North Korea (mainly on military projects), because the North Koreans were unwilling to pay for them in hard currency (Zacek 1998).

In 1993, the Russians indicated that they would accept $3.5 billion in debt repayment. But given Russian disinvestment in North Korea, it is doubtful whether the Russians will ever be repaid. However, in 1995 the two countries renewed the logging agreement that had expired in 1993 and under which North Korea continues to supply 15,000 to 20,000 laborers to Russia to work in logging camps in the Russian Far Eastern region.[52] In 1997, Russia and North Korea signed an agreement on debt repayment, and the two agreed to pursue processing on commission activities with some share of the sale proceeds deposited in a special account as a mechanism to work off the debt. About 20,000 North Koreans reside in Russia working on joint ventures in construction, agriculture, mining, and logging (Joo 1998, Moltz 2000). According to Amnesty International (1996), workers in these facilities are subject to multitudinous human rights violations by North Korean and Russian authorities.

In 1994, Russian President Boris Yeltsin announced that the mutual defense treaty with North Korea was to be revised to relieve Russia of the responsibility of defending North Korea in the event of a conflict. Indeed, Russia repaid part of its debt to *South* Korea with military hardware, including armored vehicles, ground-to-air missiles, and helicopters.[53] However, North Korea continued to suggest revisions that would

---

52. According to Joo (1998), Russia would receive an annual payment of about $57 million under the new logging agreement. However, the number of North Korean lumberjacks has fallen due to the worsening economic conditions in Russia.

53. It is unclear whether South Korea got a good deal, though. Observing that helicopters obtained from Russia were five times as costly to operate as those imported from other countries, National Assemblyman Park Chung-hoon of the National Congress for New Politics described them as "money-eating hippos" (Shim Jae-yun, *Korea Times*, 8 October 1999).

extend the mutual defense treaty, and more recently Russia has sought to reassert its political importance in Northeast Asia and adopt a more "balanced" approach to the Korean peninsula.[54] In February 2000 North Korea and Russia finally concluded a new bilateral treaty that absolves Russia of its responsibility to defend North Korea in case of attack and replaces their Cold War-era military pact. Whether the political rapprochement between Moscow and Pyongyang translates into significantly expanded economic ties remains to be seen. Russia still owes South Korea nearly $1.5 billion for an aid package that the South Koreans provided the Soviet Union prior to their normalization of relations in 1990, so it is unlikely that the Russians would press the South Koreans too hard.

Economic Relations with China

Historically, China was North Korea's second most important patron, supplying it with nearly $900 million in assistance between 1948 and 1984 (Hwang 1993, table 5.4).[55] With common interests in opposing the United States, Japan, and South Korea in Northeast Asia, the two countries claimed to be as close as "lips and teeth." Since the decline in North Korean-Russian economic relations, China has stepped into the breach, at least partially offsetting the withdrawal of Soviet assistance.[56] As Flake (1995a) observed, "in 1993 North Korea received 72 percent of food imports, 75 percent of oil imports, and 88 percent of its coking coal imports from China" (p.15). China has emerged as one of North Korea's largest providers of emergency food aid (as discussed in chapter 5).[57]

As in the case of the Soviet Union, figuring out the terms of this trade is no simple task. Apparently the Chinese initially supplied the North Koreans with oil on a significantly concessional basis, reportedly "half the world price" (Patrick 1991, 34) or "$4.50 a barrel" (C.J. Lee 1996, I.S. Kim 1998a). However, in 1991 the Chinese announced that they too would no longer continue this practice, and that all transactions would be on a cash basis at the world price beginning in 1993 (Yeon 1993a). There is some disagreement, however, over the extent to which this policy has

---

54. See Moltz (2000) for an analysis of the rejuvenation of political ties between Russia and North Korea. It was rumored that Russia would announce that it will resume supplying 400,000 to 500,000 tons of crude oil to North Korea (Noerper 1999). It is unclear how much (if any) of this assistance has materialized.

55. The same caveat with regard to assessing the value of Russian assistance apply in the Chinese case as well.

56. For an overview of North Korean-Chinese bilateral relations, see Scalapino (n.d.), Bazhanov and Moltz (2000), and the references therein.

57. China has at times supplied North Korea with as much as 800,000 tons of subsidized grain and one million tons of oil. Moreover, with mostly soft anthracite coal, North Korea needs to import Chinese coking coal to make steel (Choi 1991).

ever been implemented, and some South Korean analysts believe that perhaps 35 percent of North Korea's oil imports from China have been provided on a concessional basis. The worsening situation in North Korea in the mid-1990s and the influx into China of North Korean refugees forced the Chinese to reassess their policy. On 22 May 1996, Chinese Premier Li Peng and North Korean Vice Premier Hong Song-nam signed an agreement reportedly specifying that for five years China would provide North Korea annually with 500,000 tons of grain (half free of charge, and half at a "friendship price"), 1.3 million tons of petroleum, and 2.5 million tons of coal (Lee 1998a).[58] This largesse was provided at a time when China was moving from being a net exporter to becoming a net importer of oil, and North Korea is the only country to which China has permitted the export of its staple grains. Aid officials have indicated privately that the Chinese food goes directly to the North Korean army, a claim corroborated by the *Chochongryun*, the organization of Pyongyang-affiliated ethnic Koreans in Japan (Kirk and Hochstein 1997). Perhaps the most controversial aspect of Chinese engagement with North Korea is reports that the Chinese have assisted the North Korean missile development program in violation of the Missile Technology Control Regime (MTCR), charges that the Chinese consistently deny.[59]

In the wake of a visit led by special presidential envoy and former US Secretary of Defense William Perry to Pyongyang in May 1999, and the avoidance of another missile launch confrontation in 1999, relations between North Korea and China appear to have warmed. In June 1999 a delegation led by Kim Yong-nam, the SPA Chairman, was met by Li Peng, Chairman of the Standing Committee of China's National People's Congress, considered the most pro-Pyongyang member of the Chinese leadership.[60] This was followed by a visit by Chinese Foreign Minister Tang Jiaxuan to Pyongyang in October. Interpretation in the United States of these visits has amounted to a Rorschach test of the commentators' attitudes toward China, with some seeing Chinese designs to use the North against the United States diplomatically, while others regard

---

58. Pollack and Lee (1999) cite an unnamed Chinese military analyst to the effect that Chinese *gratis* assistance to the North in 1998 included 100,000 tons of grain, 20,000 tons of chemical fertilizers, and 80,000 tons of crude oil. According to S. Shin (1999) the 20,000 tons of chemical fertilizers were to compensate for a 50,000 to 100,000 ton reduction in direct food assistance.

59. US Secretary of State Madeleine Albright has publicly expressed concern that the Chinese continue to assist the North Koreans.

60. During this visit Chinese President Jiang Zemin reportedly told the North Koreans to put economic reform ahead of defense spending and sent them home with some grain and coal. In February 2000, the North Koreans announced that the Chinese had provided them with 150,000 tons of food and 40,000 tons of coal.

Beijing as a potentially moderating influence on North Korean behavior.[61] However, at the same time it was strengthening ties with the North, Chinese Defense Minister Chi Haotian visited Seoul, making the first official visit to South Korea by a Chinese defense minister since the Korean War.

For its part, North Korea has attempted to strengthen its ties with Taiwan.[62] It has sent missions seeking tourism and investment to Taipei, and Taiwanese textile and apparel manufacturers have expressed some interest in North Korea as a possible avenue for circumventing the Multifibre Arrangement (MFA) quotas limiting Taiwan's textile and apparel exports (North Korea has unused quotas for exports to Europe). North Korea also signed an agreement to accept 60,000 to 200,000 barrels of Taiwan's nuclear waste, reportedly for a $227 million fee. It also has appealed to Taiwan for emergency food assistance, but, given the overwhelming importance of China to North Korea, Pyongyang's ability to play Beijing off against Taipei seems rather limited.[63] Taiwan has repeatedly offered to contribute to KEDO, the international consortium that is attempting to manage the nuclear confrontation, but has been blocked diplomatically in this regard by China.

South Korean firms have been active in the Chinese provinces that border North Korea, both because of ethnic affinity and possibly to position themselves in the prospectively liberalizing North. In addition, a significant amount of illegal movement in goods and people has been apparently occurring across the China-North Korea border (though the two governments have recently made moves to halt this), with an unknown number of economic refugees exiting North Korea.[64] For all of these reasons, China is undoubtedly more important to North Korea than the raw figures would indicate, and China appears to be willing to provide significant aid in the event of a crisis that would threaten the existence of the regime.

---

61. Snyder (1997), for example, has characterized China's policy as one of encouraging North Korean economic reforms, averting collapse, and promoting North Korean dependence on China.

62. Lee (1998a) claims that Taiwan offered North Korea a $1.5 billion aid package.

63. See Glaser and Garrett (1997) and Lee (1998b) for contrasting views on this issue.

64. However, there is some evidence that the volume of two-way trade between North Korea and China's Yanbian province has declined from $310 million in 1993 to $32 million in 1998 due to a lack of goods in North Korea and the North Korean habit of defaulting (and bankrupting their Chinese counterparts) (Susan V. Lawrence, *Far Eastern Economic Review*, 26 April 1999). Kirk, Brookes, and Pica (1998) provide data consistent with this claim. Another visitor made the similar observation that cross-border exchange appears to have slackened because the North Koreans "have nothing to trade" (Snyder 1999a). S. Shin (1999), however, claims that in 1998 the volume of trade actually increased about 30 percent over the previous year, with much of it involving food and taking place in the Shinuiju-Tantung region.

Economic Relations with Japan

North Korea's economic relations with Japan are dominated by a tumultuous history—the colonial legacy of approximately 700,000 Koreans residing in Japan, military tensions, and the nuclear issue (most notably the August 1998 missile launch over Japan), the treatment of the Japanese wives of Koreans who returned to North Korea in the 1950s and 1960s, and the issue of Lee Hyon-hui (a Japanese woman who was allegedly kidnapped from Japan and forced to train the terrorist who blew up a South Korean airliner in 1987) and other abductees.[65] North Korean officials have complained about the application of statutory rather than most-favored-nation tariff rates and the prohibition against export insurance and export financing by Japan's Exim Bank on Japanese exports to North Korea. Japan also imposes COCOM restrictions on North Korea, though Japanese-made equipment was found on a North Korean submarine captured in South Korean waters.[66] Japanese firms use North Korea as a dumping ground for industrial waste.

In 1955 supporters of North Korea in Japan started their own organization, the *Chochongryun* (*Chosensoren* in Japanese), which Halloran (1998) describes as "a state within a state."[67] This group accounts for 80 percent of the foreign investment in North Korea, and much of Japan's trade with North Korea. It is through the efforts of the *Chochongryun* that North Korea at one time was able to capture a significant share of the men's suit market in Japan (S.K. Kim 1994). However, due to souring relations

---

65. The *Chochongryun* organized the repatriation of roughly 100,000 ethnic Koreans to the DPRK. Some of these people emigrated to North Korea with Japanese citizen spouses. The inability of these Japanese wives to visit or otherwise communicate with their families in Japan has become a source of diplomatic friction between Japan and North Korea. Under the stress of its food crisis the North Koreans agreed to allow these estimated 1,200 women to visit Japan in an apparent bid to soften Japanese attitudes toward additional humanitarian assistance.

As for Lee Hyon-hui, North Korean denials of this woman's existence caused the collapse of North Korea-Japan talks in 1993. See H.N. Kim (1998) on the abductee issue. For their part, the North Koreans argue that, compared to the 200,000 Korean women used as sex slaves by the Japanese military during the Second World War, a dozen or so Japanese abductees is small change.

66. This equipment, which reportedly was obtained in Hong Kong, included sonar, cameras, and ground positioning systems. In July 1999 two Diet members charged that 40 percent of the semiconductors on the Taepodong-1 missile came from Japan. In January 2000 it was reported that Japanese authorities were investigating the possibility that North Korea had obtained the sighting mechanism for an anti-tank rocket launcher from a Japanese firm, possibly via Iran, in contravention of export control regulations.

67. The *Chochongryun* is a well-organized group, reportedly with an 8,200-strong bureaucracy that administers schools, community groups, businesses, banks, and credit unions. It claims the allegiance of around one-third of the Korean residents in Japan, though a rival pro-Seoul group asserts that membership has dropped by half in recent years. The *Chochongryun* has an estimated ¥30 trillion in assets.

between the North Korean government and some of the *Chochongryun* investors, this trade appears to have declined since its peak in the mid-1990s.[68] Moreover, the *Chochongryun* itself appears to have fallen on hard times: the Korean Credit Union in Osaka, the largest of its 38 credit unions, went bust in 1997 with debts of ¥270 billion. Tokai Shoji, an important intermediary in the Japan-North Korean trade, collapsed in 1999 with liabilities of ¥6.7 billion.[69]

Trade between Japan and North Korea has been hindered by a number of impediments. As noted in "Deadbeat Debtor" (box 3.4), North Korea is in default on ¥80 billion in loans (approximately $667 million) extended by Japanese banks. As a consequence, Japanese financial institutions are reticent to become involved in financing trade activities. This in effect has imposed a "North Korea premium" on trade, as North Korean enterprises bear the risks associated with expected delays, unfulfilled payments, and exchange risk. The inability of North Korean enterprises to fulfill orders on a timely basis has been exacerbated by transportation delays due to the low volume of trade and the inefficiency of North Korean transport facilities. Agricultural goods have been mishandled in transit, causing spoilage. None of this is unique to North Korea, but is made particularly acute by the inability of foreign parties to pursue resolution of claims through conventional channels such as the International Court of Arbitration.

Aside from trade in goods, the *Chochongryun* organizes remittances to North Korea, as will be discussed in the next section. These have been estimated at anywhere from the low millions to $2 billion, with most recent estimates tending toward the lower end of that range.[70] (If the latter figure were accepted, remittances would be more than double North Korea's merchandise exports!) It is also thought that these remittances may vary considerably from year to year depending on North Korean pressure on the *Chochongryun* to raise funds for large political festivals or other events. Some have argued that they have declined in recent years due to the death of Kim Il-sung and a lessening sense of allegiance among

---

68. Among the disillusioned is the Sakura Group, a $1 billion conglomerate, which experienced considerable political interference in the operation of its enterprises in North Korea.

69. The rate of non-performing loans among the *Chochongryun* financial institutions is reportedly more than 50 percent. In 1999 two more credit associations went under and were to be merged with two healthier institutions.

70. These estimates have been made on the basis of everything from calculating the amount of currency Japanese residents visiting North Korea could take with them, to estimates of profit margins in the pachinko industry in which the *Chochongryun* have a significant presence. If the money does come significantly from the profits of the gaming industry, it may well have declined in the wake of the burst of the bubble economy in Japan and attempts by both the tax collector and major Japanese corporations to capture a share of the revenues.

the younger generation of ethnic Koreans in Japan.[71] In any case, these remittances could be important in financing North Korea's chronic trade deficits, in light of the North's inability to make use of normal financing channels due to the debt defaults.

Some Japanese banks have stopped handling transfers to North Korea, a move that the Ministry of Finance (MOF) claims is purely voluntary. The MOF also has signaled that, in case of UN sanctions, remittances would be halted.[72] However, as Sato (1993) has pointed out, for any embargo to be effective the Japanese authorities would have to prohibit Korean residents of Japan from taking money with them on trips to North Korea. The Japanese government might find this very difficult to do, though the August 1998 missile launch and threats of subsequent launches may have strengthened government resolve. In anticipation of a possible second Taepodong launch, the Diet in 1999 began bipartisan consideration of legislation that would authorize the government to block all exchanges of goods and financial transfers to a country that threatened Japanese national security. However, it is unclear whether such additional legislation would be necessary for the government to cut off remittances. Japan's Chief Cabinet Secretary Hiromu Nonaka, Foreign Minister Masahiko Komura, and Defense Minister Hosei Norota all made public statements to the effect that a second long-range missile launch would make it difficult for Japan to support the Korean Peninsula Energy Development Organization (KEDO).[73]

The activities of the *Chochongryun* go to the heart of the frequently murky world of Japanese politics. According to Sato (1993), a *Chochon-*

---

71. Katsumi Sato claims that remittances fell from a peak of ¥60 billion (around $475 million) in 1990 to ¥6 billion (less than $50 million) in 1997. The latter figure is consistent with the analysis presented later in this chapter.

72. An unnamed senior official told the Japanese press that the MOF traces all remittances and that these have declined to 5 to 6 billion yen a year. However, it has been reported that in 1994 the National Police Agency informed the Diet that about $600 million was being sent to North Korea from Japan.

73. The North responded to this (and the Diet's enactment of a law specifying the familiar *Hinomaru* as the official national flag and *Kimigayo* as the official national anthem) with a statement that was vitriolic even by North Korea's high standards of invective. A statement attributed to the "DPRK government" released by KCNA on 10 August 1999 read in part: "Japan's refusal to liquidate the past is, in essence, a revelation of the militarist design to repeat the past crimes as well as the wild ambition for reinvasion to realize the old dream of the Greater East Asia Coprosperity Sphere. . . . The militarists of Japan, an economic power of the world, are thirsty for revenge to make up for the defeat, coupled with the unchanged design of aggression. It is not hard to guess what disaster the world and human-kind will face when they launch overseas expansion, flying the *Hinomaru* and singing *Kimigayo*." After demanding compensation for past crimes, the statement goes on to make a veiled threat: "Negotiation is not the only solution to Japan's liquidation of the past. North Korea will neither wait for settlement of the issue indefinitely nor remain a passive onlooker to it."

gryun-affiliated business association has negotiated what amounts to a tax treaty with the National Tax Administration, requiring the authorities to consult with the association regarding tax matters involving pro-North Korean businesses, as well as providing tax breaks to these businesses. Japanese officials privately confirm the essence of Sato's account. Sato goes on to report that "there are rumors that in some cases Korean credit associations have simply supplied funds to Pyongyang from their deposits. . . . Informants report that in 1991, when Japan and North Korea seemed close to agreeing on diplomatic relations and a huge financial package of Japanese reparations for wartime damages on the former colony, money flowed to Japanese politicians on behalf of Pyongyang." It is indeed the case that Japanese Liberal Democratic Party (LDP) power-broker, Shin Kanemaru, visited North Korea in 1990 and indicated that Japan should give North Korea post-war compensation. Kanemaru was later indicted for corruption and left the Diet. The North Korean connection, including the seizure by investigators of gold bars stamped "North Korea," was widely reported at the time.[74]

In 1994, Japan's Social Democrat-led coalition government proposed sending another delegation to Pyongyang to resume talks that had been broken off in 1992, but splits developed within the coalition. North Korea demanded compensation for post-colonial claims before the visit and would not assure a meeting with Kim Jong-il. The proposed visit was then canceled. Clandestine visits continued, however, and the following year another leading LDP politician, Michio Watanabe, visited North Korea. This visit too got off to a rocky start with some members of the LDP opposing any kind of compensation, and both the Social Democrats and the South Koreans expressing displeasure at the LDP for getting ahead of them on an issue that they regarded as "theirs."[75] In the end, Watanabe spent two days in North Korea, but apparently little was accomplished. When the Social Democratic Party attempted to extend an invitation to a North Korean delegation in 1996, Prime Minister Ryutaro Hashimoto blocked it, citing North Korea's unwillingness at that time to participate in Four Party Talks on peace on the Korean peninsula (Hayashi and Komaki 1997).

Although relations had worsened considerably following the August 1998 missile launch over Japan, in January 1999 Hashimoto's successor, Prime Minister Keizo Obuchi, signaled the possibility of improved rela-

---

74. For detailed analyses of the *pas de deux* carried on by Pyongyang and Tokyo, see Halloran (1998), H.N. Kim (1998), B.C. Koh (1998), and Paek (1999).

75. Watanabe declared that "We cannot compensate every wartime enemy" (Halloran 1998, 239), and Social Democrat Prime Minister Tomiichi Murayama declared the earlier Kanemaru declaration "virtually shelved" (*Financial Times*, 28 March 1995). In a meeting in Copenhagen, Murayama promised South Korean President Kim Young-sam that Japan would give "proper consideration" to South Korean views (Halloran 1998, 200).

tions. Again, a potential thaw was undercut, however, this time by the March 1999 incursion of two North Korean naval vessels into Japanese waters. However, later in the year Japanese authorities once again began signaling their willingness to talk, this time in the form of a visit by former Prime Minister Murayama in the aftermath of the Perry delegation visit to Pyongyang. During the December 1999 visit, the North Koreans indicated that they were interested in restarting normalization talks. The Japanese responded by lifting their ban on humanitarian assistance for the North, and in March 2000 announced that they would supply 100,000 tons of rice to North Korea. Nevertheless, Japanese public opinion remains fairly hostile toward North Korea, and at least one observer predicted that the Japanese government would rely on *gaiatsu* (foreign pressure) from the United States and South Korea to justify its policy stance.[76]

These themes—Japan hemmed in by its own internal contradictions and an inability to come to terms with its own history on the one hand, and North Korean misbehavior and third party meddling on the other— would continue to play out in Japan's most important current arenas on economic engagement with North Korea—its support for KEDO (roughly $1 billion expected) and its provision of food assistance as discussed in greater detail in chapters 4 and 5, respectively.[77] Yet in the end, the Japanese will have to reach some settlement with North Korea (or a unified Korea) on post-colonial claims. This issue was raised by US envoy William Perry during his 1999 visit to Pyongyang, during which a Japanese aid package of billions of dollars was reputedly discussed. The Japanese government paid the South Korean government $800 million in compensation for colonial and wartime activities at the time of normalization of diplomatic relations in 1965.[78] The North Korean government expects similar compensation. Adjusting the South Korean payment for differences in population, accrued interest, inflation and appreciation of the yen since 1965, one obtains a figure in excess of $20 billion.[79] Reputedly

---

76. For the results of a public opinion poll on attitudes toward North Korea, see *Asahi Shimbun*, 14 October 1999. Masayoshi Kanabayashi, *Wall Street Journal*, 7 October 1999, cites political scientist Masao Okonogi on the issue of *gaiatsu*.

77. For an overview of these issues see Armacost and Pyle (1999).

78. The payments took the form of $300 million in grants, $200 million in development assistance loans, and $300 million in commercial credits.

79. The calculation assumes a 5 percent rate of return over 35 years, an appreciation of the yen from 360 to 120 to the dollar, the change in the Japanese price level since 1965, and the smaller North Korean population. Obviously, with different assumptions, one could obtain different figures. An additional issue raised by the North Koreans that was not included in the South Korean package is compensation for "comfort women" who were pressed into sexual slavery during the Second World War. See B.C. Koh (1998) for an analysis of the "comfort women" issue. In comparison, Yi Chong-hyok, Vice Chairman of the Korea Asia-Pacific Peace Committee, a KWP organization, indicated in remarks before a Washington audience in 1996 that $10 billion would be the minimum acceptable.

figures on the order of $5 billion to $8 billion have been discussed within the Japanese government. Such sums, properly deployed, could go a long way in restoring North Korean creditworthiness and financing economic modernization.

Economic Relations with the United States

The United States has maintained a nearly complete embargo against North Korea since its invasion of the South in 1950, and North Korea has $9.1 million in assets blocked in the United States.[80] Americans have been prosecuted for violations of these strictures.[81] If the embargo were lifted, a number of other issues would have to be resolved, such as the extension of normal trade relations status (formerly called most-favored-nation status), restrictions on US government investment guarantees, North Korea's eligibility under the Generalized System of Preferences, its participation in the Multifiber Arrangement, and export controls.

On 21 October 1994, the United States announced a number of actions to ease sanctions in the context of the US-DPRK Agreed Framework. Specifically, Washington agreed to open telecommunications channels between the United States and North Korea, allow the opening of offices by journalists, authorize North Korea to use the US banking system for transactions originating or terminating in the United States, unblock assets not connected to the North Korean government, and permit imports of magnesite from North Korea. However, as of April 2000 sanctions removal has not gone beyond these relatively limited measures. The North Koreans have complained bitterly about what they regard as the US failure to uphold its part of the Agreed Framework bargain (Harrison 1998). South Korean President Kim Dae-jung during his June 1998 state visit also urged the United States to remove sanctions. According to Flake (1999a), sanctions removal has been hindered by a bureaucratic process in which different trade sanctions have been placed into various negotiating "buckets" (a nuclear bucket, a Four Parties Talks bucket, a missile talks bucket, etc.), with different parts of the State Department bureaucracy tying partial sanctions removal to progress on their respective issues of concern.

On 17 September 1999, the Clinton Administration announced its intention to lift sanctions partially in connection with a diplomatic understanding regarding a North Korean moratorium on long-range missile testing,

---

80. North Korea faces sanctions under the Trading with the Enemy Act for being a communist country and for being on the State Department's list of countries sponsoring international terrorism. There is some dispute as to how many of the restrictions that the Administration could remove without requiring congressional legislation. For a complete analysis of the legal issues surrounding the US embargo, see Davis et al. (1994).

81. In November 1999, Mak Shea-kei, a naturalized citizen living in New York, was fined and sentenced to prison for selling speedboats to the North Korean military. He had testified that he believed the boats were bound for China.

described more fully in chapter 9. The planned relaxation of restrictions would include those on telecommunication, financial, and transportation activities, as well as lifting most controls on US exports to and imports from North Korea. Restrictions on the export of dual-use technologies under the multilateral Wassenaar Arrangement would be maintained.[82] As of April 2000, none of these sanctions had actually been removed.

The reaction to the announcement was by and large predictable. Representative Benjamin Gilman (R-New York), Chairman of the House International Relations Committee, head of a Republican study committee on North Korea, and all around thorn in the side of the Clinton Administration, denounced the action.[83] The North Koreans claimed that it was merely the long overdue fulfillment of the Agreed Framework commitment and urged further sanctions removal. Commentary in China's official *People's Daily* was favorable. The most bizarre reaction to the event came from the South Korean government's economic think tank, the Korea Development Institute, which issued a report urging the South Korean government to take preemptive measures to block the "U.S. subjugation of the North Korean economy."[84]

Sanctions removal seemed to spark some renewed interest in North Korea by perhaps the most important players, the US business community. A number of US firms, including Motorola, General Motors, Boeing, Citibank, AT&T, Coca-Cola, and PepsiCo had expressed interest in doing business in North Korea.[85] However, North Korean officials had complained vociferously that these firms have been deterred by US officials, an allegation that has been privately confirmed both by some firms and some government officials. According to a US Treasury response to a Freedom of Information Act request, nearly all approved exchanges prior to September 1999 have been for emergency food aid. Yet even

---

82. Specifically, the United States announced easing of restrictions on: sale of most US consumer goods and financial services in North Korea; ordinary transport of cargo by ship or plane; imports of most North Korean-origin products and raw materials; US investment in a variety of sectors; remittances by US nationals to North Korea; and commercial flights between North Korea and the United States. Restrictions were retained on the sale of weapons and missile-related technology, unlicensed export of dual-use technology and items that could have military uses, US support for international financial institution loans to North Korea, and unauthorized financial transactions between US citizens and the North Korean government.

83. See "Gilman Reacts to Lifting North Korea Sanctions," House International Relations Committee Press Release, 17 September 1999. Republican opposition to the move was not universal, however, as Senator John Warner (R-Virginia), Chairman of the Senate Armed Services Committee, spoke favorably about the action (Randall Mikkelson, Reuters, 17 September 1999).

84. *Korea Times* (Internet Version), 8 October 1999; reproduced as FBIS-EAS-1999-1008.

85. *Korea Times*, 11 November 1994; *Washington Post*, 2 February 1995; Flake 1995c; Eberstadt 1997a.

when US officials have allowed exchanges to proceed, deals have not always ended happily. The Cargill grain for zinc barter deal collapsed, and Quinones (1997) points to an outstanding debt of $76 million for grain purchased from an unnamed US firm between 1991 and 1994. Nevertheless, in the wake of the September 1999 action, both the American Chamber of Commerce in Korea and the Korea Society expressed plans to take US business delegations to North Korea.

US sanctions have surely prevented some exchange between North Korea and the United States. The question is, how much? If sanctions were lifted entirely today, there probably would not be a big impact on North Korean trade.[86] As will be demonstrated in chapter 7, North Korea has a comparative advantage in light manufactures and some natural resource products. North Korea regularly has unused textile and apparel quotas in Europe, where it is not subject to sanctions. That is to say, North Korea's lack of international competitiveness, not externally imposed sanctions, would appear to be the fundamental constraint on its exports.[87] This is not just true of the textile and apparel sector. Eberstadt (1997a) shows that North Korean export growth has consistently lagged other countries' exports to OECD markets (excluding the United States). Indeed, North Korean exports to the OECD have actually fallen over time.

On the other hand, as will be shown in chapter 7, if North Korea were to undertake productivity enhancing reforms, then its ability to export would improve, at which point US sanctions (were they still in place) would bite.

Today, however, it is official transfers, not commercial transactions, that account for the bulk of bilateral economic relations.[88] As will be discussed in greater detail in succeeding chapters, the United States also agreed to help supply North Korea with oil for heating and electricity to replace energy that would have been produced by the North Korean nuclear reactors. In other words, the US government maintains sanctions against North Korea that impede the ability of the North Koreans to purchase needed food on commercial terms, and then it taxes the American public so that it can provide food *gratis*. In fact, the energy assistance, food aid, and payments for the returned remains of soldiers missing from

---

86. The present author can attest to the fact that North Korean economic officials genuinely appear to hold the (mistaken) belief that US sanctions are the principal constraint on their economic revitalization. See Eberstadt (1997a) for further documentation of this observation.

87. Some have argued that the imposition of US sanctions deters investment by third parties who would like to export to the US market. But the question remains as to how important this is: North Korea faces only secondary financial sanctions in Japan (not trade barriers) and no real barriers in the European Union, the world's largest market.

88. Private transfers also play a role. According to one report, in 1998-99 US private charity to North Korea amounted to $2.5 million, while charitable giving from all non-governmental sources was nearly $10 million.

the Korean War have amounted to more than $60 million in recent years and should reach nearly $200 million in 1999.[89] This makes North Korea the largest recipient of US aid in Asia and means that, in US-North Korea exchange, aid greatly outweighs trade.

Economic Relations with South Korea

Since the mid-1990s, North and South Korea have conducted between $200 and $400 million dollars in indirect trade annually, in large part consisting of North Korean exports to South Korea via China.[90] This trade is considered internal domestic trade and is not subject to tariffs and other trade restrictions. North Korea primarily exports agricultural, forestry, and fisheries products, apparel (much of it processed on a consignment basis), and non-ferrous metals to the South; it imports chemicals and textiles. According to Yeon (1993a), this trade is carried out on an open account system—effectively a noncontemporaneous barter system—inter-mediated by the two governments. This arrangement gives the two governments enormous scope to control the pace and content of bilateral trade, a fact that is not lost on South Korean firms.[91] Prior to the presidency of Kim Dae-jung, the South Korean government was quite clear about this and conditioned permission for trade and investment in the North on resolution of political problems.[92] However, with the proclamation of the constructive engagement (neé sunshine) policy, business has been separated from politics in principle, though perhaps not in fact.

The first turning point came in 1994, when concerns about a prospective North Korean collapse and a sudden German-style unification led policy-makers to significantly loosen the controls on South Korean firms.[93] In November 1994, President Kim Young-sam announced a significant easing of restrictions on activities of South Korean firms in the North. The North Korean government's response was ferocious—publicly blasting

---

89. The United States has been paying North Korea approximately $600,000 annually since 1997 for its assistance in recovering the remains of US soldiers lost during the Korean War.

90. Different sources cite conflicting figures on inter-Korean trade. Since the South Korean authorities treat the trade as internal trade, neither import nor export figures are inclusive of transportation, insurance, etc. Additionally, a significant share of the trade is for processing on commission, and it appears that there is some double counting of reexports. See Flake (1996) for a highly informative overview of this trade.

91. According to an unnamed South Korean business executive, "when we do business in North Korea we are not really getting paid by them. We are getting paid by the [South Korean] government special fund," *Washington Post*, 29 April 1992.

92. For an example of this see *Economist*, 22 February 1992.

93. In August, Deputy Prime Minister for Unification Lee Hong-koo publicly raised the possibility of North Korean collapse and initiated a bureaucratic reorganization to strengthen reunification planning. The week following Lee's speech, President Kim Young-sam echoed this theme in a speech to the government's reunification think tank.

Kim as an "abominable flunkeyist traitor," "puppet of imperialists," and "dyed-in-the-wool, pro-American stooge"—while at the same time continuing to solicit South Korean investment.[94] In January 1995, the South Korean government announced that residents would be permitted to send small remittances to family members through third countries.

The result of these policy shifts was a flurry of private activity. Daewoo announced plans to build a seven-factory industrial park in Nampo. Lucky Goldstar accepted in principle (subject to South Korean government approval) an offer to take over the management of the Kim Chaek Iron and Steel Works, the largest in North Korea.[95] The South Korean government granted permission to six firms to go to North Korea to discuss possible investments. Ssangyong announced that it would begin importing cement from North Korea, the first direct North-South trade deal. Samsung announced plans to start buying electronics parts and to build an electronics plant in the Rajin-Sonbong SEZ. Shinawon, a textile maker, announced plans to put a garment factory in Nampo. In May 1995, the South Korean government approved the first joint venture with the North since the Second World War, a Daewoo-Samchonri venture to produce garments and bags in Nampo.[96] In January 1996, the Seoul government scrapped the $5 million limit on investments in the North, and subsequently allowed several large South Korean firms to establish larger operations. This move was widely interpreted as an attempt to induce the North Koreans to participate in the Four Party Talks, a diplomatic negotiation among North Korea, South Korea, China, and the United States aimed at securing a stable basis for peace on the peninsula.

However, while South Korean firms were aggressive in announcing plans to begin operations in the North, in reality they were considerably more cautious about committing significant amounts of capital, technology, or manpower to North Korean projects. The list of South Korean private sector overtures toward the North appears to be heavy on exploration and very light on implementation (Flake 1995b, 1998).[97] According to Flake (1999b), at the end of 1998, 40 South Korean firms had been given permission to explore business in the North, but only 15 of these had

94. One possible interpretation is that the North Korean government was still smarting over Kim Young-sam's hard-line behavior upon the death of Kim Il-sung, hence the personalized attack on the President. However, the personal antipathy between Kim Young-sam and the North Korean leadership predates Kim's election as South Korean President.

95. In this regard, the North Korean government's action would appear to undercut the notion that it was preparing for war.

96. This joint venture reportedly exports $35 million worth of goods annually.

97. In a February 1992 pact, North and South Korea agreed to negotiate over investment guarantees and avoidance of double taxation, but these negotiations have never been joined. Some have speculated that taxation and investment issues would be taken up in the planned June 2000 summit.

received South Korean approval for their proposed ventures.[98] An unknown number of these have actually been undertaken. Indeed, Daewoo appears to be the only South Korean *chaebol* to have actually begun production. Furthermore, at least one recent visitor to the North has indicated that the factories are in very bad shape and that much of the capital would have to be scrapped—raising costs to any joint venture.[99]

As in the case of the United States, this economic rapprochement was not without obstacles. A Christian relief agency run by a Korean-American in the United States was given approval to donate grain to North Korea as long as this was not used for stockpiling in preparation for war (see box 5.2). To complicate matters further, a bribery scandal erupted in South Korea in which it was alleged that South Korean firms had bribed North Korean officials in the process of investigating investment possibilities. Although no bribery was uncovered, the government's probe slowed the movement of firms to the North.[100] This was reinforced by subsequent political developments, most notably the decision by South Korean authorities to prohibit South Korean firms from participating in a September 1996 trade and investment forum held in North Korea's Rajin-Sonbong SEZ and the grounding of a North Korean submarine on the South Korean coast the following week. For all of these reasons (plus the continued decline of the North Korean economy and the 1997 crisis in the South), the gold rush fever of 1994 faded.[101] Commercial trade peaked in 1997 and actually fell in 1998.

The South Korean government's stance shifted noticeably with Kim Dae-jung's inauguration in early 1998.[102] Kim proclaimed a "sunshine

---

98. Reportedly, four of these permits were subsequently revoked.

99. In an interesting development, in February 2000, Samsung announced that it would set up a small joint venture with North Korea's Chosun Computer Center to produce computer software in China.

100. It is believed by some that the North Korean government is encouraging the South Korean firms in order to drive a wedge between the firms and the South Korean government and to avoid having to deal directly with their political opposites (e.g., Foster-Carter 1994a). In colloquial terms, the North Koreans would be gaining some (economic) hostages and some leverage over the South Korean government. At the same time, hardliners in the South Korean government can use issues such as stockpiling and bribery allegations to slow the process of integration.

101. Not all the news was bad: in 1997, the two countries agreed to allow civilian airliners passage through the Pyongyang Flight Information Region starting in 1998, and this is earning North Korea around $1.5 million annually. And in a departure from its usual attempts to micromanage private sector contacts, the South Korean government permitted the Federation of Korean Industries to send relief supplies to the North.

102. According to Flake (1999c), government-to-government initiatives include exchange of weather information, joint development of a television special on North Korea's cultural heritage, possible South Korean investment in one of the failed joint venture banks, the construction by a South Korean NGO of a pharmaceutical factory in the Rajin-Sonbong

policy," later rechristened the "constructive engagement policy," toward the North. In essence, the policy seeks to engage the North in a wide range of contacts in the hope of creating a set of interdependencies that in the long run would discourage the North from external aggression and perhaps even promote the internal transformation of the regime.[103] Initially, President Kim identified three principles in outlining this policy: no tolerance of Northern military provocation; no attempt on the Southern side to engineer North Korea's collapse or containment; and the separation of politics and economics.[104] He went even further in his "Berlin Declaration" of March 2000, indicating the South Korean government's willingness to directly support the economic rehabilitation of the North. In a clear departure from his predecessors, Kim has encouraged other countries to increase their engagement with the North, calling on the United States to end its economic sanctions against North Korea, for example. Subsequently, the South Koreans have added reciprocity to the policy mix.[105]

This perspective appears to have been born out of the conviction that the South has neither the economic, social, nor political capacity to handle a collapse of the North, and that peaceful coexistence is a preferable state of affairs. At the same time, the policy amounts to an implicit criticism of past unification policy, which had put an overwhelming emphasis on high-level government-to-government talks and, with the exception of emergency food relief, had generally discouraged nonofficial contacts.

In the economics sphere, the government immediately announced a number of business facilitation measures (mainly in the form of cutting red tape) aimed at making it easier for South Korean firms to pursue opportunities in the North.[106] For its part, the North reportedly responded

---

trade zone, and cooperation in the agricultural field, including the provision of "Super Corn" seed. Kim Dae-jung also proposed a swap of North Korean spies held in the South for Southern prisoners of war still in detention in the North. Furthermore, the South Korean government announced that it would open up South Korean airwaves to North Korean satellite television broadcasts and would permit the sale of non-political North Korean videos.

103. See G.W. Choi (1998) on the role of non-governmental organizations (NGOs) in the engagement policy.

104. As noted earlier, the June 1999 Yellow Sea naval engagement was the biggest military clash between North and South Korea since the Korean War.

105. On reciprocity, see the statement of Foreign Minister Hong Soon-young (*Yonhap*, 13 July 1999). One example was South Korea's willingness in April 1998 and June 1999 to allow fertilizer for family reunion talks to break down rather than accede to Northern demands (though announcing afterwards that private fertilizer donations would be permitted). Another was its suspension of the Mt. Kumgang tourism tours after the detention of a tourist in June 1999. (The tours were resumed in August after a bilateral accord was concluded.) See Council of Foreign Relations (1999a) for more details on the evolving engagement policy.

106. See Flake (1999c) for a list of these measures. SMEs could be a major beneficiary of the reduction in red tape. Several industry associations have made exploratory visits to Pyongyang or Rajin-Sonbong. In October 1999, however, it was reported that the South

by stationing working level commercial officers at its embassy in Beijing and reportedly at least considered a UN proposal for establishing direct rail links between the North and South (Flake 1999c). This consideration was apparently negative, however, as Pyongyang sharply rebuffed a Russian overture in early 2000 to discuss building a rail line from Russia through both North and South Korea.

Since the inauguration of this policy, there has been some increased business contact between the North and South, though it is unclear how much of this should be attributed to policy.[107] In June 1998 Hyundai founder Chung Ju Yung visited North Korea driving 500 head of cattle through the demilitarized zone (DMZ). After a second visit in October and a meeting with Kim Jong-il, an agreement was reached for a tourism project at Mt. Kumgang and the possible development of a second SEZ (in the Haeju District on North Korea's western coast just North of Inchon). This is prospectively quite important, inasmuch as the Haeju location would be vastly preferable to Rajin-Sonbong. The plan calls for Hyundai to develop the infrastructure and then lease sites to SMEs. Hyundai claims that the industrial park would take ten years to complete, could produce $4.4 billion worth of goods a year, and could generate $400 million in wages for North Korean workers.[108] The *chaebol* also reached an agreement by which it would supervise the construction of railroad cars at North Korea's Wonsan plant. It imported the first 44 of these cheap cars in May 1999. Hyundai also reportedly has discussed other projects as well, including an automobile assembly plant, a power plant in Pyongyang, a ship repair yard, offshore oil exploration, a roofing tile factory, and plans to contract North Korean workers for work on projects in third countries.[109] Chung returned with 501 more head of cattle (and 20 cars) in November 1999.[110]

One of the tenets of the policy has been the separation of business and politics. In this regard, the Kim government has been less forthcoming

---

Korean government had decided to go further and begin directly financing the activities of SMEs in North Korea through the use of subsidized loans.

107. J. Park (1998) goes so far as to argue that current policy, for a variety of reasons, will actually discourage investment in the North by the *chaebol*, but does accept the notion that there could be increased investment by SMEs. One news report (*Chosun Ilbo*, 21 March 1999) indicated that there had indeed been a decline in applications to the South Korean government for "economic cooperation" projects, but this could simply be a reflection of the depressed state of the South Korean economy at the time.

108. See Yoon (1999) for an analysis of this proposal.

109. Hyundai announced in June 1999 that it would hire the first batch of 300 North Korean workers to work on a project in Turkmenistan.

110. A number of these cattle subsequently died. North Korea chose to blame the South Korean intelligence service, asserting that the South Koreans had force-fed the cattle vinyl rope, nails, and other indigestible items before herding them north!

with official assistance than its predecessors, allowing the private sector to carry a greater share of the burden. This may in part reflect domestic politics: Kim has been tarred in the past as being "soft" on the North and, in any event, the South Korean economy has been in difficult shape since his inauguration. Nevertheless, the notion that politics and economics have been separated is not entirely credible.[111]

Take Hyundai, which has been the most prominent in North-South exchange. As is documented in chapter 6, it is in weak financial condition, and it is highly questionable whether it was in any condition to commit nearly $1 billion in payments to North Korea as called for in its agreement with the North.[112] When questioned about this, Hyundai officials have indicated that the government would "make it up to us," a claim that was verified in private conversations with government officials. Hyundai has already arguably benefited from government largesse. Government controlled banks significantly increased loans to Hyundai in 1998, and the government managed to steer the bankrupt automaker Kia out of Ford's lap and into Hyundai's (see chapter 6).[113] Similarly, many in South Korea suspect that the government helped Hyundai take over LG Semiconductor, and opposition politicians have asserted that both the semiconductor deal and the government's tolerance of Hyundai Electronics' stock manipulation (chapter 6) was a *quid pro quo* for Hyundai's activities in the North.

Probably the biggest impact of the constructive engagement policy has been the dramatic increase in the number of North and South Koreans coming into contact with each other (figure 3.6). Excluding the Mt. Kumgang tourists, nearly 3,500 South Koreans have traveled North since inauguration of the policy—more than during the entire previous period since the war. In addition, through February 2000, 150,000 tourists have visited Mt. Kumgang, though their contacts with Northerners have been highly circumscribed.

Kim's constructive engagement policy puts Pyongyang on the defensive. While the existence of a prosperous South Korea is surely an enor-

---

111. As noted earlier, the government has apparently decided to subsidize the activities of SMEs in the north.

112. According to the South Korean Ministry of National Unification, during its first nine months of operations, the Mt. Kumgang tourist projected netted revenues of around $183 million for North Korea and generated $258 million in losses for Hyundai. In addition, Hyundai agreed to ship 30,000 color television sets to North Korea on a deferred basis. The receivers are to be re-badged with a North Korean brand name (*Kumgangsan*—Mt. Kumgang) to mask their South Korean origin. The North Korean authorities had requested 25-inch televisions, but Hyundai indicated that only 20-inch models would be available.

113. At the same time, one could argue that the government's August 1998 intervention in the Hyundai Motors strike (in which it effectively sided with the strikers) and its 1999 investigation into Hyundai's "Buy Korea Fund" were against the interests of the *chaebol*.

Figure 3.6 Number of South Koreans who visited the North (excluding Mt. Kumgang tourists)

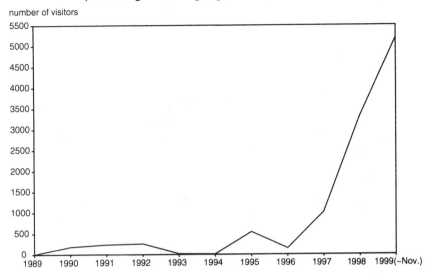

number of visitors

Sources: Ministry of National Unification.

mous advantage in terms of the North's economic development, Pyongyang is afraid of what it accurately understands as the "Trojan horse" of increased contact with the South.[114] This being so, for South Korea—like the United States—official transfers in the form of support for KEDO will outweigh private commercial exchange in its economic relationship with North Korea. (The estimated price tag for South Korea is roughly $3 billion.) This assumes that KEDO survives. Alternatively, North Korea could accept the Perry process "package deal" offer of South Korea, the United States, and Japan, which could lead to a dramatic increase in commercial exchange. Indeed, one of the most important ramifications of the "sunshine policy" has been effectively to widen Pyongyang's diplomatic options vis-à-vis third parties such as Italy and Australia. (Discussion of this possibility will be taken up in chapter 9 on "muddling through.")

Constructing a Balance of Payments, or Adventures in Unconventional Finance

This review of North Korea's principal external relations brings us back to the question raised earlier: How does it finance its chronic trade deficits?

---

114. The 31 May 1999 joint editorial of *Rodong Sinmun* and *Kŭlloja* described opening as a "Trojan horse tasked to destabilize socialism." North Korea's Charge d'Affaire at the United Nations, Kim Chang-kook, reportedly denounced the sunshine policy as an attempt to subvert the North Korean political system that could lead to open conflict and war.

One possibility is arms exports. North Korea sells small arms, training and consulting, and praetorian guard services.[115] Having been linked to nearly every major exporter of oil, it reputedly maintains the world's third largest store of chemical weapons and is alleged to have biological weapons, including the smallpox virus.[116] What has really attracted attention, however, has been its missile program.

In the 1980s, North Korea emerged as a significant player in the global arms market. The US Arms Control and Disarmament Agency (ACDA) estimated its arms exports at more than $500 million dollars at times, accounting for more than one-fourth of North Korea's exports (figure 3.3). The missile program began in the early 1960s with Soviet and Chinese assistance. The North Koreans have since entered into technical cooperation programs with a number of countries, including Egypt, Iran, and possibly Pakistan. The North Koreans also allegedly employ foreign scientists and engineers on their programs, including a number from the Ukraine, and allegations of continuing Chinese involvement have been a source of Chinese friction with the United States.[117]

The North Koreans produce a range of missiles. Single stage missiles include the medium-range Scud-B, Scud-C, and Scud-D (a.k.a. Nodong-1), while long-range multistage missiles include the Taepodong-1 (tested in August 1998), the yet untested Taepodong-2, and the Taepodong-3, which is still in development. The Nodong-1s have a range of 1000 kilometers with a 1000-kilogram nuclear or chemical warhead, putting them within striking range of both South Korea and Japan, while the Taepodong-1 is thought capable of hitting Guam and parts of Alaska. The Nodong-1s are thought to have problems with their engines and guidance systems, thus limiting their military usefulness. Nevertheless, if properly armed they could present a significant deterrent to potential adversaries.

---

115. The North Koreans have allegedly assisted the Syrians with the manufacture of chemical weapons, sold the Iraqis tunneling technology to evade detection of arms inspectors, and trained the notorious 5th Brigade associated with atrocities in Zimbabwe. According to a South Korean Defense ministry report submitted to the National Assembly, more than 400 North Korean officers are employed abroad, mostly as missile and tunnel technicians, with the largest concentrations in the Congo, Iran, and Ethiopia. It has been rumored that, in exchange for North Korean assistance in dealing with its civil war, the government of the Congo has granted the North Koreans access to its uranium mine. North Korea also has sold military hardware to Vietnam, allegedly in order to gain access to advanced Russian weaponry possessed by the Vietnamese.

116. See North Korean Advisory Group (1999) for a summary of North Korea's chemical and biological weapons programs. North Korea has reportedly produced and stored more than 5,000 tons of chemical agents (including mustard gas, phosgene, sarin, and VX agents). The North Koreans also reportedly possess significant stores of anthrax, smallpox, cholera, and bubonic plague viruses. North Korea is not a signatory to the Chemical Weapons Convention, presumably because this agreement includes a verification system.

117. Bazhanov (2000b) contains an informative history of this program.

On 16 June 1998, the North Koreans admitted what the world had long suspected: that North Korea exports missiles. Most observers believe that these exports began in the 1980s. Over the years, Iran and Syria have been among Pyongyang's most important customers, though the North Koreans also are alleged to have had dealings with Iraq, Libya, Nigeria, Pakistan, and Egypt, exchanging arms for oil, which is then resold on the international market for hard currency.[118]

Total revenues from missile sales are subject to dispute. The ACDA data displayed in figure 3.3 is broadly consistent with the Eberstadt, Rubin, and Tretyakova (1995) analysis of DPRK-Russian trade. Likewise, the South Korean defense ministry and the Stockholm International Peace Institute estimate that conventional arms sales are less than $50 million a year. Robert Einhorn, the chief US negotiator at the missile talks, reportedly described North Korea as the world's number one exporter of missile equipment and technology. A highly placed US official indicated that exports have averaged $100 million annually, with around 40 percent of these revenues plowed back into the missile development program.[119]

It appears that exports have declined over time. The lack of Cold War proxy conflicts, increasingly obsolete designs and inferior products (the Soviets stopped providing new designs and technology in 1990), shortages of necessary inputs, and shipping company fears of North Korean default have all depressed the market for North Korean goods. (Some US government officials dispute this privately and claim that arms sales have actually risen of late.) The data reported by ACDA does not support the idea that clandestine arms sales are sufficient to cover the trade gap (figure 3.3), but the military may have a purely institutional incentive to continue selling arms if the proceeds go directly to the military, even if other parts of the government would like to restrict sales for broader foreign policy reasons.

---

118. The alleged sales to Egypt were particularly problematic as they would have violated a 1990 US antiproliferation law and could have resulted in the application of economic sanctions against the second largest recipient of US aid. Sales to Pakistan have been monitored closely in light of the 1998 nuclear tests by India and Pakistan. Pakistan and North Korea have allegedly cooperated on both missile and nuclear weapons programs. In July 1999, Indian authorities detained a North Korean ship and seized missile parts thought to be bound for Pakistan as part of its nuclear program. Pakistan denied that it imports missiles from North Korea, and some evidence pointed toward Libya as the ultimate destination of the parts. Another theory was that the parts originated in China and were merely transshipped through North Korea to provide the Chinese plausible deniability. Cumings (1996) adds that North Korea possibly also transshipped Chinese "Silkworm" missiles to the Middle East.

119. A figure of $1 billion a year attributed to the US CIA sometimes appears in press reports. The truly fantastic figure of $5 billion in annual missile exports has been attributed to unnamed South Korean intelligence officials. This is surely too high. It is well above both Israel's offer in its 1992-94 attempt to buy off the North Koreans, as well as the North Korea's own contemporary demands of the United States (see chapter 4), and would make

In the previous chapter one commentator likened the South Korean economy under the Chun government to a continuing criminal enterprise. In contradistinction, the Kim Jong-il regime *is* a continuing criminal enterprise, and illicit activities—smuggling, drug trafficking, and counterfeiting, for example—offer other possibilities for financing the trade gap. It has been widely reported that North Korean embassies around the world are required to generate profits that are remitted to "Bureau 39," an organization directly controlled by Kim Jong-il.[120] During the 1990s, North Koreans, mostly diplomats, have been arrested in countries as diverse as Sweden, Finland, Estonia, Russia, Germany, Egypt, China, Nepal, Cameroon, Guinea, Kenya, Zambia, Thailand, and Cambodia for smuggling (cigarettes, alcohol, and gold), trafficking in counterfeit goods (cigarettes and CDs), endangered species, and ivory, and illegally dealing in military equipment.[121] Official North Korean involvement in ivory trafficking has been so extensive that in 1999 the secretariat of the Convention on the International Trade in Endangered Species (CITES) actually sent a *demarche* to the North Korean embassy in Switzerland. However, the big money is in drug trafficking.

North Korea has been involved in at least 30 drug trafficking incidents internationally, many involving diplomats (Perl 1999). These mainly appear to take the form of North Koreans attempting to distribute drugs produced for export in North Korea, or North Koreans using diplomatic immunity as an advantage in distributing drugs produced by non-Korean criminal cartels (see box 3.5). North Korea is believed to have begun refining opiates for export in the mid-1980s, with peak production of 50 tons of raw opium occurring in 1994. Poppy cultivation was adversely affected by bad weather and shortages of fertilizers and insecticides, however, and the North Koreans have shifted toward the production of methamphetamines in more recent years. North Korean pharmaceutical labs reportedly have the capacity to process 100 tons of opium a year. Methamphetamine production is relatively simple, and capacity virtually limitless, constrained only by the ability to finance intermediate inputs.[122]

North Korea the world's fifth largest arms exporter after the United States, the United Kingdom, Russia, and France.

120. Revenues from the Mt. Kumgang tourist project described in the next section are reportedly funneled to the same account.

121. In 1998 Russian officials seized five military helicopters that were being smuggled into North Korea by a Russian criminal gang. They had allegedly obtained them at a cut-rate price from a destitute Russian military unit (Morrison 1999, Moltz 2000). It is unknown as to whether these were intended for home use or export. The North Koreans are rumored to have been intermediaries in the Japanese Aum Shinrikyo cult's procurement of a Russian military helicopter.

122. In both cases there are more benign explanations. The North Koreans use opium to make morphine for military uses as well as for use as a traditional medicine. Given shortages of imported medicines and pharmaceuticals, opium may increasingly be used as a pain

Box 3.5 The Narco-state

In most countries gangs try to penetrate the state. In the case of North Korea, it is the other way around: it is a state attempting to penetrate the world of international criminal syndicates, exploiting its sovereign status to produce drugs at home and distribute them through embassies abroad. A few of the North Korean misadventures have included:

- June 1994. Two North Korean intelligence agents were arrested in Vladivostok in a heroin smuggling operation. The North Koreans were arrested with eighteen pounds of heroin, reportedly the first installment of a 2.2-ton deal. A Russian counter-narcotics official asserted that intelligence officials had been offered 7.7 tons in a smuggling operation that was supported by the North Korean government.

- April 1997. Japanese customs inspectors seized 154 pounds of methamphetamines, estimated value $95 million, concealed in cans labeled "honey." The customs inspectors thought it odd that a country experiencing a famine would export so much honey. At the time, it was the largest drug bust in Japanese history. In January 1999, the North Koreans broke their own record when Japanese officials seized 440 pounds of methamphetamines.

- January 1998. Two North Korean diplomats in transit from Mexico were arrested in the Moscow airport carrying 77 pounds of cocaine with an estimated value of $4.5 million. Russian authorities suspect a connection to Colombian drug cartels.

- July 1998. An Egyptian customs official insisted on inspecting the luggage of two transiting North Korean diplomats and discovered 506,000 tablets of Rohypnol, a sedative known as the "date rape" drug.

The North Korean Advisory Group (1999) provides a list of more than 40 North Korean drug trafficking incidents, many involving North Korean diplomats.

A "conservative" estimate of North Korean revenues from drug trafficking would be $71 million annually, with $59 million coming from opiates and $12 million from amphetamines, suggesting that net exports of drugs are probably of the same order of magnitude as arms (Perl 1999).[123] If the estimates of the State Department's Bureau of Narcotics Control are correct, North Korea would have the world's third highest opium poppy acreage (trailing Afghanistan and Burma by a considerable margin). Likewise, drugs would account for a lower share of exports in North Korea than in Colombia, Afghanistan, or Burma.

---

reliever in the North. Likewise, methamphetamines were originally developed for military uses, and some share of production may be devoted to officially sanctioned domestic usage.

123. In 1999, the South Korean Ministry of Foreign Affairs and Trade estimated revenues from all illegal activities (not including arms sales) at $100 million.

Counterfeiting is a third potential illicit source of revenue. Given the considerable expertise of North Korean counterfeiters, the moves to new US currency designs were reportedly undertaken in part to discourage their activities. High profile counterfeiting busts have occurred in Macau,[124] Cambodia,[125] and Russia.[126] South Korean intelligence estimates put counterfeiting revenues at $15 million a year (Perl 1999). US officials regard this estimate as high.

North Korea also receives official aid in the form of bilateral assistance, humanitarian assistance through UN agencies (principally the World Food Program), KEDO, and other channels from at least 49 countries, as documented in table 3.14. These figures indicate that North Korea has been receiving aid flows in the hundreds of millions of dollars annually, roughly one-third as large as aggregate exports, with the largest contributors typically being the United States, South Korea, China, Japan, and the European Union. However significant as these aid inflows might be for the North Korean economy, in principle they cannot be used to finance the trade deficit. The previously calculated trade deficit is defined with respect to market transactions on commercial terms. In balance of payments terms the lion's share of these aid flows are in-kind transfers. So, for example, the food aid listed in table 3.14 is distinct from and in addition to the commercial imports listed in table 3.12.[127] In theory, there is one way that these aid flows could be used to finance the North Korean trade deficit: if the North Koreans resold the aid shipments on world markets. In the past there have been allegations of "calorie arbitrage," in which the North Koreans resold high value food aid for lower quality foodstuffs on world markets. It has also been alleged that Pyongyang demands large

---

124. In 1994, police in Macau traced $600,000 of counterfeit bills to a North Korean trading company. Additional counterfeiting busts occurred in Macau in 1999. Macau appears to be the center of North Korean criminal activity abroad. For this reason, Hong Kong authorities long opposed a North Korean request to establish a consulate, but the consulate was finally opened in February 2000.

125. In a bizarre incident in 1996, Japanese Red Army member Yoshimi Tanaka (wanted on a hijacking warrant) was seized in Cambodia while traveling in a North Korean diplomatic vehicle and carrying a North Korean diplomatic passport and $200,000 in counterfeit currency.

126. In another weird incident, Russian authorities in 1998 arrested Kil Jae-young for trying to pass $30,000 in fake greenbacks. When arrested, Kil, reported to be director of "Bureau 39," Kim Jong-il's personal slush fund, followed a time-honored tradition and gave a false name and claimed to be a North Korean diplomat subject to diplomatic immunity. Kil had some experience in this regard—posted to Sweden as ambassador, he voluntarily left Sweden in 1976, allegedly after being implicated in drug trafficking.

127. In reporting inter-Korean trade, the Korea Trade Promotion Corporation (KOTRA) misclassifies KEDO contributions, in particular KEDO oil shipments, as South Korean exports to North Korea.

Table 3.14 Aid balance sheet (millions of US dollars)

	1995	1996	1997	1998	1999[a]
Argentina					
UN agencies	—	0.200	—	—	—
Other humanitarian aid	—	—	—	—	—
KEDO	—	—	—	—	2.279
Australia	5.451	1.987	6.347	2.509	—
UN agencies	—	—	—	—	—
Other humanitarian aid	—	—	—	—	—
KEDO	0.024	0.080	0.045	0.090	0.010
Austria	—	—	—	—	—
UN agencies	—	—	—	—	—
Other humanitarian aid	—	—	—	—	—
KEDO	0.007	—	—	—	—
Belgium	—	—	—	—	—
UN agencies	—	—	—	—	—
Other humanitarian aid	—	0.424	—	0.075	—
KEDO	—	—	—	—	—
Brunei Darussalam	—	—	—	—	—
UN agencies	—	—	—	—	—
Other humanitarian aid	—	—	0.002	—	—
KEDO	—	—	—	—	—
Cambodia	—	—	—	—	—
UN agencies	1.054	0.809	4.167	3.539	0.161
Other humanitarian aid	—	—	—	—	—
KEDO	—	—	—	—	—
Canada					
UN agencies					
Other humanitarian aid					
KEDO					

China	3.600	6.270	37.675	28.000	—
UN agencies	—	—	—	—	—
Other humanitarian aid	—	—	—	—	—
KEDO	—	—	—	—	—
Czech Republic	—	—	0.015	0.148	—
UN agencies	—	—	—	—	—
Other humanitarian aid	—	—	—	—	—
KEDO	—	—	—	—	—
Cyprus	—	0.003	0.005	—	—
UN agencies	—	—	—	—	—
Other humanitarian aid	—	—	—	—	—
KEDO	—	—	—	—	—
Denmark	0.872	0.509	4.274	4.044	0.557
UN agencies	—	—	—	—	—
Other humanitarian aid	—	—	—	—	—
KEDO	—	—	—	—	—
Egypt	—	—	—	—	—
UN agencies	—	—	—	—	—
Other humanitarian aid	—	—	—	—	—
KEDO	—	—	—	—	—
European Union	0.380	6.762	100.689	63.179	0.336
UN agencies	—	—	—	—	—
Other humanitarian aid	—	—	—	—	—
KEDO	—	—	—	—	—
Finland	0.117	0.189	0.774	0.304	0.814
UN agencies	—	—	—	—	—
Other humanitarian aid	—	—	—	—	—
KEDO	—	—	—	—	—
France	0.051	—	—	0.504	—
UN agencies	—	—	—	—	—
Other humanitarian aid	—	—	—	—	—
KEDO	—	—	—	—	—

(continued next page)

Table 3.14 Aid balance sheet (continued)

	1995	1996	1997	1998	1999[a]
Germany					
UN agencies	0.058	1.278	—	1.261	0.638
Other humanitarian aid	—	—	—	—	—
KEDO	—	—	—	—	—
Greece					
UN agencies	—	0.025	0.020	—	—
Other humanitarian aid	—	—	—	—	—
KEDO	—	—	—	—	—
Hungary					
UN agencies	0.008	—	0.010	—	—
Other humanitarian aid	—	—	—	—	—
KEDO	—	—	—	—	—
India					
UN agencies	0.100	—	—	—	—
Other humanitarian aid	—	—	—	—	—
KEDO	—	—	—	—	—
Indonesia					
UN agencies	0.345	0.355	—	0.325	—
Other humanitarian aid	—	—	—	—	—
KEDO	—	—	—	—	—
Iran					
UN agencies	0.100	—	—	—	—
Other humanitarian aid	—	—	—	—	—
KEDO	—	—	—	—	—
Ireland					
UN agencies	0.050	0.102	1.047	0.014	0.266
Other humanitarian aid	—	—	—	—	—
KEDO	—	—	—	—	—

Italy	0.084	0.465	0.294	—	1.821
UN agencies	—	—	—	—	—
Other humanitarian aid	—	—	—	—	—
KEDO	—	—	—	—	—
Japan	0.500	25.000	27.000	—	1,000.433
UN agencies	—	—	—	—	—
Other humanitarian aid	—	—	—	—	—
KEDO	—	—	—	—	—
Korea (Republic of)	233.982	12.412	25.527	76.366	3,244.000
UN agencies	—	—	—	—	—
Other humanitarian aid	—	—	—	—	—
KEDO	—	—	—	—	—
Luxembourg	0.018	—	0.220	0.113	—
UN agencies	—	—	—	—	—
Other humanitarian aid	—	—	—	—	—
KEDO	—	—	—	—	—
Malaysia	0.300	0.075	—	—	—
UN agencies	—	—	—	—	—
Other humanitarian aid	—	—	—	—	—
KEDO	—	—	—	—	—
Malta	—	—	—	0.020	—
UN agencies	—	—	—	—	—
Other humanitarian aid	—	—	—	—	—
KEDO	—	—	—	—	—
Mongolia	—	—	—	0.585	—
UN agencies	—	—	—	—	—
Other humanitarian aid	—	—	—	—	—
KEDO	—	—	—	—	—
Netherlands	0.626	0.825	1.849	0.268	0.237
UN agencies	—	—	—	—	—
Other humanitarian aid	—	—	—	—	—
KEDO	—	—	—	—	—

(continued next page)

Table 3.14 Aid balance sheet (continued)

	1995	1996	1997	1998	1999[a]
New Zealand	0.335	0.410	1.152	0.359	—
UN agencies	—	—	—	—	—
Other humanitarian aid	—	—	—	—	—
KEDO	—	—	—	—	0.816
Norway	0.333	2.245	6.625	3.976	—
UN agencies	—	—	—	—	—
Other humanitarian aid	—	—	—	—	—
KEDO	—	—	—	—	—
Oman	—	—	0.050	—	—
UN agencies	—	—	—	—	—
Other humanitarian aid	—	—	—	—	—
KEDO	—	—	—	—	—
Pakistan	0.150	—	—	—	—
UN agencies	—	—	—	—	—
Other humanitarian aid	—	—	—	—	—
KEDO	—	—	—	—	—
The Philippines	—	0.153	0.020	—	0.001
UN agencies	—	—	—	—	—
Other humanitarian aid	—	—	—	—	—
KEDO	—	—	—	—	—
Russian Federation	0.136	—	0.666	0.006	—
UN agencies	—	—	—	—	—
Other humanitarian aid	—	—	—	—	—
KEDO	—	—	—	—	—
Singapore	0.320	0.100	0.100	0.100	0.400
UN agencies	—	—	—	—	—
Other humanitarian aid	—	—	—	—	—
KEDO	—	—	—	—	—

Slovakia					
UN agencies	—	—	—	—	0.020
Other humanitarian aid	—	—	—	—	—
KEDO	—	—	—	—	—
Spain					
UN agencies	—	—	—	0.250	0.166
Other humanitarian aid	—	—	—	—	—
KEDO	—	—	—	—	—
Sweden					
UN agencies	2.614	1.493	3.748	3.736	4.404
Other humanitarian aid	—	—	—	—	—
KEDO	—	—	—	—	—
Switzerland					
UN agencies	3.639	0.398	7.536	6.266	—
Other humanitarian aid	—	—	—	—	—
KEDO	—	—	—	—	—
Syria					
UN agencies	5.850	—	—	—	—
Other humanitarian aid	—	—	—	—	—
KEDO	—	—	—	—	—
Taiwan					
UN agencies	—	—	0.600	—	—
Other humanitarian aid	—	—	—	—	—
KEDO	—	—	—	—	—
Thailand					
UN agencies	0.320	0.020	0.020	—	—
Other humanitarian aid	—	—	—	—	—
KEDO	—	—	—	—	—
Turkey					
UN agencies	—	—	—	0.030	—
Other humanitarian aid	—	—	—	—	—
KEDO	—	—	—	—	—

(continued next page)

Table 3.14 Aid balance sheet (continued)

	1995	1996	1997	1998	1999[a]
United Kingdom					
UN agencies	1.235	0.309	1.393	—	—
Other humanitarian aid	—	—	—	—	—
KEDO	—	—	—	—	—
United States					
UN agencies	9.725	29.171	82.748	223.732	147.000
Other humanitarian aid	—	—	—	—	—
KEDO	—	—	—	—	—
MIA Remains	—	—	2.780	—	—
Vietnam					
UN agencies	—	—	—	—	—
Other humanitarian aid	—	—	—	—	—
KEDO	—	—	—	—	—
Total Aid	272.385	92.070	317.648	419.735	4,404.173

a. Figures include multi-year commitments. KEDO contributions as of June 1999.

b. China agreed to provide 150,000 MT of food and 40,000 tons of coal.

c. 10,000 MT of rice provided to WFP.

d. 150,000 MT of food provided on concessional terms, 150,000 MT of food provided gratis. 500,000 MT in total delivered through first half of 1996.

e. "Collateral Fund" to be used as needed to support the financing of KEDO expenses in case of a liquidity shortfall.

f. Includes $1 billion contribution for light-water reactors.

g. Pakistan also provided 2000 tons of food grains according to the North Korean Central News Agency.

h. Pakistan provided 2,000 tons of foodgrains according to the North Korean Central News Agency.

i. Pakistan promised 30,000 tons of "free grain" according to the North Korean Central News Agency.

j. As of October 15, 1999. Reported by *Newsreview*.

k. The ROK provided an additional $45 million in support of KEDO activities in the form of a Korea Export-Import Bank loan.

l. Contribution for light-water reactors.

m. The US has pledged an additional 200,000 MT of food to be distributed by the WFP.

n. The US has agreed to provide 100,000 MT and 1000 MT of potato seed through PVO networks.

o. According to the Congressional Research Service, the US has paid $3.1 million since 1994 for MIA remains.

p. According to an article by Kang Joo-an in the *Joongang Ilbo* on December 6, 1999.

Sources: UN World Food Program, UN Office for the Coordination of Humanitarian Affairs, *Newsreview*, State Department, KEDO Annual Reports, *Washington Post*.

sums ($50,000 to $100,000) for Koreans in the diaspora to visit relatives in North Korea. Another possibility is that the trade deficits have been implicitly financed by China, which has permitted North Korea to accumulate large arrears in its trade account. A final possibility is that these deficits have been financed with remittances from Japan, which are sometimes reported to be in the billions of dollars.[128] The size of these remittances can be estimated as a residual of the balance of payments under a series of assumptions. An accounting identity links remittances to the other trade aggregates:

$$REM = -TB-CAP-NRT$$

That is, remittances (REM) are equal to the negative of the trade balance (TB) less net capital inflows (CAP) and whatever the balance is on non-recorded transactions (NRT), including non-recorded trade, revenues from illicit activities, and reporting errors and omissions.

In the case of North Korea, some uncertainty surrounds each of these magnitudes. In the case of the trade balance, uncertainty exists due to the difficulties in constructing North Korea's partner country trade due to incomplete or misreporting by some partner countries as previously noted. A second issue arises with respect to trade with other CPEs, since the terms of this trade may deviate significantly from market prices, and there is considerable evidence that North Korea has been allowed to run up substantial arrears in its trade with these countries. As a consequence, for the purposes of this calculation, we assume that only trade with market economies must be settled on a hard currency basis, effectively expunging China from the calculation.[129] It is assumed that North Korea does not have any outstanding balances in services trade, where data is nonexistent.[130]

Capital flow data come from the OECD. For 1993, the OECD reports the data in two breakdowns: transactions with OECD countries and transactions with non-OECD countries. For 1994, the most recent year for which this data is available, the OECD does not differentiate between OECD and non-OECD sources. The total flow concept would be appropriate if all of North Korea's trade were hard currency denominated and the capital inflows were also in hard currency form. The OECD-only formulation would be appropriate if trade with other CPEs was not

---

128. Eberstadt (1996), using an approach similar to the one adopted here, similarly concluded that these private aid flows are probably considerably smaller than claimed.

129. See Noland (1998c) for a treatment that includes trade with CPEs as well as trade with market economies.

130. The trade balance is constructed from the IMF *Direction of Trade* data, adjusted for known cases of misreporting (i.e., Mexico and Austria) and the fact that imports are reported inclusive of transport costs and exports are not.

denominated in hard currencies and was carried out on concessional or non-market terms. In this case, hard currency remittances would only be necessary to cover the hard currency deficit less hard currency net capital inflows. The situation in reality may well be somewhere between these two extremes, with some, though not all, trade with other CPEs effectively occurring on market terms.

With respect to non-recorded trade, there is no reason to believe that either smuggling or recording errors or omissions are systematically biased toward a net deficit or surplus, and in any event these cannot be observed. According to ACDA, North Korea had net arms exports of $30 million in 1993, and net arms imports of $50 million for 1994. Again, treatment of this aggregate is problematic. It may well be that the arms transactions amount to genuinely non-recorded trade and thus should be added to the balance of payments that remittances are necessary to fulfill. However, it is possible that this trade (allegedly undertaken mainly with Middle Eastern countries, some of which do in fact report trade with North Korea) is simply misreported in other commodity categories and does not represent a net addition to North Korea's balance of payments position. A third possibility is that this trade is beyond the control of the central planners, and some or all of it is being accumulated as reserves against future contingencies by either the military or the KWP.[131] If either of the latter two hypotheses is correct, then some or all of the arms exports do not represent a genuinely independent contribution to the financing gap and should not be used to calculate needed remittances. In response, two values of net arms exports are used: the ACDA estimate as a non-recorded addition to trade, and zero, under the assumption that this trade is already being counted in other commodity categories or is being accumulated as reserves. Again, reality may lie somewhere in between.

The final issue is returns to illicit activities. Perl (1999) puts revenues from the export of opiates at $59 million in recent years. (For the purposes of this calculation, methamphetamines can be ignored—North Korea did not begin exporting them in large volume until the late 1990s.) However, one faces the same problem with drugs as with guns. Presumably some of this trade is simply misreported, so that it amounts to an under invoicing by the importer, and in any event the revenues may go to foreign bank accounts and never be remitted to North Korea. So, like arms, we have two polar assumptions: the $59 million is a pure addition to the balance of payments, or it is no addition. Add in $1 million for counterfeiting revenue, and one has an even $60 million in annual revenue from illicit activity.

---

131. Alternatively, the military could use its exports to purchase parts or components that it cannot source domestically. In this case, whether military exports represent additional net financing would depend on how military *imports* are accounted for.

Table 3.15 Estimated remittances (millions of US dollars)

	Trade balance	Capital inflow	Arms sales 1	Arms sales 2	Illicit activities 1	Illicit activities 2	Estimated remittances
1993							
Case 1	−91	5	30	—	60	—	−4
Case 2	−91	5	—	0	—	0	86
Case 3	−91	5	30	—	—	0	56
Case 4	−91	5	—	0	60	—	26
Base Case	**−91**	**5**	**15**	**—**	**30**	**—**	**41**
1994							
Case 1	−209	188	−50	—	60	—	11
Case 2	−209	188	—	0	—	0	21
Case 3	−209	188	−50	—	—	0	71
Case 4	−209	188	—	0	60	—	−39
Base Case	**−209**	**188**	**−25**	**—**	**30**	**—**	**16**

Key:
Trade balance excludes trade with centrally planned economies.
Capital inflow for 1993 is from OECD sources only. Capital inflow for 1994 is from all sources.
Arms sales 1 lists the arms sales reported by the Arms Control and Disarmament Agency.
Arms sales 2 treats these as already counted in the trade balance figure.
Illicit activities 1 is the estimated revenue from illicit activities.
Illicit activities 2 assumes no additional revenue from a balance of payments standpoint.

Ten possible combinations of these alternatives are listed in table 3.15, along with a "base case" reflecting an intermediate set of assumptions. The implicit remittances generated by these calculations exhibit a range from $86 million to -$4 million in 1993 (in the latter case money would actually be flowing out of North Korea), and from $71 million to -$39 million for 1994, with the "base case" estimates being $41 million and $16 million in 1993 and 1994, respectively.[132]

One can interpret these results in several ways. If accurate, they imply that, rather than in the billions of dollars, remittances are probably far smaller—less than $100 million—on the same order of magnitude as revenues from guns and drugs. Alternatively, remittances could be much larger, as is often reported in the press, but in this case a corresponding magnitude of expenditures is missing, or North Korea is running a balance of payments surplus and exporting capital to the rest of the world.[133] Either case would be very curious, insomuch as North Korea was entering a famine during those years. Finally, a critical issue to the calculations presented in table 3.15 is the extent to which the Chinese have been implicitly providing aid by permitting the North Koreans to build up

132. Eberstadt (1996), using a similar method, obtains even lower estimates of remittances.

133. Rumor has it that North Korean officials have invested in property in Monte Carlo, and Kirk and Hochstein (1997) repeat a North Korean defector's claim that Kim Jong-il's sister controls $100 million in overseas assets.

arrears on their imports. Under the assumption that the Chinese simply barter their exports for whatever imports the North Koreans can provide and allow the difference to be built up in arrears, the remittances necessary to finance imports would be less than $100 million, which is far lower than commonly thought. However, to the extent that the Chinese are successful in extracting hard currency payments from the North Koreans, they could be soaking up whatever remittances the *Chochongryun* can provide.

Current Reforms

In keeping with the murky state of North Korean finances, its coping strategy has emphasized one-off projects that can literally and figuratively be fenced off from the rest of the economy. The first of these was the construction of an SEZ in the Rajin-Sonbong area, and the second was an opening of Mt. Kumgang to tourism.[134] Establishment of bonded export processing zones in Nampo and Wonson have also been announced.

In 1984, following visits to China by Kim Il-sung in 1982 and 1983, the North Korean government enacted a joint venture law, apparently modeled on China's (though this is denied by North Korea).[135] Initially there was a surge in investment, mainly from the *Chochongryun*, but this soon petered out, and, following another visit to China in 1991 by Kim Il-sung, the government announced the creation of an SEZ totaling 621 square kilometers in the area of Rajin, Chongjin, and Sonbong in the Tumen River delta in the extreme Northeast of the country.[136] This was

---

134. In addition to Rajin-Sonbong, North Korea has also participated in the ill-fated Tumen River Area Development Project (Flake 1995a). This was to be a joint project involving Russia, China, North Korea, South Korea, and Mongolia, under the auspices of the UNDP. Although the project has generated voluminous feasibility studies, it never really got off the ground and was subsequently downgraded to the Tumen River Economic Development Area. In light of the fact that the project involves five countries, two of which are arguably experiencing economic collapse, two of which are not market economies, and one of which does not belong to any of the multilateral development banks (which loan to governments, not projects, in any event), the likelihood of even this scaled back project having a major impact in the foreseeable future appears slight.

Projects oriented toward the mining sector have perhaps greater potential. There also has been talk of establishing a system of mining concessions to encourage inward FDI in that sector (Namkung 1998). It is claimed that North Korea is considering forming another SEZ in South Hamgyong province oriented toward the mining sector. The idea is that foreigners would rejuvenate the mining industry. The minerals could be exported via the port of Shinpo, which is being refurbished as part of the KEDO project. It has also been reported that the North Koreans are considering opening additional sites to foreign tourists.

135. See Koo 1992, S.C. Kim 1994, and S.K. Kim 1995.

136. The *Chochongryun* account for nearly 90 percent of investment nationwide since 1984, with most of these investments concentrated in light manufacturing and retailing.

expanded in March 1993 by 125 square kilometers to 742 square kilometers.[137] A spate of additional laws followed, establishing the legal framework for foreign firms operating in North Korea.[138] These laws identify sectors open to foreign investment and give foreign firms the right to own 100 percent of the capital, the right to choose the form of ownership or management, a guarantee against nationalization, the right to lease and use land for up to 50 years (a right that can be transferred and traded) with the possibility of extending the period of land usage, the right to have prices determined in the market, the right to export, the right to repatriate profits, and a no-visa system permitting foreigners free access to the SEZ.[139] Foreign funded enterprises would also receive certain preferential treatment, including tariff-free imports, a tax holiday of three years, a 50 percent reduction in profit and income taxes for two years, an income tax rate of 14 percent thereafter for firms operating in the SEZ, and free entry into the harbor for foreign ships. And for the first time, these benefits having been extended to "Koreans living outside the Republic" (Flake 1995a, 7).

On paper these conditions are better than those in the Chinese or Vietnamese SEZs (D. Lee 1993). Nevertheless, investments in the zone have remained relatively small: pledged investment has been on the order of $150 million, and gross actual investment around $30 million. Most of the investment has been for processing on consignment, with the North Koreans earning about 27 percent of the value of the exports (Y.S. Lee 1996). Difficulties encountered by investors include infrastructural problems, uncooperative low-level bureaucrats, and uncompetitive wage rates.[140] A thriving market there was reportedly shut down in September 1999, and authorities have apparently begun requiring that licenses for even small investments be issued in Pyongyang, rather than in the zone as had previously been the practice.

The Rajin port benefits from good location (the harbor conditions are relatively favorable in terms of weather, currents, climate, etc.) and good

---

137. See Hwang 1993, Yeon 1993a, and Suh and Kim 1994.

138. See Bazhanova (2000), table 7.1, for a comprehensive listing. Min (1996) provides a detailed examination of North Korean foreign investment laws. See also Koo 1992, Yeon 1993a, Y.S. Lee 1994a, Suh and Kim 1994, Flake 1995a, and S.K. Kim 1995.

139. Domestic currency receipts can in principle be converted on demand into foreign exchange at the Central Bank and remitted abroad through one of the two existing commercial banks, though one former investor indicated that in practice this can be "a bit dodgy," as sometimes the bank refuses to release foreign exchange.

140. In an attempt to jumpstart the effort, the North Korean government's Committee for the Promotion of External Economic Cooperation (CPEEC), in conjunction with the United Nations Industrial Development Organization (UNIDO) and the United Nations Development Program (UNDP), sponsored a trade and investment forum in the zone in September 1996. Three days after the conference concluded, a North Korean submarine ran aground off the coast of South Korea.

wharfs.[141] It also has considerable space for expansion. However, at present it is well below international standards. The existing structures are either of substandard quality or size and are largely unusable, as are the cranes.[142] In general, the lack of available data on the port and its traffic remains a problem. The size of a ship that can berth in the harbor is unknown, as is the current capacity utilization of the port facilities. The port of Chongjin, south of Rajin, is officially outside of the zone, but is also ranked as a free port for the zone.

Associated transportation links are also underdeveloped. There is no airport, rail links are infrequent, and overland travel is difficult even in favorable weather conditions.[143] Transportation inside the zone is also difficult. It takes nearly thirty minutes to travel the 17-kilometer distance along the single lane road connecting Rajin and Sonbong.[144] Nearly all other roads in the zone, including the essential links from Sonbong to the Chinese and Russian borders, are dirt and most likely impassable during the winter. There is no automobile bridge into Russia. The road to the Chinese border, in particular, must pass over mountains over 700 meters in height. Rail links appear somewhat better, though questions remain as to the ability of the trains to handle larger containers.[145] The trip from Pyongyang via rail takes 19 hours, and the feasibility of driving the same route is questionable.

The telecommunications infrastructure, previously functionally nonexistent, has been considerably boosted by the Loxley Pacific Company of Thailand, which has invested nearly $15 million in the zone, laying fiberoptic cables and providing phone and fax service to individual businesses. Energy requirements are currently being met by the oil-burning Sonbong power plant, courtesy of KEDO.

Until the November 1997 SEZ-only devaluation, the wage rate for unskilled North Korean labor was multiples of rates for comparably skilled labor in China and Vietnam (see box 3.3). However, with the devaluation, it is fair to say that North Korean labor is priced competi-

---

141. This discussion draws upon Noland and Flake (1997). See that source for additional details.

142. The port's cranes can only handle 20-foot containers, and not the common 40-foot containers. Moreover, shipping specialists who examined the cranes during the recent forum reported that many of the crane's engines had been cannibalized and that structural flaws in the cranes had been covered with fresh coats of paint. One possible exception to this dreary picture is a joint Russian-Japanese invested bulk fertilizer loading terminal brought up to international standard.

143. Although an airport is planned for the zone, it has not progressed beyond the planning stage. North Korean officials claim a heliport is in operation.

144. Construction of a tunnel under the mountain between Rajin and Sonbong is reportedly underway, though this was not actually observed by the present author.

145. During the course of the forum, containers were being moved to China via truck.

tively.[146] Foreign firms are forced to hire through either North Korean joint venture partners, or, in the case of greenfield investments, through the North Korean government.[147] These intermediaries in turn pay the workers and pocket the difference between what the firms pay and what the workers receive.[148] This arrangement of having hiring and compensation issues handled indirectly through North Korean intermediaries has been a source of friction. Foreign investors have indicated that North Korean intermediaries interfere with staffing decisions to the detriment of efficient management and training. They further assert that they are subjected to outrageous salary demands, and that their intermediaries drive an enormous wedge between what foreign investors pay and what workers receive.[149] In addition, North Korean labor law places significant constraints on firms' ability to dismiss workers (Min 1996).

Light manufacturing is an obvious activity for the zone.[150] Unfortunately, data on the extent of manufacturing activities in the area are

---

146. The minimum wage was $80 per month in the SEZ, and remains $150 elsewhere in the country, higher than the $60 to $80 per month in China or the $30 to $35 per month in Vietnam. However, with the devaluation the minimum wage in the SEZ has dropped to less than one dollar a month. North Korean officials argue that investors do not have to pay payroll taxes or make other social welfare contributions, though Min (1996) argues that there is a basis in North Korean law for requiring such payments.

147. In principle, there are no restrictions on the number or type of expatriate staff that foreign investors can bring to the zone. However, there is an acute lack of international standard housing within the zone, and other social infrastructure such as schools, hospitals, recreational facilities, churches or other related facilities for expatriates are nonexistent. Assignment in the Rajin-Sonbong SEZ would be a hard sell for any personnel department.

148. This same approach was used by China in the early days of the Chinese economic reforms and generated numerous complaints from the foreign investors.

149. Prior to the November 1997 devaluation, the legal minimum wage was $80 monthly. However, workers in garment factories visited by the author in September 1996 indicated that they were paid 110 brown won per month, or about $50 at the official exchange rate or about $2 at the black market rate. The devaluation appears to have simply ratified what was already occurring. The North Korean intermediaries at minimum appear to be pocketing a $30 (or 38 percent) tax at the official rate, and an even larger wedge if they are able to exploit arbitrage opportunities between brown and blue won or between official and unofficial exchange rates.

These figures are for a six-day, 48-hour work week. Regulations regarding overtime do not appear to have been codified and, given the low level of economic activity at this time, are of little immediate relevance. Employers are not expected to pay social security taxes or provide housing or transportation subsidies or other benefits. In light of the low level of activity in the zone and the ample differences between what the North Korean intermediaries receive and what the workers are paid, some observers have speculated that it might be possible to negotiate payments less than the minimum wage.

150. This is demonstrated in chapter 7. South Korea is already North Korea's second largest export market. Although nearly all of this trade is still conducted through third parties, the opening in 1995 of shipping links from Pusan to the zone is a positive development.

The Japanese and Chinese markets appear relatively open. Japan maintains relatively few barriers in the light industry sectors of North Korean comparative advantage. However, if

inadequate. The North Korean government has announced that $34 million has been invested in the SEZ. This is a gross figure and does not take into account disinvestments. Anecdotal evidence suggests that disinvestment has been considerable. Presumably most of the output would be exported rather than sold domestically. North Korea's natural export markets are South Korea, Japan, China, and the United States, in that order.[151]

Given its present state of development, the greatest potential for the zone appears to be as a center of regional transshipment trade. This will largely be driven by developments in Northeastern China and China's lack of access to the Sea of Japan (East Sea). Already, the bulk of activity at the Rajin port is transshipment trade. At present, however, the generally poor condition of the roads to China and to Russia inhibit any significant increase in transshipment activity in advance of further investments in infrastructure. Moreover, Rajin-Sonbong must compete with Russian ports for this same transshipment trade.[152] By most accounts, the port facilities in Vladivostok are in better condition, though even the Russians are keen to exploit the fertilizer handling capabilities of the Rajin port. It is hard to imagine the Rajin-Sonbong SEZ taking off without significant investments in infrastructure. The speed at which transshipping activities grow will further depend on continued economic vitality in China's Jilin Province, infrastructural investment in Rajin-Sonbong, and competition from alternative Russian ports. Even if the physical obstacles to doing business in the zone are removed, real questions remain with respect to North Korean policy and capacity.

Japanese industry were adversely affected by import surges from North Korea, Japanese officials could impose a variety of restrictions on North Korean imports. Since North Korea is not a member of the World Trade Organization (WTO), these could take the form of quantitative restrictions and other measures currently banned among WTO members.

Access to the Chinese market would appear to be largely a function of political relations. China's current strategy is to support economic reform in North Korea. Thus North Korean access to the Chinese market is likely to be good for the foreseeable future. (Indeed, in 1995 the Jilin provincial government, the Chinese Ministry of Foreign Trade and Economic Cooperation (MOFTEC), and UNIDO cosponsored a conference to promote investment in the Rajin-Sonbong SEZ.) The United States effectively maintains an embargo on trade with North Korea. Prospects for change are discussed in chapter 9.

151. This is demonstrated in chapter 7. In addition to light industry, there is a small oil refinery in Sonbong that is not currently in operation. Two Japanese firms have even produced a brochure comparing the potential development of the zone to the Kashima Waterfront Industrial Complex in Japan, though their analysis appears to be driven more by the deindustrialization of the Japanese rust belt than any real consideration of the situation in North Korea.

152. In June 1999, South Korea announced the opening of direct links between Sokcho and Posyet, a small Russian port just north of Rajin. Likewise, the Chinese have opened a new railway spur to Posyet. However, one news report claimed that conditions in Rajin-Sonbong are better than in Posyet (*Economist*, 27 June 1998).

If Rajin could develop into a viable entrepôt port for Chinese transshipping, the necessary upgrading of transportation links would also facilitate the development of commercial leisure activities in the zone. A hotel and casino constructed by the Emperor property development group of Hong Kong was opened in July 1999.[153] Outdoor activities could potentially be another source of tourist revenues. At present, the zone boasts considerable natural beauty and is relatively untrammeled by development. Given the dearth of outdoor recreational opportunities in Northeast Asia, under the right circumstances one could imagine the area becoming a regional tourist destination.

Geopolitical realities suggest that China (and by extension Hong Kong) will play a dominant role, at least in the short run. Furthermore, if the zone is to move beyond simple transshipping trade, it is generally accepted that South Korea will have to become more involved. Neither the United States nor the Japanese governments are willing to get too far ahead of South Korea on the issue of engagement with the North. The embargo effectively forecloses participation of US firms in the zone (or any other part of North Korea, for that matter). In the case of Japan, activity in the zone is dominated by firms controlled by ethnic Korean residents. Major Japanese firms have been unwilling to invest without a normalization of diplomatic relations and the extension of investment guarantees by the Japanese government. In contrast, China has a strategic interest in supporting North Korea and no qualms about doing so. In the absence of large-scale participation in the North Korean economy by South Korean, Japanese, or American firms, China has emerged by default as the driving force in the development of the zone. It is building a four-lane highway right up to the North Korean border, a development that should encourage transshipment through Rajin-Sonbong.

Placing the zone in perspective, however, even if it defies all odds and is as successful as its proponents envision, it would still have a limited

---

153. The idea appears to be to turn Rajin-Sonbong into a kind of Macau North, a place where ethnic Koreans from Jilin province (and prospectively South Korea) could engage in activities legally prohibited by their more puritanical governments. Hong Kong and Chinese investors would supply the money and management expertise, while North Korea supplies labor and political cover for these activities, with the North Koreans getting a cut above the table (and perhaps under it as well). Moreover, from the North Korean perspective these service sectors are labor-intensive. Any negative externalities associated with morally dubious activities could be kept to the relatively isolated confines of the SEZ. Indeed, it has been reported that the North Koreans initially objected to the name "Seaview Casino," inasmuch as they did not want their citizens to learn the meaning of the word "casino" (Tara Suilen Duffy, Associated Press, 30 July 1999). The prospective establishment of a bank and casino controlled by a common owner would appear to open up the possibility of gray area financial transactions such as money laundering. For more details on the casino, see (Park Jung-hoon, *Chosun Ilbo*, 25 July 1999).

direct impact on the North Korean economy.[154] The real issue is not whether the Rajin-Sonbong zone will have a significant direct impact on the North Korean economy, but rather whether it is a harbinger of things to come.[155]

The Hyundai agreement of October 1998 is important in this regard for two reasons. First, the money that Hyundai committed to pay North Korea dwarfs anything that it could plausibly earn in Rajin-Sonbong, and second, the Hyundai agreement holds forth the possibility of the construction of a new SEZ.

With respect to the former, Hyundai guaranteed North Korea $942 million over 75 months, with the payment schedule front-loaded for the first six months.[156] (Indeed, the North Koreans used brinkmanship to extract upfront payments before the first tour visited Mt. Kumgang in November 1998.) At $300 per passenger, North Korea stands to make up to $450 million annually off the tourism agreement alone if Hyundai is able to reach its target of 1.5 million visitors per year in 2005.[157] To put this in perspective, this money, if properly deployed, would be enough to close the North Korean food gap and end the famine. Unfortunately, it is believed that the funds are going into the Hong Kong bank account of "Bureau 39," a party organization controlled by Kim Jong-il, and will be used to reward his cronies and prop up his rule. If this is how the Mt. Kumgang tourism project plays out, then it will amount to a successful

---

154. As demonstrated earlier in this chapter, countries at this level of economic development typically have capital-output ratios of about 3:1. That is, it takes approximately three dollars of investment to permanently raise national income by one dollar. This suggests that, even if all the investment contracted at the 1996 trade and investment forum is actualized, the increase in GDP will only be around $100 million, or less than $5 per person. As will be argued in subsequent chapters, the rehabilitation of the North Korean economy could cost hundreds of billions of dollars. North Korea would need to have the equivalent of thousands of such zones to turn the economy around.

155. At the 1996 forum, CPEEC Chairman Kim Jong-u declined to signal a possible extension to the rest of the country of the reforms in Rajin-Sonbong. His reluctance to do so is perhaps understandable. As wider opening is not yet government policy, he likely cannot get too far out in front, even should he be inclined to do so, which is by no means certain. Furthermore, if investors thought that other, more potentially attractive, parts of the country would be opened up, they would be less likely to invest in Rajin-Sonbong.

156. It is perhaps not a coincidence that the detention of a tourist occurred in June 1999—the seventh month of the agreement—after the payments dropped to one-third their previous level.

157. North Korea and Hyundai have not always displayed a complete coincidence of interests in the project. Hyundai has reportedly been frustrated by the North's unwillingness to countenance a major expansion of non-Korean visitors. Instead, the North Koreans have apparently extracted additional funds from the South by levying heavy fines on South Korean tourists for littering, losing their passes, and other misdemeanors. See Cho (1999) for a very detailed assessment of the Mt. Kumgang project's impact—or lack thereof—on the local economy.

version of what Rajin-Sonbong is not: a regime-preserving hard currency earner with no real systemic implications for the organization of the North Korean economy or society.[158]

In this respect, the rest of the Hyundai deal might be more significant. As noted earlier, the agreement also called for the development of a second SEZ in Haeju, on the west coast north of Inchon.[159] This appears to have far greater prospects than Rajin-Sonbong. First, the geographical location is far more auspicious. Second, it has the backing of Hyundai (and presumably the South Korean government). This is critical both from the provision of the necessary infrastructure (which Rajin-Sonbong sorely lacks) as well as the imprimatur of Hyundai (and by extension the South Korean government). Thus, South Korean SMEs are far more likely to move light manufacturing operations to Haeju than to Rajin-Sonbong. Hyundai claims that the Haeju SEZ would host 850 firms, create 220,000 new jobs, and generate $20 billion in annual exports—more than 20 times North Korea's current exports. Beyond these efforts, it has also been reported that North Korea has amended its foreign investment laws to permit joint ventures outside of SEZs, but the details remain sketchy.

North Korea appears to be under serious balance of payments pressure. To the extent that the zones can contribute to generating foreign exchange, they would help relieve this pressure, but whether SEZs alone will be sufficient is another matter entirely. In most other countries that have made use of such zones with the aim of importing technology and establishing backward linkages with the rest of the economy, they have been a failure. Little integration with the rest of the economy has occurred, and the zones have amounted to little more than export enclaves to exploit locally cheap labor (Noland 1991a). The proposed mining SEZs would fit nicely into this mold. Ironically, in the case of North Korea, the regime may have little interest in integrating the SEZ with the rest of the economy, and indeed may prefer that they remain isolated enclaves.

Conclusions

Like other CPEs, North Korea initially achieved some success in mobilizing resources for development. Its uniqueness lay in the extreme degree

---

158. However, it should also be noted that the South Korean government can control the Mt. Kumgang tours in a far more direct way than it could a North Korean SEZ, a point driven home when Seoul suspended the tours after the detention of a tourist.

159. It has been widely reported that Kim Jong-il has expressed a preference for Shinuiju over Haeju, despite the latter's greater attractiveness as an economic hub. Some have argued that the choice between Haeju and Shinuiju will signal whether economics or politics are driving policy (Moon 2000). The possibility of a second Hyundai-developed SEZ, located at Tongchon on the east coast near Mt. Kumgang, also has been reported.

to which markets were repressed and decision making was invested in a single individual, Kim Il-sung. Like other CPEs, it began to stagnate when opportunities for "extensive" development had largely been exhausted, and "intensive" development and technological dynamism were required instead.

Kim's response in the 1970s was to try to circumvent this conundrum by borrowing capital and technology from abroad. This tactic failed, however, and North Korea defaulted on its debts, leaving it highly dependent on the Soviet Union. Given its lack of alternatives, the decline in relations with the Soviets and the Soviet Union's eventual collapse were blows from which the North Korean economy has never recovered.

The regime found itself in a terrible bind—its economy was failing, its primary patron was no more, and it feared that economic reform would mean the end of the regime as it had in Eastern Europe. The regime's response was essentially two-fold: engage in one-off attempts to earn foreign exchange through projects that would not affect the systemic organization of the economy (the Rajin-Sonbong SEZ and the Mt. Kumgang tourism project), while at the same time engaging in brinkmanship to extract resources from the rest of the world. The nuclear confrontation and the famine provided two opportunities to do precisely that. It is to these two crises that we now turn.

4

The Nuclear Confrontation

Today the Korean peninsula is the only place on earth where it is remotely conceivable that the United States could become involved in a major ground operation with virtually no prior warning. The US presence is a historical product of the Cold War division of the peninsula and the hot war that followed. The United States again nearly went to war with North Korea in June 1994.

North Korea faces two related but distinct problems involving energy. The first is a shortage of energy. It is dependent on imported energy, especially oil. As its economy has deteriorated, its ability to finance imports of this essential industrial intermediate input has declined, exacerbating the country's economic difficulties.

Contemporaneously, North Korea has pursued a nuclear energy development program. The characteristics of the North Korean nuclear program are such that it cannot be justified as a rational response to the nation's energy woes. Instead its *raison d'etre* must lie elsewhere, most obviously in a nuclear weapons development program. Given the North Korean regime's bellicose record of military aggression and weapons proliferation, the unnerving specter of a nuclear-armed North Korea has strongly conditioned the international community's response to the famine.

The Energy Situation

Historically, North Korea has had a high energy use economy. Von Hippel and Hayes (1998) estimate that in 1990 (probably the rough peak of North

Korean consumption) primary commercial energy use was approximately 67 giga-joules per capita, three times the level of China in 1990 and about half that of Japan (which had a GDP per capita approximately 20 times as high).[1] Energy use has been high due to inefficient use of fuels and reliance on relatively less efficient coal as a source of energy. Estimates of electrical transmission losses due to the deteriorating condition of the grid range from 16 percent to an astounding 84 percent. For the most part, it appears that, because of the lack of monitoring devices, the North Koreans have no idea how much electricity makes it to end users.[2]

Most of North Korea's energy comes from coal, with lesser amounts generated by oil and hydropower.[3] Small-scale biomass, hydropower, and wind power have been increasingly used in the rural areas. North Korea has no oil, and its domestic supplies of coal are mostly anthracite, so it needs to import coking coal for use in steel mills (Choi 1991). Because of its high intensity usage and lack of domestic resources, the North Korean economy is highly dependent on imported energy supplies.

In the past, North Korea had obtained oil from the Soviet Union at subsidized prices.[4] In the early 1990s, when the Russians began demanding payment in hard currency at world prices, China emerged as North Korea's principal supplier of both oil and coal. As China shifted from a net exporter to a net importer of oil, its willingness to finance North Korea's energy consumption withered, and it too began to demand that North Korea pay full price. The Chinese reversed course, however, once the famine intensified and large numbers of refugees began crossing into China. It now supplies North Korea with most of its food, oil, and coal imports. For its part, North Korea intensified its efforts to swap military assets for oil, but this coping strategy was not entirely successful. According to BOK statistics, between 1989 and 1994 coal production fell by more than 40 percent, crude oil imports by 65 percent, and electrical generation

---

1. The industrial sector is the largest consumer of commercial fuels—particularly coal—in North Korea. The transport sector consumes a substantial fraction of oil products, which are also used in the production of the North's most heavily used fertilizers. The military consumes a significant share of refined oil products, as well. See Moiseyev (2000) for an overview of North Korean energy policy.

2. See Von Hippel and Hayes (1998) for a detailed analysis of electrical power generation in North Korea.

3. See Young (1994), Yoo (1996), Von Hippel and Hayes (1998), and Williams, Hayes, and Von Hippel (1999) for estimates of the sources of North Korean energy.

4. Patrick (1991) cites a figure of two-thirds of the world price, though given the ubiquity of relative price distortions in socialist bloc trade it is unclear what the effective subsidy was. More recently, in an attempt to reinsert themselves into the diplomatic game, it has been rumored that Russia would begin resupplying North Korea with crude oil, possibly between 400,000 and 500,000 tons annually, though it is unclear how much (if any) of this has been delivered (Noerper 1999).

by more than 20 percent. Williams, Hayes, and Von Hippel (1999) estimate that energy supplies from all sources have fallen more than 50 percent since 1990.

The North Korean economy is highly dependent on imported energy supplies for electrical generation, transportation, and industrial uses, including the production of fertilizer. Domestic usage is extremely high due to inefficient use and wastage, especially through the electrical grid. From an economic perspective, there is an imperative that North Korea both increase the availability of supply and improve the efficiency of use. There is no reason to believe that North Korea needs a nuclear power program to address these needs. Apparently there are diplomatic advantages to conflating these issues, however.

The Nuclear Program

To construct a nuclear bomb, one needs either plutonium or enriched uranium as the fissile material. Plutonium is produced as a byproduct of nuclear fission and can be extracted from the spent fuel rods from a nuclear reactor. The amount of plutonium produced varies considerably by the type of reactor, making some designs more "proliferation-prone" than others. To fabricate a nuclear weapon, one must have some fissile material such as spent fuel rods, a facility to extract plutonium (or, alternatively, to enrich uranium to get it up to weapons grade), and a facility to actually construct the weapon. Once built, a delivery system is necessary for deployment.

North Korea began an experimental nuclear program in the 1950s, initially with help from the Soviet Union and later from China.[5] In 1967 it brought into operation at Yongdong a small experimental research reactor obtained from the Soviets, and in 1979 it began building a five megawatt reactor, which in 1986 became operational about three miles away at Yongbyon.[6] According to defectors, it was also during this period that the North Koreans began constructing nuclear weapon production facilities at an underground site nearby (Mansourov 1995).

As a condition for their help, the Soviets had insisted that North Korea accept the obligations of the Nuclear Non-Proliferation Treaty (NPT), despite the fact that they were not signatories. Beginning in 1982, US spy satellites began surveying what appeared to be the facilities necessary to construct nuclear weapons near the experimental reactor site. These facilities were surrounded by troops and antiaircraft guns.

---

5. See Mansourov (1995), Denisov (2000), Kaurov (2000), and Zhebin (2000) for histories of the North Korean nuclear program.

6. According to Mansourov (1995), the North Koreans were able to expand the original Soviet two megawatt experimental reactor to eight megawatt capacity using indigenous technology.

In 1985, North Korea began work on a 50 megawatt gas-graphite reactor at Yongbyon and later initiated construction of a 200 megawatt gas-graphite reactor at Taechon.[7] The Soviet Union agreed to supply four light water reactors on the condition that North Korea join the NPT. The North Koreans joined the NPT in December 1985, but the negotiations between the North Koreans and the International Atomic Energy Agency (IAEA), the organization tasked with ensuring treaty compliance, went on for three years. During this period, relations between North Korea and the Soviet Union deteriorated (for unrelated reasons), as the Soviet Union began its glide path toward collapse. The upshot was that the North Koreans had signed the NPT, but had not received the promised reactors.

However, in 1987, after the five megawatt reactor began operations, North Korea began building a "radiochemical laboratory" at Yongbyon, suspected by US intelligence of being a reprocessing facility used to produce plutonium in weapons-ready form from spent reactor fuel. According to Mansourov (1995), this would have been the second largest such facility in the world, after the US plant at Hanford, Washington. US intelligence estimated that the plant could produce plutonium sufficient for 30 bombs annually once all three reactors became operational.[8] In 1989, 1990, and 1991, the five megawatt reactor was periodically shut down. It is unknown whether the original fuel was extracted from the reactor and new fuel loaded—providing the raw material for producing weapons grade fissile material, as US intelligence suspected—or whether the reactor was restarted with the original fuel in place. This unanswered question is the kernel of the uncertainty surrounding the North's *existing* nuclear weapons inventory.[9]

However, the tide of history was running against the North's patrons. As the East Bloc collapsed, the nuclear program's importance as a strategic political and economic asset grew. With its own economic situation deteriorating, North Korea stepped up its efforts to barter weapons and military technology in the form of missiles, launchers, and nuclear and tunneling technology for oil with a number of countries in the Middle East, most prominently with Iran and Syria, which reportedly spent $500 million each on North Korean wares (Gerardi and Plotts 1994), and also with subsequent proliferator Pakistan, to which North Korea reportedly supplied missiles and weapons material, including warhead canisters.

---

7. In some literature, this is characterized as a 600 megawatt or an 800 megawatt plant.

8. In addition to these facilities, the North Koreans constructed more than 100 other nuclear-related facilities in the area around Yongbyon and drew up plans for three additional 635 megawatt reactors. According to Mansourov (1995), there are more than 150 nuclear scientists with doctoral degrees and over 2,400 specialists working in the North Korean program.

9. See Li (2000) for a fascinating analysis of the possible role of North Korean disinformation in contemporary Russian and US intelligence assessments of the North Korean nuclear weapons program.

As circumstantial evidence of a North Korean nuclear weapons program grew, so did calls for international inspections. These were initially rejected on the grounds that US tactical nuclear weapons were present in the South. However, when the United States stated its intention to remove these, the North Koreans added additional conditions (Bandow 1998). Then, in December 1991 North and South Korea concluded their Joint Declaration on the Denuclearization of the Korean Peninsula, renouncing the construction of nuclear reprocessing and uranium enrichment facilities and providing for mutual inspections. Although a joint commission was established, no progress was made in addressing the substantive issues (Han 1994).

Having been hoodwinked by Iraq, the IAEA was determined not to be fooled again. In May 1992, an IAEA inspection team confirmed US intelligence that the North Koreans were building facilities capable of producing weapons and had possibly extracted from the spent fuel of the existing reactors enough weapons grade plutonium to make one or two "Hiroshima-size" bombs.[10] Test data taken from the IAEA's first visit was incompatible with North Korean claims that it had only extracted plutonium from spent fuel once, and the organization requested the right to make unscheduled inspections in the future (Han 1994). The North Koreans continued to dissemble and impede follow-up inspections by the IAEA, contributing to a hardening of attitudes at the inspection organization. The UN Security Council then announced that it was prepared to undertake punitive actions to back up the IAEA.[11]

In March 1993 the North Koreans unprecedentedly threatened to withdraw from the NPT. Two months later the North test fired a potentially nuclear-capable missile, the Nodong-1, into the Sea of Japan, provoking alarm in Washington, Tokyo, and Seoul. They feared that, once the two graphite reactors under construction came on line, the amount of plutonium that North Korea could produce would increase enormously. Faced with the specter of North Korea possessing and exporting nuclear weap-

10. This narrative draws on the highly readable (and very different) accounts contained in Oberdorfer (1997) and Sigal (1998a). On this specific point, Sigal argues that subsequent evaluations suggest that the IAEA overestimated the amount of plutonium extracted and the North's bomb-making capability. See Snyder (1999b) for an insightful interpretation of the subsequent negotiations between the United States and North Korea.

11. See Dembinski (1995) for an analysis of the North Korean action regarding the nonproliferation regime. Relations between North Korea and the IAEA deteriorated in parallel with relations with South Korea and the United States. The resumption in 1993 of the "Team Spirit" joint military exercises by the United States and South Korea was characterized by the North as a dress rehearsal for invasion. In its aftermath, an attempt by lame duck South Korean President Roh Tae-woo to improve relations with the North was undercut by the South Korean Agency for National Security Planning and the presidential campaign staff of Kim Young-sam, who regarded a reduction of tension as inimical to Kim's electoral interests (Oberdorfer 1997).

ons and possibly even intercontinental ballistic missiles, the response of the Clinton Administration was to negotiate a deal that conflated the energy shortage and nuclear weapons issues.

The following month, in response to American requests, Pyongyang agreed to negotiate with Washington over its nuclear program (indeed making a proposal similar to the eventually concluded "Agreed Framework").[12] Intensive brinkmanship ensued. The United States threatened to bring a sanctions resolution to the UN Security Council, and the North Koreans responded that "sanctions are a declaration of war."[13] The IAEA pulled out its inspectors, and the UN General Assembly voted 140-1 (with China abstaining and North Korea being the lone dissenter) in favor of a resolution urging the North to "cooperate immediately." At a North-South meeting at the demilitarized zone (DMZ) truce village of Panmunjom, a North Korean negotiator stated that in the case of hostilities, the North would turn Seoul into "a sea of fire," a remark that was broadcast repeatedly over South Korean television.

In May 1994, North Korea proceeded with the removal of spent fuel rods from the experimental reactor, making the construction of an accurate nuclear history impossible under IAEA procedures.[14] The IAEA concluded that this was deliberate. Indeed, US satellite photography appeared to indicate that the North Koreans had an extra defueling machine ready to expedite the defueling process. The IAEA then requested Security Council action, and North Korea responded by releasing a statement that read in part, "sanctions mean war, and there is no mercy in war."

---

12. An important aspect of this was Pyongyang's refusal, as part of a strategy of driving a wedge between Washington and Seoul, to deal with Seoul directly but to establish an independent relationship with the United States. Although in essential terms this did not occur, the bilateral negotiations between Washington and Pyongyang did serve to increase the unease felt by Seoul and to heighten tensions in US-South Korean relations.

13. The US sanctions proposal involved three escalating stages of sanctions. The first would block arms and nuclear cooperation. The second would block remittances (largely from Japan) and oil (mostly from China). The third would have prohibited all shipping into and out of North Korea.

No one expected sanctions to be effective. North Korea's main economic partners (China, Russia, and Japan) were all lukewarm at best. The Russians wanted back into the diplomatic game and to try out its own initiative before acquiescing to sanctions. The Chinese did not want sanctions, but told the North Koreans that they would not veto a sanctions resolution in the Security Council. They counseled the North Koreans to negotiate. The incumbent government in Japan was dependent on the pro-DPRK Japan Socialist Party for support. Moreover, it wanted to avoid any unpleasantries with the pro-Pyongyang *Chochongryun*, an organization of ethnic Koreans in Japan, and indicated that it would be unable to block remittances effectively.

14. The North notified the IAEA that it was planning to do this, but rejected the IAEA demand for a comprehensive inspection of the removed fuel. Nevertheless, Sigal (1998a) argues that, with North Korean cooperation, techniques other than the procedures followed by the IAEA would have made construction of a rough nuclear history possible.

The removal of the spent fueling rods in defiance of the international non-proliferation regime was instrumental in the US policy shift from preventive to coercive diplomacy. Although the United States had lived with tens of thousands of troops arrayed along the DMZ for forty years, the specter of a cash-strapped North Korea selling nuclear weapons and delivery systems to the highest bidder was something else entirely.[15] The Pentagon began serious preparations for war on the peninsula. A plan to use air strikes and covert operations was considered and rejected: the Pentagon held grave doubts about its ability to locate, let alone destroy, the relevant facilities without spewing radioactive fallout across Japan.[16] Rather, it concluded that, in its first 90 days a war could result in 52,000 US casualties, 490,000 South Korean casualties, enormous North Korean casualties, and cost more than $61 billion, with little of this sum recoverable from allies. The Pentagon informed the Commander of US Forces Korea, General Gary Luck, that it would request the presidential authorization to begin the war buildup, commencing on 16 June 1994. North Korea indicated that a US buildup would precipitate a preemptive strike by its forces.[17]

Enter former President Jimmy Carter. For reasons of temperament or calculation, the Great Leader, Kim Il-sung, seemed to prefer the company of fellow visionaries like the Reverend Moon Sun-myung and the Reverend Billy Graham to more *realpolitik* types such as Henry Kissinger or Zbigniew Brzezinski. On his own initiative, the former President decided to pay a call on a fellow big thinker in Pyongyang. What ensued was surely one of the weirder episodes of an already strange saga. On the evening of 16 June, Pyongyang time, while General John Shalikashvili, Chairman of the Joint Chiefs of Staff, was in the White House presenting the war plan to President Clinton, Carter and Kim agreed that North Korea would freeze its nuclear activities and halt the planned expulsion of the remaining IAEA inspectors. In return, Carter would recommend that the US support North Korea's acquisition of light-water reactors (LWRs) and a resumption of the US-DPRK nuclear meetings. Carter then called the White House, interrupting Shalikashvili's presentation, to relay his conversation with Kim and inform the White House that, having

---

15. As President Clinton, in an unusual moment of clarity, put it: "it is pointless for [the North Koreans] to try to develop nuclear weapons, because if they ever use them it would be the end of their country" (quoted in Oberdorfer 1997, 288).

16. Then Air Force Chief of Staff Merrill McPeak has been quoted as telling reporters: "We can't find nuclear weapons now, except by going on a house-to-house search," and even once targets were located, "If you put them deep enough underground, we can't get to it" (quoted in Sigal 1999, 11).

17. Former President Carter was to later indicate that, on the basis of his conversations with Kim Il-sung and other high ranking North Korean officials, he believes that the North would have indeed launched a preemptive strike in the event of a United States buildup.

averted nuclear war, he was about to inform the world via a live interview on CNN.[18]

In an implicit commentary on the temperament of the National Security Council, the reaction to Carter's initiative was one of hostility.[19] In the end, cooler heads prevailed, and despite lingering anger the United States decided to send a message through Carter, adding additional conditions to the deal. Kim Il-sung acquiesced.[20]

Although the confrontation had been averted, a question would come back to haunt US policymakers: would the North Koreans have really gone to war, or was this simply a bluff on Kim Il-sung's part, one that would prove highly lucrative? While analysts were united in the view that North Korea could inflict major damage on South Korea (from shelling Seoul, if nothing else), no one seriously believed that North Korea could prevail over the United States and South Korea. If this end result were preordained, then how credible were North Korean assertions of its willingness to launch a preemptive strike? In all likelihood, not very. Nevertheless, the possibility of a horrendous war arising from ignorance, miscalculation, or irrationality on the part of the North Koreans cannot be dismissed completely. Such an outcome from this confrontation would amount to a quintessential example of a low probability event with an enormous negative payoff. While it has remained relatively easy for analysts to play Monday morning quarterback and second-guess this decision, it is difficult to imagine a reasonably risk-averse American policymaker acting differently.

Thus the United States and North Korea began preparing for a resumption of bilateral negotiations, while North and South Korea began preparing for a summit. On 7 July 1994, after conducting an on-the-spot inspection of a collective farm, the Great Leader Kim Il-sung suffered a massive

---

18. During the interview, he erroneously stated that sanctions consideration at the UN had been halted, which had the effect of doing exactly that, to the bitterness of sanctions supporters in the US government. Sigal (1999) argues that this was a deliberate action on Carter's part.

19. The atmosphere of this period should be recalled. One day prior to Carter's meeting with Kim, former Bush National Security Council (NSC) Advisor Brent Scowcroft and former Undersecretary of State Arnold Kanter, then the highest ranking US official to have ever met with the North Koreans in an official capacity, published an opinion piece titled "Korea: Time for Action" in the Washington Post. This article advocated a preemptive air strike against the North Korean nuclear facilities. The same day, Karen Elliott House, writing in the Wall Street Journal ("Korea: Raise Another Desert Shield") expressed a willingness to attack any Chinese vessel that might violate an embargo of the North.

20. In an expansive mood, Kim suggested that he and Carter repair to Kim's yacht to celebrate their accomplishment. During the boat trip on the Taedong River, Kim announced that he was willing to meet South Korean president Kim Young-sam unconditionally, and, under the prodding of his wife, Sohn Myung-soon, agreed to Carter's proposal for the establishment of joint US-North Korea teams to search for the remains of US servicemen missing in action from the Korean War.

heart attack and died. The death was to have an incalculable impact on the events that followed. South Korean President Kim Young-sam mishandled the death diplomatically, contributing to worsening relations between the North and South. With the untested "Dear Leader," Kim Jong-il, presumably at the helm, plans for the summit were postponed indefinitely. Moreover, given the younger Kim's reputation for ill health and bizarre behavior, the nuclear negotiations were evaluated under the assumption that the lifetime of the Kim regime could be measured in months, if not weeks.

As the outlines of the deal under negotiation emerged, critics in the United States correctly observed that the North Korean nuclear program was essentially *not* an energy program. If energy were the issue, there were cheaper ways of providing it than by building nuclear reactors (Galinsky 1994). The Senate, by a vote of 95-0, passed an amendment to the Foreign Assistance Act of 1995 permitting aid to North Korea only upon Presidential certification that North Korea did not possess nuclear arms and was not exporting nuclear weapons components or missile delivery systems. Despite this relatively hostile political environment, in October 1994 negotiators for North Korea and the United States signed an "Agreed Framework," a schedule of mutual commitments that address North Korea's nuclear program—but not its energy needs.

The Agreed Framework

The Agreed Framework (reproduced in Appendix A) is an ambiguous document laying out a series of reciprocal actions. The essential bargain of the Agreed Framework is that North Korea would remain in the NPT, freeze operations at the three graphite reactors and related facilities, and submit to IAEA inspections of the three graphite reactor sites. In return, it would receive two 1,000 megawatt light-water reactors by a target date of 2003 (valued at roughly $5 billion), 150,000 tons of heavy fuel oil in 1995, and 500,000 tons annually from 1996 to 2003 to replace the potential energy supply from the shut-down reactors. The two countries would also move toward normalization of economic and political relations, including the removal of US sanctions on trade and investment, establishment of liaison offices, and eventual diplomatic recognition.[21] North Korea

---

21. The issue immediately arose as to who would pay for these commitments, both internationally and within the United States. The initial oil shipment was financed by the US Defense Department (DOD), but DOD quickly made it clear that future funding would have to come from elsewhere. Although KEDO has had some success in procuring financial support internationally, it is apparent that most of the ultimate cost will be born by South Korea. Indeed, one interpretation of the agreement is that the negotiators were working under the assumption that the North Korean regime would not last until 2003. Therefore, in the context of a united Korea, the South Koreans would ultimately assume ownership of the reactors that they had financed.

would forego the reprocessing of the experimental reactor's spent nuclear fuel into plutonium, and, prior to the delivery of key LWR components, allow the IAEA to complete its appraisal of the accuracy of information earlier supplied to the IAEA by North Korea. Prior to the completion of the light-water reactors, North Korea would permit the IAEA to resume regular inspections of facilities not covered under the freeze. The United States would forego the threat or use of nuclear weapons against North Korea if the North would implement its 1991 nuclear pact with South Korea, which included mutual inspections.

In essence, the agreement traded ambiguity about past North Korean activities for a cessation of future activities—as long as the United States was confident that it had "gotten" the whole North Korean nuclear program—and kicked the can down the road roughly a decade. The crunch would come by 2003, when the United States is obligated to deliver the reactors and the North Koreans would be obligated to submit to unfettered IAEA inspections—something they had thus far been unwilling to do. The extent to which the agreement committed the North Koreans to suspension of nuclear related activities not explicitly covered in the agreement would later emerge as a source of contention.[22]

The deal was formulated as a bilateral agreed framework (or roadmap), not a treaty, and did not go through a ratification process in the US Senate. Indeed, according to Flake (1999), some congressmen regarded it as a deliberate attempt to circumvent the legislative branch. This lack of congressional "ownership" would come back to haunt the Clinton Administration as it attempted to implement the deal.[23] The election in November 1994 of a congress that was even more hostile to the Agreed Framework, and an incident the following month in which North Korean troops shot down a US helicopter that had strayed into North Korean airspace further hardened congressional attitudes.[24]

---

22. The narrow interpretation of the Agreed Framework is that it does not, as the language is couched in terms of an existing graphite reactor and the two graphite reactors under development. The broader interpretation is that North Korea's continued adherence to the NPT covers other potential nuclear sites. Some commentators also refer to unpublished "minutes" which may specify additional obligations. In a subsequent agreement with KEDO signed 15 December 1995, North Korea pledged both to freeze the existing graphite-moderated reactors and to "refrain from building the same."

23. Generally supportive commentators at the time (cf. Perkovich 1994 and Mathews 1994) worried most about the precedental effects of "buying off" a potential proliferator. Sadly, their concerns appear to have been misplaced, as events in India and Pakistan subsequently showed. For a more critical contemporary assessment of the Agreed Framework, see Galinsky and Sokolski (1994). See Cossa (1997) for a useful assessment of the agreement after several years of operation.

24. Per the Agreed Framework, the United States did undertake highly limited sanctions removal in January 1995.

In March 1995, the United States, Japan, and South Korea established the Korean Peninsula Energy Development Organization (KEDO) to oversee the construction of the two reactors and the delivery of the oil. After diplomatic maneuvering involving such issues as what firm would build the reactors (the South Koreans supported KEPCO, the Korean electrical utility, while the North Koreans preferred a non-South Korean supplier), KEDO and the government of North Korea signed a supply agreement in December 1995 for the reactors.[25] (KEDO had already begun supplying the oil called for under the Agreed Framework.) Upon completion of the reactors, North Korea would begin to repay their costs over a 20-year period (or more precisely over a 17-year period after a three-year grace period), interest free.

As might be expected, funding quickly emerged as KEDO's biggest problem. With respect to the reactors, KEDO estimated that the cost of construction would be approximately $5 billion, of which South Korea would cover roughly $3 billion, Japan $1 billion, and the remainder shared by the United States, the European Union, and other members of the consortium.[26] A second set of problems involving the inability of the parties to reach agreement on a series of protocols relating to training, warranties, and liability would emerge later as construction got underway.[27]

In addition to the reactors, KEDO must cover the costs of the oil deliveries and its own administrative costs, which together run about $65 million annually. Predictably, the provision of alternative energy supplies has proven to be controversial.[28] The US Congress has never been enthusiastic

---

25. The South Koreans reportedly insisted that they build the reactors to ease future unification of the electrical grid, while the North Koreans did not want South Korean technicians roaming North Korea (*Economist*, 11 February 1995). A highly placed US official disputes the second part of this statement. Work on the first replacement reactor began in August 1997, and the interaction of North and South Koreans in the process of reactor construction has been touted as one of the accomplishments of the agreement (Anderson 1999).

26. The exact US dollar cost is unknown, since a considerable share of the costs are in South Korean won, and the dollar equivalent fluctuates with the won-dollar exchange rate.

27. The quality assurance protocol has yet to be completed, as KEDO has refused to assign to North Korea the warranties of the project contractors and subcontractors as is the standard procedure. The training protocol has not been completed because the North Koreans refuse to permit their technicians to travel to South Korea for training on the technology that will be used in the two reactors. North Korea has yet to establish a Nuclear Regulatory Commission to act as the prudential supervisor of the LWRs and is demanding financial and technical assistance in establishing the organization. It is difficult to see how these issues and the inspection by the IAEA (which will effectively require suspension of operations for an extended period of time) are consistent with completing the project as scheduled.

28. The Clinton Administration announced concern that some of the first shipment of oil may have been diverted to industrial or military use, and the Department of Defense indicated that it would oppose buying more oil with Department of Defense funds. Diversion concerns reemerged in October 1999 with publication of a General Accounting Office report

about funding KEDO. In 1996, the House voted to give KEDO only half the money needed to purchase the heavy fuel oil and in 1998 came close to appropriating no funds at all. Key Congressmen claimed that they had been deceived in their dealings with the Administration over funding. However, Congress never killed the deal, and instead gave its tacit approval by allowing the Clinton Administration to pay for the heavy fuel oil out of a discretionary fund for "emergency" expenditures through most of 1998, averting the immediate funding crisis.

Due to the perception that this was an American-negotiated deal in which South Korea had little say, funding has also been a hard sell in South Korea, which would bear the brunt (around 60 percent) of total costs. South Korea prepared to raise electricity charges (but put these plans on hold when the financial crisis hit the country in 1997) and issued special bonds to raise the necessary funds. The government revived the tax hike idea in May 1999, after the South Korean economy began to recover, and in July 1999 signed a contract to loan KEDO $3.22 billion. For the historically minded, that South Korea should become North Korea's principal energy patron, was a stunning irony in light of the North's use of energy as a political weapon in 1948.

Even in the European Union, KEDO funding ran into difficulties, as the European Commission signed the agreement to join and fund KEDO without consulting the European Parliament. It is the Parliament which actually has to appropriate the funds, and it contains factions opposed to the agreement (Ford 1997). Former US Ambassador to the Philippines Stephen Bosworth, chosen as the first head KEDO, spent most of his tenure trying to raise money, eventually securing commitments from 24 countries to fund the annual budget (table 4.1).[29] Despite his efforts, however, the organization quickly ran into debt (in significant part due to the US Congress' fiscal year 1997 funding delay) and had to employ innovative financial techniques to ensure that it could meet its commitments to both reactor development and oil provision. It reportedly resorted to financing

---

suggesting that perhaps 5 percent of the oil deliveries had been diverted from their intended uses. In light of the fungibility of the commodity in question, the ongoing bureaucratic budget wrangling within the US government, the lack of enthusiasm for the Agreed Framework in many quarters, and the US electoral calendar, perhaps these brouhahas were to be expected. In economic terms, however, the fungibility of the oil and the militarization in the economy mean that the issue of diversion is really irrelevant.

29. Taiwan offered to contribute to KEDO, but China, despite the fact that it does not contribute, objected. (The Chinese argue that they are the largest aid contributors to North Korea and do not need to contribute to KEDO.) President Clinton in his 1998 visit to China accepted China's position on excluding Taiwan from KEDO. An official Taiwanese delegation visiting Beijing subsequently revisited the issue but was rebuffed by their hosts. Japan, which was preparing to host Chinese President Jiang Zemin, expressed "caution" at the offer (Michiyo Nakamoto, *Financial Times*, 21 October 1998).

Table 4.1 KEDO contributions

Country	Contribution	Restrictions
1995		
Australia	$5 million	Heavy fuel oil
Canada	$1.05 million	Heavy fuel oil
Finland	$93,833	
Indonesia	$324,895	Heavy fuel oil
Japan	$2.8 million	Administration
	$3 million	Pre-project
Malaysia	$300,000	
Netherlands	$500,000	
New Zealand	$334,750	Heavy fuel oil
Singapore	$300,000	
South Korea	$1.8 million	Administration
Thailand	$300,000	
United Kingdom	$1 million	For non-proliferation aspects of KEDO activity
United States	$5.5 million	Heavy fuel oil
	$4 million	Administration
1995 Total	**$26.3 million**	
1996		
Argentina	$200,000	
Australia	$1.59 million	Heavy fuel oil
Brunei	$423,691	
Canada	$735,565	
EC	$6.26 million	
Finland	$20,000	In kind—consulting services
	$2,810	Heavy fuel oil
	$100,000	
Germany	$1 million	
Greece	$25,000	
Indonesia	$325,012	In kind—Heavy fuel oil
Japan	$19 million	Collateral fund in case of liquidity shortfall
Netherlands	$290,192	
New Zealand	$343,025	Heavy fuel oil
Norway	$250,000	
Philippines	$150,000	
Singapore	$100,000	
South Korea	$2.7 million	Administration
	$6 million	Pre-project
	$165,000	Administration
Switzerland	$118,148	
United States	$22 million	Heavy fuel oil
1996 Total	**$61.8 million**	
1997		
Australia	$1.54 million	Heavy fuel oil
Canada	$906,454	
EC	$11.2 million	
	$17.2 million	

(continued next page)

Table 4.1 (continued)

Country	Contribution	Restrictions
Finland	$75,119	
	$18,780	In kind—consulting services
Hungary	$10,000	
Japan	$3.73 million	Administration
	$3.2 million	Administration
New Zealand	$321,935	Heavy fuel oil
Norway	$250,000	
Oman	$50,000	
Singapore	$100,000	
South Korea	$3 million	Administration
United States	$21 million	Heavy fuel oil
	$4 million	Administration
1997 Total	**$66.6 million**	
1998		
Australia	$1.2 million	Heavy fuel oil
Czech Republic	$127,816	
EC	$900,000	Administration
Finland	$91,193	
France	$503,778	Study on management of spent fuel
Indonesia	$325,000	In kind—Heavy fuel oil
Japan	$530,000	Administration
	$3 million	Administration
New Zealand	$258,800	Heavy fuel oil
	$355,700	Heavy fuel oil
Singapore	$100,000	
South Korea	$3.5 million	Administration
	$45 million	Korea Export-Import Bank loan
	$97,133	Administration
United States	$26.4 million	Heavy fuel oil
	$3.6 million	Administration
	$5 million	Heavy fuel oil
	$10 million	Heavy fuel oil
	$5 million	Heavy fuel oil
1998 Total	**$122.4 million**	
1999		
(as of June 1999)		
Canada	$161,447	Other
Finland	$92,333	
Italy	$1.25 million	
	$571,429	
Japan	$432,867	
	$1 billion	Light-water reactor
Singapore	$400,000	
South Korea	$3.22 billion	Light-water reactor
United States	$12 million	Heavy fuel oil
	$14 million	Heavy fuel oil
	$1 million	Administration
	$17.5 million	Heavy fuel oil
	$2.5 million	Administration

Source: Various KEDO Annual Reports.

oil purchases with loans and making credit deals with suppliers.[30] This, in turn, hampered KEDO's ability to deliver oil on a timely basis (since the North Koreans have limited storage capacity, the oil cannot be delivered all at once), and the North Koreans threatened to pull out of the agreement.[31]

The situation worsened in the spring of 1998. Prior to the second round of the Four Party Talks in March 1998, the United States presented North Korea with a potential "roadmap" for removal of US economic sanctions. The problem was complicated because sundry bits of the US government bureaucracy responsible for different sets of ongoing negotiations with the North Koreans had laid claim to various sanctions. There was a missile talks "bucket," a Four Party Talks "bucket," etc. To the North Koreans, the United States had already agreed to remove sanctions as part of the Agreed Framework. They viewed linkage of specific sanctions removals to a host of bilateral issues as an example of "salami tactics."[32]

In April North Korea suspended the process of "canning" the spent nuclear fuel rods and began threatening to resume processing. Tensions continued to increase over the summer of 1998 as a second North Korean submarine was encountered off the South Korean coast and a North Korean frogman washed up on a South Korean beach.

Funding KEDO became considerably more difficult when reports began to emerge publicly that North Korea was secretly continuing its weapons development program in violation of the agreement. In July 1998, the US General Accounting Office (GAO) reported that the North Koreans were refusing to cooperate with the IAEA and might be trying to destroy evidence of a continuing nuclear weapons program (GAO 1998). Administration credibility was further damaged by apparently contradictory characterizations of the North Korean nuclear program. During the spring, while stumping for KEDO reauthorization, the State Department had assured Congress that there was no evidence of continued nuclear activity, contradicting the private briefing given to a senior member of Congress by the National Security Agency. On 3 August, at a closed-door briefing for a select House panel, Secretary of State Madeleine Albright was casti-

---

30. Bosworth went on to become the US Ambassador to South Korea and was replaced as Executive Director of KEDO in October 1997 by another American diplomat, Desaix Anderson.

31. By the end of 1998, KEDO had fallen behind on almost half of its scheduled delivery. As in the previous year, scheduled 1998 deliveries were completed in early 1999. However, whereas KEDO owed $47 million in supplier credits at the end of 1997, by the end of 1998 this had been reduced to $21 million.

32. One North Korean negotiator reportedly exclaimed that: "We're talking national security, and they are talking about basketball players!" This was a reference to permitting a North Korean basketball player to try out for a professional basketball team in return for confidence building measures in the Korean demilitarized zone (Flake 1999a).

gated for having misled Congress. Her account of contemporaneous US intelligence assessments was flatly contradicted by Lt. General Patrick Hughes, Director of the Defense Intelligence Agency. Two weeks later, the *New York Times* reported that US intelligence had detected a secret underground complex at Kumchangri, near the frozen Yongbyon nuclear complex and believed to be for the purpose of renewing the nuclear program. The cat was publicly out of the bag.[33]

The Suspect Site and the Missile Test

As it happened, North Korea proved capable of worsening its relations with the rest of the world without the aid of the *New York Times*. The public revelation of a suspected North Korean violation of the Agreed Framework followed months of reports of increased North Korean nuclear and missile activity.[34] As noted earlier, North Korea has maintained an active missile development program and has exported missiles widely.[35] In August 1998, it publicly threatened to step up its missile exports unless the United States removed its embargo and similarly threatened to restart its nuclear program if the oil deliveries were not made on time. Once the existence of the suspected nuclear site became widely known, a period of brinkmanship followed, with both sides threatening to walk away from the Agreed Framework. US negotiator Ambassador Charles Kartman told reporters that there was "compelling evidence" of nuclear-related activities at the site (a statement he later retracted), and the South Koreans put out the line that US and South Korean scientists had discovered traces of plutonium in water and soil samples taken from the site—without revealing how such samples were obtained. North Korea, in a statement circulated by its UN Ambassador, Li Hyong-chol, characterized the US position as "like a declaration of war" and "a reckless adventure, losing all rea-

---

33. David E. Sanger, *New York Times*, 17 August 1998. The South Korean government later claimed the existence of additional underground sites as well. The Japanese press later reported that North Korea had been building three underground facilities capable of launching ballistic missiles—reports that were apparently confirmed by US spy satellites. Indeed, in the first meeting between US negotiator Ambassador Charles Kartman and North Korean Deputy Foreign Minister Kim Gye-gwan, Kim supposedly demanded $300 million for access to a *different* underground site than the one in which the United States was primarily interested. When he realized his error, he quickly retracted the offer. For a very different interpretation of these North Korean activities, see Quinones (1998).

34. Indeed, one theory was that the underground site at Kumchangri was actually a facility for testing and manufacturing the Nodong-1. The North Koreans variously characterized it as "civilian underground structures" and a "military recreational facility."

35. See Bazhanov (2000a) for an informative history of the North Korean missile program.

son."[36] Reason prevailed however, and the United States and North Korea settled down to negotiations over US inspectors' access to the site, in what one commentator characterized as another instance of "checkbook diplomacy" (Cossa 1998).[37] The North Koreans began by asking for $1 billion in "reparations" for access to the site, but through the fall of 1998 the asking price dropped to $300 million, and in March 1999 the North Koreans were instead persuaded to accept a package of 600,000 metric tons of grain with an approximate street value of $120 million (100,000 tons of which was to be provided through private humanitarian initiatives) and a potato production demonstration project.[38] In a departure from the Administration's "no compensation" line, Presidential envoy and former Defense Secretary William Perry characterized the obvious as a *"quid pro quo* for achieving our aims."[39] Yet, in another instance of following apparent progress with a provocative act, the North Koreans sent two suspicious ships into Japanese waters, prompting the Japanese Maritime Self-Defense Force to fire warning shots for the first time in 46 years. As expected, when the US team led by State Department official Joel Wit did visit Kumchangri in May 1999, it found a large underground cavern that conceivably could be used for nuclear activities, but at the time of the inspection was not so being used.

36. On threats to abandon the agreement, see Philip Shenon, *New York Times*, 6 December 1998. On Ambassador Li's statement, see Associated Press, 7 December 1998. This statement, which also contained threats to attack South Korea, Japan, and US forces stationed in South Korea, was issued while US Presidential envoy former Defense Secretary William Perry was in Asia to confer with leaders in Japan and South Korea. It was issued during a week in which the KCNA issued bellicose diatribes against the United States, Japan, and South Korea daily (see http://www.kcna.co.jp), including a threat from Army General Officer O Kum-chol "to annihilate the U.S. imperialists, Japanese reactionaries, and South Korean puppets in one stroke" (Reuters, 8 December 1998). The Perry process is discussed more generally in chapter 9.

37. The KCNA carried an editorial stating that the US demand for an inspection "slanders and blasphemes North Korea," and that if the United States wants access to the facility "they must of course pay reparations for their slander" (KCNA, 11 November 1998). US negotiator Ambassador Kartman stated that: "We have absolutely rejected the concept of compensation, so the question of the amount is irrelevant" (Reuters, 19 November 1998).

38. It is unclear what role China played in this diplomatic maneuvering. On the one hand, the Chinese Ambassador to Seoul, Wu Dawei, described the US demand for inspection based only on suspicions as going beyond international norms—a view echoed the following week by China's official news agency *Xinhua*. During US-DPRK negotiations held in Beijing, China warned the United States to "exercise prudence." On the other hand, Clinton Administration officials repeatedly indicated privately that the Chinese were being helpful, a view supported by some China watchers.

39. For the Perry quote, see David Sanger, *New York Times*, 17 March 1999. The deal was predictably attacked by former Secretary of State James A. Baker, 3rd (Baker 1999) and by the *Wall Street Journal* editorial page (*Wall Street Journal*, North Korea's Black Hole, 22 March 1999) as a likely ineffectual attempt to appease North Korea.

On 31 August 1998, while negotiations over access to the Kumchangri site were going on, the North Koreans test fired a three-stage rocket across Japan into the Pacific Ocean.[40] Whatever the motivations for the action, the rocket launch sent shock waves throughout the region.[41] Since the Japanese did not possess any independent capability to monitor the launch, they were informed of the incident by the United States in accordance with their bilateral informational exchange agreement. Once apprised, the reaction in Tokyo was embarrassment followed by fury. Japan responded by putting its military forces on alert, announcing a halt to food aid, suspending public participation in KEDO and refusing to approve KEDO financial arrangements scheduled to be signed 31 August, suspending talks on normalization of relations, and proposing to condemn North Korea in the UN Security Council.[42] Japan also expressed interest in building its own satellite reconnaissance system, cooperating with the United States in its proposal for developing a Theatre Missile Defense (TMD) system for Japan, and deepening military cooperation with South

---

40. There is considerable confusion (much of it due to bureaucratic and domestic politics) over the rocket that North Korea launched on 31 August 1998. Some have claimed that this was a test of the Taepodong-1 or a Taepodong-2 missile, while the North Koreans and some others have claimed that it was a satellite launch. Robert D. Walpole, the US Central Intelligence Agency's senior intelligence officer for strategic programs, has stated that, while a launch of the two-stage Taepodong-1 was expected, the fact that it was a three-stage rocket possibly capable of delivering a small payload across the Pacific took US intelligence analysts by surprise. The North Korean government described the US reaction as "the height of impudence" and threatened to use the rocket as a military delivery system (KCNA, 25 September 1998). It also has been reported that Deputy Foreign Minister Kim Gye-gwan, in New York for negotiations over access to the Kumchangri site, was taken by surprise by the launch.

41. A variety of explanations were proffered for the timing of the launch. Some analysts expressed the view that the North Koreans acted to express anger over the delay in shipments of fuel oil from KEDO. Others argued that this was a signal to the United States prior to the resumption of its missile talks with North Korea, citing the reported presence of past North Korean missile customers at the launch. Yet another possibility was that the launch was a symbolic propaganda act undertaken as delegates to the Supreme People's Assembly were gathering in Pyongyang for the first time in seven years. North Korean propaganda touted it as evidence of national power—a show of scientific achievement and a threat to the nation's enemies.

42. Japan subsequently agreed to renew its funding for the KEDO project in October 1998, but, when Japanese Prime Minister Keizo Obuchi met with South Korean president Kim Dae-jung, he proposed expanding the format of the Four Party Talks to include Japan and Russia. When reports of North Korean preparations for a second launch began emerging in 1999, Japanese Defense Minister Hosei Norota announced that, in the event of a second test, Japan would reconsider its support for KEDO (Reuters, 7 January 1999). He subsequently raised the possibility that Japan might engage in preemptive strikes if it believed a North Korean attack was imminent (Lee Sung-yul, *Korean Herald*, 17 March 1999). Japan signed a contract to lend $1 billion to KEDO in May 1999, shortly before Perry's visit to Pyongyang. The Diet approved the funding the following month.

Korea.[43] Indeed, the combination of North Korean bellicosity and the election of Kim Dae-jung pushed Japan and South Korea toward their closest cooperation in history.

After a brief silence, North Korea offered its own interpretation of the events, assailing Japan for being "impudent," and "bitterly denouncing" Japan for "making a fuss." North Korea explained that, rather than the test-firing of a missile, the 31 August event was a "scientific satellite" launch, sending into orbit a satellite that "is now transmitting the melody of the immortal revolutionary hymns 'Song of General Kim Il-sung' and 'Song of General Kim Jong-il' and the Morse signals '*Juche* Korea' on 27 megahertz."[44] As it went on to excoriate Japan for "slander," it asserted that Japan was using the satellite launch as a pretext for rearmament and that it had a plan for invading North Korea. It even went as far as stating in a radio broadcast that the countries were "on the verge of war."[45]

In the United States, the test firing immediately raised strategic questions, for it indicated that the North Koreans could possibly strike Japan-based US troops that were necessary for any sustained campaign on the peninsula.[46] It also raised the possibility that North Korea was developing its missiles faster than expected, and that it might have, or soon unveil, the Taepodong-2, capable of delivering warheads to Alaska and Hawaii. Predictably, the Clinton Administration policy was described as "appeasement" (Iklé 1998). House Appropriations Committee Chairman Representative Bob Livingston (R-Louisiana) recommended defunding KEDO, and the relevant House Appropriation Subcommittee voted 29 to 16 on 10 September 1998 to drop all funding. In the Senate, amendments offered by Senator John McCain (R-Arizona) and Senator Kay Bailey Hutchinson (R-Texas) to the Foreign Aid Spending Bill would have made it virtually impossible for the United States to meet its commitments under the Agreed Framework (Flake 1999a). A compromise was eventually reached in which the Congress would appropriate the necessary funds for KEDO,

---

43. Japanese concerns were heightened further in June 1999 when North Korean ships entered Japanese territorial waters before fleeing Japanese naval Self-Defense Forces. Japanese defense officials later used the existence of possible North Korean biological and chemical-armed missiles to increase funding for counter strategies.

44. KCNA, 4 September 1998. In the end, the consensus of foreign analysts was that the rocket was a failed satellite launch. This, of course, did not negate the fact that, while the 31 August 1998 delivery system may have been fitted with a satellite, subsequent rockets could be equipped with warheads.

45. Later, in an oddly timed December 1998 maneuver coming on the anniversary of the Pearl Harbor attack, North Korea threatened to attack Japan in a statement distributed by North Korean UN Ambassador Li Hyong-chol during the brinkmanship over access to the Kumchangri site.

46. The North Koreans threatened to do precisely this in a statement circulated at the UN during the negotiations over access to the suspected nuclear site at Kumchangri.

but as a *quid pro quo* the Administration would appoint an outside advisor to evaluate US policy toward North Korea and present this policy review to the Congress. In November 1998, President Clinton appointed former Defense Secretary William Perry "North Korean Policy Coordinator," with a mandate to "participate in a full and complete interagency review of U.S. policy and objectives toward North Korea."[47]

However, in negotiations the following week, after once again threatening to walk away from the Agreed Framework if the United States failed to meet its KEDO obligations, the North Koreans agreed to resume "canning" the spent nuclear fuel rods at the Yongbyon facility. The Clinton Administration responded favorably with "an unusually large" shipment of 300,000 metric tons of food. An unnamed official explained that the Administration wanted to avoid a confrontation with North Korea while enmeshed in the Monica Lewinsky scandal.[48] At the same time, the Department of Defense released its East Asia-Pacific Security Strategy, a midterm blueprint of regional security goals, which stated: "If North Korea proves unwilling to fulfill the terms of the [Agreed Framework], the U.S. will pursue its fundamental security interests through other diplomatic and security means" (Department of Defense 1998, 24).

The following month, in the separate bilateral missile talks, the United States expressed its "strong opposition" to North Korean missile exports, indicating that there would be "very negative consequences to efforts to improve U.S.-North Korea relations" if North Korea made any further attempts to test or export long-range missiles.[49] In the next set of missile talks, North Korea repeated its earlier demand for $500 million compensation for three years in exchange for an end to its export of missiles and missile technology, a figure that was later reduced to $300 million.

Having lived under direct North Korean threat for more than four decades, and having not been as acutely sensitive to the global weapons of mass destruction proliferation concerns as the United States, the initial reaction of the South Koreans was muted. Indeed, the launch was interpreted by some as a rebuke of South Korean President Kim Dae-jung's "sunshine policy" toward the North. Like the Japanese, the South Koreans announced that they were reconsidering their participation in KEDO, though unlike Japan, the South Koreans did not actually suspend participation. South Korea saw the test firing and the subsequent reactions in

---

47. Quoted from Department of State press release, "Dr. William Perry Named North Korea Policy Coordinator," 12 November 1998.

48. David E. Sanger, *New York Times*, 10 September 1998. For a chronology of US food deliveries associated with specific diplomatic negotiations, see table 5.3.

49. James P. Rubin, "U.S.-DPRK Missile Talks," 2 October 1998, press release.

Tokyo and Washington as an opportunity to advance its own strategic interests.[50]

The big loser in the midst of all of this appears to be China. Despite numerous statements from Clinton Administration officials praising China for unspecified cooperation in dealing with North Korea, China has not participated in the World Food Program (WFP) appeals, has not joined KEDO, has effectively blocked Taiwan's participation in that organization, and has turned a blind eye toward North Korean military activities at least with respect to Pakistan (which China regards as a useful tool in its rivalry with India).[51] The upshot of the August test was closer military coordination among the United States, Japan, and South Korea, as well as renewed interest in theater missile defense and the reinvigoration of Japan's satellite reconnaissance program, all of which China regards as inimical to its interests.

In January 1999, just prior to bilateral negotiations aimed at obtaining access to the suspected nuclear site at Kumchangri and another round of the Four Party Talks, North Korea, citing KEDO's delayed oil deliveries, again threatened to withdraw from the Agreed Framework. In June 1999, intelligence officials in the United States, Japan, and South Korea detected preparations for another missile test, which South Korean National Intelligence Service Director Chun Yong-taek identified as the Taepodong-2. As CIA Director George Tenet had testified before Congress, that missile could deliver small payloads to the continental United States and significantly larger payloads to Alaska and Hawaii. Deputy Assistant Secretary of Defense Kurt Campbell told reporters that the United States would regard this as "a very serious act with very real consequences" and "very

---

50. In particular, South Korea has used the North Korean action as a justification for developing missiles with ranges up to 500 kilometers, which would be in violation of the Missile Technology Control Regime (MTCR) if they proceed. See C. S. Chun (2000) for a discussion of MTCR issues.

51. For example, in an October 1997 speech, President Clinton stated that "China has helped us convince North Korea to freeze and ultimately end its dangerous nuclear program" (quoted in Jim Mann, *Los Angeles Times*, 9 September 1998). Nevertheless, unnamed White House and Pentagon sources alleged that China continued to share space technology with North Korea—even after the August 1998 missile launch.

As indicated in chapter 3, North Korea reportedly helped Pakistan develop a version of its Nodong-1 missile, and it has been speculated that Pakistan might be aiding North Korea with enrichment know-how that would permit North Korea to develop a uranium-based bomb. Unsurprisingly, analysts in India expressed concern about the implications of the North Korean missile launch. Immediately after the launch, Chinese president Jiang Zemin assured Israeli Defense Minister Yitzhak Mordechai that China would not assist Iran, another North Korean customer, in developing advanced technology that could be used to produce nonconventional weapons. Israel had earlier planned to offer North Korea $1 billion in investment and technical assistance to block an Iranian bid to purchase 150 Nodong-1 missiles, but was dissuaded from this tack by the United States and South Korea (Sigal 1998a).

real implications" for the process of normalization of relations.[52] US House International Relations Committee Chairman Benjamin A. Gilman (R-New York) launched his own preemptive strike, characterizing the Clinton Administration's policy as "appeasement," introducing legislation that would explicitly condition humanitarian aid on North Korean behavior (Gilman 1999), and later cosponsoring legislation with Representative Ed Markey (D-Massachusetts) that would make provision of key reactor components conditional on presidential and congressional certification that North Korea was in full compliance with the NPT. (The proposal passed the House, though not the Senate.)

Upon returning from Pyongyang, UN Undersecretary General Yasushi Akashi confirmed that the North Koreans were preparing for another test. Touring South Korea and Japan, US Secretary of Defense William Cohen warned that another missile launch would have "serious implications" and would imperil US support for the Agreed Framework. He agreed to increase US land, air, and naval forces around the peninsula. Attending the Association of Southeast Asian Nations (ASEAN) Regional Forum (ARF) in Singapore, Secretary Albright repeated the US formulation, stating that another long-range missile launch would have "serious negative consequences" for North Korea. The North responded by calling Cohen a "crazy war maniac" and threatening to pull out of the Agreed Framework unless the United States began to show "good faith" by lifting sanctions.[53]

At the same ARF meeting, Japanese Foreign Minister Masahiko Komura indicated that another launch would likely result in a termination of Japan's support for KEDO and passage of the economic sanctions legislation that the Diet was currently considering. Similarly, Japanese Defense Minister Hosei Norota reiterated that Japan might suspend its contributions to KEDO in the event of another North Korean missile launch. (The Japanese Diet would later take up legislation permitting the cutoff of private remittances.) As Australian Foreign Minister Alexander Downer summed it up, a second test "will not only end the Perry review initiative, and therefore the possibility of greater engagement with North Korea, but a further test will throw into doubt the whole of the Agreed Framework." South Korean Foreign Minister Hong Soon-young suggested that the international community might cut off food aid, and he added that the United States and South Korea had agreed to develop missiles with a 300-kilometer (186 mile) range. (He would later add that South Korea would delay or reduce economic cooperation as well.) The United States, Japan, and South Korea issued a joint statement at the conclusion of the ASEAN Regional Forum, urging North Korea to forego missile testing

---

52. Quoted in David E. Sanger and Eric Schmitt, *New York Times*, 1 July 1999.

53. See KCNA, 26 July 1999.

and warning of "serious consequences" if it did not. Even the UN Development Program got into the act, with Administrator Mark Malloch Brown telling the North that, while the UNDP would not close its Pyongyang office in the event of a missile launch, some donors would probably cut back funding for UNDP activities in North Korea.

As expectation of a second test grew in 1999, China hesitantly began to take a more constructive approach.[54] Although the Chinese ambassador to Seoul, Wu Dawei, once again defended Pyongyang's right to engage in "scientific launches," and at the ASEAN Regional Forum China declined to join the United States, Japan, and South Korea in their joint statement, Foreign Minister Tang Jianxuan indicated that China would "play the role it can" to deter North Korea from testing a long-range missile.[55] Nevertheless, the Chinese themselves tested a missile, arguably impeding their ability to convince the North Koreans not to do likewise.

For several weeks the world was treated to almost daily reports of North Korean missile launch preparations. During this extended buildup, North Korean rhetoric toward Japan was extreme, even by North Korea's inimitable standard, repeatedly noting the existence of the North Korean missile and demanding Japanese compensation for events of the colonial period.[56] The Japanese, however, refused either to apologize or to compen-

---

54. China allegedly demanded the removal of two North Korean missile bases near its border. These bases are reportedly dug into mountainsides facing China, requiring any attacker to overfly Chinese airspace.

55. For the "scientific launch" quote, see John Burton, *Financial Times*, 23 July 1999. For the Tang statement see Son Key-young, *Korea Times*, 25 July 1999. The Chinese continued to take this line through the September 1999 APEC summit in Auckland, New Zealand.

56. For example, the lead story from KCNA on 10 August 1999 read, in part:

"The mental, human, and material damage the Japanese imperialists inflicted upon Koreans during their occupation of Korea was something unprecedented in human history in nature, manifestation, and scale. . . . In a nutshell, the Korea policy pursued by Japan for a hundred years was aimed at exterminating, dividing, alienating, excluding and antagonizing the Korean nation. . . . Improvement of bilateral relations means, in essence, liquidating the crimes Japan committed against the Korean people in the past and, on this basis, developing new good neighborly relations. . . .

"Japan's refusal to liquidate the past is, in essence, a revelation of the militarist design to repeat the past crimes as well as the wild ambition for reinvasion to realize the old dream of the "Greater East Asian Coprosperity Sphere." An assailant, Japan is obliged to make a sincere apology and compensation to the DPRK both legally and morally for all its past crimes. A victim, the DPRK has a legitimate right to get compensation from Japan for all its past damage on the publicly recognized principle of international law and international usage. . . .

"The present Japanese authorities do not bother to conceal their scenario that the first target of their overseas aggression is the DPRK. . . . The 'threat from North Korea' on the lips of the Japanese reactionaries is a prelude to reinvasion of Korea. . . .

"Japan must stop pursuing the policy of stifling the DPRK . . . it must make a sincere apology and full compensation to the Korean people for all of its past crimes . . . if Japan dare turn to a showdown of strength in a bid to find a pretext to realize the wild ambition

sate the North Koreans. By the third week of August, the North Koreans, while continuing to demand compensation from the Japanese, stopped making repeated references to their missile, and signaled that they were reconsidering their launch.[57] Negotiations with the United States resumed in Berlin during the first week of September. Having taken a rhetorical run at Japan and having come up empty-handed, the North Koreans took the best alternative available—a moratorium on missile tests and compensation via the Perry package deal. For foregoing the test, the North Koreans obtained an announcement of partial sanctions lifting by the United States and the prospect of further concessions by Japan and South Korea. Nevertheless, they appear to have rejuvenated Japanese military modernization plans and encouraged closer cooperation between Seoul and Tokyo. The July 1999 Japan Defense Agency white paper focused almost exclusively on the threat posed by Pyongyang.

Evaluation

A number of conclusions can be gleaned from this discussion. First, North Korea has real, energy-related needs that are tied to the economy. From this perspective, neither the North Korean nuclear program nor the Agreed Framework make much sense. As Von Hippel and Hayes (1998) point out, the reactors would produce more electricity than North Korea could possibly use. Indeed, the North Korean electrical grid is in such poor shape that substantial refurbishment would be required before the reactors could be used effectively. Furthermore, the North Korean system runs on a different frequency than the systems of China and Russia, so that expensive interchanges would have to be installed before electricity could be exported to those countries. In the case of South Korea, the frequency is the same, but, because of poor frequency control and power surges in the North, a conversion station would need to be built before electricity produced in the North could be shipped South. In sum, as currently constituted, KEDO does not address North Korea's serious domestic energy problems, nor would the light-water reactors be an efficient source of export earnings. These agreements do not address the real problems that North Korea faces in the energy sector. Williams, Hayes,

---

for reinvasion, we will have no option but to take a countermeasure . . . if it repeats its crime-woven history and undertakes a reckless provocation, the DPRK will never miss the opportunity for meting out merciless retaliation but make Japan pay a high price for the blood shed by the nation and give vent to its century-old wrath."

57. In a 16 August 1999 interview with CNN, Kim Yong-sun, secretary of the KWP and a close associate of Kim Jong-il, suggested the missile launch could be delayed and transparently called for better relations between North Korea, the United States, and Japan. This was followed by a North Korean Foreign Ministry statement echoing the softer line and signaling the possibility of dealing with the Japanese abductees issue.

and Von Hippel (1999) estimate that the capital costs of rehabilitating the North Korean energy sector would be $20 to $50 billion over 20 years, though a more modest rural-oriented fix could be done for $2 to $3 billion over five years.

If the North Korean nuclear program and the Agreed Framework make little sense as energy programs, do they make sense from other perspectives? There is an extensive literature that speculates on North Korean motivations with regard to their nuclear program.[58] Several possible explanations have been put forward. The most straightforward is that the nuclear program was intended to deter the United States and South Korea. Mansourov (1995), for example, argues that the American bombing of Hiroshima and the quick way that US nuclear weapons brought Japan to surrender made an indelible impression on Kim Il-sung. Kim's respect for nuclear weapons grew into alarm upon learning that the Truman Administration had seriously considered using them against him during the Korean War. His response was to seek nuclear protection from the Soviet Union and China, but this comfort was undercut by his perception of Soviet abandonment of Cuba during the missile crisis. Mansourov argues that the decisive moment was in the late 1970s, when the North Korean government learned of the South's secret nuclear program.[59] It was one thing to face the United States, which might be expected to act with some restraint, but confronting a nuclear-armed South Korean military dictatorship was something else again. Kim decided that he needed his own nuclear capability. However, lacking an intercontinental delivery system capable of hitting the United States, Kim settled for medium-range ballistic missiles capable of striking South Korea and US forces in Japan.

Although Sigal (1998a) accepts the argument that the North Korean nuclear program may have begun as deterrence, he argues that by the late 1980s the North's leadership was more concerned about its failing economy and diplomatic isolation than about building bombs. Thus, the North's nuclear program and its subsequent negotiations should be regarded as part of an economic opening/reform process. To support this interpretation, he points to evidence that the North did not act expeditiously to develop weapons, a pattern of behavior that Mansourov (1995) ascribes to "various economic, financial, and scientific difficulties," including the inability to procure imported inputs and fund indigenous research and development activities. Nevertheless, Mansourov, too, concludes that: "In May 1992, the North Korean government had decided to abandon the military part of the nuclear program and had undertaken

---

58. See, for example, Mansourov (1995), Eberstadt (1997b), Takesada (1997), Bandow (1998), Kang (1998), and Sigal (1998a).

59. See Hayes (1993) and Englehardt (1995) on the South Korean nuclear program.

measures necessary to hide its previous actions in violation of the NPT" (Mansourov 1995, 27).

In fact, despite its collapsing economy, some regard the North Korean government strategy as masterful in that it has convincingly parlayed uncertainty about its nuclear and missile capabilities and converted a big hole in the ground at Kumchangri into major tangible benefits.[60] The problem with this view is its apparent inability to explain the suspected continuation of the North's nuclear program or its demonstrated missile program. Indeed, a darker interpretation of the "bargaining chip" hypothesis is provided by Eberstadt (1997b, 1999b), who argues: "The North Korean regime *is* the North Korean nuclear problem, and unless its intentions change, which is unlikely, that problem will continue as long as the regime is in place" (1997b, 88, emphasis in the original). Indeed, Eberstadt goes on to argue that it is in the regime's interests continually to upgrade its weapons of mass destruction and their threat of proliferation in order to extort "humanitarian" assistance from the world community.

This raises the missile issue, which, despite the separate negotiating framework, is inextricably linked to the nuclear issue.[61] The marriage of the missile and nuclear programs (or the chemical and biological weapons programs) would give the North Koreans a formidable tool with which to extort resources from the rest of the world. Without the nonconventional weapons programs, the missile program makes little sense—except possibly as a pure export good to customers who supply their own warheads.[62]

Defenders of the Agreed Framework in essence argue that the agreement was the best that could be made in a bad situation. In all probability the North Koreans had nuclear devices and the capacity for continually producing weapons-grade nuclear material from their existing reactors, posing not only a threat to their immediate neighbors, but also raising

---

60. See, for example, Cumings (1997). Commercial satellite photos released in January 2000 appear to show a very rudimentary launch site, leading some to question whether North Korea actually had the capacity for a second missile test in the summer of 1999 (Federation of American Scientists, http://www.fas.org/nuke/guide/dprk/facility/nodong.htm). US Administration sources have noted, however, that the previous launch site was equally primitive, and that North Korean launch preparations should not be compared with how the United States or Russia handle these things.

61. The multiplicity of negotiating forums (the nuclear talks, the missile talks, the Four Party talks, the negotiations over suspect nuclear sites, and bilateral negotiations over food) provides the North Koreans with numerous opportunities to extract resources from the international community.

62. On this point, in July 1998, Sigal (1998b) argued that missiles are worthless without testing, and that the failure of North Korea to test missiles is a signal that the program was not a viable option for either its own use or export; rather, the North Koreans were putting the program up for sale. Unfortunately, the firing across Japan would seem to put this line of argumentation to rest—unless it was the equivalent of a "test drive" for the assembled prospective buyers.

the likelihood of sales to other parts of the world. Other alternatives, such as economic sanctions or military strikes, would probably not receive the diplomatic support of neighboring countries and would be of questionable efficacy, in any event.[63]

Moreover, while the price extracted by the North Koreans appears high, this may be illusionary—the current North Korean regime is unlikely to outlast the KEDO reactors, and, in the end, the South Koreans will assume possession of the reactors and other infrastructural improvements for which they had largely footed the bill. In essence, the Agreed Framework is the best of bad alternatives, and, with time on our side, its temporizing nature need not be fatal.

Set against this is the notion that time may not be on our side, that North Korea may be pursuing a dual-track strategy of cooperating with the United States in dismantling its overt nuclear program (and being rewarded for doing so) while covertly continuing its nuclear weapons program and work on associated delivery systems (Drennan 1998, Armitage 1999). It may well be the case that the North Koreans have never abandoned their goal of achieving strategic deterrence against the United States and the unification of the peninsula on their terms. An intercontinental nuclear capability, together with a significant number of nuclear weapons to provide for a second-strike capability and a willingness to use them against the South, would be sufficient to alter the military balance on the Korean peninsula decisively. Kent Harrington, a former National Intelligence Officer for Asia, argues that: "Bent on achieving ultimate military power on the peninsula, North Korea has worked for 30 years to develop nuclear weapons. Its investment of resources, its risk-taking and its persistence make clear it does not intend to trade that goal for economic aid, political recognition or security guarantees. The historical record speaks for itself" (Harrington 1998). From this perspective, the Agreed Framework is at best a temporizing measure that could actually worsen any eventual confrontation (Kissinger 1994, Baker 1999).

This suggests at least four possible outcomes: successful implementation of the Agreed Framework or some modified form of the bargain; failure of the agreement due to either a North Korean breakout or provocative North Korean behavior and donor fatigue; failure of the agreement due to South Korean unwillingness to assume its back-loaded financial obligations to KEDO (for example, due to economic hardship); or collapse of the agreement through the collapse of the North Korean state. As will be argued in chapter 9, KEDO is unlikely to meet the target of completing the light-water reactors by 2003, both setting the stage for a confrontation, and, ironically, presenting the opportunity to reorient the Agreed Frame-

---

63. Future sanctions could only work if enthusiastically supported by China. This is only likely if China believes that North Korea is irredeemable and decides to throw its full backing to South Korea in anticipation of a South Korean takeover of the entire peninsula.

work in a more rational way. The stability of the North Korean regime presumably is tied to its ability to endure the famine that currently grips the country. The international community's response to that famine has been fundamentally conditioned on concerns about North Korea's weapons of mass destruction and its intercontinental delivery systems. The famine is the crisis to which we now turn.

5

The Slow-Motion Famine in the North

Prior to the partition of the Korean peninsula in 1945, the colder and more industrialized North imported food from the more fertile South. After the partition, North Korea sought food security through self-sufficiency, encouraging the production of rice in the southernmost provinces, while maize, potatoes, and other staples were grown in the northern provinces.[1] Beginning in 1959, the policy even went beyond *national* self-sufficiency, encouraging *provincial* self-sufficiency where possible.[2]

To achieve these goals, agriculture was collectivized and decision making centralized. Given unpromising objective conditions in the agricultural sector (a high ratio of population to arable land, hilly terrain, northerly latitude, and short growing seasons), the achievement of the production goals required the maximization of yields through heavy application of chemical fertilizers and agricultural chemicals, and reliance on electrically powered irrigation systems. Continuous cropping led to soil depletion and the overuse of ammonium sulfate, as nitrogen fertilizer contributed to acidification of the soil and eventually a reduction in yields. As yields declined, hillsides were denuded to bring more and more marginal land

---

1. Eventually, the goal of complete self-sufficiency was abandoned. Indeed, in recognition of the deteriorating situation, agriculture was identified as one of the oxymoronic "three first" priorities in the 21st Plenary session of the 6-term Party Central Committee in December 1993. This was repeated in Kim Il-sung's 1994 New Year's Day speech and reaffirmed in the *Rodong Sinmum's* 1995 New Year's Day editorial following his death.

2. According to H.S. Lee (1999), this was justified in terms of the unavailability of transport in time of war. Certain provinces were to achieve self-sufficiency, while others were to produce surpluses to feed urban areas.

into production. This contributed to soil erosion, river silting, and, ultimately, catastrophic flooding. Isolation from the outside world has meant that the genetic diversity of North Korean seeds have declined, making plants more vulnerable to disease.

As with everything else North Korean, some controversy surrounds the precise timing and magnitude of North Korea's agricultural decline, but the consensus is that production peaked around 1989 and has fallen significantly since (table 5.1).[3] This decline in agricultural production occurred in the context of an economy-wide crisis. The macroeconomic shocks of the late 1980s and early 1990s resulted in a reduction of industrial inputs available to the agricultural sector—that is, the economy collapsed around agriculture (table 3.2).[4] By the late 1980s, North Korea had exhausted its possibilities for extensive development and had defaulted on its international debts, effectively foreclosing its access to international capital markets. After falling afoul of its primary patron, the Soviet Union, the value of repayments on past aid exceeded the inflow of new assistance. The subsequent collapse of the Soviet Union and the breakup of the Eastern Bloc precipitated an enormous macroeconomic shock. Given the highly input-intensive nature of North Korean agriculture, this led to a dramatic fall in output.

In 1991 the government launched a "let's eat only two meals a day" campaign that was subsequently intensified. By 1993 there were persistent (though unconfirmable) reports of food riots.[5] A disillusioned China, the North's primary supplier of imported food, reduced its exports to North Korea in 1994 and 1995 (Kim, Lee, and Sumner 1998, table 7).[6] (This coincided with the period in which China went from being a net exporter to a net importer of grains globally.) This was also a time of high world prices, making it more difficult for North Korea to import on commercial

---

3. See H.S. Lee (1994a), Lee, Nakano, and Nobukuni (1995), O (1995), Kim, Lee, and Sumner (1998), Smith (1998), UNDP (1998), and Smith and Huang (2000) for discussions of North Korean agriculture in the context of the famine.

4. To give a specific example, the South Korean Unification Ministry estimated that North Korea experienced a shortage of more than one million tons of fertilizer in 1998. Output of fertilizer was estimated to be only 17 percent of capacity due to shortages of raw materials and equipment. Similarly, Smith and Huang (2000) claim that tractor usage in 1998 was only 21 percent of its level a decade earlier.

5. Again, uncertainty surrounds the onset of North Korea's nutritional problems. H.S. Lee (1999) claims that childhood stunting was admitted by Kim Il-sung as early as 1979. It has been rumored that the size of defecting North Korean soldiers has fallen in recent years—possibly implying that nutrition problems began well before the 1990s. Wolf (1998) suggests another possibility: the effects of environmental pollution, which apparently gave rise to stunting in East Germany and other Eastern Bloc states.

6. North Korea's criticism of "traitors to the socialist cause" did not help matters (Lim 1997). The subsequent famine and flood of refugees into China seems to have called China's bluff, however.

Table 5.1 Food balance estimates (milled grain equivalent million metric tons)

Source		1990	1991	1992	1993	1994	1995	1996	1997
NUB[a,b]	Production	5.48	4.81	4.43	4.27	3.88	4.13	3.45	3.70
	Demand	6.50	6.47	6.50	6.58	6.67	6.72		
	Imports	0.86	1.27	0.92	1.09	0.60	0.89		
	Uncovered requirement	−0.16	−0.39	−1.15	−1.22	−2.19	−1.70		
LNN[c]	Production	5.79	5.72	5.84	5.82	5.85	5.90	2.84	
	Demand								
	Imports	0.60	1.29	0.83	1.09	0.36	0.75	5.55	
	Uncovered requirement	0.29	0.38	−0.58	−0.46	−1.61	−1.02	−1.04	
WFP[a]	Production						4.08	2.84	
	Demand						5.99	5.55	
	Imports								
	Uncovered requirement						−1.91	−1.04	
North Korea	Production						7.64		
	Demand						3.76		
	Imports								
	Uncovered requirement						3.88		
Kim, Lee, Sumner[d]	Production								
	Demand	\multicolumn{6}{4.47 MMT (low) or 4.96 MMT (high) of rice and corn}			
	Imports	\multicolumn{5.72 MMT of rice and corn}					
	Uncovered requirement	0.52	1.26	0.92	1.35	0.40	0.89	0.97	
USDA/FAS[a,e]	Production	5.08	4.30	3.86	3.72	3.42	3.83	3.38	
	Demand								
	Imports								
	Uncovered requirement								
H. Smith[a]	Production	5.48	4.81	4.43	4.27	3.88	4.13		
	Demand	6.20	6.40	6.50	6.58	6.67	6.72		
	Imports	0.86	1.27	0.92	1.09	0.60	0.89		
	Uncovered requirement	0.14	−0.32	−1.15	−1.22	−2.19	−1.70		
P.W. Lim[a,f]	Production		4.81	4.43	4.27	3.88	4.13	3.45	3.69
	Demand								
	Imports		1.29	0.83	1.09	0.49	0.96	1.05	1.44
	Uncovered requirement								
Roundtable[a,g]	Production	7.58	7.26	7.27	7.06	7.50	5.73	2.77	1.81
	Demand								
	Imports								
	Uncovered requirement								

(continued next page)

Table 5.1 Food balance estimates (milled grain equivalent million metric tons) (continued)

Source		1990	1991	1992	1993	1994	1995	1996	1997
IMF[a]	Production								2.5
	Demand								7.8
	Imports								2.2
	Uncovered requirement								3.1
FAO/WFP[a]	Production	8.10				6.64		4.08	2.87
	Demand							5.55	4.97
	Imports							0.43	0.75
	Uncovered requirement							1.04	1.18

a. Production reported from previous year.

b. Estimates include rice, maize, other cereals, beans, and potatoes.

c. Uses NUB for production data.

d. Estimates of production and demand are based on authors' own calculations. Estimates of imports include rice, corn, wheat, and barley.

e. Estimates include rice, corn, and wheat/barley.

f. Estimates include pulses and tubers.

g. Estimates include rice and corn.

Sources: NUB = South Korean National Unification Board, various publications; LNN = Lee, Nakano, and Nabukuni 1995, table 5; WFP = World Food Program, various publications; North Korea = Chun 1996, table 2; Kim, Lee, Sumner = Kim, Lee, and Sumner 1998, tables 3, 5, and 7; USDA = US Department of Agriculture, Foreign Agricultural Service, *North Korean Grain Summary 1997/1998;* H. Smith = Smith 1998, table 9; Lim = Lim 1997, table 5; Roundtable = Thematic Roundtable Meeting on Agricultural Recovery and Environmental Protection for the DPRK, annexes M and N; IMF = IMF *Fact-Finding Report;* FAO/WFP = UN Food and Agriculture Organization/World Food Program, Special Report, various issues.

terms (Dyck 1996). By 1994 North Korean radio broadcasts had admitted the existence of hunger.[7] In May 1995, South Korean President Kim Young-sam made a public offer of unconditional food assistance to the North. Later that month the North Korean government admitted that the country was experiencing a food shortage and asked the Japanese government for assistance. In June, the North Korean government in Pyongyang reached agreements with the Japanese and South Korean governments on the procurement of emergency food aid, and, in July, the Pyongyang government announced to its public that it was receiving external assistance, though it failed to mention the South Korean role.

---

7. For examples of the anecdotal evidence emerging on hunger prior to the 1995 floods, see the *Economist,* 16 July 1994 and 22 October 1994. At the same time, it should be noted that eyewitness accounts did not paint a uniformly grim picture of the situation. Reporting on a May 1995 visit to North Korea, *Financial Times* correspondent John Burton described the people he encountered as looking "adequately fed" (*Financial Times,* 8 May 1995).

Catastrophic floods in July and August 1995 added to North Korea's suffering. The government announced that 5.4 million people had been displaced, 330,000 hectares of agricultural land had been destroyed, and 1.9 million tons of grain had been lost. The government put the total cost of the flood damages at $15 billion.[8] Although outside organizations ultimately formulated far lower estimates of these damages, in December 1995 the UN Food and Agricultural Organization (FAO) and the World Food Program (WFP) issued a joint statement that 2.1 million children and 500,000 pregnant women were on the verge of starvation. The WFP mission further warned that "starvation could possibly affect millions of people in the summer." In January 1996, the International Committee of the Red Cross (ICRC) issued a similarly bleak assessment, stating that 130,000 people were on the brink of starvation and 500,000 could be affected by the time of the autumn harvest. These floods played an important public relations role, insomuch as they facilitated the North Korean government's portrayal of the famine as a product of natural disaster, a portrayal that a number of relief agencies found to their advantage.[9]

The floods of 1995 were followed by more, though less severe, floods in July 1996 and by renewed appeals for help.[10] At the time, the WFP stated that North Korea was on the brink of a famine, though it was not until March 1997 that it provided eyewitness accounts of malnourishment (WFP 19 March 1997) (see box 5.1). Andrew Natsios of World Vision, a former US Agency for International Development (AID) official, characterized the situation in North Korea as "significantly more severe" than the Ethiopian famine of the mid-1980s, a comparison that the WFP resident representative in Pyongyang would later echo.[11] By April 1997, the WFP

---

8. The most heavily affected areas were the corn growing provinces of Chagang and North P'yongan in the northwest of the country and the rice producing area of North Hwanghae, south of Pyongyang. The consensus of outside observers is that the damage, while extensive, was not as severe as the government initially claimed. For example, a UN survey concluded that the flooding displaced 500,000 people, not the 5.4 million the government initially claimed. This information is used in the modeling work reported in chapters 7 and 8.

9. For example, the North Korean government unit charged with obtaining international assistance was renamed the Flood Damage Rehabilitation Committee. See Mansourov (2000a) for an analysis of the North Korean government's response to the floods.

10. Calamities followed in the succeeding years. In 1997 the country was hit by drought affecting rain-fed maize and tidal waves caused by Hurricane Winnie, which damaged rice crops and protective barriers along the coast. The 1997 drought reduced water levels in reservoirs, adversely affecting production in 1998. In August 1998, the country was hit by torrential rain, hail, tidal waves, and strong winds that damaged crops, though the WFP was to later assess this damage as minor (Food Aid Liaison Unit (FALU) 1998). According to North Korea's official KCNA, in 1999 the problem was again drought (KCNA 13 May 1999), followed in August by floods.

11. For the Natsios quote, see *Washington Post*, 9 February 1997. For the WFP quote, see Michael Laris, *Washington Post*, 31 January 1999.

Box 5.1 Crying Wolf?

In the aftermath of the 1995 floods, the International Committee of the Red Cross (ICRC) reported that one-third of the harvest had been lost and 40 percent of the arable land ravaged. The following year the Committee predicted that production would be 50 percent below average.

During the winter of 1995-96, Trevor Page, then the head of the World Food Program's office in Pyongyang, made a series of apocalyptic claims that were not entirely consistent with previous or subsequent statements by other observers, including other UN officials on the ground in North Korea. For example, in December 1995, Page asserted that "there are signs of famine in various parts of the country. They are everywhere. There is a food emergency" (*Korea Times,* 7 December 1995), "availability of food is below survival rations" (Associated Press, 12 December 1995) and that "the entire nation does not have enough to eat. . . . It's deteriorating every day. Malnutrition is developing all over the place . . . the availability of food is below survival rations" (*Washington Post,* 23 December 1995).

Yet Faruq Achikzad, the UNDP representative in Pyongyang who had extensively toured the flood affected areas, indicated in a series of statements that, while the damage was extensive, the situation was under control (see, for example, *Washington Post,* 13 September 1995). In March 1996, Kjell Madsen of the U.N. Department of Humanitarian Affairs said that the situation in North Korea had "moved beyond the emergency phase," that people were "working on rehabilitation," and that the media had exaggerated the situation. Madsen's statement was criticized by the World Food Program, which labeled it a misrepresentation of the situation. Likewise, Niksch (1996) cites outside observers' skepticism about the WFP and ICRC reports which were the stated basis for the US humanitarian contribution.

Given the restrictions that the North Korean government put on outside observers, it is difficult to believe that either Page or the ICRC had any real factual evidence to support their claims. Yet history may well vindicate their assessment of the situation—even if they could not substantiate these assertions at the time. It is a real tragedy that North Korean government policies have put the aid agencies in a position in which they are open to charges of crying wolf.

was characterizing North Korea as being "on the knife edge of a major famine" (WFP 18 April 1997). In September the German Red Cross characterized the famine as "the worst the world has seen since the Second World War" and said that roughly 10,000 children were dying from starvation every month.[12] By this time, the WFP reckoned that a quarter of the population was relying on international assistance. Again, these assessments have been disputed by independent observers.[13] One explanation is that conditions varied considerably by region and social group.

---

12. Conor O'Cleary, *Irish Times,* 22 September 1997.

13. See Flake (1997) and Nicholas D. Kristof, *New York Times,* 12 October 1997.

Another explanation is the seasonal variance in food availability, with fall harvest the time of greatest abundance, and early spring the time of greatest scarcity. Another is that the relief agencies have a bureaucratic self-interest in exaggerating the degree of distress—an incentive the North Korean government shares. Assessment of the true extent of distress was complicated by the widespread belief that the North Korean government maintains substantial stockpiles of grain (see box 5.2).

Given the relative scarcity and low fecundity of North Korean arable land, the drive to maximize output has involved the use of environmentally unsustainable techniques. The need to bring more and more marginal land into production has caused deforestation, which in turn has increased the rapidity of runoff, soil erosion, river bed silting, and, ultimately, of flooding.[14]

In addition to these structural problems, North Korean agriculture is beset by organizational problems, including overcentralization of decision making and an emphasis on large state farms. There have been anecdotal reports that, in response to the crisis, there has been some introduction of more incentive compatible systems, such as fixed-rent tenancies, but the extent of these changes is unclear.[15]

Although flooding may have precipitated the food crisis in North Korea, agriculture, like the rest of the economy, has been in secular decline since the beginning of the 1990s. Even without flooding, North Korea would have entered the mid-1990s with a substantial food deficit.

Yet, while there has been a decline in food production, famine in North Korea is more due to systemic crisis and a decline in income. It reflects an "entitlement failure" that Sen (1981) argues is characteristic of many famines. Sen identified the problem as a catastrophic decline in the incomes or entitlements of vulnerable groups rather than a failure to produce or supply enough food.

---

14. Kim Il-sung began encouraging the deforestation of mountainous areas in 1976, though eventually he recognized his own mistake and halted the practice in 1980 (D. Lee 1997). The practice appears to have been revived under the pressure of growing food shortages in the 1990s.

15. Agricultural operations are organized into state farms and peasant cooperatives. On the state farms, peasants are paid fixed salaries. In the case of the cooperatives, which are theoretically owned by the members, members receive equal shares paid in cash and in kind, with bonuses going to work units overfulfilling targets. "In reality, the peasants are reduced to employees in either case" (H.S. Lee 1994a, 511). Recent policy has been to increase the importance of state farms (which are considered ideologically more advanced) and to integrate the agricultural sector more firmly into the central plan, while at the same time introducing limited innovations such as the reduction of the size of work units, and introducing family or subteam responsibility systems in which families or subteams are granted responsibilities for particular subplots, subject to a fixed-rent tenancy at the farm level. It is impossible to determine the extent to which these new institutional arrangements have been adopted.

Box 5.2 The Issue of Military Stockpiling

The issue of military stockpiling is critical, since it gets at the heart of North Korea's intentions and enormously complicates the humanitarian response to the crisis. At the same time that North Korea was receiving official aid from South Korea, the United States, and other countries, North Korean propaganda was describing South Korea as "a den of thieves, people with no honor, no legitimacy" and the United States as "warmongering imperialist fascists." In 1996, North Korea's envoy to the United Nations stated that the North Korean military opposed aid on the grounds that it could be used by hostile powers to "destroy our political system." Although some US officials claimed that military stockpiles were distributed to flood victims, the possible diversion of food aid to the North Korean military has been a continuing source of concern in donor countries. South Korean President Kim Young-sam stated that most of the 150,000 tons of rice South Korea donated to North Korea had been distributed to the military. In the United States, Republican candidate Bob Dole during the 1996 Presidential campaign criticized the Clinton Administration's decision to provide aid, claiming that this was "rewarding an enemy," and that the food would go to the military.

These concerns have led both government and non-government officials into detailed analyses of the disposition of aid. On a fundamental level, however, these efforts have surely been misplaced. Food, while not perfectly fungible, is at least partly fungible, and one must assume that at least some of the benefits of increased food supplies will accrue to North Korean military. Indeed, using the model developed in chapter 7, one could calculate this.

Estimates of stockpiling range as high as two years difference between demand and supply (H.S. Lee 1994a), and some have questioned the need for external assistance in the presence of government controlled stockpiles. Niksch (1996) reports that unnamed US intelligence officials estimate that the North Korean military has enough food stockpiled to sustain offensive military operations for 90 days, while their South Korean counterparts estimate that the North Korean military has stockpiled 1.2 million tons—enough for four months during wartime. Military stockpiling has been confirmed by visiting Russian officials, and all together an estimated 15 to 20 percent of annual grain supplies goes into military stockpiles.

A slightly higher figure of 1.2 to 1.5 million tons has been given by an official at the South Korean unification think tank (Park 1996). An unnamed South Korean official put the level of military stocks as enough for ten months. South Korean Foreign Minister Gong Ro-myung asserted that these stockpiles were not being counted in estimates of North Korea's shortfall, and that the problems in North Korea had been exacerbated by the regime's unwillingness to release these stocks.

It may well be that at the onset of the crisis the military had substantial stockpiles. How much of this inventory is left, or to what extent aid has been used to replenish depleted stocks, is unknown.

Table 5.2 Rice and corn per capita daily rations

Occupation and age group	Per capita daily ration (grams)	Ratio of rice to corn Pyongyang area	Other areas
High-ranking government officials	700	10:0	10:0
Regular laborers	600	6:4	3:7
Heavy-labor workers	800	6:4	3:7
Office workers	600	6:4	3:7
Special security	800	7:3	3:7
Military	700	6:4	3:7
College students	600	6:4	3:7
Secondary school students	500	6:4	3:7
Primary school students	400	6:4	3:7
Preschool students	300	6:4	3:7
Children under 3 years	100-200	6:4	3:7
Aged and disabled	300	6:4	3:7

Source: Kim, Lee, and Sumner 1998, table 1.

One could argue that in North Korea vulnerable groups initially lost their entitlement to food due to political decisions regarding rationing through the government-run Public Distribution System (PDS) rather than through market forces. Historically, the PDS, a system through which approximately 13.5 million North Koreans (around 62 percent of the population) receive subsidized food rations, has been the primary mechanism for the distribution of food in North Korea. The main groups outside the Public Distribution System are the workers on state farms, who receive only six months' rations through the PDS, and workers on cooperative farms, who must depend on on-site production. This latter group appears to have borne the brunt of the losses due to flooding, and has been a main recipient of humanitarian assistance (WFP 1996a).

A government decree promulgated in 1952 stipulates a standard ration that all participants in the PDS are to receive (table 5.2). However, it is unclear to what extent this promise was ever fulfilled. Over the years, the ration has been reduced, ostensibly as part of various stockpiling schemes. In the course of the current crisis, consumption has been compressed further, and the standard adult grain ration has reportedly been reduced to around 400 to 450 grams per day (WFP 1996b, KDI 1999).[16] All eyewitness accounts indicate that the distribution of hardship is highly uneven, with those outside the PDS in the flood affected areas bearing the brunt of the burden.[17] Some groups and locales appear to be entirely

---

16. The South Korean government's Korea Development Institute (KDI) has estimated that average adult caloric intake is 1,600 calories, or about 410 grams (Seo Jang-soo, *Joongang Ilbo*, 22 September 1999).

17. See, for example, the statement of Dilawar Ali Khan, the UNICEF resident representative in Pyongyang (Associated Press, 26 May 1999).

unaffected by the crisis, while widespread reports of significant famine-related deaths have emerged from other areas. The North Korean government continues to deny or circumscribe access by outside observers (including humanitarian aid workers). As a consequence, it is impossible to ascertain with any degree of certainty the magnitude of hardship currently faced by the North Korean populace.

As the PDS mechanism failed and the famine intensified, food has increasingly been allocated through informal markets. In fact, the situation has come more closely to resemble past famines in market economies described by Ravallion (1987). According to research by Kim Yeon-chul of the Hyundai Research Institute, North Koreans were relying on these markets for 95 percent or more of their consumption needs.[18] According to the Food Aid Liaison Unit (FALU) of the WFP, "food supply via the Public Distribution System had run out in all areas by mid-April" 1998 (FALU 1998).[19] Eyewitnesses report that the grain in the markets is distributed in bags with international relief agency markings, and, not surprisingly, the transaction prices in the markets are far higher than the control prices. If the grain in the relief agency sacks were indeed donated food (there is some possibility that it is domestically produced grain packaged in reused sacks), it would imply that someone is capturing astronomical rents off the aid.[20]

The Food Balance

The food balance is a product of the demand for and the supply of food.[21] Demand is a function of the direct, final demand for food by the human population; indirect demand for seed, feed, and industrial uses (including the manufacture of alcohol); and losses and spoilage. Supply consists of production, imports, and any drawdown on accumulated stocks. In the

---

18. *Chosun Ilbo*, 28 September 1997.

19. FAO/WFP (1999a) would later report that "food distribution ceased in April 1999," though Paik (1999) claims that "partial food rationing began in June this year even in the remote northern provinces." While it is possible that both statements are correct, probably the best inference to draw is that lack of adequate access has made it hard for outsiders to get a clear picture of events in North Korea.

20. One press report put the price of a one kilogram of rice at 80 won, or about one month's average wage (*Korea Herald*, 5 January 1999). Kirk, Brookes, and Pica (1998) report that the farmers' price for rice is 200 times the control price. S.G. Hong (1999) and the Ministry of Unification (1999) also analyze price data by season and region.

21. This specification of "needs" or "demands" in physical terms without reference to prices or opportunity costs may strike economists as odd. This is the normal methodology used by relief agencies, however, and we will subsequently use these figures without further comment to calibrate simulation experiments in chapters 7 and 8.

case of North Korea, measures of each of these components are subject to considerable uncertainty.

Consider demand. The major component of demand is direct final consumption by humans. There are no reliable data on this demand for North Korea. Instead, analysts estimate demand by imputing a certain degree of consumption or caloric intake per capita and multiplying that estimate by the population to obtain aggregate demand. However, different population groups (children, sedentary adults, manual workers, etc.) need or desire different amounts of food. So, not only does one need information on the population size, but demographic data are essential as well.

Unfortunately, these data do not exist. The most recent population census data, which were transmitted to the UN in 1997, pertain to 1993. Prior to the release of these data, analysts and relief agencies had based their calculations on demographic data released in 1989.[22] Two US demographers analyzed these data and prepared population projections on that basis (Eberstadt and Banister 1992a). It is telling to note that the raw population estimates used by the WFP, the South Korean National Unification Board (NUB), and a team of independent researchers all differ from each other and from the Eberstadt-Banister projections. The outside world (and perhaps the North Korean government itself) does not know how many North Koreans there are, much less their distribution across different demographic categories.

Suppose for a moment that we did have good information on the North Korean population. The next step would be to estimate caloric intake and assign the sources of caloric intake to different food groups. Again, there are no data. The NUB and WFP apparently use South Korean data as a starting point and then make speculative adjustments to fit the North Korean case. In practice, differing assumptions regarding caloric needs and nutritional sources generate significantly different estimates of demand.[23] Smith (1998), for example, argues that: "The share of rice and maize in total cereal intake has historically been much lower than assumed by international agencies in assessing North Korean per capita grain consumption" (p.57).

Since there are also no data on indirect demand for seed, livestock feed, and industrial uses such as the manufacture of alcohol, these demands are imputed. To recap, not a single datum needed to estimate demand—

---

22. To cite one example, the WFP cites a population estimate around 500,000 lower than the Banister-Eberstadt projection. One is left with the impression that either North Korea had already experienced serious demographic shocks by the mid-1990s, or the only existent demographic model of North Korea is seriously flawed.

23. See Drèze and Sen (1989) for a general discussion of this issue, and H.S. Lee (1994a), Lee, Nakano, and Nobukuni (1995), and Smith (1998) for applications to the specific case of North Korea.

from population to indirect demand for seed—can be observed directly, and each must be constructed.

How about supply? Again, every relevant datum is missing. The biggest single component of supply is domestic production. Since production cannot be measured directly, outside observers impute it by combining estimates of planted acreage and yields. Setting aside the issue of land damaged by flooding, one could expect that experts could come up with tolerably accurate estimates of planted acreage. Yields are a different matter, however. The South Korean National Unification Board, for example, estimates yields by operating experimental farms in South Korea and China that mimic North Korean agricultural techniques. The WFP combines data on estimated planted acreage and selective field sampling to generate estimates of yields (WFP 1996b). Thus the potential for gross misestimation is substantial. Likewise, no hard data exist for losses from spoilage, though there are estimates (FAO 1997).

The other major component of supply is imports. In principle, one could construct reasonably accurate estimates of North Korean food imports using export statistics of North Korea's trade partners. Unfortunately, this effort faces several difficulties. Most of North Korea's food imports apparently now come from China, which has notoriously inaccurate statistics. Moreover, food aid may be misclassified in the trade statistics of China and other countries. Barter trade is not reported at all, especially barter that may involve arms or military technology. So, there is even uncertainty about supply from external sources.

Lastly, North Korea could be adding to or, more likely, running down, accumulated stocks. There is considerable disagreement as to the size of these putative stocks and the extent to which North Korea may be building upon or drawing from inventories.

To conclude, there is fundamental uncertainty about each subcomponent of North Korea's food balance. Widely cited figures unfortunately imply a degree of precision and understanding of the situation wholly unsupported by hard evidence. The outside world does not know how much food North Korea has or how much it needs (table 5.1). However, foreign aid has probably accounted for 10 to 15 percent of total consumption in recent years.

Food for Peace

The regime's active response to the crisis displayed a characteristic emphasis on technical solutions and top-down hectoring. Increased effort was put into developing high yield varieties. Norman Borlaug, father of the "Green Revolution," was invited to Pyongyang. Later, Kim Jong-il directed the mass planting of "Super Corn" developed by South Korean agronomist Kim Soon-kwon. The populace was urged to participate in

Box 5.3 "9/27 Camps"

Among the more disturbing stories that have emerged from the North Korean famine are of the existence of concentration camps or prisons to hold people found foraging for food. The camps are called "9/27 camps" after the date of 27 September 1995, when Kim Jong-il issued an edict ordering their establishment. The existence of such camps has made international aid agencies nervous, and the World Food Program will neither confirm nor deny their existence. Yet the camps have been described by scores of refugees in China, and *Medicins Sans Frontieres* (Doctors Without Borders) officials claim to have seen references to the camps in North Korean children's medical records. Indeed, it was the North Korean government's unwillingness to permit *Medicins Sans Frontieres* to visit patients in the camps that contributed to the organization's decision to withdraw from North Korea. Andrew Natsios has estimated that more than one million people pass through the camps each year. The existence of the North Korean gulag has become an international diplomatic issue, however, with United Nations High Commissioner for Human Rights Mary Robinson and United Nations High Commissioner for Refugees Sadako Ogata criticizing countries for repatriating refugees who then enter the camp system (see box 5.4).

mass mobilizations to raise rabbits, goats, and potatoes.[24] Kim Jong-il was reported to have visited a military farming complex and urged that they grow more vegetables "in order to boost combat power."[25]

At the same time, the regime acquiesced in the growth of farmers' markets, permitted farmers to begin double cropping, and tacitly removed some restrictions on mobility in order to facilitate foraging[26] (see box 5.3). Local officials took a more assertive role in procuring food supplies, and there were reports of changes in the organization of agricultural production in some local areas. These largely passive and decentralized

---

24. Paramount leader Kim Jong-il designated 1999 as the "the year of potato farming revolution" and announced that "The North Korean people might not have suffered from famine across the country if North Korea had revamped its potato raising project ten years ago." The April 1999 national planning law specifies that North Korea will "effect the revolution in potato farming and improve the farming structure on the basis of the principle of the right crop on the right soil at the right time." Kim ordered his subjects to alter their dietary habits and to consider the potato as their main food instead of rice. Shortly thereafter, the official *Rodong Sinmun* editorialized that "we should thoroughly learn about rabbits and make rabbit raising a national movement," jumpstarting the revolution. The editorial went on to observe that a rabbit can produce more than two kilograms of "delicious" meat in three months, and since it also is able to produce up to thirty baby rabbits, the rabbit will be able to produce some 50 kilograms of meat. Not content with raising rabbits, Kim Jong-il has begun urging his people to raise goats, which are good at foraging on steep hillsides.

25. Reuters, 27 June 1995.

26. See P. Kim (1999) for a description of system-fraying and coping behavior.

responses may well have been more effective in the short run than the government's more direct actions.

Finally, the government appealed for outside support.[27] While the ultimate responsibility for North Korea's predicament lies in Pyongyang, it is abundantly clear that the outside world has played politics with food. The North Korean crisis has been treated as an opportunity to extract political concessions from the North Koreans. Thus, the food crisis, while having a technical component, has also been a diplomatic issue.

By 1994 North Korea had publicly admitted a food shortage, and in February 1995 World Vision International, a California-based Christian relief organization, had secured permission from the US and South Korean governments to raise funds for humanitarian food shipments to the North. North Korea had reportedly concluded an agreement with Thailand to obtain 100,000 tons of rice in 1993 and reached a second agreement to obtain additional rice in exchange for steel.[28]

As the situation worsened, North Korea turned to Japan, its former colonial master, presumably because Japan had substantial reserve grain stocks. Plus, it would be less humiliating to accept assistance from Japan (which could be portrayed as a kind of reparations) than from rival South Korea (which had smaller reserves, in any event).[29] A positive response by Japan was opposed by the Kim Young-sam administration in South Korea, whose Deputy Prime Minister Rha Woong-bae warned Japan of "soured relations" if Japan were to provide aid in the absence of South Korean participation—a position not universally held by South Korean National Assembly members.

---

27. The government appealed to the Group of Seven industrialized countries for assistance prior to the 1995 Lyon summit. The rather paltry response elicited from these appeals reportedly undercut reformist technocrats in the government.

28. In the end, the Thais delivered roughly 160,000 tons of rice, but they refused to deliver the rest after the North Koreans defaulted on their obligations. In 1996, the director general of Thailand's Ministry of Commerce revealed that the North desired to barter weapons for rice, or, alternatively, for marble and copper. The Thais declined due to the North's prior default. North Korea also apparently concluded a cement for rice swap with Vietnam. A zinc for wheat exchange with the US firm Cargill fell through in June 1997.

29. At the same time, North Korea began accepting donations from United Nations agencies such as UNICEF and the WFP, as well as from a wide range of private charities. However, the mandate of the UN agencies was fairly narrowly drawn, focusing on particularly vulnerable groups such as children, and the volume of assistance through these channels was dwarfed by bilateral assistance. More recent WFP appeals (e.g., 6 January 1998, 18 May 1998, 16 December 1998, and 23 April 1999) have been couched in much broader terms and have targeted as many as eight million people, or more than one-third of the population.
Even fate itself seemed to conspire against the North Koreans; in March 1996 a vessel bearing the second shipment of WFP assistance (including all $2 million of US aid) sank *en route* to the North. Although the cargo was insured and could be replaced, the mishap delayed the distribution of emergency supplies.

Eventually, agreement was reached that South Korea and Japan would jointly provide assistance to North Korea.[30] According to the plan, South Korea would provide North Korea with 150,000 tons of rice in unmarked bags, while Japan would provide 150,000 tons *gratis* and another 150,000 tons on concessional terms.[31] (Japan eventually provided 500,000 tons in total.) Observers expected this deal to improve relations not only between North Korea and the donors, but also between North Korea and the United States, which had made improved North-South ties a condition of closer diplomatic relations. South Korean President Kim Young-sam predicted that the rice deal would pave the way for the planned summit meeting, which had been shelved by the death of Kim Il-sung the previous year.

This optimism was soon put to rest with the delivery of the first shipload of South Korean rice. The North Korean authorities, in contravention of the agreement, forced the ship upon entering the harbor to fly a North Korean flag and later detained the crew of another relief vessel, charging them with spying. The outrage in South Korea was predictable, and the Kim Young-sam administration, which had earlier indicated a willingness to purchase rice on the international market if additional assistance were necessary, now spoke instead of the impossibility of providing additional rice until the government purchase of the domestic crop was completed for the year. The North Koreans quickly apologized, which was interpreted in at least some quarters as an indication of their state of desperation, but already the damage had been done. The South Koreans began trying to persuade other countries not to provide additional assistance and conditioned any further assistance to the North on the opening of bilateral talks. South Korea reversed its stance in the summer of 1997, however, and began providing additional aid as it became apparent that the seriousness of the situation in North Korea was not abating. This approach was

30. See Snyder (1999b) for an account of these negotiations and subsequent negotiations between North Korea and the United States.

31. In one of the many strange twists in this strange saga, the Japanese government around this time also began providing assistance to the Palestine Liberation Organization (PLO). It was the first time Japan had provided aid to a quasi-governmental entity with which it did not have formal diplomatic relations. Some observers interpreted this as paving the way for aid to North Korea, which, like the PLO, does not enjoy diplomatic relations with Japan.

Japan subsequently announced that future aid would be conditioned on North Korea permitting Japanese wives of North Koreans to visit their families in Japan. North Korea acceded to this request, and a limited visitation program was organized through the Red Cross. See H.N. Kim (1998) and B.C. Koh (1998) for analyses of the wives issue.

Japanese aid was suspended after North Korea test-fired its Taepodong missile across Japan in August 1998. In December 1999, the government of Japan indicated that it would consider resuming humanitarian assistance, and in March 2000 it announced that it would supply 100,000 tons of rice to North Korea.

intensified following the election of Kim Dae-jung in December 1997, and South Korea continued to supply North Korea with food in 1998.

A similar evolution was occurring in the United States (table 5.3). As concern about the situation grew in early 1996, and with no diplomatic breakthroughs in sight, the United States began to adopt a slightly more assertive posture than South Korea. In June, Secretary of State Warren Christopher announced that the United States would make a small ($6.2 million) additional contribution to the WFP appeal.[32] This move was widely interpreted as an attempt to induce North Korean participation in a preparatory briefing for the Four Party Talks as well as adherence to the Agreed Framework. Although the Clinton Administration denied this intent, public statements by Representative Bill Richardson (D-New Mexico), subsequently US Ambassador to the United Nations and Secretary of Energy, seemed to bolster this interpretation.[33] Richardson had had a series of contacts with the North Koreans. The decision to provide more rice to the WFP appeal was publicly lambasted by Republican Presidential nominee apparent Bob Dole and other prominent Republicans.[34] With the crisis continuing into 1997, the United States made another, larger, $25 million donation to the WFP in the spring. In July 1997, former Senator Sam Nunn and former U.S. Ambassador to Seoul James Laney visited Pyongyang to pave the way for the anticipated August start of preliminary discussions to set the agenda for the Four Party Talks. After the Nunn-Laney trip, the United States announced a $27 million (100,000-ton) donation of grain, inaugurating a policy of "food for meetings" that would continue to the present.[35] Under this policy, the United States has

---

32. The source of these funds was the storied PL-480 ("Food for Peace") account. In the midst of the June 1996 WFP call for additional aid and diplomatic maneuvering regarding the appropriate response, press reports emerged in South Korea that North Korea received $130 million in insurance compensation for crop damage in 1994. If true, this would have dwarfed the amount of the WFP appeal and undercut the case for providing humanitarian assistance. US State Department officials expressed skepticism regarding the alleged magnitude of the insurance payment, and in the end a consensus of sorts seemed to emerge that the North Koreans had only received $13 to $25 million in insurance compensation.

33. Similarly, Japanese Foreign Ministry officials denied any linkage between the Four Party Talks and Japan's decision to follow the US lead and offer more aid. Private analysts in Tokyo asserted that this was indeed the case, however. South Korean officials, on the other hand, were more explicit about the linkage between aid and the Four Party Talks. For its part, North Korea commemorated the 46th anniversary of the beginning of the Korean War by blaming the United States for the war and pledging that the country would "annihilate all potential aggressors."

34. Former Ambassador to South Korea and China James R. Lilley, in an opinion piece titled "Underwriting a Dictatorship," characterized the Clinton policy as pouring money into a "black hole" (*Washington Post*, 19 July 1996).

35. Nevertheless, while the United States and South Korea were softening their stance toward the North, Japan maintained its distance. In July 1997, North Korea, in an apparent attempt to soften the Japanese stance, made a diplomatic concession—allowing spouses of

provided food aid in exchange for North Korean participation in a variety of diplomatic negotiations. For example, on 10 September 1998, the same day that the United States and North Korea announced resumption of suspended missile proliferation and Four Party Talks, the *New York Times* reported that the United States had agreed to send 300,000 tons of grain worth $101 million to North Korea, a report that US officials were forced to confirm publicly. To gain access to the suspected nuclear site at Kumchangri in 1999, the United States donated another 600,000 tons, 500,000 to be provided by the government and another 100,000 through nongovernmental organizations.

Looming in the background of this maneuvering has been China. When the Soviet Union withdrew support for North Korea, China emerged as its major patron, supplying in the early 1990s nearly three-quarters of its food imports (Flake 1995a, Eberstadt 1995b). China had reportedly been providing North Korea 500,000 tons of grain for free and an additional 200,000 to 300,000 tons on a concessional basis (Y.H. Park 1996). After the Chinese government indicated in 1994 that it would demand payment for future shipments, exports to North Korea subsequently dwindled.[36] However, China apparently became concerned about the worsening situation in the North and the growing numbers of North Koreans illegally crossing into China's Jilin province. In 1996 the Chinese government announced that it would send 100,000 tons of grain (see box 5.4). Chinese Premier Li Peng and North Korean Vice Premier Hong Song-nam signed an agreement on 22 May 1996 that reportedly included a Chinese commitment to ship 500,000 tons of grain annually to North Korea, half for free and half at "friendship prices."[37] One newspaper report put Chinese food exports to North Korea at 1 million tons.[38] If this report were true, this would make China North Korea's prime benefactor. What is known

---

North Koreans to return to Japan to visit their families. The Japanese had previously announced that such visits were a precondition to assistance, and they responded to the gesture by donating approximately 60,000 tons of rice.

36. Government budget pressures and a declining ability to jawbone state firms into unprofitable operations were given as the official justification for this policy change.

37. The renewal of aid was announced in July 1996 by the Secretary General of the State Council of China, Luo Gan, during a visit to Pyongyang to commemorate the 35th anniversary of the Sino-North Korean Treaty of Friendship, Cooperation, and Mutual Assistance. Observers also pointed to worsening relations between China and South Korea, as evidenced by disputes over the development of a passenger jet and fishing rights in the Yellow Sea. At the same time that China was announcing the provision of aid, North Korea sent its highest ranking delegation to Taiwan to try and procure assistance from that quarter. See Snyder (1997) for more discussion of China's relations with North Korea and the food issue. As noted in chapter 3, North Korea announced that it had received 150,000 tons of grain following a 1999 visit to China by SPA Chairman Kim Yong-nam.

38. Jim Mann, *Los Angeles Times*, 10 September 1997.

Table 5.3 Food for talks

Date	Value	Form	Channel	Diplomatic objective
February 1996	$2 million	Food	World Food Programme	Encourage North Korean adherence to the Agreed Framework during a period of increasing tension between the two Koreas.
June 1996	$6.2 million	Food	World Food Programme	Encourage North Korean flexibility with respect to a secret proposal for four-way talks between the US, North Korea, South Korea, and China.
February 1997	$10 million	Food	World Food Programme	*Quid pro quo* for North Korean agreement to participate in joint US-South Korea briefing on Four-Way Talks proposal.
April 1997	$15 million	50,000 metric tons of food	World Food Programme	*Quid pro quo* for North Korean agreement to participate in missile proliferation negotiations.
July 1997	$27 million	100,000 metric tons of food	World Food Programme	*Quid pro quo* for North Korean agreement to participate in Four-Way Talks.
October 1997	$5 million	Grant	UNICEF	*Quid pro quo* for North Korean acceptance of 10 additional food relief monitors.
February 1998	n.a.	200,000 metric tons of food	World Food Programme	*Quid pro quo* for North Korean agreement to participate in ad hoc committee meeting associated with the Four-Way Talks.
September 1998	n.a.	300,000 metric tons of food	World Food Programme	*Quid pro quo* for North Korean agreement to resume missile talks, attend the third plenary session of the Four-Way Talks, enter into negotiations over the second suspected nuclear site, and resume talks aimed at removing North Korea from the list of states sponsoring terrorism.
April 1999	n.a.	600,000 metric tons of food, 1,000 tons of potato seed	Bilateral	*Quid pro quo* for agreement on access to North Korea's under-ground construction site.

Box 5.4 Refugees

Estimates of the numbers of North Korean refugees in China and Russia vary enormously. The South Korean Institute for National Unification, the think tank of the government's National Unification Board, estimated that 200,000 North Koreans had crossed into China and Russia illegally, while Foreign Minister Hong Soon-young put the figure at 10,000 to 30,000, and the Chinese government reckons the figure is less than 10,000. A South Korean academic has estimated the number at less than 100,000 (Son 1999), while an estimate produced by a Korean NGO put it at 300,000, and Kirk (1999) cites figures as high as 500,000. It may well be the case that the relatively low estimates produced by Foreign Minister Hong and the Chinese government in the fall of 1999 represented an attempt to downplay the issue in the face of growing South Korean public concern about the situation.

It is clear that the refugees face abominable conditions in China, and that many are women sold into China in various forms of involuntary servitude. An analysis by the Korean Buddhist Sharing Movement concluded that more than three quarters of the Korean refugees in China were women, many forced into prostitution or sexual slavery.

Confronted with this situation, China's ambassador to Seoul, the ever-helpful Wu Dawei, expressed strong dissatisfaction with either official South Korean or unofficial NGO involvement in such human rights issues, terming it neo-interventionism by third parties. When asked about forcible returns of refugees to North Korea and reports of their executions and internments there, Wu blithely asserted that "their safety is guaranteed, even after their repatriation to North Korea."

South Korean human rights activists responded to Wu's remarks by demonstrating in front of the Chinese embassy and unveiling a petition with 1,180,000 signatures urging the United Nations to grant the Koreans refugee status and reminding both the Chinese envoy and the Seoul government that, under the South Korean Constitution, the refugees in China are South Korean citizens. On 13 January 2000, the United Nations High Commissioner for Refugees lodged an official protest with the Chinese government over the deportation of refugees, and that same month South Korean Foreign Minister Hong lost his job, reportedly as a result of his mishandling of the issue. The US government, however, has remained silent on this violation of international law.

is that food is entering into North Korea from China, whether on concessional, commercial, or barter terms.[39]

As the famine dragged on, two issues emerged as points of contention. First, donors (apart from China) increasingly demanded to be able to monitor aid distribution, due to the political need to assure donor constitu-

---

39. Multiple eyewitness accounts describe North Korean local officials attempting to secure food supplies in China's Jilin province. Much of this has apparently been barter trade, with the North Koreans bartering scrap metal, marine products, and trees for grain. The cutting down of trees has worsened the deforestation problem and may contribute to future flooding. However, the freelancing by local officials could be interpreted as systemic decentralization, which could be hard to reverse if and when the crisis abates.

encies that food aid was not being diverted to the military.[40] And, although donors threatened to make continued assistance conditional on monitoring, in point of fact few donors followed through with the threat. The US government, for example, made increased monitors a condition for increased aid in 1997, but actually increased its aid shipments despite the inadequacy of monitoring.[41] The following year, the World Food Program also made continued assistance conditional on greater access, and likewise increased the size of its appeals despite a lack of access to recipients. In contrast to the official agencies, however, several non-governmental organizations actually did suspend aid when the North Koreans did not keep their promises.[42]

Although understandable in political terms, this effort was essentially misplaced, in that food is fungible. Indeed, as demonstrated in chapter 7, aid is a form of balance of payments support. These incidents were probably most important not for the direct effect they had on food availability, but rather in demonstrating that the official agencies' demands were empty threats that could be ignored without penalty.

The second issue that arose was the conclusion among the donor community that there was a need to boost output as a long-run solution to the problem, and hence that there was a need to initiate development programs rather than just provide relief. As in the case of monitoring,

---

40. Privately, multilateral aid officials claim that their food is not diverted to the military because the military is fed from Chinese supplies, an account corroborated by the *Chochongryun* (Kirk and Hochstein 1997). As noted below, at least five NGOs have withdrawn from North Korea because of concerns along these lines.

41. For a statement of conditionality, see *Washington Post*, 21 October 1997. The General Accounting Office reported in October 1999 that 90 percent of the institutions receiving aid had not been visited, and that monitors had "rarely been allowed to observe the actual distribution of food to beneficiaries" (Barbara Crossette, *New York Times*, 12 October 1999).

42. In 1998, while the WFP was proclaiming conditionality, *Medicins Sans Frontieres* (Doctors Without Borders), at the time the largest relief agency operating in North Korea, discontinued its operations in North Korea on the grounds that the North Koreans denied it access to sick and malnourished children and channeled relief supplies to the children of the politically well-connected. In 1999 World Concern, a US-based NGO, halted shipments of relief supplies to North Korea after food destined for an orphanage and hospital disappeared. Oxfam pulled its five-member team out in December 1999, citing interference by North Korean authorities. They were followed in March 2000 by the French NGO Action Against Hunger (ACF), whose president, Roger Godino, cited similar interference by the North Korean authorities and claimed that "the massive UN aid effort, principally run by the World Food Programme and the United Nations Children's Fund (UNICEF) with significant US funds, is essentially a political and diplomatic operation. The United Nations is providing food aid, but not humanitarian aid" *Agence France Presse*, Paris, 7 March 2000. Less than one month later, the American NGO CARE pulled out, its President Peter D. Bell stating that "Despite a nearly four-year dialogue with the North Korean government regarding the importance of access, transparency, and accountability, the operational environment in North Korea has not progressed to a point where CARE feels it is possible to implement effective rehabilitation programs" (CARE 2000).

this is essentially misguided (as will be demonstrated in chapter 7), but it is understandable why donors would insist on actions that might reduce the apparent need to provide assistance for an indefinite period. This was also a contentious issue with the North, inasmuch as development could mean agricultural reform and a reduction of central control. In the end, South Korea, the European Union, the United States, and the UN agencies all augmented direct relief efforts with the provision of intermediate inputs such as fertilizers, high yield seed varieties, and demonstration projects.[43]

The People's Republic of Misery

As well as can be ascertained, North Korea by 2000 is into its ninth year of economic decline. It has been facing food shortages at least since the early 1990s, and is experiencing a famine of unknown severity. Robinson et al. (1999) reconstructed mortality rates for a single heavily affected province on the basis of refugee interviews and concluded that between 1995 and 1997 nearly 12 percent of that province's population had died. Non-governmental organizations, extrapolating to the entire country from a similar analysis of refugee interviews and observations on the ground, have produced estimates of famine-related deaths on the order of 2.8 to 3.5 million.[44] Likewise, US congressional staffers who visited the country concluded that from 1995 to 1998 between 900,000 and 2.4 million people

---

43. The United States, for example, donated 1,000 metric tons of potato seeds, fertilizer, and technical assistance to North Korea after gaining access to the suspected nuclear site at Kumchangri. The United States also permitted private NGOs to set up food-for-work programs as have been used in other famine situations and committed 100,000 tons of commodity food assistance to be used in these programs (USAID Press Release, 22 April 1999). This food would be provided directly, without the intermediation of US agencies. Unfortunately, the program did not seem to be operating as envisioned. One NGO representative indicated that half the food had been removed from the food-for-work program, the NGO was only able to observe two food distributions in four months, and interviews with recipients were discontinued (Gavitt 1999). This observer also reported that the military was "disbanding," as it no longer had sufficient food to feed all of the troops.

South Korea has indicated that it is prepared to provide seeds, 500,000 tons of fertilizer (worth approximately $100 million), and technical assistance. In press reports, these intentions have been linked to progress on divided family issues, though South Korean Unification Minister Kang In-duk denied any linkage. The Korean National Red Cross (KNRC) intermediated the donation of 50,000 tons of single-ingredient fertilizer, worth 16 billion won (approximately $13 million), which was donated by the South Korean government.

After visiting North Korea, the outgoing administrator of the UNDP, James Gustave Speth, indicated that his organization would focus on improving agricultural production and restoring output to its earlier peak, which, he argued, would be cheaper than providing aid in the long run. Pilot projects have involved the provision of such inputs as fertilizer and tractor tires and have resulted in rapid increases in yields.

44. See, for examples, Korea Buddhist Sharing Movement (1998) and Natsios (1999).

had died from starvation or hunger-related illnesses, with deaths peaking in 1997 (Kirk et al. 1998). South Korean sources have produced estimates of excess deaths in the range of 1.6 to 3.0 million for the period 1994-98 (Chang, 1999a), though P. Kim (1999) argues that this is probably an exaggeration. Eberstadt (1998c) observed that the number of delegates at the 1998 Supreme People's Assembly implied a mid-1998 population more than three million fewer than demographic projections made on the basis of 1989 data. Setting aside the official statement and the Robinson et al. study, which does not provide a nationwide figure, if the estimates of outside observers are accurate then they imply that a double-digit share of the precrisis population of roughly 22 million may well have succumbed.[45]

For their part, the North Koreans have not been forthcoming about the impact of the famine. High-level North Korean defector Hwang Jang-yop claimed that, prior to his defection in February 1997, he was informed by the Statistical Bureau of the Korean Workers' Party (KWP) that more than 1.5 million people had died of starvation and related illnesses in the previous two years. South Korean intelligence reportedly obtained a classified North Korean survey characterized as indicating that there had been 500,000 excess deaths annually, or 2.5 to 3.0 million since 1995, and the South Korean Unification Ministry later published an estimate of 500,00 to 800,000 excess deaths annually.[46] The North Korean Flood Damage Rehabilitation Committee called this "a whopping lie hurriedly invented and floated by the South Korean intelligence service."[47] Instead, Jon In-chen, the acting head of the Flood Damage Rehabilitation Committee, stated that there had been an increase in the mortality rate between 1995 and 1998 that would imply 55,000 excess deaths annually, or 220,000 for the period.[48] However, an earlier press report had cited a high-ranking KWP official visiting China as putting the death toll at two million.[49] Christian Lemaire, the UNDP's resident representative in Pyongyang, stated: "These three million dead are not in the areas that we monitor, and I doubt there are even three million people in total in

---

45. In addition to the apparently raised mortality rate, surveys conducted by international organizations have uncovered significant stunting among small children, and UNICEF reports that 20 percent of children suffer from iodine deficiency. However, it is unclear when the onset of this stunting began, and it may be due to environmental hazards as well as nutritional deficiencies. See Chang (1999a, 1999b) and Hoffman (1999) for informative assessments.

46. On the reputed North Korean document, see Australian Broadcast System, 17 February 1999, *Yonhap*, 17 February 1999, and Associated Press, 17 February 1999. On the South Korean estimate, see *Joongang Ilbo*, 4 March 1999.

47. Associated Press, 1 March 1999.

48. *Washington Post, Financial Times*, Reuters, Associated Press, 10 May 1999.

49. *Agence France-Presse*, 12 February 1998.

the areas that we don't monitor."[50] Yet Lemaire also disputed the emerging anecdotal evidence that the situation was improving.[51]

The dominant methodology of observing a heavily impacted region and then attempting to project onto the country as a whole would appear to be prone toward upward bias. However, if history is any indication, the situation is probably worse than we know. Eberstadt (n.d.) notes that among the worst (and least understood) famines in the past century took place in socialist countries in which governments were to a greater or lesser extent successfully able to restrict the flows of information and people both internally and externally. North Koreans have been conditioned by nearly two generations of extreme regimentation. It is not implausible, given the terrain and the instruments of social control at the disposal of the current regime, that it could prevent the mass population movements observed during famines in Africa or the Indian subcontinent. Indeed, the existence of "9/27 camps" for those arrested for leaving their villages in search of food was one of the reasons cited by *Medicins Sans Frontieres* (Doctors Without Borders) for its withdrawal from North Korea. There have been numerous reports of escapees to China being returned for internment or execution, the trafficking in women, and even instances of cannibalism.

Evidence suggests that the worst may have passed, at least temporarily, if for no other reason than the tremendous amount of international food and fertilizer aid going into the country. According to FAO/WFP (1999b), better weather and access to fertilizer contributed to an increase in food production in 1999. Kim Yong-sun, a senior official in the KWP, reportedly identified a shortage of energy, not food, as North Korea's foremost problem.

The primary agents of death in the North Korean famine are presumably tuberculosis, pneumonia, dysentery, and spontaneous abortions, not

---

50. Lorien Holland, *Agence France-Presse*, 1 February 1999.

51. Lemaire stated: "Essentially the situation is worsening. . .we are continually expanding the population that receives aid, but it is really a fire-fighting exercise that does not bring a solution" (Lorien Holland, *Agence France-Presse*, 1 February 1999). He was soon contradicted by his colleague, Tun Myat, Director of Resources for the WFP, who after visiting North Korea announced that the worst of the famine may have passed (Associated Press, 11 May 1999). A similar position was taken by Wattanapong Satatiwat, the World Vision Vice President for the Asia Pacific (Chris Johnson, Reuters, 2 June 1999). Catherine Bertini, head of the WFP, reported anecdotal evidence of improvement after visiting the country in August 1999 (Doug Struck, *Washington Post*, 16 August 1999). Erich Weingartner, the head of WFP's Food Aid Liaison Unit, indicated that malnutrition was slowly easing (*Agence France Presse*, 15 November 1999). David Morton, resident UN coordinator in Pyongyang, was quoted as stating that "the crisis peaked in the years between 1995 and 1997, and things have improved with better harvests in 1998 and 1999" (Elaine Kurtenbach, Associated Press, 14 December 1999). North Korean Vice Agricultural Minister Kim Yong-suk, in an address to the UN Food and Agriculture Organization, claimed that harvests were up by 40 percent (*Korea Herald*, 19 November 1999), but Morton denied that the crisis was over.

kwashiorkor, and we will probably only learn its full magnitude a decade hence by reading a graduate student dissertation, not by watching CNN.[52] Whatever the true numbers, the roots of this catastrophe are in political decisions made in Pyongyang, not in material resource constraints. Even taking as given the expenditure preferences of the Kim Jong-il regime, a relatively small increase in expenditure on imported food (in the hundreds of millions of dollars—not billions of dollars) would be sufficient to close the food gap. For example, if Hyundai were able to sell all of its berths on the Mt. Kumgang tour (admittedly an unlikely prospect), it would yield enough revenue to feed North Korea. Whether the revenues are used for this or other purposes is a political decision. (Conversely, as we will see in chapter 7, food aid is implicitly balance of payments support.) In this sense, the food crisis, while having a technical component, is essentially an issue of policy, both domestic and foreign. Even the World Food Program and the UN Food and Agriculture Organization have concluded that integration into the global economy is a prerequisite for the country to solve its food availability problem (FAO/WFP 1999b). Alternative North Korean policy responses to this humanitarian disaster are taken up in chapters 7 and 9, and the policy recommendations for the rest of the world are contained in the concluding chapter of this book.

---

52. North Korea is reportedly afflicted with the world's highest death rate from tuberculosis—80 persons for every 100,000. In comparison, the South Korean rate is 10.5 per 100,000 for men, and 3.7 per 100,000 for women. The World Health Organization has described the situation in the North as having "reached epidemic levels."

6

The Financial Crisis in the South

By 1996 it was clear to close observers that the South Korean economy was getting into increasing trouble.[1] An investment-led boom was coming to an end. Between 1994 and 1996, investment as a share of GDP rose by more than 2 percent, despite the fall in domestic saving. This of course simply meant that the boom was being financed by foreign capital inflow, as the current account deficit widened from 2 to 5 percent of GDP, a significant, though not historically unprecedented, level (figure 6.1).

Unlike Southeast Asia, where the investment boom was concentrated in the real estate sector, much of the capital was flowing into manufacturing, especially into the heavy industries dominated by the *chaebol*.[2] During

1. In a paper that is fascinating in retrospect, Young (1997), then head of a government think tank, addressing an audience in Washington in April 1997, accurately detailed the labor problems, the loss of political confidence, and the macroeconomic imbalances emerging in South Korea. He then dismissed concerns over the short-term debt and concluded: "There is, in fact, no economic crisis in Korea, if, by a crisis, we mean that there is imminent danger to the national economy—as was the case with Mexico in 1994" (p.4). He was not alone. As late as September 1997, IMF missions to Seoul were giving the economy a clean bill of health.

2. The South Korean banks had plunged into real estate earlier. According to Adelman (1999), in 1992 net real estate purchases by banks were nearly as large (89 percent) as total net lending. The run-up in land prices had peaked around this time, and land prices did not increase significantly in the years immediately preceding the crisis (OECD 1999). However, it appears that the channeling of investment into the traded-goods sector had one advantage—it allowed the economy to take advantage of the subsequent real exchange rate depreciation better than some of the other most heavily affected Asian economies (where the money had gone into real estate).

Figure 6.1 Saving, investment, and the current account

share of GNP (percentage)

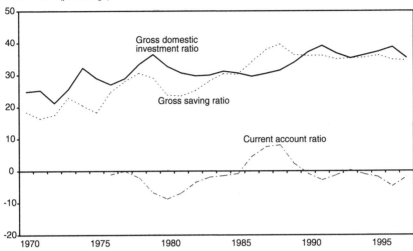

Source: Bank of Korea.

the 1994 to 1996 period, facility investment grew by 38.5 percent a year (Haggard and MacIntyre 1999). Much of it was financed by bank borrowing, which grew by more than five percentage points of GDP. Baily and Zitzewitz (1998) observe that almost half of South Korea's semiconductor capacity was installed after 1995.

This investment boom was facilitated by the ongoing financial liberalization program, in particular the phased liberalization of the capital account. While relatively more of the inflow in the previous decade had taken the form of FDI, in the mid-1990s the composition of the capital inflow began shifting toward more liquid portfolio investment and bank loans (figure 6.2). Beginning in 1993, firms were allowed to use short-term foreign currency borrowing to finance the importation of capital goods, either by borrowing directly from foreign banks or indirectly through South Korean banks. This change, in combination with relatively high interest rates in South Korea and continued restrictions on firms' ability to issue long-term foreign-currency-denominated bonds or finance through long-term foreign currency bank loans, encouraged an increased reliance on short-term finance.[3] According to Bank of International Settlements (BIS) figures, between 1994 and 1996 South Korea's foreign liabilities rose from $61 billion to $109 billion. Two-thirds of this was in the

---

3. There were restrictions on firms' ability to issue securities abroad and on contracting foreign loans at rates more than 100 basis points above LIBOR. These regulations strengthened the role of South Korean banks in intermediating external finance.

Figure 6.2 Capital inflows by type

percentage of GDP

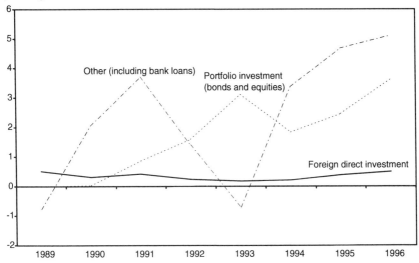

Source: Noland, Liu, Robinson, and Wang 1999, table 1.4.

form of short-term debt accumulated by South Korean banks, which was twice the level of South Korea's foreign exchange reserves at the time. Of the $109 billion liability, 34 percent was held by EU banks, 24 percent by Japanese banks, and 9 percent by US banks (IMF 1999a). The South Korean foreign debt proved to be considerably larger than these figures indicated, but even on the basis of these misleading figures one could get a picture of the situation.

Rapid growth of credit, even the rapid buildup of foreign debt, is not necessarily a bad thing as long as the capital is used to fund projects with high rates of return. The trouble was that rates of return were low. Kwack (1994) calculated that by 1990 the rate of return in South Korean manufacturing had already fallen below that in the United States. Similar results were obtained by Pyo (1999), who found that by the mid-1990s the rate of return on capital had fallen below that in Japan. Baily and Zitzewitz (1998) uncovered significant examples of industries, such as the semiconductor industry, in which capital intensity had risen to the level of the United States, but in which productivity was only half as high.

As a consequence, the rate of total factor productivity (TFP) growth began to slow, and export profit margins were squeezed (Kwack 1999). Productivity was low for a variety of reasons. One was that much of this capital was flowing into industries that were arguably characterized by excess capacity.[4] As production came on line, export volumes rose, but

---

4. See Makin (1997a, b, and c, and 1998).

Figure 6.3 Unit price of electronics and DRAMs

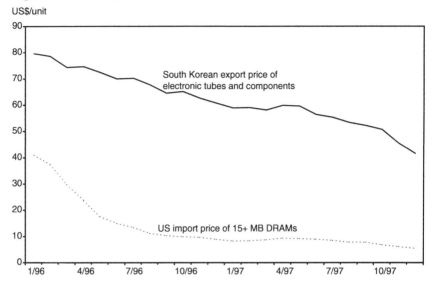

US$/unit

Sources: Bank of Korea; US Deparment of Commerce.

export prices fell. Beginning in 1994, South Korea's terms of trade began to deteriorate. The US dollar export price index for Korean electronic components fell by nearly 50 percent between January 1996 and the end of 1997, while the price of a 16MB DRAM[5] fell from more than $40 to less than $10 over the same period (figure 6.3). Part of the fall in DRAM prices surely reflected product cycle effects, but part of the fall reflected excess supply of a product characterized by enormous capital intensity in production and fabricated by firms with extremely leveraged financial structures. Anecdotal evidence suggests significant price weakening for other key manufactured exports such as steel, automobiles, and ships, though the nature of these markets makes documentation difficult.[6] As the OECD (not an organization prone to hyperbole) put it, "*Chaebol* governance structures were slow to internalize these basic changes in international competitive conditions, and *shareholder value was systematically being destroyed from the late 1980s onwards*" (OECD 1998, 23) [emphasis added].

Changing external conditions also proved to be detrimental to South Korea. Japan, its largest export market, went into recession. Moreover,

---

5. DRAM = Dynamic Random Access Memory chip.

6. Price changes for both cars and ships are difficult to document because of the differentiated nature of the products. Moreover, industry sources indicate that measured prices may not accurately reflect actual transaction prices due to rebates and other sales incentives that reportedly were employed aggressively during this period. It goes without saying that these are relatively capital intensive goods, produced by firms with fragile balance sheets.

the Japanese yen began to depreciate significantly against the US dollar—
implying an effective real appreciation of the won, which floated in a
narrow range against the dollar. This further eroded South Korean competitiveness in the Japanese market and in third country markets such as
the United States where South Korean exporters went head to head against
the Japanese.[7] As a consequence of falling external demand and falling
export prices, export growth began to slow in 1996 and turned negative
in 1997.

Financial Fragility

Adverse external conditions redounded onto the domestic economy. Profit
margins were halved; asset prices began to fall (OECD 1998). The stock
market, which had peaked in 1994, had been drifting downward for two
years, reflecting the deterioration of the real economy. It would lose one-
third of its value by the end of 1997. The financial health of the grossly
over-leveraged *chaebol* began to look increasingly dodgy. Operating cash
flow as a percentage of interest payments was only 80 percent in 1996,
raising questions about the health of the financial sector as a whole. This
all occurred in the context of a South Korean financial system increasingly
dependent on relatively liquid foreign capital inflows.

The problem was that this capital was flowing into a fragile, bank-
centered financial system that was incapable of efficiently intermediating
the capital inflow. The system was fragile for two reasons. First, similar
to the experiences of other developing countries and small industrialized
economies, South Korea exhibited more volatility in macroeconomic
aggregates and financial market indicators than larger, more diversified,
developed economies (table 6.1). At the microeconomic level this hampered risk assessment, and at the macroeconomic level it created greater
vulnerability to economic shocks.[8]

Furthermore, South Korea had a relatively concentrated financial system, with the six largest banks accounting for more than half of the
banking system. In fact, the assets of each of these six banks accounted
for about 10 percent of GDP, compared to less than 5 percent in most
other OECD countries (Claessens, Ghosh, and Scott 1999). Moreover, these
institutions tended to hold less diversified portfolios than their counter-

---

7. South Korean exchange rate policy at this juncture might be described as a quasi-peg
against the US dollar. The won followed a controlled float, but was held within a narrow
range of 770 to 800 won to the dollar from early 1993 to mid-1996, when it was allowed to
depreciate by around 10 percent. Noland, Liu, Robinson, and Wang (1999) demonstrate
that developments in Japan have a major impact on South Korea's external position due to
the strong trade links and relatively close competition in third country markets.

8. For evidence on this point, see Stiglitz (1998).

Table 6.1 Volatility of macroeconomic indicators and banking aggregates[a]

	GDP	Inflation	Bank Deposits[b]	Bank Credit to Private Sector[b]
India	2.2	4.1	3.4	4.6
Hong Kong	3.4	3.5	7.9	6.9
South Korea	**3.5**	**7.2**	**5.3**	**5.6**
Singapore	3.3	2.6	5.7	4.6
Taiwan	2.4	5.5	6.4	8.7
Indonesia	2.0	3.1	7.8	20.1
Malaysia	3.0	2.4	8.8	8.4
Thailand	2.7	4.6	6.6	6.5
Memorandum:				
United States	2.1	3.1	4.4	3.4
Japan	1.8	2.0	2.5	2.5
Germany	1.8	1.9	5.4	3.1

a. Measured as the standard deviation of annual percentage changes, 1980-95.

b. Measured as the percentage of nominal GDP.

Source: Goldstein and Turner (1996).

parts in developed countries. A higher share of assets was denominated in the domestic currency, and assets were more concentrated in terms of sectoral distribution. This relative lack of portfolio diversification contributed to financial fragility, creating vulnerability to economic downturns. Given its history of financial repression, South Korea effectively had a developing country financial system despite its relatively high income level.

In South Korea these underlying factors were exacerbated by a mismatch of assets and liabilities in both financial and non-financial sector firms. With domestic interest rates high relative to foreign interest rates, and short-run capital controls liberalized before long-run controls had been removed, the banks were induced to finance long-term domestic lending through short-term foreign borrowing.[9] This left them (and, by extension, domestic lending) vulnerable to either foreign interest rate spikes, domestic currency depreciation, or a creditor panic. In the case of

9. Notoriously, some of the newly created merchant banks simply used short-run foreign borrowing to speculate in risky markets such as the Russian bond market. Non-financial firms circumvented the capital controls by using foreign subsidiaries and affiliates to borrow when the parent could not do so under South Korean rules. These practices contributed to the chaos in December 1997, when the value of South Korean liabilities could not be ascertained with any accuracy.

South Korea, limits on foreign exchange exposure were circumvented by lending directly to firms in dollars. Unfortunately, in practice this embodied significant maturity mismatches, and when creditors panicked and refused to rollover loans, the banks were unable to liquidate their positions quickly in order to repay their creditors.[10]

Domestic policy may have contributed to financial fragility in at least two distinct ways. Financial systems such as the one in South Korea tend to be under-diversified. The presence of foreign financial institutions may effectively increase diversification and reduce fragility. For example, foreign banks tend to be less exposed to the host country's domestic economy and, thereby, in a better position to maintain lending during downturns in which host country institutions may be far more negatively impacted.[11] Lack of financial openness, therefore, can contribute to financial crises. Indeed, in South Korea, these problems were exacerbated by the relative exclusion of foreign financial institutions that could have partly offset the lack of system-wide portfolio diversification.[12]

More fundamentally, domestic policy may have contributed directly to the financial crisis by encouraging financial institutions to act in economically inefficient or irrational ways. Before the crisis broke, the South Korean government had maintained considerable involvement in the financial system. It continued to issue detailed regulations regarding corporate financial decisions, including restrictions on overseas investments, restrictions on equity finance, and restrictions on overseas finance. Participants in the financial markets were subject to a positive list system, which inhibited the introduction of innovative financial instruments and practices. The pervasive pattern of government intervention created a symbiotic relationship between the government and the private sector, eroding private sector autonomy and facilitating the corruption of the political system. Indeed, even if the liberalization program had been implemented on schedule, South Korea would still have had among the most repressed financial systems in Asia.

The banks, which had previously been government owned, had been privatized. Yet the banks retained a somewhat bureaucratic character, manifested by overstaffing and an implicit guarantee of lifetime employment. Bankers continued to set interest rates in an administered manner rather than by competition in an open marketplace. They still channeled capital to politically connected or preferred borrowers rather than to

---

10. See Aizenman and Marion (1999).

11. Indeed, in the case of South Korea, Choi and Kang (1999) in a survey of 850 firms find that precrisis access to foreign lenders was positively associated with postcrisis access to capital.

12. Foreign banks' activities were restricted, although under the reform plan they were allowed to open multiple branches.

borrowers that were independently judged to represent profitable investment opportunities with good credit risks.[13] Returns on assets were low, compared both to returns observed in other countries, and to the returns on assets of foreign banks operating in the South Korean market. Presumably this reflected the prevalence of non-economic criteria in lending decisions.[14]

These problems were not invisible. Writing in 1996, the present author observed that:

> The potential problem with the system is the implicit guarantee that banks not be allowed to fail; this, together with deposit insurance, simultaneously creates an incentive for banks to seek risk, while it relieves depositors of the incentive to monitor bank health. This problem is compounded by non-performing loan reporting requirements that the OECD describes as "weaker" than in many OECD countries. Although the banking sector is probably in better shape than in some times in the past, there has been an increase in unsecured loan defaults in recent years. The Office of Banking Supervision reports that bad loans at commercial banks totaled W2.7 trillion through the first six months of 1996, up 17 percent from the same period in the previous year. Moreover, the Korean definition of bad loans is more narrow than that commonly used abroad, and foreign bankers estimate the true bad loan problem may be three times as large as admitted. The commercial banking sector may be significantly exposed to risks associated with lending to property developers and construction companies during the stock and real estate asset bubble during the late 1980s, as well as the restructuring of small and medium-sized enterprises (SMEs) in labor-intensive manufacturing sectors. Concerns about the banking system are further aggravated by the MOFE's dual function as a promoter and supervisor of financial institutions, and legitimate questions can be raised about the degree of independence of the regulatory authorities. . . . The bottom line is that Korea should be concerned about the strength of its banking system, *and much of this concern is related to domestic financial repression and is unrelated to the issue of external financial liberalization.* Market discipline does not work when there is a lack of information, or when the notion that banks cannot fail is widely held. The appropriate responses are to deal with the structural problems of the banking system (which are likely to involve both domestic and

---

13. For example, Kang Kyung-shik, a Minister of Finance and Economy in the Kim Young-sam administration, and Kim In-ho, a former senior presidential economic advisor in the same government, were convicted in August 1999 for pressuring banks to make improper loans to ailing companies. (Some have argued that these prosecutions were politically motivated. For our purposes, prosecutorial motivation is irrelevant to the issue at hand—that state power was used to channel capital.) Another example would be the late 1996 "window guidance," which required the banks to hold on to their stock portfolios in a vain attempt to halt the decline of the stock market—thus ultimately increasing the banks' losses. In part, such interventions were made possible because the appointment of bank presidents still began with the recommendations of a committee of the Ministry of Finance and Economy (MOFE). In September 1996, the rules were changed to end the current "rubber stamp" bank president selection committees and increase the role of outside directors. Under the revised system, the outside directors would be authorized to recommend bank officers and to decide on major managerial issues. Those working for the top ten big businesses would not be eligible to be outside directors. The system was revised again following the crisis.

14. See Baily and Zitzewitz (1998) on these points.

international liberalization together with strengthened prudential supervision by public authorities) to strengthen public disclosure requirements, and to signal limits on public bailouts (Noland 1996, 12-14) [emphasis in the original].[15]

When the financial crisis broke, the official government figure on the share of non-performing loans (NPLs) was 0.8 percent, while private analysts were putting the figure anywhere from 6 percent to 30 percent, with most estimates in the upper end of this range.[16]

Outside the banking system, there was more progress. Despite unsupportive official policies, the equity market developed, but liquidity was insufficient, and a large backlog developed of companies waiting to be listed. This backlog at times exceeded more than 300 firms. Money markets and bond markets were still underdeveloped, having only a limited range of maturities and no real secondary markets. Foreign investors were subject to equity ownership ceilings in listed South Korean companies and were even more severely restricted in the bond market. The closure to foreign investors of the long-term bond market created the perverse incentive to raise capital through short-term borrowing. In part because of these restrictions, South Korean interest rates remained far above world interest rates, and the prices of foreign-owned shares in South Korean companies were above those in the domestic stock market (though this gap narrowed over time). Thus the cost of capital to South Korean corporations was higher than it would have been if there had been a full financial opening. Government interventions in the market drove up the cost of capital further still.[17]

The Bubble Story

Such financial practices may be sustainable as long as the rate of economic growth remains high, for financial institutions compensate for the low effective rate of return on loans to these preferred borrowers with high rates of return on other loans. However, with a slowing of the growth rate, the bad loan drag begins to inhibit the ability of banks and non-

---

15. In October 1996, the present author visited Seoul and gave a talk on the state of the North Korean economy that received wide press coverage. The following month the present author returned to Seoul and gave a talk on the South Korean banking system to a large audience at the Federation of Korean Industries (FKI) in which the South Korean banking system was characterized as having "Ponzi-scheme aspects." This speech received no press coverage.

16. See Aliber (1998) and *Washington Post*, 30 March 1998.

17. For example, in October 1995, the government announced that, in the case of direct investments abroad of $100 million or more by Korean corporations, at least one-fifth of the funds would have to be raised at home, where the cost was higher.

bank lending institutions to supply credit to the economy, setting off a self-reinforcing downward spiral.

In South Korea, these investments were intermediated by local banks and non-bank financial institutions in the context of the widely held belief that the South Korean government would not allow these institutions to fail.[18] Financial institutions lent for property and stock market investments, often using the very same land, real estate, and financial assets as collateral. This set up a self-reinforcing upward spiral—as financial institutions lent into these markets, the value of existing collateral increased, permitting greater lending, which in turn drove up asset prices. Lower international interest rates, together with the narrowly floating exchange rate, encouraged financial institutions to borrow foreign exchange abroad in order to convert it into domestic currency and lend it at home, or, alternatively, lend directly in foreign currencies to circumvent restrictions on foreign exchange exposure. Reckless practices were facilitated by weak prudential supervision and a culture of cronyism.[19]

Such conditions are not indefinitely sustainable. Indeed, the list of real and financial shocks that could reverse such a process is nearly endless. (Perhaps this is why such bubbles are not observed more regularly.) In particular, Aizenman and Marion (1999) argue that a key variable is foreign creditors' assessments of usable foreign exchange reserves. Foreign investors lend into emerging markets under conditions of moral hazard, expecting an official bailout if a local institution fails (see box 6.1). They may quickly reduce credit if they reassess the level of "usable" reserves relative either to the level of foreign debt or to the likelihood of repayment.[20]

Once in reverse, the process feeds on itself: asset prices begin to fall, creating both non-performing loans (NPLs) and eroding the value of collateral. Lending contracts, reducing asset prices further, create more bad loans and destroy more collateral. Foreign lending dries up, and net capital inflow turns negative as both residents and foreigners rush for the exits.

---

18. The government had intervened numerous times to rescue the *chaebol*. Similarly, it was widely believed that no South Korean bank would be allowed to fail due to the state's intimate involvement with the financial system.

19. See IMF (1999b) for details of the precrisis supervisory system.

20. One theme of the Asian financial crisis was the revelation, first in Thailand, that "usable" central bank foreign exchange reserves were lower than official reserve figures because they had been committed to forward market operations. In the case of South Korea, rumors circulated in the fall of 1997 that "usable" reserves were lower than the official figure because, like the Bank of Thailand, the Bank of Korea had committed some of them in forward market deals, and that the Bank of Korea had deposited them with the foreign subsidiaries of South Korean banks. The latter funds might not be fully recoverable if they had been used to meet the commercial banks' short-term obligations, lent-on, or seized by foreign creditors in the case of a default.

Box 6.1 Moral Hazard, the Domestic Dimension

For every borrower there is a lender. The issue at both the South Korean and international level concerns the extent to which this lending was motivated by moral hazard—the expectation that the lender would be bailed out by a third party if the borrower was unable to repay its debts. In the case of South Korea, there is a long history of the government coming to the rescue of both financial and non-financial firms, and Leipziger (1998a) argues that the extraordinary leverage of the *chaebol* was *prima facie* evidence of moral hazard, since "no respectable banker should have been lending to the *chaebol* under these circumstances were they not assured that the government would make sure that losses were managed in the event of a downturn." Haggard and MacIntyre (1999) counter that *chaebol* had been allowed to fail in the past, and they point to the bankruptcies of Hanbo and Kia as creating real uncertainty in the minds of lenders about how far the government was willing to go to rescue distressed firms.

However, the last major failure prior to the crisis, Kukje, had been more than a decade earlier, and was regarded as an exceptional case by contemporary observers (E. M. Kim 1997). The collapse of Hanbo and the political scandal it unleashed doubtlessly forced a reconsideration of the "rules of the game." But by the time Kia was nationalized and its management was dismissed in October 1997, the crisis was well underway—far, far too late to have any constructive effect on lenders' behavior. Indeed, the introduction of non-risk-adjusted deposit insurance in June 1996, under conditions of less than stellar prudential regulation, could be interpreted as providing an incentive for pre-cisely the risky behavior that South Korean banks subsequently displayed. The announcement in August 1997 that the government was considering socializing risk by guaranteeing the foreign debts of South Korean banks could also have been regarded as an invitation to "gamble for resurrection" on the part of failing South Korean banks.

These refer to precrisis moral hazards. Stiglitz (1999) argues that the crisis response program undertaken by the South Korean government and the IMF had domestic moral hazard aspects as well. Specifically, he argues that the root of the crisis was South Korea's large private foreign exchange liabilities; the decision to use high interest rates to defend the won in effect protected the firms, which held unhedged foreign exchange liabilities at the expense of firms that had hedged or simply not taken on foreign debt.

This, in turn, puts pressure on the exchange rate peg, or in this case on the narrow float or quasi-peg administered by the authorities. The conventional remedy is to raise interest rates, but given the fragile state of the domestic financial system, monetary authorities are forced to choose between maintaining the peg or the solvency of the domestic financial system. Inevitably, the peg is abandoned, and the currency collapses. For parties with a significant amount of unhedged foreign currency debt, the exchange rate depreciation means insolvency, as the domestic resource cost of debt service skyrockets. Bankruptcies cascade through the financial system. Yet, while both the real and financial sectors are contracting, inflation accelerates as the price of imports increases.

Eventually resources begin shifting into the export sector in response to this enhanced competitiveness. The economy exports its way back to full employment, suitably defined, recognizing that some part of the prior capital investment has been wasted and is unlikely ever to achieve expected returns on its installed value. Ergo, ranking *chaebol* on the basis of the book value of their assets is a mug's game.

Internal Triggers

As conditions worsened in 1996, the margin of error for the over-leveraged *chaebol* began to evaporate, and in January 1997 Hanbo Steel, the seventeenth largest *chaebol* ranked by sales, collapsed amid $6 billion of outstanding debts.[21] The collapse of Hanbo, the first major *chaebol* to go bankrupt since Kukje more than a decade earlier, was to have repercussions beyond its debts: a subsequent series of bribery arrests, culminating in the arrest and conviction of President Kim Young-sam's son and political confidante, Kim Hyun-chol, shook the political establishment and greatly damaged the elder Kim.[22]

As the spring wore on, the situation increasingly looked like a systemic crisis. In March Sammi Steel, another of the top thirty *chaebol*, went bust, driving up interest rates in the large corporate bond market and imposing negative externalities on all corporate borrowers. Sammi's failure was followed in April by the fall of yet another top thirty *chaebol*, Jinro. During the second quarter of 1997, spreads on South Korean government bonds (the excess nominal return over equivalent US Treasuries) began to widen, while, as points of comparison, those on Indonesian and Malaysian government bonds remained unchanged. The market was signaling an increase of country risk in South Korea.

The South Korean government had intervened numerous times in the past to save the *chaebol* (see box 6.1). Having adopted a more hands-off approach, however, the government did not intervene to save Hanbo's management. Hanbo was effectively nationalized, and its management

---

21. Hanbo is often referred to as the fourteenth largest *chaebol*. This is on the basis of the book value of its assets, a valuation that proved grossly misleading.

22. According to Adelman (1999), "During 1996, a costly, and ultimately unsuccessful, bailout was attempted. . . . Commercial banks were forced by politicians intimately linked to President Kim to extend new loans amounting to $7.2 billion to Hanbo, under threat of firing their presidents; those bank presidents who disobeyed the order to extend loans to Hanbo were put in jail. . . . Hanbo Steel had been started by a low-level retired tax official with no business experience but who maintained close personal relationships with many corrupt politicians who were intimates of the President. Hanbo was seriously mismanaged, had an astronomical debt-equity ratio of 16, and folded in January 1997 despite the rescue attempt." The collapse of Hanbo was the subject of investigation by the courts and the National Assembly. A number of politicians (from both parties) and bankers were jailed.

removed. With the additional failures of Sammi and Jinro, the government reverted to its old ways, and, in the words of Haggard and MacIntyre (1999), "attempted to orchestrate a more concerted response" to the growing problem of bankruptcies and defaults.

In April, South Korean banks agreed to a "voluntary" "Standstill Agreement." If a distressed firm was judged "solvent," then a consortium of banks would be bailed-in to forestall bankruptcy, despite the adverse impact that this would have on the banks' balance sheets. This, in turn, would be offset by government capital injections effected through the purchase of non-performing loans. The apparent imposition of some conditionality, together with the infusion of public money, was well received, and the stock market experienced a brief rally. The arrangement proved short-lived, however. By the end of 1997, the four firms that had come under the standstill agreement were all in some form of receivership (OECD 1998).

The real turning point in the crisis was the failure of Kia, the nation's third largest carmaker.[23] Kia's public travails began on 23 June 1997 when the firm's chairman, Kim Sun-hong, appealed to the government for assistance in obtaining a workout agreement from its creditors on $8 billion in maturing loans. What ensued was a bare knuckles political fight in which Kia's management exploited loopholes in bankruptcy laws and the government's weakening political fortunes in an ultimately unsuccessful bid to retain control. It was not until 22 October that the government finally succeeded in nationalizing Kia and ousting its management.[24] The spreads on government bonds widened further.

External Triggers

If domestic turmoil was its only problem, South Korea might have been able to avoid the conflagration that engulfed it in December 1997. Instead, South Korea was rocked by the shocks emanating from the financial crisis that had seized Southeast Asia, inaugurating its worst economic crisis in more than a generation. In July 1997, the Bank of Thailand severed the baht's link to the US dollar, allowing it to float.[25] Financial turmoil quickly spread through Southeast Asia and reached South Korea the following month as the won came under pressure. On 27 August, a high ranking

---

23. Even this was botched. The chairman of Mazda, Kia's largest shareholder, reportedly learned of the decision via a news broadcast.

24. See Haggard and MacIntyre (1999) for an insightful description of the Kia saga.

25. South Korean financial institutions had lent $173 million to Thai finance companies, most of which were not guaranteed by the Thai government. However, external developments in South Korea were dominated by the actions of foreign financial institutions, not by the direct exposure of South Korean institutions to Southeast Asia.

official of the Korean Ministry of Finance and Economy (MOFE), in one of history's weirder abuses of metaphor, told a Seoul press conference that the Bank of Korea would defend its "Maginot Line" of 900 won to the dollar. Unfortunately, this new Maginot Line was about as effective as the French original, and the level was soon breached.

Conditions continued to deteriorate through the fall. The Bank of Korea continued to intervene in the foreign exchange market in a futile attempt to defend the won. To the surprise and shock of many, Taiwan devalued its currency on 18 October. The day after Kia was nationalized, Hong Kong began to be hit by currency speculation. After authorities there raised interest rates, the fall in the Hong Kong stock market set off a worldwide wave of stock market declines. As volume dropped precipitously on the South Korean foreign exchange market, the daily exchange rate band was widened by 10 percent on 20 October (see box 6.2). By the end of October, emerging markets were being routed.

On 17 November, in a press conference that would have been farcical if not for the stakes, Ministry of Finance and Economy officials solemnly declared that they would defend their newest Maginot Line of 1000 won to the dollar. They spent billions trying, but the following day the level was once again breached, and on 19 November the Bank of Korea was forced to announce that it was once again widening the daily exchange rate band and "temporarily" suspending its defense operations. Within a month, the government was forced to abandon all pretense of controlling the exchange rate, and on 16 December authorities abolished the daily exchange rate band. The currency went into free fall, bottoming out during the final week of December at more than 1,995 won to the dollar. By then, the stock market had lost more than half its value in eight months (figure 6.4).

Developments in the currency market fed back onto the domestic financial system. As the exchange rate collapsed, financial and non-financial firms with unhedged foreign-currency-denominated debt found themselves being crushed by a mounting debt burden in domestic resource cost terms. (This was the justification for subsequent IMF policy recommendations to raise interest rates in order to stabilize both exchange rates and the domestic resource burden of outstanding foreign debt.) At the same time, foreign lenders (especially the Japanese banks) were refusing to roll over existing short-term loans, and the supply of foreign capital dried up.

The Crisis

In October 1997 policymakers initially exacerbated the situation by announcing the bailout of a small bank. The situation was worsened by a clumsily announced nationalization of the automaker Kia. The market

Box 6.2   Contagion

How much of the South Korean crisis was caused by contagion—the increase in the probability of a crisis due to knowledge of a crisis elsewhere? There are essentially two channels through which this could occur.

One is through herding. The argument is that, as global investment opportunities increase, investors' direct knowledge of local situations decreases. As a consequence, investors are forced to rely more on their observations of the behavior of other investors (who may have better or inside knowledge of local conditions) rather than on their own direct observation of local fundamentals. Hence, once one investor goes a particular direction, there is a tendency for the herd to stampede (Calvo and Mendoza 2000). It may also be the case that an event in one group of imperfectly observed countries encourages more intense scrutiny of other group members, which can lead to the transmission of a shock throughout the group (Drazen 1997). This is sometimes referred to as "the wake-up call."

Krugman (1997) argues that agents such as pension fund managers are risk averse with respect to their own income. Since their compensation is often determined relative to the performance of others, they will tend to follow the behavior of the herd. Krugman also argues that asymmetries may be at work, in that managers may face greater punishment for staying in a particular market when others are fleeing if the others are right, than rewards for better than expected performance if the agent stays in and the others turn out to be wrong.

The operational implication is that, if contagion is due to herding, it will be driven by macroeconomic or financial similarities across countries.

The other possibility is that contagion occurs due to direct and indirect trade links. If one country experiences a currency depreciation, then its competitors must also depreciate to maintain relative competitiveness or suffer the consequences. In this case, trade linkages would be the drivers.

There is not a well-developed body of empirical evidence on this issue. Glick and Rose (1998) attempt to distinguish between the two channels and find that the trade link hypothesis does a better job of explaining contagion than "the wake-up call" hypothesis.

But what about South Korea? Kaminsky and Reinhart (1999) observe that South Korean trade and financial links with the other crisis countries are generally low; linkages are the highest with Malaysia. However, Park and Song (1998) point out that, while South Korea's links to individual Southeast Asian countries might be low, in the aggregate they could be significant.

Park and Song (1998) of the South Korean bank-supported Korea Institute of Finance (KIF) then go on to produce a morass of sometimes conflicting and ultimately unpersuasive time-series econometric evidence in an attempt to demonstrate that South Korea was a victim of contagion. It does appear to be the case that, prior to the crisis, foreign investors tended to be herding, positive feedback traders (Choe, Kho, and Stulz [1999] and Kim and Wei [1999]). However, these last two sources disagree over the ability of the South Korean stock market to handle the foreigners. The former find that their presence did not have a major impact on prices, while the latter conclude that the foreigners exacerbated price movements. Kim and Wei (1999) go on to argue that local investors, who tended to be negative feedback contrarians before the crisis, joined the foreign bandwagon once the crisis was underway.

Figure 6.4 South Korea's nominal exchange rate and stock market changes

index (Jan 1996=100)

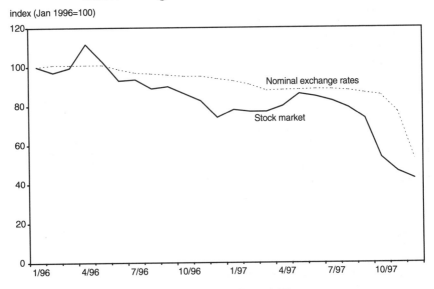

Source: Noland, Liu, Robinson, and Wang 1999, figure 1.3E.

rightly regarded this as a socialization of risk, and the spread on Korean sovereign debt began rising rapidly. Fitch IBCA, Standard & Poor's, and Moody's all downgraded Korean commercial bank debt and began issuing warnings on sovereigns as the country began drifting toward a sovereign debt crisis[26] (see box 6.3).

As the markets declined, net capital outflow was manifested in reduced roll-over rates by foreign bank creditors. These rollovers fell from about 80 percent in October 1997 to 50 percent in November to about 30 percent in December (Jwa and Huh 1998). Net foreign lending to South Korean banks fell from $18 billion in 1996 to -$6 billion in 1997 (Shin and Wang 1999, table 3). Much of this decline was due to Japanese banks, which had their own problems at home and which were possibly less "loyal" to their Korean borrowers than to subsidiaries of Japanese firms in Southeast Asia (Aliber 1998). By late November, the situation grew desperate, as Japanese banks began calling back loans and cutting off credit instead of rolling over the loans. The effect was a huge swing in net private lending, which went from $100 billion in the first nine months of 1997 to -$20 billion in the last quarter of that year (Adelman 1999). This net

---

26. The ratings agencies' failure to signal the emerging crisis earlier was not unique. As Adelman (1999) points out, between March 1993 and March 1997, South Korea's ranking on the *Euromoney* creditworthiness index actually rose from 32nd to 22nd.

Box 6.3 Moral Hazard, the International Dimension

The issue of moral hazard is not confined to domestic lenders. Some have argued that international lending, too, was affected by moral hazard (e.g., Calomis (1998), Lindsey (1998), and Meltzer (1998)). The argument is typically made that the 1997 Mexican bailout reduced international investors' appraisal of the riskiness of lending in emerging markets—if conditions turned sour, international financial institutions such as the IMF, together with national governments, would act to forestall a default or other crisis. The result was capital inflows on terms that did not reflect the true underlying risk.

The logic of this argument is unassailable. What is questionable is its relevance, and frankly the answer to the counterfactual of what would have happened under different institutional arrangements is ultimately speculative.

Nevertheless, one can examine three sorts of evidence, none of which appears to support the notion of moral hazard as a significant determinant of international lending behavior. The first is that, despite the worsening South Korean economic conditions in 1996, professional forecasters appear to have had no inkling of the impending upheaval. To illustrate, the *Blue Chip* consensus forecast of the 1998 change in the US-Korean bilateral real exchange rate is shown in figure 6.5. As late as November 1997, the *Blue Chip* consensus was real appreciation of the won in 1998. By January 1998, the consensus was for a 35 percent depreciation—a 36 percent forecast revision in two months. As for GDP growth, from February 1997 the consensus forecast for Korea remained between 5.8 percent and 6.3 percent for 1997 until significant downward revisions were made in the December and January forecasts—i.e., the professionals thought the good times would last forever. (They would probably argue that the Asian crisis was a "peso problem" phenomenon—a large impact event of low probability, and that their forecasts were accurate in discounting its likelihood in any particular forecast period.) However, moving closer to the markets does not appear to strengthen the moral hazard case.

If moral hazard considerations were motivating risk assessments, one would expect to see this reflected in the ratings of international private ratings agencies such as Moody's, Standard & Poor's, and Fitch IBCA, which take into account the possibility of international bailouts when setting their ratings. However, these firms' ratings of South Korean debt did not improve after the Mexican bailout, as one would expect if there had been a systemic reduction in risk faced by private investors. Rather, these firms' ratings remained unchanged through 1996 and were lagging indicators of the unfolding crisis in 1997. Presumably, the difficulty encountered by the ratings agencies in spotting the emerging crisis was in part due to the lack of transparency noted previously.

Well, what about actual market transactions? If the moral hazard hypothesis was the motivating behavior, then one would expect to observe a decline in spreads after the Mexican bailout in 1995. Instead, the spreads show little trend at all. Again, this is not dispositive—one would need a model of the underlying fundamentals to generate counterfactual movements in spreads to compare to the ones actually observed.

Thus, while the logic of the moral hazard argument is compelling, the evidence of its empirical significance is considerably less so. Rather than moral hazard, irrational exuberance, myopia, or just plain greed and fear appear to be more compelling explanations of investor behavior.

Figure 6.5 South Korean real GDP growth forecast and expected real exchange rate change

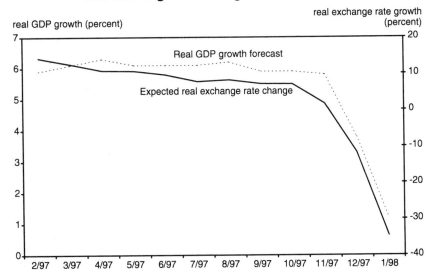

Source: Noland, Liu, Robinson, and Wang 1999, figure 1.4.

capital outflow drained official reserves and put more downward pressure on the won.

The possibility of default loomed. The IMF reports that, during the months of November and December 1997, the Bank of Korea deposited $23 billion of its foreign exchange reserves with the overseas subsidiaries of South Korean banks so that those institutions could meet their short-term foreign exchange obligations, and that by the end of November "usable" reserves had fallen to $5 billion (IMF 1999b).[27] In mid-November, in an attempt to maintain public confidence in the banking system, the government issued a blanket guarantee of all deposits until the end of 2000. This possibly bolstered public confidence, but it also created an enormous contingent liability for the government.

South Korea initially attempted to obtain non-conditioned balance of payments support from Japan and the United States, but, rebuffed by Tokyo and Washington, the government announced on 21 November that it would seek assistance from the IMF.[28]

Eleven days of tense negotiations ensued. The South Korean government constantly revised upwards its foreign debt figures, though it is

---

27. It has been claimed that much of this actually occurred earlier, even before the Thai devaluation, as the Bank of Korea lent out its reserves to support the commercial banks.

28. After South Korea initiated negotiations with the Fund, the ratings agencies cut their ratings of South Korean sovereign debt.

unclear whether this was a matter of spreading misinformation or disinformation.[29] It also leaked confidential IMF documents.[30] Uncertainty about the numbers and the quality and transparency of policymaking exacerbated the crisis. In the end, faced with potential default by a strategically important country and the world's 11th largest economy, prospects of deleterious effects on Japan's fragile financial system, and signs that the financial markets in Russia and Brazil were beginning to catch the Asian flu, the IMF blinked. On 3 December, agreement was reached on a $55 billion package, then the largest in history, nearly 20 times South Korea's quota.[31] In return, South Korea committed itself to broad, though vaguely worded, reforms, as discussed in the following section.[32]

Predictably, the candidates in the ongoing South Korean presidential election campaign denounced the program, with front-runner Kim Dae-jung announcing that he might renegotiate the pact if elected. The National Assembly refused to consider a package of financial reform legislation proposed by the Ministry of Finance and Economy, and the bank regulators marched on the National Assembly to protest their possible reorganization. Moreover, given the vagueness of the reform commitments, outside observers expressed skepticism about their eventual implementation. Market reaction was decisive: despite the provision of $59 billion in support, South Korean asset prices continued to plummet. This prompted the presidential candidates to reverse course and announce that they

---

29. Given the non-transparency of South Korean financial practices and the rapid turnover of top officials, it is plausible that senior policymakers were truly ill-informed about the state of the country's balance of payments position.

30. The Fund staff's report to its Board was leaked to the *Chosun Ilbo*, which posted the documents on its web site. There is some disagreement as to the impact of this leak. Cline (1998) argues that the IMF probably overestimated South Korea's short-run foreign debt by double counting certain items, and that the publication of this overestimate contributed to the panic. Feldstein (1998) observes that South Korea's debt ratings were cut after this report was leaked. Others argue that the private sector had already discounted the South Korean government's official figure on external debt, but that the major blow to confidence came from the realization that usable reserves were almost completely depleted (Berg 1999).

31. Of this, $21 billion came from the IMF. In a complete perversion of its mission as a provider of long-term development assistance, the World Bank pledged $10 billion for what amounted to balance of payments support to an OECD member. The Asian Development Bank chipped in $4 billion, while Japan and the United States made available contributions of $10 billion and $5 billion, respectively, as part of a "second line of defense." (The total value of the program eventually grew to approximately $59 billion as additional countries indicated willingness to provide bilateral support.) In the end, the US Treasury was extremely reluctant to permit the deployment of the "second line of defense." South Korea ultimately received less than $29 billion of the package and in fact did not draw down the entire IMF loan.

32. As the 3 December Letter of Intent notes, "circumstances did not permit a full specification of the program" (IMF 1997). South Korea and the Fund would conclude five more Letters of Intent and Memoranda on the Economic Program in the following six months.

would support the program, but this did little to restore confidence. Indeed, on 11 December, Moody's and Standard & Poor's reduced South Korean sovereign debt to junk bond status.

After being elected President on 18 December, one of Kim Dae-jung's first acts was to visit the Ministry of Finance and Economy (MOFE). On 22 December, after meeting with MOFE officials, Kim announced to the assembled press corps that the situation was worse than he had been led to believe. He blamed the situation on his predecessor, Kim Young-sam, and then began preparing the country politically for austerity, all of which was expected. However, he then went on to say, "We have no money. We don't know whether we'll default tomorrow or the day after tomorrow. . . . I am totally flabbergasted." That last unscripted bit set off a panic. Later that day in New York, William McDonough, Chairman of the New York Federal Reserve, pulled together executives of the six largest banks in the United States and convinced them to keep their credit lines open. He then managed to persuade other international banks to do likewise, providing the South Koreans with a modest bit of breathing space. Nevertheless, on 23 December, sovereign debt was downgraded again.

On 24 December, the South Korean government announced that the IMF had agreed to expedite the disbursement of $10 billion in return for accelerated implementation of the reform commitments. This infusion of official money effectively prevented a default and created a window of opportunity for South Korea to negotiate a workout with its creditors. A temporary agreement with private creditors was reached to maintain exposure, and the government initiated negotiations on rescheduling short-term debt.[33] Contemporaneously, President-elect Kim Dae-jung moved resolutely to extract concessions from both the labor unions and the *chaebol*. In the financial sector, the government closed two brokerage houses and a number of merchant banks (including some affiliated with *chaebol*). The government began the process of auctioning off two nationalized commercial banks, while putting other financial institutions on short tethers. Despite the austerity and dislocation that would accompany the process of restructuring, the financial markets responded positively to these actions with the stock market rising and the currency appreciating. As might be expected, adjustment in the real economy lagged the overshoot in the financial markets and was only made more painful by the intervention of the IMF.

---

33. During this respite, South Korea's foreign creditor banks agreed to extend the terms of short-term loans totaling $24 billion that were made to private South Korean banks. In return, the South Korean government guaranteed the new loans. The extended loans would carry interest rates higher than the original loans, but lower rates than those initially sought by the foreign banks. The South Korean borrowers would have the option of early repayment.

The Monetary Policy Response

The Christmas Eve crisis increased the Fund's leverage, and in subsequent dealings it pressed its advantage. First, the Fund demanded a tightening of the monetary stance. Money market rates, which had been around 12 percent before the crisis, were driven to 27 percent by the end of 1997. The three-year corporate bond rate reached 30 percent. The justification was that higher interest rates were needed to restrain aggregate demand, staunch capital flight, stabilize the exchange rate, and fix the domestic resource costs of servicing the foreign debt. What the Fund did not appear to realize was that South Korea was not Latin America: firms had loan-based, not equity-based, financial structures, making even efficient firms vulnerable to an interest spike. According to the OECD (1998), South Korean firms' interest costs already accounted for 17 percent of business costs—three times higher than comparable percentages in the United States or Japan—and the interest coverage ratio (the ratio of operating income before interest and taxes to net interest payments) was around 135 percent at the end of 1997, compared to ratios of 250 to 450 percent in other OECD countries. Moreover, every percentage point increase in the interest rate would drive this ratio down another 3 to 4 percentage points (Claessens, Ghosh, and Scott 1999). Financial analysts typically regard ratios over 300 percent to be healthy, and those in the 200 to 300 range as being a cause for concern. Doubling interest rates would crush these firms, and crush them it did. When the bloodletting was over, corporate insolvencies were triple their level from a year earlier. Five of the remaining top thirty *chaebol*, with assets of around $20 billion, had failed, and another eighteen of these, with combined assets of approximately $75 billion, were at risk of bankruptcy.[34] Because of the structure of South Korean capital markets, in which promissory notes issued by the big *chaebol* and discounted by banks finance the operations of small and medium-sized suppliers, the havoc cascaded throughout the system. As the terms of the notes were lengthened and discount rates rose, small and medium-sized enterprises were squeezed of liquidity and had trouble financing imported inputs (Claessens, Ghosh, and Scott 1999).[35] Indeed, there was a flight to quality among the South Korean banks. Commercial

---

34. On 18 June 1998, the FSC announced its "List of Death": 55 corporations (including 20 subsidiaries of the top five *chaebol*) were declared non-viable (in *de facto* default). Nevertheless, many observers, including Financial Supervisory Commission (FSC) head Lee Hun-jai, believed that the top five *chaebol* had been treated preferentially (Kirk 1999).

35. Choi and Kang (1999) present results from a survey of 850 firms in the aftermath of the crisis. As might be expected, they find that export-oriented firms were less severely squeezed by the credit crunch, and that precrisis access to foreign lending was a positive indicator of postcrisis access to capital. As noted previously, the latter result could substantiate the case for integrating foreign lending institutions into the local financial system so as to enhance systemic diversification and stability.

bank holdings of government bonds doubled, both absolutely and as a share of their portfolios, and the biggest *chaebol* actually increased their share of the reduced bank lending. The Fund recognized that the exchange market had stabilized and acceded to monetary relaxation in the sixth Letter of Intent (2 May 1998), but by this time considerable damage had already been done.[36]

The obvious question is whether there was any alternative to this course of action. Joseph E. Stiglitz, then the World Bank's chief economist, argued that there was, and he described the Fund's program as a "mistake" and "clearly inappropriate" for South Korea (Stiglitz 1998, 1999). His critique begins with the premise that there are good theoretical reasons to expect banks in developing countries to maintain maturity mismatches in their portfolios. One consequence, however, is that this leaves them vulnerable to interest rate spikes. He claims that the empirical evidence shows that banking crises in developing countries are associated with interest rate spikes, not with currency devaluations.

The second argument in this critique is that advocates of monetary tightening to defend the currency do so on the basis that high interest rates are needed to stabilize the currency. This in turn is designed to forestall importing inflation through higher prices for imported goods and thus strengthen economic fundamentals and confidence in the economy.

Stiglitz argues that monetary tightening would be warranted in situations in which the economy was facing excess demand and inflation. The high interest rate policy could be interpreted as a first-best response to the source of the macroeconomic disequilibria. However, in situations in which there was no prior excess demand or inflation, i.e., the South Korean case, the predominant effect would be the adverse one on the banking system and would thereby undermine confidence in the economy. In other words, if the source of the macroeconomic disequilibrium was creditor panic, then high interest rates would actually exacerbate the problem by further undermining the banking system and possibly signaling distress through the direct impact of higher interest rates and the induced response of lower aggregate demand. Or, as Stiglitz (1999) put it, "a deep downturn, especially one brought about by high interest rates, has precisely the wrong effects: it weakens firms, increases debt-equity ratios,

---

36. The Fund's own evaluation of its performance during the crisis was treated in the press as a kind of *mea culpa* (IMF 1999a). Yet the report largely exonerates Fund decisions, prosaically asserting, for example, that the monetary tightening "is unlikely to have been a major factor in the output decline" (p.121). There is not too much *culpa* in this report. At least one prominent economist, however, concurred with the IMF program. Rudiger Dornbusch visited South Korea and publicly announced his support for the IMF program (*Newsreview*, 11 July 1998). Ding, Domaç, and Ferri (1998), Feldstein (1998), and Pyo (1999) all disagree with the IMF, reaching very different conclusions with regard to the monetary tightening and supporting the analysis in the text above.

and further weakens financial institutions, making the resolution of the underlying problems even more difficult" (p.19).

The problem with this critique, of course, is that it offers little guidance for a positive response to the crisis other than to avoid monetary stringency, attempt to engineer a debt rescheduling, try to convince market participants that they are in a panic, and risk default (or be forced to impose capital controls) if market sentiment does not reverse before currency reserves are exhausted or a debt payment moratorium is imposed.[37] While it is not implausible that this was the optimal course of action in South Korea in 1997, it is understandable why risk-averse policymakers undertook the conventional remedy—as counterproductive as it might have been.

The Fiscal Policy Response

Not content just to impose monetary stringency on South Korea, the IMF demanded fiscal austerity as well. By the books, South Korea was in about the best fiscal position of any OECD country. Government expenditure was the smallest share of national income compared to other OECD countries. In 1996, its general government financial balance (inclusive of social security) was 5 percent of GDP, second only to that of Norway. Its gross outstanding debt was negligible, and the government's net debt position was actually positive (its assets exceeded its outstanding debts, though the valuation of assets was questionable). South Korea's real problem was off the books: its implicit future liabilities generated by the weak financial condition of the largest *chaebol* and the financial sector. The South Korean government expected that the impact of the crisis would be to knock the consolidated surplus down to a manageable 3.5 percent of GDP deficit—equal to Germany's and smaller than deficits observed in G7 countries such as France, Japan, the United Kingdom, or Italy (OECD 1998).

Instead, in its initial program the IMF insisted on a combination of expenditure cuts and tax increases large enough to fully offset the expected crisis-induced 1.5 to 2.0 percent increase in the cyclically-unadjusted central government budget deficit in order "to achieve at a minimum budget

---

37. Stiglitz (1999) argues that it was the debt moratorium, not high interest rates, that stopped the won overshoot and stabilized the exchange rate: "The interest rate increases did *not* seem to halt the slide in the currency, presumably because they raised the probability of bankruptcy so much that they undermined confidence in the economy and the currency. Instead, it was the debt moratorium that eventually turned around the currency. . . . Korea's exchange rate stabilized only when there was, in effect, a debt moratorium (rescheduling); arguably, if this had been done earlier, stabilization would have occurred earlier" (pp.13, 24) [emphasis in the original].

balance and, preferably, a small surplus" (IMF 1997).[38] This was justified by the need to "support external adjustment." In the fifth Letter of Intent (7 February 1998), the Fund backed off somewhat: additional expenditures on the social safety net amounting to around one-half a percent of GDP were approved, allowing the fiscal deficit target to increase to 0.8 percent of GDP, but the Fund still insisted on continuing the off-setting expenditure cuts and tax increases, partially undercutting the automatic stabilizers. In March 1998, the government increased taxes, slashed government expenditure by 2 percent of GDP (in spite of increased expenditure on the bank recapitalization described below), and cut civil servant salaries from 10 to 20 percent. The forecast growth rate dropped from 3 percent to -7 percent, and the deficit target was revised to a 5 percent of GDP central government budget deficit.[39]

In addition to the usual macroeconomic austerity, the Fund demanded other controversial changes of questionable relevance as well. Central bank independence with "price stability as its main mandate" was included in the initial 3 December Agreement.[40] South Korea agreed to international trade and financial liberalization—in particular to measures that were of special interest to Japan and the United States, such as dismantling the "import diversification program," lifting of the ban on Japanese automobile imports, and liberalizing financial services. Although trade liberalization has been another staple of IMF programs, the inclusion of these items contributed to the perception in South Korea that the IMF was simply being used as a tool of Japanese, and especially US, commercial policy. Finally, the IMF program also required labor market reforms, specifically measures that would facilitate labor shedding—proposals that

---

38. According to the IMF's calculations, a tightening of 1.5 to 2.0 percent of GDP was necessary, assuming that the costs of recapitalization were 0.8 percent of GDP. Cline (1998) carefully dissects this program, demonstrating that the Fund seriously underestimated the cyclical adjustment needed in its budget projections, and, as a consequence, imposed excessive fiscal austerity on the already weak economy. For additional criticism of the Fund's program see Pyo (1999) and Yanagita (1999).

39. With the Fund's blessing, the South Korean government reversed course and passed a supplementary budget in August 1998. However, by this point, the Ministry of Finance and Economy was more hawkish than the Fund and actually slowed the disbursement of authorized expenditures.

40. The evidence on the desirability of central bank independence is mixed. The goal of *long-run* price stability would meet almost universal acceptance among economists, though considerably fewer would support the notion that *short-run* price stability ought to be a mandate, let alone the main mandate, of the central bank. Moreover, much of the public may disagree with the perspectives of economic technocrats. As an illustration, a 1995 proposal by Senator Connie Mack (R-Florida) to amend the Federal Reserve's charter to enshrine the goal of "price stability" proved quite controversial and failed. In the case of South Korea, as Stiglitz (1999) observes, "the issue of inflation had nothing to do with the crisis, or its resolution, and it was hard to understand why it was even raised" (pp.28-29).

had proven to be enormously contentious when considered by the Korean National Assembly back in December 1996, though in contrast to the financial sector restructuring, details were left vague.

The IMF Recession

Financial markets continued to stabilize throughout the spring, helped by the 28 January 1998 agreement in principle between the South Korean government and its foreign creditors to reschedule short-term debt. By resolving the uncertainty surrounding the incidence of burden associated with the foreign debt crisis, the January agreement and the subsequent policy actions set the stage for the renewal of private capital inflows and, by extension, the revival of the South Korean economy. In February, Standard and Poor's upgraded South Korea's debt, though it was still in the junk bond category. By March, foreign exchange reserves had risen to $25 billion; the corporate bond rate had fallen to only 19 percent; and the exchange rate had stabilized at around 1400 won to the dollar. On 31 March, a debt reduction agreement was signed with South Korea's creditors. By April, progress had been sufficient for South Korea to return to international capital markets with a $4 billion bond issue.

However, conditions in the real economy continued to deteriorate. First quarter 1998 GDP growth was -3.8 percent, due to a whopping 29 percent fall in domestic demand. The current account surplus shot to roughly 14 percent of GDP, driven by a collapse of import demand. By mid-1998, capacity utilization was down 17 percent. As conditions deteriorated, the IMF reevaluated its program and in July permitted a relaxation of the fiscal and monetary constraints. The easing of the targets helped stabilize the economy, though by year's end real output was down nearly 6 percent and unemployment had quadrupled from its precrisis rate of just over 2 percent, reaching nearly 8 percent.[41] Nominal wages fell by an average of 2.5 percent in 1998, the average real wage fell by 10 percent (Lee and Rhee 1999), and the urban poverty rate reached 24 percent (Stiglitz 1999).

The unemployment rate continued to rise before peaking at nearly 9 percent in February 1999, though this indicator actually understates the extent of dislocation. Employment shrank in industry, agriculture, and services. The only sectors in which employment grew were the self-employed and public service. As employment in the core of the economy shrank, some of the decline was absorbed by the relatively informal small shopkeeper and government public works sectors. Data reported by Lee and Rhee (1999) indicate that the decline in employment disproportion-

---

41. According to Park (1999a), most of the increase in unemployment was generated by firms employing fewer than ten workers, suggesting that recession, not restructuring, was driving the process.

ately affected women, younger workers, the less educated, and first-time job seekers.

This was particularly painful, as South Korea had neither much of an unemployment insurance system nor a well-developed social safety net. Income distribution data revealed a rise in poverty, a widening of inequality, and a shrinkage of the middle class (Pyo 1999). Survey data indicated a dramatic drop in those considering themselves middle class (Hong 1999, J. S. Park 1999). This was accompanied by a withdrawal of children from school and a significant increase in non-violent crime and other social maladies (OECD 1999, J. S. Park 1999).

The South Korean crisis presented the IMF, the major finance ministries, and the multilateral development banks with a difficult situation. It occurred in the context of a cascading set of crises that threatened to spread to Brazil and Russia. The South Korean government's willingness to guarantee the short-term foreign debt of private entities socialized risk, creating moral hazard and ultimately increasing the severity of the crisis. It waited too long to approach the Fund and, once it did, engaged in unhelpful tactics. The Fund and its allies had little control over these events, and in November 1997 they confronted a situation that arguably posed a systemic risk to the international financial system.

When push came to shove, the Fund and its collaborators provided South Korea with an enormous package, far beyond the Fund's past lending practices in other cases and a timely infusion of cash that undoubtedly prevented a chaotic default. That said, the macroeconomic conditionality imposed on South Korea was too severe. It needlessly intensified the recession that came to be known colloquially as "the IMF recession."[42] The other aspects of the program, requiring specific trade and labor market reforms, were intrusive—but understandably so. As has been previously documented, the South Korean economy in 1997 had been beset with some significant structural problems, and, given the enormity of the December 1997 standby agreement, one would have to expect considerable demands for structural reform. Indeed, one could argue that the existence of such a demanding international organization allowed Kim Dae-jung to advance his own relatively liberal economic agenda more effectively than if the Fund or some similar organization had not existed.

Perhaps the lesson of the IMF's experience in South Korea is the one drawn by Feldstein (1998): IMF programs should be smaller, with less conditionality. National authorities may approach the Fund earlier, before their foreign exchange reserves are nearly exhausted, if the support they can expect, though smaller, is provided on less intrusive and hence less politically onerous terms. While containing many useful suggestions, the

---

42. It is notable that, faced with a similar set of problems, the Fund did not recommend similar policies in Japan (IMF 1998).

US government proposal (i.e., Summers 1999) may be the worst of all worlds in this respect: it calls for smaller IMF programs, but hints at even broader, and presumably more politically intrusive, conditionality. The recommendations contained in Council on Foreign Relations (1999b) steer a middle course.

Post-Crisis Developments

The IMF standby program and the South Korean electoral calendar (Kim Dae-jung would not take office until 25 February 1998) gave the country a window of roughly eight weeks to stabilize before the new National Assembly would reconvene and markets would begin expecting serious reform. In the interregnum before his inauguration, Kim performed masterfully, continuing the international negotiations from his home and in effect acting as the *de facto* President. He was abetted by the natural tendency to rally behind leaders in times of crisis, a honeymoon effect, and public political support by foreign governments.[43] One might expect sectors of society that had benefited from financial repression, including firms that had obtained preferential access to capital, politicians who had done their bidding, and bureaucrats who had wielded regulatory power, to oppose liberalization. These groups were not the President-elect's core constituencies, however. Put crudely, he did not owe them anything. His comments (following his unfortunate 22 December gaffe), his choice of advisors, and his actions during the interregnum indicated that he had reached a similar conclusion. In this crisis atmosphere, the political tide had quickly shifted to the point that considerable reform legislation was passed by the outgoing, lame-duck, National Assembly.[44]

---

43. It was not all smooth sailing for Kim Dae-jung, however. Within hours of convening, the new National Assembly rejected his nominee for Prime Minister, his coalition partner and former Park regime Korean Central Intelligence Agency (KCIA) head, Kim Jong-pil.

44. Success has a thousand fathers and failure is an orphan. Much of this legislation and the subsequent implementation of the reforms were supported by funds and technical assistance provided by the World Bank and the IMF, and indeed were specified in the December 1997 Letter of Intent and Memorandum on Economic Program and elaborated further in the February 1997 Letter of Intent and Memorandum of Economic Program. Observers have expressed considerable disagreement over how much of the reform program should be credited to the activities of these outside agencies. Some have argued that the South Korean government had evinced little real enthusiasm for reform and that it was IMF conditionality that was decisive. Others claim that the IMF in large measure provided a cover for policies that were advocated by South Korean economists in government and the think tanks, but which they had not previously been able to get accepted politically.

Financial System Reforms

Financial sector reform was described as the "centerpiece" of the IMF program, and the South Korean government acted quickly.[45] In December 1997, 15 pieces of legislation overhauling the financial system were passed. The Bank of Korea was made legally independent. The General Banking Law and the Financial Structuring Act liberalized the provision of financial services, breaking down many functional and institutional rigidities. Foreign ownership of South Korean banks was permitted. At the same time, the government's regulatory functions were consolidated into a single agency, the Financial Supervisory Commission (FSC), an independent agency reporting directly to the Prime Minister's office.

The government used international standards as its measuring stick. The rules were changed to require marking-to-market accounting, disclosure of performing loans, asset classification criteria, and foreign exchange liquidity and exposure criteria.[46] In December, 14 merchant banks, two securities houses, and one investment trust firm were ordered to suspend operations. Two large insolvent commercial banks, Korea First Bank and Seoul Bank, were nationalized and recapitalized by the authorities in January after writing off nearly all of existing shareholders' capital (table 6.2).[47] This was done in defiance of the IMF, which wanted the banks closed. By the end of 1999, the number of banks in South Korea had been reduced by ten (from 33 to 23), and overall staffing levels had been cut by 34 percent. The government had closed or suspended 21 of the 30 merchant banks, six securities houses, five leasing companies, seven investment trusts, and four insurance companies that had been in operation at the end of 1997.

Remaining institutions were strengthened. Twelve banks that had failed to meet the Bank of International Settlements (BIS) 8 percent capital adequacy standard at the end of 1997 were required to submit rehabilitation plans. In June 1998, the FSC conditionally approved seven of these plans, closed the other five institutions, and merged them into other institutions after stripping out their non-performing loans. In July 1998, more reforms were announced, including tightened rules on loan classification and provisioning, connected lending, short-term foreign borrowing, and foreign exchange exposure.[48] The deposit insurance system was strengthened and its general protection provision narrowed, with some grandfather

---

45. See IMF (1999b) for a detailed assessment of the financial sector reforms.

46. See OECD (1999) and IMF (1999b) for details on changes in prudential regulation.

47. The government eventually filed civil suits against nearly fifty executives associated with these banks, seeking to reclaim more than 777 billion won lost through malfeasance.

48. See Y. S. Park (1999) for details and Mann (2000) on the difficulty in changing institutional culture—even with the new regulatory framework.

provisions for deposits made under the old system. By the end of 1999, nearly all banks had achieved capital adequacy ratios of 10 percent.

The Korea Asset Management Corporation (KAMCO), established in November 1997 to clean up the non-performing loan problem, had been injecting money into the banking system with little conditionality, arguably throwing good money after bad. In February 1998, the system was tightened, and the government required future KAMCO purchases of non-performing loans to be conditioned on an FSC-approved rehabilitation or liquidation plan.

In May, the government announced a comprehensive 50 trillion won (W) plan (roughly 12 percent of GDP) to address financial sector problems.[49] Of this, W25 trillion was to go to KAMCO, W16 trillion for bank recapitalization, and W9 trillion to increase depositor protection. The banks were expected to raise another W20 trillion through asset revaluation and securities issues.[50] Some of these funds were expected to come from abroad in the form of foreign purchases of South Korean banks.[51] Although this plan proved to be optimistic—in September the government budgeted W64 trillion to address the situation—the government's actions revealed a degree of decisiveness largely absent from the financial restructuring efforts elsewhere in the region. After the nationalizations of Korea First Bank and Seoul Bank, and the government's interventions in Chohung, Commercial Bank of Korea, and Hanil Bank, the government controlled banks accounting for around one-third of total bank assets, or about 40 percent of GDP (table 6.2).[52]

According to the IMF, government expenditures on restructuring through mid-1999 were more than $60 billion, or about 17 percent of GDP,

---

49. These revenues were to be raised by tax increases, cuts in other government spending, and government-guaranteed bond issues by KAMCO and the Korea Deposit Insurance Corporation.

50. Asset revaluation is an adjustment in asset value, typically involving the revaluation of fixed assets at market, rather than book, value.

51. Through 1998, five South Korean banks were able to increase their capital by $678 million through foreign investment, though the sales to foreign investors of the two nationalized banks, Korea First Bank and Seoul Bank, foundered as discussed below. However, in September 1999 it was announced by KAMCO that three US fund management firms would invest at least $500 million and manage a fund of assets of local companies undergoing restructuring. This was followed in October 1999 by the announcement that Merrill Lynch and Deutsche Bank would purchase W1 trillion of KAMCO non-performing loans, and the announcement in December 1999 that KAMCO and Deutsche Bank would form a joint venture asset management company. As of the end of 1999, KAMCO had purchased W56 trillion of non-performing loans and had sold off W22 trillion of these, collecting W12 trillion in proceeds from these sales for a recovery rate of about 55 percent.

52. This figure would drop with the December 1999 sale of Korea First Bank to Newbridge.

Table 6.2 South Korean banks

Institution	FSC action	Non-performing loans (percentage)	Capital adequacy ratio (end of 1998)	Governmental participation (percentage as of end-May 1999)	Foreign participation (percentage)
Korea First	Nationalized, subsequently sold	20	-2	94	0
Seoul	Nationalized	18	-1	94	0
Daedong	Closed	—	—	—	—
Dongnam	Closed	—	—	—	—
Dongwha	Closed	—	—	—	—
Peace	Conditional approval	12	-2	42[a]	—
Chohung	Conditional approval	5	1	92	6
Korea Exchange	Conditional approval	5	8	30	35
Hanil	Conditional approval/ merged to form Hanvit	—	—	—	—
CBK	Conditional approval/ merged to form Hanvit	—	—	—	—
Hanvit	Nationalized	5	12	95	—
Koram	Assume Kyongki	3	15	35	17
Hana	Assume Chungchong and merged	3	13	46[a]	12
Boram	Merged with Hana	4	3	—	6
Kookmin	Assume Daedong and merged	6	10	15[a]	22
Housing	Assume Dongnam	8	11	40[a]	27
Shinhan	Assume Dongnam	4	15	20[a]	16
All nationwide banks		7	8	—	—
Kangwon	Conditional approval	25	-11	—	4
Chungbuk	Conditional approval	19	-5	—	—
Kyongki	Closed	—	—	—	—
Chungchong	Closed	—	—	—	—
Pusan	Management improvement recommended	6	9	—	9

(continued)

Table 6.2 (continued)

Institution	FSC action	Non-performing loans (percentage)	Capital adequacy ratio (end of 1998)	Governmental participation (percentage as of end-May 1999)	Foreign participation (percentage)
Kwangju	—	4	11	—	3
Daegu	—	8	10	—	6
Cheju	Management improvement recommended	22	12	—	58
Kyungnam	Management improvement recommended	8	13	—	6
Chonbuk	—	9	13	—	1
All regional banks		9	8	—	—
All commercial banks		7	8	—	—

a. Preferred shares.

Source: OECD 1999 table 17; IMF 1999b, table 2.

once asset swaps were taken into account (IMF 1999b, table 3).[53] As expected, the initial outlays appear insufficient to completely resolve the non-performing loan problem. In August 1999 the government announced that South Korean banks still faced nearly W26 trillion of bad loans, and a senior official indicated that additional public funds would have to be allocated before the financial sector problems could be fully resolved. Immediately following the April 2000 elections, press reports indicated that the government was calculating the supplementary amount required, though publicly the government continued to deny the need for additional funds.

Lastly, the government has attempted to bolster the capital markets. Its strategy has been to strengthen the government bond market, based on the theory that creating a liquid market in benchmark issues will convey positive externalities to the corporate markets. In September 1998, competitive bidding on initial offerings was introduced in government securities markets, with the goal of eliminating the price differential on the primary and secondary markets. Trading volume increased significantly, but problems have persisted.[54] A futures market for government

---

53. Both Aliber (1998) and Claessens, Ghosh, and Scott (1999) estimate that the ultimate costs of cleaning up the financial sector may be W125 trillion to W150 trillion, or approximately 30 to 35 percent of GDP. However, given the South Korean government's good fiscal position going into the crisis, they judge that this should be easily financible.

54. The secondary market remains thin. Banks are major holders of government debt, and tend to hold their risk-free sovereign debt to maturity to count as part of their capital base. In addition, some of the government licensed "primary bond-dealers" have ignored their obligation to supply the secondary market, retarding its growth, and inhibiting the development of benchmark issues.

bonds and other instruments also has been introduced. Furthermore, the government has been encouraging the development of rating agencies in the corporate bond market, with the hope that better monitoring, together with financial institutions no longer guaranteeing corporate bonds, will encourage the development of spreads that reflect credit worthiness relative to benchmark government bond issues. The government has also announced that it is considering allowing foreign firms to list on the Seoul bourse.

Corporate Reforms

The government has achieved less success in its attempt to reform the corporate sector. It adopted a three-pronged approach involving court-supervised insolvency procedures, voluntary debt workouts, and special procedures for the "big five" *chaebol*.[55] This had the effect of differentiating the firms by size, and amounted to extending preferential treatment to the big five.

Most attention has focused on these firms, inasmuch as the five largest *chaebol* account for around 50 percent of corporate debt and around 70 percent of external corporate debt. (The capital squeeze forced the smaller *chaebol* and small and medium-sized enterprises to restructure under duress.) In the short run, for the top five *chaebol*, the South Koreans settled on a process involving Capital Structural Improvement Plans (CSIPs), in which the big five developed their own voluntary restructuring or work-out plans that were to be approved by their lead banks. The goal was to reduce debt-equity ratios to 200 percent by the end of 1999.[56] At the end of 1999, the government announced that four of the five had attained the target. (Bankrupt Daewoo was the sole failure.) This goal was achieved through raising new capital, shedding non-core businesses, and possibly creative accounting. To facilitate debt to equity conversions, the banking law was changed to raise the ceiling from 10 percent to 15 percent on the share of equity that a bank can hold in a single firm. The top *chaebol* also reduced the number of subsidiaries from 232 at the end of 1997 to 167 by December 1999. However, the financial condition of the subsidiaries is thought to be weaker than that of the parent firms, and it would not be surprising if the debt-equity ratios once again exceed the 200 percent level when the *chaebol* are forced to report consolidated balance sheets. Despite their apparent progress, the financial condition of the *chaebol* remains weak.

---

55. The "big five" are Hyundai, Samsung, Daewoo, SK, and LG (formerly Lucky Goldstar).

56. See Graham (1999a) and Kirk (1999) for detailed assessments of the restructuring of each of the top five *chaebol*.

The CSIP approach was supplemented by high-level political intervention. Ironically, the power of the state has been used to try and create a more liberal, less interventionist economic model. In this regard, South Korea needed a true market for corporate control—that is, capital market discipline that would correct the behavior of managers who, in the OECD's words, "had systematically destroyed shareholder value" for the past decade. To accomplish this, the government needed at least five things: 1) improved accounting standards, including consolidated balance sheets, to make available accurate financial information; 2) outside directors for corporate boards and improved conflict of interest laws and protections for shareholder rights; 3) non-affiliated institutional investors who could play a true monitoring role; 4) improvements in the insolvency framework; and 5) the possibility of hostile takeovers.

For the second tier corporations (the 6th to 64th *chaebol* in size, and other large companies), the government created another process. The September 1998 Corporate Securities Law established a Corporate Restructuring Accord (CRA), designating a lead bank to negotiate the workout for each firm and specifying a set of extra-judicial rules in the case of disagreements. These would be administered by the Financial Supervisory Commission's Corporate Restructuring Coordinating Committee (CRCC). The CRA provides for preferential treatment from the banks, debt for equity swaps, and access to a 2 trillion won pool of new loans and trade finance.[57] Among the 6th to 64th *chaebol*, 198 of their 248 companies were sold, merged, or liquidated, and another 40 subsidiaries of 16 *chaebol* have gone through the workout process.[58] Another 40 large non-*chaebol* firms have also gone through the workout process. According to Graham (1999a), however, the actual amount of restructuring has been modest, and the government expects that as many as a third will require further measures.

Among smaller, third-tier firms, 56 have agreed to workouts with their creditors. One firm, Kyonggi Chemical, found its workout plan canceled after resisting its creditors' demands for a capital reduction and a debt-

---

57. See Claessens, Ghosh, and Scott (1999) and S. M. Yoo (1999) for analyses of the Corporate Restructuring Accord.

58. Hyosung (number 16), for example, spun-off some subsidiaries to foreign investors. However, as conditions in the economy have begun to improve, the *chaebol* began canceling planned deals. In the case of Ssangyong (number 6), for example, it initially told its creditors that it would sell its oil refining business to foreign investors, but has since pulled the deal off the table. Similarly, as conditions improved in the spring of 1999, Tonggook Synthetic Fibers scrapped its deal to sell its spandex yarn factory to Dupont. Indeed, even the once dead Halla, owned by the brother of Chung Ju Yung, the founder of Hyundai, managed to revive itself when its creditors (including Hyundai) agreed to write off half of its debts so that Halla could borrow additional funds. In July, Halla Heavy Engineering and Industries, the most troubled affiliate of the group, failed to resume honoring its debts as it had promised in a December 1997 bankruptcy proceeding, but its creditors simply extended the grace period by two months.

equity swap, and it was forced to file for court receivership. In most cases, however, the workout process has amounted to concerted subsidized lending to buy time until the arrival of better times. Under pressure from both labor and management, the Financial Supervisory Commission instructed creditors to be "gradual and flexible."[59] Indeed, incumbent managements are still in control and have initiated little restructuring. The FSC itself expects two-thirds of these firms to fail, leaving the banking system with W28 trillion in bad debts.

The government also has undertaken some proactive policies. According to Aiyer (1999), small and medium-sized businesses have been particularly affected by the credit crunch, since available financing has become even more concentrated among the largest firms. Seventy affiliates of the top five *chaebol* reportedly accounted for 86 percent of new rights offerings and 77 percent of corporate bonds in 1998. The government responded initially by instructing banks to roll over their loans to small and medium-sized firms and providing W33 trillion of guarantees. A small and medium enterprise Corporate Restructuring Fund of W1.6 trillion was established in October 1998.[60] In an effort to encourage the development of a market in high-yield bonds issued by smaller firms, the government has since placed ceilings on certain institutional investors' portfolio holdings of top five *chaebol* debt. In August 1999, the government announced the creation of a public venture capital fund (in partnership with four foreign venture capital firms) and other measures to promote innovative small and medium-sized enterprises.

A number of legal changes regarding corporate governance have been enacted, but these have not always had their desired effect due to problems in implementation or enforcement. As of fiscal year 1999, firms are required to produce consolidated balance sheets. The frequency of disclosure is being increased, and the practice of cross-guaranteeing debt is to be phased out by March 2000.[61] In the words of Governor You Jong-keun of North Cholla province, former special adviser to President Kim, and holder of a doctorate in economics, this practice has

> greatly contributed to the credit shortage facing many of Korea's smaller and marginal corporations. Enforcement of the existing and new laws prohibiting such practices are crucial to the successful restructuring of Korea's corporate sector and to the very survival of many small and medium-sized companies . . . [and] should produce significant benefits in terms of both resource allocation and business management. . . . Therefore the government must be willing to put more

---

59. *Newsreview*, 18 July 1998.

60. See OECD (1999) for details.

61. See OECD (1999) for details on the changes in accounting regulations. In October 1999, the Korea Fair Trade Commission (KFTC) hit the top five *chaebol* with W79 billion in fines, much of this related to cross-subsidization infractions.

teeth, including criminal prosecutions, into the laws prohibiting such practices. (You 1999, 18).[62]

Yet despite the External Audit Law of February 1998, accounting standards remain lax.[63] As of June 1998, restrictions on the voting rights of institutional investors were lifted, the legal rights of minority shareholders were broadened, and all listed firms were required to have at least one-fourth outside directors.[64] However, major firms have tried to dilute these changes by scheduling annual meetings simultaneously to discourage the participation of knowledgeable outsiders and by filling outside director seats with cronies[65] (see box 6.4).

Indeed, one effect of the financial crisis appears to be increased family control of the *chaebol*. Korea Fair Trade Commission (KFTC) data for 1999 indicated that, despite the reduction in cross-debt guarantees, the degree of cross-shareholding actually increased in the wake of the crisis, with the average degree of cross-holding among the top five *chaebol* having risen from 44.5 percent to 50.5 percent, and the average for the top ten *chaebol* having increased from 27.2 percent to 34.6 percent.[66] The *chaebol* families use the mechanism of cross-shareholding to maintain management control and evade taxes.[67]

The government responded with a three-pronged attack. One was to introduce further restrictions on cross-shareholding and to increase further the number of outside directors.[68] A second was an assault on the prerogatives of the *chaebol* "Chairman's Office," which S. M. Yoo (1999) argues actually makes restructuring more difficult by weakening the center's hold on the network of affiliated firms, while only legalizing a narrow class of holding companies. Both he and the OECD recommend a relaxation of restrictions on holding companies in order to facilitate restructuring. The third government response was a tightening of inheritance tax laws and an increase in the inheritance tax rate.

---

62. You was forced to resign from his advisor's post after a report that $120,000 was stolen from his residence, raising questions about the source of these funds and the specter of corruption.

63. See AmCham (1999).

64. See S. M. Yoo (1999) and OECD (1999) for details.

65. There is no designated procedure for nominating outside directors. It has been alleged that many of those appointed were literally on the *chaebol* payrolls before nomination (*Dong-A Ilbo*, 27 March 1998).

66. This revelation occasioned yet another meeting between the *chaebol* heads and President Kim Dae-jung.

67. See, for example, Oh Young-jin, *Korea Times*, 2 October 1999 and 5 October 1999, and Yoo Cheong-mo, *Newsreview*, 9 October 1999, for examples involving Samsung and Hanjin.

68. K. Kim (1999) argues that the *chaebol* have responded to these restrictions on intra-group finance by simply merging affiliates.

Box 6.4 Shareholder Activism

In the economics sphere, reformist activism began in 1989 with the formation of the Citizen's Coalition for Economic Justice (CCEJ), which campaigned against real estate speculation, for central bank independence, for the real-name law, and against *chaebol* domination of economic life. The CCEJ was joined in 1994 by the People's Solidarity for Participatory Democracy (PSPD) and in 1997 by its offshoot, the Participatory Economy Committee (PEC), which has used shareholder rights to promote change in *chaebol* corporate governance practices.

The non-governmental organizations (NGOs) got a boost with the crisis in 1997. The crisis and the election of Kim Dae-jung, who supported a reduction in the minimum ownership needed to propose a motion at the annual shareholders meetings to 0.01 percent, also have increased the role of foreign institutional investors. The PSPD and its charismatic leader, Korea University economics professor Jang Ha-sung, have had some notable successes of late, obtaining a court order that Korea First Bank's directors should pay W40 billion ($32.5 million) in fines for managerial failures and illegal activity associated with their role in the Hanbo Steel collapse. In another suit, Samsung Electronics was forced to pay W3 million in fines for refusing to reveal data on its illegal support of Samsung Motors. SK Telecom was forced to issue an apology for diverting profits to the largest shareholder's family and has agreed to appoint outside directors (including those effectively chosen by minority shareholders through a cumulative voting system) and outside auditors. A current target is Hyundai Heavy Industries, which illicitly channeled funds to Hyundai Motors to assist in its takeover of Kia and subsidized loss-making firms within the Hyundai Group.

Stopping management abuses by *chaebol* founders and their families has become a primary focus for the PEC. It blocked Samsung Group Chairman Lee Kun-hee from passing to his son part of his personal wealth through illegal convertible bond issues, and it has filed a suit demanding that Lee and other senior executives personally reimburse the Group W300 billion for using corporate funds for alleged illegal political contributions and cross-firm subsidies. Similarly, SK Telecom was caught trying to subsidize other SK Group subsidiaries and to funnel money to the chairman's son through procurement contracts with another unit.

Professor Jang has become a bit of a celebrity, winning praise from the World Bank and President Clinton, among others. The *chaebol* have not taken this lying down, however, and have tried to drive a wedge between the citizen organizations' grassroots supporters and their institutional investor allies. The organizations have been portrayed as tools of foreign interests, and the big five *chaebol* have scheduled their annual meetings for the same day to prevent Jang from attending all of the meetings. In a confrontation with the SK Group in August 1999, Jang and his allies were routed. Nevertheless, one gets the sense that a coalition of interests in transparency and improved corporate governance is developing, and this should constrain at least some of the more grotesque *chaebol* abuses.

Market discipline on management remains weak. A new class of institutional investors has not been created. The nascent mutual fund industry might have been expected to play this role, but it has been the *chaebol*-controlled funds, most notably Hyundai's Buy Korea Fund, that have played a prominent role, raising obvious conflict of interest concerns. In April 1999, Hyundai came under investigation for allegedly using funds from the Buy Korea Fund to buy Hyundai shares in an attempt to reduce its debt-equity ratio. Hyundai was no stranger to Financial Supervisory Commission (FSC) investigations. Earlier in the month, the FSC launched an investigation of its subsidiary, Hyundai Electronics, for manipulation of Hyundai's share prices.[69] These investigations eventually led to the arrest and conviction of Lee Ik-chi, chairman of Hyundai Securities and the mastermind behind the Buy Korea Fund, for manipulating the share price of Hyundai Electronics.[70]

In a similar case, the Korea Fair Trade Commission (KFTC) has claimed that Samsung Life insurance bought W580 billion of commercial paper from Samsung affiliates at above market prices. More generally, *chaebol*-controlled institutions in the non-banking sector have been on the rise, with their share of deposits increasing from 19 percent in 1997 to 34 percent in 1999 and their shares of overall financial sector deposits rising from 5 to 13 percent over the same period. As the barriers between financial and industrial firms have increasingly blurred, the possibility of domestic institutional investors playing an important monitoring role has receded.[71]

Since the enactment of the Corporate Restructuring Law, there has been some strengthening of the insolvency laws, including the establishment of new bankruptcy courts. Yet firms are allowed 12 or 18 months for submission and approval of reorganization plans, which has created a

---

69. For similar reasons the KFTC in June 1999 began investigating financial transactions by nine Hyundai subsidiaries and two Samsung affiliates (Hyundai and Samsung have cross-ownership through their control of investment trusts). Sixty executives eventually received reprimands. Indeed, since the crisis, all top five *chaebol* have been fined by the KFTC for these kinds of schemes, and, according to the Fair Trade Commission, the top five *chaebol* siphoned off W14 trillion to their subsidiaries in the two years after the crisis. See Oh Young-jin, *Korea Times*, 2 October 1999 for yet more examples, and K. Kim (1999) for a broader discussion of these issues.

70. Lee received a prison sentence of two years and was fined $6 million. The judge suspended the prison time on the grounds that Lee had not benefited personally from the stock price manipulation. It was variously claimed that the prosecution was a politically inspired attempt to prod Hyundai into restructuring by closing off its access to the stock market, and that prosecutors came under political pressure to end their investigation (which reportedly implicated other senior Hyundai officials) with the arrest of Lee for fear of damaging the stock market and the nascent economic recovery.

71. The LG Group possesses eight financial subsidiaries, Hyundai and Samsung have seven each, and SK has three.

disincentive for creditors to pursue foreclosure. With the passage of the Foreign Capital Inducement Act in May 1998, hostile takeovers by foreigners have been permitted, though in reality they have been impeded by an extensive web of cross-shareholdings. In fact, none have yet occurred. The process also has been marked by repeated high-level political interventions and government attempts to orchestrate the restructuring of the big five *chaebol*. On 13 January 1998, President-elect Kim met with the heads of the big *chaebol* and hammered out a five-point accord. That agreement called for improvements in transparency, elimination of cross debt payment guarantees, improvements in financial structure, specialization in core businesses, and strengthened accountability.[72] The leaders of the top thirty *chaebol* acquiesced to this agreement two weeks later.

Thus came the notion of "big deals," or business swaps among the *chaebol* as a mechanism to focus the groups on a limited number of core competencies. The top five *chaebol* agreed to consolidate businesses in seven industries and halve the number of their subsidiaries to 130. To facilitate the consolidation, South Korean labor law was amended to allow easier layoffs in the case of mergers or acquisitions. After much hectoring, the big five *chaebol* finally announced their "big deal" plans on 7 October 1998.[73] The "big deals" approach seems to make sense as a rationalization measure if interpreted as a mechanism for exploiting the changes in the labor law and social convention that had effectively granted lifetime employment to the industrial labor force. (Suppose Daewoo swapped its electronics unit for Samsung's auto business. Though Samsung might have encountered trouble downsizing its auto unit, the new owner, Daewoo, might be able to dismiss the former Samsung workers more easily.) However, the "big deals" were apparently not intended to be a rationalization measure, but rather a means of capturing scale economies. This is problematic. First, there is no reason to believe that government-led swaps of this sort boost shareholder value. Second, to the extent that these swaps were to occur, they would intensify already high levels of concentration in particular markets. For example, passenger automobiles would amount to a Hyundai-Daewoo duopoly, and Hyundai would control 95 percent of the truck market.[74] This has raised obvious competition policy concerns and would appear to require aggressive trade liberalization in order to import competition. Yet, to the extent that these potentially anticompetitive actions disadvantage foreign firms and are government-led, they

---

72. See S.M. Yoo (1999) for details of these plans.

73. See S.M. Yoo (1999), table 15 for a summary of the plans.

74. Indeed, Representative Kim Zoong-wie of the opposition Grand National Party called on the Fair Trade Commission to investigate Hyundai's price setting behavior in the auto market (*Korea Times*, 9 October 1999).

have become a source of international trade friction, as mentioned in chapter 2.

In any event, these plans have largely remained unrealized, and Governor You has argued that "by insisting on business swaps, or the so-called 'big deals,' the government has wasted time and tended to confuse people" (You 1999, 18). Dissatisfied with implementation of the plan, the Financial Supervisory Commission threatened to use the governments' increasing control of the banking system to sanction the big five *chaebol* if they did not accelerate their restructuring efforts. President Kim met again with the *chaebol* heads on 7 December 1998 (and again on 27 April 1999) to demand expedited restructuring. This meeting ended with another five-point agreement and a twenty-point action plan. Mergers were planned in nine sectors under a state-sponsored program to reduce excess production capacity and to cut overlapping investments. Announcements to form joint companies in aerospace and oil refining were made during the spring of 1999.[75] However, as subsequent improvement in the South Korean economy has shifted leverage back in favor of the *chaebol*, it is doubtful if many of these deals will ever be consummated as originally conceived. Hyundai and Daewoo in particular seemed impervious to the government's demands. Nevertheless, the "big deals" have served as a pointed reminder of the degree of concentration in the South Korean economy and the willingness of even an economically liberal government to use considerable intervention to achieve its aims.

One obvious way around this conundrum would be to encourage foreign investment. This would dilute *chaebol* dominance and increase the market responsiveness of corporate decision making. In an address to the American Chamber of Commerce during his June 1998 visit to Washington, President Kim said: "Don't tell President Clinton this, but my real reason for visiting the United States is to meet with you. If each of you were to invest $100 million in Korea, Korea's economic problems would be solved." As noted earlier, the government has undertaken a number of reforms that have greatly increased access for foreign investors.[76] In addition to those previously mentioned, it has set up a "one-stop shop," the Korea Investment Service Center, under the auspices of the Korea Trade Promotion Corporation (KOTRA).

There has been a tremendous surge in inward foreign direct investment (FDI) since the crisis began, much of this consisting of foreign firms buying

---

75. The consolidation plan to form the Korea Aerospace Industry subsequently ran into trouble involving the plans of rival foreign firms to participate in the joint development of the Korea Fighter Program and other military programs involving substantial public funds. The head of the Corporate Restructuring Committee indicated that it would request the foreigners to submit new plans and "pick the best" (Oh Young-jin, *Korea Times*, 15 June 1999).

76. See Ahn (1999), Beck (1999), Kang (1999), J. D. Kim (1999), and Yun (2000) for analyses of these reforms and data on FDI in South Korea.

out their South Korean joint venture partners (figure 2.9).[77] Among the more notable foreign acquisitions have been Philip's purchase of half of LG's flat panel display business ($1.6 billion), Volvo's purchase of Samsung's heavy equipment business ($972 million), and several foreign purchases of weak South Korean paper companies. J. D. Kim (1999) has demonstrated the beneficial effects to the South Korean economy of some of these acquisitions.

In the financial sector, Commerzbank invested $249 million in Korea Exchange Bank, obtaining a 30 percent stake largely by converting existing credits to equity. ING Bank obtained a 10 percent stake in the Housing and Commercial Bank for $280 million, and a planned $500 million investment by Goldman Sachs would make that firm the largest shareholder (16.6 percent) in Kookmin Bank. Shinhan Bank raised $400 million through issuance of global depository receipts.

However, several high profile cases involving foreign investors have raised questions about how deep this commitment goes. As noted earlier, the automaker Kia reportedly was nationalized without informing Mazda, its largest shareholder. When it came time for denationalization of Kia, Ford, one of the world's most competitive automakers, which, together with its Japanese subsidiary Mazda, held a nearly 17 percent stake, expressed keen interest in purchasing the automaker if its creditors were willing to write off half of its debt. The match made sense: Ford would consolidate its position in Northeast Asia, and South Korea would get an infusion of technology, management expertise, and global distribution capabilities. Perhaps fearing competition from a rejuvenated Kia, South Korean auto executives expressed the view that Kia should remain in South Korean hands.

In September 1998, the government refused to accept any of the bids, and then organized a second auction two weeks later. Again the court-appointed manager refused to accept any of the bids and called for a third auction the following month. At the third auction, Ford's bid was disqualified on the grounds that it had requested too large a debt write-off. Kia was awarded to Hyundai Motors, itself losing money and carrying a debt-equity ratio of more than 500 percent, but nonetheless able to obtain financing from South Korean banks.[78] Hyundai Heavy Industries was subsequently subjected to a shareholder lawsuit for funneling money to Hyundai Motors to support its bid. The government would repeat this

---

77. Foreigners have increased their friendly merger and acquisition (M&A) activity, however. According to the KFTC, in 1997 19 cross-border M&As accqunted for 4.5 percent of total M&A activity. In 1999, 132 cross-border M&As were reported to the KFTC, accounting for 27.2 percent of total M&A activity (Yun 2000). It should be observed, however, that not all of these deals will ultimately be consummated. As noted in the text, some highly publicized deals have fallen through and have not been completed.

78. See Kirk (1999) for a detailed account of Hyundai's acquisition of Kia.

pattern of holding multiple auctions in the case of Korea Life, which was at the center of the "Furgate" political corruption scandal.[79]

A similar pattern emerged in the disposal of Daewoo Motors, when Hyundai and the Federation of Korean Industries (FKI) explicitly opposed the sale of Daewoo to any foreign competitor, claiming that a foreign breach of Hyundai's bastion home market would reduce Hyundai profits in its "home playground." Even a consortium of local small businesses announced that they were preparing to enter the fray to keep Daewoo out of foreign hands. Hyundai at that time controlled more than 80 percent of the domestic market for passenger cars and had been accused of exercising market power in its pricing policies. The company later indicated that it was amenable to a joint bid with a foreign firm, and this time the government signaled that it would not oppose a foreign takeover.[80]

A second case involves the protracted sale of Korea First Bank to Newbridge Capital. The IMF had made its rescue package conditional on the sale of First Korea Bank and Seoul Bank. There are two basic interpretations of what happened. The first is that Newbridge failed to do adequate due diligence prior to signing a memorandum of understanding in January 1999. It subsequently discovered that Korea First Bank was in worse shape than it had realized, and effectively demanded a renegotiation of the terms of the agreement in an attempt to subvert it. The other interpretation is that elements of the South Korean government were uncomfortable with the notion that a South Korean bank would be taken over by a "vulture firm" and have been fighting a rearguard action. The deal began to come apart in April 1999, when Newbridge estimated that the bank's bad debts exceeded its assets by W7 trillion ($5.7 billion) and that the government had underestimated this figure by valuing the bank's assets at book rather than market value. (Korea First Bank is the prime bank for Daewoo and Hanbo Steel, among others.) Newbridge's position implied that some loans would be reclassified as non-performing, and

---

79. The scandal centered on apparent embezzlement and influence peddling by Choi Soon-young, chairman of Korea Life's parent Shindongah, and his wife Lee Hyung-ja. Like the "third-rate burglary" that set off the Watergate scandal in the United States, the initial impetus to the "Furgate" scandal was the alleged gift of an expensive fur coat to influence an ongoing investigation. After numerous twists and turns, including the first appointment of a special prosecutor in South Korea's history, Former Justice Minister Kim Tae-joung and former Presidential legal secretary Park Joo-sun were arrested in December 1999 for altering and leaking an official document. Indictments were announced for Lee Hyong-ja and her brother, Lee Hyong-ki, on charges of perjury and illegal lobbying. Three women, Yon Chong-hee (wife of former Justice Minister Kim), Bae Chong-suk (wife of former Unification Minister Kang In-duk), and Chong Il-Soon, owner of the La Sposa boutique, were indicted for perjuring themselves before the National Assembly.

80. Although the Daewoo Motors situation remains unresolved, in April 2000, the much smaller Samsung Motors became the first South Korean auto assembler to fall into foreign hands when it was sold to France's Renault.

this would increase the funds that the government would have to provide to keep Korea First Bank's assets at the stipulated level. Government officials observed that accepting Newbridge's claim would bankrupt the deposit insurance scheme.

In May 1999, Newbridge's exclusive acquisition right expired. The government indicated that it would inject W5.5 trillion into the bank and continue to negotiate with Newbridge. Sri-Ram Aiyer, the World Bank representative in Seoul, and other observers repeatedly warned that a failure of the deal to be consummated would adversely affect foreign investment, and Moody's castigated the Korean government on its handling of the sale.

As the summer dragged on, the government became increasingly concerned about allowing one of Daewoo's main creditors to fall into foreign hands—and thus affect the government's ability to manage the Daewoo restructuring. Finally, after eleventh hour brinkmanship on the part of the Financial Supervisory Commission (FSC), Korea First Bank was sold to Newbridge Capital—under the contingency that the government retain the option to buy back 5 percent of the bank after three years, thereby returning it to state control. The final contract was signed in December 1999, almost exactly two years after the IMF had made the sale of Korea First a condition in its loan package.

The other big bank denationalization, that of Seoul Bank, has proved even more problematic. In February 1999, the British financial group HSBC Holdings signed a memorandum of understanding (MOU) with the FSC to buy 70 percent of Seoul Bank, like Korea First Bank a major Daewoo creditor. Like Newbridge, HSBC insisted on using international standards for loan classification instead of the more lax standards employed by the FSC, but unlike Newbridge, according to one report, HSBC did not include this in its MOU. In August 1999 the government scuttled the negotiations, with FSC head Lee Hun-jai describing HSBC's insistence on applying international standards as irrational. His announcement reportedly perplexed HSBC negotiators. Again, observers felt that the government was concerned about allowing a major Daewoo creditor to fall into foreign hands and the ramifications for the balance sheets of Daewoo's other creditors of applying strict standards to Daewoo debt. The following week, the FSC declared Seoul Bank "financially impaired" before injecting $3.75 billion into the bank. Nevertheless, the negative reaction to the sale's collapse reportedly increased pressure on the government to come to an accommodation with Newbridge in the Korea First case. Finance Minister Kang Bong-kyun was forced to admit in December 1999 that the South Korean government did not have any prospects for a new foreign buyer for Seoul Bank.

A fourth possible case of bureaucratic hostility to foreign investment was the auction to denationalize Jinro Coors, a joint venture between the failed Jinro beverages group and Adolph Coors, the American brewery. Coors withdrew from the bidding process, characterizing it as "seriously flawed and unfair" and indicating that it had "no faith in the integrity of the process." The dispute erupted in June 1999 when OB, the largest brewery in South Korea, was permitted to resubmit its bid three days after the bidding had closed. This led Coors to suspect that its bid had been leaked to OB. The state-run Korea Development Bank, Jinro Coors' leading creditor, initially announced Coors as the winner of the auction, then reversed itself hours later and announced OB as the victor. Coors filed an injunction, claiming that OB had violated the bidding procedure, but its case was dismissed. Ironically, the employees of Jinro Coors and local public officials in Chongju, where the brewery was based, protested the decision because of fear that OB would shut down the rival brewery.

Foreign investors have expressed unease about the government's handling of labor issues, including its intervention in the Hyundai strike and in the Korea Minting and Security Printing Corporation (KOMSEP) scandal discussed below.[81] And, although foreign direct investment continues to increase, foreigners have been net sellers of South Korean equities in 1999. It appears that Korean interest in encouraging FDI waned as the economy began to recover in 1999, although FDI continues to grow at a rapid rate, reaching a record level in 1999.[82]

This has been particularly salient in light of South Korea's large state-owned enterprise (SOE) sector, which at the end of 1998 included 108 SOEs with 210,000 workers (OECD 1999). In July 1998, the government announced privatization plans for eleven large enterprises, including Korea Electric Power Company (KEPCO), Korea Telecom, Korea Tobacco and Ginseng, Pohang Steel (POSCO), Korea Gas, and 61 subsidiaries.[83]

---

81. The government's August 1998 intervention in the labor dispute at Hyundai Motors (encouraging Hyundai to back down) has been cited as a further negative signal to potential foreign investors. Similarly, the government's decision to revoke creditor responsibility for Daewoo restructuring was cited as a reason for the failure of Hanvit Bank's planned international security issue, as discussed below.

82. Approvals data released by the MOFE shows that FDI was up more than 75 percent in 1999 to a historic level of more than $15 billion. However, there appear to be large discrepancies between this data and FDI on a balance of payments basis, which in some recent years has only been around half as large. What appears clear is that FDI in South Korea is growing rapidly and is at an unprecedented level, though exactly what the level actually is, is a matter of dispute.

83. In some cases (KEPCO, Korea Tobacco and Ginseng, Korea Telecom, Korea Gas, POSCO, and Korea Heavy Industries (Hanjung)) there are aggregate or individual limits on foreign ownership. In the case of Korea Gas, it was expected that British Gas would purchase 15 percent, Osaka Gas 8 percent, and GIC 2 percent, though talks between Korea Gas and British Gas broke off in July 1999. In some cases (POSCO, Hanjung), the privatization will be complete, while in the case of KEPCO the government will retain majority ownership. See Kwak and Lee (1999) for an assessment of the privatization program.

The privatizations have not always occurred on schedule, however. As the economy recovered in 1999, the urgency of privatization waned. Other reasons include bureaucratic obstructions by ministries loath to see their captive enterprises privatized, labor disputes, and even concerns that the inflow of foreign capital could generate an exchange rate appreciation and derail the recovery. Nevertheless, through mid-1999 the government was able to raise $4.6 billion through the issuance of depository receipts abroad.

The Collapse of Daewoo

Despite the 1998 recession, Daewoo (and Hyundai) continued to expand.[84] Even according to the misleading financial information that Daewoo released, its financial condition was alarming. The conglomerate admitted that it had increased its debt 40 percent in 1998 to nearly W60 trillion ($49 billion), leaving it with a debt-equity ratio of more than 500 percent if suspect asset revaluations were excluded. Interest costs were nearly double profits. In early 1999 the watchdog Financial Supervisory Commission (FSC) estimated that Daewoo's foreign debt was $9.9 billion, with 55 percent of it falling due by the end of the year. Of the total, $3.1 billion had been borrowed from foreign banks in South Korea, $4.6 billion was borrowed from foreign banks offshore, $1.6 billion from overseas branches of South Korean banks, and $0.7 billion in overseas bond issues. Foreign banks indicated that the total actually would have been $5 billion higher if guaranteed borrowings by Daewoo's foreign subsidiaries had been included. Even this proved to be an underestimation.

In December 1998 and again in April 1999, Daewoo announced restructuring plans. The conglomerate's stated goal was to focus on the automobile business and to cut its debt in half by selling its other businesses. As part of the "big deals," it planned to swap its electronics businesses to Samsung for Samsung Motors. Daewoo also indicated that it was negotiating with Mitsui and Kawasaki of Japan to sell its shipbuilding business. Furthermore, it indicated that it would sell a considerable stake in Daewoo Motors to GM, with which it had once maintained a troubled partnership (though GM did not show much interest). Daewoo also announced that it was in negotiations with Sweden's Skania to sell its truck, bus, and large engine business, which Skania denied. Additionally, it signed a memorandum of understanding with Newbridge Capital to sell 66 percent of its stake in Daewoo Telecom (Newbridge was contempo-

---

84. Some have speculated that Daewoo and Hyundai expected favorable treatment from the government as a *quid pro quo* for absorbing the loss-making auto assemblers Samsung Motors and Kia, though in the end, Samsung Motors was sold to Renault. Similarly, it has been claimed that Hyundai expected favorable treatment in return for spearheading the government's engagement policy in North Korea.

raneously negotiating with the FSC to purchase Korea First Bank, Daewoo's main creditor) and entered into negotiations with Nippon Electric Glass to sell its Hankuk Electric Glass subsidiary.

However, many observers, including most importantly Daewoo's creditors and the ratings agencies, had trouble taking these plans seriously. The expected prices for the spin-offs were optimistic, and Daewoo's determination actually to sell these businesses was questionable. In April 1999, Standard & Poor's cut Daewoo Corporation's rating to B−.

Throughout the spring of 1999, Daewoo denied rumors that it was in financial trouble, but Fitch IBCA downgraded the rating of the Daewoo Corporation to CCC in July, indicating that "default is a real possibility." That month Daewoo narrowly averted bankruptcy when on Monday, July 19, domestic creditors agreed to extend payment on W4.5 trillion ($3.8 billion) of corporate bonds and W3 to W4 trillion of commercial paper. Among the asset management companies holding Daewoo paper were those operated by rivals Samsung and Hyundai. The asset management companies refused to extend new loans to Daewoo without government guarantees, which the government eventually did provide. Over the next week the other four large *chaebol* reportedly purchased W1.2 trillion in Daewoo commercial paper and extended concessional terms on existing holdings of Daewoo debt. This rescue effort was undertaken using in part funds deposited at the *chaebol* non-bank financial institutions, including their investment trusts.

For its part, Daewoo admitted its financial problems for the first time and pledged an additional W10.1 trillion in collateral, including W1.3 trillion owned by chairman Kim Woo-choong. Kim also offered to step down once Daewoo's auto operations were normalized, but he still clung to his goal of maintaining control of Daewoo's restructuring. The stock market rose nearly 4 percent in response. Foreign bankers protested that they were being asked to roll over loans without being provided collateral. FSC head Lee Hun-jai indicated that Daewoo should service foreign debt by selling foreign assets and that locally raised funds should not be sent abroad. On Friday, 23 July 1999, the Seoul stock market fell more than 7 percent over doubts about the Daewoo restructuring plan, leaving it down nearly 15 percent for the week.

On Tuesday, 27 July, Daewoo's creditors took control of the restructuring process and announced that they would produce a restructuring plan on 11 August. The government was responding to a threat by foreign bankers (mostly European and Japanese) to call in Daewoo's overseas debts, which would have provoked a collapse. Two days later Standard and Poor's downgraded Daewoo debt to CCC.

In a Friday, 30 July, U-turn, the government announced that responsibility for Daewoo's restructuring was being returned to Chairman Kim and his management team. The stock market fell by 3 percent after the announcement. One theory was that the government decided to hand Daewoo back over to its management rather than allow foreign bankers to participate in the restructuring. This change was regarded as a negative signal to foreign investors, and on 30 July the nationalized Hanvit bank was forced to withdraw a planned $1 billion international share offering.

On Thursday, 5 August, thirteen foreign banks sent a joint letter to Daewoo and the FSC, warning that they would not roll over loans without adequate information. The letter suggested that a Daewoo default on its foreign debt would "severely impact" the confidence of foreign investors in the South Korean economy.[85] This set off a war of words with Lee Hun-jai, head of the FSC, and these disputes between the foreign banks on the one hand and Daewoo and the South Korean government on the other would prove to be a recurring theme in the Daewoo saga. As foreign sentiment deteriorated, Hanvit was forced to accept an unprecedentedly large discount of 21 percent on its $1 billion issue of global depository receipts, unleashing a storm of criticism that the nationalized bank had conceded too much to foreign investors.

As the stock market sank, domestic interest rates rose, and Korean firms found it increasingly difficult to secure financing abroad, support for Daewoo evaporated. By mid-August 1999, the writing was on the wall for all to see. When it became clear that an aggressive sell-off was the only way to ensure the survival of Daewoo's subsidiaries, even the company union swung behind the break-up solution. On 10 August, Lee Hun-jai told the National Assembly that the FSC was prepared to allow creditors to begin disposing of assets for cash. The following day, creditors reached agreement with Daewoo to sell the conglomerate's financial units—Daewoo Securities and Seoul Investment Trust—depriving the group of its two captive sources of cash and effectively ending any possibility of staving off a breakup. On 12 August 1999, a restructuring plan was announced that effectively sheared Daewoo of all non-automobile-related businesses, and on 15 August creditors began selling off Daewoo.[86]

As might be expected, this plan did not go smoothly. More than 60 South Korean and foreign banks had claims on Daewoo, including nationalized banks directly controlled by the government. Foreign banks were excluded from the restructuring process, which was a source of constant

---

85. Indeed, US Undersecretary of Commerce David Aaron, while visiting Seoul, warned that the government's rescue package could be regarded as a subsidy, which could spark a trade dispute. By mid-August, Daewoo was reportedly in technical default on some of its overseas debt.

86. Eventually, under the Daewoo workout, GM was granted exclusive negotiating rights for Daewoo Motors. These rights expired in November 1999 without consummation of a deal. As indicated previously, Daewoo Motors' main creditor, the Korea Development Bank, has signaled that it is interested in organizing an auction that could include Hyundai, GM, Ford, Daimler-Chrysler, and Renault as participants.

irritation. Given the extensive web of inter-subsidiary financial links, bankruptcy of one subsidiary could reverberate strongly throughout the Daewoo family of firms. Despite tough talk and Kim Dae-jung's televised speech on 15 August claiming to be the first South Korean president to reform the *chaebol*, the government appeared reluctant actually to close any of the non-viable subsidiaries for fear of increasing unemployment. What was an untenable situation to be resolved by markets, increasingly appeared to be an untenable situation to be resolved by politics.

On 26 August, Daewoo's creditors effectively gave the conglomerate a reprieve, deferring debt repayments of 12 subsidiaries for three months and extending $700 million in new loans in order to avoid bankruptcy and permit due diligence and an orderly dismantling of the conglomerate.[87] The Financial Supervisory Commission then moved to sever financial ties between subsidiaries in order to prevent cross-subsidization. However, Daewoo could not come to terms with its foreign creditors, and a meeting on 27 October ended without an agreement.[88] In a reprise of earlier episodes, concerns over Daewoo were translated into a falling stock market, rising interest rates, and an inability for South Korean firms to secure finance on international markets. On 1 November, creditors rejected workout plans for two of Daewoo's bigger units, Ssangyong Motors and Daewoo Telecom, forcing Chairman Kim Woo-choong to tender his resignation. The following day domestic creditors proposed to take control of the conglomerate through a $25 billion debt-for-equity swap.[89]

Two days later, creditors received another shock when the FSC released a due diligence study indicating that Daewoo's debt stood at $73 billion— not the $49 billion previously thought. This probably makes the Daewoo collapse the largest corporate bankruptcy in history. Most of the increase came from the inclusion of debts of overseas subsidiaries which had not been previously revealed.[90] This revelation raised questions about the

---

87. This was later increased to $900 million after investment trust companies (ITCs), which held large amounts of Daewoo debt, objected to provisions to freeze interest payments on bonds (see box 6.5). The extension of new credit was led by Korea First Bank, a nationalized bank. In October, domestic creditors led by Hanvit Bank, another nationalized bank, extended Daewoo Electronics a $450 million line of credit. The bank offered this credit despite contemporaneous private estimates that put the likely loss ratio on loans to Daewoo affiliates on the order of 50 percent.

88. European banks would eventually attempt to foreclose on local Daewoo subsidiaries, seizing Daewoo cars and other assets in response to non-payment on loans.

89. Agreement on the first of these restructuring plans for Daewoo Electronics was reached on 24 November. Workout plans for eleven other major units were subsequently concluded. See Kwak Young-sup, *Newsreview*, 13 November 1999, for a summary.

90. For example, Daewoo had deleted from its books a $10 million telecom project in the Ukraine and a $58 million thermal power plant in India.

Box 6.5   The 10-11 Crisis: The Shoe That Didn't Drop

Liberalization and the fallout from the financial crisis spurred a rapid increase in the investment trust companies (ITCs). These 24 intermediaries manage funds for one in six South Koreans and account for a quarter of all deposits in the South Korean financial system. Most are owned at least in part by the big five *chaebol* (Leipziger 1999). They normally purchase about one half of the paper issued by the corporate and government sector and are big holders of Daewoo debt, which accounts for about 10 percent of their holdings.

The origins of the sector's problems extend back into the 1980s. In December 1989 then Finance Minister Lee Kyu-sung reportedly ordered the ITCs to borrow $3 billion to buy stocks and bonds in a vain attempt to shore up the market. As the market continued to decline, the ITCs were forced to borrow more and more to cover interest payments, and over the next ten years their debts grew to $6.7 billion. The Daewoo collapse was the straw that broke the camel's back.

As the crisis progressed, it became apparent that Korea Investment Trust and Daehan Investment Trust, two of the top three ITCs, were insolvent, and the government was forced to fabricate a plan to prevent a run on the whole sector. The government developed multiple lines of defense, including Korea Asset Management Company (KAMCO) purchases of unsecured Daewoo debt, a $20 billion bond stabilization fund, and a guarantee that investors who held onto their Daewoo-linked investments until 10 November would receive 80 percent of their investment. If they held on until 8 February 2000, they would get 95 percent of their money back.

On 4 November, at the same time that the government revealed that Daewoo's debt was far larger than originally thought, it also announced that it was injecting W3 trillion into Korea Investment Trust and Daehan Investment Trust to shore up those institutions in anticipation of a possible run on 10 November, meaning that two of the three largest ITCs were effectively in government hands.

When the big day came, net withdrawals were around w1 trillion, higher than the previous week, but not massively so. Nevertheless, having dodged one bullet, the ITC sector is still in weak financial shape. New regulations forcing ITCs to mark-to-market their bond holdings daily, rather than reporting book values on a monthly basis, are expected to generate liquidity crises among the weaker ITCs. In all likelihood, government entities will eventually absorb more of Daewoo's unsecured debt. Ultimately, both the management of the ITCs and the management of the entities whose paper they purchase will have to improve before the sector is out of the woods for good.

accounting practices of the other *chaebol* and possibly other unpleasant surprises to come. The most immediate effects were a reduced likelihood of an agreement with foreign creditors and an increased likelihood of a run on the investment trust companies (ITCs) (see box 6.5).

The prospects for a rapid resolution shrank even further on 6 December 1999, when Daewoo admitted to illegally funneling nearly $8 billion from the parent Daewoo Corporation to financially weak subsidiaries. The immediate impact of the revelation was to scuttle any possibility of reaching a quick deal with Daewoo's foreign creditors. The formula proposed by the Corporate Restructuring Coordinating Committee would have involved foreign creditors accepting larger losses on average than domestic creditors on their Daewoo debt because they were relatively more exposed to the parent corporation. However, foreign creditors immediately rejected the proposal after the disclosure of illegal financial transfers. In response, the FSC set up a 28-member investigation team and promised a complete accounting by June 2000.[91]

For weeks a game of chicken ensued in which the South Korean government and the Foreign Bank Standing Committee negotiated over the resolution of Daewoo's debt. Finally, on 23 January 2000, the two sides reached a tentative agreement under which foreign creditors would accept an overall write-off of 61 percent of Daewoo's debt in return for cash and warrants, which could appreciate in value if Daewoo's financial position strengthened. Approval of the deal by Daewoo's foreign creditors would permit the scheduled workouts to proceed, including the sale of Daewoo Motors.

This by no means marked the end of the Daewoo saga. Daewoo's creditors are largely South Korean financial institutions, many of which are directly or indirectly under control of the South Korean government. In effect, the state, once removed, controls Daewoo's assets. The Kim Administration will be tempted to use its leverage over the banks to keep failing Daewoo firms operating for short-run political reasons. In the longer-run, the uncertainty surrounding the resolution of the Daewoo situation impedes the state's disengagement from the financial sector by acting as a deterrent to potential private investors in South Korean financial institutions. Given this situation, in which the public, in effect, owns Daewoo, it has been argued that the government should undertake policies to create and distribute stock in Daewoo (and other firms in similar situations) to the public.[92] This possibility is taken up in the policy recommendations in chapter 10.

Labor Market Reforms

The labor market presents policymakers with a complicated set of issues. On one hand, the old rules had made labor shedding difficult for large firms, creating rigidities in the labor market by effectively guaranteeing

---

91. The revelation of illegal financial transfers had two other implications. For the first time, Daewoo founder Kim Woo-choong, who effectively had been in exile in Europe, faced the possibility of criminal sanctions, including prison. Moreover, some of the alleged illegal dealings had occurred outside of South Korea and could be prosecuted by foreign authorities beyond the political control of Seoul.

92. See, for example, Graham (1999b) and Leipziger (1999).

lifetime employment to age 58 or 60. The restrictions on labor shedding were understandable given the relative underdevelopment of the social safety net, and, in periods of high growth, the implicit costs might not have been too onerous. However, in a period of slow or negative growth, such rules can be a serious barrier to restructuring. The obvious strategy would be to expand the social safety net to compensate those adversely affected by downsizing, while removing rigidities in the labor market to encourage structural change.

Unemployment insurance in South Korea has been made more generous since the crisis in terms of both benefits and duration, but it is still well below OECD norms. In 1998 expenditures reached 2.5 percent of GDP, with nearly one percent of GDP coming directly from the government's budget (a 45 percent expenditure increase). In the initial stages of the crisis, few of the unemployed were eligible for benefits. Changes in the law, however, brought two-thirds of employees under its provisions in 1999. For most, unemployed benefits last for only two to three months, but under the pressure of the crisis the government has been forced to extend benefits on an emergency basis. Calculated on the basis of age and tenure, benefits are low, with a ceiling of half of the previous wage (subject to an absolute maximum) and a floor of 70 percent of the minimum wage (itself only around one-quarter of the average wage).[93]

Day laborers (who make up a sizeable fraction of the unemployed) are not covered under the scheme, nor are those who have left school to enter the labor force but have been unable to find work. The government therefore introduced an extensive public works program, creating 440,000 jobs in 1998 (extended through 1999), equivalent to more than one percent of the working age population.

A national pension scheme, first established in 1988, was greatly broadened in April 1999. Its funding mechanism was criticized as regressive, but changes in the pension contribution schedules, along with income tax reductions for low and middle income households, have increased the degree of progressivity of the tax system.

With respect to labor market rigidities, the severity of the recession has forced an increase in flexibility. As D.G. Shin (1999) points out, the yearly job turnover rate is 35 percent, close to the 40 percent observed in the United States, and average tenure is actually lower than in the United States. The government has allowed an expansion of temporary worker agencies, increased support for job placement centers, and stepped up vocational training. At the same time, the government increased the sub-

---

93. In addition to unemployment insurance, there are some public assistance programs in which participants are subject to strict means tests. These include limits based on income, assets, and the availability of family support. An able bodied person is ineligible for cash transfers and only eligible for in-kind transfers. See Wang and Zang (1998), S. I. Park (1999b), and OECD (1999) for details.

sidy for firms to retain redundant workers. While this could be regarded as a sensible policy if the changed economic conditions are expected to be temporary or transitional in nature, the subsidization program does work against the long-run efficient reallocation of resources.

Industrial relations continue to be a major focus of policy, despite the fact that the unions account for a shrinking share of the labor force (figure 2.7).[94] An innovation of the Kim Dae-jung government was the formation of a Tripartite Commission, which was designed to try to reach a new social consensus on labor relations. In February 1998, this group announced a Social Agreement in which provisions for mass dismissals were included. Armed with a domestic political basis for the changes demanded under the IMF program, the National Assembly passed labor law revisions making labor shedding easier, especially in cases of mergers and acquisitions.[95] Even with these amendments, however, layoffs undertaken by ongoing enterprises require 60 days of discussion with enterprise unions and, for large layoffs, a 30-day notification to the Ministry of Labor.

As a consequence of these concessions, the leadership of the Korean Confederation of Trade Unions (KCTU) received considerable criticism from its membership and was replaced. The new leadership withdrew from the Tripartite Commission in February 1999, and the larger Federation of Korea Trade Unions (FKTU) also withdrew in April. (The Korean Employers Federation—representing management—also quit, claiming that the forum was not impartial.) The more conservative FKTU (and the employers' federation) later returned to the fold, but the KCTU stayed out.

In 1999, labor unrest increased as the economy began to bottom out and public sector unions entered the fray. A threatened general strike in April fizzled, however, underlining the dual nature of the labor market, the relatively privileged position of the industrial unions in it, and the lack of broader public sympathy for their cause. However, public passions were re-ignited in June when it was revealed that government agent provocateurs had fomented an illegal strike at the state-owned Korea Minting and Security Printing Corporation (KOMSEP) to facilitate a crackdown on union activities there and at other state-owned companies. After

---

94. Even in the midst of the recession, South Korea was subject to significant labor turmoil, including mass strikes in July 1998. Hyundai's automobile assembly plant was shut down for more than one month, and it was only high-level political intervention that averted a bloody denouement. The government's intervention in the Hyundai strike was criticized by South Korean industrialists at the time. The planned number of layoffs was reduced from 5,000 to 1,500 as a result of the strike. In the end, Hyundai dismissed only 277 workers (167 from the plant cafeteria), and the rest will be permitted to return to work within 18 months. See Kirk (1999) for an account of labor relations at Hyundai.

95. The IMF was subsequently sued in Seoul District Court by the Korean Federation of Bank and Financial Labor Unions for W480 million in damages. This is thought to be the first such suit against the IMF by citizens under a Fund program.

staging separate warning strikes, the FKTU and the KCTU agreed to join forces, and two citizens' groups, the Citizen's Coalition for Economic Justice and the People's Solidarity for Participatory Democracy (see box 6.4), joined them in demanding that a special independent prosecutor be appointed to investigate the affair. The KCTU then filed a complaint with the International Labor Organization (ILO), the UN body tasked with promoting equitable labor relations. Bowing to public pressure, Kang Won-il, a former prosecutor, was appointed as special prosecutor in October 1999 to investigate the strike-rigging scandal, and Choi Byung-mo, a former judge, was tasked with getting to the bottom of the "Furgate" scandal. These were the first such special prosecutor appointments in Korean history.[96] Radicalized, and feeling more confident with a tightening of the labor market, labor unrest picked up in the second half of 1999, with protests aimed at blocking privatizations and derailing implementation of the December 1997 labor law revision.

Public Sector Reforms

The financial crisis and the election of a reformist government stimulated attempts at public sector reform. South Korea faced essentially three problems. First, the government had historically engaged in extensive intervention in the economy. Although progress had been made since the early 1980s in regularizing the tools of industrial policy, the private sector was still subject to selective and at times highly politicized interventions that were both economically inefficient and encouraged outright corruption. Second, given that many of the institutions of South Korean governance had been inherited from the Japanese, these institutions embodied a high degree of centralization, as might be expected from an imperial colonial administration. Since sub-national units had little autonomy, there was little popular control over decision making at the local level. Third, the government bureaucracy had grown large and unwieldy. K. Choi (1999) cites the remarkable fact that the number of agricultural civil servants had grown 500 percent in the previous three decades, despite the fact that the farm population had declined by 30 percent.

The Kim Dae-jung government identified three administrative reform goals when it took power: reduce the size of the government; increase its responsiveness; and increase its efficiency both at the macro level through reorganization and at the micro level by introducing competitive principles into personnel practices. It sought to increase the coherence of governmental operations by combining duplicative organs, privatizing certain

---

96. In the end, Kang Hi-bock, the former president of KOMSEP, was jailed for the plot, and the scandal-ridden Kim Tae-joung, the Minister of Justice, was forced to resign. In addition, a number of presidential advisors eventually resigned for politically mishandling the scandal, although they were not directly implicated in the original strike rigging.

organizations and activities, and devolving certain responsibilities to local governments.

Between February 1998 and May 1999, the government undertook a fairly extensive reorganization and embarked on a significant reduction of public sector employment.[97] At the same time, the budgetary process was streamlined, with the heads of agencies given greater flexibility in the allocation of expenditures. A "carryover" system also was introduced to eliminate the bureaucratic incentive for mindless splurges at the end of each fiscal year.

South Korea maintains an extensive array of state-owned enterprises, and privatization is potentially an important component of the public sector reform. In July 1998, the government announced a multiyear plan to privatize many of these enterprises, though in some cases implementation has been delayed. The main obstacles appear to be a decreased sense of urgency due to the economy's recovery, opposition from the public sector unions, and a reluctance to take on the unions with an election approaching in 2000. In addition, the government appears to have shown some ambivalence about the role of foreign investors in its privatization scheme.

The government also has announced ambitious plans for regulatory reform. In February 1998, it established the Regulatory Reform Commission, which scrapped 5,000 regulations in its first year of operation. The government has used South Korea's commitments under the WTO and OECD to push the process of deregulation along in the face of special interest opposition.

Less progress has been made on decentralization. The power of the purse has remained predominately in central government hands. With a strong central government continuing to set national standards and controlling access to funds, the scope for local government initiative remains relatively constrained.

Recovery

The economy continued to deteriorate through 1998. GDP bottomed out in the fourth quarter of 1998, with the level of GDP nearly 6 percent lower than a year earlier. Beginning in the first quarter of 1999, positive income growth resumed, and the rate of growth accelerated for the remainder of the year. The recovery was led by a strong increase in private consumption from the extremely depressed levels of 1998 and by inventory restocking by private firms. Private facilities investment began growing as well,

---

97. Through mid-1999, the number of civil servants (excluding police and teachers) had been reduced by around 11 percent, with another 5 percent reduction to be implemented by 2002. See K. Choi (1999) for details.

though new construction remained depressed. In addition, the government undertook a policy of fiscal stimulus and monetary ease. As a result, interest rates were pushed below their precrisis levels by August 1998, and the lower interest rates fed into the revival of private investment.

As would be expected, the private sector recovered less rapidly than the economy as a whole (reflecting the positive contribution of the increases in public consumption). Manufacturing output, for example, did not bottom out until February 1999. Total employment hit its trough the same month, when the unemployment rate peaked at 8.6 percent. Even as the unemployment rate began to fall, employment in the core sectors of the economy—industry, agriculture, and services—remained weak. For the first half of 1999, the increase in employment from the trough reflected increases in public employment (mainly through public works schemes) and increases in self-employment. In essence, public works programs and the small shopkeeper sector were absorbing labor that had been shed from the core sectors of the economy. Industrial employment and wages began to rise in the second half of 1999, but remained relatively weak. As of November 1999, employment had not returned to its precrisis level. Nevertheless, the trend heading into 2000 was positive, and the World Bank predicted that the urban poverty rate would fall to nearly its precrisis level by the end of that year (Stiglitz 1999).

South Korea continued to run large trade surpluses, which actually became a drag on growth in 1999, as an increase in imports from the compressed levels of 1998 reduced net exports. What had set South Korea (and to some extent the Philippines) apart from the other Asian countries was that the domestic lending boom had largely gone into creating excess capacity in the tradables sector. When exchange rates collapsed at the end of 1997, these countries were able to take advantage of their large exchange rate depreciations to boost exports.[98] While initially some of the increases in export volume were offset by decreases in price, a revival of the electronics industry led to a firming of electronics prices, particularly semiconductor prices, beginning in late 1998. This was to South Korea's benefit.[99]

By September 1999, GDP had returned to its precrisis level, and by December 1999 things were so improved that on 3 December, the second anniversary of the IMF bailout, President Kim Dae-jung felt sufficiently confident to declare the crisis officially over.

Yet this recovery is partly illusionary. It has been driven largely by: traditional short-run Keynesian stimulus through government fiscal expenditure; recovery of private consumption from its extremely low

---

98. Lee and Rhee (1999) present some econometric evidence supporting this contention.

99. South Korea was aided in this regard by the earthquake that shook Taiwan in October 1999 and disrupted semiconductor production there.

levels of 1998; inventory restocking; and a trade surplus. None of these factors are sustainable in the long run. The government will eventually have to rein in spending; consumers' buying habits will adjust back to normal; firms will achieve their desired inventory levels; and a reduction of the trade surplus will act as a net drag on the economy. Indeed, the consensus among forecasters is a slowing of growth in 2000 and beyond.

As a consequence, both the crisis and the recovery may prove more ephemeral than anticipated. As economic conditions have improved, however, interest in reform has slackened, for it can be disruptive in the short run and adversely affect the interests of those privileged under the *status quo*, though beneficial to the economy as a whole. In the long run, South Korea will need to come to terms with the underlying problems that contributed to the crisis in the first place.

Conclusions

The South Korean economy, circa 1980, was characterized by a symbiotic relationship between government and business in which business acumen was a necessary, though not sufficient, condition for economic success. Instead of screening loans, banks merely wrote the checks for government-sponsored ventures. Risk was socialized. Firms were not subject to market discipline; rather, they were subject to politically motivated punishment. Faced with a macroeconomic shock in the form of a precipitous decline in the terms of trade associated with the second OPEC oil shock, the system began to fail. Wages went unpaid, and labor violence erupted. Faced with a crisis, the government restored social stability at the point of a gun and permitted the technocrats to begin a reform process that was short-circuited by a North Korean act of terror.

Unfortunately, in 1997 the South Korean economy retained a number of the characteristics of that earlier period. The over-leveraged *chaebol* got fat on bank loans. When the country was hit by an external shock—this time a precipitous decline in the terms of trade associated with a collapse in export prices—the economy once again began to contract.

However, this time two things differed. First, South Korea had already partly liberalized its capital account, but the way that it had done so—liberalizing short-term before long-term flows without strengthening prudential supervision—arguably made the country more susceptible to shocks from abroad, be it the panic in Southeast Asia or the Japanese banking crisis. Second, South Korea had become a democracy. It was inconceivable that the military could or would step in and force acquiescence at the point of a gun.

South Korea now faces the task of building on the economic policy reforms that it has undertaken during the past two decades. Ironically, the international trade sector probably requires the least reform, because the existence of well-specified international norms and institutions have provided both the road map and the diplomatic environments to facilitate such reforms. It is the "domestic" product, labor, and financial markets that need the most work, and where the international community cannot provide the same kind of technical and political support as it has in the international trade sphere.

As of mid-1999, resolution of the crisis had cost South Korea 17 percent of GDP, and the bills continued to mount. One effect of the crisis had been to reverse the process of the government's disengagement from the financial system. Coming out of the crisis the government owned a large portion of the banking system and was tempted to use this control for political ends.

The collapse of Daewoo is critical in this regard. As long as the status of Daewoo debts remain unresolved, denationalization of the financial system will be impeded. Moreover, Daewoo's ability to continue to muddle through with indirect state support increases resistance to reform among the other *chaebol* and discourages rational decision making in the financial sector.

Nevertheless, it is important that South Korea continue the reform process, both for its own purposes and as a preparation for contingencies involving the North. As will be discussed in the next three chapters, events in the North could have profound effects on both the South Korean economy and its politics. It is to these prospective developments that we now turn, returning in the final chapter to policy recommendations for South Korea.

7

The Prospect for Successful Reform in the North

The capitalist market economy is a corrupt anti-people economy that reduces human beings to slaves of money and materials.... We should have a correct understanding about the true nature of the capitalist market economy as an anti-people [sic] and thoroughly reject any illusions about it. And we should resolutely protect and defend our *chuch'e*-based socialist economic system, which is the most successful in the world, and bring the superiority of the socialist planned economy into fuller play.

—Hwang Kyong-o, *Pyongyang Kyonje Yongu*,
20 August 1998, 37, FBIS translation

When thinking about the future prospects of North Korea, one is immediately confronted with two fundamental problems. First, there is an extreme lack of knowledge. Despite the efforts of scholars and intelligence analysts, remarkably little is known about the inner workings of the North Korean regime—its motivations, decision-making processes, or capabilities. A vast gulf exists between fragmentary, anecdotal evidence on the one hand and highly uncertain estimates of macroeconomic aggregates on the other.

Second, we really have no reliable theory linking economic distress or deprivation to political change. Even a reasonably persuasive analysis of the economy does not necessarily provide much guidance as to political decision making, much less regime stability. Nevertheless, there must be some utility in sharpening our understanding of the North Korean economic predicament. At a minimum, this analysis should inform our subjective appraisal of the likelihood of alternative outcomes and the advisable set of policies for decision makers inside and outside of North Korea to consider.

Finally, although what happens on the Korean peninsula will largely be determined by Koreans, outside powers will have an influence as well, and their actions and motivations must be factored into any analysis.

The strategy over the next three chapters will be to analyze future prospects in terms of two fundamental and polar opposite scenarios: successful reform of the North Korean economy by a fully functioning North Korean state (the present chapter); its collapse and absorption into South Korea (chapter 8); and a middle way of muddling through (chapter 9). These alternatives are obviously not exhaustive. Other possibilities such as war, descent into anarchy, or partitioning are possible, but effectively beyond the analytical scope of this book.[1] Nor is this to say that successful reform or collapse is even likely in the foreseeable future. But having established the intellectual "extreme bounds," we are then in a position to work backward and identify what the critical points of similarity and divergence are between the two extreme scenarios—especially from the standpoint of South Korea. We then evaluate the likelihood of each of these scenarios coming to pass and what the future may indeed hold.

Reform in the North

Our country is well organized. There are no riots, no strikes, no differences in opinion.

—Kim Mun-sung, then Deputy Chair of the Committee for the Promotion of External Economic Cooperation[2]

As argued in the previous chapters, North Korea is an economy in crisis. Although the regime has undertaken some reforms in response to the crisis (establishment of the Rajin-Sonbong special economic zone (SEZ), the Mt. Kumgang tourism project, permission for limited private initiative in agriculture, and allowance of greater scope for private markets outside the plan in the distribution of consumer goods), the consensus of a wide range of observers is that the current reforms are insufficient to pull North Korea out of its predicament. Current policies arguably amount to a series of short-term tactical adjustments without any overarching vision or rationale. If these moves prove inadequate to cope with the crisis at

---

1. For a careful consideration of the whole range of possible outcomes, see Ahn (1998) and Pollack and Lee (1999).

2. Quoted in the *Financial Times*, 27 September 1995.

hand, then the regime will be forced to make a choice of whether to accelerate and widen the reforms or to stand pat and try to ride out the current difficulties, risking collapse if the situation worsens. At some point in the future, policymakers may conclude that the status quo is unsustainable absent fundamental changes, forcing them to confront the issue of whether and how to accelerate and deepen the economic reforms. We begin by examining what successful reform might entail and the prospective economic payoffs to this strategy. The purpose is to establish what is at stake economically in North Korea.

Internal Reforms

A true self-initiated reform strategy would include reforms of labor and capital allocation schemes or markets, a reform of the price structure to reflect genuine scarcity or opportunity costs, fundamental reforms of the planning mechanism (with the goal of encouraging greater reliance on market signals to inform the decision making of economic agents and of promoting competition between domestic enterprises in product markets), and introduction of the family responsibility system or a similar scheme to de-bureaucratize agriculture.[3] In a relatively industrialized economy such as North Korea's, clarification of property rights and a strengthening of the rule of law would also be necessary, at least in the long run. In principle, defined property rights would not necessarily require a shift toward private property. It might be possible to maintain forms of non-private ownership, such as the township and village enterprises in China. The critical requirement is that enterprises respond to market signals.

The experiences of other transitional economies suggest that considerable increases in productivity can be attained through de-bureaucratization of agriculture. In the most well-known case, that of China, peasants have not been assigned alienable private property rights to land, but have been extended contractual rights. A similar change in property rights has been undertaken in Vietnam. While rights to the land (and some communally applied inputs) continue to be vested in the state, and the state continues to exercise control over some planting decisions (as it does in many countries), individual families exercise a much greater degree of control over production and marketing decisions. This, combined with the introduction of a more rational price structure for agricultural output, has generated tremendous increases in agricultural productivity, not only raising domestic output, but also critically freeing labor for reemployment elsewhere in the economy. North Korea already appears to be headed down this road, at least to a limited extent.

---

3. Consideration of certain issues unique to a rapid collapse and absorption scenario are postponed until chapter 8.

Things are more complicated in the industrial and service sectors of the economy. There are two ways to raise productivity. The first is to create new high-productivity enterprises. The second is to improve the productivity of existing ones. While the latter has been the focus of considerable analysis of enterprise restructuring, it is important to keep in mind that it has been the former that has generated most of the growth in the industrial and service sectors of transitional economies.

With this in mind, there are essentially three ways to improve enterprise management. The first is to improve managerial incentives by tying managers' compensation more closely to the economic fortunes of the enterprise. A second is to improve information flows within the enterprise and generate improved decision making on the part of managers. This improvement can be facilitated by reducing the size and hierarchy of the large managerial bureaucracies that typically characterize state-owned enterprises (SOEs). Lastly, and probably most importantly, management of existing enterprises can be improved by installing new managers.

Indeed, a survey by McMillan (1997a) found that improving incentives and introducing new managers was complementary—that is to say, improvements in enterprise performance were the greatest when both the incentives and the management were changed. Although privatization is not essential in this regard, the process of privatization, especially privatization involving new foreign owners, often has accomplished both (Dyck 1997, Frydman et al. 1999).[4]

A related task is to improve the allocation of capital, which fundamentally requires that the allocation be depoliticized and that "hard" budget constraints be imposed on firms. McMillan (1997a) argues that this reform would be best achieved through decentralization of the capital allocation mechanism; in practice, successful reform could involve a decentralization of the banking system or the introduction of capital markets. The idea here is that, in the highly concentrated financial systems of centrally planned economies (CPEs), lenders effectively have little choice in making loans. The move to a more decentralized system that consists of a larger number of lenders (each accounting for a smaller share of total lending) would facilitate greater selectivity on the part of lenders.

The functioning of post-reform banking systems is intimately related to developments in product markets. In the simplest sense, competition in product markets is necessary to spur allocative efficiency and to constrain the exercise of market power by monopolistic or oligopolistic state-owned enterprises. Given the market-dominant positions of many SOEs,

---

4. See Stiglitz (1994) for an analysis that is more sympathetic to the maintenance of existing relationships within the firm and more skeptical about the advisability of privatization. The issue of privatization is taken up in more depth in chapter 8 in the context of policy lessons from German unification.

legalization of new entry is a necessary, though not sufficient, requirement to foster competition.

However, new entrants and increased competition in product markets may disadvantage incumbent state-owned enterprises and their lenders. A problem encountered by many economies in transition has been the use of the state-controlled banking system to funnel implicit subsidies to loss-making SOEs. Indeed, the dual problem of lagging productivity and mounting losses among SOEs on the one hand, and the growing incidence of non-performing loans in the banking sector on the other, has emerged as the single biggest economic policy problem confronting China, underscoring the necessity of depoliticizing lending. Privatization may be helpful in this regard if it leads to a decrease in the political influence of the enterprise. However, it is no panacea, as demonstrated by the continued subsidization of loss-making privatized enterprises in Russia.

A final source of productivity improvement for existing enterprises is technological upgrading. This advancement requires investment, which immediately raises the issue of property rights. China and Vietnam have been able to achieve significant productivity gains in agriculture through the introduction of contractual rights instead of property rights. Moreover, China has witnessed a spectacular increase in industrial output concentrated in light manufactures without the benefit of well-defined property rights or commercial law. This system appears to work in part because of reputational considerations in the context of a repeated game (i.e., no one will do business with you if you renege on your deals.) When reputation is insufficient to insure adherence to agreements, private coercion can be employed to ensure compliance.[5]

Nevertheless, the expansion of the non-state-owned sector does not demonstrate that the absence of property rights or legal means to adjudicate disputes is desirable. One does not know the answer to the counterfactual of what might have occurred during the past twenty years if China had developed a more fully functional legal system. Presumably, the reliance on reputation and private enforcement raises transactions costs, and close observers of China question whether its current set of institutions is sufficient for a more complex economy in which longer-run strategic decision making and commitments are necessary (Gelb, Jefferson, and Singh 1993). The ability successfully to introduce legally enforceable property rights and commercial codes appears to be correlated with the historical legacy of the pre-socialist period.[6] In this regard, North Korea does not appear to be well placed, either in theory or practice. Although

---

5. McMillan (1997a) contains an enlightening discussion of these issues.

6. See Sachs (1995) on this issue.

it apparently has demonstrated interest in improving its commercial legal system, in reality the system appears to be still non-functional.[7]

Returning to the issue of technological upgrading, while privatization is not required, investment is essential. As in the case of managerial incentives, it is natural to think of infusion of capital and new technology coming from private and quite possibly foreign investors (Sinn and Sinn 1992, Dyck 1997).[8] Eickelpasch (1998), in a survey of East German enterprises, found that foreign affiliation not only facilitated better access to capital, but better access to sales distribution networks as well. Frydman et al. (1999) found that the new owners make an enormous difference: enterprises under new "outside" ownership greatly outperform SOEs or privatized enterprises controlled by "insiders," possibly for the reasons that Eickelpasch identified. As one might expect, the empirical evidence on the ability of transitional economies to raise the productivity of state-owned enterprises is mixed.[9]

Similarly, the empirical evidence on the benefits of the speed of transformation is mixed. However, the preponderance of evidence suggests that, *given initial conditions*, rapid transformations are no more costly and can be more successful than slow transformations. Since this analysis appears to contradict the popular view (especially in Asia) that "gradualism" is preferable to "shock therapy" or "big bangs," it is worth explaining why.

The empirical evidence from the entire universe of transitional economies suggests that rapid reform is preferable to slow, gradual, or piecemeal reform, fundamentally because it is more politically sustainable. The reason is that swift restructuring offers the smallest scope for opportunistic rent-seeking behavior by the *nomenklatura* and, in democratic societies, makes the political differences between pro and anti-reform forces most stark.[10] Moreover, democracy and economic reform can be self reinforcing.

---

7. Chiddy (1997) provides two examples: the inability or unwillingness of North Korean officials to specify which state-owned enterprise commitments are backed by the state, and ING Bank's inability even to call in loans on a local bank that is 50 percent owned by overseas Koreans.

8. Sinn and Sinn (1992) argue that in the German case privatization was key: "Without privatization there is no incentive for capital formation, and without capital formation there can be no upswing." See Johnson (1997) for a contrary view. See the World Bank (1996), chapter 3, for a summary of the broader international experience with privatization. The issue of privatization will be revisited in the chapter 8 discussion of the German experience and its relevance to Korea.

9. On this point, see Groves et al. (1994, 1995), Woo et al. (1994), Choi and Woo (1996), and Kong, Marks, and Wan (1999) for contrasting assessments of China's experience in raising the productivity of SOEs.

10. The most comprehensive empirical analysis on this point is by Åslund, Boone, and Johnson (1996). One of the things that they observe is that "gradual" reformers actually have a higher probability of being voted out of office in favor of former communists than do "radical" reformers. See also Heybey and Murrell (1999) for a discussion of the relationship

As Åslund, Boone, and Johnson (1996) observe, "reformers have found the creation of new political institutions that provide new norms as well as checks and balances to be a valuable means of locking in reform" (p.227).

How, then, can one explain the popularity of the notion that "gradual" reform has been more successful than "rapid" reform? The answer can be summed up in a word: China. However, a close examination of the Chinese case (and the similar case of Vietnam) suggests that initial conditions played a critical role in their reform experience. Among economies in transition, pre-reform macroeconomic stability has been associated with favorable outcomes, whatever the reform strategy adopted. However, gradual, slow, or piecemeal reform can only be undertaken under conditions of macroeconomic stability. Conversely, under conditions of macroeconomic instability, "shock therapy" and the acceptance of a certain degree of chaos in the reform process may be the only option. That is to say, examples of successful gradual reform began from relatively favorable macroeconomic initial conditions, while rapid reform has been undertaken from a variety of starting points. There are no cases of countries experiencing pre-reform macroeconomic instability that successfully introduced gradual reform—though there are some that tried and experienced more or less continual decline in output.[11]

The second initial condition that appears to be highly correlated with successful reform is the existence of labor-intensive agriculture.[12] This relationship exists for two reasons. Raising productivity in the agricultural sector is easier than raising it in the industrial sector. Relatively agrarian economies such as China and Vietnam (both with more than 70 percent of their labor forces in agriculture at the time that they initiated economic reforms, as shown in table 3.7) were able to initiate reforms in the agricultural sector. In these cases the price liberalization provoked rapid efficiency gains, freeing up low productivity surplus agricultural labor to be absorbed by the emerging, non-state or semi-private light manufacturing and service sectors. In theory, this sector then could be taxed to provide

---

between rapidity of reform and its success. They find that initial conditions (most importantly, pre-liberalization growth performance and the initial level of liberalization) strongly condition growth performance in the first four years of transition. Their results also suggest that, if anything, causality runs from growth performance in the initial stages of transition to liberalization speed, not the other way around.

11. See Åslund, Boone, and Johnson (1996) on this point.

12. The modifier *labor-intensive* is important. One could imagine countries such as Russia or the Ukraine (similar to the United States, Canada, and Australia), which have large agricultural sectors, where the more land and capital-intensive nature of production would be less amenable to simple decentralization reforms than labor-intensive production in China or Vietnam.

the resources necessary to cushion the restructuring of the old state-owned heavy manufacturing sector.[13]

However, the initial conditions of China and Vietnam are not reproducible, and such a path does not appear to be viable for more industrialized centrally planned economies.[14] Piecemeal reforms have not been successful in industrialized CPEs facing economic crises. The more highly interdependent nature of industrial enterprises means that a whole host of reforms (macroeconomic stabilization, introduction of rational pricing, liberalization of international trade and introduction of a convertible currency, tax, bankruptcy, and social safety net reforms, etc.) are a seamless web and must be done simultaneously for reform to be successful economically and sustainable politically.

The experiences of Poland, the USSR, and Vietnam are instructive in this regard. All three attempted gradual reforms in the 1980s. In the first two cases, the non-state sector did not emerge quickly enough to ease the burden of restructuring the industrial state-owned enterprises. The Polish private sector only began to grow rapidly after radical reforms in 1990. In the case of Russia, it attempted radical reform, but in fact followed no coherent policy in the aftermath of the breakup of the Soviet Union.

Vietnam actually began a process of gradual reform in 1986 under Soviet encouragement. Although reform was relatively successful, Vietnam subsequently was forced to undertake shock therapy in March 1989 when the collapse of the USSR severely squeezed its finances. In the process, it removed legal prohibitions on many business activities, slashed subsidies, decontrolled prices, unified its multiple exchange rates, devalued the currency, and liberalized trade. Economic structure, in particular its large, labor-intensive agricultural sector, not "gradualism," has been the key to its relatively successful performance.

Political economy provides another reason why the more agrarian reformers have done relatively well. In an economy characterized by surplus labor in the agricultural sector, liberalization, which raises agricultural incomes and increases absorption of labor into higher productivity manufacturing jobs, is less likely to generate popular opposition from the masses. (In technical economic terms, it is more likely to be Pareto-improving—that is, everyone is made better off.) In contrast, in an economy in which state-owned heavy industry plays a significant role, reform is likely to create significant losers—at least in the short run. As a consequence, the surplus agricultural labor reform path is likely to generate

---

13. This is simply the famous Lewis (1954) two-sector model of development with unlimited supplies of labor in action. See Lau, Qian, and Roland (2000) for a very different interpretation of the Chinese experience.

14. See Lipton and Sachs (1990), Riedel (1993), Sachs and Woo (1994), Sachs (1995), Kemme and Marrese (1997), Leipziger (1998b), and Lee and Montes (1999).

less political opposition as compared to one in which the restructuring of existing industrial enterprises is central. In the latter case, rapid reform might well be more sustainable since, while it would generate dislocation, it would be less likely to generate macroeconomic instability than a gradual program that could involve the prolongation of soft budget constraints. As Sachs and Woo (1994) and Sachs (1995) point out, China and Vietnam were blessed by having a far smaller share of their labor forces employed in industrial state-owned enterprises than did the European centrally planned economies. Moreover, in the case of China, the introduction of reforms in 1978 followed a period of falling incomes and deprivation; the masses were ready for a change. In this last respect, contemporary North Korea could be ripe for reform.

This raises a final issue, that of the sequencing of reforms, in particular the relative advisability of the Russian model (*"glasnost"* before *"perestroika"*) or the Chinese model (economic reform under continued Communist Party rule). Again, as in the previous discussion of "gradualism" versus "shock therapy," there is a certain superficiality to this debate. One can think of political outcomes as being a product of demands on the state and of the state's capacity to carry out its core responsibilities without succumbing to particularistic demands of special interests, i.e., political demand and supply.

Again, initial conditions matter. As shown in Sachs and Woo (1994) and Sachs (1995), the social welfare system in the European centrally planned economies was far more extensive than in China or Vietnam, where state provision of social services outside the urban areas was scant. Consequently, the post-reform European governments had to contend with higher expectations about the delivery of services than did the reforming governments of China and Vietnam. This situation had two implications: higher social welfare expenditures in Europe were a source of strain on government budgets, contributing to macroeconomic instability, and provision of services was a focus of popular discontent, which contributed to political instability. Presumably, the degree of political openness affects the manifestation of discontent, but not its existence. One must use the modifier "presumably" because, of course, in politically repressed societies there is no way of gauging it directly.

Moreover, gradual reform creates heightened opportunities for rent-seeking and criminal behavior. A strong state may be capable of implementing a gradual reform process while keeping these impulses in check, or at least restraining them. A weak state cannot. A weak state that attempts gradual reform will likely end up with a disfunctional mix of both macroeconomic instability and opportunistic behavior by *appartachik* or criminal groups, regardless of the degree of political openness.

The point is that a weak state that is incapable of resisting opportunistic behavior of *apparatchik* or criminal groups will be unable to implement

Table 7.1 Alternative reform scenarios

Opening without reform
Opening with reform
    —Non-preferential opening
    —Opening with restrictions on North-South integration (China-Taiwan model)
    —Preferential North-South opening
        —Free trade area (direct trade, no internal barriers)
        —Customs union (common external barriers)
        —Economic union (free movement of productive factors)
        —Monetary union (common currency)
        —Social union (common labor rules, social security systems, etc.)
    —Political unification

gradual reform successfully, and, indeed, may be unable to implement rapid reform successfully, also. Rapid reform that may undercut the sources of power of the *nomenklatura* and promote the development of new, reform oriented groups, may actually have a better chance of succeeding in this case. A strong state will have a greater degree of latitude in implementing reform policies. It may be able to undertake gradual reform successfully, though the evidence on the desirability of this course of action is ambiguous at best.

An oft-heard syllogism goes "there are two ways to reform a centrally planned economy: the unsuccessful European big bang approach and the successful Asian gradual approach. North Korea is an Asian country, ergo it will adopt the successful, gradual approach and grow at 10 percent a year upon commencement of reform." A careful examination of the evidence supports a different view. The most important lesson for North Korea is that initial conditions may constrain significantly the policy options that would-be reformers may fruitfully pursue. The most relevant of these conditions appears to be the structure of the economy, the degree of macroeconomic stability, the degree of state capacity at the time that reform is initiated, and the willingness of the population to undertake change. Of these four factors, the absence of a surplus labor agricultural sector along the lines of China or Vietnam is preordained, and the others, while not predetermined, may well be *fait accompli*.

External Reforms

The discussion thus far has focused on internal reform measures. If the North Korean regime were willing to undertake such reforms, it would face a number of alternatives with respect to its external relations (table 7.1). It could, for example, simply open to all foreigners in a non-discriminatory fashion, treating them equally in terms of trade and investment policy. (This would be consistent with the precepts of the World Trade Organization.)

Alternatively, North Korea could open preferentially—discriminating among foreigners on the basis of nationality. One variant would be to open to the rest of the world, but retain restrictions on trade and investment with South Korea, restrictions similar to those that exist for trade and investment between Taiwan and China. This might be attractive if the regime were concerned about being, in effect, absorbed by the South.

North Korea also could take the opposite tack, opening preferentially to the South.[15] Successively deeper forms of integration would include: a free trade area (goods would move freely within the Korean peninsula); a customs union (North and South Korea would maintain a common set of trade policies toward the rest of the world); a common market or economic union (in which productive factors as well as goods could flow freely); a monetary union (a common currency); a social union (common social insurance systems); or political union and the complete dissolution of North and South Korea as separate sovereign nations.[16]

In reality, these alternatives would not be entirely exclusive. A decision to pursue non-discriminatory opening might result in a predominance of trade and investment with South Korea, for example. South Korean firms might be less risk averse than their non-Korean competitors about doing business in the North due to common language, culture, geographic proximity, etc. Also, in light of North Korea's tradition of central planning and the ubiquity of discriminatory trade practices in Northeast Asia (among Japan, South Korea, and Taiwan, for example) it would not at all be surprising if nominally non-discriminatory policies had a substantial discriminatory element.

The question naturally arises: what would the North Korean economy look like if it were to undergo successful reform? For one thing, there would be a reallocation of factors according to comparative advantage. If reform were accompanied by a reduction of political hostilities with the South, there could also be a significant demobilization of the military and a release of productive factors for alternative uses. Based on the experience of other transitional economies, one would expect significant

---

15. A number of observers have noted that the tariff-free treatment of North Korean trade probably violates South Korea's WTO obligations, if any of its trade partners would be so churlish as to make a case of this. This issue might arise if a significant number of firms entered the North Korean market as a back door to the South, though even in this eventuality a WTO case would seem unlikely.

16. For more on these types of schemata, see Chun (1993) and S.M. Lee (1993). For its part, North Korea has proposed a Confederal Republic of Koryo, to be governed by a national assembly consisting of an equal number of representatives from North and South Korea. For details of this proposal, see Han and Choe (1995) and Yu (1997). For highly informative interpretations of North Korea's unification policy see H.S. Park (1993) and Eberstadt (1998d). In a 1999 meeting at the Council of Foreign Relations in New York, North Korean Foreign Minister Paek Nam-sun reportedly indicated that North Korea could consider a "one country, two systems" model along the lines of Hong Kong and China.

Table 7.2 Actual and "natural" North Korean trade shares, 1990

	Actual trade share		"Natural" trade share
China	23	South Korea	35
Japan	21	Japan	30
South Korea	10	China	13
Russia	4	U.S.	7
Rest of world	42	Rest of world	15
Memorandum:			
Share of total trade in GDP	12		71

Note: Intra-Korean trade counted as international trade; GDP in current dollars from Bank of Korea.

reorientation of international trade away from socialist allies and toward natural trading partners. One way to get a sense of how North Korea might look as a "normal" country is to use a standard "gravity" model of bilateral trade to simulate its post-reform trade pattern. The regression model, originally estimated by Frankel and Wei (1995), characterizes the volume of trade as a function of size, income level, proximity, adjacency, participation in regional economic integration schemes, and cultural similarity. North Korean values of these explanatory figures were then substituted into the gravity model regression to generate North Korea's "natural" pattern of trade.

According to the results reported in table 7.2, North Korea's natural trade partners would be South Korea, Japan, China, and the United States, in that order. South Korea and Japan alone would account for nearly two-thirds of North Korea's trade. Moreover, the share of international trade in national income would roughly quintuple, as indicated in the memorandum item (though the resource reallocation associated with such a large increase in trade would almost certainly boost income significantly as well). This gives some indication of the potentially dramatic scope for change in North Korea.

North Korea's prospective comparative advantage is analyzed using disaggregated trade and investment data for North Korea, South Korea, and Japan. Initially, data for North and South Korea are subjected to five filters: 1) sectors in which North Korea had a "revealed" comparative advantage, defined as the ratio of North Korea's share of world exports of a particular commodity category to its share of world exports as a whole; 2) sectors in which "revealed" comparative advantage had increased between 1980 and 1992; 3) sectors in which South Korea has declining "revealed" comparative advantage; 4) sectors in which Noland (1991b) projected South Korean export shares to fall; and lastly 5) sectors in which the growth of South Korean outward FDI has exceeded that of

Table 7.3 Prospective sectors of comparative advantage
(based on analysis of North and South Korean data)

SITC	Description
0342	Fish, frozen (excluding fillets)
0360	Crustaceans and molluscs, fresh, chilled, frozen, etc.
0542	Beans, peas, lentils, and other leguminous vegetables
0545	Other fresh or chilled vegetables
2613	Raw silk (not thrown)
2731	Building and monumental stone not further worked
2733	Sands, natural, of all kinds, whether or not colored
2786	Slag, dross, scalings, and similar waste, n.e.s.
2815	Iron ore and concentrates, not agglomerated
2816	Iron ore agglomerates (sifters, pellets, briquettes)
2881	Ash and residues, contain. metals/metallic compounds
2911	Bones, horns, ivory, hooves, claws, coral, shells, etc.
3221	Anthracite, whether/not pulverized, not agglomerated
5621	Mineral or chemical fertilizers, nitrogenous
6512	Yarn of wool or animal hair (including wool tops)
6672	Diamonds, unworked cut/otherwise worked, not mounted/set
761a	Television receivers
8421	Overcoats and other coats, men's
8422	Suits, men's, of textile fabrics
8423	Trousers, breeches, etc., of textile fabrics
8429	Other outer garments of textile fabrics
8431	Coats and jackets of textile fabrics
8451	Jerseys, pull-overs, twinsets, cardigans, knitted
8997	Basketwork, wickerwork, etc., of plaiting materials
9410	Animals, live, n.e.s., incl. zoo animals

Note: SITC = Standard International Trade Classification.

the economy. The list is debatable—one might not expect North Korea's current exports, in essence the residual of the plan, necessarily to be the exports in a reformed, market economy. Nonetheless, this seems like a reasonable place to start. Twenty-five of the original 465 sectors meet all five criteria. They are reported in table 7.3.

The most promising sectors for North Korea are primary products such as fish and minerals, and manufactured goods such as textiles and apparel. Although South Korea had been the rice bowl in the past, if trade were opened today North Korea might end up being a net exporter of agricultural goods to the South, especially if capital markets were relatively unified and labor markets were not.[17] This is a very conservative list. By loosening the criteria to include, for example, sectors where Japanese FDI has been high, the list of candidate sectors is lengthened. Additional goods

---

17. O (1995) asserts that a reformed North Korea could have a comparative advantage in fruits, vegetables, dairy products, and meat (including beef, chicken, and pork).

Table 7.4 Prospective sectors of comparative advantage
(based on analysis of North Korean and Japanese data)

SITC	Description
0577	Edible nuts (excl. nuts used for the extraction of oil)
0811	Hay and fodder, green or dry
2238	Oil seeds and oleaginous fruit. N.e.s.
2471	Sawlogs and veneer logs, of coniferous species
2472	Sawlogs and veneer logs, of non-coniferous species
2820	Waste and scrap metal of iron or steel
2924	Plants, seeds, fruit used in perfumery, pharmacy
6821	Copper and copper alloys, refined or not, unwrought
6841	Aluminum and aluminum alloys, unwrought
6861	Zinc and zinc alloys, unwrought
7752	Refrig. Hh, fd frz, e/o
8981	Pianos and other string musical instruments

Note: SITC = Standard International Trade Classification.

that meet an analogous filter for Japan are reported in table 7.4.[18] There are no big surprises here either: the additional 12 products are mostly natural resource products.[19]

Since North Korea's current exports might not provide a useful signal of its future exports, the data are reanalyzed focusing exclusively on the South Korean and Japanese data. A similar set of criteria are employed: sectors in which both countries have "revealed" comparative advantage; sectors in which this "revealed" comparative advantage is declining over time; sectors in which both countries are forecast to lose competitiveness; and sectors in which the rate of outward FDI in both countries is higher than national income. The additional fourteen sectors that meet these criteria are listed in table 7.5. With the exception of two agricultural categories, these are all light industry sectors. In summary, an analysis of the North Korean, South Korean, and Japanese trade and investment data suggest that North Korea's prospective comparative advantage would largely be in primary products sectors, in which North Korea's natural resources convey a comparative advantage, and light manufactur-

---

18. The criteria were: 1) sectors where North Korea had a "revealed" comparative advantage; 2) sectors where North Korea's "revealed" comparative advantage had increased between 1980 and 1992; 3) sectors where Japan has declining "revealed" comparative advantage; 4) sectors in which Noland (1990) projected Japanese net exports to fall; and 5) sectors in which the growth rate of Japanese outward FDI has exceeded that of the economy.

19. The inclusion of the two raw wood sectors is problematic. North Korea currently is exporting raw wood to China, but this does not appear sustainable. Moreover, the original North Korean data do not include imports from Russia or probable illegal imports from Indonesia and the Philippines. As a consequence, North Korea's comparative advantage in wood products is probably weaker than table 7.4 would suggest.

Table 7.5 Prospective sectors of comparative advantage
(based on analysis of South Korean and Japanese data)

SITC	Description
0561	Vegetables, dried, dehydrated or evaporated
0565	Vegetables, prepared or preserved, n.e.s.
6514	Yarn containing 85 percent synthetic fibers
6517	Yarn of regenerated fibres, not for retail sale
6531	Fabrics, woven of continuous synthetic textile materials
6539	Pile & chenille fabrics, woven of man-made fibers
6560	Tulle, lace, embroidery, ribbons, & other small wares
8471	Clothing accessories of textile fabrics
8942	Children's toys, indoor games, etc.
8947	Other sporting goods and fairground amusements
8982	Other musical instruments
8983	Gramophone records and similar sound recordings
8998	Small-wares and toilet articles, feather dusters, etc.
8999	Manufactured goods, n.e.s.

Note: SITC = Standard International Trade Classification.

ing industries, which are declining in Japan and South Korea but could be competitive in lower wage North Korea.

This analysis has been done partly on the basis of historical experience. It is possible that, with appreciation of the yen, the future industries of greater capital intensity (auto parts, for example) than listed in tables 7.3 through 7.5 could be candidates for relocation to North Korea.[20] Overall, these sectors are consistent with the sectors identified by Hyundai for its prospective Haeju SEZ.[21]

Nevertheless, the preceding analysis, along with the huge increase in trade indicated in table 7.2, would imply an enormous change in the composition of North Korean output away from heavy toward light industry. Recovery of land damaged in the natural disasters of the 1990s could be expected to lead to increased agricultural output and employment. This would mean significant adjustments for many North Korean workers and enterprises. At the same time, the expanding industries would be

20. GM, for example, has expressed interest in constructing an auto parts plant in Rajin-Sonbong (*Financial Times*, 17 June 1995).

21. At a press conference on 1 November 1998, Hyundai Chairman Chong Mong-hon identified light industrial products, shoes, clothes, needlework, woven goods, spinning, toys, kitchen wares, assembled metal products, precise machines, metal machine tools, plain operating machines, leather goods, bags, and textile goods as promising sectors for investment in the North on the basis of their labor intensity. In addition, TV assembling, radios, fans, electronics parts, plastic goods, synthetic rubber processing, and machine parts have been declining in competitiveness in the South and could be produced "with mutual cooperation." Beverages, food, cigarettes, and pulp, for which raw materials are "easy to obtain," could also be produced in the North. See also S.Y. Lee (1998), who performed an analysis similar to the one above—and obtained similar results.

labor intensive, which would facilitate the transition by absorbing displaced labor (especially if military demobilization were to release a large number of workers for non-military activities).[22]

A General Equilibrium Perspective on Reform

Noland, Robinson, and Wang (2000a,b,c) use a series of computable general equilibrium (CGE) models to analyze the economy-wide repercussions of the recovery of land damaged in the flooding, the provision of food aid, the liberalization of international trade, the change in technology, the "obsolescence shock" associated with opening to the outside world, and, lastly, the potential "peace dividend" from military demobilization. These models have a standard neoclassical specification, except that they incorporate disequilibrium in grain markets and severe quantity controls in exports and imports with concomitant distortions in domestic product and factor markets.[23] The markets for goods, factors, and foreign exchange are assumed to respond to changing demand and supply conditions, which in turn are affected by government policies, the external environment, and other exogenous influences. The models can be considered medium-to-long run, in that all factors are assumed to be intersectorally mobile. They are Walrasian in that only relative prices matter. Sectoral product prices, factor prices, and the exchange rate are determined relative to an aggregate consumer price index, which defines the numeraire. The results presented in this chapter are comparatively static in nature—that is, there is no explicit time dimension. Results from some simple dynamic models are presented in the following chapter.

The models have eleven sectors: rice, maize, other agricultural, forestry and fisheries products, mining, light manufacturing, industrial intermediates, capital goods, construction, public administration, the military, and services. There are three "demanders": a single aggregate household that buys consumer goods; a government that spends on goods and public administration; and an aggregate capital account that purchases investment goods. The government is the sole, and completely price inelastic, demander of military services (defined narrowly as distinctly military "war-fighting" activities, as opposed to the broader range of activities in which the Korean People's Army (KPA) engages). All goods and services

---

22. As noted earlier, perhaps half of the military is already engaged in non-military activities, leaving half available for effective demobilization.

23. Coles and Hammond (1995) develop a rigorous general equilibrium model of famine and demonstrate that famine is possible even in a perfectly competitive Walrasian economy and that all of the classical existence and efficiency theorems apply. Noland, Robinson, and Wang (2000b) is, to the present author's knowledge, the first application of CGE modeling to an actual famine.

are traded internationally with the exceptions of construction, public administration, and the military. Domestically produced and traded goods are specified as imperfect substitutes, which provides for a realistic continuum of "tradability" and allows for two-way intersectoral trade.

Primary factors of production include three types of land, capital, agricultural labor, high-skill urban labor, and low-skill urban labor. Aggregate production functions were estimated for aggregate capital and labor using data reported in Hwang (1993) and Y.S. Lee (1994b). The results are remarkably robust and plausible given the quality of the underlying data. Constant elasticity of substitution (CES) specifications yielded estimates of the substitutability between capital and labor of around unity. The hypothesis that the aggregate production function was Cobb-Douglas could not be rejected. In most specifications, North Korea exhibited slightly negative total factor productivity (TFP) growth, which is typical of many pre-reform socialist economies. In the computable general equilibrium (CGE) model, sectoral production technology is represented by a set of Cobb-Douglas functions of the primary factors, with the exception of the mining and military sectors, which use CES functions with lower substitution elasticities. Intermediate inputs are demanded according to Leontief fixed input-output coefficients. Labor and capital are intersectorally mobile; land is specific to agriculture, but mobile within the three agricultural sectors. Migration is permitted between rural and urban low-skill labor markets.

The Loss and Recovery of Arable Land

Total arable land in North Korea is 1.85 million hectares. Following the FAO (1997) and the UNDP (1998), the models incorporate three types of land: high quality land (0.4 million hectares) that is permanently irrigated, medium quality land (0.65 million hectares) that is not permanently irrigated, but capable of supporting rice production, and non-irrigated lower quality land (0.8 million hectares), suitable only for the production of other cereals. Since the late 1980s, rice and maize have been produced on 0.58 million and 0.6 million hectares of land, respectively. The remaining arable land has been used to produce other agricultural goods. All rice production has occurred on irrigated, high quality or medium quality land. Of the 0.6 million hectares allocated for maize, only one-third is irrigated. Most of the remaining maize has been grown on medium quality or low quality land that does not have permanent irrigation.

By using the county data from the UNDP (1998), land lost in the 1995-96 floods has been estimated county by county and class by class. About 15 percent of arable land was destroyed, with the incidence of flooding being higher on high quality land (28 percent) than on medium and low quality land (13 percent). The post-flood land distribution is then used as the base in simulations; this land is costlessly restored in the "land recovery" scenario. It should be noted that land recovery is not evenly distributed across the three types, and, to the extent that different crops use the three types of land in differing intensities, the Rybczynski effects on the three types of crops are also unequal.[24]

The Role of Food Aid

To account for the current famine conditions, it is assumed that there is an infinite demand for grains at the base price up to the WFP/FAO/UNDP minimum human needs target of 3.7 million metric tons. (These organizations put "normal" human demand at 4.8 million metric tons, and they estimate total demand including seed, livestock, and industrial uses at 7.8 million metric tons.) Beyond this human minimum, demand is elastic and the market-clearing price falls. This approach implies that production up to 3.7 million metric tons could be absorbed by the economy without a fall in prices received by farmers or any possible adverse supply response.[25] This specification also provides us the benchmark for concessional assistance in an aid-oriented scenario: "small" amounts of aid—up to the minimum human needs level—are essentially absorbed into the economy with no effect on prices. Beyond this level, however, aid depresses prices and begins to crowd out both domestic production and imports on commercial terms. The issue of the fungibility of aid and its role as implicit balance of payments support can be examined in this way.

Quantity Controls in Trade

The major distortions in the economy are assumed to be quantitative controls on both imports and exports.[26] Demanders are assumed to treat

---

24. The Rybczynski effect refers to the impact of a change in a factor endowment on output quantities. In an "even" international trade model in which the number of goods equals the number of factors, an increase in a factor endowment will lead to an increase in the production of at least one good and a decrease in the production of at least one other. This simple version of the theorem breaks down when the model is "uneven," in that it includes nontradables and differentiated products, as in the case at hand. Nevertheless, as an empirical matter, one may still obtain the counterintuitive result that an increase in an endowment can cause a decrease in an output quantity.

25. Technically, this is modeled as an increase in government (PDS) demand, which leaves prices unchanged as the supply curve shifts. In the North Korean context, one could imagine this as simply an increase in Public Distribution System (PDS) deliveries back toward some previous survival ration.

26. Data on aggregate revenue from turnover taxes are reported in table 3.4. Since these taxes are assessed on the basis of the legal status of the transacting enterprises, sectoral tax rates *per se* do not exist. In the modeling work, these receipts were allocated more or less evenly across the industrial sector, with a mild degree of escalation by degree of processing, as typically has been the case in other centrally planned economies.

imports and domestically produced goods as imperfect substitutes (the Armington assumption). They have a sectoral import demand function that depends on the relative prices of imports and domestically produced goods on the domestic market. These demand functions are parameterized according to the "normal" levels of sectoral imports that one would expect North Korea to have without any rationing, given the results from the gravity model. Then we assume that the difference between desired imports and observed imports is due to the imposition of quantity rationing by the government.[27]

The model also specifies sectoral export supply functions in which the export supply ratio depends on the ratio of the export price to the price on the domestic market. The supply functions also are parameterized, so that the desired ratio is consistent with the results from the gravity model. Symmetric with the treatment of imports, quantity controls are specified, so that actual exports are less than desired. The result is that demanders are forced off their import demand curves and producers are forced off their export supply curves. The distortions are quite large, indicating large potential gains from liberalizing trade and allowing markets to clear. The trade rationing contributes to major distortions in the domestic price system on top of explicit internal taxes.

Technical Change

Recent research suggests that the world is characterized by international technological spillovers. These are quite important in the case of developing countries, which benefit from technological developments abroad transmitted through international trade. In the case of North Korea, the parameters estimated by Coe, Helpman, and Hoffmaister (1996) indicate that complete liberalization would result in total factor productivity (TFP) gain of approximately 18 percent as a result of economic opening and importation of capital equipment embodying new technologies from abroad. (Indeed, the results reported in Noland, Robinson, and Liu (1999) imply that this is a conservative estimate.)[28] This treatment of technological change is provisional. The issue will be reexamined in the following chapter in the context of North-South economic integration and the possibility of technology transfer from the South to the North.

---

27. The degrees of sectoral quantity rationing are given in Noland, Robinson, and Wang (2000a), appendix 3.

28. See Noland, Robinson, and Liu (1999) for further discussion as well as an analysis of sectorally non-uniform changes in TFP. In all likelihood, importation of capital equipment would not be the only avenue of TFP enhancement associated with opening. Dyck (1997) argues that the introduction of new management practices was critical in the East German case.

The "Obsolescence Shock"

A final issue concerns the valuation of the post-liberalization capital stock. There are three points to consider. First, due to the nature of technology, the capital stock accumulated under one set of output and factor prices is likely to be sub-optimal for different relative prices. While this is true for all economies, the impact is particularly acute for transition economies in which the relative prices under central planning were wildly different from those observed in world markets. Second, economies sheltered from international trade may manufacture products that are essentially worthless in world markets. Think of televisions or radios without tuners—both of which are produced in North Korea. To the extent that capital is product specific, this capital would be effectively worthless when the economy is opened up to trade.[29] Third, as pointed out by Wolf (1998), in the case of German unification there was a once and for all culling of the worst environmental polluters among the East German enterprises. Some of the observed stunting of the North Korean population may actually be due to environmental degradation—not the famine. South Korean pollution standards might not be up to German levels of rigor, but if the collapse and absorption scenario were to obtain this would provide a third justification for the obsolescence shock to the capital stock. Although not directly relevant to the case at hand, this should be kept in mind.

Sinn and Sinn (1992) report that one-half to two-thirds of East Germany's capital stock was worthless after unification. If lack of exposure to international trade is taken as a proxy for internal distortion, then the North Korean economy is likely to be even more distorted than was the East German economy. On the basis of the East German experience, Noland, Robinson, and Scatasta (1997) calibrated this shock as one-half to two-thirds of the value of the 1990 pre-opening capital stock. In the current model, calibrated to 1996, the capital stock has already shrunk, and the obsolescence shock is assumed to be smaller, or 25 percent.[30]

---

29. This treatment is obviously a stylized one. One way to think of it is that there are goods with positive prices in autarky and a world price of zero. When the economy is opened up, product specific capital depreciates instantly.

30. There is a counterargument that the North Korean capital stock might not decline by as much as East German capital stock did. Two reasons are given. First, it is argued that the decline in the value of the East German capital stock was partly a result of West German transfers, which facilitated the shift in demand from formerly East German home goods to imports from the West. If the North Koreans were to receive fewer transfers, they would be forced to continue buying home goods, maintaining the value of the North Korean capital stock.

Second, the East Germans had lost their major markets in other CPEs, which contributed to the decline in the capital stock. In contrast, some suggest that China could represent a viable market for cheap, low quality North Korean manufactured goods. If one accepts

Military Demobilization

North Korea is the most militarized society on earth, devoting an estimated 25 percent of GDP to military activities and maintaining more than one million men under arms. As noted earlier, these stylized facts may be a bit misleading. Probably half of North Korea's armed forces are engaged in non-war-fighting activities that would be performed by the civilian sector in most other countries. In our model, half of the army is allocated to non-military activities, leaving a sizable share of the economy's resources tied up in military activities. Assuming that trade and other reforms were undertaken, military demobilization could generate additional welfare gains as resources previously devoted to the military were released into higher productivity activities.

Data

The models utilize two main databases: a macroeconomic and a microeconomic Social Accounting Matrix (SAM) of North Korea for 1996, the most recent year for which data are available. The SAM is a consistent array of economic transactions among agents that reconciles the input-output data and national accounts.[31] In estimating the SAM, we had to draw on a variety of sources, including incomplete national accounts, sectoral production and trade data, and estimates of government accounts. These data are not only incomplete, but they also are probably replete with serious measurement errors.

For the modeling exercise, various share coefficients from the matrix, such as sectoral intermediate-input and value-added shares (for production functions) and expenditure shares (for consumption functions), are needed. Our problem is to estimate these coefficients, which requires estimating a consistent Social Accounting Matrix for the base year of the model using scarce data measured with unknown error. Using standard econometric methods, the problem is essentially hopeless—there are not enough data to provide the degrees of freedom necessary to estimate the parameters, even if one were willing to make very strong assumptions about the error generation process, (which the author is not). However, in contrast to the usual situation in econometrics, we have a great deal of prior information about the parameters to be estimated. The structure of the SAM imposes powerful adding-up constraints, and information is available about the likely values of the various coefficients from a variety

---

these arguments, then one should focus on the previously described scenarios in which the value of the North Korean capital stock is implicitly maintained.

31. See Noland, Robinson, and Wang (2000a, b, c) for more detail on the construction of the social accounting matrices, the actual SAMs employed, and complete algebraic renderings of the models.

of sources, including comparative data from past periods and other similar countries. The issue is how to use this information efficiently.

In this application, an estimation approach (which Golan, Judge, and Miller (1996) call "maximum entropy econometrics") is employed that draws on information theory. The estimation philosophy is to use all the information available, including information about the coefficients to be estimated, but not to assume any information that is unavailable. The particular estimation approach is described in Golan, Judge, and Robinson (1994) and Robinson, Cattaneo, and El-Said (1998). It incorporates assumptions of estimation errors (errors in variables) and prior knowledge about parts of the SAM (such as various macro aggregates). First, this prior information about the structure of the SAM is incorporated by specifying an initial SAM that reflects all the information available (even if inconsistent). Second, a new SAM is estimated that is not only "close" to the old SAM, minimizing a "cross entropy" measure of the deviation between the two, but also: 1) satisfies all the adding-up constraints inherent in the definition of a SAM; 2) includes any other constraints, such as knowledge, about parts of the SAM (e.g., some of the national accounts or other aggregates); and 3) incorporates stochastic information about constraints involving measurement error. The method is both flexible and powerful when dealing with scattered and inconsistent data.

With respect to the microeconomic SAM, the inter-industry relations from the Noland, Robinson, and Scatasta 1990 micro-SAM were used as the proto-SAM. These were then updated to reflect the apparent reduction in the capacity utilization rate (or, alternatively, decline in the value of the North Korean capital stock) and to obtain consistency with the macro-SAM.[32]

Urban workers are classified as either high-skilled (professional, technical, and managerial) or low-skilled (the remainder). The initial starting point for industry employment structures was taken from pre-reform Chinese data. The wage premium is calculated on the basis of South Korean data. While one might expect *a priori* that wage dispersion in the North would be less than in the South, at this level of sectoral aggregation, the skilled wage premium obtained from the South Korean data is within the dispersion observed in fragmentary data on North Korean wages.

Land is allocated across the three agricultural activities as described in the previous section. The share of land in value added is initially estimated

---

32. The input-output coefficients contained in the 1990 proto-SAM were in turn derived from a pre-reform (1979) Chinese input-output table compiled by the World Bank. This table was constructed to UN System of National Accounts (SNA) standards, expanding on the material product accounts (World Bank 1985). The assumption is that a starting point (or prior) for the inter-industry input-output relations in North Korea is pre-reform China, reflecting their common links to 1970s vintage Soviet manufacturing technology. See Noland, Robinson, and Scatasta (1997) for sensitivity analyses.

from cross country comparisons, yielding reasonable starting estimates of "rental rates" for different types of land.

Results

In Noland, Robinson, and Wang (2000a), the model is used to run five basic scenarios. In the first, North Korea costlessly recovers land damaged in the 1996-97 floods. In the second, quantity rationing of international trade is removed. The next three scenarios are in some sense extensions of the second. In the third, the North Korean economy experiences an 18 percent sectorally uniform increase in TFP as a result of its economic opening and its importation of capital equipment embodying new technologies.[33] The fourth scenario subjects the North Korean economy to an "obsolescence shock" to its capital stock as a result of economic opening, exposure to new technologies, and changes in relative prices of inputs and outputs. Finally, Noland, Robinson, and Wang (2000a) examine the issue of military demobilization and the "peace dividend." In this scenario, the North Korean military is demobilized by 70 percent, until the share of the military in national income approximates the 3 percent exhibited in South Korea.[34] Each of these scenarios is implemented in 10 steps or experiments. In addition to scenario 1 (land recovery) and scenario 4 (systemic reform), Noland, Robinson, and Wang (2000b) in a famine-focused paper report additional scenarios involving the provision of international food aid together with varying degrees of limited reform in the agricultural sector.

North Korean GDP results from Noland, Robinson, and Wang (2000a) are shown in figure 4. Base GDP is calculated to be roughly 32 billion North Korean won, which is higher than the officially reported 23 billion won figure shown in table 3.2. The reason is two-fold. First, the officially reported figure appears to exclude the military and unofficial markets outside the central plan.[35] Second, the officially reported data do not appear to be internally consistent when entered into a consistent social accounting matrix. Even if one were to assume the occurrence of little investment and the shrinkage of the capital stock, the 1996 figures would imply a tremendous decline in output relative to the 1990 SAM constructed

---

33. The possibility of sectorally non-uniform increases in TFP is taken up in the next chapter in the context of collapse and absorption, though this is obviously not the only mechanism by which this could occur.

34. In the model, it is assumed that half of the army is engaged in activities (construction, manufacturing, etc.) that normally would be performed by the civilian sector of the economy, and that half of the army is engaged in "war-fighting" activities. Demobilization is modeled as a reduction of resources devoted to strictly military activities.

35. Michell (1998) estimates that the unofficial economy is 20 percent of the actual economy.

Figure 7.1 Model simulation results

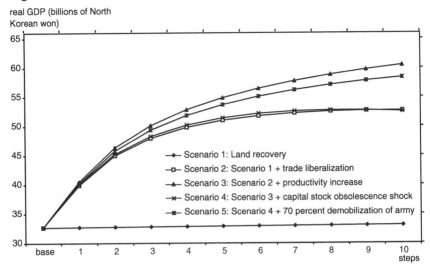

real GDP (billions of North
Korean won)

by Noland, Robinson, and Scatasta, suggesting that there were very big
reductions in factor supplies or that much of the economy was operating
at 10 to 15 percent of capacity. The simplest way to generate a consistent
SAM was to raise output.[36] While it may well be the case that floods,
famine, and the practice of scrapping capital and bartering it for food
have reduced factor supplies, and that utilization of remaining capacity
has been low, there also are reasons to believe that the actual output is
higher than reported by the authorities.[37]

In scenario 1, North Korea costlessly rehabilitates flood-affected lands
in ten successive steps. As can be seen in figure 7.1, the impact on GDP
would be minimal, increasing it by less than 2 percent. Domestic production of rice and other agricultural commodities would increase by around
4 percent and corn production would rise by 12 percent. However, as

---

36. For modeling convenience, the remaining decline was handled as an exogenous fall in
the level of total factor productivity (TFP). Alternatively, one could explicitly model the
less than complete utilization of resources by introducing unemployed resources explicitly,
but the gains associated with this strategy did not appear to warrant the great increase in
model complexity. The author is under no illusions that North Korea is a Walrasian economy.

37. First, the North Korean authorities have an incentive to understate output so as to
increase international aid flows. Second, as mentioned in the text, the official data appears
to refer only to output or resources controlled by the central planners. Evidence indicates
that both military and economic activity outside the plan have increased, or at least have
not decreased as rapidly as formal activity under the plan. Finally, aid flows, which in
recent years have probably accounted for 10 to 15 percent of food consumption, do not
appear to be included in the official figures.

Figure 7.2 Food availability

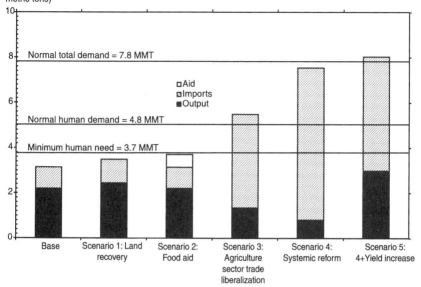

food availability (millions of metric tons)

shown in figure 7.2, domestic food availability would remain below the quantitative target established by the UNDP, the FAO, and the WFP.[38] At first glance this might seem odd—that increasing the arable land endowment of a famine-afflicted country would not have a bigger macroeconomic impact. Two things should be kept in mind, though. First, North Korea was already experiencing a famine prior to the floods that commenced in July 1995. Second, only around 15 percent of the arable land was affected by the floods. So, while natural disasters may have exacerbated the food availability problem, the famine is not a product of bad weather.[39] Rather, systemic mismanagement and a lack of intermediate inputs such as fuel and fertilizer are its proximate cause. The shortage of intermediate inputs, in turn, has been due to severe balance of payments constraints and policy decisions about the use of foreign exchange—areas that are fundamentally outside the agricultural sector. Nevertheless, this

---

38. One can think of at least two possible channels through which the impact of the floods could be underestimated. First, if one assumes high substitutability among primary inputs, then labor and capital could simply substitute for land. Second, some of the capital stock in the agricultural sector were destroyed in the floods. As a mental experiment and check on robustness, we ran a variant of the first experiment in which the agricultural capital stock was augmented as land was recovered. The addition of capital along with land did indeed increase the output response, but the impact on GDP was still only around 2 percent.

39. On the basis of econometrically estimated agricultural yield, Smith and Huang (2000) functions reach the same conclusion.

result underlines a critical issue: If only a relatively modest component of the decline in output can be attributed to flood-related declines in agriculture, then what explains the rest?

Scenario 2 addresses the main distortion in the model, the severe repression of international trade. The gravity model results suggest that in 1990 the total share of imports and exports in North Korean GDP would have been roughly 70 percent if North Korea had exhibited the economic behavior of a "normal" country. With the economy now smaller, the expected trade share should be even higher. In scenario 2, the quantitative restrictions on trade are relaxed in ten steps, and the impact on GDP is shown in figure 7.1. (Qualitatively similar results are obtained in Noland, Robinson, and Wang (2000c) when North Korea liberalizes preferentially and forms a customs union with South Korea.)[40] As shown in this figure, the impact of the relaxation of the constraint would be greatest at the beginning and would decline thereafter, as could be expected on the basis of microeconomic theory. A complete freeing of this constraint would increase GDP by 40 to 60 percent due to static reallocation of factors alone, depending on the precise specification of the model and whether liberalization is on a non-preferential or preferential basis. Domestic availability of rice and corn on commercial terms would increase by 80 to 90 percent.[41]

This static reallocation effect would not be the only impact of liberalizing trade. Results derived from Coe, Helpman, and Hoffmaister (1996) indicate that TFP might increase by 18 percent. As shown in figure 7.1, these gains would be almost exactly offset by the negative impact of an assumed

---

40. In the customs union scenario, integration with the North would have a modest positive impact on South Korea. Trade with North Korea would mostly substitute for trade with other countries and, given the small economic size of North Korea relative to South Korea, trade creation and diversion would have a trivial impact on South Korea. Only three sectors would experience percentage changes in output of more than one percent, and South Korean GDP would rise by less than one-half of one percent. These results are consistent with the results from a one-country model of South Korea (in which North Korea is simply represented by a set of export and import demand and supply equations) reported by Chang (1997). Formation of the customs union would be a Pareto-improvement: returns to all factors would either increase or remain unchanged. The distributional implications would be trivial. This conclusion changes dramatically, however, if factor markets are allowed to integrate— an issue explored in the collapse and absorption section of the next chapter.

In contrast, formation of a customs union would amount to a significant movement toward free trade for North Korea relative to its previous external barriers and would generate results similar to those discussed above for the non-preferential opening scenario. Trade with both South Korea and the rest of the world would increase, and, from the standpoint of the whole peninsula, the customs union would be strongly trade creating. GDP for the peninsula as a whole would rise by 1.5 percent.

41. In some sense this result is reminiscent of Stewart (1986), who argues that cash relief may be preferable to direct provision of food aid, in that cash relief may have the desirable benefit of sustaining the economic infrastructure of the famine-affected region.

obsolescence shock to the capital stock of 25 percent (Scenario 4). Obviously one should not attach too much weight to the exact figures derived from this modeling exercise. Rather, these results are probably best interpreted as an indication that, in an economy as distorted as North Korea's, even a relatively simple move such as an increase in the economy's openness to international trade could have enormous macroeconomic effects, dwarfing the impact of a flood.

The final scenario is a 70 percent military demobilization, in which North Korea's expenditure on the military is reduced to a share of GDP similar to that of the South's. Obviously there would have to be major diplomatic breakthroughs for this to occur, but the experiment is presented as a heuristic exercise to illustrate the size of potential payoffs. In some sense, this experiment, too, is dependent on the trade liberalization experiment. Without liberalization, it is unclear where the demobilized resources would be redeployed; however, with liberalization, they can be redeployed to their highest efficiency uses.

Figure 7.1 illustrates that redeployment of resources on this scale at the margin could add another 8 to 10 percent to GDP. The five scenarios, undertaken together, increase real GDP by 40 to 80 percent from the base, depending on specification and whether liberalization was undertaken on a preferential or non-preferential basis. Domestic food availability would exceed the UNDP/FAO/WFP target for "normal total demand" in the unilateral liberalization scenario and would exceed the "normal human demand" in the customs union scenario.[42] With non-defense government spending held constant in nominal terms, the other components of GDP would rise. Real consumption would nearly triple, investment would nearly double, and international trade would expand enormously. With the trade balance held constant, the real exchange rate would experience a modest appreciation. If the real exchange rate is held constant, then the trade deficit would expand somewhat.

The composition of output would change enormously (figure 7.3) as light manufacturing, mining, construction, and services expand, while industrial intermediates, capital goods, and the army contract in response

---

42. Noland, Robinson, and Wang (2000b) also report a "complete recovery" scenario, in which agricultural yields are raised to their precrisis level as a function of the increased availability of intermediate inputs. The main difference between this and the previous "systemic reform" scenario is that, due to increased yields, rice production in North Korea actually rises, increasing 20 percent from the base. Maize production more than doubles. (The production increase is tilted toward maize, because North Korea's comparative disadvantage is less intense in maize production. Under free trade, some land formerly used to grow rice is converted to maize production.) The increase in grain yields boosts the agricultural wage, thus moderating some of the rural-urban migration and reducing the increase in income inequality that arises, though it should be emphasized that this increase in inequality occurs as all three categories of labor more than double their wage rates relative to the base.

Figure 7.3 Output by sector

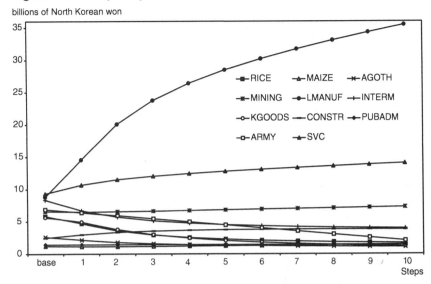

billions of North Korean won

Legend:
- ■ RICE
- ▲ MAIZE
- ✳ AGOTH
- ✳ MINING
- ● LMANUF
- + INTERM
- ○ KGOODS
- — CONSTR
- ◆ PUBADM
- □ ARMY
- ▲ SVC

X-axis: base, 1, 2, 3, 4, 5, 6, 7, 8, 9, 10 — Steps

Y-axis: 0, 5, 10, 15, 20, 25, 30, 35

to changes in the relative price structure and the decline in government demand for military services (figure 7.4).[43] Within agriculture, maize output would fall, then expand, as the highly inefficient production of rice is abandoned and land is increasingly devoted to the production of maize.

Light manufacturing would experience an export explosion, with exports increasing 40-fold; mining exports would increase more than three-fold. Imports would rise in all traded-goods categories, led by a 15-fold growth in capital goods imports. The composition of output would change enormously, as light manufacturing, mining, construction, and services expand, while industrial intermediates, capital goods, and the army contract. These qualitative results hold whether liberalization is on a most-favored-nation basis or on a preferential basis with South Korea. Even in the case of large financial inflows from abroad that drive up the real exchange rate, the traded-goods sector of North Korea expands relative to the base (Noland, Robinson, and Wang 2000c).

These changes in composition would have profound effects on factor usage and returns (figure 7.5). In the maximum reform scenario, 2.5 million workers would leave the agricultural sector and another 350,000 would leave the army, with the bulk reemployed in the light manufacturing sector. (Even in the agricultural sector, the employment and wage changes would be greater under economic reform than through land recovery.) Employment also would increase in the mining, construction, and service

---

43. For the sake of brevity, the remaining discussion refers to scenario 5, step 10—i.e., the maximal reform case.

Figure 7.4   Relative price of output by sector

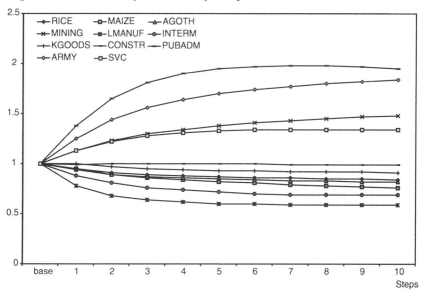

Figure 7.5   Percent change in average factor price

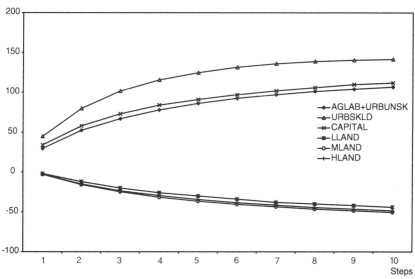

sectors. The real wages of all three classes of labor would more than triple, with the largest increases experienced by the highly skilled. The rate of return on capital would also more than triple. The rate of return on land would fall, however, as the increased availability of imported agricultural goods reduce domestic scarcity and with it the implicit returns to land. There would be some shift in the distribution of income away from land and toward urban high-skill labor.

Noland, Robinson, and Wang (2000b) report one additional scenario of interest, under which, in the absence of reform, North Korea is provided food aid until the UNDP/FAO/WFP "normal human demand" target is reached. The result would crowd out both domestic production and imports on commercial terms. (Indeed, according to South Korean Ministry of Unification figures, aid as a share of total food imports has risen from nil in 1994 to more than 80 percent in 1999.) The aid in effect acts as implicit balance of payments support, and import demand for all traded goods increases. Public administration and military expenditures are held constant by construction. If this modeling assumption is relaxed, however, these activities, too, would presumably expand in response to the provision of aid. Food aid is fungible.[44]

These results are speculative and subject to a certain degree of spurious precision. Moreover, the results presented thus far are derived from static models in which there is no explicit consideration of time. It might well be the case, for example, that while the long-run results would be along the lines sketched out in this chapter, the complete attainment of these outcomes could take a considerable length of time (as infrastructural investments were undertaken, for example). Indeed, it is possible to generate a "J-curve" adjustment path, in which output initially falls and then rises, by subjecting the North Korean economy to an instantaneous obsolescence shock to its capital stock while phasing in the trade reform and technological upgrading (cf. Noland, Robinson, and Liu 1998). Frankly, the relative dynamics of these effects are not clear, though it is quite possible that output would fall in the short run even under propitious conditions.

---

44. An issue that could be relevant in North Korea is that the local intermediary (the PDS) could act as a rent-extracting monopolist rather than a competitive supplier of aid. Coate (1989) discusses the role of intermediaries in the context of a formal model of famine relief, focusing solely on the efficiency of alternative famine relief policies. In the case of North Korea, concerns have been expressed among donors that the North Korean government might expropriate rents to support additional military expenditures, and this has been used as an argument in favor of in-kind food aid. Also of relevance is McGregor (1998), which analyses both targeted and non-targeted food distribution and public works famine relief strategies in a general equilibrium context without reaching robust analytical conclusions. Donors, who apparently expect targeting, have expressed concern that the North Korean government might divert humanitarian aid to the military and other favored groups. Indeed, the possible use of the Public Distribution System as a rent-extraction mechanism provides an additional argument for the trade-enabling strategy.

Nevertheless, the modeling work conveys a number of important points. First, even when defined narrowly in terms of domestic food availability, the payoffs to reform dwarf the impact of more narrow efforts to raise productivity in agriculture. In addition, the provision of aid may have unintended consequences, such as implicitly supporting increased military activities. Second, there would be massive shifts in the composition of output under fundamental reform. Millions of workers would switch jobs, for example. Third, with reform the importance of international trade would increase tremendously. Fourth, the military acts as a significant drag on the North Korean economy, suggesting that demobilization could have significant economic benefits.

The Likelihood of Reform

These results indicate that there are potentially gigantic benefits to reform. Yet there are economic and presumably domestic political obstacles to reform. Ahn (1998) sets out a number of preconditions: 1) a reformist leadership (which he implies excludes Kim Jong-il); 2) pragmatism and demilitarization; 3) structural economic reforms; 4) an "extended opening" to the outside world and the multilateral development institutions; 5) North-South reconciliation, including peaceful coexistence, confidence building and arms control measures, confederation and cross-recognition, North-South interdependence, and "a mini-Marshall Plan;" and 6) Chinese support and cooperation.[45]

Even without this extensive list of diplomatic precursors, North Korea's reform path would be more difficult than the ones traversed by China and Vietnam, Asia's two other major transitional economies. Successful gradual reform of a centrally planned economy requires resources to cushion adjustments in the heavy manufacturing sector. Propitious initial conditions have facilitated successful results by relatively agrarian reformers such as China and Vietnam.[46] At the time they initiated reforms, China and Vietnam had more than double the share of population employed in the agricultural sector than North Korea apparently has today, and their reform strategies were made possible by the existence of this enor-

---

45. One might imagine a reformist military coup, for example. The problem is that the North Korean populace has essentially been ruled for more than two generations by the Kim dynasty, and a non-Kimilsuugist regime would face problems of legitimacy. An obvious solution would be to keep Kim Jong-il on as window dressing, and given his lack of contact with the non-military public this might be feasible. There is no real evidence, however, that the North Korean military is interested in governing or in reform. See K. W. Kim (1996) for more sophisticated speculations along these lines.

46. See Oh (1993), Choi and Woo (1996), Naughton (1997), and McMillan (1997b) for more on the relevance of China's reforms to the North Korean case.

mous pool of low productivity labor.[47] In these countries, the state-owned heavy industry sector was initially relatively small (table 3.7), and, even in these cases, adjustment in the old state-owned heavy industry sector has proven to be difficult.[48] This agriculture-driven transition path is simply not available to North Korea, which in economic terms more closely resembles some of the economies of Eastern Europe than it does China or Vietnam.

The second hurdle that North Korea faces is ideological. Consider the case of Vietnam. The North Vietnamese government and its Vietcong allies defeated the South Vietnamese government in a civil war, allowing them to claim an ideological monopoly in the united Vietnam. Likewise, while China has contended with the rump government on Taiwan, no one has seriously claimed that the Taiwanese historically represented an ideological threat to the Chinese government. The point is that reformers in both China and Vietnam were relatively free to construct tortured rationalizations about how their market-oriented reforms were what Marx, Mao, or Ho really had in mind.

The ideological terrain faced by the current North Korean regime is very different. Rather than monopolist purveyors or dominant definers of national ideology, the North Koreans clearly are junior partners on the peninsula, both in size and achievement. Moreover, the dynastic aspects of the Kim regime make it even more difficult for the son to disavow the legacy of the father. And while the ideologues of Pyongyang can certainly try to reinterpret North Korea founder Kim Il-sung's *juche* philosophy to mean market-oriented reform, the existence of a prosperous, democratic South Korea makes their task very difficult. After all, why be a second-rate imitation South Korea when one can head south and be the real thing?

This, of course, raises a third point. The sheer scale change that is likely to accompany significant liberalization is tremendous. North Korea is probably the most distorted economy in the world. Liberalization would mean huge changes in the composition of output and employment. International trade would become far, far more important, and most of that trade would be with South Korea and Japan, two countries with which

---

47. Ironically, North Korea's extreme centralization may prove advantageous in at least one regard. Whereas in other CPEs many benefits, most importantly pensions and housing, are provided through the enterprise (and thus give workers an incentive to oppose enterprise reform, in North Korea these are provided directly by the state. As a consequence, North Korean workers may be more mobile and oppose enterprise reform less than their counterparts in other CPEs in some future reform situation, though as one observer has put it, the politics of the iron rice bowl are hard to break.

48. As noted earlier, much of the efficiency gains modeled in the previous section presumably would be realized through the creation of new enterprises, not the privatization of existing SOEs. This could be especially important in the case of North Korea, given the scope for existing enterprises to exercise anti-competitive market power in a post-reform environment.

North Korea maintains highly problematic relations. While today's North Korean economy has unexploited latent potential, its isolation means that there is no institutional mechanism through which this latent potential can be transformed into products that the rest of the world would want to buy. Even in the case of China, a significant part of the vitality of China's international trade sector can be attributed to foreign-invested enterprises, which account for as much as 40 percent of Chinese exports (Naughton 1996, table 3). In prosaic terms, North Korean enterprises need blueprints and worldwide distribution and marketing networks.

Foreign direct investment (and through it an infusion of new technology and management) would undoubtedly play a key role in creating institutional linkages between potential output and world markets. The most likely investors in North Korea are firms from South Korea and Japan. (In this respect, the potential for North Korea to draw upon South Koreans and Koreans in the diaspora is a strength, similar to the advantage that China has had with respect to Taiwan and the overseas Chinese.)

Continued exclusion from international financial institutions and international capital markets, as well as US economic sanctions, are all disincentives for potential investors of all nationalities. It is unlikely that either Japan or the United States would normalize relations with North Korea unless there were significant improvements in North-South relations. Normalization with Japan would permit the Japanese investment guaranty agency to insure Japanese investments in North Korea and to pave the way for mainstream Japanese firms to make large-scale investments. As noted in chapter 3, the most immediate issue that Japan and North Korea would confront would be the settlement of post-colonial claims. It would not be surprising if the final agreed upon figure was in the billions of dollars, spread over some period of time.[49]

Normalization with the United States would permit the termination of the embargo.[50] Even with the "right policies," a series of diplomatic tum-

---

49. Presumably Japan would seek to obtain credit for its contribution to KEDO as well as any expenditures on the recapitalization of *Chochongryun*-affiliated financial institutions. See Okonogi (n.d.) for an interpretation of Japanese interests that is largely sympathetic to support for engagement with the existing North Korean regime.

50. If the United States were to implement its announced intention to lift the embargo on North Korea, it would have to establish a policy toward the treatment of textile and apparel imports. These are currently subject to bilateral quotas under the Multifiber Arrangement (MFA). It has been argued in some circles that, if North and South Korea treat inter-Korean trade as domestic trade, then any imports of textiles and apparel from North Korea would have to be counted against the current South Korean quota. It would immediately raise the difficult issue of devising a quota allocation mechanism or formula between North and South Korea. Rather than counting North Korean imports against the South Korean quota, it would be politically more expedient to allocate North Korea a small quota (which might be offset fully or partially from a US perspective through South Korean acquiescence in the reduction of its quota). In the case of Europe, North Korea does not currently fill its existing MFA quotas.

blers would have to fall into place for such a reform strategy to work. As hard as it may be for an economist to admit, this analysis suggests a case for the primacy of politics over economics in resolving this crisis.

In this respect, the Asian financial crisis has made Pyongyang's tasks even more difficult. The decline in dollar production costs throughout Asia, together with rising bankruptcies, means that purchase of existing assets has become more attractive to foreign investors relative to the establishment of new greenfield facilities. In other words, if one wants to manufacture garments, there is no reason to build a factory in North Korea when you can buy an existing one in Thailand (where you are already familiar with local laws and customs) at fire sale prices. Moreover, the primary potential investors in North Korea, namely South Korean and Japanese firms, themselves are in dire straits, and their banking systems are unlikely to want to lend to speculative ventures in North Korea.

Finally, it is hard to imagine North Korea undertaking significant reform without a more secure external environment. The military is probably the most coherent institution in the society, with privileged access to economic assets. It could possibly be a prime beneficiary of reform, but it may well oppose reform if it believes that this will endanger the nation's military security. This suggests that economic reform is unlikely to occur before some rapprochement with South Korea. Taken together, these considerations suggest that North Korea is unlikely to undertake wide-ranging reforms of its own volition.

There is little sign that the North Korean regime is contemplating such output boosting reforms. Policymakers view the current crisis as a product of the "diplomatic environment"—specifically the collapse of the USSR and the US embargo—rather than any kind of domestic systemic failure. As a consequence, there appears to be a disconcerting degree of inertia and drift in North Korean economic policy. The postponement of decisive action is likely to mean continued deterioration in the economy, raising the specter of economic collapse. It is to this possibility that we now turn.

8

The Implications of North Korean Collapse

Aban eɛgu a, ɛfiri yam. (If the state falls, it is from the belly.)

—Akan proverb

The previous chapter explored the potential economic payoffs of fundamental reform. Unfortunately, there is little evidence that the North Korean regime is contemplating reforms on this scale. Policy stasis under conditions of growing economic distress raises the possibility (though not the necessity) of collapse and absorption along the lines of the German experience.[1] This chapter first reviews the German unification experience and then compares Germany prior to unification with the situation today on the Korean peninsula. The quantitative implications of this scenario are then explored using a computable general equilibrium (CGE) model. The chapter concludes with some ruminations on what a collapse on the Korean peninsula that did not occur as smoothly as East Germany's might imply.

---

1. See Ahn (1998) and Pollack and Lee (1999) for a careful analysis of how a North Korean collapse might come about.

The German Experience

The remarkable thing about German unification is the rapidity with which it occurred. Rumors of a Soviet deal on Germany initially surfaced in May 1987, but they were generally discounted. Two years later, the rumors were widely circulating in the press, and, in May 1989, Hungary began allowing East Germans to transit to the West, thereby releasing a wave of emigration.[2] Mass demonstrations against the East German regime began in September of that year, and by November the Berlin Wall had come down and the borders had opened.[3] Shortly thereafter, the communist regime began to implode, and West German Chancellor Helmut Kohl made a series of decisive overtures to the East. What proved to be a transitional elected East German government under Christian Democratic leader Lothar de Maizière took office in April 1990. A currency reform took place in July, and by October 1990, less than a year after the Wall came down, East Germany had ceased to exist. No one predicted it (though a theory of unanticipated revolutions does exist [Kuran 1989, 1991]).

Economic logic pushes centrally planned economies (CPEs) toward dictatorship. The maintenance of internal prices far at variance from those of the rest of the world necessitates a massive police apparatus to prevent people from exploiting the latent gains from trade. This point could be seen most clearly in East Germany, which had only to look west to see the alternative. Sinn and Sinn (1992) argue that the Marxist emphasis on materialism was ultimately the East German regime's undoing. Once it was clear to all that capitalism would generate greater material prosperity than socialism, the *raison d'etre* of the socialist state evaporated. Indeed, they attribute the bloodless collapses of the communist regimes throughout Central Europe to the communist authorities' respect for the iron laws of history: Once the masses were in opposition, resistance was pointless. Ironically, the sudden reversal of fortune recalls Lenin's remark to Trotsky on the Winter Palace balcony: "*Es schwindelt!*" (It's dizzying!).

Economic Policies

Confronted with a collapsing East Germany, West German economic policy had a number of possibly conflicting goals.[4] Among these were to

---

2. In the 18 months between January 1989 and June 1990, East Germany lost 7 percent of its working population, with the losses concentrated among the young and skilled (Flassbeck 1994).

3. If the USSR and Hungary effectively were able to pull the plug on the East German regime, China could presumably do the same to North Korea if so inclined.

4. For useful analyses of German unification see Lipshitz and McDonald (1990), Sinn and Sinn (1992), Dornbusch and Wolf (1994), Carlin and Meyer (1994), Thimann and Breitner (1995), Hughes Hallett, Ma, and Melitz (1996), Dyck (1997), von Hagen (1997), and Lange

stem the flood of immigrants and to protect West German wages. Another was to achieve restitution for property owners whose assets had been seized by the communist regime.[5]

The standard prescription for economies in transition from central planning to the market is macroeconomic stabilization, liberalization of domestic trade and prices, current account convertibility, privatization, creation of a social safety net, and the creation of a legal framework for commercial transactions. Through monetary union and absorption into West Germany, most of these goals were achieved in a decisive fashion. The outstanding issues for East Germany concerned the terms of the monetary union and the method of privatization.

Monetary union occurred in July 1990. The goals of the monetary union were threefold: to establish a competitive wage; to give the new economy the right amount of liquidity; and to give East German residents sufficient capital for their participation in the unified economy. Under the terms of the agreement, an exchange rate of 1:1 between East and West German currencies (ostmark and deutsche mark) was adopted for wages, government transfers, and savings accounts up to certain limits. An exchange rate of 2:1 was adopted for remaining household savings, enterprise and government deposits, debts of the state, enterprises, and individuals, and 3:1 for accounts outside East Germany. Pensions were based on East German wages but calculated using West German formulas.

Most observers thought that the 1:1 exchange rate was probably too high. They thought the overvaluation of the ostmark would generate uncompetitive costs in the East and a bout of consumption-led inflation (cf., Cline 1990, Sinn and Sinn 1992, and Yeon 1993b). In reality, inflation did not occur, though a peacetime depression in East Germany unparalleled in modern history did.

Product Market Adjustment

In East Germany, GDP fell by 30 percent, industrial output by 67 percent, and the unemployment rate rose to 30 percent (Sinn and Sinn 1992, Dornbusch and Wolf 1994). Economically, this was worse than the situation during the Great Depression.

---

and Pugh (1998) among others. See Sinn and Sinn (1996), Watrin (1998), and Wolf (1998) for Korea-oriented summaries of the German experience.

5. The then West German Foreign Minister and leader of the junior government coalition partner, the Free Democrats, Hans-Dietrich Genscher, spearheaded the push for restitution. The transitional East German government of Lothar de Maizière supported compensation but opposed restitution, seeking to preserve East German residents' effective control of assets in East Germany. Revelations of connections between de Maizière and the *Staasi* secret police weakened his government, which in the end was forced to accept the principle of restitution. In hindsight, the pursuit of restitution was undoubtedly one of the blunders of German unification.

Why did output collapse so precipitously? There were several contributing factors. The East German economy was in bad shape at the time of the currency union. The flood of emigration had taken away many of the best and brightest. As a result of these skilled labor shortages, both the government and the enterprises were having trouble functioning prior to the currency union. In addition, the *Treuhandanstalt* had closed some uncompetitive enterprises, contributing to the decline of output and the rise of unemployment.[6]

These direct impacts, though non-negligible, were not the fundamental reasons for the depression, however. More fundamentally, the centrally planned East German economy was not ready to compete in the market. Incentives were not conducive to success in competitive markets; the structures of enterprises (in terms of horizontal and vertical integration) were not appropriate; and the enterprises were engaged in a variety of social welfare activities that typically would be handled by other institutions in a market economy.

Moreover, the technical aspects of production (techniques, input mix, output mix) were sub-optimal for a market economy facing world prices. Sources cited in Sinn and Sinn 1992 estimate that anywhere from 50 to 67 percent of the East German capital stock was obsolete. In addition, the state guarantee of employment led to disguised unemployment. (To cite but one example, in East Germany 260,000 workers worked 14,000 kilometers of rail lines; in West Germany 230,000 workers operated 27,000 kilometers of track [Yeon 1993b].) Given the nature of technology, resources could not be reallocated instantly or costlessly, even under the best of circumstances.

To compound these problems, the economy was hit with a series of macroeconomic shocks. Two were on the demand side. First, the economy suffered from declines in trade with its former partners in the COMECON. (Though given the relatively low reliance of East Germany on COMECON trade, this trade shock was actually smaller than what hit the other Central European transitional economies.)

Second, and more important, was a temporary autonomous fall in the domestic demand for home goods. East German consumers began buying Western-made goods that had been previously unavailable but were known to East Germans via the West German media (table 8.1). Dornbusch and Wolf (1994) note that this shift away from home goods was greater in East Germany than in the other Central European transitional economies. They ascribe this to the greater familiarity of East German consumers with Western products and to the relatively powerful marketing and distribution push by large West German consumer products firms in the East German market.

---

6. The *Treuhandanstalt* was a trust agency created in March 1990 to oversee all state-owned firms in East Germany. It was dissolved at the end of 1994.

Table 8.1 Western goods penetration

Product	Western product share of East German sales, Sept. 1990
Margarine	35
Cooking Oil	41
Detergent	53
Black Tea	66
Cooking Fat	76
Dishwashing Liquid	81
Fruit Yogurt	90
Canned Soup	94
Chocolate	96

Sources: Sinn and Sinn (1992), Dornbusch and Wolf (1994).

On the supply side, the East German economy was hit both by relative price shocks and by a massive real exchange rate appreciation engendered by the 1:1 exchange rate and the subsequent high wage policy. The conventional wisdom at the time of the monetary union held that the 1:1 exchange rate priced East German producers out of the market and was a fundamental mistake of unification policy—a view that still holds popular currency. In hindsight, the situation looks more complicated.

A number of studies summarized in Sinn and Sinn convincingly demonstrate that the purchasing power exchange rate at the time of unification was probably something on the order of 1:1. (The much higher black market rate at the time of unification reflected not only the usual black market premium but also the steady fall in value of the ostmark as speculators bet against the East German currency.) The problem was that the relative prices existing in Germany at the time not only reflected the lower relative prices of nontradables typically found in low income countries, but also reflected an additional distortion imposed by the central planners (table 8.2). The shadow price of foreign exchange (which appears to have varied significantly across exporters) was on the order of 4:1 (Sinn and Sinn 1992, Dornbusch and Wolf 1994, Flassbeck 1994). As a consequence, when the currencies were unified at 1:1, the traded-goods sector suffered a massive cost shock *and* suddenly had to compete against foreign producers who could in effect provide an infinite supply of goods at the going prices.

The price shock was compounded by subsequent wage policies. (Indeed, both Sinn and Sinn and Dornbusch and Wolf argue that the wage policies would have been sufficient to price East German producers out of the market regardless of the conversion formula at the time of monetary union.)[7] In the non-traded sector, it was politically difficult to

---

7. Dornbusch and Wolf write: "The one to one conversion had no lasting effect on relative wages: since the conversion, relative wages in the East have increased steadily, and outright parity is the avowed objective of the unions on both sides" (p.159). This does not mean,

Table 8.2 East German relative prices

Product	Ratio of East German to West German prices, May 1990 (percent)
Tape recorder	600
Pineapple	550
Camera	530
Women's nylons	510
Calculator	490
Refrigerator	390
Coffee beans	390
Chocolate	310
Electricity	24
Housing	18
Coal (for heating)	17
Newspaper	17
Bread	16
Haircut	15
Streetcar fare	10
Kindergarten fees	5

Source: SPD-Bundestagfraktion, Wochentext No. 10 (19 May 1990) cited in Lim (1996).

resist the demand for equalization of wages, especially in the public sector.[8]

In the traded goods sector, West German unions pressed for a high wage policy in the East to prevent an eastward migration of jobs.[9] At the same time, wage negotiations in the East were subject to a particularly pernicious principal-agent problem: since no one was negotiating for the future (privatized) managements of East German enterprises, the incumbent lame duck managers simply gave in to demands for higher wages.[10] The *Treuhand*, which might have acted to halt this, did not participate in wage negotiations because it saw itself as representing the state, not capital, and the state was not supposed to participate in private wage negotiations under German law. Moreover, under German law the dominant parent company in a group is responsible for the debts accrued by insolvent subsidiaries. The *Treuhand* wanted to ensure that it was not held

---

however, that the conversion rate is irrelevant in all circumstances. Under a different set of wage policies (such as those that might obtain in Korea) it could be quite important.

8. Wolf (1998) cites the example of East Berlin bus drivers who demanded the same pay as their West Berlin counterparts.

9. Sinn and Sinn argue that either there should not have been a monetary union (thereby preserving the exchange rate as an adjustment mechanism), or the wage increases should have been legally prohibited.

10. As Soltwedel (1998) aptly put it: "There was a severe principal-agent problem in the wage policy in the last months of the GDR; in fact, there were no principals at all" (p.276).

liable as the parent of these enterprises and their debts (Scheremet and Zwiener 1994).

Privatization

These problems were compounded by delays in privatization. The key was not privatization *per se*—the evidence from other transitional economies is ambiguous on this point, but that without privatization one would not get investment, and *investment* was the key for at least two reasons.[11] First, at the microeconomic level, new investment would be the mechanism by which new market-competitive products and processes would be introduced at the level of the firm. Second, from an economy-wide standpoint, in contrast to the existing allocation of capital, new investment would be carried out on market principles and hence would be the mechanism for the sectoral and regional restructuring of the economy (Lange and Pugh 1998).

In point of fact, the privatization of the East German economy proceeded slowly for two reasons. Restitution claims were one.[12] As Lange and Pugh (1998) observe, by mid-1991, 1.5 million restitution claims had been filed, simply overwhelming the administrative capacity of the system. In Dresden, for example, only 700 of 40,000 claims had been decided.

Another contributing factor was the *Treuhand's* preference for selling firms to single buyers and normally requiring payment in cash.[13] The *Treuhand* in effect tried to sell the entire East German economy to individual bidders for cash. Not surprisingly, it did not find too many takers. (Even if it had, the process of putting so many assets on the market at

---

11. See Sinn and Sinn (1992) on the German case and World Bank (1996) chapter 3 and Nellis (n.d.) for summaries of the broader international experience with privatization. In a very interesting paper, Frydman et al. (1999) present evidence from a large panel of Central European firms that the ownership of the privatized enterprise is critical: enterprises under "outside" ownership show markedly improved performance, while those under "insider" ownership are indistinguishable from state owned enterprises. This could be related to the observation of Eickelpasch (1998) that East German enterprises in the traded goods sector transferred to "outside" owners had better access to financing and distribution channels. Indeed, Frydman et al. (1999) find that it is revenue growth, not cost reduction, that differentiates enterprises sold to outsiders. In any event, the experience in most transitional economies (including Romania, as discussed in the following chapter) is that increased industrial output has come from new firms—not from newly privatized existing firms.

12. In 1991 the German Constitutional Court separated in principle the issue of claims of dispossessed previous owners from the issue of compensation. Other countries, such as Hungary, have either rejected the restitution principle or narrowed its application. See Barna (1998) for more discussion.

13. See Sinn and Sinn (1992), Carlin and Mayer (1994), and Lange and Pugh (1998) for extensive reviews of *Treuhand* practices.

once would have surely pushed prices down to fire sale levels for the benefit of the largely West German investors.)

Indeed, residents of East Germany were effectively frozen out of this process. The paucity of financial instruments in East Germany prior to unification meant that the portfolios of East German households were extremely concentrated in cash and demand deposits. East German households had very few financial claims on state or enterprise assets. Sinn and Sinn estimate that the limits on the 1:1 convertibility of bank accounts wiped out almost one-third of household financial wealth. Indeed, Sinn and Sinn estimate that about half of this loss (or one-sixth of East German household financial wealth) ended up in the coffers of the *Bundesbank*, which actually made money off of the currency unification. Given their lack of financial resources (and consequent inability to borrow) and the *Treuhand's* preference for single buyers, only 6 percent of industrial properties had been sold to East German buyers through 1991 (Carlin and Mayer 1994, table 14.4).[14] This was truly unfortunate, since the East Germans were likely to be among the most interested, informed, and motivated potential buyers.[15] Foreigners only accounted for another 2 percent of sales. A vast majority of the industrial assets in East Germany were sold to residents of West Germany.

The *Treuhand* also took responsibility for restructuring enterprises and breaking up the giant *Kombinaten*, which lengthened the time to market and created more enterprises to be privatized.[16] The consensus (by no means unanimous) among economists is that this policy was mistaken. Given that speed was of the essence, it would probably be better to allow markets to value and restructure these assets.[17] (Parenthetically, this would have given the East German managers an advantage, especially since they probably understood both the enterprises and the local environment better than outsiders.)

The pace of privatization was further slowed by concerns about anti-competitive effects. There was an understandable tendency for West Ger-

---

14. This is in contrast to other transitional economies, where "spontaneous privatizations" by the *nomenklatura* have been closer to the norm.

15. The potential parallels to the North Korean case, in which financial assets are even more likely to be concentrated in cash, is obvious.

16. Lichtblau (1998), in a very interesting paper, argues that the *Treuhand* understood the costs of delay and tried to expedite the process as best it could, but was organizationally incapable of doing so.

17. Again, another principal-agent problem potentially arises, this time between the government selling authority (the *Treuhand*) and the dispossessed property owner. The seller recognizes a social cost associated with the existence of non-privatized enterprises and, as a consequence, has a higher rate of time discount than the dispossessed owner interested in compensation. In other words, the seller prefers to sell the property, while the dispossessed owner prefers to hold out for a higher price.

man firms to attempt to purchase potential rivals in the East, either to operate them or, more likely, shut them down or turn them into sales offices. Potential sales of this sort were disallowed by the Cartel Office. (Given the extreme degree of concentration in the South Korean economy, unification might present a good opportunity to increase competition in some sectors. It is hard to imagine the Korea Fair Trade Commission blocking enterprise sales, though.)

The economic environment in East Germany created a final disincentive for potential buyers. A survey of potential investors found that poor infrastructure, especially transportation and telecommunications infrastructure, was a major disincentive for investment (Sinn and Sinn 1992). This disincentive would be particularly acute if production were to be characterized by close horizontal and vertical networking of firms. Networks would create economies of agglomeration, which would likely work against "pioneers" in relatively inaccessible environs.[18] As pointed out by Soltwedel (1998), regional development priorities had influenced the East Germans' construction of the *Kombinaten*—in essence, industrial plants were located with no regard for regional comparative advantages or transport costs. The *Treuhand* administrators were faced with the unenviable task of privatizing East German industrial assets without completely closing local economies. A similar problem is likely to confront future attempts to restructure North Korea, where the geographic pattern of economic activity has been strongly conditioned by non-economic criteria.

Labor Market Adjustment

As a result of the fundamental lack of competitiveness, combined macroeconomic shocks, and slow privatization, East Germany experienced a dramatic decline in output and employment. East German employment was 9.8 million in 1989. More than 3.5 million jobs in East Germany were subsequently lost, though only about one-third of these turned up on the unemployment rolls. Approximately one-third found jobs in West Germany, either as commuters or migrants, and about one-third either entered training programs, took early retirement, or simply left the labor force.[19] Survey data reported in Dornbusch and Wolf indicate that willing-

---

18. In part, this can be overcome by strengthening links between the core and the border region of the periphery. The relevance of this for the Korean case is obvious: The North Korean infrastructure is abysmal and provides a disincentive to investors. However, strengthened links between North and South Korea would enhance the attractiveness of both North and South as locations for production. (The South would no longer effectively be an island if one could transport goods via rail directly to Western Europe.)

19. In this regard, it is notable that a large share of those exiting the labor force were women. It is impossible to determine to what extent this was an expression of underlying personal preference or to what extent this reflected social pressure or coercion. By extension it is impossible to determine whether women were better off after unification or not. There is

ness to migrate was driven first by fears of unemployment, second by environmental concerns, and only third by wage differentials. Ironically, the high wage policy, which narrowed income differentials but at the cost of unemployment, probably increased migration.[20] Given the proximity of Seoul to the border, it is hard to imagine that Korean unification would be accompanied by insufficient southward migration.

Despite these problems, by 1991 production in East Germany was expanding even in some tradable sectors such as nonmetallic minerals, parts of iron and steel, printing, plastics processing, and some processed foods. These were typically sectors that had been engaged in exporting prior to unification. They were less dependent on collapsing domestic demand and presumably knew something about international markets and competition. While East German growth has continued to be concentrated in nontradables, some tradable sectors also have continued to expand.[21]

All in all, the experience in Germany has proved to be more protracted and costly than analysts anticipated at the time of unification, with transfers running at 6 to 10 percent of GDP annually.[22] Although macroeconomic variables have been moving in the right direction (the economy of the former East Germany grew nearly 10 percent in 1994, the fastest rate in Europe), the economy remains plagued by high unemployment. Transfers have been larger (net of taxes, they account for 40 percent of East German income) and have gone on longer than expected.[23] Even with this largesse, East Germany has gone through a truly wrenching transformation.[24] While the replacement of the socialist centrally planned

---

no natural rate of employment independent of incentives. Relative to West Germany, East Germany prior to unification tied more social benefits to employment, while providing benefits such as child care that facilitated women's participation in the labor force. It is not surprising, then, that East Germany exhibited high labor force participation by women. Under the West German system, benefits were not tied to employment, and the facilitating devices were absent. Thus, it is not surprising, that fewer women chose to work. Under which regime their welfare was higher is impossible to tell.

The potential parallels to the Korean case, in which North Korean women exhibit extremely high labor force participation rates, are clear.

20. To be clear, this does not mean that the elasticity of migration with respect to wages was zero. Even so, Sinn and Sinn argue that generous transfers created a stay put premium, with the result that the amount of westward migration was sub-optimal.

21. See Eickelpasch (1998) for a detailed analysis of enterprise restructuring and the sectoral pattern of recovery.

22. See Yang (1998a) for figures on public expenditure and net financial transfers from West to East.

23. See Heilemann and Rappen (1997).

24. Eberstadt (1994c) reports very sobering demographic data indicating that the immediate effect of unification and the ensuing depression was a collapse in the birth rate and a rise in the mortality rate at levels completely unprecedented in German history (including the

society with a democratic capitalist one will undoubtedly benefit East Germans in the long run, after reviewing the demographic data, one cannot help but come away with the impression that the transition has been extraordinarily costly in human terms.

Relevance to Korea

Any attempt to draw lessons for Korea from the German case must start with a comparison of the two pairings. In some ways, the Korean case presents a gloomier picture than the German case: North Korea is larger and poorer relative to South Korea than East Germany was in comparison to West Germany; North Korea's economy is probably more distorted than East Germany's was; and South Korea is not as rich as West Germany. On the other hand, demographically, the combined Korea is younger than the combined Germany, and North Korea has a younger demographic profile than East Germany.

Size

At the time of unification, East Germany's population was roughly one-quarter of West Germany's. Today, North Korea's population is about half that of South Korea. Moreover, under current demographic trends, the ratio of South Korean to North Korean population would fall from 2:1 to 1.7:1 by 2010 (Chun 1994).

Per capita income comparisons are quite hazardous, due mainly to the fundamental problem of comparing output baskets of widely differing composition and quality, and the differences in national accounting conventions between the two systems. Estimates from Germany indicate that per capita income prior to unification was perhaps one-half to one-third that of West Germany, though this cannot be determined with any real precision. Comparisons for North and South Korea are even more speculative due to the paucity of reliable statistical information about the North. Yet, as argued in chapter 3, the ratio of per capita income is probably something on the order of 8:1 to 11:1 and growing by the day.

Demographics

While North Korea is bigger and poorer than East Germany, it has the advantage of having a younger population. Today, the median age in the

---

inter-war years and the period of military defeat) and comparable only to disasters such as China's Great Leap Forward. Though some of the declines in marriages and births presumably represent time-shifting and not permanent reduction, the same cannot be said for the increase in mortality rates. In addition, social maladies such as racist and neo-Nazi groups have grown in the fertile ground of anomie and alienation.

combined Korea would be around 26 years, while in Germany at unification it was around 38 years. The share of the North Korean population under 15 is around 29 percent, while in East Germany it was around 20 percent (Chun 1994).

This latter point is quite important since, in the case of East Germany, it has been estimated that 80 percent of workers will have to undergo retraining (Eberstadt 1995a). The younger population of North Korea would make it possible to handle more of this retraining through the conventional educational system, minimizing both economic costs and personal dislocation.

At the other end of the life cycle, the combined Korea would be carrying fewer retirees than the combined Germany. Eberstadt (1995a) reports that the ratio of workers to retirees was 5:1 in Germany, while it is 15:1 in Korea. There would be more workers in Korea available to finance the costs of unification.

Economic Dislocation

As noted earlier, a combination of fundamental competitiveness problems, macroeconomic shocks, and poor policy choices initially caused an enormous fall in output and employment in East Germany. Obviously, one cannot predict what would happen in North Korea. Nevertheless, one can point to some comparisons.

With respect to competitiveness, the North Korean economy is probably even more distorted than the East German economy was. Its exposure to international trade, which might be taken as a proxy for competitiveness, is lower than that of East Germany. The shifts in relative prices in response to liberalization reported in figure 7.4 are on the same order of magnitude as the shifts actually experienced by East Germany. Moreover, the degree of industrial concentration may well be even greater than the degree of concentration in East Germany.

North Korea exhibits the same extremely high rates of labor force participation as East Germany did prior to unification, which probably reflects disguised unemployment. The infrastructure is in poor condition. A report by the Korea Transport Institute concluded that it would cost $30.6 billion to refurbish the North Korean transportation infrastructure and integrate it with the South's in the event of unification. It is not difficult to imagine North Korean dinosaur-like enterprises—subject to massive relative price shocks, exposed for the first time to international competition, burdened with excess labor and working with decrepit infrastructure—failing.[25]

In addition, North Korea is the most militarized society on Earth, with 1.05 million men under arms, fully one-fifth working age men. As pre-

---

25. Indeed, Bazhanova (1992) cites a disconcerting number of instances in which shoddy North Korean products were not accepted even by other centrally planned economies!

viously noted, this figure may be a bit misleading, however, as the North Korean military engages in many non-military activities that would be performed in the civilian sector in other countries. Nonetheless, it would not be too much of a stretch to say that unification accompanied by demobilization would probably generate a significant number of new entrants into the labor market, though this could generate a considerable peace dividend as well.

Three obvious channels of labor market adjustment exist. First, as demonstrated in the previous chapter, the production of labor-absorbing light manufactures would grow in a liberalized North Korean economy. Second, as in the case of Germany, there might well be a reduction in labor force participation, especially of women. The final channel for labor market absorption would be migration.

Both the relatively young structure of the North Korean population and the proximity of Seoul to the border would appear to encourage southward migration, though some have suggested that the DMZ could be maintained as a barrier.[26] An alternative to migration would be commuting, which could be encouraged by strengthening the transport links between North and South Korea. This would facilitate commuting from North Korea to jobs in the South, and the relocation of production from the South to the North.

Home ownership has been robustly and negatively correlated with willingness to move. Prior to unification, more than half of East German farmland and nearly half of the housing stock was privately owned (Yeon 1993b). In contrast, private ownership in North Korea is practically nonexistent. Yeon (1994) suggests that North Koreans should be given title to their housing to discourage migration. Another possibility would be to tie property rights to housing (and other assets) to some specified period of post-unification residence or employment.

The eventual equilibrium distribution of the population across the two regions is contingent on the policies applied. As a point of reference though, Chun (1994) observes that the per capita income of the poorest region of South Korea is only 60 percent of the richest area, and the simple average provincial income is only 76 percent of that of the richest. Within West Germany, wage differentials of 70 percent have existed without inducing large-scale migration. In the United States, the poorest state has income per capita only around half as great as the richest. Presumably, a united Korea could maintain substantial regional difference in per capita income without undue social strain.

---

26. Various researchers have attempted to estimate the possible number of migrants that might head south if the border were opened. These estimates range from 1.4-2.8 million to 4 million (Hyundai Research Institute 1997). Compare Foster-Carter 1992, Koh 1994, and Young, Lee, and Zang 1998.

Table 8.3 Inter-German and inter-Korean exchange

Inter-German exchange	1970	1980	1990
Trips (thousand)[a]	1,254	2,746	2,410
Migration (thousand)[b]	12.5	8.8	11.5
Two-way trade			
(million DM)	4,411	10,873	14,014

Inter-Korean exchange	1989	1990	1991	1992	1993	1994	1995	1996	1997	1998
Trips[c]	1	474	412	360	na	na	na	146	1015	3337
Two-way trade										
(million $)	18.7	13.6	111.8	174.5	187.4	196.4	293.7	259.0	319.9	234.9

a. Number of trips from West to East Germany.

b. Migration from East to West Germany.

c. Trips in both directions.

Sources: Yeon (1993b); Ministry of National Unification.

Imponderables

Finally, there are a whole series of points of comparison that are difficult to analyze but could have a major impact on final outcomes. The most obvious qualitative difference between the German and Korean cases is the much greater degree of isolation of North Korea. East Germans were in the middle of Central Europe, with Berlin serving as a point of contact between the East and West. Many East German residents could receive West German radio and television broadcasts and had a fairly good idea of conditions in their western neighbor. Table 8.3 reports some data on inter-German personal contacts prior to unification and inter-Korean contacts today. In comparison to the German figures, the numbers for Korea are vastly smaller—even with the recent increases due to the South's engagement policy.

How this relatively greater isolation will play out is hard to predict. Analyzing the path to unification, Foster-Carter (1992, 1994a, b), for example, makes much of the lack of political passivity that the North Koreans may display when the truth of their relative deprivation becomes clear. Knowledge is a necessary precondition for this to come about, however, and there is no reason to believe that the average North Korean is particularly well-informed.

Similarly, knowledge of the West surely contributed to the surge of migration that occurred when the borders were initially opened in Germany. Those migrants were not sailing off into the unknown: They had a pretty good idea of their destination. Indeed, Dornbusch and Wolf argue that the East German residents' pre-unification familiarity with West German products contributed to the temporary demand shock that the East German economy suffered at the time of monetary union. North Koreans are undoubtedly more ignorant of conditions in the South than East Germans were of conditions in West Germany, so their expectations may be lower. This potentially means less migratory responsiveness and less of a shift away from home goods.[27] South Korean policy could affect both of these developments.

It is interesting to ponder Sinn and Sinn's observation about East Germany: "It is possible that the problem engendered by the difference in living standards might have been less severe if the communist government had been able to indoctrinate the people with a self-denying idealism that would have made them resistant to the lure of material prosperity" (p.7). In the case of North Korea, it has been argued that the *juche* ideology of Kim Il-sung replaces the Marxist emphasis on materialism with an emphasis on purity of spirit (see box 3.1). Indeed, references to Marxism-Leninism have been expunged from the constitution. Perhaps North Korea will prove ideologically more resilient and less enticed by the creature comforts of the South.

The issue of expectations raises the final imponderables—politics, attitudes, and spirit. Germany and Korea differ considerably in history and political culture; German unification was shaped by specific characteristics of the German situation, and Korean unification will be shaped by its unique circumstances as well.

Several characteristics strongly shaped German decision making about unification. First, Germany is a democracy, and West German Chancellor Helmut Kohl saw the East Germans as potential voters. (Indeed, he was criticized in 1990 by his predecessor, Helmut Schmidt, for promising unification without increasing taxes in the West and for not making a "blood, toil, and tears" appeal for sacrifice.) Second, Hans-Dietrich Genscher and the Free Democrats were an important focal point for restitution demands. Third, the West German unions were an important interest group in German politics and were successful in pursuing their own interests. Lastly, and intriguingly, Sinn and Sinn argue that the Germans approached the task of reunification with a lack of patriotism:

> The wave of patriotism that could have triggered a vigorous policy of rebuilding was nowhere to be seen. Some people reacted skeptically to the poor Eastern relatives, responding to the appeal of the outstretched hands by nervously protecting their wallets. Others, conveniently forgetting the fortunate circumstances of their own success, arrogantly and wrongly attributed the poverty of their Eastern relatives to differences in mentality rather than to differences in systems. Most

---

27. Unlike the East German case, North Korean consumers presumably are not especially familiar with Western consumer goods. However, like the German case (and in contrast to the situation in countries such as Poland, the Czech Republic, and Hungary), the South Korean *chaebol* are probably in a good position in make a marketing push into North Korea in the event of unification. If maintaining production in the North is a high priority, the South Korean government might want to discourage this.

people, however, acted as if the whole thing was no business of theirs and deceived themselves into thinking that German unification would in no way disturb the even tenor of their ways (p.xii).

Certain prospective similarities and differences exist in the Korean case. Unlike Germany, the unions in Korea are relatively weak. South Koreans have been unable to restrict the government's right of eminent domain, suggesting that the politics of South Korea are such that it might be able to avoid the twin pitfalls of the high wage policy and the principle of restitution that bedeviled German unification policy (Mo 1994).

Mo (1994) argues further that Helmut Kohl (the most powerful German Chancellor since Bismarck) acted too hastily because of his insecure domestic political position. In contrast: "A South Korean leader will have a secure domestic power base . . . and if the German experience is any indication, North Koreans will vote for the ruling South Korean party" (pp. 61-62). Foster-Carter (1992, 1994a,b) similarly claims that North Korean voters will be a conservative force in Korean politics.

An alternative interpretation of the German experience is that in a democracy an incumbent leader facing a potential third or more of the electorate (which is what the North Koreans will be) will be relatively responsive to their interests and, at least initially, will be rewarded. Beyond this, the recent electoral trends in Central Europe suggest that the newly enfranchised voters will remain conservative free-marketeers until shortly after the subsidies run out. Regionalism has long played a role in Korean politics, and it is not hard to imagine an essentially regional response dominating any particular ideological orientation.

The closer relationship between business and government in South Korea should allow the South Korean government to guide the activities of South Korean firms to a greater extent than the West German government could. It is not difficult to imagine the *chaebol* being encouraged to rehabilitate failing North Korean enterprises.

Unfortunately, the malaise with which Sinn and Sinn claim the average German greeted unification appears to have gripped South Korea as well. Lim (1996) writes that the "unification fever" of 1989 "has all but evaporated, and disillusionment has begun to set in" (p.1). Indeed, a review of the literature on the costs of unification suggests that Korean economists interpret the German experience as a costly failure.[28] This view appears to be shared by the general public. Han (1998) and Yang (1998b) both cite

---

28. Yeon (1993b) is typical: "It is difficult to identify economic gains that rapid unification and elimination of the border could entail for the South Korean people. When free flows of commodity and production factors, including labor, are allowed, the economic gain could only be the consequence of eased labor migration. Thus, if a significant labor shortage, especially for unskilled labor, prevails in the South, it may derive a small benefit from rapid unification. Otherwise, an important influx of labor will simply raise severe social problems" (p.29).

results of a 1997 public opinion survey conducted by the Sejong Institute, a South Korean think tank. Although nearly 90 percent of those South Koreans surveyed regarded unification as "somewhat" or "very" important, they did not appear to be ready to pay much for it. More than 70 percent of the respondents agreed with the view that "since unification can create many problems, it must proceed slowly," and, when asked about the appropriate tax increase to finance unification, more than half supported the view that it should be "only to the extent that it does not burden the average household, even if the amount is insufficient to help reconstruction" (Han 1998, tables 2, 3 and 4).

A General Equilibrium Perspective on Collapse and Absorption

Noland, Robinson, and Wang (2000c) extend the computable general equilibrium (CGE) model described in the previous chapter to include both North and South Korea in a Korean Integration Model (KIM).[29] They use this model to analyze the impact of the formation of a customs union on the Korean peninsula in the context of a "preferential opening" reform strategy on the part of North Korea. Since the North Korean economy is so distorted, the main result is that the formation of a customs union with South Korea would amount to a tremendous move toward free trade on the part of North Korea. The qualitative results obtained in the preferential and non-preferential opening scenarios are similar from the standpoint of North Korea. From the standpoint of South Korea, the formation of the customs union and integration of product markets would not have much effect because of the relatively small size of the North Korean economy.

However, if North Korea were to collapse and be absorbed by South Korea, one would expect at least partial integration of factor markets. In this section, the results that Noland, Robinson, and Wang (2000c) obtain using the Korean Integration Model are reviewed for a number of interesting issues: the integration of product markets, the integration of factor markets, and the impact of foreign capital inflows in the context of simple comparative static experiments in which there is no explicit reference to time.[30] Dynamic issues of South-North technology transfer, income

---

29. See Noland, Robinson, and Wang (2000c) for an algebraic rendering of the model.

30. The KIM is used to examine alternative famine relief strategies, the static reallocation gains to trade liberalization, the obsolescence shock to North Korean capital stock, and the potential peace dividend to military demobilization, as outlined in the previous chapter. See Noland, Robinson, and Wang (2000c) for details.

convergence, and the costs and benefits of unification are taken up in subsequent sections.[31]

Finally, it is worth noting that the results reported in this section, while motivated by a collapse and absorption scenario, strictly speaking are not logically dependent on collapse and absorption. Although it is unlikely, an independent North Korea could decide to enter into a monetary union with the South, or the South could decide to allow an inflow of a substantial number of Northern immigrants. The results in this section could thus be interpreted as an extreme version of the preferential opening strategy described in the previous chapter.

Product Market Integration

As indicated in the previous chapter, the formation of a customs union would have a significant positive effect on North Korea and a modestly beneficial impact on the South. Economic integration of this sort would presumably require an enormous reduction in political tensions (or even political integration). If, in this circumstance, North and South Korea (or a unified Korea) were to reduce military expenditures to the OECD average of 2.5 percent of GDP, this would generate for South Korea a small "peace dividend" of less than $300 million.[32] However, for the far more

---

31. Given that much of the preceding discussion has been based on the German experience, it is worthwhile to indicate how this has been incorporated into this modeling work. Given the KIM's medium-to-long-run orientation, the focus is primarily on sectoral adjustment issues in the context of a simple macroeconomic framework. For two principal reasons a number of interesting macroeconomic issues, such as exchange rate overshooting, that have been prominent in the literature on German unification are not addressed. First, the dissimilarity of factor endowments is far more pronounced in the Korean case than in the German case, and, as a consequence, integration may have more dramatic sectoral implications in the Korean case compared to the German case. This fact, combined with the far larger differences in economic size between the two Koreas compared to pre-unification Germany, suggests that in certain respects the North American Free Trade Area (NAFTA) may be a closer analogue to the prospective Korean situation than the German experience. The KIM is well suited for examining these integration issues.

Second, history does not operate by analogy. There is no particular reason to believe that adjustment issues that arose in the German case (which were at least partly due to avoidable policy mistakes, such as the wage equalization policy), would occur in the Korean case. Indeed, the Koreans can learn from the German experience and avoid some of the German errors. To cite a specific example, in contrast to the German wage equalization policy, most Korean analysts expect the maintenance of the existing DMZ to control population movements after economic integration. They also expect the perpetuation of greatly differing wage structures in the two halves of the peninsula for some extended period of time (cf. Young, Lee, and Zang 1998). These "lessons" from the German experience are taken up in the final chapter on policy recommendations.

32. This is the efficiency gain associated with military demobilization. The direct budgetary impact would be higher. Bae (1996) estimates that, with unification, the elimination of duplicative intelligence operations, diplomatic missions, etc., might generate budgetary savings of around $500 million for the peninsula as a whole.

militarized North Korea, the impact would be much larger, adding another 10 percent to GDP on top of the gains from joining the customs union. For the peninsula as a whole, the peace dividend would be 0.3 percent of GDP. In this scenario, North Korea would achieve the FAO/WFP/UNDP total normal demand food target of 7.8 million metric tons. Per capita income in the North would remain less than a tenth of that in the South under this scenario.

Factor Market Integration

This basic picture—a large impact on North Korea, a small impact on South Korea—would change considerably if factor markets were allowed to integrate. In the case of exchange rate or monetary unification, it is natural to expect the capital market, if not the labor market, to integrate. For heuristic purposes, however, a hypothetical case initially considered in which the inter-Korean labor market integrates, but the inter-Korean capital market does not (that is to say, labor flows from North to South, but capital does not flow in the other direction). This could happen if, for example, North Korea suddenly were to collapse *a la* East Germany before political rapprochement and cross-border capital flows had occurred. To examine this possibility, consider a situation in which labor migrates until per capita income in the North is 60 percent that of the South, as previously discussed. In this case, North Korea would be virtually depopulated (more than 90 percent of the population would migrate) before the 60 percent per capita income target was attained. This extreme result serves to underscore the critical importance of generating capital inflows into North Korea.[33]

In the more plausible converse case (capital flows North and North Korea adopts South Korean technology, but labor is not permitted to move South), nearly $700 billion of new investment (more than a quarter of the South Korean capital stock) would be required to move in order to attain the per capita income target, underlining the implicit trade-off between capital and labor flows as equilibrating adjustment mechanisms.[34]

Having established the extreme bounds of the cross-border factor mobility necessary to achieve the per capita income convergence target, it is useful to focus on an intermediate case in which there is a degree of cross-border movement in both labor and capital. J. Park (1997), on the basis

---

33. It is assumed that this migration solely takes the form of North to South Korea. It is quite possible that in reality there might also be emigration to other destinations, in particular to China. If this were the case, it would obviously affect the precise calculation of migration necessary to achieve the income convergence target.

34. The capital movement has been treated as a pure grant. It is also possible to calculate the rents and impute them to South Korean national income as remitted profits, as is done in the following section.

of the German experience, estimates that with unification, two million North Korean workers might migrate south. Koo (1998) obtains a similar result, estimating that under contemporaneous labor market conditions in the South, 1.4 million to 2.8 million North Koreans might migrate south, while B. S. Lee (1998) puts the figure at 2.1 million. The Hyundai Research Institute (1997) estimates that the figure could be four million, mostly from the "hostile" or dissident class. Assuming that two million workers did cross the border and that total factor productivity (TFP) increased by 18 percent, South Korea would have to invest more than $500 billion in the North (more than a fifth of the South Korean capital stock) for North Korea to attain the 60 percent per capita income target.[35] If this transfer were to occur over ten years, it would imply a transfer of roughly 10 percent of GDP annually—a share comparable to that in the German case.

In this scenario, real GDP would rise tremendously in North Korea and fall slightly in South Korea in response to these factor movements. Output would rise in all sectors in North Korea, except in the public administration and military sectors, which, by construction, remain constant. Conversely, output would fall in all sectors in South Korea (except in public administration and the military).[36]

However, the existence of cross-border factor flows raises the possibility that GDP could differ significantly from GNP if migrants were to remit wage income or if foreign investment were to generate repatriated profits.[37] In the extreme case in which all incomes earned by migrants and

---

35. In the North, the increases in the capital-labor and land-labor ratios, together with the increase in TFP, would generate a considerable increase in North Korean agricultural wages, which would converge to the South Korean level. Urban wages in the North would remain significantly below the South Korean level, however. In this sense, the attainment in this scenario of the 60 percent per capita income target and the posited implications for cross-border migration and social stability may be a bit misleading. For most North Koreans, wage income would still be far less than that earned by equivalent labor classes in the South.

36. Chang (1997), using a CGE model of South Korea in which North Korea is represented as a set of import and export demand and supply equations, examines two scenarios involving factor movements. In the first, 10 percent of the North Korean labor force (roughly one million workers) migrates to South Korea. The result is to increase South Korean real GDP by 5 percent and increase output in all sectors. In the second scenario, South Korea transfers 10 percent of its capital stock to North Korea. South Korean real GDP falls by just over 5 percent, and output falls in all sectors except textiles and apparel. This last result presumably reflects the reduction in South Korea's capital-labor ratio, together with the assumption of capital mobility across sectors.

37. One could think of the transfer of capital from South to North Korea taking the form of grants or private investment. In the former case, capital would be transferred to the North, and there it would remain, providing economic benefits to the Northern economy. In the latter case, Southern investors would retain ownership, and the investments would yield a stream of remitted profits adding to Southern income. In the event of unification, actual transfers would probably reflect a mix of grants (perhaps funding public infrastructure) and private profit-making investments (factories, etc.).

foreign investment are remitted to their sources, profits from investment in the North largely would offset the negative impact in the South of the monetary union with the North. The North would still come out substantially ahead. Income for the combined Koreas would rise as the returns to factors are equalized in the two economies, and the combined income would exceed the base by roughly 12 percent.

Foreign Capital Inflow

In the comparative static simulations thus far, the process of capital transfer literally amounts to taking capital from the South Korean capital stock and moving it north. It would be desirable to model external capital inflows as well. In the comparative statics setup, one could model capital inflow as either an exogenous increase in the capital stock (which would not affect the current account balance) or an exogenous increase in the trade or current account deficits (which would not affect the capital stock). One could think of the latter as representing the moment when imported capital goods are purchased, and the former as representing the moment when they are installed.

In the extreme case, all investment in North Korea could come from abroad. In this scenario, more than $600 billion of capital inflow (together with the emigration of two million workers) would be necessary to reach the per capita income target. More capital would be necessary than in the previous internal transfer case, since the South Korean capital stock would be unaffected, and South Korean per capita incomes would be commensurately higher.

A key issue is the effect of the inflow of foreign capital on the real exchange rate. To explore this issue, Noland, Robinson, and Wang (2000c) took the unified exchange rate and subjected it to a series of trade balance shocks that would leave the measured capital stocks in the two countries unaffected. (These should be thought of as medium-to-long-run effects, abstracting from short-run monetary shocks that the KIM is poorly suited for modeling.) The experiments are summarized in figure 8.1, which depicts the real exchange rate appreciation in response to foreign capital inflows. Suppose the $600 billion inflow were to occur at a steady linear rate over a decade (i.e., $60 billion annually). As the real exchange rate appreciated, the level of output in the South Korean traded goods sectors would fall, while the non-traded goods sectors (construction and services) would exhibit increases in output (figure 8.2). (Public administration and the military are fixed by assumption and show no output response.) The real exchange rate appreciation also would adversely affect the traded goods sector in North Korea, though some traded goods sectors such as light manufacturing and mining would continue to register significant increases in output relative to the highly distorted base (figure 8.3).

Figure 8.1 Capital inflow and exchange rate appreciation

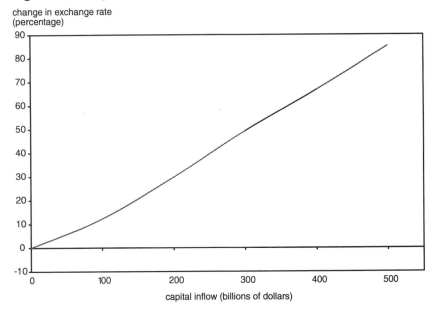

change in exchange rate
(percentage)

capital inflow (billions of dollars)

Figure 8.2 External capital inflow case: composition of output change in South Korea

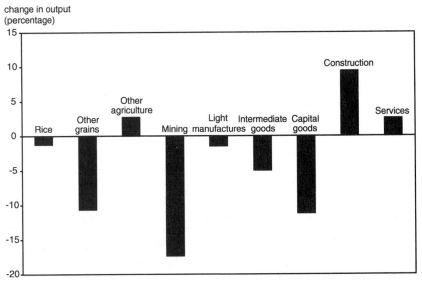

change in output
(percentage)

Figure 8.3 External capital inflow case: composition of output change in North Korea

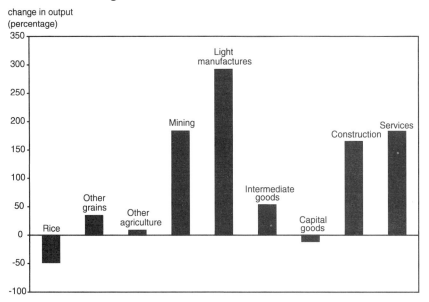

change in output
(percentage)

Conceptualizing the Costs and Benefits of Unification

A veritable cottage industry devoted to the estimation of the prospective costs of Korean unification now exists. These "costs" are typically found to be in the hundreds of billions of dollars. (Some of the more notable studies are summarized in table 8.4.) Most existing studies have adopted one of two conceptually inadequate approaches. The first is to apply data from the German experience to the Korean case (S. M. Lee 1993, Bae 1996). Costs are measured in terms of budgetary expenditures, which are relatively straightforward to calculate, and benefits are viewed through a similarly narrow prism of offsetting possibilities for budgetary expenditure reduction (primarily through military demobilization). For example, in the case of German unification, one can measure net transfers from the West to the East (i.e., expenditures less taxes paid). Likewise, budgetary benefits associated with things like military demobilization, reduction in expenditures on duplicative diplomatic activities, etc., can be measured in terms of spending. These are the initial direct budgetary impacts. Most analysts, Bae (1996) for instance, stop there.[38] This is not the end of the

---

38. Bae (1996) concludes that, in the mid-1990s, the annual "peace dividend" for the two economies, broadly defined, would have been on the order of $7 billion. However, this estimate (like earlier ones) is based on military budget expenditures rather than on the more

Table 8.4 Estimated costs of unification

Source	Methodology	Definition of cost	Unification date	Results
Hwang	Income Target	Total investment (including private)	1990	$300 billion, over (1993) undefined period[a]
			1995	$700 billion, over an undefined period[a]
			2000	$1,200 billion, over an undefined period[a]
S.M. Lee (1993)	German Comparison	Government Expenditure	2000	$200 billion over 10 years
Yeon	Income Target	Government Expenditure	2000	$230-250 billion over (1993) 10 years
Y.S. Lee	Income Target	Government Expenditure	1990	PDV $330 billion over (1994) 40-50 years
		South Korean Income Foregone		PDV $841 billion over 40-50 years
Bae	German Comparison	Government Expenditure	1993	$488 billion over 5 (1996) years
Noland, Robinson, Scatasta (1996)	Income Target	Total investment	1990	$600 billion
	(CGE model, North Korean capital-output ratio)		1995	$1,378 billion
			2000	$3,172 billion
	(CGE model, market economy capital-output ratio)		1990	$319 billion
			1995	$754 billion
			2000	$1,721 billion
Noland, Robinson, Liu (1998)	Dynamic CGE	PDV of national income relative to no unification base	1997-2006	Difference between without unification PDV and with unification PDV range from $35 billion to −$541 billion.

a. This figure can be doubled to include the cost of "socio-economic adjustment."

story, however. Take the example of military demobilization. Both East and West Germany maintained conscript armies (as do both North and South Korea). Conscripts are presumably paid less than what they could earn in other activities in the civilian economy. Their wages are not the true measure of the cost to the economy of maintaining the army; the wages they would have otherwise earned are. So, when the army demobi-

---

appropriate opportunity or shadow cost measure of resources used by the military. The modeling work reported below implicitly embodies the latter approach in its treatment of the reallocation of resources in the context of economic integration.

lizes, labor and other resources are released from relatively low productivity activities (the army) into relatively higher productivity activities in the civilian economy. National income increases. So does the tax base. In other words, those lowly paid conscripts leave the army, join the civilian economy, and begin paying taxes on their higher wages.

This logic applies to the whole economy, not just to the government budget. The process of unification will be accompanied by a reallocation of resources throughout the economy as factors are deployed in more productive ways. The result is an increase in national income and an increase in tax receipts. Calculations such as Bae's, which ignore these general equilibrium effects, systematically underestimate the benefit side of the cost-benefit calculus.

Even if one were to implement the budgetary analysis properly, it is not at all clear that budgetary saving is the best measure of net benefits. The government's budget balance in and of itself is not very interesting. What is relevant is not the size or direction of any imbalance, but rather its implications for income and consumption growth, which are the ultimate measures of economic welfare. For example, most people would choose a future of slight budget deficits and steady robust growth over one characterized by fiscal balance and negative growth.

The second set of studies, which measure the costs of unification in terms of overall resource transfers, could be interpreted as heading in this direction. They measure the transfer costs necessary to raise North Korea to some share of South Korean income, but they do not measure the benefits (Hwang 1993, Yeon 1993b, Y. S. Lee 1994b, Noland, Robinson, and Scatasta 1997). Cost in these studies is measured in terms of resource transfers, typically taking the form of investment capital or government expenditure. Benefits are usually ignored. For example, if the transfers were to take the form of investment in the North by Southern owners of capital, then those investments would yield a stream of profits remitted to Southern investors that would directly add to Southern income. Moreover, to the extent that the rate of return on capital investment is higher in the North than in the South, those investors will earn higher returns than if they had invested in the South. More generally, the opening of exchange between the North and South could be expected to be accompanied by a reallocation of resources that would raise the level of income in both economies. Unfortunately, none of these studies attempt to measure the impact of economic integration in either the narrow or broader sense noted above. With one exception, all are based on simple spreadsheet calculations; only Noland, Robinson, and Scatasta (1997) use a behavioral model as the basis of calculation.

A conceptually superior measure of the costs and benefits of potential unification would be the present discounted value (PDV) of income (or consumption) under alternative scenarios about unification. Noland, Robinson, and Liu (1998) calculate precisely this measure using a CGE model calibrated to 1990 (the most recent year for which the requisite data were available at the time that study was undertaken) and updated to 1996 on the basis of the Bank of Korea's estimates of North and South Korean growth in the interim. They find that under one scenario, the South Korean PDV income stream is higher than the one associated with the baseline scenario of no unification.[39] This scenario, in which unification yields positive net benefits to South Korea, is characterized by relatively low levels of South Korean private investment in the North, combined with relatively high levels of North-South labor migration. The result depends on two critical assumptions: first, that capital invested in the North take the form of profit-generating private investment that yields returns to its South Korean owners; and second, that the rate of technological convergence is relatively rapid. Nevertheless, this result highlights two crucial points. First, it indicates that a wide range of outcomes is possible, and that the policies applied have a significant impact. Second, it makes an apparently plausible case for the possibility of a Pareto-improving unification scenario in which everyone is potentially made better off.

Noland, Robinson, and Wang (2000c) reexamine this result using a model calibrated directly to 1996 and find that the earlier result rested on two problematic foundations. First, the situation in North Korea had deteriorated more than originally thought, and, as a consequence, the income gap to be closed had widened significantly. Second, the result depended critically on the rapidity of technological convergence between the North and South. In the potentially Pareto-improving case, the North adopts South Korean technology over a decade, attaining not only Southern levels of total factor productivity, but the Southern input mix as well.[40] Noland, Robinson, and Wang (2000c) reexamine these issues making use of new data that had become available since the earlier study and the considerable literature on the rate of technological convergence emerging from the studies on German unification.

Dynamic Results

Thus far, the process of economic integration has been analyzed using comparative static models to examine a number of key issues. The integration process, however, is inherently time dependent, for investment and technological upgrading cannot occur instantaneously. The divided country nature of the case at hand distinguishes it from the generic case

---

39. It also should be noted that they report seven scenarios in which unification leaves South Korea worse off.

40. It appears that North Korea wastes a lot of intermediate inputs, as is typical of centrally planned economies.

of technological convergence in two ways. First, North Korea would presumably be converging on South Korean technology, not just in terms of the level of total factor productivity, but in terms of primary factor and intermediate input usage as well. In other words, one would expect North Korea to more or less adopt South Korean technology.[41] Second, the literature on German unification suggests that, in the context of such a fundamental regime change, the rate of technological upgrading could be much more rapid than is usually the case.

With respect to the first issue, the discussion thus far has treated technological change as a sectorally uniform process, and the amount of total factor productivity increase has been calibrated from the work of Coe, Helpman, and Hoffmaister. However, the Korean situation may differ importantly from the generic phenomenon they analyzed. For the purposes of their regression model, Coe, Helpman, and Hoffmaister classify South Korea as a developing country. Thus no technological spillovers would be attributed to the importation of South Korean capital goods. Moreover, in the exchange rate unification and monetary union simulations, one would expect cross-border factor flows; in particular, one would expect capital to flow from South to North Korea. In this case, it would be plausible to expect that the North would adopt the South Korean technologies embodied in the capital. The rationale is that, as the two economies integrated, the relative price structure of the smaller North Korean economy would begin to converge toward that of the larger South Korean economy. Moreover, as new plants in North Korea were built using South Korean capital, and new production technologies were adopted in the North, this process would change the allocation of basic inputs and produced intermediates. As South Korean techniques become the norm, the input-output coefficients in the North should converge to those of the South. These coefficients would presumably be optimal, given the existing factor prices and distortions in South Korea, so their adoption by North Korea would imply the elimination of those internal distortions that were not modeled explicitly.[42] Operationally, the parameter shift of the North's production functions (its productivity level) would increase to the level of the South's, and the North would adopt South Korea's intermediate input mix in the form of the South's input-output coefficients.[43]

---

41. Obviously there would be investment and technological transfers from non-South Korean sources as well, most probably from Japan. This already occurs to a limited extent today.

42. One could also rationalize the linkage of capital investment and productivity convergence along the lines of the management perspective of Dyck (1997), who argues that, in the German case, replacement of East German managers with West German managers was key to enterprise rehabilitation and viability.

43. Noland, Robinson, and Liu (1999) develop a decomposition, a graphical explication, and some modeling results pertaining to these two effects. In the interests of brevity, only the case in which North Korea adopts South Korean technology is reported here.

That said, cross-border investment and technological change will not occur instantly, so the speed of technological convergence is a crucial issue. Barro and Sala-i-Martin (1992, 1995) present evidence that countries with low initial levels of per capita income tend to exhibit higher per capita income growth than countries with initially higher per capita income levels. That is, there is a tendency toward per capita income convergence. Indeed, Barro and Sala-i-Martin argue that, in a variety of contexts (among US states, among members of the OECD, among all countries) there is a tendency for the incomes of poorer regions to converge on the incomes of richer regions at a rate of roughly 2 percent annually.

Yet this "2 percent rule" is probably inadequate for the task at hand. Rather than convergence based on the steady state growth paths of regions with access at least to similar production technology, the economic integration of North and South Korea would arguably put North Korea on a new growth path, at least transitionally. The critical question concerns the rapidity at which this convergence would occur. Evidence from the German case suggests that the speed of technological convergence between East and West Germany has been considerably higher than 2 percent annually. The estimates of this vary enormously, with upper end estimates of technological convergence on the order of 10 to 12 percent annually.[44]

The economic implications of this uncertainty are illustrated in figure 8.4, which displays the results obtained when the Korean Integration Model is run by imposing 2 percent to 12 percent annual technological convergence, with both the sectoral level of TFP and the input-output mix in North Korea converging to the South Korean norm over a period of ten years. The amount of capital transfer necessary to reach the 60 percent benchmark was then calculated for each of these cases. This calculation assumes that the rate of technological convergence and the volume of capital flows are independent—at least above an investment threshold. Assuming 2 percent technological convergence and no labor migration, it would take more than $600 billion of investment in the North to reach the 60 percent per capita income benchmark after ten years. This figure falls by more than half, to less than $300 billion, if 12 percent convergence is assumed. Indeed, convergence rates of less than 10 percent imply larger transfers as a share of GDP than in the German case.[45]

---

44. See Hughes Hallet and Ma (1992), Burda and Funke (1993), Herz and Roger (1995), Sinn (1995), Schalk and Untiedt (1996), Boltho, Carlin, and Scaramozzino (1997), Keller (1997), Rummel (1997), and Lange and Pugh (1998). The estimates of convergence appear to vary for two reasons. First, it is difficult to disentangle productivity gains from the large increase in public and private investment in East Germany that had occurred post-unification. Second, the sample period is relatively short. Hence the coefficient estimates appear to be sample and specification sensitive.

45. This comparison is a bit inexact, in that the transfers in the German case are measured as public transfers, while in our case the figure could include private investment flows.

Figure 8.4 Rate of convergence and capital investment requirement

Capital investment necessary to reach
60 percent per capita income target

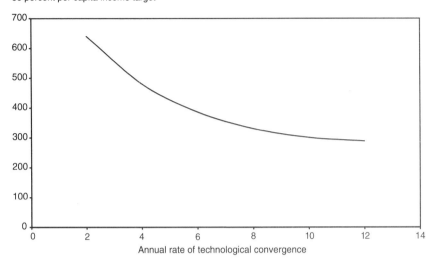

Annual rate of technological convergence

This treatment is not fully satisfactory for two reasons. It is inadequate in that it is not a truly dynamic model. It is simply the imposition of a temporal pattern of technological change on the comparative statics model, and the choice of a ten-year period is arbitrary (though Kwon (1997) argues that this was sufficient for convergence in Germany). Furthermore, as demonstrated in the previous section, labor migration can act as a substitute for capital investment, and so migration must be taken into account in estimating investment requirements. In a final set of experiments, a simple recursive dynamic model was specified in which labor force growth is set on the basis of demographic projections, capital is accumulated as a constant share of output, and the rate of TFP change is set exogenously.[46]

Suppose that monetary or exchange rate union occurred instantaneously in 1996 (the year for which the model is calibrated) and that over

46. The labor force growth of the two economies was set exogenously, based on the basis of economically active labor force projections released by the Ministry of National Unification. TFP growth rates were set exogenously on the basis of econometric estimates. Capital accumulation was calibrated to reproduce the pattern of economic growth observed over the period 1991 through 1996. The KIM is essentially a long-run equilibrium model and is not designed to capture short-run cyclical effects. The assumption is that the cross-border factor flows occur at a constant rate over the course of a decade. In reality, these could occur with considerable abruptness. Endogenization of the cross-border factor flow is an obvious direction for future research.

Figure 8.5 North Korea: GDP and GNP

GDP and GNP (billions of dollars)

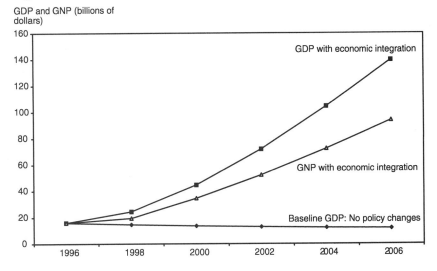

the course of ten years, two million North Koreans migrated to South Korea, technological convergence occurred at the mid-range estimate of 6 percent a year, and a portion of South Korean capital accumulation was invested in the North until the rate of return on capital equalized in the two Koreas.[47] This would imply a transfer in excess of $600 billion over ten years or about 11 percent of South Korea's annual GDP, which is significantly more than the value of public transfers in the German case.[48]

As shown in figures 8.5 and 8.6, this scenario would amount to a tremendous (to the point of implausibility) positive shock to the North Korean economy, a modestly negative shock to the South Korean economy, and a moderately positive shock from the perspective of the peninsula as a whole.[49] At the end of ten years, output on the Korean peninsula

---

47. It was assumed that the transfers to the North come completely at the expense of investment in the South (i.e., there is complete crowding out of investment, and no crowding out of consumption or FDI). This scenario would generate a bit more slowing of South Korea's rate of capital accumulation and growth than if investment in the North were allowed to crowd out all components of absorption. In this experiment, the role of foreign capital, which was discussed in a previous section, is ignored. To the extent that foreigners financed the capital accumulation in the North, the burden on South Korea would be commensurately less.

48. See Heilemann and Rapen (1997).

49. Meade (1997), using an input-output model imbedded in an exogenous macroeconomic framework, obtains a smooth adjustment path similar to that depicted in figure 8.5 (and aggregate results generally consistent with those reported here). East Germany actually exhibited a "J-curve" pattern in which industrial output initially fell by two-thirds before rising. A "J-curve" adjustment path can be generated in which output initially falls and

Figure 8.6 South Korea: GDP and GNP

GDP and GNP (billions of dollars)

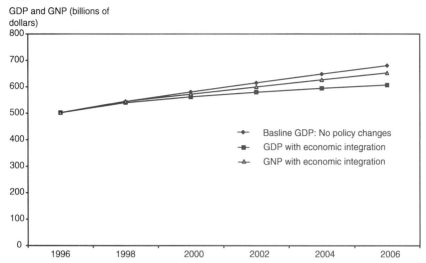

would be around 7 percent higher than under the baseline projection. In South Korea, monetary union and cross border factor flows would reduce the rate of GDP growth in South Korea by about one percentage point a year. If one were to attribute to North Korea the income of all the migrants who went to the South, and assume that all profits on investment in the North were repatriated to South Korea, then the impact would be moderated, and the growth rate of South Korean GNP would fall by only about 0.5 percent.

Compared with the German experience (and indeed the experiences of most transitional economies) these results appear quite optimistic. Why is this the case?

Two specifics of this modeling differ from the German case. First, the level of transfers is somewhat higher. Second, the transfers are modeled as additions to the North Korean capital stock—not as supplements to current consumption. If Korean economic integration takes the form of integration by two sovereign states, then the predominant form of transfer would presumably be private direct investment—not grants or consumption transfers, and the model scenarios are probably broadly correct (though the magnitude of capital flows is probably overstated if private investment is the sole channel). However, if there were a collapse and absorption as in Germany, there might well be political pressures for

then rises by subjecting the North Korean economy to an instantaneous obsolescence shock to its capital stock while phasing in the trade reform and technological upgrading (cf. Noland, Robinson, and Liu 1998). In reality, the trajectory of output would be determined by the relative dynamics of these, and other, effects.

consumption transfers, even though the Koreans have had the opportunity to learn from the German experience.[50]

More fundamentally, the neoclassical nature of the model generates relatively frictionless adjustment, especially in the reallocation of factors across sectors, and the experience of the past decade with other transitional economies suggests that considerable institutional and policy reform are required to support successful adjustment. In this sense, the model results are surely overoptimistic.[51] Yet the existence of South Korea (and the Korean diaspora beyond the peninsula) provide the North Koreans advantages in terms of potential investors, opportunities for technological transfer, and access to worldwide distribution networks largely absent in the cases of other transitional economies (with the possible exceptions of East Germany and China).

This latter point raises the issue of distribution. There are three ways to think about the distributional effects in this setup: comparisons between North and South Korea, comparisons between the outcomes after economic integration relative to the 1996 base, and comparisons between these outcomes and what is projected without integration. The first is the simplest and possibly the most important: Rates of return for capital and labor would (partly) converge between North and South Korea, but the convergence would not be sufficient to attain the 60 percent per capita income target (figure 8.7). (The ratio of per capita incomes at the end of the period would be about 55 percent.) This result implies that, even in this relatively optimistic scenario, per capita income in North Korea would remain well below the level in South Korea for an extended period of time. This implies the need for either some method of restraining migration or, alternatively, higher levels of migration than contemplated in this experiment. Indeed, under the assumptions of a 6 percent rate of technological convergence and two million migrants, the capital transfers necessary to hit the 60 percent per capita income target would drive the rate of return on capital in North Korea below that in South Korea. If a more rapid rate of technological convergence (say, 12 percent instead of 6 percent) is assumed, it would be possible to attain the 60 percent target before the rates of return on capital were equalized. Allowing some of the North Korean capital accumulation to be financed by foreign capital inflows would reduce the direct burden on South Korea, but make achieving the 60 percent target more difficult. It would mean less crowding out of South Korean domestic investment, more rapid South Korean growth, and, as a consequence, a higher level of target income.

---

50. See Heilemann and Rappen (1997) for a breakdown of the composition of West German transfers to East Germany.

51. Similarly, formal modeling work on German unification tends to underestimate the severity of the fall in output and the persistence of fiscal transfers (Gagnon, Masson, and McKibbin 1996).

Figure 8.7   Factor return equalization

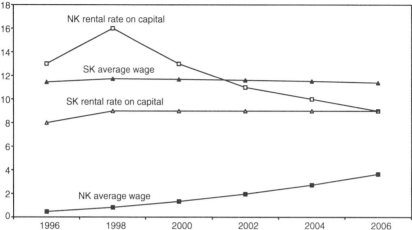

rental rate on capital (percent) and
average wage (thousands of US dollars per worker)

Figure 8.8   South Korean distribution of income

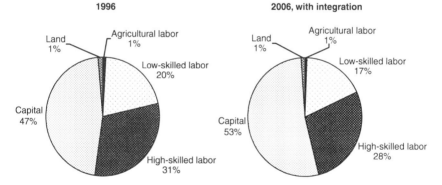

In South Korea, economic integration with North Korea would generate a shift in income away from labor toward capital, regardless of whether transfers to the North were considered grants or profit-making investments, and within labor away from less skilled groups and toward higher skilled groups (figure 8.8). To the extent that higher skilled labor groups tend to be the predominant owners of capital, this result implies that, absent some compensatory redistribution policies, the process of economic integration would be accompanied by increased income and wealth inequality in the South. In comparison to the no-integration base, all classes of labor would lose. However, compared to the base of 1996, the wages of low-skilled labor would fall, while the wages of the higher skilled would rise (albeit less than in the no-integration scenario). Capital would benefit in both comparisons.

In addition to these effects, increased government expenditures would have to be financed either through taxes or bonds. In the case of taxes, the costs may not be borne equally, depending on tax incidence.[52] In the case of bond finance, there will be a redistribution from taxpayers to bondholders. Presumably the median taxpayer will be poorer than the median bondholder. More generally, a rise in real interest rates would benefit savers to the detriment of borrowers.

Thus unification will have an impact on income distribution through a variety of channels. The bottom line is that, if one is a low-skilled worker in South Korea, then unification could have some negative implications. If, on the other hand, one is a South Korean construction company executive with money to invest in unification bonds, then unification could be very, very good for you. Presumably, these differences in perspective will be reflected in South Korean politics. This issue will be revisited in the concluding chapter of this book.

Policy Lessons of the German Experience for South Korea

The lessons of the German unification experience are of two types: first, identification of mistakes to avoid and, second, identification of policy changes that can be made in anticipation of unification.

The first set of lessons is relatively straightforward. The consensus among economists is that the 1:1 exchange rate was not the primary cause of the depression in East Germany, but that the wage policy was. On the contrary, the overvaluation (if any) could be justified as a one-time wealth transfer to the East German population, which was entering the market economy with few financial assets.[53] Despite the fact that the increase in the money supply may have been greater than what would have been justified on the grounds of providing liquidity to the East German economy, inflation did not materialize. The lesson for Korea (if there is one) is that competitiveness problems are likely to be so severe that a little extra liquidity may not be a bad thing. It might help to attempt to dollarize North-South trade to try to get an idea of the real North Korean exchange rate and the North Korean shadow price of foreign exchange.

---

52. On tax incidence, see Bahl, Kim, and Park (1986).

53. In fact, at a symposium held in Seoul, Deputy Minister of Finance and Economy Uhm Rak-yong argued that a mild overvaluation of the North Korean won at the time of unification should be undertaken precisely to effect the wealth transfer, discourage mass migration, and alleviate social discord. See SaKong and Kim (1998).

Rather than misspecifying the exchange rate, the Germans made two obvious mistakes. The first was the policy of driving East German wages beyond productivity. This policy had the effect of depressing output in East Germany (and probably encouraging westward migration). Labor union pressure was one reason for this error. The relative weakness of unions in North and South Korea suggests that this may not be a major problem in the Korean case. The other contributors to this outcome were the compliant managements of pre-privatized enterprises. These considerations simply reinforce the point that, when it comes to privatization, speed is of the essence.[54]

In this regard, the practice of restitution was a disaster.[55] It slowed the process of assigning property rights, thereby impeding investment and rehabilitation. Although compensation may be acceptable, restitution is to be avoided.[56]

Third, most observers have criticized the decision not to write off or otherwise reduce East German enterprise debt. The argument is that these debts reflected transactions based on the arbitrary internal prices and fundamentally irrational practices of East Germany's central planning system, and they left enterprises that otherwise might have been viable hobbled by financial liabilities which in turn made them very difficult to privatize. Blanchard et al. (1991) and Dornbusch and Wolf (1994) recommended simply wiping out East German enterprise debt, while Sinn and Sinn (1992) presented a proposal for reducing these debts. The *Treuhand* eventually adopted a procedure of constructing "confirmed" balance sheets, which involved writing off approximately three-quarters of enterprise debts (Carlin and Mayer 1994).

Beyond the debt write-offs, there is less consensus on how privatization should be carried out. Dornbusch and Wolf (1994) and Nölling (1994)

---

54. In dissent, John Williamson has argued that maximum speed privatization "is a platitude that does not stand up to scrutiny," as the fastest growing Central European economy, Poland, has been the slowest to privatize large enterprises. Rather than privatizing, simply forcing enterprise managers to face a hard budget constraint prior to privatization creates the proper incentives and minimizes the principal agent problem. The drawback, as Williamson admits, is that this is not a steady-state equilibrium solution. Indeed, as the pre-privatization period lengthens, the enterprises are likely to look increasingly unattractive to potential buyers as their capital stocks are run down due to lack of investment. Moreover, as the extensive firm-level analyses of Eickelpasch (1998) and Frydman et al. (1999) show, enterprises sold to "outside" owners significantly outperform state owned enterprises or enterprises sold to "insider" managements.

55. In a bizarre twist, it was reported that former Nazis were using the procedure to re-acquire assets that they themselves had stolen from Jews during the Third Reich (*Financial Times*, 4 May 1994).

56. Jung and Park (1998) examined this issue in the context of land ownership in North Korea and concluded that both compensation and restitution should be rejected. They also presented survey data that suggest that most South Koreans agree with this stance.

argue for maximum speed transformation, including shutting down non-viable enterprises and extending unemployment benefits to individual workers, as the only way to free up resources for viable enterprises and for the necessary resource shifts. They note that, while outside observers put the share of non-viable enterprises at around 30 percent, the *Treuhand* only shut down 10 percent. They recognize that, due to the extreme industrial concentration of centrally planned economies, shutting down some enterprises would be tantamount to shutting down a town or a region, and that this externality may lead to a divergence between private and social costs, a point emphasized by Carlin and Mayer (1994). This problem may be particularly acute in the case of North Korea, where anecdotal evidence indicates that industrial concentration is on a mind-boggling scale (cf. H. S. Lee 1994b). At the same time, Frydman et al. (1999), in an extensive analysis of Central European enterprises, found that the main effect of privatizing former state owned enterprises to "outside" managements was to increase revenue, not reduce costs. This suggests that the employment impact of privatization could be less than previously thought.

Sinn and Sinn (1992) present a privatization proposal that would allow agents who did not possess enough cash to purchase an enterprise outright or to take partial ownership by bringing some new asset (such as proprietary technology) to the table. The Czech system of voucher privatization is another possible alternative that in the Czech case has benefited the mass of the citizenry, improved corporate governance, and made its architect, Vaclav Klaus, Prime Minister.[57] C. H. Lee (1994) contains a detailed proposal for how a voucher system might work in North Korea. A final option would be simply to turn assets over to the user, formalizing the "spontaneous privatizations" that have occurred in other transitional economies.

Thinking Beyond the German Case

While a process of gradual, peaceful, integration may be desired, abrupt, possibly violent, disintegration and collapse might occur. The two gravest threats would be an external lashing out of force by North Korea or a collapse into civil war or anarchy in which one faction might appeal to one of the surrounding states for support, leading to intervention by and

---

57. Eighty-two percent of adult Czechs participated in the voucher privatization program, which fostered the creation of banks and investment funds as financial intermediaries. These intermediaries have played an important institutional investor monitoring role, and, indeed, have organized networks of financially related industrial groups along the lines of German *konzern* or Japanese *keiretsu*, though perhaps at the cost of large transaction expenses, corruption, and non-transparency. See Claessens, Djankov, and Pohl (1996), Johnson (1997), and Mertlík (1998) for evaluations of the Czech experience.

possible confrontation among outside powers. The key in dealing with both situations is deep, serious, and high-level consultation and coordination among the militaries of the region, especially South Korea, the United States, and China. South Korea and the United States already maintain a high level of coordination, so the real issue is drawing the Chinese military into serious contingency planning. With respect to the explosion scenario, it is crucial that China communicate to North Korea that it will not condone any North Korean military adventures and will not oppose any retaliatory actions on the part of South Korea and the United States. At the same time, China potentially could play a very constructive role by offering, in advance, a comfortable safe haven to Kim Jong-il and his retinue. Such offers of asylum have played important roles in facilitating the exeunt of such dictators as East Germany's Erich Honneker (Chile), Haiti's Jean-Claude ("Baby Doc") Duvalier (France), and Brigadier General Raoul Cédras (Panama), to cite a few examples. Although it may go against political tendencies in South Korea, pre-announced amnesties for high-ranking North Korean officials might play an important role in defusing a potentially explosive situation.

Even more dangerous would be the civil war scenario, which creates the possibility of a military confrontation between China and South Korea (and possibly the United States). Probably the safest course of action would be an *ex ante* agreement that no outside power will intervene in internecine struggles within North Korea. The problem, of course, is that such commitments are not entirely credible and may not be completely verifiable. This situation simply underscores the importance of extensive military-to-military consultations prior to any emergency on the peninsula.

Even if North Korea's denouement is merely an implosion instead of an explosion, coordination among the region's militaries will be critical. The reason is simple: an implosion would undoubtedly be accompanied by large scale refugee movements, a breakdown of law and order, and possibly famine and pandemics. The militaries are the only social institutions with the logistical and management capability to take on such tasks on a rapid-response emergency basis.[58] It is important to engage China. Even the best case variant of this scenario—an international emergency relief operation invited into North Korea by a functioning North Korean government—would in all likelihood require South Korean, US, and Chinese military units to enter North Korean territory. This raises the possibility of confrontation between these forces and rogue elements of the (North)

---

58. For an analysis of this issue from the standpoint of handling refugees, see Pilkington (1998). Hufbauer (1996) makes a number of interesting and provocative suggestions, including maintaining KPA units under South Korean command and providing short-term income and employment guarantees to members of the North Korean military in order to smooth a likely chaotic transition.

Korean People's Army (KPA) or, even more dangerously, between US and Chinese forces. This scenario underlines the imperative of close precrisis coordination among the military forces of South Korea, the United States, and China.[59]

In the previous chapter, it was argued that self-initiated fundamental reform in North Korea, while desirable, is unlikely. The bottom line of this chapter is that, even in the best case, a collapse of North Korea would raise a host of tremendously important long and short-run economic and political issues for South Korea and its partners. Many find this prospect so daunting that they hope for a less cataclysmic outcome in the North. It is to this possibility that we turn.

---

59. Hufbauer (1996) observes that coordination of police activities with authorities in Japan and the United States will also be necessary to deal with the problems of organized crime that are likely to attend the social chaos. This could be particularly acute in light of the importance of illicit activities such as drug trafficking and counterfeiting in the North Korean external economy.

9

Can the North Muddle Through?

Production was focused on quantity, not quality or cost-effectiveness. Wastage of material and energy was phenomenal. Romanian industry used four to five times as much energy per unit of output as the EC average. As a result, industry absorbed 90 percent of Romania's entire energy consumption, an extraordinary figure which left the population literally in the cold and darkness. The industrial plant is badly run down due to a lack of maintenance and spare parts, neither of which was adequately provided for in the Plan. The country's infrastructure is abominable. Roads are primitive, communications are inadequate (there are only 300 international telephone lines for the whole country), and buildings are in serious disrepair. Worker motivation was destroyed. Working people's energies were focused on scrounging food and supplies from the factory or using work time to hunt them down outside it.

—former US Ambassador to Romania Roger Kirk.[1]

Between the extremes of successful reform and collapse in North Korea lies the more prosaic, and perhaps more likely, path of muddling though—a path of making ad hoc adjustments as circumstances dictate but without any overarching strategy or rationale. One could also interpret this path as a minimalist strategy undertaken by a regime cognizant of its need to improve material conditions, but fearful of the destabilizing changes that could be unleashed by more fundamental reforms. In this regard, examining the recent history of Romania would perhaps be more instructive than looking back at the experience of Germany. After all, North Korea

---

Roger Kirk. 1991. The U.S. and Romania: Facing a Difficult Future. Washington: The ᴺntic Council of the United States, April, p.11.

and Romania are similar in population, income, social indicators, and composition of output. And both have experimented with socialism in one family.

Socialism in One Family

Rising to power in 1965, Nicolae Ceauşescu continued and intensified Romania's symbolically independent line in foreign and economic affairs, which was reminiscent in some ways of Kim Il-sung's attempt to steer an independent course between Moscow and Beijing. In 1967 Romania established full diplomatic relations with West Germany, and Ceauşescu later became the first Eastern Bloc head of state to visit West Germany since the Second World War. Ceauşescu subsequently hosted US President Richard Nixon (twice) and French General Charles de Gaulle.

Romania's foreign policy independence was not limited to courting capitalists. Although Romania was a member of the Warsaw Pact, it did not participate in Warsaw Pact military exercises. Romania broke ranks in 1967, refused to join other East Bloc governments in condemning Israel for its actions during the Six Day War, and openly sided with the "Prague Spring" reformers. This independence was later repeated when, in 1979, Ceauşescu denounced the Soviet-backed Vietnamese invasion of Cambodia, and, a year later, the Soviet invasion of Afghanistan. Romania subsequently refused to join the Soviet Union in boycotting the 1984 Los Angeles Olympics.

In economic policy, Romania pursued a similar combination of internal orthodoxy and symbolic independence in external relations. The economy was dominated by the state. By 1985, the state-owned enterprises (SOEs) accounted for 95 percent of output. State and collective farms controlled 80 percent of agricultural land. Ninety percent of investment was channeled to the state sector, and the state owned virtually all of the capital stock (Earle and Oprescu 1995).

Planning was carried out in quantity terms down to minute levels. To facilitate planning, an extreme degree of horizontal and vertical integration was encouraged, creating huge enterprises. Although Romania had been a largely agrarian economy at the end of the Second World War, heavy industry was so emphasized that by the 1980s light industry output was actually falling as resources were being transferred to the heavy industry sectors.

Furthermore, the state maintained a monopoly on external trade. W'
it carried out Stalinist orthodoxy internally, Romania attempted tc
its reliance on commerce with the communist bloc and joined V
institutions such as the General Agreement on Tariffs and Trade
Though this policy may have marginally oriented Romanian tr

the West, the country was reliant on the subsidized supplies of coal, oil, and gas from the Soviet Union.

Despite its attempts to differentiate itself from other Soviet bloc societies, Romania remained essentially a communist country. After visiting China and North Korea in 1971, Ceauşescu attempted to introduce a cultural revolution by building a personality cult around himself and his family. In 1973, his wife Elena was elevated to the Communist Party's executive committee, in which family relations and cronies assumed positions of power.

In the aftermath of the first oil shock, Western bankers, with petrodollars to recycle, began pushing loans. Some went to communist states, including Romania and North Korea. Romania began borrowing large sums from abroad to finance a series of grandiose endeavors, including a nuclear power plant, massive steel and aluminum complexes, and white elephant infrastructural projects such as the Transfagarasan Highway, the Danube Canal, and the Bucharest Metro.

Eventually, the foreign debt came due. Like North Korea, Romania was unable to service the debt, and it was rescheduled in 1981. Since much of the money had been plowed into projects with low economic rates of return, resources had to be extracted from elsewhere in the economy to free up funds for debt repayment. Ceauşescu's solution was to suppress consumption. (In contrast, the North Koreans simply defaulted on the debts.) By 1981, standards of living were falling. Economic hardship intensified during the winter of 1985, when Romania experienced an extremely cold season. Faced with a severe energy shortage, Romanians were forced to live and work in freezing conditions. Farm animals were substituted for mechanical machinery in agriculture. A popular joke went: "What did Romanians use to light their homes before candles?" Answer: light bulbs.

Economic hardship continued unabated, and mass civil unrest broke out for the first time two years later (November 1987) when workers in Brasov, Romania's second largest industrial region, went on strike. The rioting was put down violently by the military, but mass unrest occurred again the following year in response to a government plan to forcibly displace 8,000 villages.

Despite this turbulence, Romania finished paying off its foreign debt in April 1989. By this time, however, anti-Ceauşescu sentiments were being expressed by elements of the Romanian elite. On the ground, violent protests broke out among ethnic Hungarians in the city of Timisoara in December. These were put down by the secret police at the cost of approximately 100 lives, but within days the fighting spread to Bucharest and other cities. Stunned, Ceauşescu attempted to address a mass rally organized to mobilize support. An angry mob hooted him off his balcony, an event broadcast live on national television. On 22 December 1989, with the army in revolt, the Ceauşescu government was removed in an intraelite coup by the National Salvation Front (NSF). On Christmas Day, Nicolae Ceauşescu, his wife Elena, and their three children, including Nicu, the political heir apparent, were tried in secret by the military. The elder Ceauşescus were sentenced to death and summarily shot. A tape of the executions was broadcast on state television.[2]

Life After Ceauşescu

In a move to halt the worst excesses of the Ceauşescu regime quickly, the Communist dominated National Salvation Front (NSF) named Ion Iliescu as President and Petre Roman as Prime Minister. Iliescu and Roman were elected in a landslide over a badly disorganized opposition in May 1990, though it soon became apparent that the NSF was more interested in preserving the perquisites of Communist Party functionaries than in effecting revolutionary change in Romanian society.[3] Iliescu's Party of Social Democracy (PDSR) was closely linked to the former Communist *nomenklatura* and led a series of weak governments in coalition with extreme nationalist and far left groups.

Despite having been elected in a landslide, Iliescu and the PDSR did not appear to represent any real ideology beyond opportunism. Nor was the election a real mandate for reform. Moreover, the bureaucracy, which had seen its influence wane under the vagaries of Ceauşescu's rule, asserted itself and attempted to "nationalize" rather than replace the communist apparatus (Tismaneanu 1993). A 1991 survey cited by Kirk (1991) found that 41 percent of workers wanted to work in a state owned enterprise, 37 percent in a mixed public-private enterprise, and only 27 percent preferred to work in a private enterprise. Thirty-eight percent thought that economic reform was being implemented too fast, while a plurality (49 percent) thought that it had proceeded too slowly. The politics of the iron rice bowl were alive and well in the Carpathians.

Given the PDSR's political base and the lack of popular consensus for change, economic reforms were pursued hesitantly. Many Romanians became worse off materially than under Ceauşescu. At the same time, the half-reformed nature of the economy gave rise to large rents, of which a considerable share was captured by a wealthy elite of former Communist Party *apparatchiks*, further increasing public cynicism and distrust.

In the November 1996 elections, Iliescu was turned out of office in favor of a more genuinely reformist center-right coalition government led by

---

2. The three children were given prison terms and have since been released. Nicu Ceauseşcu, a hard-drinking playboy, died of cirrhosis of the liver in Vienna in 1996.

3. Roman eventually split with Iliescu and formed his own opposition group, the Social Democratic Union. A parade of obscure figures served as Prime Minister under Iliescu for the remainder of his term.

Figure 9.1 North Korean and Romanian growth rates

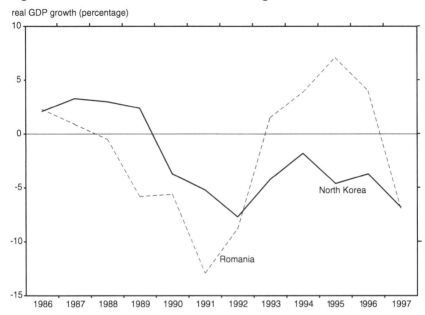

real GDP growth (percentage)

Sources: Bank of Korea; IFS.

President Emil Constantinescu and Prime Minister Victor Ciorbea. They promised "shock therapy" and, under the tutelage of the IMF, undertook an economic reform program that soon had the economy shrinking. This did not promote stability in the bickering coalition (which included the traditionalist Peasant Party, the more liberal and technocratic Democratic Party, the regionally-based ethnic Hungarian Party, and the Liberal Party). Ciorbea was sacrificed politically and replaced by Radu Vasile in 1997 as Prime Minister. He, in turn, was sacked and replaced by former central bank governor Mugur Isarescu in 1999.

Economic Policy and Performance

The Iliescu regime inherited an already deteriorating centrally planned economy (CPE) (figure 9.1). It was soon hit by trade shocks associated with the dissolution of the communist Council for Mutual Economic Assistance (COMECON) in 1991 and the decline of traditional Eastern Bloc markets. These developments intensified the economic contraction, and the government's timid response contributed to growing macroeconomic disequilibria (table 9.1).

Central planning was formally abandoned in 1990. In the late 1980s, the Ceauşescu regime had run budget and external surpluses to service

Table 9.1 Romanian macroeconomic indicators

	1985	1986	1987	1988	1989	1990	1991	1992	1993	1994	1995	1996	1997
Real GDP growth	−0.1	2.3	0.8	−0.5	−5.8	−7.4	−13.0	−10.0	1.3	3.4	6.9	3.9	−6.6
Budget balance (as percent of GDP)						−0.5	−2.0	−4.6	−0.4	−1.9	−2.6	−4.0	−3.6
Inflation rate				2.6	0.9	4.7	161	199	296	62	28	57	152
Current account balance (US$ billions)	1.4	1.4	2.0	3.9	2.5	−3.3	−1.0	−1.5	−1.2	−0.5	−1.8	−2.6	−2.3

Source: National statistics, International Monetary Fund.

the foreign debt. In the face of falling output and external shocks, the Iliescu regime allowed the budget to go into deficit in order to finance industrial subsidies and inter-enterprise arrears that had grown by 1991 to 50 percent of GDP (Khan and Clifton 1992). Loss of fiscal control, the maintenance of negative real interest rates, and structurally driven price increases associated with non-competitive domestic markets contributed to the acceleration of inflation, which reached nearly 300 percent in 1993. At the same time, maintenance of negative deposit rates, together with the failure to float the domestic currency, the lei, contributed to a loss of competitiveness manifested in the emergence of a current account deficit and a move into foreign-currency-denominated accounts. For reasons that are not fully understood, unlike other countries in the region, labor force participation actually increased. Women's labor force participation rose from 76.2 percent in 1989 to an astounding 85.2 percent in 1992, the same rate as for men (Earle and Oprescu 1995). Although employment grew, it did not grow fast enough to keep pace with the growing labor force, and unemployment rose to more than 10 percent.

At the industry level, the economy deindustrialized, with industrial output falling between 1989 and 1993 in all sectors (Jackson 1994). An unknown share of the capital stock was rendered worthless by the shift in relative prices and the collapse of demand for Romanian products. (The relative success story was the furniture sector. It suffered a relatively small decline in output (13 percent, peak to trough) and was the fastest to revive, driven by export sales.) However, these changes were measured against a status quo that, like the East German and North Korean cases, undoubtedly embodied a larger industrial (and smaller services) sector than would have been generated by a market economy.

In response to the crisis, the government attempted a number of reforms. Agriculture was decollectivized, and, in contrast to the industrial sector, measured output remained relatively stable. (Gross output may have fallen in response to input supply disruption and the like, but a smaller share of gross output was retained for on-farm consumption.) In the industrial sector, the government announced policies of privatization and restructuring, but made little progress.[4] The private enterprises that subsequently emerged were developed mainly through entrepreneurs entering the services sector.[5]

---

4. A State Ownership Fund (SOF) was established to handle the privatization of SOEs. Privatization proceeded slowly. Investors reported that they experienced difficulty concluding deals with the SOF, and that intervention by senior government officials was usually required. There was ample opportunity for corruption. A voucher plan similar to the Czech model was attempted, but made little progress.

5. Private enterprises at this time accounted for only 18 percent of industrial production. The share has risen substantially since the privatizations of 1997.

The state continued to intervene in the market in a variety of formal and informal ways. This was manifested in continuing large internal price distortions as well as sluggish labor market adjustment. Both of these effects were reinforced by the extreme concentration of Romanian industry and the opportunities to exercise monopoly or oligopoly power. Between interventions to alter relative prices, the extension of soft budget constraints to favored sectors and firms, foreign exchange controls, and the absence of any real competition policy, the Romanian authorities in effect pursued an active industrial policy.

The net effect of these interventions retarded restructuring, especially with regard to state-owned industrial enterprises. Although net industrial employment in SOEs declined, data analyzed by Earle and Oprescu (1995) indicated that there was considerable labor flow both into and out of industrial SOEs. Certain firms and sectors appear to have been systematically granted more favorable treatment, allowing them to maintain employment levels. They concluded that: "Large-scale labor reallocation appears to be necessary, yet the current structural policies seem to be ineffectual in bringing this about" (p.235).

The fundamental problem was that, although the authorities announced progressive policies relating to marketization and property rights (at one point even proclaiming "shock treatment"!), the lack of political consensus behind the reforms and the governing party's political base in the *nomenklatura* meant that the government lacked credibility. The private sector was weak and unresponsive in light of the government's tepid commitment to reform.

Externally, the state monopoly of international trade was dissolved in 1990, though the maintenance of exchange controls and a dual exchange rate still gave the state plenty of scope for influencing international trade. The pattern of trade shifted dramatically. In 1989, European market economies supplied 14.4 percent of Romanian imports and absorbed 33.9 percent of Romanian exports, while centrally planned economies supplied 53.6 percent of the imports and absorbed 40.1 percent of its exports. In 1995, Western Europe accounted for more than half of both imports and exports. Trade shares with the former centrally planned economies had fallen to less than half of their previous levels, though some of this decline was undoubtedly due to economic difficulties in the former communist bloc.

Export statistics provide some indication of Romania's emergent comparative advantage. In 1989, minerals (19.4 percent), metals (16.2 percent), machinery (16.1 percent), and transportation equipment (13.1 percent) were the largest export sectors. By 1995, export specialization had changed considerably: textiles (19.7 percent) was now the leading sector, followed by metals (18.5 percent), minerals (9.6 percent), and chemicals (9.4 percent). In essence, textiles and chemicals had replaced engineering products in Romania's export basket.

With the support of the World Bank and the IMF, the new government inaugurated in early 1997 undertook economic reform with a greater sense of urgency. Initially, the Ciorbea government made strong progress. It floated the exchange rate, abolished domestic price controls, and downsized the politically sensitive coal mining industry. It also privatized more state owned enterprises in its first year than the Iliescu government had in the previous six, though critics observed that this still amounted to less than 20 percent of the State Ownership Fund's portfolio. Trade reform boosted the fortunes of the export-oriented agricultural sector. As the coalition government began to weaken, however, the pace of reform slowed significantly. The government faced problems related to the soft budget constraints imposed on loss-making SOEs in both the state budget and the banking sector. The Russian crisis of August 1998 was an external shock to the economy and led to a ratings agency downgrade.

The economic and political legacy of Ceauşescu's misrule has proven to be a very heavy burden. A decade after his fall, the Romanian economy and polity seem to have settled into a rough equilibrium in which economic conditions are not catastrophic, but difficult. Setting aside the former Soviet Union, the country has lagged other large Eastern European countries in making a successful transition to the market. Decades of mismanagement of the industrial sector have contributed to macroeconomic imbalances and difficulties in achieving sustainable non-inflationary growth. The country has chronic balance of payments difficulties, which are financed largely through World Bank and IMF lending. Three International Monetary Fund programs have been suspended for Romanian non-compliance with program conditionality, and relations with the IMF are strained.

Politically, Western-oriented reformers are weaker in Romania than in the rest of Eastern Europe, and the political and business class is still dominated by Ceauşescu-era *apparatchiks*. The country continues to face problems of corruption but has made enormous strides since the dictatorial rule of Ceauşescu. The year 2000 will bring elections and more foreign debts to be repaid. Only optimists and criminals run for office.

Relevance for North Korea

The striking parallels between the Romanian and North Korean cases provide a number of potential lessons for North Korea. The most obvious is that sufficient economic mismanagement can bring down a Communist regime, even if led by someone as ruthless and despotic as Nicolae Ceauşescu. Both countries have suffered from central planning and its attendant maladies. Both got into debt trouble in the 1970s. One striking difference is that Ceauşescu made the fateful decision to repay the debt, while Kim Il-sung simply defaulted on his Western creditors. (The lesson here may be that, if one has to displease a constituency, foreign bankers are a better choice than the local populace.)

In the Romanian case, living standards began to fall in the early 1980s as domestic consumption was compressed to free up resources for debt repayment. Conditions worsened in 1985 when the country was hit by severe weather while coping with an energy crisis. Yet the first mass unrest did not appear until 1987, six years after the decline in living standards began, and it was not until 1989, when other socialist regimes began to collapse and the economy began to enter free fall, that the Ceauşescu regime toppled. This suggests caution in drawing too deterministic a link between economic hardship and political failure—a caveat reinforced by the contemporary experiences of countries as diverse as Cuba, Iraq, and Mobutu-era Zaire. The willingness of foreign powers to support the incumbent regime also differs greatly in the Romanian and North Korean cases, as will be argued below.

Moreover, Ceauşescu's removal had more the air of a regime-preserving coup than of a genuine revolution. Subsequent Romanian experience suggests that muddling through may indeed be a viable strategy. Figure 9.1 plots Romanian and North Korean growth rates, with the implicit caveat that these figures are subject to enormous uncertainty for reasons already elaborated. However, it is striking that both countries grew at 2.5 percent in 1985. Romania subsequently suffered a deeper contraction in output than North Korea has experienced. However, once the reform process was initiated in 1990, the Romanian economy began to stabilize. By 1993, it was registering positive, though unspectacular, economic growth. Still, it will be years before Romania will recoup the fall in output experienced during the period 1988 to 1992.

It is not difficult to imagine similar economic (and in some circumstances political) developments occurring in North Korea. The initial economic reform strategy in Romania was strongly influenced by the political and economic interests of the former Communist Party embodied in Iliescu's PDSR. The state continued to be the dominant force in the economy. Political power was used to create and allocate rents, which were then channeled to politically influential groups and individuals either directly or informally through corruption. The process of restructuring has proceeded at a slow pace. It is not difficult to imagine Kim Jong-il (or his successor) adopting a similar set of policies in response to the exigencies of economic hardship on the one hand and the requirement of satisfying the regime's political base on the other. In the case of North Korea, these favored constituencies would presumably be the Kim clique, along with the military and possibly the Korean Workers' Party (KWP).

While communism bequeathed Romania an unenviable legacy with which its policymakers continue to grapple, democratization eventually led to the replacement of Iliescu with the more reformist Constantinescu.

Although the economic prospects for Romania do not look particularly bright, domestic political debate has revealed an awareness of the implications of economic policy choices and of the need for institutional reform. Romania has become a much more "normal" country. Indeed, these changes lend credibility to the analysis of successful reform in chapter 7: comparative advantage has been maintained in certain natural resource-oriented sectors and has emerged in light manufacturing, while the engineering products sector has been hit hard. The pattern of trade has begun to be determined more by markets and less by politics, shifting trade toward Romania's natural partners in Western Europe. The major difference with the earlier analysis of successful reform is that Romania has pursued these reforms in a timid and hesitant fashion. Consequently, the extent of these changes do not match the dramatic potential presented in the earlier analysis.

Muddling Through in Our Own Style

How might the North Korean regime pursue a "satisficing" policy of economic improvement with minimal institutional change and minimal likelihood of spawning discontent? The most obvious organizational response would be to redouble efforts on existing strategies—in this case one-off projects that would generate foreign exchange (such as the Rajin-Sonbong special economic zone (SEZ) and the Mt. Kumgang tourism project) and the external threat and extortion tactics most plainly manifest in the long-range missile test. While the Rajin-Sonbong SEZ has been a failure, the contract with Hyundai has also signaled the possible development of a new, more attractive SEZ at Haeju.

Beyond these moves, one might expect the North Koreans to ratify the kind of system-fraying that has been occurring in response to the crisis. This might include greater decentralization of decision-making authority at the planning level, which would give local authorities increased responsibility. (Kim Jong-il did, after all, write his dissertation on the role of the county in economic development.) Enterprise managers could also be given greater autonomy and promote the current tendencies toward the formation of multi-enterprise affiliated groups under some common management coordination or control.[6] The military and party could be prominent in this process.[7]

Moreover, the present regime may prove to be more resilient than some other communist regimes. It has more closely aligned itself with

---

6. See Michell (1998) for a more detailed analysis of these prospective changes.

7. Levin (1997) discusses some of the internal and external ramifications of a successful muddling through strategy by North Korea.

nationalism than most of the communist parties of Eastern Europe were able to do. Moreover, as pointed out by Chung (1991), the general populace has been highly isolated from outside contacts. The state has a near perfect monopoly of the mass media and completely regiments everyday life. There are no disaffected ethnic minorities as was the case in Romania, nor are there groups in the civil society capable of offering an alternative program as did Poland's Solidarity or Czechoslovakia's Civic Forum.[8] There is no real civil society in North Korea today. Rather, political change in North Korea may be of a more incremental nature. Scalapino (1992) envisions the possibility of an "authoritarian but pluralist stage, in which politics is still constrained but a civil society of sorts emerges and the economy has a prominent market factor. There may be joint civilian-military control, or more military, but order is kept. At least it seems to me that this is just as probable as the collapse scenario, and it has ample precedent, including here in South Korea" (pp.4-5).[9]

An obvious question is whether this could come through a non-Kimil-sungist regime. Kim Jong-il appears to rely increasingly on the military to govern. As Ahn (1998) observes, 38 of his 58 public appearances in 1996 and 39 of 59 public appearances in 1997 were military-related, and military figures are increasingly prominent in the government hierarchy. Indeed, when Kim Jong-il formally assumed power in August 1998, it was not as head of state, but rather as Chairman of the newly created National Defense Commission. A US intelligence official with longstanding expertise on North Korea has indicated that Kim appears to depend increasingly on the military to govern, while the Korean Workers' Party withers.

This suggests at least three possibilities. One would be a straightforward military coup.[10] Were it successful, the military regime would face immedi-

---

8. Chung (1991) cites the move from *juche*, with its emphasis on national self-reliance, to the more open-ended *Kimilsungism* as the kind of ideological shift that would allow the regime to begin opening economically to the outside and avoid an ideological crisis of contradictions.

9. The experience of Taiwan may be instructive in this regard. Chiang Ching-Kuo, another autocrat's son with ties to the party and military, served as a transitional figure, paving the way for the evolution of the political system from the authoritarianism of his father, Chiang Kai-Shek, to the democracy of his successor Lee Teng-Hui. Some North Korea watchers aver that Kim Jong-il is no Chiang Ching-Kuo, however.

10. Rumors abound of disloyalty among army officers and unsuccessful coup attempts, though it is unclear how much credibility should be attached to these stories. Gertz (1999) reproduces a secret State Department cable that refers to "extensive evidence of a major coup attempt by elements of the VI Corps in 1995, which appears to have been crushed only with some difficulty" (p. 264). The State Department has not denied the authenticity of this cable. According to Oberdorfer (1997), after the uprising the corps, based in the famine-stricken northeastern city of Hamhung, "was disbanded, its leadership purged, and its units submerged into others under circumstances suggesting disarray in the ranks" (p.375).

ate questions of legitimacy. One possibility would be to install another Kim, such as half-brother Kim Pyung-il, as titular head of state and attempt to work with Kim family loyalists. A more radical approach would be to abjure the window dressing and attempt to root out the Kim family loyalists from the military, the government, and the Party, in the process seeking to make a clean break with the past. Without any of the traditional trappings of legitimacy, however, such a regime would have to deliver material improvement very quickly or risk serious mass discontent. Presumably, such reformist authoritarians would not find it difficult to obtain material support from abroad.[11]

Perhaps the most intriguing option is made possible by Kim Jong-il's very public reticence. The military could stage a coup, but allow Kim Jong-il to reign—but not rule—as a symbol of continuity, tradition, and legitimacy. Kim's very lack of public accessibility and the frequency of his appearances in military settings would facilitate this approach. The striking thing about this scenario is that, from external appearances, it would be observationally little different from the status quo. Indeed, in some sense it may have already occurred.

All this is to say that one can construct models in which the North Korean government acts rationally and could decide to pursue economic reform without necessitating an internal crisis. Shirk (1995) argues that domestic political considerations, not economic considerations, were the driving force behind the Chinese economic reforms and the gradualist, decentralized, and particularistic form that they took. In her interpretation, economic reform was a means of strengthening political control, not threatening it. While North Korea is not China, such a view has obvious relevance to the North Korean case.

Minimum Survival Requirements

The North Korean economy desperately needs two things to meet the minimum survival requirements of its population: food and energy. It may well be that the country generates enough through production or aid to attain the minimum survival basket, but chooses not to do so (i.e., the regime has a strong preference for guns over butter). Taking these preferences as given, how much additional income would the country need to achieve the minimum survival basket? The analysis in chapter 5 suggests that, under current conditions, North Korea runs a structural

---

11. Indeed, in the midst of the August 1999 missile launch scare, TV preacher, former Republican Presidential candidate, and all around fan of the apocalypse Pat Robertson raised just this issue (which has been a subject of theological controversy since at least the time of Thomas More), asking would it not be better just to "take out" Kim Jong-il than to "spend billions of dollars on a war that harms innocent civilians and destroys the infrastructure?" (Hanna Rosin, *Washington Post*, 10 August 1999).

food deficit of around two million tons. For the last five years, this gap has mainly been closed through the provision of international assistance.

In addition to food, North Korea needs energy. It relies on imported oil to generate fuels and fertilizer for use in transportation and agriculture. Electricity is mainly generated using coal and hydropower. Generation has been hampered by difficulties in extracting increasingly inaccessible and low quality domestic coal reserves. Beyond this problem, the power grid (largely underground for security purposes) is said to suffer from extraordinarily large transmission losses. Assuming continued implementation of the Agreed Framework, North Korea's energy problems would be partly addressed through the provision of fuel oil during the construction of the light-water reactors. Nevertheless, North Korea would need energy inputs beyond those specified in the Agreed Framework even to reattain 1991's estimated level of electrical consumption.

If these estimates are correct, and the Agreed Framework is fully implemented, then the actual cost of purchasing the estimated shortfalls in grain and energy, as well as desperately needed supplies of fertilizers, pharmaceuticals, etc., would not be very large, less than $1 billion dollars (Michell 1998). Assuming no more interruptions in service, the Hyundai Mt. Kumgang deal guarantees North Korea a minimum of nearly $150 million annually. North Korea receives a payment for each visitor, and if Hyundai were to fill all the berths on its ships, then North Korea would stand to net approximately $450 million per year—or enough to cover its grain deficit on commercial terms. Moreover, other South Korean firms have expressed interest in similar tourist ventures. If the North Koreans went through with the other projects in the Hyundai agreement, including the establishment of a new SEZ at Haeju, this could generate additional revenues.

Michell (1998) argues that for $2 billion one could sufficiently fix the North Korean economy that it would generate rising living standards and presumably reduce discontent.[12] Around half of this would be for recurrent consumption expenditures, and around half would be for industrial and infrastructural investments that could be self-financed through export revenues. This is not a lot of money—less than the cost of one of the two light-water reactors that the United States is committed to build. These sums are nearly within the margin of error of what we think we know about the North Korean economy. It may well be that North Korea can survive (in a biological sense, at least) without any (or with relatively modest) external assistance.

---

12. As hardship does not necessarily mean instability, rising living standards do not necessarily mean contentment. Political change seldom occurs during famines; people's energies are consumed by the needs of survival. Political change comes after famines—when culpability is reckoned. See Huntington (1968) for more on the relationship between economic growth and political stability.

North Korea is not Romania, and so one should not push such analogies too far. Most pertinently, the existence of a prosperous, democratic South Korea would seem to make it much more difficult for Kim Jong-il (or his successors) to pursue *apparatchik* capitalism as a long-run development strategy. (Indeed, even in Romania, Iliescu's party was driven from power after one election.) Nor does ad hoc coping ensure success—some of the "muddlers" among the states of the former Soviet Union have experienced output declines of 50 to 80 percent. Nevertheless, the experience of Romania suggests that muddling through may last for years before there is a more permanent turn toward reform or chaos, especially if external powers find that this solution is in their interests.

Friends in High Places

In the short run, China, Japan, or South Korea could keep North Korea afloat (in this narrow sense). Both Japan and China at present appear to have surplus government grain stocks that could be used to make up the North Korean shortfall with minimal expenditures. It may well be the case that China, Japan, and Russia would prefer a muddling, domesticated North Korea to a unified, capitalist, and possibly nuclear armed state on the Korean peninsula.[13] China (and, for similar reasons, Russia and Japan) may prefer continued economic engagement with South Korea and would be willing to expend some resources to maintain North Korea as an allied buffer state. China has begun to pick up some of the slack left by Russia, North Korea's former patron, though the extent to which current Chinese exports of food and other essentials are on concessional terms is unclear. Nor is it known what kind of economic or foreign policy conditions are attached to these flows. The dual goals of continuing support for the North and enhancing economic engagement with the South present Beijing with a delicate diplomatic conundrum.

Unification along the lines of the German model would complicate the strategic planning of China and Japan, and would further reduce Russian influence in the region. At least in the short to medium run, one can envision China providing North Korea with aid and technical assistance, South Korea engaging China (and possibly North Korea) economically, while being protected by the American security umbrella, and Japanese concerns of a Sino-Japanese military imbalance allayed by the American counterweight.

In contrast, the United States would bear little of any unification's direct costs. Unification would eliminate the direct threat posed by North Korea to US troops currently stationed in Northeast Asia and end North Korean proliferation of weapons of mass destruction. While there may be some

---

13. See Okonogi (n.d.) for a Japanese perspective.

benefit to the United States in playing the role outlined above, long-run US interests are surely better served by unification. In this regard the United States may be unique.[14]

It is precisely this divergence between the interests of the United States and the other relevant powers that has put the United States in the awkward position of looking for second-best solutions. From a US perspective, the first-best solution would be the elimination of the Kim Jong-il regime and its absorption into a democratic, capitalist Korea. Unfortunately, even if the other relevant powers supported this goal, for geographical reasons, if for no other, they would be more risk averse in pursuing it. So, the United States is impeded from seeking its first-best solution and forced into politically unsatisfying, fallback positions, as demonstrated by the US response to the nuclear confrontation and the famine and further evidenced by the lack of domestic political consensus in support of those policies.

The Perry Report and the Package Deal

Choosing among second-bests is always difficult, and, in this case, it is complicated by the need to coordinate with others. American interests and those of South Korea and Japan do not exactly coincide. North Korea has 10,000 forward-deployed artillery tubes that have effectively held Seoul hostage for years. While the North Korean nuclear and missile programs pose a threat to South Korean security (largely by threatening US forces based in Japan that would be critical in any conflict on the Korean peninsula), it is a second-order threat. In the case of Japan, it is the Nodong missile, not the Taepodong, that poses the most immediate threat to Japanese security. Moreover, the United States, with its far-flung global interests, is the country most impacted by North Korean exports of missiles and weapons of mass destruction. This is simply to say that, while the United States, South Korea, and Japan share common interests, their priorities are not identical.

The Clinton Administration has done a good job coordinating with Japan and South Korea; its ability to coordinate a response with China has been less evident, but this may well be a function of basic Chinese attitudes toward the peninsula. This coordinated approach has been manifested in the Perry policy review, or the so-called "package deal." As discussed in chapter 4, the Perry policy review had its origins in a political compromise over congressional skepticism about the Clinton Administration's North Korea policy. It was seized upon by Kim Dae-jung as a way to get the United States and Japan more firmly behind his policy of engagement.

---

14. See Jannuzi (1998) for a discussion from an American perspective.

The Perry review did not get off to an auspicious start. When the former defense secretary accepted in November 1998 President Clinton's request that he conduct such a review, it was understood that Perry would present his report in April 1999. In March, he informed Congress that his report could be expected the following month.[15] The report was again postponed to June after Perry and a US delegation visited Pyongyang in May. However, in a June meeting with senior members of Congress, Perry indicated that the report would not be ready for another four to six weeks. By late summer, the rumor circulating around Washington was that the "report" might not be a "report" as the word is conventionally understood, but rather an oral briefing delivered to the President. Republicans in Congress were understandably angered by these developments, and on 23 August the Republican House Leadership formed a "North Korea Advisory Group" under the chairmanship of House International Relations Committee Chairman Benjamin A. Gilman (R-New York).[16] A process aimed at mollifying congressional antipathy toward the Administration's North Korea policy had actually inflamed it.

When it was presented to the President in September 1999 (and released in an unclassified form the following month), Perry's report identified North Korean nuclear weapons and long-range missile-related activities as the key priorities for US attention (Perry 1999). Perry then went on to make specific policy recommendations under three basic assumptions: 1) that North Korea is here to stay (i.e., collapse is not imminent); 2) that war is not an option; and 3) that the United States should not act to undermine or supplant the Agreed Framework. (The justification for the last was that the quickest and most effective way for the North Koreans to step up nuclear weapons activities would be through the unfreezing of their facilities at Yongbyon. Adherence to this proposition is not universal.) The report found that the central US interest in its relations with North Korea was ending North Korea's nuclear and long-range missile-related activities.[17] The best way of achieving US nuclear and missile-related objectives would be through increased bilateral cooperation through "a new comprehensive and integrated approach" eventually leading to a normalization of economic and political relations, including

---

15. Opening statement of Chairman Benjamin A. Gilman, Hearing: US Policy Towards North Korea and the Pending Perry Review, House International Relations Committee, 24 March 1999.

16. The North Korea Advisory Group sent its report to the Speaker of the House on 29 October 1999.

17. Note that the United States identified the *long-range* Taepodong missile program (i.e., the one which could potentially threaten the United States directly) as its main priority, not the shorter range Nodong, which would be of more direct relevance to South Korea and Japan.

easing of economic sanctions. Privately, Perry compared this approach to the US normalization of relations with Vietnam.

No US policy could succeed without the active cooperation of South Korea and Japan. Indeed, unstated in the publicly released report, but included in Perry's message to Pyongyang in May 1999, was a statement that a settlement of post-colonial claims against Japan, which are far more valuable to the North Koreans than the easing of US sanctions, would be attainable through the cooperative approach. Whether this would succeed would ultimately depend on North Korea's response. Without prejudging Pyongyang's likely response, the Perry report concluded that the United States should be prepared to pursue unspecified "second path" policies in case the cooperative approach failed.

Pyongyang did not respond with alacrity. With regard to the feasibility of the cooperative approach, the report indicated that a senior North Korean official (identified in numerous press reports as First Vice Minister Kim Sok-ju) would probably visit Washington in the fall of 1999. State Department officials indicated privately that the visit would occur in October. When it did not, the date of the putative visit was pushed back to mid-2000. Hedging his bets, Perry acknowledged that North Korea might reject the proffered hand of cooperation and that "the United States should keep its powder dry."[18]

One could excuse the North Koreans for a certain degree of skepticism about the Perry proposal. After all, removal of economic sanctions and the establishment of liaison offices as a stepping stone to complete diplomatic recognition already are part of the Agreed Framework. The United States has not opposed North Korean involvement with the international financial institutions, and South Korea has actively supported North Korean efforts in that regard.

Vietnam does not receive normal trade status (most-favored-nation treatment) in its trade with the United States, and it is not a member of the World Trade Organization, so it is largely excluded from the US market in the critical textiles and apparel sector. Thus it is unclear what additional economic concessions the United States is offering North Korea in return for it to forgo its missile program. In effect, the Perry offer appears to amount to the normalization of North Korean relations with Japan and the provision of Japanese money in return for the North Korean missile program. It is no wonder that the North Koreans threatened a second long-range missile test while demanding compensation from Japan (chapter 4). Why not see if one can drive a wedge between Japan and the others to extract a better deal? The fact that the Japanese did not strike a separate deal immeasurably strengthened Perry's hand. The subsequent North Korean interest in reopening normalization talks with Japan,

---

18. Stephen Fidler, *Financial Times*, 30 November 1999.

expressed during former Prime Minister Murayama's December 1999 visit to Pyongyang, could be interpreted as a positive response to the Perry offer. At the same time, it opens up the possibility that, after it extracted concessions from Japan through the normalization process, North Korea could resume its previous brinkmanship-extortion strategy.

Ultimately, any serious resuscitation of the North Korean economy will require significantly expanded interaction with South Korea. Recognizing this reality, the US reacted positively to the April 2000 announcement of a North-South summit planned for June. The extent of economic inducements that Kim Dae-jung has in mind and his willingness to make these conditional on progress in attaining US strategic aims is less clear, however. South Korean moves to increase economic assistance (whether under the guise of economic cooperation or as outright assistance) could undercut the US position. At the same time, increased South Korean corporate involvement with North Korea is likely to further complicate government-business relations in South Korea, impeding the South Korean government's attempt to disengage constructively from direct intervention in its own corporate sector.

If North Korea were to accept the Perry review's terms of engagement, the last carrot that the United States and its allies could hold out would be membership in the international financial organizations and the prospect of multilateral economic assistance. Pyongyang has periodically expressed interest in joining the IMF, the World Bank, and the Asian Development Bank (ADB). Membership talks have never made much progress, however, for they have snagged both on North Korea's unwillingness to permit the kind of access to economic data and information required for membership in these organizations and on Japanese opposition relating to unresolved political issues, most notably the alleged kidnapping of Japanese citizens. Under normal circumstances, if North Korea were to join these organizations it would be unlikely that the multilateral development banks would make significant loans in the absence of considerable reorientation in North Korea's domestic economic policies. However, given the political importance of North Korea to the United States and Japan (influential shareholders in the World Bank and the dominant shareholders in the ADB), one would expect that North Korea might receive favorable treatment. As Leipziger (1998b) makes clear in his thoughtful analysis of the international financial institutions' prospective role in North Korea's economic reconstruction, the impact of the multilateral development banks would depend highly on the North Korean government's commitment to reform. Technical advice and assistance would really be more important than direct lending activities, which would ultimately only complement the activities of private investors.[19] Working

19. It is possible that North Korea could access IMF or multilateral development bank loans under some circumstances even if it were not a member. For example, the World Bank maintains a special program for peace and sustainable development in the Middle East

from the case of Vietnam (another Asian transitional economy in which the government undertook rapid economic reforms) and scaling down the multilateral development banks' lending program for the smaller size of the North Korean population, one obtains lending on a scale of $150 million to $250 million annually. While this is not trivial, it is not enough to finance even Michell's bare-bones recovery program. More money might be available if South Korea, Japan, and others set up a special fund for North Korea at the World Bank or the ADB. Such a fund might be particularly useful as a way of politically laundering Japanese reparations.

Sustainability

It is questionable whether a "muddling through" strategy on the part of North Korea, and a counterpart engagement strategy on the part of the United States, South Korea, and Japan, would be sustainable. Such a strategy could fail for economic, diplomatic, or domestic political reasons. The Perry report identified North Korea's nuclear weapons and long-range missile-related activities as the dual fulcrums on which the US bilateral relationship moved. In both cases there are reasons to believe that the status quo is not sustainable in the long run.

During the weekend following the delivery of the Perry report, the United States and North Korea concluded a round of negotiations in Berlin over North Korea's missile program. In a verbal agreement, the United States agreed to lift most of its economic sanctions against North Korea in return for a North Korean moratorium on long-range missile testing. US negotiators claimed that the flight-testing moratorium would significantly impede the further development of North Korean missiles. National Security Advisor Sandy Berger indicated that the agreement would remain in force for the duration of bilateral talks aimed at achieving a broader missile accord. Juxtaposed against Perry's recommendation for a "new, comprehensive approach," the agreement was denounced as representing precisely the opposite: engaging a piecemeal negotiation through which North Koreans could use brinkmanship (threat of another

---

through which it makes loans in the areas controlled by the Palestinian Authority. It also has adopted a policy that allows it to assist countries that are emerging from crises, even though they are not members in good standing of the Bank. This policy was adopted after the Bank was precluded from lending to Cambodia because of a debt arrearage problem. The key attributes in these cases appear to be a cooperative recipient government and strong support from major institutional shareholders. An April 2000 public statement to this effect in Seoul by IMF resident representative David T. Coe sparked an immediate denunciation by Rep. James Saxton (R-New Jersey). Bank staff also have expressed the view privately that an independent, poor North Korea probably would be able to access more lending than a unified, middle-income Korea. Lee and Morrison (1995) even raise the possibility of asking APEC for money!

Taepodong launch) to obtain real concessions—the lifting of US sanctions.[20]

The real issue seems to be the reversibility of the sanctions lifting. If the sanctions could be imposed and removed by executive fiat, then the policy could be interpreted as a kind of confidence-building measure in the context of a possible broader agreement covering not only testing of long-range missiles, but also their production and export, as well as potential restrictions on shorter range missiles. However, if the removal of sanctions were to be relatively irreversible, then North Korean brinkmanship would seem to have obtained the removal of US sanctions at no real cost to itself. The sanctions that the United States apparently agreed to remove were restrictions originally imposed under the Trading With the Enemy Act. These can be administratively removed (and reimposed) by the President. There is thus no legal irreversibility to the sanctions removal. Some might argue that there is a degree of political or policy irreversibility, though it is hard to imagine that there would be much opposition to reimposing sanctions if North Korean testing of long-range missiles were resumed. (However, the one aspect of this deal that does embody some potential irreversibility would be settlement of post-colonial claims against Japan.) Thus, at least on the question of missiles, there is a plausible case to be made that the cooperative strategy is working. The real issue is what price is the United States willing to pay to circumscribe the North Korean missile program to its liking. As in all market transactions, there is no guarantee that the two sides will find a mutually acceptable price that will clear the market.

The other principal focus of US policy is North Korea's nuclear weapons activities. Here, despite the existence of a written document, the Agreed Framework, and a billion-dollar multinational consortium—KEDO—to carry out its central mandate, the horizon is clouded. The Agreed Framework contains only one date, 2003, the target date for the completion of the light water reactors (LWRs). Before the delivery of key components to complete the project, North Korea must come into compliance with IAEA plutonium safeguards.[21] Under current circumstances, both the timetable and North Korea's compliance are problematic.

---

20. For examples of public commentary along these lines, see the editorial of the *Los Angeles Times*, 14 September 1999, and op-ed pieces by Jim Mann, *Los Angeles Times*, 15 September 1999, and Nicholas Eberstadt, *Chosun Ilbo*, 13 September 1999.

21. According to the agreement, "when a significant portion of the LWR project is completed, but before the delivery of key nuclear components, the DPRK will come into full compliance with the IAEA (INFCIRC/403), including taking all steps that may be deemed necessary by the IAEA, following consultations with the Agency with regard to verifying the accuracy and completeness of the DPRK's initial report on all nuclear material in the DPRK." See appendix A for the complete text of the Agreed Framework.

Problems with the timetable reflect the fact that the Agreed Framework is ultimately a diplomatic project, not an economic one. Financing has been problematic from the start. Setting aside the financing issues, implementation has been highly politicized. KEDO has refused to assign to North Korea warranties from the project contractors and subcontractors (per standard practice), and this has slowed the completion of the Quality Assurance Protocol. For its part, North Korea has refused to send technicians to South Korea for training, slowing the Training Protocol, and it has demanded a tremendous increase in the wages paid to North Korean workers on the project, threatening demobilization if their demands are not met. As part of the Safety Protocol, North Korea is to establish a Nuclear Regulatory Commission, but issues remain unresolved: Who will finance the creation of this organization? Will it be given unfettered access to the site and empowered to shut down the reactors (possibly permitting the diversion of nuclear materials)? A Liability Protocol similarly remains unresolved.[22]

Even if these issues could be successfully resolved, the project faces enormous hurdles with the Delivery Schedule Protocol and with bringing North Korea into compliance with the IAEA safeguards regime. The IAEA inspections could take as long as two years and would require that work on the LWRs largely be halted in the interim. Once the IAEA completes its investigation, several outcomes are possible. One is that the IAEA could admit that it was wrong and that no diversion took place. Alternatively, the North Koreans could admit that they were lying all along and then hand over the diverted plutonium. Neither of these outcomes is very likely. Instead, the most likely outcome is that the IAEA will reach an indefinite conclusion about North Korea's past nuclear activities, couching its conclusion in language to the effect that there is an "x percent" probability that no diversion took place.[23] Whether "x percent" is sufficient certainty for the project to proceed will then be a political issue. There is no guarantee that the United States and its KEDO partners will agree. Some have suggested an even more sinister variant in which the IAEA will come under political pressure to reach certain conclusions, as has been alleged with regard to inspections by the UN Special Commission (UNSCOM) in Iraq.

These scenarios suggest that KEDO is unlikely to make its 2003 target. The North Koreans already have begun signaling what it would take to prevent a break-out under these circumstances: "immediate diplomatic

---

22. See Mansourov (2000b) and Reiss (2000) for further details on the practical obstacles confronting North Korea and KEDO in completing the project.

23. Mansourov (2000a) raises the possibility that the floods of the mid-1990s, which affected the nuclear installations, may prevent the construction of an accurate nuclear history even if the North Koreans were to cooperate.

recognition, signing a peace treaty, an across-the-board-lifting of sanctions, and removal of the DPRK from the list of terrorist countries" (M.C. Kim 1999). Additional demands will surely be forthcoming. The planned North-South summit, dramatically fulfilling the North Korean pledge to resume dialogue with South, will increase their negotiating leverage vis-à-vis the United States. In the language of bureaucracy, the can has been kicked down the road.

10

Conclusions

In Korean there is a saying, "two enemies will meet on a one log bridge." On the Korean peninsula today, two rivals tied together by history, geography, and nationality face off along the world's most militarized border. South Korea has been described as the first developing country to achieve developed country status. It has made the transition from military authoritarianism to a fragile and still maturing democracy. Yet even as policymakers in developing countries look to the "Korean model" for insights, the crisis that rocked South Korea at the end of 1997 is forcing a reassessment of this approach.

In stark contrast, North Korea is arguably the strangest political regime in existence today. It is perennially ranked last in *Euromoney's* annual assessment of country risk. The world's first example of dynastic Stalinism has endured a decade of economic decline and has experienced famine, yet it has continued to pour resources into the development of weapons of mass destruction and their delivery systems. This crisis is fundamentally systemic, not a period of aberrant performance due to bad weather or unfavorable external shocks, though both have contributed to the North's current predicament. Yet, to paraphrase Mark Twain, reports of the regime's collapse have been exaggerated, and its durability has confounded numerous observers.

This confrontation is terribly important, not only to the Koreans themselves, but to the rest of the world. North Korea has a history of external violence, and during the past century the Korean peninsula has been contested by the United States, Russia, China, and Japan. The outcome on the Korean peninsula will have enormous implications for the long-run economic, political, and military development of Asia and the US role in that part of the world.

North Korea

North Korea has a dysfunctional economy and a political regime that appears to place an extremely high value on military expenditure relative to the well-being of its populace. Unwilling or incapable of resolving its internal problems, it has pursued a policy of international brinkmanship to extract resources from the international community. However, the two principal creations of this policy, the Korean Peninsula Energy Development Organization (KEDO) and the multinational famine relief effort, do not address the country's essential economic problems and indeed may be politically unsustainable in the outside world. KEDO is a creature of diplomacy masquerading as an energy development program that is unlikely to make much real contribution to resolving North Korea's acute energy problems. In a somewhat similar fashion, the multinational famine relief effort is driven largely by diplomatic considerations. At best, it only ameliorates the manifestation of the North's economic collapse. It neither addresses its underlying causes nor promotes the needed solutions. Thus, in the case of North Korea, the world confronts an ongoing foreign policy problem driven by an apparent refusal of the Kim regime to deal with its own internal difficulties.

There are solutions to North Korea's economic problems. As demonstrated in chapter 7, economic reform could have enormous payoffs, increasing domestic food availability and, more generally, addressing the pressing material needs of the people. The real issue is not whether reform would be beneficial—it would, though the technical difficulties of reforming the North Korean economy should not be minimized. The real issue is whether reform would be compatible with the continued existence of the Kim Jong-il regime and, if not, what the world should expect. The key questions relate to the intentions of the regime. How much internal transformation can it tolerate? And how will the regime use its newly obtained wealth?

With respect to the first question, the signals are mixed. Over an extended period of years the regime has engaged in an extremely cautious opening to the outside world. It has emphasized forms of interaction (special economic zones and tourist projects in isolated parts of the country) that appear to be designed to maximize foreign exchange earnings while minimizing contact with foreigners and the transformative possibilities of these interactions. Marginally broader forms of opening have been discussed as well. This is a kind of "quarantined" opening, consistent with official propaganda, which has likened market relations to a "germ" that is to be warded off.

Yet even this hesitant opening has a "two steps forward, one step back" character. At times, North Korea has engaged foreigners in cooperation while simultaneously denouncing such cooperation internally or engaging in provocative actions that undercut the possibility of such cooperation. This behavior could reflect genuine ideological divisions within the regime or simply bureaucratic politics in which different organs pursue their own missions without regard to any broader coherency. Presumably, the resolution of such problems is made more difficult by the extraordinarily repressive nature of internal politics. Ultimately, the rest of the world has little influence on the pace and content of economic change within North Korea. However, the world does have a very large stake in how the regime spends its money.

One can imagine at least two North Korean strategies for this endgame. The first is for the North Korean elite to accept that they are on the wrong side of history. The South Koreans are bigger and richer and have the Americans in their corner. The peninsula is not going to be unified forcibly on North Korean terms. The North's proposal for a Confederal Republic of Koryo is a dead letter. Its preconditions for North-South dialogue: discontinue the South's military association and exercises with foreign powers; abolish the South Korean National Security Law; and eliminate restrictions on private movements for national unification will not be met.[1] Even a "one country, two systems" model along the lines of China and Hong Kong may be unworkable. After throwing in the towel politically, the goal of the regime could become self-enrichment. The elite's one real card is their control over the levers of power in a sovereign state. From this derives their ability to channel to themselves the lion's share of economic gains generated by reform. The most efficient way to improve their own material condition (as well as that of the broader North Korean society) would be to engage with foreigners and begin acting cooperatively. Such maneuvers must be done carefully however, so as not to jeopardize the elite's hold on power.

From this perspective, a certain investment in weapons of mass destruction and, more importantly, delivery systems capable of hitting targets beyond the Korean peninsula, is probably warranted to keep the South Koreans and Americans in check. Investments would be made in relatively inexpensive defensive systems to confound any external threats. For example, tunneling has been used to decrease the effectiveness of US and South Korean munitions, deter accurate targeting, and create diversionary or decoy targets. Other possibilities would include electronic countermeasures, such as jamming equipment (to interfere with US and South Korean weapon guidance systems, mobile surface to air missiles, and advanced naval mines), and the rebasing of air assets near the Chinese border to

---

1. See the *People's Korea*, 15 December 1999, and H. W. Lee 2000.

deter US and South Korean attacks. (Remember: without sovereignty, they are nothing.) Massive forward-deployed conventional forces are an unnecessary burden, however, and represent a real drag on the economy. In this characterization, North Korea is a porcupine in the forest, repelling aggression, not a tiger rapaciously hunting in the jungle.

This vision has real operational implications for both North Korea and the rest of the world. Externally, North Korea should maintain deterrence, which implies continued production, testing, and deployment of missiles capable of striking Japan and South Korea at a minimum, though not necessarily their export. Internally, reform should be pursued to the fullest extent consistent with social stability and the generation of rents for the ruling class. Conventional forces could be significantly demobilized to capture the "peace dividend," as demonstrated in chapter 7. While unilateral partial demobilization would make sense in purely self-interested terms, it would be worthwhile to engage South Korea and the United States to see what they would be willing to pay. This initiative might be undertaken in the context of a renegotiation of the Agreed Framework. The light water reactor project does not address North Korea's real energy problems. In this "golden parachutes" scenario, North Korea would be willing to forego the construction of the LWRs (and all the problems they would entail) in return for genuine economic assistance. Together, South Korea and Japan already have pledged $4 billion to KEDO, and more funds could be obtained from the multilateral development banks. These funds, invested efficiently rather than squandered on LWRs, could go a long way toward restoring stability, if not prosperity, to the North Korean economy. Thus, a "golden parachutes" strategy would have concrete implications for the operation of the North Korean economy, including its expenditure patterns, its military deployments, and its diplomatic engagements.

An alternative scenario would be "playing for time." In this case, internal reforms would be kept minimal, since regime preservation, not material improvement, would be the fundamental goal. Economic openings and diplomatic engagements would be expedient means to an end, not ends in themselves. Economic gains would be plowed back into a broad program of military modernization.[2]

While the jury is still out, the preponderance of recent evidence supports the "playing for time" interpretation of North Korean behavior. Despite the fact that the Hyundai deal is bringing in hundreds of millions of dollars in hard currency revenues, making it possible for North Korea to import food on commercial terms, North Korea has increased its dependence on external assistance for food and has used the Hyundai revenues for other purposes. According to the South Korean National Defense

---

2. See Bennett (1999) on North Korean military capabilities and unification strategies.

White Paper (1999), North Korea has increased its reserves of chemical weapons, boosted army manpower by 10,000 troops, created a missile division, and added 10 submarines to its fleet. In August 1999, it was revealed that North Korea had purchased roughly 40 aging MiG-21 fighters and eight military helicopters from Kazakhstan. It was subsequently reported that North Korea was trying to obtain more advanced MiG-29 and SU-30 fighters as well.[3] In September 1999, a classified US Air Force report allegedly describing continued North Korean work on its Taepodong missile was leaked to the press. In March 2000, in testimony before the Senate Armed Forces Committee, General Thomas Schwartz, Commander, US Forces Korea, stated that North Korea had accelerated its arms buildup and was forward-deploying artillery and rocket-launchers in hardened sites.[4] In a public briefing the following day, Admiral Dennis Blair, Commander-in-Chief, US Pacific Forces, indicated that North Korean military exercises during the winter of 1999-2000 had been the most extensive in recent years.[5] Russian observers claim that North Korea is emphasizing "high impact" arms over conventional weapons.

Of course, this evidence does not prove that the North Koreans are playing for time. It is possible that the appeals for food assistance are purely opportunistic—after all, why pay for something if others are willing to provide it for free? It is surely easier politically for the United States to provide food aid than other kinds of assistance. In this respect, food assistance may be the manifestation of a kind of diplomatic mutual dependency syndrome between the Kim Jong-il regime and the Clinton Administration. Likewise, the fighter purchases could be rationalized as simply the North Korean military spending revenues it obtains through its own arms sales rather than the product of considered strategic planning. Even statements from the US military could be interpreted in a similarly self-interested light, though it is harder to rationalize away the Russian report. The announcement of the North-South summit, just days before a South Korean election in which the incumbent government was trailing in the polls, could be interpreted as either signalling a strategic shift, or simply a tactical move to maximize concessional assistance. If "golden parachutes" for the Northern elite means "unification by acquisition" by the South, it certainly does not appear that the North Koreans are positioning themselves as a friendly takeover target.

---

3. The MiG-21 sale eventually resulted in the sacking of the Kazakh defense minister and the imposition on Kazakhstan of some minor economic sanctions by the United States. North Korea has reportedly undertaken other buying missions as well.

4. "Statement of General Thomas A. Schwartz, Commander-in-Chief United Nations Command/Combined Forces Command and Commander, US Forces Korea," Senate Armed Services Committee, 7 March 2000.

5. Department of Defense news briefing, 8 March 2000.

South Korea

The internal problems that South Korea faces are of a fundamentally different nature. In the South, heavy government intervention in, and coordination, of private sector economic activity has largely outlived its usefulness, even though this has been a significant aspect of South Korean economic policy since the inception of the Republic. The challenge now is to develop political and economic policies for constructive disengagement between government and the private sector. Through such an undertaking, the state would retreat from some of its more dirigiste policies, while at the same time strengthening its capacities as a guarantor of property rights, a prudential regulator, and, ultimately, a disinterested facilitator or referee of economic life.

The modifiers political *and* economic are used intentionally in this regard. There are very clear economic problems facing South Korea in areas such as financial market regulation, competition policy, labor relations, and trade policy. These policies cannot be viewed in isolation either from each other or from the historical and political context in which they have arisen. Put crudely, government interventions in the economy have generated rents that have been allocated politically, establishing a symbiotic relationship between the political and business worlds much more pronounced than observed in most other countries. As a result, economic policy decisions not only have economic ramifications, but they also have major political consequences that go to the heart of South Korea's young, and still not entirely mature, democracy.

Successfully implementing a policy of constructive disengagement would be a daunting task under any circumstances. The existence of North Korea adds an extra dimension of complexity to the challenge facing South Korea. Fortunately, the reforms that would be desirable from a purely internal perspective also are reforms that will better position South Korea to deal with contingencies involving the North.

However, the ability of South Korea to implement such a policy of constructive disengagement successfully is by no means assured. The rapidity of the country's recovery from the financial crisis may actually reduce the likelihood of it making this transition. In this regard, the recent policies of the South Korean government have been uneven. Through preference or lack of other means, the government has resorted to relatively illiberal means in its attempt to achieve a more liberal, efficient, and equitable South Korean economy. At least compared to its Asian neighbors, relatively good progress has been made in cleaning up the banking system. Less headway has been achieved on the interrelated issues of structural reform, corporate governance, and product market competition. The government has displayed an ambivalent attitude toward inward foreign direct investment (FDI), on the one hand liberalizing laws and permitting greatly increased FDI flows, while on the other discouraging foreign investment in a number of high-profile privatizations. Current concern is growing over *chaebol* domination of non-bank financial institutions.

In the short run, South Korea's relatively relaxed approach to continued cleanup of the financial sector and corporate restructuring will probably not greatly imperil its recovery. The single biggest component of demand has been household consumption, which has been financed largely by dissaving and a reduction in the household saving rate from an abnormally high level in 1998. As long as there are no major disruptions in the financial sector (which could cause panic and a jump in precautionary saving), households will be able to self-finance consumption. Likewise, firms should be able to continue to operate successfully, barring a major mishap in the domestic financial system. They have been financing much of their current investment in plant and equipment out of retained earnings, which are, to a certain extent, immune from impairment of the financial sector. Furthermore, throughout the crisis, exporters had relatively good access to finance through their ties to less affected foreign financial institutions. Thus they escaped the brunt of the credit crunch in 1998. In the short run, the risks to the South Korean economy may stem more from renewed inflation and labor unrest than from impairment of the financial sector.

The real financial and corporate problems are long-run in nature. They relate to how the South Korean government will extricate itself from the financial sector and what impact this disengagement will have on the decision making of the financial sector and corporate managements. Without behavioral changes, South Korea faces the possibility of another costly financial crisis in the not-too-distant future.

The *chaebol* are at the center of the reform agenda. These huge conglomerates are in many respects creatures of government policies. Successive Korean governments have had extreme difficulty in balancing sometimes conflicting goals of equity, efficiency, and political expediency regarding the *chaebol* and competition policy generally. The government now faces the very difficult challenge of devising a set of policies that will reduce the degree of government intervention in the economy without either destroying these firms or allowing them to completely dominate South Korean economic and political life.

This can be seen most acutely in the financial sector, where the symbiotic relationships between the *chaebol* and the state have contributed to the weakening and corruption of the South Korean financial system, fostering a higher likelihood of systemic crisis than is either necessary or advisable. The recent financial crisis has provided the country and its political leadership an opportunity to develop a more flexible banking system and more robust money, bond, and stock markets. Considerable progress has been made, though far more remains to be done.

To recover successfully from the crisis and prevent another recurrence, the major systemic reform goal is relatively easy to identify: Subject firms to real capital market discipline and a real market for corporate control. Similarly, the means to attain this goal are not hard to identify. They include: adoption of improved accounting standards; installation of outside directors; reduction of state involvement in bank lending decisions (together with increased emphasis on direct finance); and promotion of independent institutional investors capable of monitoring management. This set of measures is not controversial—they have been identified by the South Korean government in one form or another. The problem is how to get from here to there given South Korea's economic and political institutions, particularly the overwhelming presence of the *chaebol*.

Upon reviewing South Korean economic history, two lessons stand out. First, progress in policy reform has been the greatest where international involvement has been the highest. Over the course of the last 50 years, international trade policy has stood out as the arena of most successful policy reform. It also has been the area in which there has been the greatest consensus about and articulation of international norms (such as free trade in goods). Moreover, this has been the area in which international institutions, such as the World Trade Organization, have been the most developed.[6] In the financial arena, there has been less consensus about best practices with regard either to domestic institutions or external relations, and the international institutions (the Bank of International Settlements and the International Monetary Fund) have been relatively less successful in promoting an international consensus about desirable norms. In areas such as labor policy, there has been little consensus beyond some minimal standards (i.e., prohibitions on forced labor or child labor), and the international institution (the International Labor Organization) is weak. Similarly, in the area of competition policy, there has been little consensus about desirable practices, and no international organization (except perhaps the OECD) has really addressed these issues.

Perhaps it is not surprising, then, that South Korea has made the greatest progress in international trade liberalization, arguably has performed next best in financial reform, and probably has achieved the least in the largely "domestic" arenas of labor and competition policy. The reasons are straightforward: The existence of international norms gives policymakers a goal at which to aim, and the existence of the international institutions (and other avenues of international diplomatic pressure) help in overcoming the historical weakness and parochialism of South Korean political institutions.

A second lesson is that rules are better than discretion. Economists typically regard simple and transparent rules as preferable to discretion,

---

6. Bilateral and regional pressures have contributed to liberalization as well. See Noland (1993b, 1998b) and J. Yang (1999) for discussions of US-South Korean bilateral trade relations.

in that rules tend to reduce uncertainties about future policies. The stabilization of expectations then enables decision making on the part of private agents, thereby contributing to more efficient economic outcomes.

Such rules-based systems are difficult to develop in countries with weak democratic political institutions, yet the payoffs can be considerable. In the aftermath of the crisis, the relatively liberal government of President Kim Dae-jung has, at times, undertaken relatively illiberal policies to promote economic restructuring and recovery. This is perhaps best exemplified in the ongoing to-ing and fro-ing over the so-called "big deals"— the government's attempt to engineer a restructuring of the *chaebol* by pressuring them to swap business assets and consolidate production in particular industries.

In this environment, it is desirable to promote rules-based changes that involve foreigners and foreign institutions whenever possible. The emphasis on rules and the inclusion of non-Korean actors should help overcome the weaknesses of South Korean political institutions and push change in a constructive direction.

Internal Reforms

South Korea needs to continue its process of internal reform, both because of the beneficial direct impact on the well-being of South Koreans, and because it will improve South Korea's preparation for contingencies involving North Korea. In the financial sector, the continuing rehabilitation of banking is central. The costs of cleaning up the financial sector may ultimately reach 30 to 35 percent of GDP. This amount can be financed. The real question is whether, at the end of the day, the standard operating procedures of the South Korean corporate and financial sectors will have changed. If not, a recurrence of the crisis is possible.

In this regard, a lot is at stake in the resolution of the Daewoo collapse. There are at least two channels through which the Daewoo case will influence the future development of the South Korean financial sector. The first is that the unresolved nature of the Daewoo situation discourages the denationalization of the banks, thereby impeding foreign involvement in the South Korean banking system and extending government influence over the sector. The reason is straightforward: South Korean banks hold Daewoo debt. Until the Daewoo situation is resolved, foreign investment in a South Korean bank will amount to buying "a pig in a poke." Under such circumstances, power remains in the hands of politicized bureaucrats rather than in the hands of efficient foreign bankers. This arrangement may be good for patronage, but it is not good for economic rationality.[7]

---

7. To cite but one example, in August 1999, as bond prices fell in the wake of the Daewoo collapse, the government forced South Korean banks to contribute 20 trillion won to a fund to buy bonds. The government was aided in this undertaking by the fact that at the time

The other channel through which the Daewoo case will influence future developments is its effect on other *chaebol* managements and their lenders. If, at the end of the day, the Daewoo management remains largely intact, then the lesson that will be learned by the other *chaebol* managements is that the financial risks that Daewoo took and the illegal behavior in which it allegedly engaged may well have been worth it. This would be the domestic moral hazard problem discussed in box 6.1, in spades.

One solution to this conundrum would be to de-emphasize indirect finance channels prone to political intervention. Personal and corporate tax changes are needed to reduce favorable treatment of debt and thereby encourage equity finance. In debt markets, greater differentiation of risk should be encouraged through the creation of benchmark issues to encourage a secondary market, and rating activities by both South Korean and foreign ratings agencies should be promoted. A high-yield bond market should be fostered for firms that traditionally have not been among the government's preferred borrowers and that suffered disproportionately in the 1998 credit crunch.

With a greater emphasis on direct finance, there is a parallel need to promote the activities of independent institutional investors who are capable of monitoring corporate management decisions and exerting capital market discipline on incumbent managements. A source of current concern is *chaebol* domination of the nascent mutual fund industry. Three reinforcing means of addressing this issue come to mind. One method would be to create fire walls and separate the financial and non-financial *chaebol*. While this approach goes against trends elsewhere, given the predominant role of the largest *chaebol* in the South Korean economy, the exclusion of industrial *chaebol* from participation in the financial sector is warranted. As it now stands, the *chaebol* own significant stakes in merchant banks, securities companies, investment trusts, and insurance companies.[8]

Another strategy would be to encourage foreign financial firms in fund management. They have expertise currently lacking in South Korean firms and are unencumbered by the web of connections and obligations characteristic of the South Korean financial sector.

A third approach would be along the lines of proposals by Graham (1999b) and Leipziger (1999) for a swap of suitably written-down nonperforming loans for government bonds, followed by a mandatory corporate debt-for-equity swap, and then sale of government-held shares to the public. This approach would in effect democratize the ownership of the *chaebol*. It also could be used to foster the development of independent

---

it owned the three biggest commercial banks (Hanvit, Chohung, and Seoul) and had a majority stake in three others (Housing and Commercial, Kookmin, and Korea Exchange Bank). As pointed out in chapter 6, a similar undertaking in 1989 to prop up share prices contributed to financial sector weakness in the 1990s.

8. See Leipziger 1999, table 5.

institutional investors. Last, but not least, there is a need to improve the transparency of accounting and the functioning of South Korea's bankruptcy procedures.

A final question involves the optimal policies for the capital account. The South Korean financial crisis had its origins in fundamentally flawed financial market policies that socialized risk on a massive scale for an extended period of time. One flaw in the system was poorly designed liberalization of the capital account, which created perverse incentives for short-term borrowing. This mistake was but one of a series of mistakes, and a crisis eventually would have occurred under any set of capital account rules. The particular policies in place in 1997 accentuated the importance of foreign debt during the crisis and contributed to its timing. However, external considerations were not the primary cause of the crisis.

Given that more complete markets are presumptively superior to less complete markets, one could argue that the crisis would have been less severe if South Korean markets had been more open to long-term investment. The liberalization program adopted since the crisis has tended to increase the openness of South Korean financial markets and to ameliorate some of the perverse incentives embodied in precrisis policies. The real issue is whether greater openness is enough. Some (e.g., Stiglitz 1999) have called for "surge suppressors," such as Chilean-style taxes, to dampen excessive capital inflows. These are no panacea, as they appear mainly to affect the composition, not the volume, of capital inflows, though their imposition would probably do little harm and might do some good.[9]

What is known for sure is that South Korea needs better regulation and supervision of its financial institutions. The 1990s liberalization amounted to putting regulators with automobile drivers' licenses into the cockpits of jumbo jets. Relative to other countries in the region, considerable improvements in the regulatory framework have been achieved, but more needs to be done. This area is one in which the United States, South Korea, and international institutions such as the World Bank can continue fruitful collaboration.

The final issue that South Korea faces in this regard is the organization of the international financial system. Unlike the national-level reforms noted above, South Korea cannot resolve this issue on its own. It will require cooperation with the United States, Japan, and others to advance its interests in the redesign of the international financial architecture.

In product markets, there is a real threat of anti-competitive behavior due to increased concentration coming out of the crisis—a development actually encouraged by the government's policy of promoting "big deals" and industrial consolidation. For example, Hyundai-Kia now holds

---

9. See Edwards 1999.

72 percent of the passenger automobile market, 77 percent of the bus market, and 95 percent of the truck market.

The standard remedy in this case is a hortatory call to strengthen the Korea Fair Trade Commission (KFTC) and to engage in cooperative international competition policies either bilaterally or multilaterally. In fact, the KFTC has increased its level of activity in the wake of the crisis. Yet "strengthening the KFTC" cannot be accomplished overnight. As a consequence, it is imperative that South Korea aggressively liberalize international trade to "import" competition, especially in sectors such as motor vehicle products, in which the potential for abuse of market position appears the greatest. The idea would be to use the threat of imports to maintain the contestability of markets, while strengthening domestic procompetitive forces. In this respect, liberalizing international trade does not mean just cutting tariffs, which in the case of South Korea are often reasonably low. It also includes undertaking a variety of ancillary actions that would facilitate the presence of foreign firms in the market through trade or investment.[10]

South Korea's labor markets have a reputation for rigidity, despite the fact that, by standard indices such as job turnover or real wage variability, economy-wide they are the most flexible in the OECD. The segment in which rigidity is a valid concern is employment in the largest *chaebol*. For them, current employment regulations make labor a quasi-fixed factor of production, discouraging hiring while encouraging the adoption of inappropriately capital-intensive techniques of production, and stigmatizing the unfortunates who do lose their jobs. The appropriate response is a two-track strategy of reducing labor market regulation (making it easier to dismiss employees) and strengthening the unemployment insurance system and social safety net. This set of issues is complex, as currently a whole basket of benefits (including pensions and housing) are not entirely portable and are contingent on employment.

These reforms would generate changes in the South Korean economy— the democratization of finance, increased competition in product markets, and more flexible labor markets—that would create a more dynamic entrepreneurial economy. Beyond the present crisis, the government should err on the side of a tight fiscal policy in anticipation of future liabilities associated with unification.

Policies with Respect to North Korea

From a South Korean standpoint, North Korea can be regarded as a huge contingent liability. Fortunately for South Korea, the actions that address

---

10. For an example of this, see the analysis of the automobile sector by the American Chamber of Commerce (1999).

its own internal problems in the wake of the financial crisis are some of the same actions that are advisable in preparation for future eventualities involving the North. Some of these actions are contingent on particular outcomes in the North, some are not.

Setting aside the possibility of war, the worst case would be an abrupt collapse of North Korea that could require hundreds of billions of dollars in expenditures to resolve. There are two obvious responses. One would be to prepare for this contingency by strengthening public finances and building up reserves for such a rainy day. The operational implication is that, as the immediate financial crisis in South Korea is surmounted, the government should return to its historical policy of fiscal rectitude and build up its government surpluses. Such an approach would contribute to funding the costs of unification by providing reserves and facilitating additional borrowing.

The other obvious response would be to try and head off collapse. The Kim Dae-jung administration has broken from past history by explicitly announcing that it will not undertake measures to subvert North Korea. Instead, its stated preference is for peaceful coexistence. Not all modes of peaceful coexistence are equally attractive, however. Rather than simply accepting North Korea as is, Seoul should structure its economic engagement with Pyongyang in ways that promote systemic transformation of the North and strengthen the relatively progressive forces within North Korea. If one were to rank South Korean economic interaction with North Korea by the possibility for promoting systemic change, projects like the Mt. Kumgang tourist project would rank at the bottom—contact between North and South Koreans is highly restricted, and the project can be fenced off from the rest of the North Korean economy and society, literally as well as figuratively. This sort of project largely serves to generate foreign exchange earnings for the North Korean central government (if not for Kim Jong-il personally) without posing any significant challenges to how the regime operates. The Mt. Kumgang project was probably a necessary confidence-building measure for broader forms of economic interaction. That said, it appears to involve implicit subsidies on the part of the South Korean government. Additional ventures along these lines should be assessed with a skeptical eye.

Marginally more desirable are the proposals for foreign mining concessions. These projects are classic enclave economies that again would be fenced off from the rest of the economy, literally and figuratively. Interaction would largely involve the central government's mining ministry. Special economic zones, while also geographically limited (especially in the case of the isolated Rajin-Sonbong zone), at least involve interactions between foreign firms and a broader range of North Korean institutions and enterprises. Special economic zones, export processing zones, or bonded warehouses in more desirable urban locations could potentially involve higher degrees of contact and, for this reason alone, would be better still.

The most desirable form of engagement would be foreign direct investment outside of specified zones. This type of interaction would involve the most extensive contact between North Koreans and outsiders, and competition among North Korean institutions and enterprises to attract FDI could have enormous learning and demonstration effects. This would be the form of engagement most likely to generate systemic change. The North Koreans have described economic opening "as a Trojan horse tasked with destabilizing socialism." They are right, of course.

Lastly, the South Korean government should support North Korean entry into international financial institutions. Contact with these institutions might promote learning about the modern global economy, its institutions, and its practices, and generally serve to socialize North Korean policymakers in desirable directions. Involvement with the international financial institutions might also have the added benefit of being less prone to the vagaries of bilateral relations than other modes of engagement.

Unification

Although South Korea proclaims that it is not interested in absorbing the North, and although its own official unification scheme is gradual in the extreme, ultimately its vision of a protracted consensual unification may not come to pass. Instead, events in the North may necessitate a much more precipitous process than Seoul may prefer. Thus it is worthwhile thinking about what such a scenario might entail.

The specific form of the North's breakdown would have enormous implications for the undertakings required. The commonalities across scenarios would be that close coordination among South Korea, the United States, and China would be essential, and that their respective militaries would play critical roles due to their rapid response and logistical capabilities. Once the situation on the ground was stabilized, broader economic and political policy decisions would be required.

At the time of unification, the South Korean government will have multiple (and potentially conflicting) policy objectives. On the one hand, maintenance of economic activity in the North on market-consistent terms will be a top priority. At the same time, the government should seek to effect a one-time-only wealth transfer to the current North Korean population, since they will have to adjust to market institutions with virtually no household wealth. One can imagine a multi-pronged approach:

- Adopt dual rate monetary conversion. Aim for slight undervaluation of the North Korean won to maintain competitiveness, thereby making

North Korea an attractive location for investment. Convert personal savings at an overvalued rate (effecting a wealth transfer).

- Deed land to the tiller and the housing stock to its occupants, contingent on maintaining use for some specified period of time.

- Maintain some kind of temporary, emergency, non-market social safety net in the North.

Having given the land to the tiller, one must confront the issue of property rights claims by past owners or their descendants and the more general issue of assignment of property rights to commercial or industrial assets. Lessons learned from the experience of Germany and other former centrally planned economies are instructive in this regard:

- Avoid the policy of restitution for seized assets. Monetary compensation for seized assets might be considered, though even some South Korean analysts have argued that this would be a mistake.

- Privatize quickly and avoid the cash-on-the-barrelhead model. Abolish inter-enterprise debts.

- Emphasize investment, not consumption, transfers.

- Accept assistance from foreigners, including the Japanese.

With respect to privatization, the experience of East Germany and other centrally planned economies suggests that it would be best to move quickly and avoid the cash-in-advance model, since it would severely restrict potential buyers. Attempts to restructure these enterprises before privatization should also be avoided. That is better left to the market. Inter-firm debts, which are a legacy of irrational policies under the centrally planned regime, should be written off. Debt-equity swaps could be used to pay off external debt and simultaneously create a stake in the viability of North Korean enterprises for South Korean or foreign firms.

Given these considerations, there appears to be one institution in South Korea ideally suited for the task of making North Korea competitive: the *chaebol*. Unfortunately, one policy goal (to get the North Korean economy functioning as rapidly as possible) and another policy goal (to clean up business-government relations in South Korea) would conflict. It goes without saying which one will receive the greater weight. The *chaebol* are probably ideally suited for refurbishing the North Korean economy. However, saddling them with unproductive North Korean enterprises would have an economic price in terms of reducing *chaebol* competitiveness internationally and possibly encouraging anti-competitive behavior domestically. There would also be a political price in the form of the *quid pro quos* that the *chaebol* could be expected to extract. This complication in business-government relations is probably an unavoidable by-product of increased economic integration between North and South Korea in any scenario.

The other important actors whose roles would have to be defined are the North Koreans themselves. Presumably, a unified Korean government would want to avoid the German-style monetary and privatization policies that effectively froze East Germans out of privatization. If not addressed, then the same problem could arise in an even more severe way in the Korean case, especially given the greater divergence in income levels and the probably even smaller outstanding claims on productive assets that North Korean residents would have at the time of unification.

It would be desirable to create new businesses in North Korea, as start-ups rather than restructured existing enterprises have generated most of the revival of industrial output in other transitional economies. There could be a role for fiscal incentives here. As Cheong and Lee (1996) point out, South Korean firms already have been relocating labor-intensive activities abroad. However, investment in the North may be associated with a positive externality, since it would presumably reduce unification costs. Hence there is a divergence between the private and social rate of return on South Korean foreign direct investment and scope for government intervention.[11] Wage subsidies in the North would be another obvious alternative.[12] Given the South Korean government's interventionist bent, it would be surprising if policies like this were *not* undertaken.[13]

The use of fiscal incentives raises the broader issue of financing. There are a couple of obvious points to be made. Since South Koreans fear the impact of absorption on their own economy, minimizing the burden on South Korean taxpayers has to be an imperative of South Korean govern-

---

11. A similar argument for tax breaks prior to unification could be made, though the advisability of investment insurance prior to unification is less clear. Tax incentives would apply only if a South Korean firm were to own and operate a facility in the North, and if it did not expose the government to expropriation risk (borne by the firm). Insurance guarantees could create South Korean government exposure to North Korean expropriation and generate some serious moral hazard problems.

Agreements between the North and South governments on such things as avoidance of double taxation, dispute settlement, and standards harmonization would be appropriate, however.

12. See Koo (1998) for a wage subsidy proposal.

13. Yeon (1994), for example, writes, "The government could use a number of policy tools in order to encourage private sector decision making in directions it considers desirable, including special tax treatment, low-interest loans, channeling public funds towards certain investment, and providing information and advice. Government intervention would also be needed in order to influence the rate of industrial and rural development, as well as to control speculative and rent-seeking behavior on the part of both the public and private sectors" (p.394).

ment policy.[14] This means that attracting private capital, especially foreign private investment, will be of the highest priority.

South Korea's need to prepare for the contingencies of unification with North Korea coincides with its need to strengthen its financial system in the wake of its own financial crisis. In the event of unification, there is absolutely no reason to finance the construction of infrastructure out of current tax receipts. Instead, the government will want to use both taxes and bonds to finance unification expenditures. Hence the development of a robust government bond market prior to unification should be a priority. A second priority would be the rejuvenation of South Korea's flagging privatization program: There is no reason why the privatization agenda in the North should be more aggressive than the one in the South.[15]

With respect to trade, the unified Korea would presumably operate under South Korean trade policies, including tariffs, quotas, etc. This would result in substantial de-protection for North Korean enterprises (though prior to unification one could imagine a variety of halfway houses that would permit North Korean producers to operate under greater protection). Treatment of agriculture could be particularly problematic relative to the German case: Agriculture is more important to North Korea than it was to East Germany, and, unlike South Korea, the Germans had little autonomy in agricultural policy since it was determined within the context of Germany's membership in the European Union. Moreover, South Korea's agricultural policies are even more distortionary internally than those of the European Union.[16] Extending costly South Korean agricultural policies to farmers in the North would be so expensive that, rather than doing so, the unified Korea might be pushed into reform.

As shown in table 7.2, a liberalized North Korea would trade most intensively with South Korea (accounting for 35 percent of its trade) and Japan (an additional 30 percent). With unification, the single biggest share of trade (the 35 percent with South Korea) would be internal and not subject to WTO rules. Some observers have advocated the internal application of dumping rules to protect South Korean producers. This approach would be a mistake, since the priority would undoubtedly be on maintaining production in the North.

---

14. Yeon (1994), for example, writes: "The financial cost of Korean reconstruction and restructuring could amount to $230-250 billion over a ten year period. . . .North Korea is in no position to finance any portion of the costs of rapid unification. This means that the financial burden associated with Korean economic, monetary, and social integration would have to fall almost entirely on South Korea" (p.395).

15. Bae (1996) makes recommendations to improve tax collection. He raises the possibility of privatizing South Korean government assets as a means to finance unification as well.

16. Von Cramon-Taubadel (1998) discusses prospective issues relating to agriculture in the context of unification.

The second largest share of trade would be with Japan, and this trade would be subject to WTO rules, which constrain the use of safeguards. It would not be surprising, given the prevalence of discriminatory arrangements within Asia and the unresolved issue of Japanese post-colonial claims, if some bilateral understanding was reached between the unified Korea and Japan on this issue.

Lastly, and perhaps most importantly, is the issue of labor market adjustment. Unification would create big incentives to migrate, especially if unification was accompanied, as expected, by demobilization of the huge North Korean army. Some advocate maintaining the DMZ as a form of influx control, but it is questionable as to how politically sustainable such a plan would be. (North Koreans will make up about a third of the electorate.) If the German case holds any lessons for Korea, it is that the decision to migrate is strongly influenced by employment security. This lesson simply underscores the need to implement privatization and restructuring as quickly as possible. A structured program for temporary commuting might be a politically feasible halfway house between unfettered migration and the maintenance of the DMZ.

Migration also could be discouraged by policies that would award property rights to housing and productive assets to users (conditional on their continued residence in the North), or by policies to distribute aid only to households at their original place of residence. More generally, social policies will affect the incidence of migration. Retraining is certainly an area for government involvement (optimally in conjunction with prospective private employers). These programs can be located in the North.

A more difficult issue involves the social safety net. Koo (1998) argues that a wage subsidy policy could be a substitute for the non-existent unemployment insurance program. However, this policy could be only a partial remedy. The government will have to face issues such as whether health care should be on the North Korean socialized basis or on the South Korean private insurance model. There are good arguments for the private insurance model, but one must recognize that, under this system, the quality of health care is strongly related to income level. Adoption of the private approach, in the context of low North Korean incomes and the wrenching dislocation that would accompany unification, could mean that demographic shocks in North Korea could be even more severe than those observed in post-unification East Germany.

All of this suggests that the political rights afforded to the residents of North Korea are the key determinants of economic outcomes. Per capita income differences are large, the North Korean population is young, and Seoul, glowing like a beacon, lies just south of the DMZ. Unless they are forcibly restrained, one must assume that large numbers of North Koreans will head south. Even if they were temporarily restrained, pressures for cross-border migration would persist until the income gap was substan-

tially reduced. This could require considerable capital investment and technological transfer.

Ultimately, Korea will have to deal with issues relating to political integration. How this integration occurs will in part be a function of how unification occurs—whether through a negotiated process by two functioning sovereign states, an explosion, or an implosion. Nevertheless, some fundamental issues will arise in virtually any context.

At the most basic level are the issues of accountability, retribution, and justice. Three issues stand out: human rights abuses, the initiation and conduct of the Korean War, and state-sponsored terrorism.[17] In each case, international, as well as national, tribunals could claim jurisdiction. The relevant authorities will have to decide how far up (or down) the chain of command responsibility lies. Likewise, victims of crime and abuse of power are entitled to rehabilitation and compensation under UN Declarations of which both North and South Korea are signatories.

The real problem that will confront Korea, as has been encountered by other societies undergoing similar political transformations, is how to balance claims of justice against broader societal interests in facilitating and smoothing a desired political transition.

These issues are likely to be particularly acute in the Korean case. As bad as East Germany was, it did not compare to North Korea. Having fought a horrific civil war, the Koreans will have to confront a legacy far more poisoned than the one faced by the Germans in 1989. For both substantive and cultural reasons, retribution will be a far more important issue in Korea than it was in Germany. Truth and reconciliation commissions such as those used in Argentina and South Africa may be able to play some role.

It will be imperative for Northerners to be incorporated into the political life of the unified Korea.[18] The legal basis of their claim to full participation appears to be strong: Article 4 of the present South Korean constitution implies that even current residents of the North are citizens of the Republic of Korea. Political inclusion in a democratic Korea will require a "de-Nazification"-like process for the elites, together with proactive policies for the masses. The South will have to accept that long-run maintenance of the DMZ as a method of population control is not sustainable and that the perpetuation of significant differences between the North and South is not in the long-run interests of the current population of the South.

The issue then becomes: What will be the form and character of the polity of a united Korea?[19] While trends are positive, it is not clear that

---

17. See C. B. Park (1997). This discussion will proceed as if only North Korea was in the dock. In some contexts, North Korea could plausibly raise similar issues concerning South Korea.

18. Moon (1999) raises for consideration an extensive set of tasks and issues along these lines.

19. See N.Y. Lee (1998) for a detailed discussion of prospective political institutions of a unified Korea.

today South Korea is a *Rechtsstaat* (a state governed by law) in the same way that Germany is. The government of a unified Korea will have to confront troublesome issues of respect for law, the role of the judiciary, and local government autonomy. The latter issue is particularly salient given the history of regionalism in Korean politics and the centralization of both the North and South Korean states today.[20] More broadly, a unified Korea will have to deal with the questions of who sets the rules? To give a prosaic example, who will set school curricula? Will it be set centrally (as is done today in both North and South Korea), or will it be done locally? How will Korean history, including the history of the past five decades, be treated in that curriculum?

A unified Korea will be riven by regional and class cleavages. In the case of Germany, strong political parties have acted as a mechanism for trans-partition political integration. In contrast, political parties in South Korea are weak, and, given the isolation of North Korea (again worse than the East German case), there is no evidence that any mainstream South Korean politician has any significant mass following in the North. It is within the realm of reason that the (North) Korean Workers' Party could emerge as the largest (or at least the most disciplined and coherent) political party in a unified Korea. The point is that the country will face an enormous task, both in revitalizing the North Korean economy and in extending the emerging liberal political culture of South Korea.

Lastly, something will have to be done with the gigantic North Korean military, its missile program, and its weapons of mass destruction. Even accepting the "shrimp among whales" metaphor, one would have to expect a significant demobilization of forces in a unified Korea, and the modeling work presented in chapter 8 suggests that the "peace dividend" could be considerable. Nonetheless, decisions about the military will be enormously sensitive both within Korea and vis-à-vis its neighbors. Ultimately, this issue will call into question the presence of US forces on the peninsula. The range of possibilities runs from reconfiguration and redeployment (most likely as a regionally-oriented force based in the far southern part of the peninsula or off the peninsula altogether) to withdrawal and demobilization.

What happens on the Korean peninsula will largely be determined by Koreans. Although the United States, Japan, China, other countries, and international institutions have important roles to play, Korean history will ultimately be written by Koreans. The appropriate role of the outside world will be to support the Koreans in their attempt to strengthen liberal

---

20. See Steinberg (1998), N.Y. Lee (1998), and Moon (1999) for contrasting views on the desirability of greater decentralization of the government of a unified Korea. As noted in chapter 6, the present South Korean government has undertaken a limited process of decentralization of authority.

democratic institutions in the face of what could be an enormous political and economic shock.

Other Actors

The United States

The United States has a broad set of interests on the Korean peninsula. The Korean War cost more than 33,000 US lives, and the United States continues to maintain a military presence in South Korea and Japan as a legacy of that involvement. Today, South Korea is America's ninth largest trade partner, accounting for roughly $50 billion in two-way trade annually. South Korea is an important US ally, and the United States has a large stake in its national security as well as in its economic and political development. In the economic sphere, the main US task is to support South Korea's ongoing economic recovery from the financial crisis. In this regard, there are two principal arenas in which the two countries interact: international trade and international financial policy.

With respect to the former, the biggest contribution that the United States can make in the short run is to keep its market open. Access to the US market will continue to be an important part of South Korea's economic recovery for the foreseeable future. The ability to export to the United States could become even more important if South Korea's recovery was to falter or if recession in the United States were to be accompanied by demands for protection. In the longer run, South Korea's growth and its increasing integration with the rest of Asia mean that its dependence on the US market is likely to decline in relative terms. Although South Korea remains significantly dependent on the US market (especially in this immediate post-crisis period), and although it will certainly seek to maintain a good relationship with the United States for the foreseeable future, the degree of asymmetry in terms of dependence is lessening. Past trade conflict between South Korea and the United States has been played out in excessively bilateral and politicized forums. In the future, with democratization and growth, South Korea should begin to play a more prominent role in international organizations. What have been largely bilateral issues may be submerged in more multilateral forums. The traditional US approach—unilateral demands backed by the implicit threat of market closure—will probably become increasingly ineffective in the future due both to this fundamental shift in the relationship and to the formation of the World Trade Organization. The WTO can be expected to play a greater role in intermediating conflict in the future. In this regard, the failure of the WTO to launch a new round of trade negotiations at its biennial ministerial in Seattle in 1999 was a setback.

The second economic policy area in which South Korea and the United States interact involves international financial policy and what has come to be known as the international financial architecture. Both countries are in the "Group of 20," a group of large industrial economies and systemically significant developing countries that has come together to discuss reforms of the current system. The United States would be well advised to consider South Korean views on these issues carefully. After all, South Korea was the recipient of the largest bailout package in history, which nonetheless was neither widely popular nor necessarily regarded as appropriate either by South Korean economists and officials or by some outside observers. The United States, in particular, is regarded in many quarters as having used the conditionality embodied in the IMF program for its own mercantilist purposes without ever actually spending a dime of its own commitment to the "second line of defense." The most recent US proposal for architectural reform (Summers 1999) appears to advocate both a toughening of the terms on which the IMF lends and a broadening of the terms of conditionality. The terms of conditionality were regarded as politically controversial and politically intrusive in the South Korean case.

Beyond these issues, the United States has an important role in questions relating to North Korea. The US political system has two goals with regard to North Korea. The first is to reduce the threat it poses to US security interests in Northeast Asia and elsewhere around the world. The second is to alleviate the humanitarian tragedy of the famine. Different groups and individuals within the political system place different emphases and priorities on these two goals, but it is safe to say that, in the long run, actions to address the famine will be politically unsustainable without progress in addressing the security threat.

Washington's relations with Pyongyang have been marked by an almost Pavlovian pattern, in which the North Koreans create a crisis and the United States responds by essentially trying to bribe North Korea into acceptable behavior. This pattern was arguably established in 1994 with the signing of the Agreed Framework, which committed the United States to a costly and questionable scheme to build light water reactors (LWRs) in North Korea in return for North Korean compliance with the Nonproliferation Treaty. In the case of the Agreed Framework, at least the United States could claim that it was getting something demonstrable in return—the freezing of North Korean nuclear activities at Yongbyon. More generally, the *modus operandi* has been that North Korea provokes a confrontation and then invites in the World Food Program (WFP), which has a humanitarian and bureaucratic interest in erring on the side of generosity in dealing with the North Korean famine. The WFP then issues an appeal for international humanitarian assistance, and the United States uses it as multilateral cover for what can only be described as diplomatic bribery. In the case of the inspection of Kumchangri, the United States did not even go through the motions of contributing via the UN, but simply paid off the North Koreans directly.[21]

The result has been a string of North Korean tactical victories—it has successfully used extortionary tactics to extract resources from a timid and compliant United States which, at the end of the day, would prefer to temporize and appease the North Koreans rather than confront them. From a US perspective, this result presents two problems. First, there is no real evidence that these US responses to North Korean brinkmanship have furthered US strategic interests on the peninsula. Second, rather than transforming North Korea in ways that the United States would find more desirable, they actually reward bad behavior.

The goal of US policy in this regard should be to play to our strength— our lucrative market—and avoid our weakness—our comparative disadvantage in negotiating with opaque totalitarian states.[22] The United States should therefore attempt to shift the locus of its relations with North Korea away from the State Department and toward the market—or, in the language of US politics, get North Korea off welfare and onto workfare. The Perry report and the "package deal" could be interpreted as moving partly in this direction, at least by attempting to avoid North Korean "salami tactics." Operationally, this "tough love" approach would have two components. First would be sanctions removal, which the United States has announced but not actually implemented. (This would not include the COCOM sanctions under the Wassenaar Agreement.) Conditional on North Korea refraining from terrorist acts—it has been more than a decade now since any significant North Korean terrorist incident— removal from the State Department's list of countries supporting terrorism would open eligibility for North Korean participation in US economic programs such as Export-Import Bank trade loans and OPIC investment guarantees. The United States also would want to provide North Korea with textile and apparel import quotas, inasmuch as textiles and apparel are among North Korea's most promising sectors. The idea would be to encourage North Korea to participate in legitimate international commerce.

At the same time, the United States would scale back its participation in WFP appeals. Food is fungible, and food aid amounts to unconditional balance of payments support. There is no reason that the United States should provide this to North Korea in perpetuity, especially if the US is opening its doors to legitimate commercial exchange. The amount of foreign exchange necessary to close the North Korean food gap is rela-

---

21. US officials reputedly have expressed frustration with the WFP's apparent inability to issue appeals quickly enough to satisfy US desires to provide food assistance linked to political negotiations.

22. See Snyder (1999b) for a comprehensive analysis of US-North Korean negotiations.

tively small—on the order of hundreds of millions of dollars. Current US policy embodies the bizarre contradiction that the United States discourages commercial activity by which Pyongyang could earn the dollars to buy food from American farmers, but instead taxes US citizens to provide the same food *gratis*. US policy should aim to get North Korea off international welfare and into the global marketplace.

Furthermore, to the extent that the United States wants to deliver humanitarian aid to North Koreans, there is no reason that it must be done in North Korea. Under the status quo, China, the poorest of North Korea's neighbors, bears the brunt of North Korea's refugee exodus. In addition to the direct costs of absorbing refugees, China prefers not to see an increase in the ethnic Korean population of its border provinces of Jilin and Liaoning. The obvious solution would be a multinational effort to bear the costs of refugee resettlement. At a minimum, this effort could amount to defraying the costs of housing and feeding refugees in China. More equitably, South Korea, Japan, and other countries (including the United States) could take in refugees for resettlement.

The final aspect of a more constructive US policy toward North Korea would be a willingness on the part of the United States to reopen the Agreed Framework. The Agreed Framework in essence trades some ambiguity over North Korea's nuclear history for the ending of its ongoing nuclear weapons program. The problem with this bargain (setting aside the verifiability of North Korean compliance—itself a significant issue) is that it sets up a likely confrontation among the United States and its partners (principally South Korea and Japan) with North Korea around 2002-03. The nub of the problem is that the agreement commits the United States to completing the LWRs in 2003, though the United States will assuredly argue that this is merely a target. Under current circumstances, completion is unlikely to occur by that date, leading to the United States arguably being out of compliance with the agreement. Moreover, before sensitive reactor components are installed, the International Atomic Energy Agency (IAEA) must verify North Korea's past nuclear history. There is likely to be ambiguity in that determination, which can open up disagreement between South Korea and Japan on the one hand and the United States on the other (since the United States puts a greater priority on proliferation concerns). Heavy fuel oil donor fatigue on the part of Congress is another potential source of friction with Pyongyang, Seoul, and Tokyo. The planned North-South summit, a dramatic fulfillment of North Korea's pledge to resume talks with the South, will strengthen North Korea's hand and put additional pressure on the United States and its allies. Implementation of the Agreed Framework is a train wreck in the offing.

The United States ought to recognize this likely sequence of events, get ahead of the curve, and indicate a willingness to reopen the agreement.

The idea is that the United States and its partners would scrap the commitment to build the light water reactors and instead use the funds committed to KEDO to address the real economic and energy problems that North Korea faces. This shift could involve replacing the LWRs with more sensible coal-fired plants, rehabilitating the North Korean electrical grid, building transformers (which would permit North Korea to export electricity to South Korea and China), and financing other kinds of infrastructural investment.[23] If the North Koreans are truly interested in rejuvenating their economy, then these measures will be far more useful than a couple of light water reactors. There is no guarantee that the North Koreans would respond positively to such an offer—after all, they were the originators of the basic deal underlying the Agreed Framework. Nevertheless, it is surely worth raising this possibility. If their true interests lie in building nuclear weapons, then they will hold the United States to its 1994 commitment. Such a response by the North Koreans would presumably increase the attractiveness of missile defense systems to the United States, Japan, and South Korea.[24]

Japan

Like the United States, Japan's policy toward the Korean peninsula can be thought of as having two aspects: promotion of continued economic recovery in South Korea and support for a process of domesticating North Korea. In both instances, Japan has a key role to play. Japan's own economic trouble helped precipitate the financial crisis in South Korea, when weak Japanese banks began to call in lines of credit in 1997 and refused to roll over loans. Prior to its own crisis, Japan was South Korea's largest trade partner, and its economic weakness of late has adversely affected South Korea. Modeling work by Noland et al. (1999) has demonstrated that developments in Japan have a considerable impact on economic activity in South Korea, both through direct trade linkages between the two countries and through competition in third country export markets such as the United States and the European Union. Either renewed recession in Japan or a weak yen strategy of export-led recovery would have a detrimental impact on South Korea. From this standpoint, the best thing that Japan could do for South Korea would be to strengthen its own financial system to enable it to play a more constructive role as a source

---

23. Oddly enough, the Pyongyang-affiliated journalist M.C. Kim (1998) comes to some similar conclusions with regard to how the US failure to implement its Agreed Framework commitments might play out.

24. See Garwin (1999), O'Hanlon (1999), Lewis, Gronlund, and Wright (1999-2000), and Payne (2000) for differing assessments of missile defense schemes. The North Koreans have indicated that, if the United States proceeded toward installing a missile defense system, then they would reconsider their moratorium on flight testing missiles.

and intermediator of international capital flows and to promote domestic demand-led recovery within Japan.

For want of robust military capability, Japan's policy toward North Korea has a similar economic focus. The big money issue outstanding between North Korea and the rest of the world is the settlement of post-colonial claims with Japan. Taking the 1965 accord between South Korea and Japan as a base, and adjusting for changes in price levels, differences in population, accrued interest, etc., one can obtain a figure on the order of $20 billion in today's dollars. Given relative negotiating positions and the current state of Japanese public finances, it is unlikely that the North Koreans will be able to extract anything approaching this sum from Japan. Internal Japanese discussions revolve around figures that are less than half as large. Nevertheless, Japanese reparations are the one large monetary claim that North Korea has on the rest of the world. Moreover, settlement of this issue would be less reversible than removal of the US embargo.

Japan will certainly argue that its billion-dollar contribution to KEDO should be counted against this charge. Some have speculated that Japan will even try to claim credit for the costs of recapitalizing bankrupt *Chochongryun*-controlled financial institutions in Japan. Contributions to a "North Korea Fund" administered by the World Bank or the Asian Development Bank would be another way of handling reparations. In any event, the sum that North Korea could ultimately call upon is likely to be bigger than anything that it can expect to receive from other countries or the international financial institutions. As a consequence, settlement of this claim is a sensitive political issue. It is of utmost importance that Tokyo coordinate very closely with Washington and Seoul on this matter. This settlement was reputedly put on the table during the May 1999 Perry mission to Pyongyang as a consequence of close consultation between Washington, Tokyo, and Seoul. Presumably, it will be raised again in bilateral talks between Tokyo and Pyongyang.

The December 1999 visit of former Prime Minister Murayama to Pyongyang has led to renewed Japanese food assistance. As mentioned earlier, it is not necessary that food assistance to needy North Koreans be provided in North Korea. Japan bears a significant historical responsibility for the situation on the Korean peninsula. Although it might cause some political discomfort in Japan, acceptance of refugees for resettlement could take some pressure off China and would make a significant contribution to alleviating the suffering of the North Korean population.

China

China occupies the most ambiguous position of any of the major powers in the region. The conventional thinking in China is that it benefits from the maintenance of a divided peninsula and a fraternally allied socialist state on its border. The senior Chinese leadership includes a significant number of Korean War veterans who have a personal bond to North Korea. In 1999, China apparently stepped up military cooperation with North Korea, and US Secretary of State Madeleine Albright has publicly questioned Chinese assistance to North Korea's missile development program. China has steadfastly avoided participation in KEDO or the WFP food program, preferring to act alone and with little transparency, yet Clinton Administration officials from the President on down praise China's cooperation on Korea-related issues.

That said, China has been the major loser in developments on the peninsula over the last several years. The August 1998 North Korean missile test spurred an unprecedented degree of military cooperation between Tokyo and Seoul, encouraged increases in military expenditures and a more assertive national security posture in Japan, and undercut Chinese diplomatic efforts in opposition to the development and deployment of Theater Missile Defenses (TMD) in Northeast Asia.[25] The development of longer-range North Korean missiles and the deployment of North Korean missile batteries in areas near the Chinese border have dismayed the Chinese. Lastly, and perhaps most importantly, from the Chinese perspective North Korea's reluctance to adopt Chinese-style economic reforms perpetuates a potentially unstable situation in which China could be inundated with unwanted refugee flows as it was in the mid-1990s, or, worse yet, be drawn into a second confrontation with the United States on the Korean peninsula.

In some respects, China's interests with regard to North Korea are similar to those of South Korea and Japan: It would like to see a stable, non-threatening North Korea that could act as a buffer state, without continually upsetting strategic calculations in Northeast Asia. Its role is distinct, in that the domestic political basis for underwriting the Pyongyang regime is more robust in Beijing than in Tokyo or Seoul. As a consequence, Beijing is Pyongyang's most reliable ally and prospectively an important tutor in economic reform, despite differences in the two countries' situations.

The absence of significant constructive change in North Korea may put these ties at risk, however. Although the older generation of Chinese leaders may feel ideological and historical bonds with North Korea, the younger generation, many of whom were victimized in the Cultural Revolution, regard the personality cult around the Kims with a mixture of revulsion and derision. As many of them have observed, Beijing maintains

25. For an interesting analysis of the TMD issue, see Cha (1999).

a cordial and prosperous relationship with Seoul.[26] The sticking point, of course, is the presence of US troops on the Korean peninsula.

Although supporting the North Koreans may be China's first-best option, at some point China may conclude that North Korea is irredeemable and that the maintenance of a divided peninsula is unsustainable. At this point, China may switch strategies, seeking to achieve a second-best alternative of a unified Korea strategically removed from the US orbit. China could play a role similar to the one played by Gorbachev and the Hungarians in the case of East Germany. It could, in essence, pull the plug on the Kim Jong-il regime by cutting off assistance, opening the border, and taking up a multinational coalition's offer to fund refugee resettlement. The issue is what price they could extract from Seoul. Presumably, the Chinese would request removal of US troops from the Korean peninsula and the nullification of the US-South Korea mutual defense treaty, although intermediate solutions might be possible (no US troops in the northern part of the peninsula). In the extreme case, South Korean policymakers could face a choice between national unification on the one hand or continued military alliance with the United States on the other. In this circumstance, it is not at all clear how South Korea would choose.

Others

In addition to the United States, Japan, and China, other actors may play significant roles on the Korean peninsula. The European Union has considerable diplomatic and financial resources and participates in the KEDO consortium. However, it is far away, and the Korean peninsula is relatively peripheral to its strategic interests.

In contrast, Russia, which borders North Korea, has expressed interest in raising its diplomatic profile in Northeast Asia but has few financial resources. This limits Russia's capacity for playing a significant role in Korean affairs. Were Moscow to have a major impact on events on the Korean peninsula, it most likely would be as a spoiler, providing North Korea diplomatic support and frustrating the plans of the United States and others in order to obtain diplomatic concessions on other issues of more direct Russian interest, such as its economic interactions with the West. However, others argue that, by giving the Russians enough "face," they could be persuaded to play a constructive role vis-à-vis North Korea.

Either way, there are two obvious areas of concern for the rest of the world. Russia is likely to continue to downsize its military, thereby generating redundant personnel and equipment. Given the Soviet mili-

---

26. Bazhanov and Moltz (2000) provide vivid examples of such Chinese attitudes toward North Korea.

tary's historical ties to Pyongyang, Russia could become an ongoing source of specialist personnel and hardware for North Korea's military modernization, whether officially sanctioned by Moscow or not.

A second area of concern has to do with illicit activities, specifically cooperation between North Korean state-sponsored criminal enterprises and Russian transnational criminal groups. North Korea has exploited the breakdown of law and order in Russia to conduct criminal activities, including drug trafficking, arms smuggling, and counterfeit dispensing on Russian soil. Continued weakness in Russia and penetration of the state by Russian criminal groups could foster a supportive environment for North Korean transnational criminal activities.

Finally, international organizations could have a significant impact on the Korean peninsula. Technically, the current division of the peninsula reflects the UN-supervised armistice agreement, which ended fighting during the Korean War, and the presence of US troops on the peninsula is a legacy of the US participation in the United Nations police action in Korea. One gets the impression that New York is unenthusiastic about the continued UN role in Korea, however titular. In the end, any peace treaty or other significant political changes on the peninsula is likely to reflect the diplomacy of key national players, not the United Nations.

Of potentially greater importance could be the activities of the International Monetary Fund, the World Bank, and the Asian Development Bank. Of course, they do not act completely autonomously, and their activities to a significant extent will reflect the diplomatic consensus among the United States, Japan, and South Korea. Also, their direct lending activities in North Korea (or in a united Korea) are likely to be relatively modest. Nevertheless, these institutions could play a constructive role by offering relatively non-politicized technical advice and support and complementing the activities of private investors. They could play an even bigger role if interested parties were to pool their resources and establish a "North Korea Fund" within one or both of the development banks.

Final Thoughts

Koreans sometimes describe themselves as a "shrimp among whales," and during the past century Koreans and foreigners have clashed violently over control of the Korean peninsula. The result of these struggles is a peninsula divided between an increasingly prosperous and democratic South Korea and an increasingly destitute and totalitarian North Korea. Even if the North did not exist, the South would face great economic and political challenges in its own process of economic development and political maturation. The existence of the North creates an additional layer of complexity to the challenges that South Korea confronts, posing both a threat to its economic prosperity and to its political democratization, while at the same time creating an opportunity to extend those same achievements to 20 million more Koreans.

Foreign powers have been a significant force in these developments, acting constructively at times and malevolently at others. Although Koreans will ultimately write their own history, foreigners will continue to exercise significant influence on events on the peninsula. One can only hope that they play a more unambiguously positive role in this new century than they did in the last.

References

Adelman, Irma. 1999. The Korean Crisis of 1997/1998 and its Implications. In *Visible and Invisible Hand: The Economic Development of Korea*, ed., Irma Adelman and Song Byung-nak. Singapore: Scientific Press, forthcoming.

Ahn Byung-joon. 1998. Let's Engage North Korea with Contingency Planning. In *Managing Change on the Korean Peninsula*, Seoul: Seoul Press.

Ahn Choong-yong. 1999. Assessing Foreign Direct Investment in Korea. *Joint U.S.-Korea Academic Studies* 9: 247-65.

Aiyer, Sri-Ram. 1999. The Search for a New Development Paradigm. *Joint U.S-Korea Academic Studies* 9: 21-49.

Aizenman, Joshua and Nancy Marion. 1999. *Reserve Uncertainty and the Supply of International Credit*. NBER Working Paper 7202. Cambridge, MA: National Bureau of Economic Research.

Aliber, Robert Z. 1998. Transforming Korean Values. In *Korea's Economy 1998*. Washington: Korea Economic Institute of America, 14:28-32.

American Chamber of Commerce (AmCham) in Korea. 1996. *Korea: US Trade and Investment Issues 1996*. Seoul: American Chamber of Commerce in Korea.

American Chamber of Commerce (AmCham) in Korea. 1999. *Improving Korea's Business Climate*. Seoul: American Chamber of Commerce in Korea.

Amnesty International. 1996. Pursuit, Intimidation, and Abuse of North Korean Refugees and Workers. *Report—ASA* 24/06/96.

Anderson, Desaix. 1999. KEDO in the Strategic Context of Northeast Asia, in *Korea's Economy 1999*. Washington: Korea Economic Institute of America: 107-12.

APEC, 1995. *Survey of Impediments to Trade and Investment in the APEC Region*. Singapore: APEC Secretariat.

Armacost, Michael H., And Kenneth B. Pyle. 1999. Japan and the Unification of Korea: Challenges for US Policy Coordination. *NBR Analysis* 10, 1(March):5-38.

Armitage, Richard L. 1999. A Comprehensive Approach to North Korea. *National Defense University Strategic Forum*. Washington: Institute for National Strategic Studies 159 (March).

Armstrong, Charles K. 1998. A Socialism in Our Style: North Korean Ideology in a Post-Communist Era. In *North Korean Foreign Relations, ed.* Samuel S. Kim. Hong Kong: Oxford University Press.

Armstrong, Charles K. 2000. DPRK Energy. NAPSNET Discussion. Berkeley: The Nautilus Institute (16 April).

Åslund, Anders, Peter Boone, and Simon Johnson. 1996. How to Stabilize: Lessons from Post-Communist Countries. *Brookings Paper on Economic Activity* 1996, 1: 217-313.

Babson, Bradley. n.d. North Korean Economy Today (North Korea on the Brink). Washington: East Asia and Pacific Region, World Bank, processed.

Bae Jin-young. 1996. The Fiscal Burden of Korean Reunification and Its Impact on South Korea's Macroeconomic Stability. *Joint U.S.-Korea Academic Studies* 6: 185-202.

Bahl, Roy, Kim Chuk-kyo, and Park Chong-kee. 1986. *Public Finances During the Korean Modernization Process.* Cambridge: Harvard University Press.

Baily, Martin and Eric Zitzewitz. 1998. Extending the East Asian Miracle: Microeconomic Evidence from Korea. *Brookings Papers on Economic Activity,* Microeconomics 1998: 249-308.

Baker, James A., 3rd. 1999. North Korea Wins Again. *New York Times,* 19 March.

Balassa, Bela. 1990. *Economic Policies in the Pacific Area Developing Countries.* London: Macmillan.

Balassa, Bela and John Williamson, 1990. *Adjusting to Success: Balance of Payments Policy in the East Asian NICs* (rev). Institute for International Economics: Washington.

Bandow, Doug. 1998. Nuclear Issues Between the United States and North Korea. In *North Korea After Kim Il Sung, ed.* Suh Dae-suk and Lee Chae-jin. Boulder: Lynne Rienner.

Barna, Brian J. 1998. An Economic Roadmap to Korean Reunification. *Asian Survey,* XXXVIII, 3 (March): 265-90.

Barro, Robert J. and Xavier Sala-i-Martin. 1992. Convergence. *Journal of Political Economy* 100, 2 (April): 223-51.

Barro, Robert J. and Xavier Sala-i-Martin. 1995. *Economic Growth.* New York: McGraw-Hill.

Bazhanov, Evgeniy P. 2000a. Russia's Policies Toward the Two Koreas. In *The Two Koreas and the United States, ed.* Dong Won-mo. Armonk: M.E. Sharpe.

Bazhanov, Evgeniy P. 2000b. Military-Strategic Aspects of the North Korean Nuclear Program. In *The North Korean Nuclear Program, ed.* James Clay Moltz and Alexandre Y. Mansourov. New York: Routledge.

Bazhanov, Evgeniy P. and James Clay Moltz. 2000. China and the Korean Peninsula. In *The North Korean Nuclear Program, ed.* James Clay Moltz and Alexandre Y. Mansourov. New York: Routledge.

Bazhanova, Natalie. 1992. Between Dead Dogmas and Practical Requirements: External Economic Relations of North Korea, 1945-1990, processed.

Bazhanova, Natalya. 2000. Economic Factors and the Stability of the North Korean Regime. In *The North Korean Nuclear Program, ed.* James Clay Moltz and Alexandre Y. Mansourov. New York: Routledge.

Beck, Peter M. 1999. Foreign Investment in Korea: From Exclusion to Inducement, *Joint U.S.-Korea Academic Studies* 9: 221-45.

Bennett,Bruce. 1999. The Dynamics of the North Korean Security Threat. *International Journal of Korean Studies* 3, 1 (Spring/Summer): 1-34.

Berg, Andrew. 1999. *The Asia Crisis: Causes, Policy Responses, and Outcomes.* Working Paper 99/135. Washington: International Monetary Fund.

Blanchard, Olivier Jean, Rudiger Dornbusch, Paul Krugman, Richard Layard, and Lawrence Summers. 1991. *Reform in Eastern Europe.* Cambridge: MIT Press.

Boltho, Andrea, Wendy Carlin, and Pasquale Scaramozzino. 1997. Will East Germany Become the New Mezzogiorno? *Journal of Comparative Economics* 24 (June): 241-64.

Bosworth, Barry P. and Gur Ofer. 1995. *Reforming Planned Economies in an Integrating World Economy.* Washington: Brookings Institution.

Burda, Michael and Michael Funke. 1993. *Eastern Germany: Can't We Be More Optimistic?* CEPR Discussion Paper 893. London: Centre for Economic Policy Research.

Buzo, Adrian. 1999. *The Guerilla Dynasty: Politics and Leadership in North Korea.* Boulder, Colorado: Westview Press.

Calomis, Charles. 1998. *Harmful Bailouts.* Washington: American Enterprise Institute. January.

Calvo, Guillermo a. and Enrique G. Mendoza. 2000. Rational Herd Behavior and the Globalization of Securities Markets. *Journal of International Economics,* forthcoming.

CARE, 2000. CARE to withdraw from North Korea Consortium. http://www.care.org/ info_center/newsroom/2000/apr_2000_news.html

Cargill, Thomas F. 1999. Economic and Financial Crisis in Korea, the Japanese Financial Regime, and the Need for a New Financial Paradigm. *U.S.-Korea Academic Studies* 9: 111-30.

Carlin, Wendy and Colin Mayer, 1994. The *Treuhand*anstalt: Privatization by the State and the Market. In *The Transition in Eastern Europe Volume 2,* eds. Olivier Jean Blanchard, Kenneth A. Froot, and Jeffrey D. Sachs. Chicago: University of Chicago Press: 189-207.

Central Intelligence Agency, 1994. *Handbook of Economic Statistics.* Washington: CIA.

Cha, Victor. 1999. Berlin: What Have We Learned, and Where Do We Go From Here? *NAPSNET Policy Forum Online #99-07.* Berkeley: The Nautilus Institute.

Chang Nam-soo. 1999a. Status of Food Shortage and Malnutrition in North Korea. *Korea Focus* 7, 1 (January/February): 47-55.

Chang Nam-soo. 1999b. Nutrition of North Korean Children. In *Nutritional Problems of North Korean Children.* Seoul: KDI School of International Policy and Management.

Chang Suk-in. 1997. The Effects of Economic Integration Between North and South Korea, *International Economic Journal,* 11, no. 4 (Fall): 1-16.

Cheong Kwang-soo and C. H. Lee. 1996. Toward Korean Unification: A Policy Proposal for Investment in North Korea. University of Hawaii at Manoa, January, processed.

Chiddy, Keith. 1997. Speech, 7th Meeting of the Northeast Asia Economic Forum, Ulaan Baatar, Mongolia, 17-21 August.

Chiddy, Keith. 1998. Doing Business in the DPRK. *ERINA Report,* vol. 23: 6-10.

Cho, Dongchul and Youngsun Koh. 1996. "Liberalization of Capital Inflows in Korea: Big Bang or Gradualism?" National Bureau of Economic Research Working Paper Series. 5824.

Cho Dong-ho. 1997. Labor Policy After Reunification. *Economic Bulletin.* Seoul: Center for Economic Information, Korea Development Institute, Ministry of Finance and Economy 19, 6: 31-8.

Cho Soon. 1994. *The Dynamics of Korean Economic Development.* Washington: Institute for International Economics.

Cho Myung-chol and Zang Hyoung-soo. 1999a. North Korea's Budgetary System. Paper presented at a World Bank seminar, Washington (7 December).

Cho Myung-chol and Zang Hyoung-soo. 1999b. North Korea's Education System. Paper presented at a World Bank seminar, Washington (9 December).

Cho Seong-kyu. 1999. The Effects of Mt. Kumgang Tour Business on the National and Local Economy. *The Economics of Korean Unification* 4, no. 2 (Fall): 154-68.

Choe Hyuk, Kho Bong-chan, and René Stulz. 1999. *Do Foreign Investors Destabilize Stock Markets? The Korean Experience in 1997,* January, processed.

Choi Gi-woo. 1998. The Role of NGOs in the Korean Unification Process and Policy Implications. *Peace Forum* 14,.26 (Winter): 185-205.

Choi Iyong-gae and Wing Thye Woo. 1996. Lessons for North Korean Economic Reform from China? In *Middle Powers in the Age of Globalization,* ed. Hwang Byong-moo and Yoon Young-kwan. KAIS International Conference Series 5, Seoul: Korean Association of International Studies.

Choi Jin-wook. 1998. North Korean Local Politics Under the New Constitution. *Korea and World Affairs*, Winter: 569-91.

Choi Jin-wook. 1999. New Constitution and the Status of the Party, Military, and Government, *NAPSNET Special Report*, 11 January.

Choi Kwang. 1999. Public Sector Reform in Korea. *Korea Focus* 7, 5 (September/October): 66-77.

Choi Nak-gyoon and Kang Du-yong. 1999. *A Study on the Crisis, Recovery, and Industrial Upgrading in Korea*. February, processed.

Choi Soo-young. 1991. Foreign Trade of North Korea, 1946-1988: Structure and Performance, dissertation, Northeastern University, Boston, September.

Choi Wan-kyu. 1998. The Current State and Tasks of the Study of Change in the North Korean Political System. In *Understanding Regime Dynamics in North Korea*, ed. Moon Chung-in. Seoul: Yonsei University Press.

Choi Won-ki. 1999. Dealing With North Korea 'As It Is', Nautilus Policy Forum Online (#99-07). Berkeley: The Nautilus Institute.

Chun, Chae-sung. 2000. Missile Technology Control Regime and North Korea. *Korea Focus* 8, 1 (January-February): 15–29.

Chun Hong-tack. 1992. Estimating North Korea's GNP by Physical Indicators Approach. *Korea Development Review* 14, no. 1: 167-225 (In Korean).

Chun Hong-tack. 1993. *A Gradual Approach Toward North and South Korean Economic Integration*. KDI Working Paper 9311. Seoul: Korea Development Institute, November.

Chun, Hong-tack. 1997 "Economic Conditions in North Korea and Prospects for Reform" in Thomas H. Henricksen and Jongryn Mo, eds. *North Korea after Kim Il-Sung*. Sanford: Hoover Institution Press.

Chung, Joseph S. 1974. *The North Korean Economy*. Stanford: Hoover Institution Press.

Chung, Joseph S. 1991. *Potential Future Scenarios for the North Korean Economy*. International Commission for the Peaceful Reunification of Korea. Washington: Summit Council for World Peace.

Citizens' Alliance to Help Political Prisoners in North Korea. 1999. *Human Rights Light to North Korea*. Seoul: Citizens' Alliance to Help Political Prisoners in North Korea.

Claessens, Stijn, Simeon Djankov, and Gerhard Pohl. 1996. Ownership and Corporate Governance: Evidence from the Czech Republic. Paper presented at the International Symposium on Capital Markets and Enterprise Reform, Beijing, China (8-9 November).

Claessens, Stijn, Swati Ghosh, and David Scott. 1999. Korea's Financial Sector Reforms. *U.S.-Korea Academic Studies* 9: 83-110.

Clifford, Mark. 1997. *Troubled Tiger* (revised edition). Singapore: Butterworth-Heinemann Asia.

Cline, William R. 1990. *German Currency Unification*. Washington: Institute for International Economics, July, processed.

Cline, William R. 1995. *International Debt Reexamined*. Washington: Institute for International Economics.

Cline, William R. 1998. *IMF-Supported Adjustment Programs in the East Asian Financial Crisis*. IIF Research Paper No. 98-1. Washington: Institute for International Finance.

Coate, Stephen. 1989. Cash Versus Direct Food Relief. *Journal of Development Economics* 30 (April): 199-224.

Coe, David T., Elhanan Helpman, and Alexander Hoffmaister. 1996. North-South R&D Spillovers. *Economic Journal* 107, 440 (September): 134-49.

Coles, Jeffrey L. and Peter J. Hammond. 1995. Walrasian Equilibrium Without Survival: Existence, Efficiency, and Remedial Policy, in *Choice, Welfare, and Development: a Festschrift in Honor of Amartya Sen*, eds. K. Basu, P. Pattanaik, and K. Suzumura. Oxford: Clarendon Press.

Commander, Simon and Fabrizio Coricelli. 1995. *Unemployment, Restructuring, and the Labor Market in Eastern Europe and Russia*. Washington: World Bank.

Committee on Armed Services and Committee on Foreign Relations, United States Senate. 1951. *Military Situation in the Far East, Part 4*. Washington: Government Printing Office.

Cossa, Ralph A. 1997. Monitoring the Agreed Framework, Special Report, Honolulu: Pacific Forum CSIS, October.

Cossa, Ralph A. 1998. US-North Korea Talks: Time to Break a Bad Habit. *Korea Times* 3 (December).

Council on Foreign Relations. 1999a. *U.S. Policy Toward North Korea: A Second Look*. http://www.foreignrelations.org/public/pubs/NKoreaTask.html.

Council on Foreign Relations. 1999b. *Safeguarding Prosperity in the Global Financial System*. New York: Council on Foreign Relations.

Cumings, Bruce. 1996. The Historical Origins of North Korean Foreign Policy. Paper presented at the Conference on North Korean Foreign Policy in the Post-Cold War Era, Colombia University, New York, (31 May-1 June).

Cumings, Bruce. 1997. *Korea's Place in the Sun*. New York: W.W. Norton.

Davis, Zachary S. et al. 1994. Korea: Procedural and Jurisdictional Questions Regarding Possible Normalization of Relations with North Korea. Washington: US Congressional Research Service *Report to Congress*, November 29.

Dembinski, Matthias. 1995. North Korea, IAEA Special Inspections, and the Future of the Nonproliferation Regime. *The Nonproliferation Review* 2, 2(Winter): 31-39.

Denisov, Valery I. 2000. Nuclear Institutions and Organizations in North Korea. In *The North Korean Nuclear Program*, eds. James Clay Moltz and Alexandre Y. Mansourov. New York: Routledge.

Department of Defense. 1998. The United States Security Strategy for the East Asia-Pacific Region, 1998. *East Asia Strategy Reports 1998*. Washington: Department of Defense.

Dervis, Kemal, Jaime de Melo, and Sherman Robinson. 1982. *General Equilibrium Models for Development Policy*. New York: Cambridge University Press.

Deutsch-Koreanische Industrie und Handelskammer. 1991. *Nordkorea: Einblicke in Wirtschaft und Lebenweise*. Seoul: Deutsch-Koreanische Industrie und Handelskammer.

Ding, Wei, Ilker Domaç, and Giovanni Ferri. 1998. *Is There A Credit Crunch in East Asia?* Policy Research Working Paper 1959, Washington: World Bank, East Asia and Pacific Region. August.

Dobson, Wendy and Pierre Jacquet. 1998. *Financial Services Liberalization in the WTO*. Washington: Institute for International Economics.

Dollar, David, and Kenneth Sokoloff. 1990. Patterns of Productivity Growth in South Korean Manufacturing Industries 1963-1979. *Journal of Development Economics* 3,2(October).

Dornbusch, Rudiger and Holger C. Wolf. 1994. East German Economic Reconstruction, in Olivier Jean Blanchard. In *The Transition in Eastern Europe Volume 1*, ed. Kenneth A. Froot and Jeffrey D. Sachs. Chicago: University of Chicago Press: 155-90.

Drazen, Allan. 1997. *Contagious Currency Crises*. College Park: Center for International Economics, University of Maryland, processed.

Drennan, William. 1994. *Student Radicalization and Anti-Americanism in the Republic of Korea*. Catholic University, March 2, processed.

Drennan, William. 1998. Mistrust and the Korean Peninsula: Dangers of Miscalculation. Washington: United States Institute for Peace Special Report, November.

Drèze, Jean and Amartya Sen. 1989. *Hunger and Public Action*. Oxford: Clarendon Press.

Dyck, I.J. Alexander. 1997. Privatization in Eastern Germany: Management Selection and Economic Transmission. *American Economic Review* 87, 4 (September): 565-97.

Dyck, John. 1996. North Korean an Emerging Market for Food Trade, APEC Agriculture and Trade. Washington: USDA Economic Research Service: May, 22-23, *Agricultural Economic Report* #734.

Earle, John S. and Gheorghe Oprescu. 1995. Romania in Simon Commander and Fabrizio Coricelli editors, *Unemployment, Restructuring, and the Labor Market in Eastern Europe and Russia*, Washington: World Bank: 253-288.

Easterly, William and Stanley Fischer. 1994. *The Soviet Economic Decline: Historical and Republican Data*. NBER Working Paper 4735. Cambridge, Massachusetts: National Bureau of Economic Research.

Eberstadt, Nicholas. 1994a. Reform, Muddling through, or Collapse? In *One Korea?*, ed. Thomas H. Henriksen and Lho Kyong-soo. Stanford: Hoover Institution Press.

Eberstadt, Nicholas. 1994b. Inter-Korean Economic Cooperation: Rapprochement Through Trade? *Korea and World Affairs* 18, 4: 642-661.

Eberstadt, Nicholas. 1994c. Demographic Shocks After Communism: Eastern Germany, 1989-93. *Population and Development Review* 20, 1(March): 137-152.

Eberstadt, Nicholas. 1995a. *Korea Approaches Reunification*. Armonk, New York: ME Sharpe.

Eberstadt, Nicholas. 1995b. China's Trade With the DPRK 1990-1994. *Korea and World Affairs* 19:4 (Winter): 665-685.

Eberstadt, Nicholas. 1996. How Much Money Goes from Japan to North Korea? *Asian Survey* XXXVI, 5 (May): 523-542.

Eberstadt, Nicholas. 1997a. Prospects for US-DPRK Economic Relations. *Korea and World Affairs* 21, 4 (Winter): 534-67.

Eberstadt, Nicholas. 1997b. Hastening Korean Unification. *Foreign Affairs* 76, 2 (March/ April): 77-92.

Eberstadt, Nicholas. 1998a. North Korea's International Trade in Capital Goods. 1970-1995: Indications from 'Mirror Statistics', *Journal of East Asian Affairs* XII, 1 (Winter/Spring): 165-223.

Eberstadt, Nicholas. 1998b. A Quantitative Comparison of Current Socioeconomic Conditions in North and South Korea. Paper presented to the Second Conference of the International Interdisciplinary Project on Nation-Building for Korean Unification. Honolulu, Hawaii, 21-25 January.

Eberstadt, Nicholas. 1998c. Development, Structure, and Performance of North Korea Economy: Empirical Indications. Paper presented at the conference Developing Social Infrastructure in North Korea for Economic Cooperation between the North and the South. Seoul, Korea, 9-10 November.

Eberstadt, Nicholas. 1998d. North Korea's Unification Policy: 1948-1996, in *North Korean Foreign Relations*, ed. Samuel S. Kim. Oxford: Oxford University Press.

Eberstadt, Nicholas. 1999a. 'Our Own Style of Statistics': Availability and Reliability of Official Quantitative Data for the People's Republic of Korea. Paper presented at Advancing Statistics for the Next Millennium, Taejon, Republic of Korea, 16-18 September.

Eberstadt, Nicholas. 1999b. *The End of North Korea*. Washington: American Enterprise Institute.

Eberstadt, Nicholas. n.d. The D.P.R.K. As An Economy Under Multiple Severe Stresses: Analogies and Lessons from Past and Recent Historical Experience, processed.

Eberstadt, Nicholas, and Judith Banister. 1992a. *The Population of North Korea*. Berkeley, CA: Institute of East Asian Studies.

Eberstadt, Nicholas, and Judith Banister. 1992b. Divided Korea: Demographic and Socioeconomic Issues for Reunification. *Population and Development Review* 18, 3(September): 505-531.

Eberstadt, Nicholas, Marc Rubin, and Albina Tretyakova. 1995. The Collapse of Soviet and Russian Trade with North Korea, 1989-1993: Impact and Implications. *The Korean Journal of National Unification* 4, 1995: 87-104.

Eberstadt, Nicholas, Christina W. Harbaugh, Marc Rubin, and Lorraine A. West. 1995. China's Trade with North Korea, 1990-1994: Pyongyang's Thrifty New Patron. *Korea and World Affairs* 19,4 (Winter): 665-685.

Eckert, Carter J. 1991. *Offspring of Empire*. Seattle: University of Washington Press.

Edwards, Sebastian. 1999. *On Crisis Prevention: Lessons from Mexico and East Asia*. NBER Working Paper No. 7233. Cambridge: National Bureau of Economic Research.

Eickelpasch, Alexander. 1998. Enterprise Restructuring in East Germany. *Economic Survey of Europe* No. 2. Geneva: UN Economic Commission for Europe.

Engelhardt, Michael J. 1995. Rewarding Nonproliferation: The South and North Korean Cases. *The Nonproliferation Review* 3,3(Spring-Summer): 31-37.

FALU. 1998. Pyongyang Activity Report, Rome: World Food Program Food Assessment Liaison Unit Steering Committee, November 15.

Feldstein, Martin. 1998. Refocusing the IMF. *Foreign Affairs* 77, 2 (March/April): 20-33.

Flake, L. Gordon. 1995a. North Korea's External Economy. Paper presented at the Sixth Annual Convention of the Congress of Political Economists (COPE), International, Seoul (5-10 January).

Flake, L. Gordon. 1995b. Seoul Discussions on North Korea's Economy. Washington: Korea Economic Institute of America, 18 January, memo.

Flake, L. Gordon. 1995c. International Economic Linkages of North Korea. Paper presented at the Symposium on North Korea and Prospects for Korean Unification, University of California, San Diego, LaJolla, California, 25-27 May.

Flake, L. Gordon. 1996. Recent Trends in Inter-Korean Trade and Economic Relations. *Korea Economic Update* 7:3 (June), Washington: Korea Economic Institute of America.

Flake, L. Gordon. 1997. *Korea Economic Institute of America, Research Analysis: Personal Views on the Food Shortage and the Stability of the Regime.* Washington: KEI, 22 April.

Flake, L. Gordon. 1998. Inter-Korean Economic Relations. *Korea's Economy 1998* 14: 131-35.

Flake, L. Gordon. 1999a. The Geneva Agreed Framework and the Ryugyong Hotel: Lessons in Maintenance. Washington: Atlantic Council of the US, processed.

Flake, L. Gordon. 1999b. Inter-Korean Relations Under the 'Sunshine Policy'. In *Korea's Economy 1999* 15: 100-106.

Flake, L. Gordon. 1999c. Patterns of Inter-Korean Economic Relations. Washington: Atlantic Council of the US, processed.

Flassbeck, Heiner. 1994. The Transition of the GDR into a Market Economy. Paper presented at the KDI-DIW Joint Seminar, The German Economy Four Years After Unification and Its Implication for Korea, Seoul (12 May).

Food and Agriculture Organization. 1997. Special Report: FAO/WFP Crop and Food Supply Assessment Mission to the Democratic People's Republic of Korea, 25 November 1997.

Food and Agriculture Organization/World Food Program. 1999a. Special Report: FAO/WFP Crop and Food Supply Assessment Mission to the Democratic People's Republic of Korea, 29 June.

Food and Agriculture Organization/World Food Program. 1999b. Special Report: FAO/WFP Crop and Food Supply Assessment Mission to the Democratic People's Republic of Korea, 8 November.

Ford, Glyn. 1997. KEDO Supporters on Thin Ice in Europe. *Japan Times,* 2 November.

Foster-Carter, Aidan. 1992. Korea's Coming Unification. *Economist Intelligence Unit Special Report* M212, April.

Foster-Carter, Aidan. 1994a. North Korea After Kim Il-Sung. Economist Intelligence Unit. *Research Report.*

Foster-Carter, Aidan. 1994b. Korea: Sociopolitical Realities of Reuniting a Divided Nation, in *One Korea?*, ed. Thomas H. Hendricksen and Lho Kyong-soo. Stanford: Hoover Institution Press.

Frankel, Jeffrey A. and Wei Shang-Jin. 1995. Is A *Yen* Bloc Emerging? *Joint U.S.-Korean Academic Studies* 5: 145-175.

Frydman, Roman, Cheryl Gray, Marek Hessel, and Andrzej Rapaczynski. 1999. When Does Privatization Work? *Quarterly Journal of Economics* 64, 4 (November): 1153-91.

Gagnon, Joseph E., Paul R. Masson, and Warwick J. McKibbin. 1996. *German Unification: What Have We Learned from Multi-Country Models?* IMF Working Paper 96/43. Washington: Research Department, International Monetary Fund.

Galinsky, Victor. 1994. No Quick Fix on Korea. *Washington Post,* 2 August.

Galinsky, Victor and Henry Sokolski. 1994. Korea Accord: What Is It? *Washington Post*, 23 November.

Garwin, Richard L. 1999. Effectiveness of Proposed National Missile Defense Against ICBMs from North Korea. *NAPSNET Special Report*, 26 March.

Gavitt, Christy. 1999. Presentation organized by the Korea Economic Institute of America, Washington, 5 August.

Gelb, Alan, Gary Jefferson, and Inderjit Singh. 1993. Can Communist Economies Transform Themselves Incrementally? The experience of China. *Economics of Transition* 1, 3(1993): 401-35.

General Accounting Office (GAO) 1998. Nuclear Nonproliferation, Report to the Chairman, Committee on Energy and Natural Resources, U.S. Senate. July.

Gerardi, Greg J., and James A. Plotts. 1994. An Annotated Chronology of DPRK Missile Trade and Developments. *Nonproliferation Review* 2, 1(Fall): 65-98.

Gertz, Bill. 1999. *Betrayal*. Washington: Regnery Publishing.

Gilman, Benjamin A. 1999. Gilman Reaction to Prospective North Korea Missile, press release, Washington, 17 June.

Glaser, Bonnie and Banning Garrett. 1997. Chinese Assessments of the Korean Peninsula. 28 January, processed.

Gleysteen, William H., Jr. 1999. *Massive Entanglement, Marginal Influence: Carter and Korea in Crisis*. Washington: The Brookings Institution.

Glick, Reuven and Andrew Rose. 1998. *Contagion and Trade: Why Are Crises Regional?* NBER Working Paper Series 6806. Cambridge: National Bureau of Economic Research.

Golan, Amos, George Judge and Douglas Miller. 1996. *Maximum Entropy Econometrics: Robust Estimation with Limited Data*. New York: Wiley.

Golan, Amos, George Judge and Sherman Robinson. 1994. Recovering Information from Incomplete or Partial Multisectoral Economic Data. *The Review of Economics and Statistics* LXXVI, 3 (August): 541-549.

Goldstein, Morris and Philip Turner. 1996. *Banking Crises in Emerging Market Economies: Origins and Policy Options*. BIS Economic Papers 46. Basel: Bank for International Settlements, October.

Graham. Edward M. 1996. *Competition Policies in the Dynamic Industrializing Economies*. Working Paper Series 96-6. Washington: Institute for International Economics.

Graham, Edward M. 1999a. Reform of the *Chaebol* since the Onset of the Korean Financial Crisis. Paper presented at the US-Korea 21st Century Council Meeting. Washington, 18-19 October.

Graham, Edward M. 1999b. *A Radical but Workable Restructuring Plan for South Korea*. International Economic Policy Briefs 99-2. Washington: Institute for International Economics, January.

Groves, Theodore, Yongmiao Hong, John McMillan, and Barry Naughton. 1994. Autonomy and Incentives in Chinese State Enterprises. *Quarterly Journal of Economics* CIX, 1 (February): 183-209.

Groves, Theodore, Yongmiao Hong, John McMillan, and Barry Naughton. 1995. Productivity Growth in Chinese State-Run Industry. In *Reform of China's State-Owned Enterprises*, ed. Fureng Dong, Cyril Lin, and Barry Naughton. London: Macmillan.

Gustavson, Kristin R. and Jinmin Lee-Rudolph. 1997. Political and Economic Human Rights Violations in North Korea, in *North Korea After Kim Il Sung*, ed. Thomas H. Hendricksen and Jongryn Mo. Stanford: Hoover Institution Press.

Haggard, Stephan. 1990. *Pathways from the Periphery: The Politics of Growth in the Newly Industrializing Countries*. Ithaca: Cornell University Press.

Haggard, Stephan. 2000. *The Political Economy of the Asian Financial Crisis*. Washington: Institute for International Economics, forthcoming.

Haggard, Stephan and Andrew MacIntyre. 1999. The Politics of Moral Hazard: The Origins of Financial Crisis in Indonesia, Korea, and Thailand. University of California at San Diego, processed.

Halloran, Richard. 1998. North Korea and Japan. In *North Korea After Kim Il Sung,* ed. Suh Dae-suk and Lee Chae-jin. Boulder: Lynne Rienner Publishers.

Han Seung-soo. 1994. The North Korea Nuclear Issue. *Korea Economic Update* 5:1 Spring.

Han Song-ryol. 1995. Industrial Development in Korea, document distributed at the Symposium on North Korea and Prospects for Korean Unification, University of California at San Diego, LaJolla, 25-27 May.

Han Song-ryol and Choe Tong-u. 1995. Perspectives of Issues by the DPRK, New York: DPRK Mission to the UN, processed.

Han Tae-joon. 1998. Notes on the Burden of Korean Unification. In *The Political Economy of Korean Unification,* ed. Yang Un-chul. Seoul: The Sejong Institute.

Harrington, Kent. 1998. *30 Years in the Making,* The Washington Post. editorial, 9 September 1998.

Harrison, Selig S. 1998. "U.S. Policy Toward North Korea" in Dae-Suk Suh and Chae-Jin Lee eds., *North Korea After Kim Il Sung.* Boulder, CO: Lynne Rienner Publishers, Inc.

Hayashi, Kazunobu and Teruo Komaki. 1997. *Kim Jong-Il's North Korea.* Tokyo: Institute of Developing Economies, March.

Hayes, Peter. 1993. The Republic of Korea and the Nuclear Issue. In *Asian Flashpoint,* ed. Andrew Mack. Canberra: Allen & Unwin. 51-83.

Hayes, Peter. 1994. Enduring Legacies: Economic Dimensions of Restoring North Korea's Environment. Paper presented at the Fourth Annual International Symposium on the North Korean Economy, Seoul (18 October).

Hayes, Peter and David von Hippel. 1998. Ecological Crisis and the Quality of Life in the Democratic People's Republic of Korea. In *Understanding Regime Dynamics in North Korea,* ed. Moon Chung-in. Seoul: Yonsei University Press.

Heilemann, Ullrich and Hermann Rappen. 1997. *The Seven Year Itch? German Unity from a Fiscal Viewpoint.* AICGS Research Report 6, Economic Studies Program, American Institute for Contemporary German Studies, The Johns Hopkins University.

Herz, Bernhard and Werner Roger. 1995. Economic Growth and Convergence in Germany. *Weltwirtschaftliches Archiv* 131, 1: 132-43.

Heybey, Berta and Peter Murrell. 1999. The Relationship Between Economic Growth and the Speed of Liberalization During Transition. *Journal of Policy Reform* 3: 121-37.

Hoffman, M. Elizabeth. 1999. The'Flower Swallows': North Korean Children's Development During a Time of Crisis. In *Nutritional Problems of North Korean Children.* Seoul: KDI School of International Policy and Management.

Hong Seong-guk. 1999. The State of Farmers' Markets in North Korea and Its Implications. *The Economics of Korean Unification* 4, 2 (Fall): 57-66.

Hong Seong-min. 1999. Korea's Dwindling Middle Class. *VIP Economic Report* 5: 13-4.

Hong Soon-jick. 1999. Environmental Pollution in North Korea and Inter-Korean Cooperation. *The Economics of Korean Unification* 4, 2 (Fall): 67-84.

Hufbauer, Gary. 1996. What Role Might the International Community Play in the Process of Korean Unification? Paper presented at the International Conference on the International Implications of Korean Unification, Seoul (28-29 June).

Hughes Hallet, Andrew, and Yue Ma. 1992. "East Germany, West Germany and Their Mezzogiorno Problem," CEPR Discussion Paper 623. London: Centre for Economic Policy Research. February.

Hughes Hallett, Andrew J. and Yue Ma. 1997. *East Germany, West Germany, and their Mezzogiorno Problem: an Empirical Investigation.* CEPR Discussion Paper No. 623, Centre for Economic Policy Research: London (February).

Hughes Hallett, Andrew J., Yue Ma, and Jacques Melitz. 1996. Unification and the Policy Predicament in Germany. *Economic Modeling 13* (October): 519-44.

Huh Moon-young. 1996. The Stability and Durability of the Kim Jong-Il Regime. *The Korean Journal Of National Unification* 5: 65-81.

Hunter, Helen-Louise. 1999. *Kim Il-song's North Korea.* Greenwood.

Huntington, Samuel P. 1968. *Political Order in Changing Societies*. New Haven: Yale University Press.

Hwang Eui-gak. 1993. *The Korean Economies*. Oxford: Clarendon Press.

Hyundai Research Institute. 1997. Policy Response to Increase in North Korean Escapees (Refugees), *VIP Report*, 10 February.

Iklé, Fred C. 1998. U.S. Folly May Start Another Korean War. *Wall Street Journal*, 12 October.

Illarionov, Andrei, Richard Layard and Peter Orszag. 1994. The Conditions of Life. In *Economic Transformation in Russia*, ed. Anders Åslund. London: Pinter.

International Monetary Fund (IMF). 1997. *Letter of Intent. http://www.imf.org/external/np/loi/120397.htm*.

IMF. 1998. Public Information Notice (PIN) 98/60: IMF Concludes Article IV Consultation with Japan. Washington: International Monetary Fund (13 August).

IMF. 1999a. IMF-Supported Programs in Indonesia, Korea, and Thailand: A Preliminary Assessment. Washington: International Monetary Fund, processed.

IMF. 1999b. Financial Sector Crisis and Restructuring: Lessons from Asia. Washington: International Monetary Fund (September).

Jackson, Marvin. 1994. Political Incredibility and Bureaucratic Transition in Romania in East-Central European Economies in Transition. Study Papers submitted to the Joint Economic Committee, Congress of the United States. Washington: Government Printing Office (November): 552-578.

Jannuzi, Frank. 1998. Can the US Cause the Collapse of North Korea? In *Managing Change on the Korean Peninsula*, ed. Kim Kyung-won and Han Sung-joo. Seoul: Seoul Forum.

Jeong In-soo. 1999. Employment Adjustment Policy and Its Problems: Comparing Korea and other OECD Countries [in Korean]. *Journal of Labor Economics*: (December) 255-76.

Jeong Kap-yeong. 1993. Comparing the North Korean Level of Economic Development by Principal Components Analysis. In *North Korea's Reality and Unification*, ed. Lee Young-sun. Seoul: Center for East and West Studies, Yonsei University. [In Korean].

Johnson, Gale. 1995. Integration of East Asian Agriculture into the World Trading Community. *Joint U.S.-Korea Academic Studies* 6:51-69.

Johnson, Simon. 1997. Does Privatization Matter? Evidence from Eastern Europe and the former Soviet Union. In *The System Transformation of The Transition Economies*, ed. Lee Doo-won. Seoul: Yonsei University Press.

Jones, Leroy P. and SaKong Il. 1980. *Government, Business, and Entrepreneurship in Economic Development: the Korean Case*. Cambridge: Harvard University Press.

Joo Seung-ho. 1998. Russia and Korea. In *The Korean Peninsula and the Major Powers*, ed. Hahn Bae-ho and Lee Chae-jin. Seoul: The Sejong Institute.

Jung Hee-nam and Park Heon-joo. 1998. A Proposed Reform Program on Land Ownership After Reunification of Korea. In *Policy Priorities for the Unified Korean Economy*, ed. SaKong Il and Kim Kwang-suk. Seoul: Institute for Global Economics.

Jwa Sung-hee, and Huh Chan-guk. 1998. *Risk and Returns of Financial-Industrial Interactions: The Korean Experience*. KERI Working Paper 9801. Seoul: Korea Economic Reseach Institute.

Kaminsky, Graciela L., and Carmen M. Reinhart. 1999. On Crises, Contagion, and Confusion. *Journal of International Economics* (forthcoming).

Kang, David. 1998. North Korea's Security Policy. In *North Korean Foreign Relations*, ed. Samuel S. Kim. Hong Kong: Cambridge University Press.

Kang In-soo. 1999. Foreign Direct Investment in Korea: Trends and Prospects. *Korea's Economy 1999* 15: 64-8.

Kang Wi-jo. 1997. *Christ and Caesar in Modern Korea*. Albany: State University of New York Press.

Karatnycky, Adrian. 1999. *The Comparative Survey of Freedom, 1989-1999*. Washington: Freedom House.

Kaurov, Georgiy. 2000. A Technical History of Soviet-North Korean Nuclear Relations. In *The North Korean Nuclear Program*, ed. James Clay Moltz and Alexandre Y. Mansourov. New York: Routledge.

Keller, Wolfgang. 1997. From Socialist Showcase to Mezzogiorno? Lessons on the Role of Technical Change from East Germany's Post-World War II Growth Performance. University of Wisconsin: Madison, processed (May).

Kemme, David M., and Michael Marrese. 1997. Economic Transition and Economic Performance: Lessons from Eastern Europe and the former Soviet Union. In *The System Transformation of the Transition Economies*, ed. Lee Doo-won. Seoul: Yonsei University Press.

Khan, Mohsin S., and Eric V. Clifton. 1992. Inter-Enterprize Arrears in Transforming Economies: The Case of Romania. Washington: International Monetary Fund (July).

Kim Chung-soo. 1990. Labor Market Developments in Macroeconomic Perspective. In *Korean Economic Development*, ed. Jene K. Kwon. New York: Greenwood Press.

Kim, E. Han. 1990. Financing Korean Corporations: Evidence and Theory. In *Korean Economic Development*, ed. Jene K. Kwon. New York: Greenwood Press.

Kim Eun-mee. 1997. *Big Business Strong State*. Albany: State University of New York Press.

Kim Hong-nack. 1998. Japan in North Korean Foreign Policy. In *North Korean Foreign Relations*, ed. Samuel S. Kim. Hong Kong: Oxford University Press.

Kim Il-pyong J. 1998. China in North Korean Foreign Policy. In *North Korean Foreign Relations*, ed. Samuel S. Kim. Hong Kong: Oxford University Press.

Kim Jong-gie, and Son Jae-young. 1997. Rural-Urban Disparity and Government Policies for Rural Development. In *The Strains of Economic Growth: Labor Unrest and Dissatisfaction in Korea*, ed. David L. Lindauer et al. Cambridge: Harvard University Press.

Kim June-dong. 1999. *Inward Foreign Direct Investment Regime and Some Evidences of Spillover Effects in Korea*. Working Paper 99-09. Seoul: Korea Institute for International Economic Policy.

Kim June-dong. 2000. Foreign Direct Investment: Trends and Policies. *Korea's Economy 2000* 16. Washington: The Korea Economic Institute of America.

Kim June-dong, and Hwang Sang-In. 1998. *The Role of Foreign Direct Investment in Korea's Economic Development: Productivity Effects and Implications for the Currency Crisis*. Seoul: Korea Institute for International Economic Policy.

Kim Kwang-suk, and Michael Roemer. 1979. *Growth and Structural Transformation*. Cambridge: Harvard University Press.

Kim Kyung-won. 1996. No Way Out: North Korea's Impending Collapse. *Harvard International Review* XVIII, 2 (Spring): 22-71.

Kim Ky-won. 1999. *Chaebol* Reform: Rationale and Contradictions. *Korea Focus* 7,6:74-91.

Kim Myong-chol. 1998. *The Day of Korean Unification by Kim Jong-Il*. Tokyo: Kojinsha [In Japanese].

Kim Myong-chol. 1999. *US Will End Up in a Shotgun Marriage with DPRK*. Nautilus Institute Policy Forum Online (99-07) Berkeley: The Nautilus Institute (22 October).

Kim Nam-doo. 1996. *Measuring the Costs of Visible Protection in Korea*. Washington: Institute for International Economics.

Kim Phi-lo. 1999. The Social Impact of the Food Crisis in North Korea. In *Nutritional Problems of North Korean Children*. Seoul: KDI School of International Policy and Management.

Kim Pyung-joo. 1995. *Money and Banking System in North Korea*. Seoul: Korea Institute of Finance.

Kim Pyung-joo. 1998. Monetary Integration and Stabilization in the Unified Korea. In *Policy Priorities for the Unified Korean Economy*, ed. SaKong Il and Kim Kwang-suk. Seoul: Institute for Global Economics.

Kim Sang-kyom. 1994. Opening North Korea's Economy. In *Northeast Asian Economic Cooperation*, ed. Yoo Jang-hee and Lee Chang-jae. Policy Studies 94-08. Seoul: Korea Institute for International Economic Policy.

Kim Sang-kyom. 1995. *North Korean Economy: Prospects for Opening and Inter-Korean Coopera-tion*. Seoul: Korea Institute for International Economic Policy, processed.

Kim Sung-chull. 1994. Is North Korea Following the Chinese Model of Reform and Opening? *East Asia Institute Reports*. New York: East Asia Institute, Columbia University (December).

Kim Sung-chull. 1996. The Development of Systemic Dissonance in North Korea. *The Korean Journal Of National Unification* 5: 83-109.

Kim, Samuel S. 1998. In Search of a Theory of North Korean Foreign Policy. In *North Korean Foreign Relations*, ed. Samuel S. Kim. Hong Kong: Oxford University Press.

Kim Tae-kwon, and Koh Hyunwook. 1994. A New Perspective on Economic Reform in North Korea. *Depth* 4.

Kim Woo-chan, and Shang-jin Wei. *1999. Foreign Portfolio Investors Before and During A Crisis*. NBER Working Paper Series 6968. Cambridge: National Bureau of Economic Research.

Kim Woon-keun, Lee Hyun-ok, and Daniel A. Sumner. 1998. Assessing the Food Situation in North Korea. *Economic Development and Cultural Change* 46,3: 519-34(April).

Kirk, Donald. 1999. *Korean Crisis: Unraveling of the Miracle in the IMF Era*. New York: St. Martin's Press.

Kirk, Mark, and Amos Hochstein. 1997. Trip Report. Washington: International Relations Committee, U.S. House of Representatives, processed.

Kirk, Mark, Peter Brookes, and Maria Pica. 1998. Mission to North Korea and China August 11-23, 1998. International Relations Committee, U.S. House of Representatives, Washing-ton, processed.

Kirk, Roger. 1991. *The U.S. and Romania: Facing a Difficult Future*. Washington: The Atlantic Council of the U.S. (April).

Kissinger, Henry. 1994. No Compromise, But a Rollback. *Washington Post, 6 July*.

Koh, B.C. 1998. Japan and Korea. In *The Korean Peninsula and the Major Powers*, ed. Hahn Bae-ho and Lee Chae-jin. Seoul: Sejong Institute.

Koh Il-dong. 1994. The Future of the Two Korean States. *Internationale Politik und Gesellschaft* 4, 1994: 343-350.

Koh Il-dong. 1998. Policy Options for the Privatization of North Korea's State Owned Enterprises. In *Policy Priorities for the Unified Korean Economy*, ed. SaKong Il and Kim Kwang-suk. Seoul: Institute for Global Economics.

Kong, Xiang, Robert E. Marks, and Guang Hua Wan. 1999. Technical Efficiency, Technologi-cal Change and Total Factor Productivity Growth in Chinese State-Owned Enterprises in the Early 1990s. *Asian Economic Journal* 13, 3 (September): 267-81.

Koo Bon-hak. 1992. *Political Economy of Self-Reliance*. Korean Unification Studies Series 14. Seoul: Research Center for Peace and Unification in Korea.

Koo Seung-yeal. 1998. Prospect and Policy Measures for North-South Migration. In *Policy Priorities for the Unified Korean Economy*, ed. SaKong Il and Kim Kwang-suk. Seoul: Institute for Global Economics.

Korea Buddhist Sharing Movement. 1998. Witnessed by 1,019 Food Refugees. Seoul: Korea Buddhist Sharing Movement (June).

Korea Development Bank. 1998. *North Korea's Industry and Technology*. http://www.kol.co.kr/~kdbmst/focus/nk__it.html

Korea Development Institute (KDI). 1999. *Nutritional Problems of North Korean Children*. Seoul: KDI School of International Policy Management.

Kornai, Janos. 1992. *The Socialist Economy*. Princeton: Princeton University Press.

Krugman, Paul R. 1997. Currency Crises. Cambridge: Department of Economics, MIT, pro-cessed.

Kuark, John Y.T. 1992. A Comparative Study of Foreign Trade in North and South Korea. University of Denver (March), processed.

Kuran, Timur. 1989. Sparks and Prairie Fires: A Theory of Unanticipated Political Revolution. *Public Choice* 61, 1 (April): 41-74.

Kuran, Timur. 1991. The East European Revolution of 1989: Is It Surprising that We were Surprised? *American Economic Review* 81,2 (May): 121-125.

Kwack Sung-yueng. 1994. The Rates of Return on Capital in the United States, Japan, and Korea, 1972-1990. In *The Korean Economy at a Crossroad*, ed. Kwack Sung-yeung. Westport: Praeger.

Kwack Seung-yueng. 1999. Total Factor Productivity Growth and the Sources of Growth in Korean Manufacturing Industries, 1971-1999, processed.

Kwak Yong-sun, and Kowun Audrey Lee. 1999. Restructuring of Public Enterprises and Its Prospects. *VIP Economic Report* (September).

Kwon Goo-hoon. 1997. Experiences with Monetary Integration and Lessons for Korean Unification. Washington: International Monetary Fund, processed.

Kwon, Jene K. 1986. Capital Utilization, Economies of Scale, and Technical Change in the Growth of Total Factor Productivity: An explanation of South Korean manufacturing. *Journal of Development Economics* 24, 1(November): 75-89.

Lange, Thomas, and Geoffrey Pugh. 1998. *The Economics of German Unification*. Cheltenham: Edward Elgar.

Lau, Lawrence J., Yingi Qian, and Gérard Roland. 2000. Reform Without Losers: An Interpretation of China's Dual-Track Approach to Transition. *Journal of Political Economy* 108,1 (February): 120-43.

Lee Bun-song. 1994. Sex Discrimination in Korea's Job Market. In *The Korean Economy at a Crossroad*, ed. Kwack Sung-yeung. Westport: Praeger.

Lee Bun-song. 1998. Comments. In *Policy Priorites for the Unified Korean Economy*, ed. SaKong Il and Kim Kwang-suk. Seoul: Institute for Global Economics.

Lee, Chae-jin. 1996. *China and Korea: Dynamic Relations.* Stanford. Hoover Institution Press.

Lee Chae-jin. 1998a. The Evolution of China's Two-Korea Policy. In *The Korean Peninsula and the Major Powers*, ed. Hahn Bae-ho and Lee Chae-jin. Seoul: Sejong Institute.

Lee Chae-jin. 1998b. China and North Korea. In *North Korea After Kim Il-Sung*, ed. Suh Dae-sook and Lee Chae-jin. Boulder: Lynne Rienner.

Lee Chan-woo, Tsutomu Nakano, and Makoto Nobukuni. 1995. *Estimate of the Supply and Demand for Grain in the Democratic People's Republic of Korea: 1995*. Niigata, Japan: Economic Research Institute for Northeast Asia (ERINA), Research Division (July), processed.

Lee Chong-sik. 1994. The Political Economy of North Korea, 1994. *NBR Analysis* 5:2 (September).

Lee, Chung H. 1994. A Note on Unifying the Two Korean Economies. *Seoul Journal of Economics* 7,1:77-89.

Lee, Chung H., and Charles E. Morrison. 1995. *APEC and Two Koreas*. Manoa: University of Hawaii (December), processed.

Lee Doo-won. 1993. Assessing North Korean Economic Reform: Historical Trajectory, Opportunities and Constraints. *Pacific Focus* VIII, (Fall) 3: 5-29.

Lee Doo-won. 1995. Inter-Korean Economic Relation: Rivaled Past, Unbalanced Present, and Integrated Future. *Yonsei Economic Studies* 2,1. (Spring).

Lee Doo-won. 1997. *Democratic People's Republic of Korea: Structure of the Welfare System and Expected Impact of Marketization*. Seoul: Yonsei University, processed.

Lee Doo-won. n.d. Lessons of Transitional Economies' Reform for North Korea. Seoul: Yonsei University, processed.

Lee Hwal-woong. 2000. *A Regional Approach to Korean Security*. Nautilus Policy Forum Online (#00-01). Berkeley: The Nautilus Institute.

Lee Hy-sang. 1991. Inter-Korean Cooperation: Realities and Possibilities. In *Korea in the 1990s*, ed. Steven W. Mosher. New Brunswick, New Jersey: Transaction Publishers: 15-36.

Lee Hy-sang. 1994a. Supply and Demand for Grains in North Korea. *Korea and World Affairs* XVIII, 3 (Fall): 509-554.

Lee Hy-sang. 1994b. Breeding Earthworms for Poultry and Swine in North Korea: A Quintessential Case of *Juche* Agriculture. Paper presented at the 23rd Annual Meeting of the Mid-Atlantic Regional Association of Asian Studies, Pittsburgh, 21-23 October.

Lee Hy-sang. 1994c. Economic Factors in Korean Reunification. In *Korea and the World*, ed. Kihl Young-whan. Boulder: Westview Press: 189-215.

Lee Hy-sang. 1999. North Korea: Strange Socialist Fortress, processed.

Lee Jong-wha, and Rhee Chang-yong. 1999. Macroeconmic Impacts of the Korean Financial Crisis: Comparison with the Cross-Country Patterns. Paper presented to the Conference on the Korean Currency Crisis, Cambridge, 1 February.

Lee Joung-woo, and David L. Lindauer. 1997. The Quality of Working Life. In *The Strains of Economic Growth: Labor Unrest and Dissatisfaction in Korea*, ed. Lindauer et al. Cambridge: Harvard University Press.

Lee Kuen, and Manuel Montes. 1999. Comparative Analysis of the Chinese Economic Reform and Growth. In *Comparison of Korean and Chinese Economic Development*, ed. Lee Doo-won and Jason Z. Yin. Seoul: Yonsei University Press.

Lee Nae-young. 1998. Political Integration and Political Institutions in a Unified Korea, in *The Political Economy of Korean Unification*, ed. Yang Un-chul. Seoul: The Sejong Institute.

Lee Sang-man. 1993. A Study on Patterns of Economic Integration Between South and North Korea. *East Asian Review* 5,3: 91-113.

Lee Shi-young. 1998. Prospects for Trade Between the Two Koreas. In *The Political Economy of Korean Unification*, ed. Yang Un-chul. Seoul: The Sejong Institute.

Lee Yang, and Kim Joon-hyung. 1994. *Peace Building on the Korean Peninsula*. Washington: United States Institute for Peace. (December).

Lee Young-sun. 1994a. The Current Status of the North Korean Economy and Prospects for Reform. *Osteuropa-Wirtschaft* 39, 2 (June): 135-145.

Lee Young-sun. 1994b. Economic Integration of the Korean Peninsula: A Scenario Approach to the Cost of Unification. In *The Korean Economy at a Crossroad*, ed. Kwack Sung-yeung. Westport: Praeger.

Lee Young-sun. 1995. Is Korean Unification Possible? *Korea Focus* 3,3 (May/June): 5-21.

Lee Young-sun. 1996. Economic Integration in the Korean Peninsula: Effects and Implications. In *Korea-United States Cooperation in the New World Order*, ed. C. Fred Bergsten and SaKong Il. Washington: Institute for International Economics.

Lee Young-sun. 1997. Kim Jong-il and Economic Reform: Myth and Reality. *Korea Focus* 5, 6 (June/July): 70-83.

Leff, Nathaniel A. 1978. Industrial Organization and Entrepreneurship in the Developing Countries. *Economic Development and Cultural Change* 26,4(July): 661-675.

Leipziger, Danny. 1988. Industrial Restructuring in Korea. *World Development* 16, 1(January): 121-35.

Leipziger, Danny. 1998a. *Public and Private Interests in Korea: Views on Moral Hazard and Crisis Resolution*. Working Paper. Economic Development Institute of the World Bank.

Leipziger, Danny M. 1998b. Thinking About the World Bank and North Korea. In *Economic Integration on the Korean Peninsula*, ed. Marcus Noland. Washington: Institute for International Economics.

Leipziger, Danny M. 1999. The Global Standards and Korea's Economic Reform. Paper presented at the conference Debates on the Global Standards and Their Implications to Korea, Seoul, 1 November.

Leipziger, Danny M., And Peter A. Petri. 1993. *Korean Industrial Policy*. East Asian & Pacific Region Series, World Bank Discussion Papers 197. Washington: International Bank for Reconstruction and Development.

Levin, Norman D. 1997. What if North Korea Survives? *Survival* 39,4(Winter 1997-98): 156-74.

Lewis, George, Lisbeth Gronlund, and David Wright. 1999-2000. National Missile Defense: An Indefensible System. *Foreign Policy* 117 (Winter): 120-137.

Lewis, W. Arthur. 1954. Economic Development with Unlimited Supplies of Labour. *Manchester School* 22: 139-91.

Li, Vladimir F. 2000. North Korea and the Nuclear Nonproliferation Regime. In *The North Korean Nuclear Program*, ed. James Clay Moltz and Alexandre Y. Mansourov. New York: Routledge.

Lichtblau, Karl. 1998. Privatization of State-owned Enterprises in Former Socialist States: Lessons from the German Experience. In *Policy Priorities for the Unified Korean Economy*, ed. SaKong Il and Kim Kwang-suk. Seoul: Institute for Global Economics.

Lim Eul-chul. 1999. North Korea's Missile Program: Assessment and Future Outlook. *Korea Focus* 7,5 (September/October): 1-11.

Lim Won-hyuk. 1997. North Korea's Food Crisis. *Korea and World Affairs* 21,4 (Winter): 568-85.

Lim Won-hyuk. 1996. Preparing for Korea's Unification. Seoul: Korea Military Academy, processed (January).

Lim Young-il. 1999. *Technology and Productivity*. Cambridge: MIT Press.

Lind, Jenny. 1995. *Gambling With Globalism*. MITJP 95-07. Cambridge: MIT Program on Science Technology and Management.

Lindsey, Lawrence B. 1998. *The Benefits of Bankruptcy*. Washington: American Enterprise Institute (January).

Lindauer, David L. 1997. Introduction. In *The Strains of Economic Growth: Labor Unrest and Social Dissatisfaction in Korea*, ed. David L. Lindauer et al. Cambridge: Harvard University Press.

Lipschitz, Leslie, and Donough McDonald. 1990. *German Unification*. International Monetary Fund Occasional Paper 75. Washington: International Monetary Fund.

Lipton, David, and Jeffrey Sachs. 1990. *Creating a Market Economy in Eastern Europe: The Case of Poland*. Brookings Papers on Economic Activity 1990,1. Washington: The Brookings Institution: 75-148.

Makin John H. 1997a. *America Reflates While Asia Deflates*. Washington: American Enterprise Institute (September).

Makin, John H. 1997b. *Two New Paradigms*. Washington: American Enterprise Institute (October).

Makin, John H. 1997c. *Asian Deflation Threat Grows Ugly*. Washington: American Enterprise Institute (December).

Makin, John H. 1998. *The Painful Death of the Japanese Model*. Washington: American Enterprise Institute (January).

Mann, Catherine L. 2000. Korea and the Brave New World of Finance. *Joint U.S.-Korea Academic Studies* 10.

Mansourov, Alexandre Y. 1995. The Origins, Evolution, and Current Politics of the North Korean Nuclear Program. *The Nonproliferation Review* 2,3(Spring-Summer): 25-38.

Mansourov, Alexandre Y. 2000a. The Natural Disasters of the Mid-1990s and Their Impact on the Implementation of the Agreed Framework. In *The North Korean Nuclear Program*, ed. James Clay Moltz and Alexandre Y. Mansourov. New York: Routledge.

Mansourov, Alexandre Y. 2000b. North Korea's Negotiations with the Korean Peninsula Energy Development Organization (KEDO). In *The North Korean Nuclear Program*, ed. James Clay Moltz and Alexandre Y. Mansourov. New York: Routledge.

Mathews, Jessica. 1994. A Sound Beginning With North Korea. *Washington Post*, 21 October.

McGregor, Pat. 1998. Famine: A Simple General Equilibrium Model. *Oxford Economic Papers* 50 (October): 623-43.

McMillan, John. 1997a. Markets in Transition. In *Advances in Economics and Econometrics*, ed. David M. Kreps and Kenneth F. Wallis. Volume II. Cambridge: Cambridge University Press.

McMillan, John. 1997b. What Can North Korea Learn from China's Market Reforms? In *The System Transformation of the Transition Economies*, ed. Lee Doo-won. Seoul: Yonsei University Press.

Meade, Douglas S. 1997. The Impact of Korean Unification on North Korea, INFORUM: College Park, Maryland, processed.

Meltzer, Allan H. 1998. *Moral Hazard Goes Global: The IMF, Mexico, and Asia*. Washington: American Enterprise Institute (January).

Mertlík, Pavel. 1998. The Czech Privatization and Subsequent Structural Changes in Capital Ownership and Property Rights. *Economic Survey of Europe*, No. 2. Geneva: UN Economic Commission for Europe.

Michell, Anthony R. 1995. Reconstruction of the D.P.R.K. Beijing: Euro-Asian Business Consultancy Ltd., processed.

Michell, Anthony R. 1998. The Current North Korean Economy. In *Economic Integration of the Korean Peninsula*, ed. Marcus Noland. Washington: Institute for International Economics.

Min, Timothy J., II. 1996. North Korean Foreign Investment Laws. Washington, processed.

Ministry of Defense. 1999. *White Paper*. Seoul: Ministry of Defense.

Ministry of Unification. 1999. Price Variations in North Korea. *Korean Unification Bulletin* 13: 4-5.

Mo Jong-ryn. 1994. German Lessons for Managing the Economic Cost of Korean Unification. In *One Korea?*, ed. Thomas H. Hendricksen and Lho Kyong-soo. Stanford: Hoover Institution Press.

Moiseyev, Valentine I. 2000. The North Korean Energy Sector. In *The North Korean Nuclear Program*, ed. James Clay Moltz and Alexandre Y. Mansourov. New York: Routledge.

Moltz, James Clay. 2000. The Renewal of Russian-North Korean Relations. In *The North Korean Nuclear Program*, ed. James Clay Moltz and Alexandre Y. Mansourov. New York: Routledge.

Moon Chung-in. 1999. Korean Unification and Political & Administrative Foundation. Paper presented to the Conference on Two Koreas: Toward One Economy, Washington, 4-5 October.

Moon Chung-in. 2000. Korea and Asian Security in the 21st Century. *Asian Voices: Promoting Dialogue between the United States and Asia*. Washington: Saskawa Peace Foundation USA.

Moon Pal-yong. 1998. Agrarian Reform Scenarios for North Korea. In *Policy Priorities for the Unified Korean Economy*, ed. SaKong Il and Kim Kwang-suk. Seoul: Institute for Global Economics.

Morrison, Charles. 1999. *Asia Security Outlook 1999*. Tokyo: Japan Center for International Exchange.

Murooka, Tetsuo. 1999. North Korean Economic Policy and Implications for Japan's Economic Assistance. In *Japan and Korean Unification*, ed. Lee Young-sun and Masao Okonogi. Seoul: Yonsei University Press.

Nam Sang-woo. 1992. *Korea's Financial Reform Since the Early 1980s*. KDI Working Paper 9207 (March). Seoul: Korea Development Institute.

Nam Sang-yirl. 1999. *Total Factor Productivity Growth in Korean Industry and Its Relationship to Export Growth*. Working Paper 99-34. Seoul: Korea Institute for International Economic Policy.

Namkoong Young. 1994. Assessment of the North Korean Economy: Status and Prospects, in *US-Korean Relations at a Time of Change*. Seoul: Research Institute for National Unification.

Namkoong Young. 1995. An Analysis of North Korea's Policy to Attract Foreign Capital. *Korea and World Affairs* (Fall): 459-481.

Namkoong Young, and Yoo Ho-yeol. 1994. North Korea's Economic System. In *Prospects for Change in North Korea*, ed. Ok Tae-hwan and Lee Hong-yung. Seoul: Research Institute for National Unification.

Namkung, K.A. 1998. US Leadership in the Rebuilding of the North Korean Economy. In *Economic Integration of the Korean Peninsula*, ed. Marcus Noland. Washington: Institute for International Economics.

Natsios, Andrew. 1999. "The Politics of Famine in North Korea" *Special Report*. (2August) Washington: United States Institute of Peace.

Naughton, Barry. 1996. *China's Emergence and Prospects as a Trading Nation*. Brookings Papers on Economic Activity 2: 273-344. Washington: The Brookings Institution

Naughton, Barry. 1997. Economic Reform in China: Macroeconomic and Overall Performance. In *The System Transformation of the Transition Economies*, ed. Lee Doo-won. Seoul: Yonsei University Press.

Nellis, John. n.d. *Time To Rethink Privatization in Transition Economies?* International Finance Corporation Discussion Paper 38. Washington: International Finance Corporation.

Niksch, Larry. 1996. North Korean Food Shortages: U.S. and Allied Responses. CRS Report to Congress. Washington: Congressional Research Service, 11 April.

Noerper, Stephen E. 1999. Toward a New Stability: Challenges and Change on the Korean Peninsula. *Northeast Asia Peace and Security Network (NAPSNET) Special Report* (3 June).

Noland, Marcus. 1990. Prospective Changes in Japan's Trade Pattern. *Japan and the World Economy* 2 (September): 211-238.

Noland, Marcus. 1991a. *Pacific Basin Developing Countries: Prospects for the Future*. Washington: Institute for International Economics.

Noland, Marcus. 1991b. Prospective Changes in the Commodity Composition of U.S.-Korea Trade. *Joint U.S.-Korea Academic Studies* 1.

Noland, Marcus. 1993a. Selective Intervention and Growth: The Case of Korea. Washington: Institute for International Economics, processed.

Noland, Marcus. 1993b. The Origins of U.S.-Korea Trade Frictions. In *Shaping a New Relationship: The Republic of Korea and the United States*, ed. Mo Jong-ryn and Ramon H. Myers. Stanford: Hoover Institution Press.

Noland, Marcus 1996. *Restructuring the Korean Financial System for Greater Competitiveness*. Working Papers in Asia-Pacific Economic Cooperation 96-14. Washington: Institute for International Economics.

Noland, Marcus. 1998a. Introduction. In *Economic Integration of the Korean Peninsula*, ed. Marcus Noland. Washington: Institute for International Economics.

Noland, Marcus. 1998b. U.S.-South Korea Economic Relations. In *The U.S. and the Two Koreas*, ed. Park Tong-whan. Boulder: Lynne Rienner.

Noland, Marcus. 1998c. The External Economic Relations of North Korea and Prospects for Reform. In *North Korean Foreign Relations*, ed. Samuel S. Kim. Hong Kong: Oxford University Press.

Noland, Marcus, and L. Gordon Flake. 1997. Opening Attempt: North Korea and the Rajin-Sonbong Free Economic and Trade Zone. *Journal of Asian Business* 13, 2 (Spring): 99-116.

Noland, Marcus, LiGang Liu, Sherman Robinson, and Zhi Wang. 1999. *Global Economic Effects of the Asian Currency Devaluations* (revised). Washington: Institute for International Economics.

Noland, Marcus, Sherman Robinson, and LiGang Liu. 1998. The Costs and Benefits of Korean Unification. *Asian Survey* XXXVIII, 8 (August): 801-814.

Noland, Marcus, Sherman Robinson, and LiGang Liu. 1999. The Economics of Korean Unification. *Journal of Policy Reform* 3: 255-99.

Noland, Marcus, Sherman Robinson, and Monica Scatasta. 1997. Modeling North Korean Economic Reform. *Journal of Asian Economics* 8, 1 (April): 15-38.

Noland, Marcus, Sherman Robinson, and Tao Wang. 2000a. Rigorous Speculation: The Collapse and Revival of the North Korean Economy. *World Development*. forthcoming (September).

Noland, Marcus, Sherman Robinson, and Tao Wang. 2000b. Famine In North Korea: Causes and Cures. *Economic Development and Cultural Change*. forthcoming.

Noland, Marcus, Sherman Robinson, and Tao Wang. 2000c. Modeling Korean Unification. *Journal of Comparative Economics*. forthcoming (June).

Nölling, Wilhelm 1994. Comment. In *The Transition in Eastern Europe Volume 2, ed.* Olivier Jean Blanchard, Kenneth A. Froot, and Jeffrey D. Sachs. Chicago: University of Chicago Press: 208-211.

North Korean Advisory Group. 1999. *Report to the Speaker of the U.S. House of Representatives.* http://www.house.gov./international_relations/nkag/report.htm (November).

O Won-chol. 1995. A Response to North Korea's Food Crisis. Revised and edited English translation of *Ssalboda nonsabop wonjo p'ilyo Sin Tong-A* (September): 460-476. Canberra: Australian National University.

Oberdorfer, Don. 1997. *The Two Koreas.* Reading: Addison-Wesley.

Organization of Economic Cooperation and Development (OECD). 1996. *OECD Economic Surveys Korea.* Paris: OECD.

Organization of Economic Cooperation and Development (OECD). 1998. *OECD Economic Surveys Korea.* Paris: OECD.

Organization of Economic Cooperation and Development (OECD). 1999. *OECD Economic Surveys Korea.* Paris: OECD

Oh Kong-dan, and Ralph Hassig. 1999. North Korea Between Collapse and Reform. *Asian Survey* 39,2 (March/April): 287-309.

Oh Seung-yul. 1993. Economic Reform in North Korea: Is China's Reform Model Relevant to North Korea? *The Korean Journal of National Unification* 2: 127-151.

Oh Seung-yul. 1996. Prospects for Economic Reforms in North Korea and Policy Recommendations. *The Korean Journal of National Unification* 5: 133-151.

O'Hanlon, Michael. 1999. Star Wars Strikes Back. *Foreign Affairs* 78, 6 (November/December): 68-82.

Okonogi, Masao. n.d. Korean Unification and Japan's Position. Tokyo: Keio University, processed.

Pacific Economic Cooperation Council (PECC). 1995. *Survey of Impediments to Trade and Investment in the APEC Region.* Singapore: APEC Secretariat.

Pack, Howard, and Larry E. Westphal. 1986. Industrial Strategy and Technological Change: Theory versus Reality. *Journal of Development Economics* 22,1 (June): 87-128.

Paek Tae-youl. 1999. Korean Unification and Japan's Foreign Policy. In *Japan and Korean Unification,* ed. Lee Young-Sun and Masao Okonogi. Seoul: Yonsei University Press.

Paik Hak-soon. 1999. Comments by Haksoon Paik. *Nautilus Policy Forum Online* (#99-07), Berkeley: Nautilus Institute. (28 September).

Park Chan-bong. 1997. The Prospects for Political Reform and Transitional Justice in North Korea. Seoul: Ministry of National Unification, processed.

Park Han-shik. 1993. North Korea's Ideology and Unification Policy. In *The Prospects for Korean Unification, ed.* Jay Speakman and Lee Chae-jin. Claremont: Keck Center for International and Strategic Studies.

Park, Han S. 1998. Human Needs, Human Rights, and Regime Legitimacy. In *Understanding Regime Dynamics in North Korea,* ed. Moon Chung-in. Seoul: Yonsei University Press.

Park Jin. 1997. The Economic Impacts of Migration After Unification. Seoul: Korea Development Institute, processed.

Park Jin. 1998. Inter-Korean Economic Relations in the IMF Era. *Korea Focus* (March-April): 66-80.

Park Jin-soo. 1999. Household Income Up, But Many hardships Remain. *Korean Business Review* 224 (December): 16-18.

Park Se-il. 1990. Industrial Relations Policy in Korea: Its Features and Problems. In *Korean Economic Development,* ed. Jene K. Kwon. New York: Greenwood Press.

Park Se-il. 1999a. Remarks at the Brookings Institution. Washington (5 April).

Park Se-Il. 1999b. Labor Market Reform and the Social Safety Net in Korea. *Joint U.S.-Korea Academic Studies* 9: 201-20.

Park Seung-rok and Jene K. Kwon. 1995. Rapid Economic Growth with Increasing Returns to Scale and Little or No Productivity Growth. *Review of Economics and Statistics* 77, 2 (May): 332-51.

Park Yoon-shik. 1999. Financial Sector Restructuring in Korea. *Korea's Economy 1999,* 15: 27-31.

Park Young-ho. 1996. North Korea's Food Supply Situation. *Korea Focus* 4, 1 (January/February): 36-45.

Park, Yung Chul, 1995. "Korea's Experience with Managing Foreign Capital Flows." Korea University and Korea Institute of Finance, September, processed.

Park, Yung Chul and Chi-Young Song. 1996. *Managing Foreign Capital Flows: The Experiences of Korea, Thailand, Malaysia and Indonesia*. Jerome Levy Economics Institute Working Papers No. 163. Annandale-on-Hudson: Bard College, May.

Park Yung-chul, and Song Chi-young. 1998. The East Asian Crisis: A Year Later. Paper presented to the East Asian Workshop, Institute of Development Studies, University of Sussex (13 July).

Patrick, Hugh. 1991. *Peace and Security on the Korean Peninsula: Reflections on the Economic Dimension*. Working Paper Series 56. Center on Japanese Economy and Business, Graduate School of Business, Columbia University.

Payne, Keith B. 2000. *National Missile Defense: Why Now?* WIRE 8:1. Philadelphia: Foreign Policy Research Institute.

Perkovich, George. 1994. The Korea Precedent. *Washington Post*, 28 September.

Perl, Raphael. 1999. North Korean Drug Trafficking: Allegations and Issues for Congress. Congressional Research Service (9 March), processed.

Perry, William J. 1999. *Review of United States Policy Toward North Korea: Findings and Recommendations*. http://www.state.gov /regions/eap/991012_northkorea_rpt.html.

Pilkington, Jeffrey S. 1998. Refugee Issues Relating to Three Scenarios for the Future of the Korean Peninsula. In *Economic Integration on the Korean Peninsula*, ed. Marcus Noland. Washington: Institute for International Economics.

Pollack, Jonathan, and Lee Chung-min. 1999. *Preparing for Korean Unification*. Santa Monica: RAND.

Pyo Hak-kil. 1989. Export-led Growth, Domestic Distortions, and Trade Liberalization. Paper presented at the United States-Korea Financial Policy Discussions, Washington (12 December).

Pyo Hak-kil. 1999. *The Financial Crisis in Korea and Its Aftermath: A Political-economic Perspective*. Seoul National University, processed.

Quinones, Kenneth. 1997. The Agricultural Situation in North Korea. *Korea's Economy 1997*, 13: 97-103.

Quinones, C. Kenneth. 1998. North Korea's New Nuclear Site—Fact or Fiction? *International Journal of Korean Studies* 2,1 (Fall/Winter): 45-51.

Ravallion, Martin. 1987. *Markets and Famines*. Oxford: Clarendon Press.

Reese, David. 1998. The Prospects for North Korea's Survival. *Adelphi Paper* 323. International Institute for Strategic Studies. Oxford: Oxford University Press.

Reiss, Mitchell. 2000. Testimony before the Committee on International Relations, U.S. House of Representatives, 16 March.

Research Institute on National Unification (RINU). 1996. *White Paper on Human Rights in North Korea 1996*. Seoul: RINU.

Rhee, Yung-whee, Bruce Ross-Larsen, and Gary Purcell, 1984. *Korea's Competitive Edge: Managing the Entry into World Markets*. Baltimore: Johns Hopkins University Press.

Rhee, Yung-whee, 1989. "Managing Entry into International Markets: Lessons from the East Asian Experience." Paper presented at the Seminar on Manufactured Export Expansion of Industrializing Countries in East Asia, Hong Kong, 7-9 June.

Rhee Yung-whee. 1994. Managing Entry into International Markets: Lessons from the East Asian Experience. In *Manufactured Exports of East Asian Industrializing Economies*, ed. Yang Shu-chin. Armonk: M.E. Sharpe: 53-84.

Riedel, James. 1993. Vietnam: On the Trail of the Tigers. *World Economy* 16, 4 (July): 401-422.

Robinson, Joan. 1974. Korea, 1964: Economic Miracle. Originally published in the *Monthly Review*, January 1965, reprinted in *Collected Papers Volume 3*. Oxford: Basil Blackwell.

Robinson, Sherman, Andrea Cattaneo, and Moataz El-Said. 1998. *Estimating a Social Account-ing Matrix Using Cross-Entropy Methods*. Trade and Macroeconomics Division Discussion Paper 33. Washington: International Food Policy Research Institute.

Robinson, W. Courtland, Lee Myung-ken, Kenneth Hill, and Gilbert Burnham. Mortality in North Korean Migrant Households: A Retrospective Study. *Lancet 354* (July-December 1999): 291-295.

Roy, Denny. 1998. North Korea as an Alienated State. *Survival* 38,4: 22-36.

Rummel, Ole J. 1997. Why East Germany Failed to Become an Economic Tiger: Sobering Convergence Lessons from German Unification. *Economic Policy in Transition Economies* 7, 3: 37-65.

Sachs, Jeffrey. 1995. Reforms in Eastern Europe and the Former Soviet Union in Light of the East Asian Experience. *Journal of the Japanese and International Economies* 9 (December): 454-85.

Sachs, Jeffrey, and Woo Wing Thye. 1994. Structural Factors in the Economic Reforms of China, Eastern Europe, and the Former Soviet Union. *Economic Policy* 18 (April): 101-145.

SaKong Il. 1993. *Korea in the World Economy*. Washington: Institute for International Eco-nomics.

SaKong Il, and Kim Kwang-suk. 1998. Introduction and Summary. In *Policy Priorities for the Unified Korean Economy*, ed. SaKong Il and Kim Kwang-suk. Seoul: Institute for Global Economics.

Sato, Katsumi. 1993. Japan: Stop funding KIS! *Far Eastern Economic Review* (29 July).

Scalapino, Robert A. 1992. Trends in North-South Relations: An External Perspective. *RINU Newsletter* 1:1.

Scalapino, Robert A. n.d. China and Korean Reunification—A Neighbor's Concerns. Berke-ley: University of California, Berkeley, processed.

Schalk, Hans J., and Gerhard Untiedt. 1996. *Technologie im neoklassichen Wachstumsmodell: Effekte auf Wachstum und Konvergenz. Jahrbücher für Nationalokönomie und Statistik* 215, 5 (September): 562-85.

Scheremet, Wolfgang, and Rudolf Zwiener. 1994. The Economic Impacts of German Unifica-tion. Paper presented at the KDI-DIW Joint Seminar on The German Economy Four Years After Unification and Its Implication for Korea, Seoul (12 May).

Sen, A.K. 1981. *Poverty and Famines: An essay on entitlement and depression*. Oxford: Claren-don Press.

Shin Dong-gyun. 1999. Labor Market Reform. *Korea's Economy 1999* 15: 39-42.

Shin In-seok, and Wang Yun-jong. 1999. *How to Sequence Capital Market Liberalization: Lessons from the Korean Experience*. Working Paper 99-30. Seoul: Korea Institute for International Economic Policy.

Shin Sang-jin. 1999. Pyongyang-Beijing Relations and China's Policy Toward North Korea. *Vantage Point* 22, 4(April): 38-47.

Shirk, Susan L. 1995. Beyond Particularism: The Challenges of the Next Stage of China's Foreign Economic Reforms. *Joint U.S.-Korean Academic Studies* 5: 115-144.

Shishido, Shuntaro, and Mitsuru Hamada. 1998. Northeast Asia in the 21st Century—Per Capita Income and the Real Scale of the Economy in the year 2025 as a Macro-Economic Framework. *ERINA Report* 24. 2-7. Niigata: The Economic Research Institute for North-east Asia.

Sigal, Leon V. 1998a. *Disarming Strangers*. Princeton: Princeton University Press.

Sigal, Leon V. 1998b. For Sale: North Korea's Missile Program, processed.

Sigal, Leon V. 1999. Cooperative Security with North Korea. In *Mixing Honey and Vinegar: Incentives, Sanctions, and Foreign Policy*, ed. Richard Haass and Meghan O'Sullivan. Washington: The Brookings Institution. forthcoming.

Sinn, Gerlinde, and Hans-Werner Sinn. 1992. *Jumpstart*. Cambridge: MIT Press.

Sinn, Gerlinde, and Hans-Werner Sinn. 1996. What Can Korea Learn from German Unifica-tion? In *Middle Powers in the Age of Globalization*, ed. Hwang Byong-moo and Yoon

Young-kwan. KAIS International Conference Series 5. Seoul: Korean Association of International Studies.

Sinn, Hans-Werner. 1995. Staggering Along: wages policy and investment support in East Germany. *Economics of Transition* 3, 4 (December): 403-26.

Smith, Heather. 1998. The Food Economy: Catalyst for Collapse? In *Economic Integration of the Korean Peninsula*, ed. Marcus Noland. Special Report 10. Washington: Institute for International Economics.

Smith, Heather and Yiping Huang. 2000. What Caused North Korea's Agricultural Crisis, Canberra: Australian National University, processed.

Snyder, Scott. 1997. *North Korea's Decline and China's Strategic Dilemmas*. Washington: United States Institute for Peace (October).

Snyder, Scott. 1999a. Personal communication (10 July).

Snyder, Scott. 1999b. *Negotiating on the Edge: North Korean Negotiating Behavior*. Washington: United States Institute for Peace.

Soltwedel, Rüdiger. 1998. Restructuring the Manufacture (sic) Sector: The Experience from United Germany. In *Policy Priorities for the Unified Korean Economy*, ed. SaKong Il and Kim Kwang-suk. Seoul: Institute for Global Economics.

Son Chu-whan. 1999. North Korean Refugees: Problems and Considerations. *Korea Focus* 7,3: 1-12.

Steinberg, David I. 1998. South Korea: Preparations Awaiting Unification—The Political Components. In *Economic Integration on the Korean Peninsula*, ed. Marcus Noland. Washington: Institute for International Economics.

Stewart, Frances. 1986. Food Aid: Pitfalls and Potential. *Food Policy* 11, 3 (November): 11-22.

Stiglitz, Joseph E. 1994. *Whither Socialism?* Cambridge: MIT Press.

Stiglitz, Joseph E. 1998. More Instruments and Broader Goals: Moving Toward a Post-Washington Consensus. *WIDER Annual Lectures 2*. Helsinki: WIDER.

Stiglitz, Joseph E. 1999. The Korean Miracle: Growth, Crisis, and Recovery. Paper presented to the International Conference on Economic Crisis and Restructuring in Korea, Seoul, Korea (3 December).

Suh Dae-sook. 1988. *Kim Il Sung*. New York: Columbia University Press.

Suh Jae-jean. 1998. Class Conflict and Regime Crisis in North Korea. In *Understanding Regime Dynamics in North Korea*, ed. Moon Chung-in. Seoul: Yonsei University Press.

Suh Jae-jean, and Kim Byoung-lo. 1994. Prospects for Change in the Kim Jong-Il Regime. *Series No. 2 Policy Studies Report*. Seoul: The Research Institute for National Unification (RINU) (3 December).

Summers, Lawrence H. 1999. The Right Kind of IMF For a Stable Global Financial System. Remarks to the London School of Business, London (14 December).

Summers, Robert, and Alan Heston. 1991. *Penn World Tables (Mark 5.6)*, Quarterly Journal of Economics, 106:2 327-68.

Takesada, Hideshi. 1997. The North Korean Military Threat Under Kim Jong Il. In *North Korea After Kim Il Sung*, ed. Thomas H. Hendriksen and Mo Jong-ryn. Stanford: Hoover Institute Press.

Takesada, Hideshi. n.d. Civil-Military Relations in North Korea, processed.

Tarullo, Daniel. 1996. "US-Korea Economic Relations." In C. Fred Bergsten and Il SaKong, *Korea-United States Cooperation in the New World Order*. Washington: Institute for International Economics.

Thimann, Christian, and M.H. Breitner. (1995). Eastern Germany and the Conflict between Wage Adjustment, Investment, and Employment: A Numerical Analysis. *Weltwirtschaftliches Archiv* 131, 3: 446-69.

Tismaneanu, Vladimir. 1993. The Quasi-Revolution and Its Discontents: Emerging Political Pluralism in Post-Ceauşescu Romania. *East European Politics and Societies* 7, 2(Spring): 309-48.

Trigubenko, M. (1991), "Industry of the DPRK". Paper presented at Korea Development Institute Symposium, Seoul, ROK, October, 1991. Quoted in The Economist Intelligence Unit (1993?), China, North Korea Country Profile 1992-1993. The Economist Intelligence Unit, London, United Kingdom.

UNCTAD. 1994. Handbook of International Trade and Development Statistics. Geneva: United Nations Commission on Trade and Development.

UNDP. 1994. Human Development Report. New York: United Nations Development Program.

UNDP. 1998. Thematic Roundtable on Agricultural Recovery and Environmental Protection in DPR Korea, Geneva: United Nations Development Program. (28-29 May), processed.

UNESCO. 1993. Statistical Yearbook. Geneva: United Nations Economic, Social, and Cultural Organization.

United States Arms Control and Disarmament Agency. 1998. World Military Expenditures and Arms Transfers 1993-94. Washington: Department of State.

United States Department of State. 1999. Democratic People's Republic of Korea Country Report on Human Rights Practices for 1998. Bureau of Democracy, Human Rights, and Labor (26 February).

United States Trade Representative (USTR). 1995. 1995 National Trade Estimate Report on Foreign Trade Barriers, Washington: USTR.

United States Trade Representative (USTR). 1997. 1997 National Trade Estimate Report on Foreign Trade Barriers, Washington: USTR.

United States Trade Representative (USTR). 1999. 1999 National Trade Estimate Report on Foreign Trade Barriers, Washington: USTR.

Vogel, Ezra F., and David L. Lindauer. 1997. Toward A Social Compact for South Korean Labor. In The Strains of Economic Growth: Labor Unrest and Social Dissatisfaction in Korea, ed. David L. Lindauer et al. Cambridge: Harvard University Press.

von Cramon-Taubadel, Stephen. 1998. The Transformation of Agriculture in East Germany and Central Eastern Europe: Lessons for North Korea. In Policy Priorities for the Unified Korean Economy, ed. SaKong Il and Kim Kwang-suk. Seoul: Institute for Global Economics.

von Hagen, Jürgen. 1997. East Germany. In Going Global, ed. Padma Desai. Cambridge: MIT Press.

Von Hippel, David, and Peter Hayes. 1995. DPRK Energy Efficiency Scoping Study: Report on Work in Progress. Paper presented at the Symposium on North Korea and Prospects for Korean Unification, University of California at San Diego, LaJolla (25-27 May).

Von Hippel, David, and Peter Hayes. 1998. DPRK Energy Sector: Current Status and Scenarios for 2000 and 2005. In Economic Integration of the Korean Peninsula, ed. Marcus Noland. Special Report 10. Washington: Institute for International Economics.

Wang Yun-jong, and Zang Hyoung-soo. 1998. Adjustment Reforms in Korea since the Financial Crisis. Policy Paper 98-02. Seoul: Korea Institute for International Economic Policy.

Watrin, Christian. 1998. Monetary Integration and Stabilization Policy: The German Case. In Policy Priorities for the Unified Korean Economy, ed. SaKong Il and Kim Kwang-suk. Seoul: Institute for Global Economics.

Westphal, Larry E., Yung W. Rhee, and Garry Purcell. 1981. Korean Industrial Competence: Where it Came From. World Bank Staff Working Paper 469. Washington: International Bank for Reconstruction and Development.

Westphal, Larry E., and Kim Kwang-suk. 1982. Korea, in Bela Balassa and associates, Development Strategies for Semi-Industrial Economies. Baltimore: Johns Hopkins University Press.

Westphal, Lawrence, Linsu Kim, and Carl Dahlman. 1985. "Reflections on Korea's Acquisition of Technological Capability," in Nathan Rosenberg and Claudio Frischtak, eds. International Technology Transfer. New York: Praeger.

Wickham, John A. 1999. Korea on the Brink: From the '12/12 Incident' to the Kwangju Uprising, 1979-1980. Washington: The National Defense University Press.

Williams, James H., Peter Hayes, and David Von Hippel. 1999. Fuel and Famine: North Korea's Rural Energy Crisis. Paper presented to the Pentagon Study Group on Japan and Northeast Asia, Washington (22 October).

Wolf, Holger. 1998. Korean Unification: Lessons from Germany. In *Economic Integration of the Korean Peninsula*, ed. Marcus Noland. Washington: Institute for International Economics.

Woo Jung-en. 1991. *Race to the Swift*. New York: Columbia University Press.

Woo Wing Thye, Wen Hai, Yibiao Jin, and Gang Fan. 1994. How Successful Has Chinese Enterprise Reform Been? *Journal of Comparative Economics* 18, 3(June): 410-37.

World Bank. 1985. *China: Economic Structure and International Perspective*. Washington: International Bank for Reconstruction and Development.

World Bank. 1996. *World Development Report 1996*. Washington: International Bank for Reconstruction and Development.

World Food Program. 1996a. Special Alert No. 267. Rome: World Food Program (May).

World Food Program. 1996b. Special Report: FAO/WFP Crop and Food Supply Assessment Mission to the Democratic People's Republic of Korea. Rome: World Food Program (6 December).

Yanagita, Tatuo. 1999. IMF Conditionality and the Korean Economy in the Late 1990s. Paper presented at the Brookings Institution, Washington (5 April).

Yang Jun-sok. 2000. Korea's Trade Relations: Conflict and Opportunity. *Joint U.S.-Korea Academic Studies* 10: 105-38.

Yang Un-chul. 1998a. The Political Economy of Korean Unification. In *The Political Economy of Korean Unification*, ed. Yang Un-chul. Seoul: The Sejong Institute.

Yang Un-chul. 1998b. Investment Needs for Korean Unification: Ideal and Reality. Paper presented at National Bureau for Asian Research conference, Washington (19-23 October).

Yeon Ha-cheong. 1993a. *Practical Means to Improve Intra-Korean Trade and Economic Cooperation*. KDI Working Paper 9301. Seoul: Korea Development Institute (January).

Yeon Ha-cheong. 1993b. *Economic Consequences of German Unification and Its Policy Implications for Korea*. KDI Working Paper 9303. Seoul: Korea Development Institute (April).

Yeon Ha-cheong. 1994. Economic Consequences of German Unification and its Policy Implications for Korea. *Perspectives of Global Responsibility*. New York: InterAction Council.

Yoo Jong-goo. 1990. Income Distribution in Korea. In *Korean Economic Development*, ed. Jene K. Kwon. New York: Greenwood Press.

Yoo Jung-ho. 1993. The Political Economy of Protection Structures in Korea. In *Trade and Protectionism*, ed. Takatoshi Ito and Anne O. Krueger. Chicago: University of Chicago Press.

Yoo Jung-ho, Sung-hoon Hong, and Jae-ho Lee. 1993. *Korea's Industrial Protection and Distortion of Incentive System*. Seoul: Korea Development Institute [In Korean].

Yoo Jung-ho. 1994. South Korea's Manufactured Exports and Industrial Targeting Policy. In *Manufactured Exports of East Asian Industrializing Economies*, ed. Yang Shu-Chin. Armonk: ME Sharpe.

Yoo Seong-min. 1995. Korean Business Conglomerates: Misconceptions, Realities, and Policies. *Korea's Economy 1995*. Washington: Korea Economic Institute of America.

Yoo Seong-min. 1999. Corporate Restructuring in Korea. *Joint U.S.-Korea Academic Studies* 9: 131-199.

Yoo Young-ock. 1996. North Korean Economic Situation, and the Possibilities for South-North Economic Cooperation. *East Asian Review* VIII, (Spring) 1: 62-78.

Yoon Deok-ryong. 1999. Economic Effects of the Development of Industrial Complexes in North Korea and Strategies for Successful Development. *The Economics of Korean Unification* 4,2: 139-53.

You Jong-kuen. 1999. Paradigm Shift in Korea. *U.S.-Korea Academic Studies* 9: 9-20.

Young Soo gil. 1989. Korean Trade Policy. In *Economic Relations Between the United States and Korea: Conflict or Cooperation?* ed. Thomas O. Bayard and Young Soo gil. Washington: Institute for International Economics.

Young Soo gil. 1997. The End of Korea's Economic Miracle? Paper presented at the Congressional Roundtable luncheon, Washington (30 April).

Young Soo gil, Lee Chang-jae, and Zang Hyoung-soo. 1998. Preparing for Economic Integration of Two Koreas: Policy Challenges to South Korea. In *Economic Integration of the Korean Peninsula*, ed. Marcus Noland. Washington: Institute for International Economics.

Yu Suk-ryul. 1997. Problems for Korean Reunification. Paper presented at the Joint Conference of the Council for U.S.-Korean Security Studies and the International Council On Korean Studies, Arlington, Virginia (4-23 October).

Yun Mi-kyung. 2000. Foreign Direct Investment: A Catalyst for Change? *Joint U.S.-Korean Academic Studies* 10: 139-74.

Zacek, Jane Shapiro. 1998. Russia in North Korean Foreign Policy. In *North Korean Foreign Relations*, ed. Samuel S. Kim. Hong Kong: Oxford University Press.

Zhebin, Alexander. 2000. A Political History of Soviet-North Korean Nuclear Cooperation. In *The North Korean Nuclear Program*, ed. James Clay Moltz and Alexandre Y. Mansourov. New York: Routledge.

Appendix

Agreed Framework between
the United States of America and
the Democratic People's Republic of Korea

Geneva, October 21, 1994

Delegations of the Government of the United States of America (U.S.) and the Democratic People's Republic of Korea (DPRK) held talks in Geneva from September 23 to October 21, 1994, to negotiate an overall resolution to the nuclear issue on the Korean Peninsula.

Both sides reaffirmed the importance of attaining the objectives contained in the August 12, 1994 Agreed Statement between the U.S. and the DPRK and upholding the principles of the June 11, 1993 Joint Statement of the U.S. and the DPRK to achieve peace and security on a nuclear-free Korean peninsula. The U.S. and the DPRK decided to take the following actions for the resolution of the nuclear issue:

I. Both sides will cooperate to replace the DPRK's graphite-moderated reactors and related facilities with light-water reactor (LWR) power plants.

1) In accordance with the October 20, 1994 letter of assurance from the U.S. President, the U.S. will undertake to make arrangements for the provision to the DPRK of a LWR project with total generating capacity of approximately 2,000 MW(e)[1] by the target date of 2003.

---

1. MW(e) refers to megawatts of electricity.

—The U.S. will organize under its leadership an international consortium to finance and supply the LWR project to be provided to the DPRK. The U.S., representing the international consortium, will serve as the principal point of contact with the DPRK for the LWR project.

—The U.S., representing the consortium, will make best efforts to secure the conclusion of a supply contract with the DPRK within six months of the date of this Document for the provision of the LWR project. Contract talks will begin as soon as possible after the date of this Document.

—As necessary, the U.S. and the DPRK will conclude a bilateral agreement for cooperation in the field of peaceful uses of nuclear energy.

2) In accordance with the October 20, 1994 letter of assurance from the U.S. President, the U.S., representing the consortium, will make arrangements to offset the energy foregone due to the freeze of the DPRK's graphite moderated reactors and related facilities, pending completion of the first LWR unit.

—Alternative energy will be provided in the form of heavy oil for heating and electricity production.

—Deliveries of the heavy oil will begin within three months of the date of this Document and will reach a rate of 500,000 tons annually, in accordance with an agreed schedule of deliveries.

3) Upon receipt of the U.S. assurances for the provision of LWR's and for arrangements for interim energy alternatives, the DPRK will freeze its graphite-moderated reactors and related facilities and will eventually dismantle these reactors and related facilities.

—The freeze of the DPRK's graphite-moderated reactors and related facilities will be fully implemented within one month of the date of this Document. During this one-moth period, and throughout the freeze, the International Atomic Energy Agency (IAEA) will be allowed to monitor this freeze, and the DPRK will provide full cooperation to the IAEA for this purpose.

—Dismantlement of the DPRK's graphite-moderated reactors and related facilities will be completed when the LWR project is completed.

—The U.S. and the DPRK will cooperate in finding a method to store safely the spent fuel from the 5MW(e) experimental reactor during the construction of the LWR project, and to dispose of the fuel in a safe manner that does not involve reprocessing in the DPRK.

4) As soon as possible after the date of this Document U.S. and DPRK experts will hold two sets of expert talks.

—At one set of talks, experts will discuss issues related to alternative energy and the replacement of the graphite-moderated reactor program with the LWR project.

—At the other set of talks, experts will discuss specific arrangements for spent fuel storage and ultimate disposition.

II. The two sides will move toward full normalization of political and economic relations.

1) Within three months of the date of this Document, both sides will reduce barriers to trade and investment, including restrictions on telecommunications services and financial transactions.

2) Each side will open a liaison office in the other's capital following resolution of consular and other technical issues through expert-level discussions.

3) As progress is made on issues of concern to each side, the U.S. and DPRK will upgrade bilateral relations to the Ambassadorial level.

III. Both sides will work together for peace and security on a nuclear-free Korean peninsula.

1) The U.S. will provide formal assurances to the DPRK against the threat or use of nuclear weapons by the U.S.

2) The DPRK will consistently take steps to implement the North-South Joint Declaration on the Denuclearization of the Korean Peninsula.

3) The DPRK will engage in North-South dialogue, as this Agreed Framework will help create an atmosphere that promotes such dialogue.

IV. Both sides will work to strengthen the international nuclear non-proliferation regime.

1) The DPRK will remain a party to the Treaty on the Non-Proliferation of Nuclear Weapons (NPT) and will allow implementation of its safeguards agreement under the Treaty.

2) Upon conclusion of the supply contract for the provision of the LWR project, ad hoc and routine inspections will resume under the DPRK's safeguards agreement with the IAEA with respect to the facilities not subject to the freeze. Pending conclusion of the supply contract, inspections required by the IAEA for the continuity of safeguards will continue at the facilities not subject to the freeze.

3) When a significant portion of the LWR project is completed, but before delivery of key nuclear components, the DPRK will come into full compliance with its safeguards agreement with the IAEA (INFCIRC/ 403), including taking all steps that may be deemed necessary by the IAEA, following consultations with the Agency with regard to verifying the accuracy and completeness of the DPRK's initial report on all nuclear material in the DPRK.

—*Kang Sok Ju, Head of the Delegation for the Democratic People's Republic of Korea, First Vice-minister of Foreign Affairs of the Democratic People's Republic of Korea*
—*Robert L. Gallucci, Head of the Delegation of the United States of America, Ambassador at Large of the United States of America*

Index

Aaron, David, 240n
ACDA. *See* Arms Control and
  Disarmament Agency (ACDA)
Achikzad, Faruq, 176
Action Against Hunger (ACF), 190n
ADB. *See* Asian Development Bank
  (ADB)
administrative reforms, 246-247, 352
advertising, 48-49
aerospace industry, 233, 234n
Agency for International Development
  (AID), 175
Agency for National Security Planning,
  147n
Agreed Framework, 151-158, 368
  actual text, 401-404
  congressional attitudes toward, 151-
    154, 157-158, 161-162, 339
  establishment of, 5
  evaluation of, 166-170
  light-water reactors (*See* light-water
    reactors)
  renegotiation of, 350, 370-371
  sanctions removal, 107, 108
  suspected Korean violations of, 158-
    166
Agreement on Government Procurement
  (WTO), 46
agricultural chemicals, 171
agricultural output

North Korea, 69f, 70, 84
  boosting of, 83, 87, 171n, 190-191,
    193, 253, 255, 265
  decline in, 171-172
  effect on reform, 257-259
  under general equilibrium model,
    274, 278
  lack of data on, 182
  price structure for, 253
  structural problems, 177
South Korea, 25, 26f
agricultural products
  customs clearance delays for, 44-45
  trade protection of, 41f, 41-44, 44t
agricultural wages, 177n, 277n, 304n
agriculture
  collectivization of, 63-65, 171, 177
  de-bureaucratization of, 252-253
  decollectivization of, in Romania, 329
  and Korean unification, 363
  labor-intensive, effect on reform, 257n,
    257-259, 266, 282
AID. *See* Agency for International
  Development (AID)
Aiyer, Sri-Ram, 236
Akashi, Yasushi, 164
Albright, Madeleine, 100n, 157-158, 164,
  373
alienated state, 7

American Chamber of Commerce (Korea), 109, 233
ammonium sulfate, 171
Anderson, Desaix, 11*n*, 157*n*
anticompetitive practices
  of *chaebol*, 33*n*, 33-34, 232, 353
  and German unification, 292-293
"anti-consumption" campaign, 48*n*
antidumping suits, 43
Antitrust Act, 34
Antitrust and Fair Trade Law, 50*n*
ANU. *See* Australian National University (ANU)
APEC. *See* Asia-Pacific Economic Cooperation (APEC)
appartachiks, 259-260, 326, 331, 337
"apple" class, 73
ARF. *See* Association of Southeast Asian Nations (ASEAN), Regional Forum (ARF)
Armington assumption, 269
Arms Control and Disarmament Agency (ACDA), 117-118, 131
arms trade (North Korean)
  with China, 100, 373
  incentives for, 72
  with Middle East, 117-118, 146
  missiles, 4-5, 8, 117-118
  with Soviet Union, 97-98
  statistics, 92, 93*t*, 131
ASEAN. *See* Association of Southeast Asian Nations (ASEAN)
Asia Foundation, 86
Asian Development Bank (ADB), 213*n*, 341-342, 372, 375
Asian financial crisis, 7, 207-209, 249, 284
Asia-Pacific Economic Cooperation (APEC), 44*n*
asset bubbles, 54*n*-55*n*, 58, 202, 203-208
asset prices, 204, 213
asset revaluation, 223*n*
Association of Southeast Asian Nations (ASEAN), Regional Forum (ARF), 164-165
AT&T, 108
"August 3 campaign for people's goods," 83-84
Aum Shinrikyo, 119*n*
"austerity" campaign, 48*n*
Australian National University (ANU), 86
authoritarian paternalism, 38
automobile industry. *See also specific automaker*

competitiveness concerns, 232
export/import trade, 29, 46-48, 48*n*
government intervention in, 24, 207, 234-235
liberalization of, 46-48
price weakening in, 198
automobile loan market, 48*n*, 52
automobiles, taxes on, 40

bad loans. *See* non-performing loans
baht, 7, 207
Baker, James A., 159*n*
balance of payments, North Korea, 88, 116-133
bank credit, 52
bank failure, prevention of, 53, 202, 204*n*, 212
bank financing, corporate, 32
banking aggregates, South Korea, 199, 200*t*
banking system
  North Korean, 254-255
  South Korean, 19, 49, 52-54, 199-200, 255
bank loans, South Korea, 196, 197*f*
Bank of International Settlements (BIS), 53, 196, 222, 354
Bank of Korea (BOK)
  commercial bank supervision, 53
  economic growth estimates, 79, 81, 310
  foreign exchange reserves, 7, 204*n*, 208, 212
  independence of, 222
Bank of Thailand, 7, 204*n*, 207
bankruptcy, 33, 207, 215, 231-232, 241
banks. *See also specific bank*
  commercial (*See* commercial banks)
  foreign (*See* foreign banks)
  foreign lending to, 210
  local, 204
  merchant, 52*n*, 200*n*, 214, 222, 356
  nationalization of, 214
  privatization of, 53, 201-202
  state-owned, 52, 57, 65-68
  statistical data, 224*t*-225*t*
barter trade, 89, 90, 92, 97, 109
  food, 182, 184, 189*n*
beef quotas, 41*n*-42*n*, 46
Beijing University, 86
Bell, Peter D., 190*n*
Berger, Sandy, 342
Berlin Declaration (Kim Dae-jung), 113
Berlin Wall, fall of, 286
big bang therapy. *See* shock therapy

"big deals" *(chaebol)*, 35, 232-233, 355
biological weapons, 8, 117
biomass power, 144
birth rate, and German unification, 294*n*-295*n*
BIS. *See* Bank of International Settlements(BIS)
black market
  currency exchange, 68-69
  sale of food aid on, 180
Blair, Dennis, 351
Boeing, 108
bonded warehouses, 28, 359
bond markets, 55-56, 353, 356
  corporate, 55-56, 215, 219, 226
  and economic crisis, 203, 206, 215-216, 353, 356
  foreign participation in, 56
  government, 55-56, 215-216, 225-226, 356-357, 363
  long-term, 55-56
border areas
  China-North Korea, 101, 165*n*, 187, 189, 349, 370, 373
  migration across *(See* migration; refugees)
  Russia-North Korea, 189, 374
Borlaug, Norman, 182
Bosworth, Stephen, 154, 157*n*
bribery, 35, 55, 112
British Gas, 237*n*
Brown, Mark Malloch, 165
Brzezinski, Zbigniew, 149
budget balance, and Korean unification, 307-309
Bundesbank, 292
Bureau 39, 118, 139
business training, exchange programs for, 86, 87
Buy Korea Fund (Hyundai), 115*n*, 231

caloric intake, North Korea, 179*n*, 181
Cambodia, 342*n*
CAMEL system, 53
Campbell, Kurt, 163
"9/27 camps," 183, 193
capacity utilization, 219
capital, rate of return on, 197, 280, 309, 316, 317*f*
capital account, phased liberalization of, 196, 249, 357
capital allocation, decentralization of, 254
capital channeling, 6, 19-20, 30-31, 51
capital flows, 56, 210

foreign *(See* foreign direct investment (FDI))
  and Korean unification, 303-305, 305, 306*f*-307*f*, 311-312, 313*f*
  South Korea, 56, 195-196, 197*f*, 199, 357
capital gains, on land ownership, 38*n*
capital goods imports, 93
capitalism, *versus* socialism, 286, 299
capital market discipline, need for, 354, 356
capital markets, 54-56, 215
  bolstering of, 225-226
  corruption of, 55
  and Korean unification, 301-302
capital-output ratios, North Korea, 78*t*, 80
capital stock
  and German unification, 288
  international comparisons, 78, 78*t*
  manufacturing, 28
  North Korea, 77, 77*t*
  post-liberalization, 270
  Romania, 329
Capital Structural Improvement Plans (CSIPs), 226-227
capital utilization, 29
CARE, 190*n*
Cargill grain for zinc barter deal, 109, 184*n*
carryover system, 247
cars. *See* automobiles
Carter, Jimmy, 149-150
CCEJ. *See* Citizen's Coalition for Economic Justice (CCEJ)
Ceausescu, Nicolae, 324-326, 331-332
Cédras, Raoul, 321
census, North Korean, 74, 181
central bank independence, 218
Central Intelligence Agency (CIA), 97, 160*n*, 163
centrally planned economies (CPEs), 61
  capital-output ratios, 80
  dictatorships in, 286
  financial systems of, 254
  initial economic growth in, 60*n*
  national accounting principles, 76
  North Korea debt to, 93
  North Korean trade with, 130-131
  reform experiences, 255-260, 320
  social welfare systems, 259
  turnover taxes, 71
centrally planned national accounting system, 76

central plans, 65, 66t-67t
  versus military economy, 71-73
Central State Agriculture Committee, 63
certification requirements, for imports, 46
CES. *See* constant elasticity of
    substitution (CES)
CGE models. *See* computable general
    equilibrium (CGE) models
chaebol. See also specific firm
  anticompetitive concerns, 33-34, 232,
    353
  attempted rescue of Daewoo, 239
  "big deals," 35, 232-233, 355
  "big five," 226n
  "Chairman's Office," 229, 356
  competition among, 19
  competitive policy restraints imposed
    on, 34-35, 50
  corporate financing, 31-33
  definition of, 16n
  diversification of, 30, 38
  exclusion from financial sector, 32, 356
  failure of, 205, 206, 215
  family control of, 229
  financial fragility of, 199, 217
  government rescue of, 204n, 206
  industrial involvement of, 24
  investment in North Korea, 114n
  and Korean unification, 361-362
  labor-management disputes, 36-38
  management abuses, 229-230, 231n
  manufacturing investment boom, 195-
    196
  market dominance of, 33
  and moral hazard, 205
  North Korean equivalent of, 63
  origin of, 16, 30
  ownership of, democratization of, 356-
    357
  political involvement, 35
  product market involvement, 30, 352-
    353
  ranking of, 206
  rankings of, 32n
  restructuring of, 226-238, 353
  role in Korean unification, 299n, 300
  shareholder values, 198
  share of GDP, 21, 31
  specialization of, 34-35, 232-233
  systemic defects, 33
chemical weapons, 8, 117
Chemical Weapons Convention, 8, 117n
Chiang Ching-Kuo, 334n

Chiang Kai-Shek, 334n
chicken plants, 64
Chi Haotian, 101
China
  aid to North Korea, 88, 90, 100, 121,
    130, 144, 337-338
    food, 172, 182, 187-189, 337-338
  border area with North Korea, 101,
    165n, 187, 349, 370, 373
  business training in, 86
  economic relations with North Korea,
    90-91, 99-101, 182, 187, 262
  history of relationship with Korea, 2
  investment in North Korean SEZs,
    137n, 138
  Korean policy overview, 372-374
  Korean unification policy, 321, 337,
    360, 374
  military confrontation with South
    Korea, 321
  Ministry of Foreign Trade and
    Economic Cooperation (MOFTEC),
    137n
  North Korea as tributary of, 13
  North Korean economic reform policy,
    281, 337
  North Korean refugees in, 187, 189,
    193, 303n
  nuclear program assistance, 145, 158,
    159n, 163, 165, 169n, 373
  oil/coal exports to North Korea, 99-
    100, 144
  reform experience, 255, 257-259, 281-
    282
Chin Ung-won, 63n
Chochongryun, 3n, 190n, 283n, 372
  definition of, 100
  investment in North Korea by, 102-
    105, 133
  organization of, 102n
  Park assasination attempt, 19
  repatriation project, 102n
Chohung Bank, 223, 356n
Choi Byung-mo, 246
Choi Soon-young, 235n
Chollima movement, 63n
Chong Il-Soon, 235n
Chongjin, 135
Chong Mong-hon, 265n
Chosensoren. See Chochongryun
Choson, 69
Cho Soon, 16
Chosun Computer Center, 112n

debt service to exports ratio, 94
debt workouts, corporate, 226, 228
DEC. *See* Dialogue for Economic
    Cooperation (DEC)
decentralization, 86, 247, 333, 366*n*
defection, of North Korean soldiers, 172*n*
Defense Intelligence Agency, 158
deforestation, 177, 177*n*
de Gaulle, Charles, 324
Delivery Schedule Protocol, 344
de Maizière, Lothar, 286-287, 287*n*
demanders, 266
demilitarized zone (DMZ), 114, 148-149,
    157*n*, 297
democracy
    effect on economic reform, 256-257,
        352
    and German unification, 299-300
Democratic Party (Romania), 327
Democratic People's Republic of Korea
    (DPRK). *See* North Korea
democratization pledge, 24-25
demographic data
    North Korea
        compared to East Germany, 295-296
        famine-related morbidity/mortality,
            192
        lack of, 181
    North/South comparison, 74, 74*t*
Department of Defense (DOD), 151*n*,
    153*n*, 162
Department of State, 157
deposit insurance, 53, 53*n*, 202, 212, 222-
    223
deposit taking institutions, 52
depression, East German, 287, 294*n*-295*n*,
    318-319
deregulation, 247
Deutsche Bank, 223*n*
deutsche mark, 287
Dialogue for Economic Cooperation
    (DEC), 44*n*, 47
disease, famine-related, 192-194
DMZ. *See* demilitarized zone (DMZ)
Doctors Without Borders (Medicins Sans
    Frontieres), 183, 190*n*, 193
DOD. *See* Department of Defense (DOD)
Dole, Bob, 178, 186
Dornbusch, Rudiger, 216*n*
Downer, Alexander, 164
DPRK (Democratic People's Republic of
    Korea). *See* North Korea
DRAMs, 198, 198*n*

drought, 175*n*
drug trafficking, 118-121, 131, 322*n*
duty-free imports, 18, 18*n*
Duvalier, Jean-Claude, 321
dynasticism, 62

earthworm breeding scheme, 64
East Asia-Pacific Security Strategy, 162
East Bloc. *See also specific country*
    collapse of, 4, 88, 146, 172, 286
East Germany. *See also* German
    unification
    demographic data, 295-296
economic collapse. *See* North Korean
    economic collapse
economic dislocation, during German
    unification, 296-297
economic hardship, link between
    political failure and, 332, 336*n*
Economic Planning Board (EPB), 23, 34
economic reform, North Korea. *See*
    North Korean economic reform
economic union (North-South), 261
education
    compulsory, 27*n*, 75, 75*t*
    professional, 86, 86*n*
educational attainment rates, North/
    South comparison, 75, 75*t*
Egypt, 118
Einhorn, Robert, 118
electrical power needs, North Korea, 144-
    145, 166, 171, 336
electronic countermeasures, 349
electronics industry, 248. *See also specific
    firm*
elite, North Korean, 9, 11, 73, 349
embargo, 91, 94, 107
    lifting of, 107-109, 113, 151, 157, 166,
        283-284, 342-343, 369
employment. *See also under labor*
    and German unification, 293-296
    and Korean unification, 363
    and North Korean reform scenarios,
        265, 278-280, 282-283
energy imports, North Korea, 144-145
energy usage, North Korea, 143-145, 166,
    193, 335-337
engineering market, 48
enterprise restructuring, 254
entitlement failure, 177
environmental degradation, 84, 171,
    172*n*, 177
EPB. *See* Economic Planning Board (EPB)
equity markets, 52, 203

standards and requirements for, 46-47

Inchon airport, 46*n*

income

international comparisons, 78, 78*t*

North Korean, estimation of, 77-78

present discounted value of, 309-310

income convergence, and Korean unification, 312, 364

income distribution

and German unification, 297

and Korean unification, 317*f*, 317-318

North Korea, 73, 280

South Korea, 38, 38*n*, 220, 317*f*, 317-318

Independent Accounting System, 63

industrial development, North Korea, 82*n*, 84-85, 254

Industrial Development Law, 23

industrial employment, under SAM model, 272-273

industrial employment rate, 248

industrial labor relations, 35-36, 245. *See also* labor unions

industrial output. *See also* manufacturing

North Korea, 69*f*, 70, 81, 82, 265

boosting of, 83, 87

Romanian, 329

South Korea, 248

industrial promotion policies, South Korea, 19-22

industrial waste, 102

industrial wholesale prices, 65

industries

priority, tax incentives for, 20

trade protection for, 20

infant mortality rate, North/South comparison, 74, 74*t*

inflation

Romania, 329

South Korea, 353

information flows, within enterprise, 254

infrastructure, North Korean, 84, 135, 137, 293*n*

ING Bank, 234, 256*n*

ING-Northeast Asian Bank, 67-68

inheritance tax, 229

insurance, 52, 67

deposit, 53, 53*n*, 202, 212, 222-223

investment, prior to unification, 362*n*

reform of, 49

unemployment, 244, 244*n*

insurance companies, 57, 356

interest coverage ratio, 215

interest payments, corporate, tax code and, 31*n*

interest rates, 203

deregulation of, 23, 53-54

high, 216

lowering of, 15, 19

real, 19, 20*f*, 22

Romania, 329

world, fall in, 24

inter-Korean trade

actual and natural, 262, 262*t*

comparative advantage in, 263*t*-265*t*

constructive engagement policy, 110-116, 359-360

and reform scenarios, 283

statistics, 91, 91*n*, 297, 298*t*

and unification, 363

international aid (North Korea), 13, 121-130, 122*t*-129*t*. *See also* food aid (North Korea)

from China, 88, 90, 100, 121, 130, 144, 337-338

from European Union, 121, 191

from Japan, 121, 130, 213*n*, 337-338

maintainence level, 337-338

nuclear program as leverage for, 5-6, 10, 85, 159, 168, 187, 333, 341-343, 348, 368-369

omission of data from North Korea trade figures, 92

to South Korea, 16

from United States, 13, 109-110, 213*n*

International Atomic Energy Agency (IAEA), 146-149, 151-152, 157, 343-344, 370

International Committee of Red Cross (ICRC), 175-176

International Court of Arbitration, 95, 103

international financial institutions, role in Korean peninsula, 341-342, 375

international financial system, organization of, 357

International Labor Organization (ILO), 38, 246, 354

International Monetary Fund (IMF), 354

aid to Romania, 327, 331

exchange rate policy, 208

fiscal policy demands, 217-219

and moral hazard, 205, 211

North Korean macroeconomic data, 69*f*, 69-70

North Korean membership in, 341*n*, 341-342

North Korea trade statistics, 89*n*, 90*n*
recession caused by, 219-221
role in Korean peninsula, 375
South Korea debt obligation report,
212
standby package, 7, 212-221
International Olympic Committee (IOC),
24
international trade. *See also* trade policy
North Korea (*See* North Korean
international trade)
Romania, 324-325, 330
South Korea (*See* South Korean
international trade)
investment, 49-50
foreign (*See* foreign direct investment
(FDI))
during German unification, 291
inter-Korean, 110-114
and Korean unification, 303-305,
304*n*, 309-314, 313*f*, 361-362
North Korean, decline in, 70, 70*n*
private facilities, 247-248
as share of GDP, 195
and taxation issues, 111*n*
investment boom, South Korea, 195-196,
196*f*
investment insurance, prior to
unification, 362*n*
investment market, 52, 356
investment trust companies (ITCs), 241*n*,
242, 356
IOC. *See* International Olympic
Committee (IOC)
Iran, 117*n*, 118, 146, 163*n*
Iraq, 118
irrigation system, electrically powered,
171
ivory trafficking, 118

Jang Ha-sung, 230
Japan
aid to North Korea, 121, 130, 213*n*,
337-338
food, 174, 184-185, 185*n*-187*n*, 337-
338, 372
August 1998 missile launch over, 104,
105, 147, 160*n*, 160-161, 185*n*, 340,
373
automobile exports, 47-48, 218
economic relations with North Korea,
91, 91*t*, 102-107, 198-199, 262
comparative advantage, 264*t*-265*t*
and reform scenarios, 283, 364

economic relations with South Korea,
198-199, 218
invasion by North Korean naval
vessels, 106, 161*n*
involvement in KEDO, 153-158, 160*n*,
160-161, 164-166, 283*n*, 350, 372
Korean policy overview, 371-372
Korean supporters in (*See*
Chochongryun)
Korean unification policy, 337, 361
Liberal Democratic Party (LDP), 105
national security issues, 338
normalization of North Korean
relations with, 340-341
North Korean debt to, 95, 103
North Korean military confrontation
with, 159
post-WWII compensation to Korea,
105-107, 106*n*, 283, 340, 364, 372
Social Democratic Party, 105
Japanese banks, investment in South
Korea, 197, 210
Japanese occupation, 2
Japanese *yen*
appreciation of, 24, 54*n*, 265
depreciation of, 199
J-curve pattern, 314*n*-315*n*
Jiang Zemin, 100*n*, 154*n*, 163*n*
Jinro, 206, 207
Jinro Coors, 236-237
Joint Declaration on Denuclearization of
Korean Peninsula, 147
joint venture laws, North Korean, 133
joint ventures, 233-234, 234*n*, 236-237
inter-Korean, 111-112
North Korea/Russia, 98, 98*n*
Jon In-chen, 192
juche, 61, 82, 334*n*
and economic reform, 282, 299
environmental protection ideology, 84
and foreign trade issues, 87-88
and rate of urbanization, 75
as theology, 62
juche agriculture, 64
juche calendar, 62

KAL007, Soviet downing of, 23
KAMCO. *See* Korea Asset Management
Company (KAMCO); Korea Asset
Management Corp (KAMCO)
Kanemaru, Shin, 105
Kang Bong-kyun, 236
Kang Hi-bock, 246*n*
Kang In-duk, 191*n*

remains of US soldiers from, 91, 109-110, 110n, 150n

Korean Workers' Party (KWP), 11n, 166n, 332, 334, 366
  assets controlled by, 73
  Central Committee, 59
  Fourth Central Committee, 71
  rebuilding of, 61
  Statistical Bureau, 192

Korea Society, 109
Korea Telecom, 237, 237n
Korea Tobacco and Ginseng, 237, 237n
Korea Trade Promotion Corporation (KOTRA), 17, 89, 90n, 121n, 233
Korea Transport Institute, 296
Korea University, 230
KPA. *See* Korean People's Army (KPA)
KSIC. *See* Korean Standard Industrial Classification (KSIC)
Kukje, 32n, 206
Kulloja, 59, 86, 87, 116n
Kumchangri, 158, 158n, 159, 160, 160n, 161n, 163, 168, 187, 368-369
Kumgangsan, 115n
KWP. *See* Korean Workers Party (KWP)
Kyonggi Chemical, 227

labeling, of imports, 46
labor
  prices (*See* wages)
  rate of return, 316, 317f
labor disputes, 36-37, 37f, 237, 245n, 245-246, 249, 353
  involvement of "third parties" in, 36, 38
labor force
  distribution of, 75, 76t
  North Korean, 70
labor force participation rates
  East German/North Korean comparison, 296
  women, and German unification, 293n-294n, 297
labor laws, 232
  North Korea, 136-137
  South Korea, 17-18, 36, 38-39, 244
labor market
  during German unification, 293-295, 297
  and Korean unification, 301-302, 364
  Romania, 330
labor market policy, South Korea, 35-39, 58, 243-246, 354, 359

labor movement, dualistic structure of, 36, 36n
labor relations, industrial, 35-36
labor unionization rate, 36, 37f
labor unions. *See also* industrial labor relations
  banning of, 36
  and German unification, 299-300, 319
  organization of, 17-18, 36
  reorganization of, 36
land
  rate of return on, 280
  types of, 267
land allocation
  post-flood, 267-268
  under SAM model, 272-273
land ownership
  capital gains on, 38n
  foreign, 50, 56-57
  and Korean unification, 361
  North Korea, 253, 297, 319n
land prices, 195n
land recovery, under general equilibrium model, 267, 273-276, 274f
land reform
  North Korea, 59
  South Korea, 15
land values, 38n
Laney, James, 186
layoffs, restrictions on, 38
leadership, reformist, 281n, 281-282, 300, 335
Lee Hong-koo, 110n
Lee Hun-jai, 215n, 236, 239, 240
Lee Hyong-ki, 235n
Lee Hyon-hui, 102, 102n
Lee Hyung-ja, 235n
Lee Ik-chi, 231, 231n
Lee Kun-hee, 230
Lee Kyu-sung, 242
Lee Sung-yul, 160n
Lee Teng-Hui, 334n
legal system
  abuse of, 17n
  commercial, 255
  and corporate governance, 228-229
leisure activities, commercial, in special economic zones, 138, 138n
Lemaire, Christian, 192-193
lenders, motivation of, 205, 211
lending, state banks in, 52
"let's only eat two meals a day" campaign, 172

as deterrence, 168-169, 349-350
history of, 4-5, 145-151, 167
international inspection of, 147-149,
    151-152, 157-159, 187, 343-344, 348,
    368-369
and Korean unification, 366
as leverage for international aid, 5-6,
    10, 85, 159, 168, 187, 333, 341-343,
    368-369
link to missile program, 168
missile testing, 107, 158-166
suspected sites, 158-166
US confrontation over, 5
nuclear program (South Korea), 167
Nuclear Regulatory Commission, 344
nuclear waste, 101
Nunn, Sam, 186

OB, 237
obsolescence shock, 266, 270, 273, 274f,
    277
Obuchi, Keizo, 105, 160n
O'Donnell, Eugene, Jr., 1
OECD. *See* Organization of Economic
    Cooperation and Development
    (OECD)
Office of Banking Supervision, 202
Office of Bank Supervision, 53
Office of State Affairs, 65
    Economic Bureau, 63
Ogata, Sadako, 183
oil, energy derived from, 144
oil imports, 97-98, 99n, 99-100, 100n, 144,
    336
    under KEDO, 153, 154n, 157, 163
oil prices, 24
oil refining industry, 233
oil shocks, 19, 22, 23, 249
O Kum-chol, 159n
Olympics, Seoul, 24-25
Organization of Economic Cooperation
    and Development (OECD), 198, 354
    agricultural subsidy monitoring, 42,
    43t
    financial system codes, 57
    labor law revisions, 38-39
    North Korea capital flow date, 130
    North Korea debt to, 93
    South Korean application to join, 49,
    52, 56
    stock market capitalization, 54
Organization of Petroleum Exporting
    Countries (OPEC), oil shocks, 19, 22-
    23, 249

ostmark, 287, 289
output
    during German unification, 293-296
    North Korea, 68
        composition of, 69f, 70, 277-278,
        278f-279f, 281-283
        military share of, 72, 72n
    Romania, 329, 332
    South Korea, structure of, 25, 26f
Oxfam, 190n

pachinko industry, 103n
package deal. *See* Perry report
Paek Nam-sun, 261n
Page, Trevor, 176
Pakistan, 118, 118n, 146, 163, 163n
Palestine, 342n
Palestine Liberation Organization (PLO),
    185n
Panmunjom, 148
Pareto-improving case, 258, 310
Park Chung-hee
    assassination of, 22
    chaebol under, 30
    economic policies, 16-22, 27, 51, 58
Park Chung-hoon, 98n
Park Joo-sun, 235n
Participatory Economy Committee (PEC),
    230
Party Central Committee, 83
Party of Social Democracy (PDSR), 326
patent laws, 46
PDS. *See* Public Distribution System
    (PDS)
PDV. *See* present discounted value
    (PDV)
peace dividend, 266, 274f, 277. *See also*
    military demobilization
    and Korean unification, 302n, 302-303,
    307n-308n, 307-309, 366
peasant cooperatives, 63, 177n, 179
Peasant Party (Romania), 327
PEC. *See* Participatory Economy
    Committee (PEC)
pensions, 244, 287
People's Daily, 108
People's Solidarity for Participatory
    Democracy (PSPD), 230, 246
PepsiCo, 108
per capita income
    North Korea, 60, 76-78, 78n
        comparison with East Germany, 295
    North/South comparison, 78-79, 79t,
    303, 316

North Korea, 84, 135
North Korea-Russia link, 114, 137*n*
North-South link, 114
Rajin-Sonbong special economic zone,
    67-69, 85, 88, 111-112, 114, 133, 252,
    333, 359
  infrastructure of, 137
  reforms in, 139-140
  transportation within, 135, 137
Rangoon bombing, 95
real estate, 195*n*
"real name" law, 53
recession, IMF, 219-221
Rechtsstaat, 366
"Red Banner" campaign, 85*n*
Red Cross
  German, 176
  International Committee, 175-176
  Korean National, 191*n*
reformist leadership, 281*n*, 281-282, 300,
    335
refugees, 187, 189, 193, 303*n*, 321*n*, 370,
    373
regulatory reform, 247
Regulatory Reform Commission, 247
religious cult, *juche* as, 62
remittances
  accounting identity links, 130
  estimated, 132, 132*t*
Renault, 235*n*, 238*n*, 240*n*
rents, state-generated, 15, 280*n*
rent-seeking behavior, 259-260, 280*n*
Republic of Korea (ROK). *See* South
    Korea
resource reallocation, and Korean
    unification, 309
restitution
  during German unification, 287*n*, 319,
    361
  and Korean unification, 365
retail prices, 65
retirees, ratio of workers to, 296
reunification, 9, 12, 94, 110*n*, 169
  forms of, 261
  and trade reforms, 261
Revitalization *(Yushin)* constitution, 19
Rha Woong-bae, 184
Rhee, Syngman, 15-16, 16, 22, 36
rice, trade protection, 42*n*, 44*t*
rice imports, 185, 185*n*
rice production, 267, 274, 277*n*, 278
rice rationing, 179, 179*t*, 181, 276
Richardson, Bill, 186

rioting, 22, 24, 172
risk, socialization of, 30-31
Robertson, Pat, 335*n*
Robinson, Joan, 60
Robinson, Mary, 183
Rodong Sinmun, 59, 86, 87, 116*n*, 171*n*,
    183*n*
Roh Tae-woo, 7, 23*n*, 97
  democratization pledge, 24-25
  election of, 24
  labor law under, 36-38
  relations with North, 147*n*
ROK (Republic of Korea). *See* South
    Korea
Roman, Petre, 326
Romania, 323-331
  after Ceausescu, 326-327
  under Ceausescu, 324-326
  economic policy and performance,
    327*f*, 327-331, 328*t*, 332-333
  foreign debt, 325
  foreign policy independence, 324
  relevance for North Korea, 331-333,
    337
Russia
  aid from South Korea, 99
  border area with North Korea, 189, 374
  economic relations with North Korea,
    91, 91*t*, 95-99
  history of relationship with Korea, 2
  Korean policy overview, 374-375
  North Korea refugees in, 187, 189
  reform experience, 258-259
Rybczynski effect, 268, 268*n*
Ryugyong Hotel, 82*n*

Safety Protocol, 344
Sakura Group, 103*n*
SAM. *See* Social Accounting Matrix
    (SAM)
Sammi Steel, 206, 207
Samsung, 24, 111, 112*n*, 231*n*
  business swaps, 232
  subsidiaries, 231*n*, 234
Samsung Electronics, 230
Samsung Life insurance, 231
Samsung Motors, 230, 235*n*, 238, 238*n*
Sanger, David E., 159*n*, 162*n*
savings rate, South Korea, 195, 196*f*
Saxton, James, 342*n*
scale economies, 27, 29, 232
Schmidt, Helmut, 299
Schwartz, Thomas, 351
Scowcroft, Brent, 150*n*

South Korean international trade, 354
    and contagion, 209
    with Japan, 198-199
    with North Korea (See inter-Korean
        trade)
    trade policy, 39-50, 218, 354, 358
    with United States, 199
South Korean National Defense White
    Paper, 350-351
South Korean National Intelligence
    Service, 93
South Korean National Unification
    Board, 182
South Korean policymakers, importance
    of, 27
South Koreans
    travel to North Korea by, 115, 116f
    view of unification, 300-301
South Korean Unification Ministry, 172n,
    191n, 192, 280
South Korea/US joint military
    maneuvers, North Korean reaction
    to, 72n, 147n, 349
Soviet Union
    collapse of, 4, 88, 88n, 90, 172, 258, 284
    downing of flight KAL007, 23
    economic relations with North Korea,
        95-99
    and German unification, 286, 286n
    joint ventures with North Korea, 98,
        98n
    mutual defense treaty with North
        Korea, 98-99
    North Korea debt repayment to, 98
    North Korean aid from, 90, 96t, 97
    nuclear program assistance, 145-146
    reform experience, 258-259
SPA. See Supreme People's Assembly
    (SPA)
spare parts, lack of, 84
special economic zones (SEZ), 133n, 133-
    140, 348, 359
    commercial leisure activities in, 138,
        138n
    Haeju District, 114, 139, 140n, 333, 336
    Rajin-Sonbong (See Rajin-Sonbong
        special economic zone)
    Shinuiju, 140n
    wages in, 135-136, 136n
specialization policy, 34-35, 34n-35n
Speth, James Gustave, 191n
Ssangyong, 111, 227n
Ssangyong Motors, 241
Standard & Poor's, 210, 211, 214, 219, 239

standards, for imports, 46-47
Standstill Agreement, 207
state banks, 52, 57
state farms, 63-64, 84, 177, 177n, 179
state-generated rents, 15
state-owned banks, North Korea, 65-68
state-owned enterprises (SOEs)
    North Korean, 61-63, 71, 254, 255
    privatization of
        in centrally planned economies, 320
        in North Korea, 254-255
        in Romania, 329n, 329-330
        in South Korea, 237n, 237-238, 247
    restructuring of, 258
        in Romania, 324
State Ownership Fund (SOF), 329n, 331
State Planning Commission, 65, 71
state-run markets, 65
Stiglitz, Joseph E., 216
stock futures contracts, quota system, 55
Stockholm International Peace Institute,
    118
stock market capitalization, 54
stock markets, 203, 207, 353
    changes, 208, 210t
    and collapse of Daewoo, 239-240
    foreign participation in, 55, 55n
    Hong Kong, 208
strike-rigging scandals, 246, 246n
strikes, banning of, 18
subcontracting, 28
submarine incidents, 85, 85n-86n, 112,
    157
Suh Sang-chul, 23
sunshine policy, 110, 112-116, 116n, 162
"Super Corn" seed, 113n, 182
Supreme People's Assembly (SPA), 87,
    100, 192
surge suppressors, 357
Syria, 117n, 118, 146
System of National Accounts (SNA),
    272n

Taechon, 146
Taepodong-1 missile, 102n, 104, 117,
    160n, 351
Taepodong-2 missile, 117, 160n, 161, 163,
    185n, 343
Taepodong-3 missile, 117
Taiwan, 101, 334n
    currency devaluation, 208
    earthquake, 248n
    exclusion from KEDO, 154n, 163
    food aid to North Korea, 187n

Tanaka, Yoshimi, 121*n*
Tang Jianxuan, 100, 165
tariff barriers, in agriculture, 41*f*, 41*n*-
    42*n*, 41-43
tariff-rate quota (TRQ) schemes, 42, 42*n*
tariff rates, cutting of, 39-40, 40*f*, 358
tax audits, and imported cars, 48*n*
tax code, and corporate interest
    payments, 31*n*
taxes
    on automobiles, 40
    increase in, 217-218
    inheritance, 229
    and investment issues, 111*n*
    and Korean unification, 309, 318, 362*n*-
        363*n*
    luxury, 40
    personal, North Korea, 71*n*
    turnover, 71, 268*n*
    wage, North Korea, 71*n*
tax incentives, for priority industries, 20
tax policies
    and debt, 31*n*, 54*n*
    South Korean, 356
tax treaties, 105
technical assistance
    to North Korea, 97, 100
    provided by North Korea, 117*n*, 117-
        118, 146
technological change (North Korea), 85,
    255
    and economic reform, 269
    and Korean unification, 303, 310-313,
        312, 313*f*
technology transfer, 28, 28*n*, 29, 108, 269
telecommunications channels, US/North
    Korea, 107
telecommunications system, North
    Korean, 84, 135
Tenet, George, 163
terms of trade, South Korea, 198
terrorism, 8, 23, 23*n*, 95, 365, 369
testing, of imports, 46
TFP. *See* total factor productivity (TFP)
Thai *baht*, 7, 207, 212*n*
Thailand, 184*n*, 204*n*, 207*n*
Theatre Missile Defense (TMD), 160, 373
"third parties," involvement in labor
    disputes, 36, 38
"three blessings," 24
"three firsts," 83, 87, 171*n*
"three lows," 15
Tokai Shoji, 103

"tomato" class, 73
Tonggook Synthetic Fibers, 227*n*
total factor productivity (TFP), 21, 29,
    197-198
    and Korean unification, 304, 310, 313*n*
    and North Korean economic reform,
        267, 269, 273, 274*n*, 274*f*, 276-277
tourism projects. *See* Mt. Kumgang
    tourism project
trademark laws, 46
trade policy
    and Korean unification, 363
    North Korea, 88-116, 268-269, 273, 274*f*,
        276, 281
    South Korea, 39-50, 218, 354, 358
trade protection
    agricultural products, 41*f*, 41*n*-42*n*, 41-
        44, 44*t*
    effective and nominal rates of, 43, 44*t*
    factors affecting, 40*n*
    for industries, 20
    manufacturing, 43, 44*t*
    reversal of, 23
trade shares, North Korea, actual and
    natural, 262, 262*t*
trade shocks, South Korea, 6-7
trade unions. *See* labor unions
trading companies, and export boom, 28,
    28*n*
trading firms, North Korea, 88
Trading with the Enemy Act, 107*n*, 343
transitional economies, 281-282, 287
    speed of reform in, 256-258
transportation facilities, North Korean,
    84, 135, 137, 138, 138*n*, 296
travel, inter-Korean, 115, 116*f*, 298, 298*t*
Treuhandanstalt, 288, 288*n*, 290-293, 292*n*,
    319, 320
Tripartite Commission, 245
Truman Administration, 167
Tumen River Area Development Project,
    133*n*
turnover taxes, 71, 268*n*
two meals per day campaign, 172

Uhm Rak-yong, 318*n*
UN. *See* United Nations (UN)
UNDP. *See* United Nations Development
    Program (UNDP)
unemployment
    and German unification, 288
    Romania, 329
unemployment insurance, 244, 244*n*
unemployment rate, 219*n*, 219-220, 248

UNICEF, 184*n*
UNIDO. *See* United Nations Industrial
 Development Organization (UNIDO)
United Nations (UN)
 Department of Humanitarian Affairs,
  176
 Food and Agricultural Organization,
  175, 194
 humanitarian aid to North Korea, 121,
  191, 194
 involvement in Korean civil war, 3
 North Korean membership in, 60, 60*n*
 North Korean nuclear program
  confrontation, 5, 148, 148*n*, 150*n*
 North Korea trade statistics, 89*n*, 90*n*
 North-South rail links proposal, 114
 role in Korean peninsula, 375
 Security Council, 147-148, 160
 socioeconomic data collection, 74
 System of National Accounts, 272*n*
United Nations Development Program
 (UNDP), 69, 79, 79*n*, 81, 134*n*, 176,
 191*n*, 192
United Nations Industrial Development
 Organization (UNIDO), 134*n*, 137*n*,
 165
United States. *See also* Clinton
 administration
 Agreed Framework with North Korea
  (*See* Agreed Framework)
 aid to North Korea, 13, 91, 93*n*, 121,
  213*n*, 370
  food, 108-110, 121, 159, 162, 186-187,
   190-191, 351, 369-370
 aid to South Korea, 16
 Dialogue for Economic Cooperation,
  44*n*, 47
 disputes over South Korean trade
  barriers, 41*n*, 46*n*, 46-47
 economic relations with North Korea,
  107-110, 262
 economic relations with South Korea,
  199, 218
 educational exchange program, 87
 embargo against North Korea, 91, 94,
  107
  lifting of, 107-109, 113, 151, 157, 166,
   283-284, 342-343, 369
 history of relationship with Korean, 2
 Korean policy overview, 367-371
 Korean unification policy, 337-338
 normalization of relations with North
  Korea, 11*n*, 151, 283-284

North Korean nuclear program
 confrontation, 5, 148*n*, 148-150, 149*n*
 private investment in North Korea
  from, 108-109, 109*n*
 remains of Korean War soldiers, 91,
  109-110, 110*n*, 150*n*
 removal of troops from South Korea,
  9, 374
 South Korean joint military maneuvers
  with, 72*n*, 147*n*, 349
United States banks, investment in South
 Korea, 197
United States-Korea mutual defense
 treaty, nullification of, 374
United States Trade Representative
 (USTR), 46
uranium, 145
urbanization rate, North/South
 comparison, 74*t*, 74-75
Uruguay Round, 39, 42, 42*n*, 43*n*, 47, 50
USSR. *See* Soviet Union

Vasile, Radu, 327
Vietcong, 282
Vietnam
 loss of Soviet aid, 88*n*
 normalization of relations with U.S.,
  340
 North Korean arms transfers to, 117*n*
 property rights changes, 253
 reform experience, 255, 256-259, 257*n*,
  281-282, 342
Vietnam War, 16
Vinalon, 82*n*
Volvo, 234

wages
 agricultural, 177*n*, 277*n*, 304*n*
 industrial, 248
 and Korean unification, 304*n*, 317-319
 nominal, 219
 North Korea, 63, 135-136
  under economic reform model, 272-
   273, 277*n*, 278-280
 wage-setting policy, 36
  during German unification, 289-290,
   289*n*-290*n*, 294, 297, 318-319
 wage taxes, North Korea, 71*n*
 "wake-up call," 209
 Wall Street Journal, 150*n*, 159*n*
 Walpole, Robert D., 160*n*
 warehouses, bonded, 28, 359
 warrants, 56
 Warsaw Pact, 324